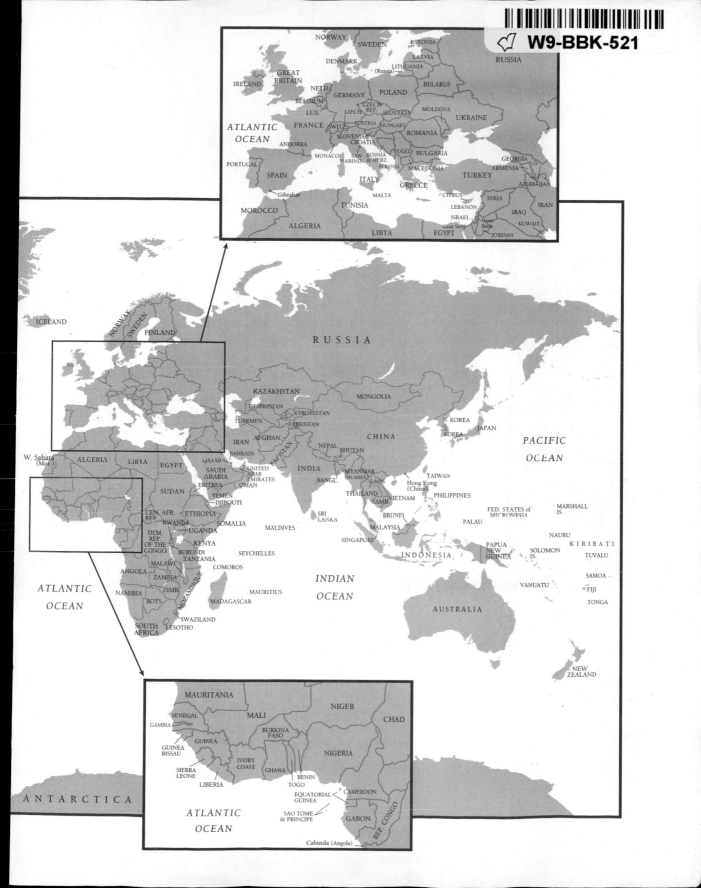

WORLD POLITICS

THE MENU FOR CHOICE

WORLD POLITICS

THE MENU FOR CHOICE

Sixth Edition

Bruce Russett

Yale University

Harvey Starr

University of South Carolina

David Kinsella

American University

BEDFORD/ST. MARTIN'S
Boston ♦ New York

For Bedford/St. Martin's
Political Science Editor: James R. Headley
Senior Editor, Publishing Services: Douglas Bell
Production Supervisor: Dennis Conroy
Project Management: Stratford Publishing Services, Inc.
Marketing Manager: Charles Cavaliere
Cover Design: Lucy Krikorian
Cover Art: Andrew Judd/Masterfile
Composition: Stratford Publishing Services, Inc.
Printing and Binding: Haddon Craftsman, an R. R. Donnelley & Sons Company

President: Charles H. Christensen
Editorial Director: Joan E. Feinberg
Director of Editing, Design, and Production: Marcia Cohen
Manager, Publishing Services: Emily Berleth

Library of Congress Catalog Card Number: 99-62364

Manufactured in the United States of America.

5 4 3 2 1 0
f e d c b a

For information, write: Bedford/St. Martin's, 75 Arlington Street, Boston, MA 02116   (617-399-4000)

ISBN: 1-57259-752-6

Acknowledgments

PREFACE

World politics is a fascinating subject. It is also a vast and complex subject. The student of world politics is asked to master, in varying degrees, history, current affairs, political and economic theory, principles of social science research, and ethics. Through five editions this book has been providing students with the tools they need to get started on their journey, and this substantially revised sixth edition will do the same for students whose journey starts with the turn of a new century.

World politics is constantly changing, and no one can hope to absorb fully these changes as they are occurring. We believe that a broad and self-conscious theoretical orientation remains the best resource for comprehending and coping with change, now and in the years ahead. Thus, this book includes a substantial component of theory, from both older and newer sources. The study of world politics is also constantly changing. In recent decades we have altered the ways we think about the subject; standards of concept formation, of logic, and of evidence are markedly different from what they were, and even now they are in a state of flux. Advances in the study of world politics can only be consolidated when we have the pedagogical skill and tools to educate the next generation. The consolidation we have tried for in *World Politics* is inclusive rather than exclusive: we have sought to synthesize the best of older traditions with newer approaches.

Students must learn something about how theory is constructed and tested, so we deal to some extent with the social scientific method, providing some "how to" material and guidelines for recognizing well-executed research. We stress the importance of cause-and-effect statements, encourage a respect for evidence, and help students recognize the type of statements for which evidence is not altogether relevant. To succeed in a rapidly changing world as active citizens rather than passive objects of historical forces, students must develop a good set of basic concepts and questions, a taste for analysis, a healthy bit of skepticism regarding the "conventional wisdom" of the "authorities" on the subject, and some tolerance for ambiguity when our understanding is, at best, incomplete.

We also provide a great deal of historical and contemporary factual material about world politics. One kind of fact is, simply, information about what is, and what has been, "out there" in the world. History and information about the contemporary world system are essential, so the book includes material on the characteristics of the major participants in world politics and the scope and function of major international instutions. We always introduce or punctuate our theoretical discussions with details on how the "real world" seems to work or has worked in the past. To supplement the wealth of factual material in text, we provide two appendixes: a chronology of major events from the Napoleonic wars to the present, and a set of comparative data on the characteristics of modern nation-states.

Another kind of fact is the evidence needed to support or refute major theoretical statements about world politics. We have tried to give the student some sense of the volume and quality of evidence relevant to various statements. When we feel that the evidence is reasonably solid, we have tried to document it. When we consider the evidence sparse or ambiguous, we have tried to indicate that, too. We also give references to empirical research, so that students — and instructors — will not have to take our statements on faith. At the same time, we have tried not to burden students with excessive technical detail or pedantry.

We feel strongly that the study of world politics should concern itself with values, and not just theories and facts: with how the world should work as well as how it does work. In world politics there are often both winners and losers. There is nothing natural or inevitable about who wins and who loses. Rather, these outcomes are products of the choices made by state leaders and by ordinary citizens. Students need guidance on how choices can be made, or perhaps avoided, while at the same time taking into account the consequences in terms of peace, security, equity, justice, and respect. These are values that many of us — maybe most of us, to varying degrees — hold dear. All choice involves ethics, and serious reflection on such matters is an important component of the study of world politics.

Changes in the Sixth Edition

Those who have used previous editions of *World Politics* will notice that the changes for the sixth edition begin on the front cover, with the addition of a third author. David Kinsella brings to this ongoing project a set of intellectual and pedagogical commitments consistent with those reflected in previous editions of the book, but from a different generational perspective. We suspect that veteran users of *World Politics* will see evidence of both in the current edition.

For this edition, we have undertaken a significant reorganization and consolidation of previous material, and we have added much new material. Part I explores the analytical dimensions of world politics, as previous editions have, although this part is shorter now, consisting only of seven chapters. It still introduces the student to the modern study of world politics, as organized according to the six levels of analysis we find useful: world system, interstate relations, society, government, roles, and the individual. It also introduces and develops our perspective — reflected in the book's subtitle, *The Menu for Choice* — that actors' decisions are constrained by the set of options presented by both global and domestic conditions. In Part I we discuss and illustrate how influences at various levels affect the process of policy making and choice.

As in previous editions, the analytic themes developed in Part I are woven through the remainder of the book. Each of the remaining chapters explores a broadly defined issue area in contemporary world politics, but we now organize these into three separate parts. Part II consists of four chapters on international conflict and cooperation, covering domestic and interstate war, armament and disarmament, international law and organization, and the causes of peace. Part III, also four chapters, is devoted to international political economy, including the political economy of national security and defense, economic interdependence, regional integration and globalization, and the North-South development gap. Part IV of the book is oriented toward the future, with a chapter on global ecology and the capacity of planet earth to sustain a burgeoning human population, plus a concluding chapter that examines three scenarios for world politics in the twenty-first century.

We have found that certain key theories and concepts help to frame what can often appear to first-time students of world politics as a jumble of facts and disagreements about the way the world works. Therefore, we introduce three broad theoretical perspectives at the beginning of the book — realism, liberalism, and radicalism — and return to these frequently throughout the book to help students realize that most of the fundamental debates in world politics are not erratic or haphazard, but usually reflect competing worldviews. Other key concepts that surface at various points in the book include the prisoner's dilemma and collective goods, concepts that reflect the continuing influence of the rational choice approach in the study of world politics. Since we ask students to take these concepts seriously, it is incumbent upon us to explain such game-theoretic notions as equilibrium, suboptimal outcome, and expected utility clearly and concisely, and without resort to detailed mathematics. We think we have. Those instructors who are adept at game theory can fill in the technical details for their students if they wish. For others, our treatment of this material will be sufficient to provide their students with some basic tools for comprehending certain forms of international interaction from a rational choice perspective.

Finally, the text, tables, and figures have been thoroughly updated. Those familiar with the fifth edition will find a lot of new material distributed throughout the book, but we do want to point out a few substantial additions. Chapter 8, on military conflict and warfare, collects and expands relevant discussions that had appeared in multiple chapters in the fifth edition. All of Chapter 12 is devoted to the political economy of national security and defense, and most of that is new to this edition. Chapter 14, on regional integration, includes a much expanded discussion of the European Union and its evolution, as well as all-new material on emerging economic blocs in other regions. The three global futures presented in Chapter 17 are also new. Finally, previous users of *World Politics* will notice many new tables and figures, each of which illustrates an important point made in the text.

World Politics and the Web

Since its inauguration in 1996, the *World Politics: The Menu for Choice* homepage has provided a variety of supplemental resources catered specifically to this textbook and to a first course on world politics. These resources include a set of chapter summaries, photographs with captions, chapter quizzes with feedback, and numerous links to Web sites that are relevant to the topics covered in each chapter. All of these resources can be found at the book site for *World Politics,* which can be accessed through the Bedford/St. Martin's Political Science homepage at <www.bedfordstmartins.com/polisci>.

In the sixth edition, readers will encounter many references to Web-based sources. We have found the Internet to be an invaluable resource for the latest information about world politics, and this has allowed us to provide readers with information that really is as up-to-date as it can be. When we cite a Web source, we have tried to do so in a consistent fashion. The elements of our Web citations are, in this order: the author (person or institution), the title of the Web page, the date that the page was last updated (if available), the date we accessed it, and the Web address. Mindful of the fact that Web pages come and go, and of the related problem of "link rot," we will endeavor to maintain a current list of Web sites referenced in each chapter on the *World Politics* homepage.

Acknowledgments

We owe thanks to innumerable colleagues and students who have assisted us over the years as we have worked toward producing and improving this book. Rather than single out some for expressions of gratitude here, we will pass over those who in the past contributed to the formation of our thinking. Many of them, thought not all, will find themselves footnoted in the text. We do want to thank explicitly all those who have read and commented on parts of all of this book in its journey from the first to the sixth edition: Francis Adams, William Avery, Andrew Bennett, Bruce Bueno de Mesquita, Steve Chan, Claudio Cioffi-Revilla, Delane Clark, David Clinton, Robert Dorf, Raymond Duvall, Nader Entesser, Michael Francis, John Freeman, Scott Sigmund Gartner, F. Gregory Gause, Guy Gosselin, Rober Hamburg, Robert Harkavy, Jeffrey Hart, Terrance Hopmann, Darril Hudson, Patrick James, Robert Jervis, Brian Job, Robert Keohane, Robert Mandel, Zeev Maoz, Douglas Nelson, Rene Peritz, James Ray, J. Rogers, J. David Singer, Randolph Siverson, Patricia Stein Wrightson, Michael Stohl, Richard Stoll, Stuart Thorson, Herbert Tillema, and Dina Zinnes. Thanks also to Susan Finnemore Brennan, senior editor at W. H. Freeman and Company, publisher of the first five editions of *World Politics,* and to James Headley, former executive editor at Bedford/St. Martin's, the book's new home as of this sixth edition. We greatly appreciate the hard work of our research assistants during the preparation of the sixth edition, Anita Dey, Todd Kennedy, Karl Riber, and Stephanie Schalk-Zaitsev, and we owe a special thanks to Mike Ward for bringing the *World Politics* web page online and for maintaining it while the book was in its fifth edition. Parts of the book represent research done with the aid of grants from the Carnegie Corporation, the Ford Foundation, the John D. and Catherine T. MacArthur Foundation, the National Science Foundation, the United States Institute of Peace, and the World Society Foundation (Switzerland). Over the course of six editions our home universities — Yale, Indiana, South Carolina, and American — have provided truly fine environments for research and reflection. We hope that all these people and institutions will in some degree be pleased with the outcome; any embarrassment with it must be ours alone.

Bruce Russett
Harvey Starr
David Kinsella

CONTENTS

ABOUT THE AUTHORS

Bruce Russett (Ph.D., Yale University, 1961) is Dean Acheson Professor of International Relations and Director of United Nations Studies at Yale University. Since 1972 he has edited the *Journal of Conflict Resolution* and has been president of the International Studies Association and the Peace Science Society (International). He has also taught at Columbia University, M.I.T., and the Free University of Brussels, and was Visiting Professor of International Capital Markets Law at the University of Tokyo. In addition, he has held research appointments at the University of Michigan, University of North Carolina, the Richardson Institute in London, the Netherlands Institute for Advanced Study, and the University of Tel Aviv. He has had numerous research grants from the National Science Foundation, and from the Carnegie Corporation of New York, the Center for Global Partnership of the Japan Foundation, the Ford Foundation, the Guggenheim Foundation, the Naval War College, the U.S. Institute of Peace, and the World Society Foundation of Switzerland. His publications include 21 books and approximately 200 articles.

Harvey Starr (Ph.D., Yale University, 1971) is the Dag Hammarskjold Professor in International Affairs and Interim Chair of the Department of Government and International Studies at the University of South Carolina. He is the former president of the Conflict Processes Section of the American Political Science Association (1992–95) and APSA vice president (1995–96). The editor of *International Interactions* since 1991, he specializes in international relations theory and method, international conflict, geopolitics, and foreign policy analysis. His most recent books are *Anarchy, Order and Integration: How to Manage Interdependence* (Univeristy of Michigan Press, 1997), *Agency Structure and International Politics* (Routledge, 1997, with Gil Friedman), and the edited volume, *The Understanding and Management of Global Violence* (St. Martin's, 1999).

David Kinsella (Ph.D., Yale University, 1993) is Assistant Professor of International Politics and Foreign Policy at American University, where he teaches courses on international relations theory and methodology. He is former president of the International Studies Association Midwest Region. He has taught at the University of Missouri and held a Mershon postdoctoral fellowship at Ohio State University. His areas of research include the arms trade, Third World arms production, political economy of national defense, and international conflict processes. His articles have appeared in *International Studies Quarterly, Journal of Conflict Resolution, Journal of Peace Research, American Journal of Political Science*, and elsewhere.

WORLD POLITICS

THE MENU FOR CHOICE

I

ANALYZING WORLD POLITICS

I would rather understand a single cause than be king of Persia.
— DEMOCRITUS OF ABDER

1

World Politics: Levels of Analysis, Choice, and Constraint

Three Momentous Events

Dropping the Atomic Bomb

On August 6, 1945, the U.S. bomber *Enola Gay* dropped an atomic bomb on the Japanese city of Hiroshima. Coupled with the explosion of another bomb over Nagasaki three days later, this act precipitated the Japanese surrender and the end of World War II. Nearly 200,000 people, most of them noncombatant civilians, ultimately died from the explosions. These two bombings represented the first, and so far the last, time nuclear weapons were used against enemy targets. Exploding a bomb of this magnitude (about 4,000 times more powerful than the biggest conventional World War II explosive) marked an enormous leap in "killing ability." At the same time it brought forth the age of nuclear deterrence, when peace among the great powers was kept, at least in part, by the awesome threat of mutual annihilation. At the time of these bombings, both scientists and statesmen realized that they were engaged in an act that would fundamentally change the future; the nuclear physicist J. Robert Oppenheimer, on watching the first test explosion a month before Hiroshima, quoted to himself the phrase from the Hindu scripture, the *Bhagavad Gita,* "I am become death, destroyer of worlds."

Despite the magnitude of this act and the precedents it set, there was remarkably little discussion within the American government as to whether the bomb should be used in war. Questions of morality were either ignored or quickly stilled with the argument that, overall, using the bomb would save lives. The only alternative to the use of the bomb to force Japan's surrender seemed to be an American invasion of the Japanese home islands, in which tens of thousands of Americans and hundreds of thousands of Japanese casualties could be expected. U.S. Secretary of War Henry L. Stimson later wrote that the reasons for dropping the atomic bomb "have always seemed compelling and clear, and I cannot see how any person vested with such responsibilities as mine could have taken any other course or given any other advice to his chiefs." British Prime Minister Winston Churchill reported that "the decision whether or not to use the atomic bomb to compel the surrender of Japan was never even an issue. There was unanimous, automatic, unquestioned agreement."[1] How can we explain this?

Particular characteristics of President Harry Truman may have made some difference. Before President Franklin Roosevelt's death in April 1945, it was assumed that the atomic bomb would be used in combat, although Roosevelt had not entirely ruled out the possibility of first warning the enemy and demonstrating the power of the bomb in a test. However, Truman was inexperienced and uninformed about foreign affairs; when he became president he was not even aware of the atomic bomb project. He was therefore in no position to challenge the existing basic assumption about the bomb's intended use or to dissent sharply from the military and foreign policy plans that had been put into effect by the advisers he had inherited from Roosevelt. Only one adviser (Admiral William Leahy, whose opinion had already been devalued due to his prediction that the bomb would not work at all) did not accept the consensus. There was some disagreement among the nuclear scientists who had produced the bomb, but in the end the prevailing scientific opinion was that they could "propose no technical demonstration likely to bring an end to the war; we can see no acceptable alternative to direct military use."[2]

Truman was caught up in the near unanimity around him; Roosevelt, although more experienced and politically stronger, probably would not have behaved much differently. Bureaucratic momentum carried matters along, and it would have required either a very unusual president or an exceptionally open structure of decision making to slow it. Furthermore, the alternative seemed technically and politically dangerous. The Japanese could be warned and the bomb tested publicly in some deserted spot, but there was a risk that the bomb would not go off or not look very impressive. The enemy would be uncowed, and, some advisers feared, Congress would be in a political uproar over the fizzled demonstration and consequent American casualties suffered in an invasion. Nowhere — in the executive branch, in Congress, or in the public at large — was there much disagreement over the need to end the war as soon as possible, princi-

---

[1] Henry L. Stimson, "The Decision to Use the Atomic Bomb," *Harper's* 194 (February 1947): p. 106; Winston S. Churchill, *Triumph and Tragedy* (Boston: Houghton Mifflin, 1953), p. 639.
[2] Scientific report quoted in Stimson, "The Decision to Use the Atomic Bomb," 101.

pally to spare American lives. Consequently, there were few moral restraints on the use of atomic weapons in war. Certainly there had been little objection earlier to the massive conventional bombing of civilian targets in Germany and Japan.

The basic constraints, therefore, stemmed from the international situation: a war waged against a determined opponent in an era when the moral and legal restrictions on warfare were few. Moreover, the international balance of forces likely to emerge after the war reinforced this perspective. The wartime Soviet-American alliance was deteriorating rapidly, especially in the face of severe disagreements about who should control Eastern Europe. Most American decisionmakers welcomed the atomic bomb as a master card of "atomic diplomacy," which would impress the Russians with American power and encourage them to make concessions to the American view about how the postwar world should be organized. Additionally, the Soviet Union had not yet entered the war with Japan. If the atomic bomb could force a Japanese surrender before the Russians were to attack Japan (in fact, the surrender came after that attack), it would help to limit Russian intrusion into Japanese-controlled portions of the Far East. American foreign policy decisionmakers largely agreed on these perceptions, as did most members of Congress and most opinion leaders in the American public.[3]

Ending the Cold War

In November 1988 Margaret Thatcher, then British prime minister, proclaimed, "The cold war is over." Events since then have dramatically confirmed her judgment. The cold war, which had dominated world politics for more than forty years, enforcing political domination on hundreds of millions of people and threatening to bring war on billions, was indeed over. The basic values of the West (democratic government and free-market economics) had triumphed — and the end of the cold war was then confirmed, even initiated, by the leader of the "losing" state, Soviet President Mikhail Gorbachev.

The events came in a cascade. First, Gorbachev made limited political and economic reforms in the Soviet Union. Then, free elections ousted the communist governments in most of Eastern Europe, and Gorbachev made no move to intervene in their support. In November 1989, the Berlin Wall was breached, and by October, 1990 East and West Germany were united. Moreover, Gorbachev took no military or political action to save what had been the Soviet Union's most important and loyal ally. In response to demands from the new anticommunist governments, Gorbachev withdrew all Soviet military forces from Czechoslovakia and Hungary in 1991 and concluded a major arms reduction agreement with the West. Nearly all the formerly antagonistic North Atlantic Treaty Organization (NATO) and Warsaw Pact countries agreed to reduce their military forces, with the Soviets accepting disproportionately deep cuts. Soviet forces assumed a defensive posture, unable to mount any threat of

---

[3] A valuable study is Barton J. Bernstein, "The Atomic Bombings Reconsidered," *Foreign Affairs* 41, 1 (January/February 1995): pp. 135–152; for the relevance of diplomacy toward the Soviet Union, see, contrastingly, Gar Alperovitz, *Atomic Diplomacy: Hiroshima and Potsdam*, 2nd ed. (London: Penguin, 1985), especially the new introduction; and McGeorge Bundy, *Danger and Survival* (New York: Vintage, 1988), chap. 2.

invading Western Europe. Even the Warsaw Pact between the USSR and its former East European satellites — the linchpin of Soviet security and control — was disbanded in 1991, as was the Council for Mutual Economic Assistance (COMECON), which had regulated trade among these countries for over forty years. Gorbachev announced that Soviet troops would come home, without victory, from the war in Afghanistan, and he insisted that Soviet-dependent governments like that in Nicaragua face the consequences of elections. At home, open dissent and secessionist movements emerged in many Soviet republics; free elections resulted in anticommunist governments in several and brought the end of the communist monopoly on power everywhere. In fact, by the end of 1991, the Soviet Union itself had dissolved as a single entity, ultimately leaving the state of Russia and fourteen other successor states of the former Soviet Union (FSU).[4] Gorbachev twisted and turned like an adroit slalom skier, but the slope he was on seemed to be leading ever nearer to drastic economic and political changes. After a reactionary coup against Gorbachev in August 1991 failed, Boris Yeltsin forced even more radical changes.

The end of the cold war, as initiated by Gorbachev's actions, was as astonishing as it was swift. It was one of those world-shaking turns that few theories either clearly anticipate or explain well after the fact. Nevertheless, we must grope toward an understanding, and in doing so we can at least offer some possible explanations, even if we can prove little.

In one clear sense, Gorbachev's personal characteristics deserve much of the credit. Following a series of aging leaders in ill health (his predecessors, Leonid Brezhnev, Yuri Andropov, and Konstantin Chernenko, all died within a three-year period), Gorbachev was only fifty-three when he came to power. He was vigorous, a skilled politician, and committed to reforming (but not necessarily to revolutionizing) the Soviet system. His fresh perspectives, energy, drive, and intelligence were essential to the task. Previous leaders might have seen the need for some reforms but were unable or unwilling to make dramatic changes.[5]

Exclusive attention to Gorbachev's personal qualities, however, leaves much out. He changed Soviet domestic and foreign policies because they hadn't worked, even by standards widely accepted among communist leaders. The Soviet economy was stagnant, with per capita income showing essentially no growth since the late 1970s, and the life expectancy of Soviet citizens was dropping. The insular and centrally planned Soviet economy, dependent on heavy industry and collective farms, was increasingly unable to compete in a world market based on innovation and driven by high technology and the free flow of goods, capital, and information within and between states. The burden of military spending bore down ever more painfully on Soviet living standards, as did Soviet expenditures to prop up allies in Africa, Asia, and Central America. The USSR had overreached itself globally, acquiring weak clients and eroding its own security. Something had to give — but why did it give then, rather than later, or sooner?

---

[4] The collapse of the Soviet Union is well recounted by Robert V. Daniels, *The End of the Communist Revolution* (London: Routledge, 1993).

[5] For an in-depth look at the personal background and qualities of the man who saw things differently from his predecessors, see Gail Sheehy, *The Man Who Changed the World: The Lives of Mikhail S. Gorbachev* (New York: HarperCollins, 1990).

Another element was surely the increasingly assertive political and military competition the Soviet Union faced from the United States, which intensified in the decade or so before Gorbachev made his big changes. In the last years of the Jimmy Carter administration, and more dramatically in the Ronald Reagan years, the United States and its allies began a spurt of additions to NATO military capabilities, especially by the development and deployment of high-tech weapons that exploited Western scientific advances. American military assistance to opponents of Soviet-backed regimes in Afghanistan, Angola, Cambodia, Nicaragua, and elsewhere raised the costs to the USSR of supporting those governments. Again, the Soviet Union had always been technologically behind the West and had long borne heavy costs. Why could it have not maintained itself longer? In addition, the United States was also feeling the burdens of the cold war and by 1986 was no longer increasing its own military expenditures. American willingness to respond carefully to Soviet overtures — not exploiting Soviet weakness so as to risk "enraging a cornered bear" — played an important part in allowing Soviet liberalization to continue.

Yet another influence was the spread of information across international borders, and especially in both directions across what had been known as the Iron Curtain. Citizens of communist countries could now know more and more about the prosperity and political liberties enjoyed by their counterparts in the West. By the 1980s most East Germans could regularly watch West German television, and informal personal contacts between Western and Eastern peoples were increasingly difficult to regulate. Under pressure of the human-rights provisions of the wide-ranging Helsinki Accords of 1975, communist governments increasingly had to tolerate dissident movements. Western news agencies regularly operated in East European and Soviet cities; any violent crackdown on dissent would have been shown immediately on hundreds of millions of television screens around the globe. Technological and cultural changes in the world were making communist efforts to insulate their people from world developments ever more anachronistic, ineffective, and costly. Furthermore, relaxation of the Soviet grip in Eastern Europe interacted with relaxation at home.

All these factors — the nature of the Soviet leadership, domestic political and economic decay, international political competition, global information flows — suggest reasons why the cold war ended. But no single explanation completely dominates the others, nor does it explain why the end came just when it did. If Gorbachev himself was essential to the changes, that still begs the question of why he was ready to change, even at enormous personal and national risk. Gorbachev faced opportunities and constraints; he was willing to make certain choices and was given very little latitude to make others. The reasons we list suggest a portion of the range of influences on world politics that any serious analyst must consider.

The Asian Financial Crisis

In 1995, the U.S. dollar began to climb in value relative to the currencies of other industrialized countries, including Japan. Over the next two years the Japanese yen lost about one-third of its value compared to the dollar, and in May 1997 Japanese officials seriously considered increasing interest rates in order to stem the yen's decline. In the end they didn't, but these were the first symptoms of a financial uncertainty that spread like the flu throughout Asia and beyond. It started in Southeast Asia. During the 1990s, many Southeast Asian currencies were "pegged" to the U.S. dollar, meaning that when the dollar appreciated, so did the Thai baht, the Indonesian rupiah, the Malaysian ringgit, and the Philippine peso. In Thailand, the feeling among local investors that the Thai currency was overvalued — that its face value was more than its true worth — led to the widespread trading of bahts for foreign currencies, especially dollars and yen, whose values inspired more confidence. Foreign investors followed suit, as did speculators hoping to profit from the changing currency values. The result was a massive sell-off of bahts. The Thai central bank did what it could to purchase bahts in order to maintain the baht's value against the dollar, but was quickly overwhelmed. In July 1997, Thailand was forced to let the value of its currency fall to levels determined by the financial market, and the baht plummeted.

The scenario was repeated in Indonesia in August 1997, and similar events unfolded in Malaysia and the Philippines. The financial crisis then spread to East Asia. In October, the South Korean won plunged in value, sending the world's eleventh largest economy reeling. Despite heroic efforts by the Korean central bank to prevent the won from breaching the psychologically important barrier of 1,000 to the dollar, what one Korean official said would "never, never, never" happen *did* happen in November, when the won was allowed to close at 1,008.6. The pressure on the won reverberated: the Singapore and Taiwanese dollars also sank to new lows, while the value of the Hong Kong dollar remained steady only as a result of intensive intervention by Hong Kong central bankers in the currency market.

The implications of falling Asian currency values were serious. Indeed, a former U.S. official called the financial crisis "one of the gravest of modern times."[6] Everyone holding these currencies, or assets denominated in them, had their wealth suddenly diminished. Those who were unable to liquidate their holdings were stuck. Although foreign investors could run for the exit, and did, local investors and consumers could not. The currency crisis threatened severe economic dislocation in each of the affected countries and, in some cases, forecast economic collapse as it became clear that some major corporate institutions would not be able to meet financial obligations to their creditors, their customers, or their workers. Thailand, Indonesia, South Korea, and the Philippines each turned to the international community for help. Before long more than $110 billion had been pledged to these countries on behalf of the International Monetary Fund (IMF), the World Bank, and other sources (primarily the U.S. and Japanese governments). In return, the recipients promised to undertake various economic and financial reforms.[7] The prospect of an international bailout had immediate, though in some cases temporary, effects: all the Asian currencies had begun to recover in value by January 1998.

---

[6] Laura D'Andrea Tyson, "Leadership in a Crisis," *Washington Post,* January 22, 1998.

[7] The responses of the IMF and World Bank to the Asian financial crisis are detailed in International Monetary Fund, "Factsheet: The IMF's Response to the Asian Crisis," April 1998; available from <http://www.imf.org/External/np/exr/facts/asia.htm> (April 24, 1998), and Sven Sandström, "The East Asia Crisis and the Role of the World Bank: Statement to the Bretton Woods Committee," February 13, 1998; available at <http://www.worldbank.org/html/extdr/extme/ss3speech.htm> (April 26, 1998).

The unfolding of the financial crisis amply demonstrated the interconnectedness of the Asian financial markets, but the potential reverberations of the crisis were not limited to Asia. The gloomiest forecasts predicted a sharp downturn in Japanese economic growth — already slow for several years — and possibly even a stock market crash. If the Japanese economy, the world's second largest, was engulfed by the crisis, the global repercussions would be impossible to contain. Consequently, once the free fall in currency values had been arrested, international efforts to manage the crisis turned to Japan. The government of Prime Minister Ryutaro Hashimoto was criticized for not doing more to prevent the financial meltdown in Southeast Asia, and international pressure mounted for Japan to stimulate its own growth and open its markets in order to help pave the way for the region's economic and financial recovery. The chairman of Japan's own Sony Corporation went so far as to assert that the Japanese economy was on the verge of collapse and compared Hashimoto to U.S. President Herbert Hoover, whose policies were blamed by many for the Great Depression of the 1930s. In April 1998, the Japanese government announced an unprecedented $128 billion domestic program, consisting of major government spending and substantial tax cuts, to stimulate its economy.

Much debate ensued about the causes of the Asian financial crisis. There were two main camps. One placed the blame on factors internal to Asian societies. Long before the crisis, many Asian governments were criticized in the West for their authoritarian political practices. Dismissing these criticisms as the West's failure to appreciate "Asian values" was relatively easy when the Asian governments had an enviable record of delivering economic prosperity to their citizens.[8] Now the tables were turned, however. Critics could now point to the *economic* downside of "Asian values": poor regulation, high corporate debt, favoritism, even corruption. The multibillion-dollar financial empire controlled by Indonesian President Suharto and his family stood as a potent symbol of the excesses of Asian "crony capitalism." This was essentially the IMF's perspective on the crisis, which is why the fund insisted on economic and financial reform as a condition for its bailout.

The other camp looked instead to external factors, seeing in the crisis the classic characteristics of a financial panic. There may have been elements of cronyism and other weaknesses in the Asian economies, but they were basically healthy, according to this view. It was just that the enthusiasm with which international investors sought to profit from the so-called "Asian miracle" was a bit excessive, and it created a bubble of confidence. The bubble burst in summer 1997, investors panicked, and the exodus of capital from the region left currency values in the gutter. Despite the soundness of the Asian economies, international investors participated in a self-fulfilling prophecy. It was their own actions, more than internal economic weaknesses, that undermined the economic and financial stability of the region.[9] From this perspective, the IMF's insis-

---

[8] One firm believer in the differences between Western and Asian values is Singapore's former prime minister, Lee Kuan Yew. See Fareed Zakaria, "Culture Is Destiny: A Conversation with Lee Kuan Yew," *Foreign Affairs* 73, 2 (March/April 1994): pp. 109–126.

[9] See, for example, Jagdish Bhagwati, "The Capital Myth: The Difference between Trade in Widgets and Dollars," *Foreign Affairs* 77, 3 (May/June 1998): pp. 7–12; see also Robert Wade and Frank Veneroso, "The Asian Crisis: The High Debt Model vs. the Wall Street–Treasury-IMF Complex, *New Left Review* 228 (March/April 1998): pp. 3–23.

tence on economic and financial reform in some ways may have contributed to the panic by further drawing attention to weaknesses instead of strengths.

We are not yet aware of the full ramifications of the financial crisis in Asia, and it may still be too early to judge the best explanation for those events. The path of future economic and financial recovery in the region will help settle some differences of opinion, as will developments in these countries' domestic politics. Whatever the final verdict, the events of 1997 and 1998 did illustrate some important features of international relations at the turn of the twenty-first century. The boundary between domestic affairs and foreign affairs was once again called into question. Although the free flow of capital across national boundaries was nothing new — Asian economies benefited from large capital inflows during the years prior to the crisis — the sheer magnitude and speed of the capital outflow in fall 1997 was staggering. Moreover, the decisions that affected this outflow were made primarily by foreign investors. The consequences of their actions for domestic economies in the region were immediately apparent, and may or may not turn out to be long-lived. But their actions also had an impact on domestic *politics* in Asia. In addition to forcing a major policy change on a reluctant ruling party in Japan, the financial crisis helped clinch electoral victory for long-time political outsider Kim Dae Jung in Korea and triggered a series of violent riots in Indonesia, which ultimately toppled President Suharto after more than three decades in office.

The Asian crisis was yet another illustration of the ineffectiveness of government intervention in financial markets. With the exception of Hong Kong, none of the Asian central banks succeeded in preventing huge devaluations of their national currencies. In the aftermath, there were renewed calls to regulate capital flows in hopes that this would enhance the limited leverage exercised by governments (Malaysia imposed controls in September 1998). The crisis also provided an opportunity for the IMF to expand its own role in world affairs, as it had during the Latin American debt crisis of the 1980s and the East European transition to market capitalism in the early 1990s. The policies of the IMF during the Asian crisis were criticized in some quarters, but the high profile of this and other international organizations has become a significant feature of contemporary international relations. Any restructuring of the global financial system to incorporate lessons learned from the Asian financial crisis is likely to include the IMF as an integral component.[10]

Levels of Analysis

The preceding three sketches — of the United States in 1945, the Soviet Union at the end of the cold war, and Asia from fall 1997 — are taken from very different times, treat richer and poorer countries, and deal with military, political, and economic matters. The quality of evidence for explaining policy choice varies from one case to another, as

---

[10] For some proposals for reform, see Martin Feldstein, "Refocusing the IMF," *Foreign Affairs* 77, 2 (March/April 1998): pp. 20–33; Jeffrey E. Garten, "Lessons for the Next Financial Crisis," *Foreign Affairs* 78, 2 (March/April 1999): pp. 76–92.

does the plausibility of our speculations. Political scientists usually find it difficult to predict a single event, such as the American decision to drop the atomic bomb or the revolution in East Germany in 1989, and economists cannot predict market panics or manias, as occurred in Asia in 1997. More often we try to understand why certain classes of events occur — for example, why states may engage in acts of violence. Most analysts see their job as one of trying to detect comparable preceding events that seem to produce similar types of behavior. The patterns we see often describe what Dina Zinnes has called a puzzle: "pieces of information, the belief that the pieces fit together into a meaningful picture, but the inability to fit the pieces together initially."[11]

How can states and other actors existing within the same environment behave so differently? To address such puzzles we need to describe what international systems look like, how they change over time, and how they affect the behavior of the entities within them. We also need to look at the internal, or domestic, makeup of states. Doing so helps us understand puzzles about the different behaviors of states at different times or in different circumstances — the conditions in which they will cooperate or coordinate their actions with other international actors, and those in which conflicts will develop, escalate, and even lead to violence. We wish to understand what processes — cooperative or opposing; economic, diplomatic, or military — result in what patterns of outcomes. We wish to understand the causes of the patterns we find.

In our attempts to uncover causes, or significant preceding events, we have found it useful to distinguish between **levels of analysis** — points on an ordered scale of size and complexity. These levels include units whose behavior we attempt to describe, predict, or explain, as well as units whose impact on individual decisionmakers we examine. That is, a level may refer to the actors themselves, to the states or individuals whose actions we are trying to explain, or (as in our discussions so far) to different kinds of influences on those actors. In our earlier examples, we used influences from various levels of analysis to explain decisions made by national leaders.

The International System and the Nation-State

In a well-known article J. David Singer introduced the idea of levels of analysis and discussed two broad levels: the international system and the nation-state. By so doing, he highlighted a major distinction used in discerning influences on foreign policy: (1) internal, or domestic, influences, which originate within the boundaries of the nation-state, and (2) external influences, which arise outside the state's boundaries.

The international-system level is the most comprehensive level of analysis. It permits the observer to study international relations as a whole; that is, to look at the *overall* global patterns of behavior among states and the level of interdependence among them. These include the overall distribution of capabilities, resources, and status in world politics. The nation-state level of analysis allows us to use a decision-making approach and to investigate in far more detail the conditions and processes within states that affect foreign policy choices. Thus, although the international-system level provides a more comprehensive picture of patterns and generalizations, the nation-

---

[11] Dina Zinnes, "Three Puzzles in Search of a Researcher," *International Studies Quarterly* 24, 3 (1980): pp. 315–342.

state level provides a picture of greater depth, detail, and intensity. Singer summarized the level-of-analysis problem with this set of analogies:

> In any area of scholarly inquiry, there are always several ways in which the phenomena under study may be sorted and arranged for purposes of systematic analysis. Whether in the physical or social sciences, the observer may choose to focus upon the parts or upon the whole, upon the components or upon the system. He may, for example, choose between the flowers or the garden, the rocks or the quarry, the trees or the forest, the houses or the neighborhood, the cars or the traffic jam, the delinquents or the gang, the legislators or the legislature, and so on.[12]

In international relations it is possible to study the flowers/rocks/trees/ houses/ cars/delinquents/legislators, or to shift the level of analysis and study the garden/ quarry/forest/neighborhood/traffic jam/gang/legislature. Thus, we may choose to study international phenomena from a "macro" or a "micro" perspective: Is it the international system that accounts for the behavior of its constituent state units, or the states that account for variations in the international system? Do we look at the state or at its societal components — ethnic groups or classes or specific economic interests? Do we look at the government or at the bureaucracies that comprise it? Do we look at bureaucracies or at the individuals that comprise them? Do we look at the system or its constituent parts?[13]

The macro, or inclusive, system forms the environment for its parts. As we will discuss in the next section, the ultimate constituent parts, surrounded by a set of environments, are individuals who act as governmental decisionmakers. These decisionmakers, in turn, constantly try, insofar as possible, to shape and control those environments.

Distinguishing among various levels of analysis helps us with the different aspects of explanation and understanding. The macro approach tells one story, explaining what has occurred because of outside factors; the micro approach tells another story, attempting to explain the significance of events from the point of view of people within the units. Using different levels of analysis thus helps us clarify what kinds of questions we want to ask and what kinds of questions might be answered most profitably from which perspective.

The international-system level lets us see, for example, under what conditions dropping the atomic bomb would be likely or under what conditions the cold war could end. Analysis at that level is concerned with questions about the impact of the distribution of military power, or about the impact of the changing distribution of

---

[12] J. David Singer, "The Level-of-Analysis Problem in International Relations," in Klaus Knorr and Sidney Verba, eds., *The International System: Theoretical Essays* (Princeton, N.J.: Princeton University Press, 1961), p. 77. See also Kenneth N. Waltz, *Man, the State, and War: A Theoretical Analysis* (New York: Columbia University Press, 1954), who refers, not to levels of analysis, but to "images" of international relations; and see the critique by William B. Moul, "The Level of Analysis Problem Revisited," *Canadian Journal of Political Science* 6 (1973): pp. 494–513.

[13] This perspective is outlined by Martin Hollis and Steve Smith, *Explaining and Understanding International Relations* (Oxford: Clarendon, 1990). They note, "At each stage the 'unit' of the higher level becomes the 'system' of the lower layer" (p. 8).

wealth in the world economy. Looking at Truman or Gorbachev, their particular situations and characters, gives us a better understanding of how such conditions were perceived and interpreted and leads us to questions about the importance of the individual decisionmaker in policy choices. In all three of the cases discussed, we can also see how questions are linked across levels. In particular, the various sets of factors involved in managing changing economic and financial conditions illustrate how different domestic and international levels blend into one another and link together.

Six Levels of Analysis

Singer's distinction is valuable, but, as we have already seen, his two levels can be elaborated on. In later work, analysts found a more useful scheme, which identifies six levels.[14] They are: (1) **individual decisionmakers** and their characteristics, (2) the **roles** occupied by the decisionmakers, (3) the structure of the **government** within which the decisionmakers operate, (4) the **society** the decisionmakers govern and within which they live, (5) the sets of **relations** that exist between the decisionmakers' nation-state and the other international actors, and (6) the **world system** (see Figure 1.1).

Individual Decisionmakers　At the micro, or most disaggregated, level of analysis we have individual decisionmakers. In what ways — education and socialization, personality traits, or physical health — does the particular occupant of a major role in making foreign policy differ from other individuals who have held or might have held the

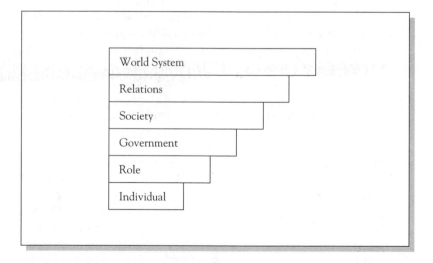

FIGURE 1.1　Levels of Analysis in World Politics

---

[14] This analytical scheme is adapted from the one presented in James N. Rosenau, *The Scientific Study of Foreign Policy,* rev. ed. (London: Pinter, 1980), chap. 6. The six levels presented in this book, their added complexity, and our use of them also address a number of points in Moul's critique (see note 12).

position in the past? Explanations at this level must relate differences in the characteristics of decisionmakers to differences in the decisions they make — for example, what can be explained by contrasting Truman's or Gorbachev's foreign policy inexperience with the foreign policy of such experienced predecessors as Franklin Roosevelt or Leonid Brezhnev?

Roles of Decisionmakers   Relations between individual decisionmakers are heavily affected by the individuals' roles. When acting on behalf of an organization, a decision-maker is the focal point of innumerable pressures and constraints. At this level of analysis, the decisionmaker is seen to act in a particular way because of his or her role in the societal and political system. We would, for example, expect an air force chief of staff, regardless of differences in personality or ideology from other top military officers, to be concerned with protecting the air force as an institution — to see that it receives a fair share of budgets, equipment, and talented personnel and is assigned missions that will improve its operating capabilities but not overtax them in hopeless causes.

Any individual — military or civilian — placed in charge of an institution has a responsibility to look out for the interests of that institution. He or she must also consider the interests of other people and institutions, of course, and not pursue the organization's interests completely to the exclusion of all others. At heart, however, the person in charge knows that if he or she does not protect his or her own institution, no one else will. Other institutions are also protected through the pursuit of their own enlightened self-interest and by the existence of institutions at higher levels that include them. Thus, the U.S. secretary of defense must arbitrate among the interests of the three military services (and the civilian defense bureaucracy), and the president must somehow reconcile the interests of the numerous, competing military and civilian groups. As part of our examination of the individual's role, we must consider the small-group environment (a president and advisers or a prime minister within the cabinet setting) within which the individual acts and ask how group interaction affects both perceptions and actions.

We must also assume that people tend to acquire other interests and perspectives from their roles in society. For example, corporate executives typically acquire a set of attitudes and perspectives that are not necessarily specific to the particular companies they run but are broadly shared with other executives and distinct from those of labor union officials. Soviet Communist party leaders who had shared common experiences of the Bolshevik Revolution, Marxism, the Western intervention after World War I, and the German invasions of two world wars, as well as the experiences of trying to hold together a multiethnic empire, had a set of shared perspectives very different from those of Latin American military officers trying to resolve pressures for political participation and economic development while being buffeted by the world economy (or, indeed, from those of the post–World War II generation of political leaders in Latvia, Lithuania, or Estonia).

Governmental Structure   Another set of influences on decisions is determined by the structure of the government — or organization — in which the decisionmakers operate. Most obviously, a democratic system of government with frequent and truly competitive elections will pose a different set of opportunities and constraints for decision-makers than will an authoritarian government. In the former, it is probably necessary for a leader to build a wider base of approval for his or her actions, yet he or she is likely to be held accountable for those actions at elections held at regular, specified intervals. In an authoritarian system, a leader can work from a narrower political base to repress opposition, but the fear of a coup or revolt by one's opponents is always present. Subtler differences in types of government are also important. Gorbachev attempted in vain to maintain political direction over a form of government that was changing from a tightly controlled authoritarian system to a presidential system based on free elections. As the government became increasingly open, Gorbachev and other high officials had to operate under ever greater constraints, both from the public and from entrenched interest groups, having opened a Pandora's box of change, in both government and society, which ultimately could not be controlled.

Characteristics of the Society   Expanding our set of influences still further, we come to nongovernmental characteristics of the society as a whole that affect or condition choices. Governments of rich countries have far more material resources at their disposal than do those of poorer countries (see Appendix B and compare the United States and Thailand); they can afford large quantities of modern weapons and can offer economic assistance to other states, while their citizens expect a high and ever-rising standard of living. Again, changing economic conditions in the Soviet Union, through its dissolution and the emergence of the Russian successor state, provide an example of the impact of domestic factors on foreign policy: as the domestic picture worsened, the USSR/Russia moved from its position as an apparently wealthy superpower competitor of the United States to a new role as supplicant for aid and trade from the developed Western states.

Big countries, though they may be relatively poor, still have more resources at their disposal than do small countries. China and India can afford nuclear weapons far more readily than can Laos and Ireland. Small and poor countries are especially likely to be deeply penetrated by other countries or by nonstate actors like multinational corporations. What a leader can do and wants to do are substantially determined by the kind of country he or she represents.

Different forms of economic organization may have foreign policy effects. Various theories treat the requirements and results of capitalism. Are capitalist economies driven by military-industrial complexes? Does capitalism lead to imperialism? Seeking evidence, we might ask whether most capitalist countries have been significantly more prone to war than most socialist countries, and if so, why.

International Relations   The actions of states toward each other are affected by the relationship between them, which, in turn, is determined by the characteristics of the two states. These characteristics help shape the nature of influence between the states — how it is attempted, how successful it is, and what outcomes are produced. A small, weak country will act differently toward a neighboring small, weak country than it will toward a neighboring superpower. Democracies may maintain peaceful relations with each other, but the differences between a democracy and a neighboring dictatorship may bring them into conflict. Rich and poor countries are likely to develop a relationship of dominance or dependence vis-à-vis each other that looks very different depending on which country you inhabit.

The World System   Finally, it is essential to consider the wider international, regional, or global system in which a decisionmaker must operate. A **system** is simply a *set of interacting elements.* A world with two dominant elements — superpowers — differs in very important ways from a world with four or five powers of essentially equal strength; and both differ from a unipolar world with only one dominant element. A world of two superpowers tends to focus world fears and antagonisms between those two countries; a world of several equal powers produces at least the possibility of shifting alliances or coalitions to balance power without creating permanent antipathies. A unipolar world — as some people think has emerged with the dissolution of the Warsaw Pact and the Soviet Union, the continued Russian preoccupation with internal problems, and the demonstration of American military dominance in the Gulf War and in Yugoslavia — considerably reduces the possibility of effective military alliances (but perhaps not economic ones).

Another aspect of the larger system that makes a difference is the degree of wealth and, especially, of technological development. As an environment for political decisionmakers, the contemporary world is a far different place from the world of the eighteenth century. Rapid communication, swift transportation, and techniques of mass destruction have revolutionized the character of warfare and the means of seeking national security. These technologies — and the enormous structure of industry and commerce supported by the wealth of the modern world — also have created a far more interdependent system than existed decades or centuries ago. A cutback in Middle East oil production, the collapse of a major stock market, or atmospheric pollution from a nuclear accident can produce virtually instant, and often drastic, worldwide repercussions. Thus, as part of the world system, we shall also have to discuss nonstate actors like intergovernmental organizations (for instance, the IMF), as well as nongovernmental organizations (such as religious groups, terrorist bands, and multinational corporations).

Actors in World Politics

The six basic levels of analysis will serve as organizing principles for most of this book. In Part I we shall proceed systematically through these various levels, identifying some of the most important ideas or theories about how these levels affect national decision making by providing constraints and opportunities. We shall focus primarily on the policies adopted by the governments of nation-states, as influenced by various entities at different levels of analysis within each state's total environment. This focus is typical of the field of study known as international relations or international politics. States usually have control over territory, dominion over the the people on the territory, and a monopoly over the use of military force within that territory. In many ways the state remains the most significant single type of actor in determining conditions of war and peace, as well as the distribution of income and resources.

There are good reasons, nevertheless, to refer to our field of study as *world* politics (rather than as *international* relations or *international* politics), thus acknowledging the importance of actors other than nation-states. This distinction is observed in the title of this book, and we shall refer many times to nonstate actors. A decisionmaker typically acts, not merely on his or her own behalf, but also on behalf of some group or organization. One such group is the nation-state itself, for which a president or prime minister may act; other organizations relevant to world politics include (1) private organizations operating within a nation-state, such as interest groups and banks; (2) parts of national governments, such as the British ministry of defense or the Republican leadership of the U.S. House of Representatives; and (3) transnational organizations, such as Amnesty International, the International Red Cross, or the Roman Catholic Church.

Within nation-states there also exist numerous *subgroups* based on ethnic, racial, linguistic, religious, cultural, regional, or economic identifications. The process by which subgroupism fragments states and by which subgroups strive for independence as separate international actors (for example, the breakup of the Soviet Union into Russia and fourteen other independent units, none of which wished to remain attached to Russia; the violent fragmentation of what had been Yugoslavia; or the peaceful separation of Czechoslovakia into Slovakia and the Czech Republic) or transnational actors (for example, the Kurds, who are spread across five different nation-states) gives such groups an important place in world politics. James Rosenau includes such subgroups with all the other nonstate actors in his discussion of the rise of a "multicentric" world of politics, which he claims now coexists with the "state-centric" world.[15]

The key point is that *all* these groups are important agents, or actors, in world politics. Although we shall give special attention to the state as actor, we must always remember that it acts within an environment that includes the multicentric world of individuals and group actors of many different types. A careful use of a levels-of-analysis perspective, focusing both on different entities and on different forms of interaction, will identify other major actors important to world politics. Multinational corporations, for instance, need stable and predictable (if not necessarily completely peaceful) relations between major powers if they are to pursue global profits safely. In turn, multinational corporations may create an economic interdependence among states that very seriously inhibits the latter from making war, which would sever the bonds of trade and prosperity. Multinational corporations change the relative size and power of social groups and classes wherever they invest; for example, they increase the labor force in some industries and expand the middle class of technicians and managers. In turn, the political demands of these people, such as attracting more foreign corporations or nationalizing those that are already in the country, are strengthened. In any case, actors interact across separate levels of analysis.

The complexity of interactions is denoted by the term *system*. When we speak of a global or regional system, we imply that the major elements or influences at different levels of analysis affect one another. We shall see that this *interdependence* is a key element of systems. Nation-states affect multinational corporations or component communal groups, and vice versa; states develop new military technologies and in turn are constrained by the destructive capabilities of those technologies.

---

[15] See James N. Rosenau, *Turbulence in World Politics: A Theory of Change and Continuity* (Princeton, N.J.: Princeton University Press, 1990).

It is not too extreme to say that the interdependent interactions of a system mean that everything affects everything else. If you kill a single butterfly, you reduce the stock of genetic material in the next generation of butterflies and therefore change the pattern of evolution for future butterflies — and for predators that feed on butterflies. Over millions of years of evolution you will exert an unknowable effect on life, and even on the physical environment that life modifies. Probably those effects will be trivial, but they could be very large: chaos theory suggests that small changes in initial conditions may produce large changes in the ultimate behavior of the system. One mark of a good analyst is the ability to simplify a complex reality in a way that concentrates on the most important relationships and at least temporarily ignores the others. Jacob Bronowski explained:

> I believe that there are no events anywhere in the universe which are not tied to every other event in the universe. . . . But you cannot carry on science on the supposition that you are going to be able to connect every event with every other event. . . . It is, therefore, an essential part of the methodology of science to divide the world for any experiment into what we regard as relevant and what we regard, for purposes of that experiment, as irrelevant.[16]

Any simplification leaves something out. Any level of analysis ignores something important, and another simplification — another level of analysis — will tell us something a little different. In examining the Asian financial crisis, we did not look at the specific personality characteristics of leaders of the various countries; in looking at the atom bomb decision, a role explanation will be different from one based on Truman's personality, and still different from an explanation based on the global power structure or the U.S.-Soviet relationship. But we have to start somewhere. Certain questions about national decisionmakers' behavior are more readily answered from one level than from another. Questions that can be answered from various levels allow different perspectives on the same issue and require different kinds of evidence. Micro information on the perceptions of individual leaders and their true preferences may, for instance, be very hard to obtain. One may contend that nearly all leaders of poor and weak countries have the same preferences in a given situation; thus, detailed information on preferences is not needed so long as one has adequate information at the societal level of analysis and the aim is macro explanation.

The choice of level of analysis is therefore determined by one's theory and by the availability of data, but the choice cannot be capricious. Several different classes of influence (levels of analysis) must be identified in every analytical instance, as was clearly illustrated by all three of our brief cases. Explanations from different levels need not exclude each other. They may be complementary, with each making a contribution to our understanding. To some degree, estimates of the relative weight of each contribution can be compiled through the techniques of data gathering and analysis typical

---

[16] Jacob Bronowski, *The Origins of Knowledge and Imagination* (New Haven, Conn.: Yale University Press, 1978), p. 58. A related interdependence phenomenon, studied in chaos theory, is known as the Butterfly Effect — "the notion that a butterfly stirring the air today in Peking can transform storm systems next month in New York." See James Gleick, *Chaos: Making a New Science* (New York: Penguin, 1987), p. 8.

of modern social science. However, beyond that point we remain in the realm of speculation, intuition, and informed wisdom.

The "Menu": Choice and Constraint in World Politics

Opportunity and Willingness

How can we use levels of analysis to help us understand the choices of decisionmakers
who direct international actors? We have noted that at each level we have some sort of
system made up of its constituent units. We can study what goes on inside each of
these units and the ways in which their behavior is constrained by the surrounding
system. As Martin Hollis and Steve Smith put it, "Whatever the unit, its activities
can be explained from without or understood from within. Every unit has a decision-
making process. Those making the decisions are influenced from outside and from
inside." Ultimately, then, we are concerned with the possibilities and constraints that
face decisionmakers **(opportunity)** and with the choices that they make in light of
these possibilities and constraints **(willingness).**[17]

The willingness of the decisionmaker to make certain choices is constrained by her
or his own nature (the individual level), as well as by the decisionmaker's place in the
governmental structure (role); the nature and form of the government within which the
decisionmaker operates; the resources, makeup, and politics of the society that houses
the decisionmaker and the government; the web of influence relations that the decisionmaker's state has with other world actors; and the structure of the world system. Each
level affects the opportunities available to decisionmakers; each affects the images decisionmakers hold and the ways in which they make choices. Exactly how each of these
levels affects opportunity and willingness is developed in Chapters 4 through 7.

Opportunity and willingness force us to consider both the world system, or
broader environment, and the process of decision making that goes on within that system's constituent units. The various levels of analysis are thus linked by thinking of a
decisionmaker as an entity who must behave within the very complex environment
that surrounds her or him. Each level of analysis describes one of the environments
within which the decisionmaker must operate.[18]

---

[17] These two concepts were originally developed by Harvey Starr and later elaborated in Benjamin A.
Most and Harvey Starr, *Inquiry, Logic and International Politics* (Columbia: University of South Carolina
Press, 1989), chap. 2. The quote is from Hollis and Smith, *Explaining and Understanding International
Relations*, p. 42.

[18] How to choose between explanations that emphasize decisionmakers' willingness ("agency") and
those that emphasize constraints beyond their immediate control ("structure") is hotly debated. See
Alexander E. Wendt, "The Agent-Structure Problem in International Relations Theory," *International
Organization* 41, 3 (1987): pp. 337–370; Walter Carlsnaes, "The Agency-Structure Problem in Foreign
Policy Analysis," *International Studies Quarterly* 36, 3 (1992): pp. 245–270; and Gil Friedman and Har-
vey Starr, *Agency, Structure, and International Politics* (London: Routledge, 1997).

Opportunity　"Politics is the art of the possible." The environments of decision-making entities provide a structure of opportunities, risks, and potential costs and benefits, which constrain decisionmakers. How are all these elements captured by the concept of opportunity?

First, the environment *makes possible* certain opportunities, and not others. Here the environment is seen as a set of constraints on what it is actually possible for the entity to do in the environment. Napoleon could not threaten Moscow with nuclear destruction, nor could Franklin Roosevelt coerce the Japanese in 1941 with the atomic bomb — but Truman, with that possibility at hand, had to decide how to use the opportunity it provided. In the eighth century, the Spanish could not draw on the resources of the New World to repel the initial Islamic invasion of Iberia because no European knew there was a New World; the economically besieged countries trying to deal with the Great Depression of the 1930s could not call on the IMF for assistance because it did not exist. The list is endless.

Possibility includes two dimensions. First, the phenomenon must already exist somewhere in the world system. The phenomenon — be it nuclear weapons, or telecommunications satellites, or Protestantism, or Marxism, or railroads — must have been "invented" so that it is available as a possibility to at least some actors in the system. The second dimension is the distribution of this possibility in the system. Nuclear weapons do exist; however, most states cannot "take advantage" of them because they have neither the wealth nor the expertise to produce their own. The technology needed to place telecommunications satellites in space is widely known but is not affordable by all. Though a possibility may exist, limits on resources will affect the ability to make use of it.

The unequal distribution of possibilities also makes it *probable* that certain opportunities will be taken. Environmental constraints in any situation make certain behavior more or less likely — there is some normally expected behavior in the situation under consideration. Given that interaction between states is possible, what is the probability that they will act in certain ways? For example, what was the probability that the United States and the USSR, the only two superpowers after World War II, would become rivals? What was the probability of interaction between Thailand and Bolivia, small powers in different regions of the world that are separated by thousands of miles? Given the characteristics of the domestic environment (a country's size, wealth, form of government, and ethnic diversity), what is the probability of certain behavior? For example, what was the probability that Britain, Japan, or America would become a naval power? Or that the Swiss would follow a policy of neutrality? Given a terrible war drawing to a close, the impatience of a democratic electorate to end that war, and the existence of a new weapon that could hasten surrender, what is the probability that the weapon will be used?

To summarize, opportunity requires three related conditions: (1) an international environment that permits interaction between states, (2) states that possess adequate resources to be capable of certain kinds of actions, and (3) decisionmakers who are aware of both the range of interactions and the extent of capabilities available to them. Opportunity can be illustrated with a reference to Lewis Fry Richardson, one of the pioneers of the study of war and peace. Richardson, who was concerned with "deadly quarrels," drew a parallel between war and murder. Asking why people in one country tended to murder each other more often than they murdered foreigners, he drew the simple conclusion that they had much less opportunity to murder foreigners since they had far fewer contacts with them.[19] In fact, police records indicate that a person is most likely to be murdered by a close relative or a friend, presumably because constant contact and high levels of interaction provide the opportunity for murder. Similarly, Thailand and Bolivia are *unlikely* to fight each other because their range of interaction is too limited to allow a conflict to develop. Opportunity is the possibility of interaction because of objective conditions, which may be perceived in varying ways by different decisionmakers.

Willingness Willingness is a concept concerned with the motivations that lead people to avail themselves of opportunities. Willingness deals with the goals and motivations of decisionmakers and focuses on why they choose one course over another. Willingness is therefore based on perceptions of the global scene and domestic political conditions. It derives from calculations of the costs and benefits of alternative courses of action, based, not only on objective factors but also on perceptions (for instance, of threat) and emotions (for instance, fear, insecurity, or a desire for revenge). Willingness thus depends on *choice* and *perception*. People react according to what they think they can do and also according to what others expect them to do.

Decisionmakers behave on the basis of their perception of the world, which in fact may be very different from what the world is actually like. Such differences may be brought home in many ways when a decisionmaker attempts to implement a policy in the real world: in effect, if someone thinks a glass patio door is open when it is not, the consequences of operating on such a belief can be shattering. Neville Chamberlain, the British prime minister, believed that Adolf Hitler could be appeased and his aggression ended, and so gave in to him at Munich in 1938; the result was further Nazi expansion. History also provides us with the picture of Hitler some years later, isolated in his Berlin bunker, moving divisions on a map — lost divisions that were real only to him and that had no impact on the Red Army as it moved inexorably toward the German capital. One argument for dropping the atomic bomb stemmed from the perception that a demonstration of its power would restrain the Soviet Union from expansion.

Thus, when we study different environments or levels of analysis, we are also interested in how they affect the image of the world that decisionmakers hold. Willingness involves all the factors that affect how decisionmakers see the world, process information about what they see, and make choices.

It is important to understand that *both* opportunity and willingness are required for a given behavior to occur; they are *jointly necessary conditions*. Wishing for something to happen is not enough — the capabilities to act for its fulfillment must be available. Simply being able to do something does not mean it will happen unless you also have the will to take action. Successful deterrence, for example, requires both

---

[19] Lewis F. Richardson, *Statistics of Deadly Quarrels* (Chicago: Quadrangle Books, 1961), p. 288.

appropriate weapons — the opportunity — and the willingness to pay the political and military costs of using the weapons. The development of the atomic bomb made its use a possibility, but analysts since 1945 have been studying the willingness of state leaders to use it.[20]

The Menu

Opportunity, willingness, and the relationships between the decision-making entity and its environment can be summarized and brought together through the analogy of a **menu.** The person (entity or actor) who enters a restaurant is confronted by a gastronomical environment — the menu. The menu provides a number of behavioral opportunities, not determining the diner's choice but constraining what is possible (pizza, lasagna, and linguini are possible in an Italian restaurant, but chicken chow mein and matzo ball soup are not). The menu also affects the probability of the diner's choice through price, portion size, side dishes, specials, and the restaurant's reputation for certain foods. In the Italian restaurant whose menu proclaims that it has served pizza since 1910 and offers over fifty varieties at low prices today, a diner is most probably going to order a pizza. The restaurant, however, offers other selections as well, and the probabilities they will be ordered are affected by how the diner sees those choices. Though the restaurant may not be known for its lasagna, which may be extraordinarily expensive, lasagna is still a possibility. A patron who is Russian and unable to read English (and even may be unfamiliar with the Latin alphabet) may order the lasagna believing that he or she is ordering pizza. A patron who is rich and is obsessed with lasagna of any quality may also make this selection. Thus, knowing of a patron's resources and individual decision-making process in relation to the menu, as well as the diner's perception of the menu, permits us to analyze his or her restaurant behavior.

The key to understanding the menu analogy is to understand that the opportunities of international actors are constrained in various ways and that these constraints affect the willingness of decisionmakers to act. Constraints can be external or they can be internal. Most constraint in international relations is self-constraint. For more than two decades the academic writings of former U.S. Secretary of State Henry Kissinger have stressed the domestic and international constraints on the foreign policy decision-maker. The true diplomat, Kissinger has emphasized, understands these constraints and learns to work within them to achieve his or her desired aims.[21]

---

[20] The joint necessity of having both opportunity and willingness for some action to occur is formally developed by Claudio Cioffi-Revilla and Harvey Starr, "Opportunity, Willingness, and Political Uncertainty: Theoretical Foundations of Politics," *Journal of Theoretical Politics* 7 (1995): pp. 447–476.

[21] See, for example, Henry Kissinger, *Diplomacy* (New York: Simon & Schuster, 1994), as well as the most recent volume of Kissinger's memoirs, *Years of Renewal* (New York: Simon & Schuster, 1999).

Plan of the Book

Most of Part I will follow the levels-of-analysis presentation from the preceding pages. First, however, we give a brief overview, in Chapter 2, of how world politics can be studied; we stress a social scientific approach. Before moving on to discussions of the different levels of analysis, we discuss, in Chapter 3, the various actors on the world stage. We give much attention to the development of the contemporary nation-state system, nations, and nationalism, and consider how the nation-state compares with other international actors.

The following discussion will begin with the most comprehensive context or environment and work its way down to the most specific. Chapter 4 deals with the world system and how the global environment affects the behavior of international actors. Chapter 5 looks at relations among states and the ways states interact. Chapter 6 covers the domestic environment of states and the effects of societal and governmental factors on foreign policy and world politics. Finally, Chapter 7 explores the behavior of decisionmakers — people who are constrained by their roles and whose individual characteristics affect the way they perceive the world. Part I thus offers an understanding of the complex set of environments within which foreign policy decisionmakers work.

In Part II we focus on issues of international conflict and cooperation. Although people often think of the international arena as a realm of conflict, a remarkable amount of neutral or cooperative behavior also occurs there. We therefore examine not only the causes of conflict and war but also factors that contribute to cooperation and the willingness to address shared problems, including the activities of international organizations. In doing so we summarize the theory and research of many recent efforts. We also refer often to historical examples of cooperative and antagonistic behavior, trying to show how current behavior is conditioned by the past experience of world history and how decisionmakers interpret that experience.

It is impossible to fully grasp world politics without a basic understanding of its economic dimensions. In Part III we focus on such issues, which are referred to collectively as "international political economy." Matters involving international trade and finance, including the sorts of developments that set the stage for the Asian financial crisis described earlier in this chapter, fall under this rubric. The disparity in wealth between the global north and south, the emergence of regional economic blocs, and the economic aspects of national defense are other topics we discuss in this part of the book. (A full understanding of international political economy also requires a background in cooperation and conflict, such as that provided in Part II.) In Part IV we consider the ecological challenges confronting the human race and the global environment. Given these new challenges to global interdependence and order, we discuss alternative ways to manage such interdependence. Finally, we speculate about the future of world politics in the new century.

2

Thinking About World Politics: Theory and Reality

Realists, Liberals, and Radicals

World War I left leaders and ordinary people aghast. The balance of power — the relative equality of strength among all the contending major states and the shifting alliances to preserve equilibrium when one state threatened to become dangerous — had provided a very substantial degree of peace in Europe since the end of the Napoleonic Wars in 1815. That system then was violently upset by a war that lasted four years and left 9 million soldiers dead. Many, perhaps foremost among them U.S. president Woodrow Wilson, concluded that the balance-of-power system was fatally flawed and a new world order had to be constructed. These people became known as idealists because they had a vision, or ideal, of how a new and peaceful world order might be constructed. The idealists supported the formation of the League of Nations and other institutions of international law, hoping to build a system of collective security in which democratic nations would be especially peace-loving and in which all nations would band together to defeat unjust aggression. The events leading to World War II, however, disillusioned many of the idealists. Democracy was overthrown in

Germany, Italy, Spain, and elsewhere. The United States never joined the League. The United States and members of the League failed to band together against the fascists and Nazis until it was almost too late.

After World War II, people once again vowed that global wars must be prevented. Idealists supported the creation of a new organization — the United Nations (UN) — to replace the League of Nations. Once again they emphasized the benefits of collective security and the rule of international law, which limited countries' actions. This time the United States would join the international organization and the members, perhaps having learned a lesson, would cooperate. They continued to trust in democratic forms of government, which respected individual rights, and they hoped that the spread of democracy would lead to more peaceful relations among states. These people, many of them intellectual descendants of the idealists, are often called **liberals.** Their faith in human progress and social harmony was extended to the "society of states," an arena where institutions and other linkages between states could facilitate and promote cooperation, coordination, and nonviolent modes of conflict resolution. Those linkages may need to be strengthened, but, the liberals believe, they are already much more than some distant "ideal." This perspective on world politics also goes by other names, including *liberal internationalism, liberal institutionalism,* and *transnationalism.*[1]

Another perspective, however — the one held by **realists** — is more skeptical. Their insistence that the worst of World War II could have been avoided by earlier resistance to Hitler derived from a "realistic" understanding of conflict and power in international politics. According to realism — which has been the central approach to the study of international politics for several decades and perhaps even today — people are self-interested and selfish and seek to dominate others. They cannot be depended on to cooperate, and if they do cooperate, they will stop when it no longer serves their immediate interests. This is a conservative view of human relations, which the realists extended to relations between states. They do consider nation-states by far the most important actors in world politics, with international organizations like the United Nations only as important as their most powerful members wish them to be. States are assumed to be rational, unitary actors pursuing essentially the same goals of national interest, regardless of their form of government or type of economic organization. According to realists, a system of competing nation-states is basically an anarchic system; literally, a system without a government or ruling authority. States struggle with one another for power, must look out for their own interests, and ultimately depend upon "self-help"; they cannot appeal to some higher authority to ensure their national security. The realist view of international relations is also known as the *power politics perspective,* or *realpolitik.*[2]

---

[1] For an overview of the basic tenets of liberalism and how they flow from Wilsonian idealism, see Charles W. Kegley, Jr., "The Neoliberal Challenge to Realist Theories of World Politics: An Introduction," in Charles W. Kegley, ed., *Controversies in International Relations Theory: Realism and the Neoliberal Challenge* (New York: St. Martin's, 1995), pp. 1–24. This entire volume provides a useful presentation of the liberal challenge to the descriptive, explanatory, predictive, and prescriptive adequacies of the realist perspective.

[2] For early, and now truly classic, statements of realist thought, see Edward Hallett Carr, *The Twenty Years' Crisis, 1919–1939: An Introduction to the Study of International Relations* (London: Macmillan, 1939), and Hans J. Morgenthau, *Politics Among Nations: The Struggle for Power and Peace,* 2nd ed. (New York: Knopf, 1954).

The realist picture is in many ways an accurate description of the world in which we live. But anarchic does not necessarily mean disorderly. On the contrary, there is a great deal of order and predictability in the behavior of nation-states. Usually states do obey international law, not because they are particularly "good," but because it is in their interest to be law-abiding and to encourage others to obey the law as well. Nation-states work together in many ways, including in the peaceful conduct of trade and finance, the movement of people across national borders, the exchange of information, and medical cooperation. Without this cooperation, the substantial peace and prosperity we know would be completely impossible. Realism as an approach to international relations helps to explain why states fight or threaten each other, but it is less effective in explaining much of the cooperative behavior we see — the order within the anarchy. It sees any cooperation as stemming only from temporarily converging self-interests. More important, it says little about how more order can be created without imposing some dominating authority, either a world empire or at least one dominant country that can impose its will on others. It is that need to explain order and to seek greater order in a dangerously armed world that compels us to move beyond realism and to pay attention to actors other than nation-states (especially international organizations) and issues other than the pursuit of military power (such as trade, development, and environmental management).

Both realists and liberals possess important, but limited, truths about the world; each side has a powerful answer to excessive reliance on the other's argument. The world is a dangerous place; we cannot reshape it as we like; and being "good" will not necessarily make a nation safe. Yet moral principles provide goals toward which to strive and transnational linkages do moderate the excesses of power politics. Just as realism was a reaction to the idealist failure to control Nazi Germany, liberalism was a reaction to the dangers of overemphasizing power politics and the naked pursuit of self-interest in a world that includes not only weapons of mass destruction, but also abject poverty and injustice.

A third perspective that paints a coherent picture of how the world works should be distinguished from both realism and liberalism. **Radicals,** whose views often stem from Marxist thought, share with realists the convictions that people are motivated largely by self-interest and are ready to dominate others, and that those who would oppress must be resisted. Like realists, radicals consider states to be very important actors in world affairs, but they also emphasize the conflicting interests of social classes. Classes (capitalists, workers, peasants) clash for control of state policy within countries, and the government pursues not some overall national interest, but the interest of the dominant class or classes. States are not unitary actors. Classes exist within and across national boundaries; capitalists, for example, may cooperate internationally to maintain a political and economic environment that is hospitable to investment by multinational corporations. Where realists see anarchy, radicals see a hierarchy of classes and states in which the weak are subordinated to the strong. Like realists, they see individuals as acting from a kind of rationality, but one that is often distorted by false consciousness regarding their interests — by acceptance by the weak of perspectives and values propagated by the strong. Like liberals, radicals are dissatisfied with the global status quo and hope to transform world politics so as to make the system more equitable and just. Imperialism and wars, they believe, are caused by capitalists' attempts to maintain their power to exploit other classes, by their competition with capitalists in rival states, and by their efforts to dominate noncapitalist states that would challenge the system. To have general peace, capitalism must be abolished, or at least radically tamed. As with the other views, this one gets labeled in various ways: some refer to it as the *Marxist perspective,* or as *socialism* or *socialist internationalism.*

Full-blown Marxist radicalism is no longer very popular, chiefly because of the economic and political failures of communism and socialism. Radicals are generally not considered to have a credible model for the organization of society. Nevertheless, as a critique of the excesses of capitalism and power politics, radicalism still has something to say. Regardless of whether one accepts its basic philosophical premises, it provides an important antidote to complacency about contemporary world conditions.

These three perspectives offer different predictions and theoretical explanations about world politics. In each case, some of the beliefs are not easily confirmed or refuted by evidence. The perspectives lead their proponents to ask different questions, and they stress different levels of analysis in their explanations. Nevertheless, they often lead to contrasting explanations or predictions that can be tested and found to be more or less correct. At various points in this book we will contrast explanations or predictions derived from the three perspectives; at other points you may wish to try to construct and contrast such arguments.

Recent Challenges

It is fair to say that twentieth-century world politics — both theory and practice — have been dominated by the realist and liberal perspectives, each ascendant at different times. Radicalism has always presented a serious alternative view, however, one adopted by many prominent scholars and, of course, world leaders. Together these three perspectives constitute "mainstream" thinking about world politics. They are more than worldviews or even schools of thought, for they have also motivated the vast majority of theorizing and research on international relations. They are, in other words, the field's dominant *paradigms.*[3]

In recent years there have emerged new challenges to mainstream thinking in its various forms. These new perspectives do more than challenge the typical explanations of world politics offered by realism, liberalism, and radicalism to describe what states and other international actors do, and why they do it. They also reject the modes of theorizing and research that have become so widespread in universities, research institutes, and policy circles — that is, the field's dominant *epistemologies.* Some challenges, like "critical" international relations theory, do take some of their insights from mainstream theory (Marxism, in this case). Others, like postmodernism, are more alien

---

[3] Perhaps the most studied comparison of these three perspectives, and especially of their roots in political philosophy, is Michael W. Doyle, *Ways of War and Peace* (New York: Norton, 1997). Other useful overviews include K. J. Holsti, *The Dividing Discipline* (Boston: Allen & Unwin, 1985), and Paul R. Viotti and Mark V. Kauppi, *International Relations Theory: Realism, Pluralism, Globalism,* 3rd ed. (Boston: Allyn & Bacon, 1999). On the historical evolution of contemporary thinking about world politics, see Torbjörn L. Knutsen, *A History of International Relations Theory* (New York: Manchester University Press, 1992), esp. part 3.

to the field, adopting approaches developed outside the social sciences (especially the humanities). Still other challenges, like feminism, include some variants that are perfectly compatible with mainstream approaches to theory and research, and others that are less compatible.

We do no more than mention these perspectives at this point as they defy simple summary. They represent part of the field's "cutting edge." As with any literature, some contributions will surely endure the test of time; others may not. However, each perspective has generated key insights into world politics and the study of world politics, and we will draw upon them at times in this book.[4]

Social Scientific Study of World Politics

Just as there have always been different views about the current or desired nature of world politics, there have also been different views about how world politics should be studied. In the debates over the causes of the first and second world wars, the realists, with their insistence on the overwhelming importance of nation-states as actors, stressed the study of diplomatic history — the study of actions by national governments. The idealists attended primarily to the study and development of international law. Both approaches were highly descriptive, providing a detailed record of how states *actually* behave. They were also often prescriptive, setting forth ways in which states *should* behave, sometimes with legalistic or moral/ethical arguments.

Historical and legal approaches stressed the description of unique events and sought to explain them. Given the crucial world problems that appeared after 1945, many scholars and analysts felt that only a more systematic understanding would lead to solutions. Problems of war and peace took on new meanings with the advent of nuclear weapons. The interdependence and complexity of the world became greater as the Western colonial empires broke up, scores of new states were created, and political and economic hierarchies around the world were reordered. The traditional methods of explanation seemed inadequate.

The post–World War II intellectual reaction to these approaches was to seek instead to try to study international relations in a scientific manner, using procedures and methods borrowed from the physical sciences. Other disciplines of study, such as economics and psychology, had borrowed from the physical sciences, and the tactic seemed to be paying off in the accumulation of knowledge. The idea was to stress comparability rather than uniqueness — to look for recurring patterns and to understand

---

[4] A good overview of critical and postmodern international relations theory is Jim George, *Discourses of Global Politics: A Critical (Re)Introduction to International Relations* (Boulder, Colo.: Reinner, 1994); see also Pauline Rosenau, "Once Again into the Fray: International Relations Confronts the Humanities," *Millennium* 19 (1990): pp. 83–110. Feminist approaches to world politics are reviewed in V. Spike Peterson and Anne Sisson Runyan, *Global Gender Issues* (Boulder, Colo.: Westview, 1993); see also Craig N. Murphy, "Seeing Women, Recognizing Gender, Recasting International Relations," *International Organization* 50, 3 (Summer 1996): pp. 513–538.

particular events as emerging from these larger patterns or processes.[5] The new "social scientific" approach, then, assumed that knowledge could be acquired by investigating patterns of *social behavior* — which is why the social sciences are sometimes called the behavioral sciences — and that includes international behavior. These patterns may be investigated cross-nationally (that is, by comparisons of several states at a particular time) or longitudinally (that is, by comparisons of conditions in one or more states at several points in time). This approach to world politics assumes that over the long run, many historic parallels will transcend the specific times, places, and people involved.

In approaching the study of international relations in this way, stress was placed on finding and developing tools for organizing the intellectual complexity of the field: the development of concepts, frameworks, and theories. These tools represent the most basic elements of science. We have already noted that events, situations, or social phenomena *can* be compared. Although in many respects events and people have unique aspects that will never reoccur, all of them bear similarities to broader concepts or classes of events. To "think theoretically," we must always be ready to look at some phenomenon and ask, "Of what is this an instance?"[6]

Thus, in a very basic way, the social scientific method distinguishes the study of international relations or politics from the study of international history. Some critics, including some historians, believe that humanity is the least promising area for scientific study because social behavior and events — especially international events — are too complex and singular. Denying the existence of regularities would leave us to study only singular cases or to produce detailed descriptions, with no cumulation of knowledge for the scholar or policymaker. If every historical event is truly unique, and thus noncomparable, the gulf between the social scientist and the critic is indeed unbridgeable. Some scholars appear to hold this position; however, we don't believe it (and probably neither do they). Everyone has compared two events at some time. By comparing things, we admit the possibility of certain similarities across events. Using a single event to illustrate some more general phenomenon reveals the same agreement with the principle of comparison and the possibility of patterns. The most basic rationale for the study of social relations — that the past can be used as some sort of guide to the future — must also rest on the similarities of events and the existence of regularities: in short, on the possibility of comparison.

While science believes that things are comparable and that we should search for explanations that cover many cases, it is a false characterization of science (even the physical, or "hard," sciences) to believe that it promises general laws that explain everything and will predict exactly what will happen. All science is based on models,

---

[5] Thus many scholars feel that science, at its core, is about *comparison*. A good treatment of comparative social science is found in Charles C. Ragin, *The Comparative Method* (Berkeley: University of California Press, 1987).

[6] James N. Rosenau, "Thinking Theory Thoroughly," in James N. Rosenau, ed., *The Scientific Study of Foreign Policy*, rev. ed. (London: Frances Pinter, 1980), pp. 25–26. For an excellent discussion of the social scientific approach to the study of international relations, see Michael Nicholson, *Causes and Consequences in International Relations: A Conceptual Study* (London: Pinter, 1996). A useful general introduction to methods of social scientific research is Earl Babbie, *The Practice of Social Research*, 8th ed. (Belmont, Calif.: Wadsworth, 1998).

propositions, or laws that are contingent — that will hold only under certain conditions. As the world approximates such conditions, the probabilities that the events proposed by a model or theory will occur will vary. That the study of international relations does not now and may never look like physics, with its apparently "universal laws," does not mean that international relations cannot be scientific. As Rosenau warns us, "To think theoretically one must be tolerant of ambiguity, concerned with probabilities, and distrustful of absolutes." Using **probabilistic explanation** is what Jacob Bronowski called the "revolution" of thought in modern science: "replacing the concept of the inevitable effect with that of the probable trend. . . . History is neither determined nor random. At any moment it moves forward into an area whose general shape is known, but whose boundaries are uncertain in a calculable way."[7]

To understand world politics we need to have a high tolerance for uncertainty, the imperfect state of human knowledge, and the whys of human society and politics. The phenomena are extraordinarily complex, and we know far less than we would like. You will doubtless yearn at times for more certainty, more conviction, than the authors of this book can give about the causes and possible solutions of various problems. But knowing what it is that you don't know, why you don't know it, and what you might do to remedy your ignorance is a part of wisdom and maturity.

Theory and Evidence

A key element in science is the development of **theory.** Theory is an intellectual tool that provides us with a way to organize the complexity of the world and helps us to see how phenomena are interrelated. Theory simplifies reality, thus helping to separate the important from the trivial by pointing out what we really wish to look at and what is unimportant enough to ignore. Theories are sometimes called *models,* and they serve much the same purpose as the model airplanes used by aeronautical engineers in wind tunnels. In order to study the effects of different wing designs on the maneuverability of aircraft under conditions of air turbulence, engineers need not replicate every detail of real aircraft in their models; they can, for example, ignore the interior layout of the plane and the electrical and communication systems. Since they concentrate on one aspect of air travel — the maneuverability and structural integrity of an aircraft in flight — their theories and models simplify all of the aspects of air travel that are not relevant to this concern. No aeronautical engineer would suggest that these other aspects of air travel are unimportant, only that they are not relevant when studying wing designs. This is why theory is so central — it affects not only which answers we come up with, but also what questions we ask in the first place! What questions would a realist, liberal, or radical ask about the end of the cold war? We will see in the following discussion.

---

[7]Rosenau, "Thinking Theory Thoroughly," p. 28; Jacob Bronowski, *The Common Sense of Science* (London: Heinemann, 1951), pp. 86–87. See also Benjamin A. Most and Harvey Starr, *Inquiry, Logic and International Politics* (Columbia: University of South Carolina Press, 1989), chaps. 1, 5.

Theories, if they are to be evaluated scientifically, must be stated in a clear and precise way. A good theory is one that can be supported or rejected using information, or *data,* about the world. Obviously, we prefer that our theories are supported by the data, but a theory that cannot be tested at all — that cannot be disproved in any conceivable way — will not get us very far. Think, for example, of the proposition, "People always act to advance their own self-interest, no matter how much they delude themselves or others into thinking they are acting in someone else's interest." Since the proponent of such an argument can always support the argument ("The people in question are deluding themselves about their motives"), and since that statement cannot be checked against evidence (we cannot look inside a person's mind), the self-interest proposition cannot be disproved, or "falsified." It is not a scientific statement because any evidence can be interpreted as agreeing with it.

Where do theories come from? Some of the most sophisticated and elaborate theories are the result of painstaking study and deep familiarity with the subject matter. However, even these theories often start out as hunches about the way the world works. Theories come from all aspects of human experience, and many of the most successful scientists, such as Louis Pasteur or Thomas Edison, had a creative knack by which they could look at things differently and draw analogies where others could not.

Theories tell us what to look at and how the things we look at relate to each other. Because we can argue an opposite and plausible reason for almost every aspect of human interaction (for example, either "absence makes the heart grow fonder" or "out of sight, out of mind"), we need systematic **evidence** to test a theory. Science assumes that at least some of the patterns described by our theory can be observed and measured in some way. The evidence used must be objective. It must be collected in such ways as to be relevant to the question at hand and to avoid biasing the results. The procedures by which the evidence has been collected must be made *explicit.* Otherwise, it will be difficult to judge whether the analysis has been slanted or biased in some way, and consequently, the evidence will lack credibility. Science thus is a systematic way of obtaining information and making generalizations.

> Scientific observation is deliberate search, carried out with care and forethought, as contrasted with the casual and largely passive perceptions of everyday life. It is this deliberateness and control of the process of observation that is distinctive of science, not merely the use of special instruments.[8]

As some experienced social scientists point out, much of what we know about social phenomena is "ordinary knowledge," not derived from systematic scientific endeavors. Ordinary knowledge, or common sense as it is sometimes called, is "that on which people can agree at a particular time and place."[9] It might include the fact that

---

[8] Abraham Kaplan, *The Language of Inquiry* (San Francisco: Chandler, 1964), p. 126. Quoted, with further discussion, in Charles E. Lindblom and David K. Cohen, *Usable Knowledge: Social Science and Social Problem Solving* (New Haven, Conn.: Yale University Press, 1979), pp. 15–16.

[9] See Karl W. Deutsch, "The Limits of Common Sense," in Nelson W. Polsby, Robert A. Dentler, and Paul Smith, eds., *Politics and Social Life: An Introduction to Political Behavior* (Boston: Houghton Mifflin, 1963), pp. 51–58.

there are many countries in the world, that there is a war going on somewhere at virtually all times, and that very big states usually have larger armies than do very small states. However, we must also know when to doubt what passes as ordinary knowledge, when to question it, and how to supplant or supplement it by scientific knowledge when needed. Common sense can be untrue, as were the formerly held beliefs that the world is flat or that light is white. Common sense may be simply the result of changing intellectual fashions, as in the relationship between Isaac Newton's physics and previous knowledge or that between Einstein's physics and the earlier, Newtonian beliefs. Most important, as already pointed out, common sense is often contradictory. Social science should be directed at key points of inquiry where ordinary knowledge is suspect.

Hypotheses and Assumptions

Theoretical statements that relate to possible observations are called **hypotheses.** The testing of hypotheses — checking their predictions against the observed data — is a central activity of science. Hypotheses that are confirmed in virtually all the classes of phenomena to which they are applied are often known as *laws.* In the social sciences, interesting laws are quite rare. The phenomena of social science are so complex, with so many different influences or causes acting on a particular event, and our knowledge of these complex phenomena is still so imperfect that few laws have been established. As we have emphasized, even with much more theory and research, we are likely to have only *probability statements,* which assert that most phenomena of a given class will behave in a certain way most of the time. This is why social scientists find it hard to predict how particular events will develop; for example, which Soviet leader, at what specific point in time, would be willing to let the East European states go their independent ways. At best, the social scientist can indicate a probability that a particular action (a threat, a promise, a concession) will be followed by a specific result (armed conflict, capitulation, compromise).[10]

When we say that we hope to make general statements about phenomena in international relations, we do not necessarily mean generalizations that apply to all countries at all times. Such generalizations may be approximated in physics, but they are hard to make in political science. Even when states are widely observed to react to certain stimuli, like an increase in their rivals' military power, they may do so in any number of ways — by building their own military power, by joining an alliance, or by launching a preemptive strike, for example. In other words, one reaction may "substitute" for another, depending on the state's opportunities (whether military resources or powerful allies are available) and its willingness to act on those opportunities. In

---

[10] See John Lewis Gaddis, "International Relations Theory and the End of the Cold War," *International Security* 17 (Winter 1992/93): pp. 5–58; and James Lee Ray and Bruce Russett, "The Future as Arbiter of Theoretical Controversies: The Scientific Study of Politics and Predictions," *British Journal of Political Science* 26, 4 (1996): pp. 441–470. For a recent "real-time" prediction (made in April 1999) regarding the likely effects of NATO's air attacks on Serbia and Serb targets in Kosovo, see Jon C. Pevehouse and Joshua S. Goldstein, "Serbian Compliance or Defiance in Kosovo? Statistical Analysis and Real-Time Predictions," *Journal of Conflict Resolution* 43, 3 (August 1999): pp. 538–546.

different contexts, therefore, the same cause will have different effects. In May 1998, after India tested five nuclear bombs, there was virtual certainty that India's arch-rival, Pakistan, would react in some way, but it was not a foregone conclusion that it would react by detonating its own nuclear devices. Though in the end they were unsuccessful, many countries sought to convince Pakistan to pursue an alternative course of action, and one opportunity available to that nation in the aftermath of India's nuclear tests might have been to enhance its conventional military strength by acquiring advanced weapons from the United States. Theoretical statements that specify the set of contingencies that usually lead to one type of foreign policy response versus another have been called "nice laws."[11]

If statements have been supported by empirical study, it is also important that they identify the *process* or *causal relationship* that underlies the observed patterns. For example, the statement, "young drivers have more traffic accidents than do somewhat older drivers" is an empirically correct statement of fact — a correlation — but it tells us little of interest about causality, about *why* young drivers tend to crash their cars more often. Often it is very difficult to uncover the process of causation that underlies an observed correlation. In this example, is it because younger drivers are more reckless or less experienced? Or might it be because they drive older cars, with fewer safety features?

All theories include **assumptions.** In contrast to hypotheses, we do not systematically test assumptions against actual data. This is either because our assumptions are fairly straightforward statements about the world, with which many people agree, or because examining the accuracy of these statements must be deferred until later, at which time they can be treated as hypotheses to be tested. Assumptions simplify the task of theory building, and we sometimes make assumptions that we know are not correct or not fully correct. For example, we can assume that the speed of a falling body is not slowed by friction with the air. Sometimes this assumption is close enough to reality that it does do not affect our conclusions about the acceleration of objects of different weights. For example, the resistance encountered by iron and lead balls may be minimal when they are dropped from the Leaning Tower of Pisa. But if the assumptions were wildly incorrect for a particular set of problems, the results would be irrelevant at best, and disastrous at worst. What if we assumed that air resistance would make no difference in the speeds of a feather and a lead ball dropped from the tower? By following the precepts of scientific inquiry, a careful analyst will always be alert to the nature of his or her assumptions, to ways in which they may differ from reality, and to the conditions under which the difference may be significant. A careful analyst will want to know what has been simplified and have some sense of how that simplification may compromise his or her predictions.

We suggested earlier that the realists treat all nation-states as rational, unitary actors — that is, they *assume*, for purposes of building a realist theory of world politics, that states are rational and unitary entities. Of course, realists know that states consist of many societal groups, which may have an impact on the process of foreign policy making, and that the parties directly involved in policy making sometimes make

---

[11] See Most and Starr, *Inquiry, Logic and International Politics,* esp. chap. 5.

miscalculations and adopt what appear to be irrational strategies. However, for the realists, these details are unimportant when explaining and predicting state behavior; when all is said and done, states behave *as if* they were rational, unitary actors. Because most realists agree with this assessment, it is a common assumption in realist theories of world politics. Liberals and radicals are not generally willing to make such an assumption, so their explanations and predictions can look quite different.

Specifying and Testing Hypotheses

Social scientists often proceed in the following way:

1. Start with some behavior that needs to be explained.

2. Offer some tentative hypotheses, perhaps derived from some theory purporting to explain that behavior.

3. Evaluate the hypotheses in light of available evidence.

4. If the evidence supports the hypotheses, consider the implications — the additional statements (or predictions) that can be deduced from these confirmed hypotheses.

5. Treat these new statements as hypotheses and evaluate them in light of available evidence.[12]

Sometimes an analysis along these lines is referred to as a "thinking experiment." It is a purely analytical exercise, unlike clinical or laboratory experiments, in which one varies actual conditions to see what effect the changes have. With citizens and nations, we simply cannot conduct a real-life experiment. Nor are we able, in this chapter, to gather and document systematically a substantial body of rigorous empirical data on the case we will discuss. Instead, we shall proceed with a very tentative analysis, proposing hypotheses that would require much more research to confirm but that meanwhile may produce some intriguing suggestions. Still, this exercise highlights another hallmark of science — that propositions must confront evidence and should then be revised or abandoned on that basis. As Rosenau notes, to think theoretically one must be ready to be proven wrong.

Our example is Gorbachev's decision not to use Soviet troops to suppress the dissidents of East Germany in 1989 and thus save its Communist government. This was one of the most dramatic and important decisions that permitted an end to the cold war. The discussion illustrates some approaches to the great guessing game about the sources and stability of Soviet policy up to that point. Different hypotheses can be derived from the realist, liberal, and radical perspectives.

Hypothesis 1   Gorbachev did not use force to support the East German government because he feared a NATO military response, which might culminate in World War III.

---

[12] This basic procedure comes from R. E. Lipsey, *Introduction to Positive Economics* (New York: Harper & Row, 1963), as reported by Martin Hollis and Steve Smith, *Explaining and Understanding International Relations* (Oxford: Clarendon, 1990), chap. 3 See also Charles A. Lave and James G. March, *An Introduction to Models in the Social Sciences* (New York: Harper & Row, 1975), chap. 1.

A realist might say that the NATO allies could not have resisted the opportunity to gain a critical power advantage; in this case, to bring all East Germany under their control. A radical might say much the same thing but give as the reason the capitalist world's continuing wish to expand the realm of capitalism and to bring down the competing system of economic and political organization.

Evaluation   One problem with either version of this hypothesis is that the NATO countries had passed up similar opportunities in the past. When the Soviet Union crushed the Hungarian revolution in 1956 and the liberalization of Czechoslovakia, known as the Prague Spring, in 1968, the West did virtually nothing. NATO countries implicitly acknowledged that the Soviet Union had the right to do as it wished within Eastern Europe, which was its own sphere of influence, and that the risks involved in any NATO military response were much too great. There is little reason to think that in 1989 they would have judged the situation in East Germany differently.

Hypothesis 2   Gorbachev did not use force because he secretly held goals different from those of other Soviet leaders. Perhaps he really was a "closet democrat" who wanted noncommunist governments in East Germany and the rest of Eastern Europe (a liberal explanation), or perhaps he really was an agent of the U.S. Central Intelligence Agency (CIA) whose aim was to betray communism (a radical explanation).

Evaluation   There are virtually no facts to support either version of this hypothesis. Gorbachev acted much more like a reformer of communism, with no fully formed goal in mind, than like someone who wanted to do away with the communist system entirely. He came out of much the same set of party and government experiences as did other Soviet leaders and gave no hint of a desire to make a complete break with the past. As for deliberately betraying the system as a Western agent, that belief requires very great faith in the CIA. We find both versions of this hypothesis implausible.

Hypothesis 3   Gorbachev feared he could no longer make repression effective and that the effort to do so would only hasten the spread of revolution across Eastern Europe (a liberal hypothesis).

Evaluation   This hypothesis draws its strength from the increasing growth of transnational communications links that carried new information and ideas into and out of Eastern Europe. It implies the idea that people would rise up in support of those ideas and in support of one another, even in the face of terrible costs. Perhaps the Soviet people and Soviet troops would also have rebelled rather than permit wholesale repression. It is true that transnational linkages had grown substantially, yet comparatively recently, in Czechoslovakia in 1968, they had had little effect. While one cannot completely dismiss this hypothesis, it is implausible as a primary explanation.

Hypothesis 4   Gorbachev knew that the use of force would alienate the Western countries, on which he was relying for technological and military assistance to rebuild the Soviet economy. No Soviet leader with such a goal could afford to do something that would cut off the possibility of trade with the West (another liberal hypothesis).

Evaluation   This hypothesis also has some plausibility, but it does not fit all the facts well. Western responses to previous Soviet crackdowns on dissent had not been very strong. When, in December 1981 the Communist government of Poland violently repressed the Solidarity movement with Soviet approval and encouragement (but no Soviet troops), there was only a partial and ineffective Western trade embargo; the same was true in response to the Soviet military intervention in Afghanistan. Gorbachev might have thought that once again the West would accept the Soviet sphere of influence and not enforce severe economic sanctions.

Hypothesis 5   Gorbachev did not intervene because Eastern Europe had become not an asset but was rather a serious drain on Soviet resources; he thought that the national interest of the Soviet Union would be better served economically and politically by letting the satellites go (a realist hypothesis).

Evaluation   There is a lot of evidence that Eastern Europe had long been an economic drain, receiving many hidden subsidies, such as cheap Soviet oil, for barter rather than having to purchase them at world market prices for dollars. On the one hand, such considerations had earlier had little effect; on the other hand, we now know that the Soviet economy was in far worse shape than suspected by most analysts. More important for the evaluation of theory, national-interest explanations can too easily be created after an event. Almost anything can be described as being in the national interest, but the national interest is not something self-evident, on which all objective observers would agree.

Hypothesis 6   Gorbachev did not intervene because the Soviet Union no longer needed the political and military buffer that Eastern Europe had provided. Gorbachev no longer, if he ever had, feared a NATO attack (another realist hypothesis).

Evaluation   Gorbachev might finally have decided that the West did not wish to attack his country. But it is not clear why Western intentions should have so recently — in the years of tough rhetoric from the Reagan administration about the Soviet "evil empire" — come to seem more benign, or why Gorbachev in particular should have reached that conclusion. Evidence for the realist view may be found in the growing Soviet and American realization that in a world of nuclear parity, nuclear weapons could not be used credibly for anything but the defense of one's homeland, and certainly not to coerce another superpower. Thus, as long as the Soviet Union retained a rough nuclear parity with the United States, it could protect itself without allies or the kind of in-depth defense that a shield of reluctant East European satellites might provide. After 1986 Gorbachev abandoned most of his previous rhetoric in favor of totally eliminating nuclear weapons from the world, and he may have come to see them as even more necessary than the satellites.

New Propositions and Possible Tests   We did not totally reject any of the hypotheses, although the first two seem least compelling. Even the last two, which are probably the strongest, are expressed in ambiguous terms and cannot be confidently either accepted or rejected. The important part of the exercise, however, is not to make a definitive choice among them but to confront various hypotheses and consider the kind of logic and evidence that would make one more plausible than another. Each hypothesis stresses different variables, and even different levels of analysis. For example, the individuality of Gorbachev is stressed in hypothesis 2 (a micro explanation based on understanding how a particular individual views the world). Hypothesis 5 emphasizes economic conditions within formerly communist-ruled areas, and hypothesis 6 focuses on superpower military relations in an international system with bipolar nuclear capabilities (these are both macro explanations based on factors from the global political environment). Making the hypotheses more precise, with sharper definitions of economic burdens or the nuclear balance, would make it clearer how — and whether — they could be tested by confronting systematic evidence from the real world.

They might be tested in several ways. One would be to look more systematically at the several times during the cold war era in which Soviet leaders had to decide whether to use military force to suppress a rebellion. This would have to include not only instances when the Soviet government did use force, but also instances when it did not (for example, when Yugoslav president Tito took his country out of the Soviet orbit in 1948). One could compare the different objective conditions, and also the different public statements and reasons given for Soviet actions. Public statements may not, however, give real reasons; ultimately, new scholarly access to Soviet government archives may give us a better, but still imperfect, measure of the real reasons. Better still would be to treat the hypotheses as general statements about all major military powers and alliance leaders, and not just the Soviet Union, to see how widely they apply. Alternatively, one could look at analyses of the peaceful breakup of the Soviet Union itself for additional evidence (or even hypotheses).

Facts and Values

Science can help us in understanding the world. Every day political decisionmakers take actions that affect the lives and happiness of millions of people, but they do not always know what the effects of their acts will be, nor do their advisers. While recognizing that action is necessary, we must retain a sense of humility about the knowledge base of our actions. Similar self-consciousness is needed for statements of value. We make such statements all the time: one painting is more beautiful than another; one act is morally right, and another wrong. We all make these judgments, with varying degrees of confidence, and we often disagree about them. The systems of thought by which we deduce statements about goodness and beauty may start from very different premises. A Buddhist, a Sunni Muslim, an evangelical Christian, and an atheistic Marxist may well agree that certain elements of life, such as decent living conditions and essential liberties, constitute, in some sense, "basic human rights." However, they will differ in how they arrive at that common conclusion, about the specific forms those rights should take, and about the relative importance of each.

Rosenau warns us, "To think theoretically one has to be clear as to whether one aspires to empirical theory or value theory."[13] In adopting a social scientific approach to the study of world politics, one decides to concentrate on empirical theory — constructing and evaluating models of what international actors do, how they do it, and why. The rightness or wrongness of what they do, the justice or injustice of the outcomes, are the concerns of value, or *normative,* theory. Of course, matters of right and wrong do affect the choices that leaders make and even the menu of alternatives from which they choose. In that sense values are an important element of many empirical theories in international relations. However, when, as students of world politics, we attempt to judge right and wrong in world politics, we have entered the realm of normative theory. Religion, ethical systems, and other elements of culture, as well as economic conditions, influence people's values and ethical judgments. The methods of social science can establish the impact of different sets of values on actual behavior, but they cannot determine the superiority of one set of values over another.

Most, but not all, research in contemporary international relations has been guided by empirical theory, but this has not always been the case. Normative theory has a long and distinguished pedigree in political philosophy, and some of the issues we discuss in this book — the ethics of war, human rights, global poverty — are, first and foremost, matters of international justice.[14] Knowing the empirical "facts" about these issues, such as which sets of values are reflected in which states' foreign policies, is important, but that knowledge can, and should, be used to inform one's normative judgments.

The line between empirical and normative theory can indeed be a fine one. Many of the individuals who are most committed to an objective, scientific approach to world politics have strong ethical views about the subject they study. In conducting our research, we may be relatively successful in not allowing our ethics to cloud the collection of data and the evaluation of our hypotheses. But, as we have seen, our values can be reflected in the very questions we ask about world politics. There is nothing inherently wrong with this; indeed, it is what attracts many people to the study of world politics in the first place. It is wrong, however, to pretend that a social scientific approach is completely value free. Critical, postmodern, and some feminist theories start with this realization about the study of world politics and go on to explore the implications of asking some questions and not others, of gathering some types of evidence and not others, and of evaluating that evidence in some ways and not others. In examining such previously unexamined issues, they hope to shed new light on the incompleteness — or worse, the bias — of our current understanding of world politics.

---

[13] Rosenau, "Thinking Theory Thoroughly," p. 22.

[14] An excellent introduction to contemporary normative theory in international relations, including its philosophical foundations, is Chris Brown, *International Relations Theory: New Normative Approaches* (New York: Columbia University Press, 1992). See also Terry Nardin and David R. Mapel, eds., *Traditions of International Ethics* (Cambridge: Cambridge University Press, 1992).

The Study and Practice of World Politics

We can analyze a decision or event from the perspectives of different approaches to world politics and at various levels of analysis. In the next chapters we focus on characteristics of the global system (Chapter 4) and the relations between nation-states (Chapter 5). We emphasize the large-scale, highly aggregated units of analysis, working with theories that hold that the most important, persistent influences on war and economic distribution are found at the highest levels. This kind of analysis is part of the grand sociological tradition shared, in different ways and with different theoretical details, by writers such as Émile Durkheim and Karl Marx. The case for this perspective is well argued by Nazli Choucri and Robert North in their analysis of the conditions that brought about World War I:

> The dynamics of national growth and expansion, the conflict of national interests, patterns of growth in military expenditures, alliance-formation, and violence-behavior . . . were not the immediate cause of WWI. The processes set the stage, armed the players, and deployed the forces, but they did not join the antagonists in combat. They created the conditions of an armed camp within which the assassination of the Austrian archduke was sufficient to trigger an international crisis and a major war.[15]

Even if the particular crisis of August 1914 had been resolved by wiser decision-makers, from this perspective the underlying international dynamics of national expansion were certain to create further crises, and one or another of them was very likely to escalate out of control. Thus, it is important to understand the great forces that regularly produce situations fraught with the threat of war rather than to study the behavior of decisionmakers alone. Although individuals may be able to extricate themselves from one crisis, they cannot be expected to do so repeatedly in an environment where basic systemic forces continually produce such situations.

A social scientist works at a level of analysis different from that of a policymaker faced with immediate decisions. This difference can be illustrated by comparing the situations of a medical researcher and a practicing physician both concerned with coronary illness. Research scientists have established that a number of personal characteristics and environmental conditions contribute to heart disease. They now know that an individual's probability of suffering a heart attack is greater if that person is male and middle-aged or older and if one or both parents suffered heart attacks. Factors that increase the likelihood of heart disease include being overweight, smoking, consuming a diet high in cholesterol-rich fats, and not getting enough exercise. High blood

---

[15] Nazli Choucri and Robert North, *Nations in Conflict: National Growth and International Violence* (San Francisco: Freeman, 1975), p. 9. In contemporary international relations theory, this macro perspective is most often associated with the work of Kenneth N. Waltz. See his *Man, the State and War: A Theoretical Analysis* (New York: Columbia University Press, 1954) and *Theory of International Politics* (Boston: Addison-Wesley, 1979).

pressure also contributes to this likelihood, as do stress and anxiety in the working or living environment. Finally, some people with aggressive, hard-driving personalities appear especially prone to heart disease. For the scientist, all these influences may seem interesting, and provide information that may, at some point, prove important.

For the physician who must treat patients, however, different influences are not of equal interest. Some are beyond the control of the individual patient or doctor: the patient cannot stop growing older, is unlikely to change gender, and cannot change biological parents. A patient, to some degree, may be able to change a lifestyle or even quit a stressful job, but most people cannot do much about their basic personality. A doctor may actually increase the danger of a heart attack by frightening an already worried or anxious patient.

Other influences, however, can be more readily controlled. High blood pressure or high cholesterol, for instance, can be reduced by medication. A patient can be told to lose weight, stop smoking, change diet, or get more exercise. Controlling just one of these conditions may be enough, especially if two contributing influences interact (if, for example, smoking and obesity together pose a much greater danger than either one alone). In a particular patient, heart disease may be "overdetermined"; that is, *any one* of the several contributing conditions is sufficient to produce a high risk of disease, and therefore all must be eliminated. Here, very careful theory, as well as detailed understanding of a particular case, are essential for responsible treatment. Patients who refuse to take any steps to reduce their risks can at least be advised to keep their life insurance paid up — prediction is of some value, even without control over the medical events! Finally, some ethical considerations may also apply. Suppose a patient also suffers from a painful and terminal cancer. Should that patient be saved from a heart attack only to be faced with a difficult death from cancer shortly thereafter? Neither the doctor nor the patient can be indifferent to such a question, whatever their answers.

In our concern with world politics, we must take into account many considerations similar to those facing the physician.[16] At times the student of world politics proceeds chiefly with the kind of concern typical of scientists; at times, with that typical of policymakers, policy advisers, or citizen activists. A social scientist wants to understand the causes of a particular outcome. Since both the causes and the outcome vary (they are "variables"), we hope to find those causes (or "independent variables") that make the greatest difference in bringing about that outcome (the "dependent variable"). In other words, certain causes may account for most of the variation in the outcome; these causes, therefore, should figure most prominently in our theory. The social scientist may not be immediately concerned with whether those causes identified as most important are readily manipulable by policymakers. If pure knowledge is what interests us, then, in principle, there should be no reason for preferring an explanation that highlights one set of independent variables over another. Of course, since any scientific endeavor is driven partly by normative concerns, the social scientist will care about finding practical ways to make a difference (say, in promoting peace or justice). But the social scientist is not necessarily looking to put acquired knowledge to immediate use.

---

[16] Johan Galtung has also argued the parallels with medical science. See his "Twenty-five Years of Peace Research: Ten Challenges and Some Responses," *Journal of Peace Research* 22 (1985): pp. 141–158.

The policymaker, by contrast, is centrally concerned with putting information to use, especially with an eye toward changing outcomes from what they might otherwise be. To *change* outcomes, the policymaker must identify not just important, but also manipulable, variables. Explanations that identify causes that are controllable are more useful to policymakers than those that identify broad historical forces over which policymakers have little control. They are likely to be much more interested in explanations about how a crisis can be resolved short of war than in knowing about forces that brought about the crisis. While "knowledge for knowledge's sake" drives social science research, the fruits of that research are not always useful or popular among foreign policymakers.

Suppose we showed that states with large, unwieldy bureaucracies are more prone to making war, or that great powers with system-wide interests are more likely to be involved in world-endangering crises. Would a policymaker for such a government want to reduce the power of the state bureaucracy, or fundamentally alter the state's alliances and other international relationships, even if the necessary steps could be identified? An explanation of how decisionmakers perceive and act under crisis conditions may seem more interesting. The decisionmaker may, in fact, have little control over the external environment but may believe that it is possible to exert substantial influence over the decision-making process that operates in times of crisis in order to improve it.

Most people who deal in world politics — theorists, researchers, and practitioners — share elements of the perspectives we have characterized as those of scientists versus policymakers. They want to understand and to effect change. In the long run, even what appear as givens in world politics are subject to change: great powers rise and fall; entrenched systems decay. Sometimes all it takes is a nudge by citizens who care enough. Occasionally, change is spontaneous and far-reaching, as happened when democratic revolution spread throughout Eastern Europe and helped bring about the collapse of the cold war system. More often, perhaps, change is slow and arduous, like the process initiated by Europeans who, in the decades after World War II, promoted economic and political integration through the creation of organizations like the European Coal and Steel Community, which led to the present-day European Union and a fundamental transformation of European politics.

In this book we attempt to offer some understanding of world political phenomena without necessarily providing readily manipulable levers to solve problems. We shall address basic questions about war, peace, development, governance, and justice, which will be around for many decades and will require concerted, long-term effort. We shall look at explanations of why wars occur, how crises can be managed to peaceful conclusions, and why crises arise at all. We shall look at arms races, and why they can escalate or be restrained; at problems of economic and political interdependence among the rich industrialized countries of the world; and at how inflation or depression can spread and constrain national governments. We shall look at relations between rich and poor countries; from one perspective, they are seen as questions of access to resources and of promoting growth in national income, and from another, as questions of dependence, national autonomy, and internal distribution of economic and political rewards. We shall also look at problems of global resource availability and distribution, population pressures, pollution, and alleged limits to growth. And all these questions will be considered in light of the global growth of democracy and its effects on both military and economic relations.

Some of these problems would have been discussed in a textbook written twenty or thirty years ago; others are quite new. Part of the change may be attributed to very important changes in empirical reality in the world around us. Global pollution, for example, certainly is perceived as far more threatening now than it was a few decades ago. Yet pollution has been carried across international borders for centuries, like the industrial pollutants swept down the Rhine River, without being considered a major political issue. Small countries have always been dependent on big ones, but theories about the causes and consequences of that dependence have become widely adopted only with the great increase in the number of politically sovereign states during recent decades. The Soviet Union is gone, and with it the cold war, which had dominated international politics since 1945. However, major powers or empires have come and gone throughout world history. One might argue that democracy has been on the menu of the international system since 1776, but only now, for the first time, could a near-majority of state actors in the system be called democracies.

Thus, facts change, values change, problems change, and theories change. At a very basic level, we shall try to teach you *how to think* about world politics. This will aid your understanding of particular contemporary problems. But it will also give you a set of analytical tools to apply to new problems many years from now. Then you will have to search for your own manipulable levers — levers appropriate to your circumstances, your political resources, your understanding, and your values.

3

International Actors: States and Other Players on the World Stage

Humans in Groups: Nationalism and the Nation

Now that we have provided some basic conceptions of world politics and how the subject is studied, one further preliminary issue must be discussed: Exactly what sorts of groups of people are we concerned with — whose behavior interests us? We must start our discussion of the actors on the world stage at the most basic level. World politics begins with the idea of *relations,* which are activities between social entities. Thus, we must start with the notion of humans forming *groups.*

Perhaps one of the things that makes us human is our need to affiliate into groups. Aristotle observed that people are social animals, a view supported by such disciplines as anthropology and sociology (and also ethology, the study of animal behavior). Because our evolutionary heritage provides us with the genetic material most open to the forces and influences of the environment, we also require a *social environment* for the brain to develop and for potential skills like speech and written communication to be realized. Human beings as animals — as physical and physiological creatures — appear to require society and throughout their existence have formed groups.

The comfort, security, and other advantages that a group provides for its members are central to the study of sociology and psychology. Given the limitations of the human animal, people must form groups to meet physiological and psychological wants and needs. Thus, along with the idea of the group goes the idea of identification. Individuals will identify with groups, give their loyalty to them, and act to maintain their character, security, and survival; the group identity gives individuals a basic sense of "belongingness" and self-esteem. We can say that a group of individuals has developed a group identification and a group loyalty when a certain amount of "we-feeling" exists — when members feel more like "we" than like some other "they."[1]

The group is defined and held together by complex nets of *social communications* among people. Barriers to social communication (because of distance, language, or different belief systems about how the world works, based on such things as religion, ideology, or different historical experiences) help create differentiated groups of people. The more easily social communication flows, the greater the probability that such feelings of "we-ness" and identity will develop. These notions of social communication and the development of we-feeling and loyalty underlie group identification from the smallest social organization to the nation-state.[2] When people identify with groups, they become cut off from people not in those groups. Much of what occurs in world politics boils down to this separation of "we" and "they." *They* are different; therefore, they are not normal, are inferior in some way, and so on. *They* always want something that we have. Can *they* be trusted? What do *they* really want?

In discussing the nation-state, we start with the idea of a **nation,** a people who feel themselves part of some large identity group. Ernest Renan, the nineteenth-century French philosopher, captured the essence of a nation when he wrote:

> A nation is a soul, a spiritual principle. Two things, which in truth are but one, constitute this soul or spiritual principle. One lies in the past, one in the present. One is the possession in common of a rich legacy of memories; the other is present-day consent, the desire to live together, the will to perpetuate the value of the heritage that one has received in an undivided form.[3]

Nationalism refers to the complex set of psychological, cultural, and social forces that drive the formation of a nation. The development of the concept and reality of the state is similarly complex. Historically, as we shall see, state building occurred in Europe over a period of several hundred years before 1648, when the Treaty of Westphalia was signed to end the Thirty Years' War. Kings and princes extended their central authority

---

[1] For the psychological role that group identity plays for humans (e.g., "belongingness") see Harold Isaacs, *Idols of the Tribe: Group Identity and Political Change* (New York: Harper & Row, 1975), pp. 32–33.

[2] These ideas were developed in Karl Deutsch's classic work, *Nationalism and Social Communication* (Cambridge, Mass.: MIT Press, 1953).

[3] Ernest Renan, "What Is a Nation?," translated by Martin Thom, in Homi K. Bhabha, ed., *Nation and Narration* (London: Routledge, 1990), p. 19.

over territories that had formerly been a disconnected hodgepodge of feudal fiefdoms. Centralization and consolidation continued throughout Europe until World War I. Each group that identified itself as a people sought representation through the **state** — a legal entity consisting of a government that manages the affairs of a population in a given territory. That is, peoples who identified themselves as nations sought their own states, resulting in what we now call **nation-states.** Although *nation, state,* and *nation-state* do have specific meanings, the three terms are often used interchangeably.

State building can take the form of unification; for example, neither Italy nor Germany was finally united into a nation-state until the latter half of the nineteenth century, when war and diplomatic maneuvering were used to forge single units out of many smaller states. Other European nationalities sought to establish their own states by separating themselves from the larger empires that dominated much of Europe until World War I. These imperial entities included the Turkish Ottoman Empire, which had begun its spread westward into Eastern and Central Europe in the early 1300s and then retreated only slowly after its defeat before the gates of Vienna in 1683. The Austro-Hungarian Empire was the descendant of the Austrian Empire, and before that, the Holy Roman Empire of the Hapsburgs. Under Charles V, Holy Roman Emperor from 1519 to 1558, the Hapsburg territories dominated the Continent. When his Hapsburg inheritances were combined with the areas under nominal control of the Empire, Charles's dominions included what is now Spain (and its New World possessions at that time), the Netherlands, Belgium, most of Italy, Austria, and many of the states of Central Europe. A third multiethnic, or multinational, grouping was the Russian Empire. Turkish rule in Europe was ended with the two Balkan wars of 1912–1913. The process by which nations separated from larger entities to form their own states culminated, in the aftermath of World War I, with the dissolution of all three of the empires already noted, as well as of Imperial Germany.

The desire of national groups to separate from larger empires and form their own states was the dominant process reflecting nationalism until the end of World War II. Nationalistic separatism has vigorously reemerged over the past decade or so as a crucial issue in world politics, as modern-day "empires" such as the Soviet Union, or multiethnic states such as Yugoslavia, have similarly disintegrated. Other groups with national consciousness but without states, such as the Kurds and the Palestinians, have had important effects on world politics.

It is crucial to note that this process may work in reverse. As we have seen in the post–World War II period of decolonization, it is possible for states to govern populations that do not possess single national identities — these are states without nations. This condition is found in areas outside Europe, and especially in Africa, where territorial boundaries were artificially drawn by Western colonial authorities. Thus, in states such as Nigeria or India, the process then becomes one of creating a nation — a we-feeling — to match the already existing state.

So far nationalism has been discussed primarily in terms of we-feeling — a condition of mind, a feeling of identification or loyalty to some group of people. This is probably the crucial factor — that people *feel* themselves to be American or German or Canadian or Bulgarian or Cuban. What produces the we-feeling? A number of factors have been identified. One is regionalism, sharing a common territory. People living and interacting in the same area, facing similar problems and challenges, often develop a common feeling and identity. Closely related to regionalism is the effect of common economic activities, of relying on the same resources, engaging in the same types of activities, and having common sets of economic interactions. All these provide people with a similar view of the world and common interests.

Obviously, when we speak of groups as large as nations, direct face-to-face interaction occurs only among small subgroups of individuals. Common experiences in the absence of direct interaction often do not extend much farther. What can account for the development of these larger national identities, or what one scholar has called "imagined communities"?[4] A second set of factors is related to cultural similarity. A common language is an extremely important aspect of nationalism. Indeed, in attempting to increase national cohesion, political leaders have reinstituted languages that were dead or had been used only infrequently. The resurrection of the Welsh language by nationalists in Wales is at best only a partially successful attempt to use a language to reinforce or create nationalistic feelings, whereas the use of Hebrew in Israel has been quite successful in drawing together a diverse people. Other common cultural factors that have proven particularly powerful in today's world are a common ethnic background and a common religion. Last, and maybe most important, is the existence of a set of historical experiences and backgrounds perceived as a common history. What Ernest Renan observed over a century ago about the importance of "a rich legacy of memories" is still highlighted by contemporary students of nationalism.[5]

Nationalism involves loyalty to a group — an imagined community — and, as we can see, contemporary world politics is witnessing a growth of loyalties to nonstate groups based on communal ties of various kinds. It is increasingly clear that "maps which show the world neatly divided into countries, each with its own boundaries and territory, convey a misleading image of people's political identities."[6] The rise of religious fundamentalism is one example of the forces of fragmentation confronting the nation-state today. For example, an individual may identify first as a Shiite, then as a Muslim, and then as an Iraqi, in a loyalty chain that finds the state last on the list. One observer sees fragmentation as a major force in world politics that will increase the number of independent actors and shrink the size of many existing states.[7] For example, having expanded from a small area around Kiev in the ninth century, "Russia" first became the Russian Empire and then expanded further into the USSR; now, it is again Russia (but with only about half the population and three-quarters of the land area of the Soviet Union).

---

[4] See Benedict Anderson, *Imagined Communities: Reflections on the Origin and Spread of Nationalism*, 2nd ed. (London: Verso, 1991).

[5] Two good collections of readings on nationalism are John Hutchinson and Anthony D. Smith, eds., *Nationalism* (Oxford: Oxford University Press, 1994); and Geoff Eley and Ronald Grigor Suny, eds., *Becoming National* (New York: Oxford University Press, 1996).

[6] Ted Robert Gurr and Barbara Harff, *Ethnic Conflict in World Politics* (Boulder, Colo.: Westview, 1994), p. 1.

[7] See James N. Rosenau, *Turbulence in World Politics: A Theory of Change and Continuity* (Princeton, N.J.: Princeton University Press, 1990).

The State as International Actor

Despite a number of trends to the contrary, the state (or the nation-state) has been, and remains, the primary actor in the global system. The number of states in the system has risen steadily since the end of World War II. In the twenty years from 1973 to 1993, the number of states in the international system grew by a full one-third. Another indicator is the growth in the membership of the UN: in 1945 there were 51 charter members of the UN; in 1994 the admission of Palau capped a burst of new members (28 from 1990 to 1994), increasing the membership to 185. Of the 28 members joining after 1990, a full two-thirds were the result of the drive for separatism, especially the fragmentation of formerly communist systems. Six other new members were microstates such as Andorra, which had long been part of the international system (to be discussed later). The addition of 134 new members since the UN's establishment illustrates the continuing desire of groups to achieve statehood in the contemporary system, no matter their size or previous status.

The Modern State System

There have been large-scale political organizations for 7,000 years, starting with the city-states and empires of the Tigris and Euphrates and the Nile. However, the state, or nation-state, in its present form is relatively new. While many scholars date the modern nation-state from 1648 and the Treaty of Westphalia, the state as it existed in the seventeenth century was the result of a convergence of processes that had been occurring for over 500 years before Westphalia. The 200 years from about 1450 to 1650 mark the transition from one historical epoch to another, when the combination and interaction of political, economic, technological, and religious factors were decisive in bringing about the shift to the **modern state system.**[8]

For hundreds of years before this transition period, Europe consisted of a complex system of feudal entities. With the disintegration of the Roman Empire during the fifth century, the Germanic tribes that overran Roman settlements in western Europe remained organized on only the most local level, cutting their political or economic ties to the Mediterranean region. The Frankish empire of Charlemagne, established in 800, began to create the outlines of what we now know as Europe, but it, too, was overrun by barbarians from the East. Even after the fall of Rome, the Church maintained a presence and spiritual authority across Europe, and both waves of invaders were assimilated into Christianity. By the eleventh century, a system composed of large numbers of local political entities was in place, based on the feudal relationships between lord and vassal and involving little interaction with other parts of the world. At the geographic and political center of the European system was the successor to Charlemagne's empire, the Holy Roman Empire.

---

[8] See Geoffrey Barraclough, *An Introduction to Contemporary History* (New York: Penguin, 1964), for an introduction to these ideas of transition and interaction. Barraclough also reminds us to look for the differences and discontinuities in history.

The leaders of these various feudal entities, and their subjects, were enmeshed in a web of multiple loyalties. The various levels and ranks of nobility were both lords and vassals, receiving fealty (loyalty or obedience) from those below them and giving fealty to those above them. In principle such loyalty culminated in two figures: the Holy Roman Emperor, in regard to secular authority and leadership, and the pope, in regard to spiritual authority and leadership. Thus, in stark contrast to the state system that was to develop, the principle of authority was *hierarchical*. At the same time, actual authority was diffuse: the ability of those at the top of the hierarchy to exercise their authority over large territories was in fact limited.

European politics during this time was more about the interaction of nobles and princes than it was about dynastic relations among European monarchs, or about relations between the monarchs and the Holy Roman Emperor or the pope. But what would characterize the fifteenth and sixteenth centuries was the gradual growth of monarchical power and influence. Scholars studying the rise of the nation-state in western Europe focus on two central elements: capital and coercion.[9] As monarchs struggled against the feudal nobility in their efforts to expand, centralize, and consolidate their control over large swaths of territory, they needed economic and especially military resources. Certain factors provided the opportunities that enabled kings to engage in this process, and ultimately to succeed against the nobles.

One key factor was economic. Manufacturing, trade, and communication had become increasingly concentrated, resulting in the growth of cities and towns. Eventually, a money economy developed to replace the system of barter that characterized feudal exchange, and a merchant class began to emerge. Each town or city came to represent a larger regional economy, encompassing the surrounding areas of agriculture. The merchant class, whose newfound wealth derived from its commercial activities, desired continued growth and expansion of these regional economies, including greater trade with the agricultural areas and with other towns and cities. This expansion required security and order: an authority to provide for roads and communication and otherwise reduce barriers to economic expansion.

Here is where the interests of the merchant class and the monarchy coincided. If the kings were to effectively challenge the military power of the nobility, they needed to raise their own mass armies. To do so, they needed to extract resources from the prosperous urban areas, drawing especially on the wealth of the commercial classes. Merchants, bankers, and others benefiting from economic expansion could, for their part, enjoy the order and stability that came with the establishment of a single political authority in their territory.

To raise and support armies, monarchs needed bureaucrats. Elaborate bureaucracies evolved in order to extract resources, in the form of taxes, and to administer military camps and hospitals. Raising mass armies was a substantial undertaking; only

---

[9] See Charles Tilly, "Reflections on the History of European State-Making," in Charles Tilly, ed., *The Formation of National States in Western Europe* (Princeton, N.J.: Princeton University Press, 1975), pp. 3–83; as well as his *Coercion, Capital and European States, A.D. 990–1990* (Oxford: Blackwell, 1990); William H. McNeill, *The Pursuit of Power* (Chicago: University of Chicago Press, 1982); Michael Mann, *States, War, and Capitalism* (Oxford: Blackwell, 1988); and Perry Anderson, *Lineages of the Absolutist State* (London: Verso, 1979).

monarchs had at their disposal the necessary resources (and the ability to extract them). The nobility continued to rely on much smaller, mainly mercenary, forces led by warriors drawn from the aristocratic classes. Technological factors were also crucial. Advances in military technology, especially gunpowder and the cannon, made it possible for individuals with enough resources to overcome the castle strongholds of knights and other nobility. As victory brought more territory under monarchical control, that territory in turn needed to be administered by increasingly larger bureaucracies. We can see in this expansion of bureaucracy the origins of the formal administrative institutions that have come to characterize the modern state. The process was summarized well by Charles Tilly: "The state makes war, and war makes the state."[10]

The interrelationships among the commercial class, monarchs, and the bureaucracy in Europe promoted the rapid development and use of the military technology that also made possible European expansion to the rest of the globe. In fact, Paul Kennedy attributes the "European miracle," or the rise of Europe rather than areas seemingly more advanced, to the interaction of all these factors. The continual wars and rivalries between kings and nobles, and then among kings, pushed each to find some advantage in arms or wealth and led to rapid technological and scientific innovations (in areas such as weaponry, transportation, navigation, and cartography), as well as innovations in commerce, finance, administration, and bureaucratic structure. The upward spiral occurred not only in arms, wealth, and power, but also, and perhaps more important, in scientific knowledge. All these factors promoted a European expansion, which in turn provided another source of wealth for the European states.[11]

Sovereignty and the Nature of the State

A final element that created the opportunity for the rise of the state system was religion, which connected all these interrelated elements. In 1517 Martin Luther challenged the spiritual authority of the pope and the Church of Rome. Luther's challenge was taken up by a number of German princes; Lutheranism spread across much of Central Europe and resulted in a series of increasingly destructive religious conflicts, which dominated the history of the sixteenth and early seventeenth centuries, and culminated in the Thirty Years' War. That war began in 1618 when Ferdinand II, a member of the Catholic Hapsburg dynasty of Austria and the sitting Holy Roman Emperor, sent imperial forces into Bohemia to quash a challenge to his authority by Protestant princes. With help from Philip IV of Spain, also a Hapsburg, the first phase of the war saw the reimposition of Catholicism in central Germany, but not before raising concerns among the other monarchs in Europe about Ferdinand's larger designs. Denmark entered the war against the Hapsburgs, followed by Sweden and then France. After thirty years of destructive warfare, the attempt to assert imperial authority on

---

[10] Tilly, *Coercion, Capital and European States*, chap. 1.

[11] Paul Kennedy, *The Rise and Fall of the Great Powers* (New York: Random House, 1987), chap. 1. McNeill argues that China lost the advantages of its earlier developments in technology and organization because the Chinese bureaucracy actually opposed the interaction between commercial interests and political centralization, including military uses of new technology. See his *The Pursuit of Power*, chap. 3.

behalf of the Hapsburg dynasty had been defeated, but all parties were exhausted. The war ended with the **Peace of Westphalia** in 1648, and it is with this event that we usually date the birth of the modern state system. Indeed, we often refer to ours as the *Westphalian state system.*

The central principle of the Peace of Westphalia was apparently simple: *cuius regio, eius religio* — he who rules a region determines its religion. This principle had been articulated as early as the Peace of Augsburg in 1555, which had sought to end the religious strife of the Reformation. Despite its simplicity, this principle had enormous consequences: the major issue of the day — religion — was to be determined by the local ruler, *not* by an external authority, whether the Holy Roman Emperor or the pope. No longer was there even the pretense of religious or political unity in Europe. Authority was dispersed to the various kings and princes. In each territory there were no longer multiple loyalties and authorities; there was only one: loyalty to the authority of the king or prince. The territory and the people in that territory belonged to the ruler, who did not have to answer to an external authority. Thus the Westphalian state system distinguished itself not only from the earlier feudal principle in Europe, but also from similar principles of suzerainty that existed elsewhere at that time — in India, China, the Arab Islamic world, and the Mongol-Tatar system.

The key elements of the modern nation-state were now all available: a people, a territory in which they lived, and a bureaucracy administering the affairs of the king, whose authority over the people of his territory was established by international law (the treaties signed at Augsburg and Westphalia). The king, with his administrative bureaucracy, was recognized as the agent of the *state* — a *legal* entity having the special status of **sovereignty.** The very term *state,* which arose in the sixteenth century, derived from the Latin *status,* meaning "position" or "standing" — in this case, the position or standing of a sovereign, or ruler.[12]

We can now begin to answer the question of why the state was, and is, the main international actor. The notion of separate secular and spiritual entities disappeared, and the authority that had been vested in both was assumed exclusively by the state. Consequently, the international norms and laws that developed provided the state with a status enjoyed by no other actor. Perhaps the operative word here is *law.* The state is a legal entity; it has been invested with a legal status and a legal equality with all other states that have been denied to other actors on the international or global scene. Like a corporation, the state technically has no concrete existence; it is a legal abstraction. Its agent is a government, and representatives of that government undertake legal commitments, both rights and responsibilities, on behalf of the state: signing treaties, joining organizations, and the like.

Sovereignty should be seen as indicating a special, theoretical relationship between each state and all other states. Hedley Bull noted that sovereignty includes both "internal sovereignty," meaning supremacy over all other entities within one's territory, and "external sovereignty," meaning independence from authorities outside

---

[12] The exact meaning of sovereignty and the state, and the implications of differing definitions, are complex and subject to debate among scholars. For a review of that debate, see Joseph A. Camilleri and Jim Falk, *The End of Sovereignty* (London: Elgar, 1992), and Alan James, *Sovereign Statehood* (London: Allen & Unwin, 1986).

that territory.[13] During the period preceding the Peace of Westphalia, the monarchies of western Europe had pretty much established their internal sovereignty vis-à-vis the nobility within their own territories (though it was a continuing process). It was really external sovereignty that was consecrated at Westphalia: no other national or international entity can legitimately dictate a state's activities; *there is no authority above the state*. This is the essence of the **anarchic** international system we have today.

In principle, this means that there is a monopoly over the control of the means of force within the state. No other authority has a right to exercise force or maintain order within the territory of the state. Similarly, through international law, the state has been given a legal monopoly on the use of force in the global arena. Piracy and nonstate terrorism are considered illegal because they entail the use of force and violence by actors other than a state. When implemented by a state, force can be pinpointed, responsibility can be assigned, and other rules of conduct can be invoked. For example, until the creation of the League of Nations after World War I, international law was concerned with how states behaved during a special legal condition called war. This condition could exist only between two equal units — equal in the legal sense of being sovereign states. Once this condition existed, belligerents were designated by declarations of war, and neutrals by declarations of their neutrality. Each category had rights and responsibilities of behavior toward other states, according to the status they had declared. The various structures of international law were rarely seen to apply to peoples who were outside the system of states, such as aboriginal populations and non-European areas, which were to be conquered, colonized, and dominated by the European nation-states.

In addition to its special legal status, the state has another important characteristic that is basic to its dominance of the international system: territory. The government of the state represents a group of people who inhabit a piece of territory. Commentators who argue that the state is no longer dominant in the world system must confront the fact that every person lives in territory controlled (at least nominally) by a state. No other form of international actor controls territory. Governments consider territory to be of overriding importance, and the stakes involved in the loss of territory are intimately related to the onset of war.[14]

We have been reminded by John Herz that "Throughout history that unit which affords protection and security to human beings has tended to become the basic political unit."[15] This proposition can be applied to the feudal knight and the protection his castle provided to the villagers. This changed with the advent of gunpowder and the larger military forces developed by kings. The basis of the state was its ability to protect people through its size — its physical territory, which created a "hard shell" around the population in an era of gunpowder and the professional armies of monarchs. Although weapons of mass destruction (nuclear, biological, and chemical) and

---

[13] Hedley Bull, *The Anarchical Society: A Study of Order in World Politics* (London: Macmillan, 1977), p. 8.
[14] See Gary Goertz and Paul Diehl, *Territorial Changes and International Conflict* (London: Routledge, 1992), and K. J. Holsti, *Peace and War: Armed Conflicts and International Order 1648–1989* (Cambridge: Cambridge University Press, 1991).
[15] John Herz, "Rise and Demise of the Territorial State," *World Politics* 9 (1957): pp. 473–493; see also Herz's rethinking of the subject, "The Territorial State Revisited — Reflections on the Future of the Nation-State," *Polity* 1 (1968): pp. 11–34.

modern delivery systems make the hard shell of the state obsolete, in general the *territoriality* of the state still protects its citizens from most conflicts with other states.

Sovereignty and territoriality provide the state with major advantages over non-state actors in the global arena. The European version of the state expanded throughout the world because it had first won out in the European competition. To survive in Europe, a country needed large amounts of capital, a large population, and significant military forces. European states controlled about 7 percent of the world's territory in 1500; by 1914 they controlled 84 percent. Tilly summarizes our arguments:

> Because of their advantages in translating national resources into success in international war, large national states superseded tribute-taking empires, federations, city-states, and all their other competitors as the predominant European entities, and as the models for state formation. . . . Those states finally defined the character of the European state system and spearheaded its extension to the entire world.[16]

Beyond Anarchy: The State System since Westphalia

The anarchic system of states recognized by the Peace of Westphalia has not survived without challenge. Its initial principle of internal sovereignty incorporated the institution of dynastic succession; that is, the inheritance of royal authority from one generation to another. The ruler embodied that sovereignty. However, the French Revolution of 1789 challenged all that. The notion of popular sovereignty — boldly asserted half a world away in the American Declaration of Independence — was gaining favor over the divine right of kings. The ultimate source of governmental authority was said to reside in the people — the public — and not the monarch. This "republican" principle proved a powerful organizing and empowering force; it fueled the enthusiasm for enlistment of a huge army of citizens, which proved to be far larger and displayed more ideological fervor than that shown by previous professional armies serving royal authority. Its strength enabled revolutionary France to turn back the forces of its neighbors, which had tried to reinstate the old regime, and then to expand French power by appealing directly to its neighbors' populations.[17]

When Napoleon Bonaparte seized power, France retained the republican spirit of governance even as Napoleon consolidated his own authority by proclaiming himself emperor. However, while enhancing his internal sovereignty, Napoleon challenged the principle of external sovereignty: he sought hegemony. Not content with maintaining French security by balancing power with other European monarchs, in his military campaigns he tried to make France the dominant power in Europe. Napoleon absorbed some of his neighbors into France and attempted to reduce the rest to vassals. The Napoleonic Wars were to determine whether the Westphalian system would survive.

The system did survive, with the victory by a coalition of all the other great powers — Britain, Russia, Prussia, and Austria. Yet the victors recognized their close call.

---

[16] Tilly, *Coercion, Capital and European States,* pp. 183, 160.

[17] On the evolution of sovereignty in the international system, see Mark Zacher, "The Decaying Pillars of the Westphalian System," in Ernst-Otto Czempiel and James Rosenau, eds., *Governance without Government: Order and Change in World Politics* (Cambridge: Cambridge University Press, 1992).

They learned from the failure of the old system and tried to revise it even as they reinstituted it. Like the parties that signed the treaties at Westphalia, those participating in the Congress of Vienna in 1815 sought to provide for an era of peace following a catastrophic period of continent-wide warfare. They tried to restore dynastic authority, but in a form tempered to the republican spirit, which could not be erased from Europeans' consciousness. The great powers allowed France to recover and reenter the system, essentially within its pre-1792 borders, and to participate as an equal partner in great power politics. The *Concert of Europe* expressed certain normative principles of proper behavior: states had a right to security and independence; states should respect one another's legitimacy and should observe international law; differences should be settled by negotiation. Military power was to back up these hopes; no state was again to aspire to dominance, nor to be permitted to make the effort. An expansionist state was to be "balanced" (actually, overpowered) by the combination of all others. In this constellation Britain and Russia, as the most powerful states, played key roles. Britain was the world's leading naval and industrial power; Russia was Europe's leading land power, with the largest population and army. Insofar as the two powers pursued expansionist aims, those aims were concentrated outside Europe. They did not directly threaten other major European powers and, because of their geographic separation, they could not substantially threaten each other. As long as Britain and Russia were basically in agreement, no other state could hope to dominate Europe.[18]

This restored, but modified, Westphalian system worked reasonably well for a full century. A wave of popular and nationalist revolution swept much of central Europe in 1848, but most of the revolutionary movements were put down by force or tempered in practice. There were only two major wars during the century, neither of which approached the scope or ferocity of the Napoleonic Wars. Britain and France fought Russia in the Crimean War of 1854, but in a limited locale and for limited goals. More far-reaching in its effects was the Franco-Prussian War of 1870, which capped the unification of Germany as the most powerful state on the European continent. Furthermore, by its territorial settlement — which transferred the provinces of Alsace and Lorraine from French to German control — it left a legacy of bitterness and demand for revenge in France. Even so, there was no further war between any of the major powers in Europe until 1914, when everything seemed to collapse. Tensions increased, and alliances rigidified. New military technology appeared to favor offense over defense and fed regional arms races. Long-term demographic and industrial trends threatened to enhance German or Russian power, to the endangerment of their neighbors. A Continent-wide war, expanding to world war, was the result. It reached a level of killing that surpassed even the Napoleonic Wars.

Again the victorious powers recognized that the system had failed in its most important purpose — preserving peace and the sovereignty of most of its constituent states. American President Woodrow Wilson championed the rights of national groups to self-determination — internal sovereignty now seemed to mean the right of an ethnically homogeneous people to govern itself. Some new states in central Europe had

---

[18] See Paul Schroeder, *The Transformation of European Politics 1763–1848* (New York: Oxford University Press, 1994), and Adam Watson, *The Evolution of International Society: A Comparative Historical Analysis* (London: Routledge, 1992).

their boundaries drawn to reflect those principles. However, the ethnic map of Europe did not fit easily into any kind of political map. Peoples were mixed together in ways that defied the creation of any neat or territorially defensible border. Some peoples' aspirations were deliberately submerged to those of more powerful groups. In legitimating an outburst of demands for national self-determination that could not be satisfied, Wilson helped promote a force that would be as disruptive as it was pacifying.[19]

The victorious powers were also looking for a principle of international relations by which to restore order and security. Wilson's vision was of a system of collective security, embedded in a League of Nations, by which all members would agree to oppose jointly a threat to the security of any one of them, from any quarter. But this vision fit badly with the view that the threat to peace stemmed primarily from a few particular states, especially Germany. This view, which was expressed most vigorously by France, required cutting territory away from Germany and imposing economically debilitating war reparations in order to weaken that nation (and also excluding it, at least initially, from the new League of Nations). In the negotiations leading to the signing of the Treaty of Versailles in 1919, this latter view predominated. Furthermore, the U.S. Senate — by then representing the world's strongest power and the one potentially best able to restrain any possible hegemonic aggressor — refused to ratify the treaty, thus precluding American membership in the League. The attempt to institute a new set of rules for the system failed at the outset. Germany recovered its power and nurtured its sense of injustice at the Versailles settlement. Eventually Hitler came to power at the head of a totalitarian government that was determined to impose a new order on Europe and perhaps the world. Britain, France, and the Soviet Union could not agree on how to resist him; the Americans stood aside, while Italy and Japan allied with him. In 1939 began the most dangerous bid for dominance since Napoleon, which was driven by an odious ideology of German racial superiority. It ended with 15 million dead in battle and a much greater number of civilian dead.

Yet again, in 1945, the victors met to pick up and rearrange the pieces. The United Nations was to replace the League. This time the United States would join. Again the world organization was founded primarily on the principle of collective security, including the intention of providing the UN with a permanent force of military units earmarked for its use in keeping the peace. By the charter of the new organization, the UN Security Council was empowered to authorize and carry out collective military action against anyone it declared to be a threat to international peace. The principal victors — Britain, the Soviet Union, and the United States (with China and France added as something of a courtesy) — were declared to be permanent members of the Security Council. As such, each was given the power to veto any military or other action against a state. The reasons for giving them this veto power were straightforward. First, the major victors insisted on it. Second, the founders of the UN were practical; they understood that for the foreseeable future, the permanent members would have to provide most of the military muscle. Moreover, if a great power felt that a particular proposal for UN action violated its vital interests, it would surely oppose such

---

[19] See Daniel Patrick Moynihan, *Pandaemonium: Ethnicity in International Politics* (Oxford: Oxford University Press, 1993).

an action, whether or not it had a veto. A UN that tried to go ahead with such an action would risk world war anyway. Thus, the veto merely recognized the realities of power. Smaller powers were given no veto. Many of them did not like this two-tiered distinction — it smacked of great-power privilege, like the earlier Concert of Europe — but they could not effectively resist it.

In creating the Security Council with its veto power, the founders were not being naive, but pragmatic. As it happened, the hope for great-power cooperation did not last long. The cold war was thoroughly underway by 1948, and the Soviet Union had already exercised its veto many times. In effect, the Security Council could act only in those disputes in which the permanent members had no vital interests at stake. No UN military force could be created. The council did, however, prove able to authorize action in cases where the great powers' vital interests did not conflict or where their interests would be endangered if the conflict were not contained (as in the Middle East).

The end of the cold war (often dated from the symbolically striking fall of the Berlin Wall in 1989) provided yet another opportunity to revise and strengthen these principles of international organization. The Soviet Union (and its successor state, Russia) cooperated with the Western powers and almost entirely stopped using its veto. China could be persuaded, by a variety of positive and negative means, not to use its veto. Thus it became possible for the Security Council to agree that important events or actions constituted a threat to international peace and security and to authorize collective action to deal with them. The most spectacular such action was the 1991 war against Iraq to restore the independence of Kuwait, by an international coalition as authorized by the Security Council. But unity in the Security Council was short-lived.

Sovereignty, the principle of interstate relations enshrined by the Peace of Westphalia, has been a central issue in world politics ever since. The great struggles between states, and the agreements that concluded them, have often demonstrated both the dangers of an anarchic international system and the fragility of efforts to move beyond anarchy. Whether, in the aftermath of the cold war, the members of the international community have the will or the capability to make a new set of rules to bring more order to this enduring anarchic system is an open question, and one as yet unanswered.

All States Are Equal (But Some States Are More Equal Than Others)

In *Animal Farm*, George Orwell's satire of the Russian Revolution and its betrayal, the last and most important of the seven principles of "Animalism" was that "all animals are equal." The pigs, however, were able to capitalize on their advantages over other animals and before long came to dominate the farm. The seven principles were reduced to one: "all animals are equal but some animals are more equal than others."

By the principles of sovereignty and in the eyes of international law, all states are equal. But one of the truisms in world politics is that nothing is distributed equally on the face of the globe — not people or their talents, not resources, not climate or geo-graphic features, not technology, not air quality. In fact, many things are distributed in a highly unequal manner. The differences between nation-states in terms of resources, capabilities, available menus, and their ability to exploit and choose from those menus can be staggering. In Chapter 5 we shall discuss in detail the concepts of power and influence, the whole range of state capabilities, and the ways in which states attempt to exert their power and influence on others. Here, however, we may simply point out that states range widely in size, from the Russian Federation, with 6.5 mil-lion square miles (more than 1.8 times the size of the United States), to Nauru, with 7.7 square miles; the smallest member of the United Nations is Monaco, with about 0.6 square miles (only 368 acres). Similarly, the People's Republic of China had a 1996 population of more than 1.2 *billion* people, whereas in that same year, microstates like Nauru and Tuvalu had populations of around 10,000; San Marino, the smallest mem-ber of the UN in population, had about 24,000 people.

Sovereignty carries with it only the *principle* of independence from outside author-ity; it does not ensure equality in capabilities or independence from the outside inter-ference of others. Sovereignty has also come to imply that the government of a state has the capacity and ability to carry out the internal responsibilities of a sovereign state. This has led some to differentiate between "juridical statehood," the rights and respon-sibilities accorded to sovereign states by international law, and "empirical statehood," the state's capacity to enforce its external independence and provide for internal stabil-ity and well-being. No official authority controls states in the contemporary world sys-tem, but many are subject to powerful unofficial forces, pressures, and influences that penetrate the supposed hard shell of the state. Moreover, many of these same states can scarcely provide the internal security that we have come to expect of sovereign states. Indeed, they have been called "quasi-states."[20]

The question of the relationship between small and large states has been perennial. Although there are any number of ways to divide states so as to categorize and classify them, one division has always existed and been used in interstate interactions: the hier-archy of size and power. We may always find large and small units, the strong and the weak, the influential and the ineffectual. The largest states of today are *proportionately* neither larger nor smaller than they were 2,000 years ago.[21] Like the debates at the Con-stitutional Convention in Philadelphia over the representation of states in the U.S. Congress, the major conflicts in setting up the United Nations were over size: "The basic argument in 1944–45 was not between the Russians and the Western Allies, although there were crises in that field too. It was between the big powers and the rest." The small countries "contested very strongly any departure from the principle of one country, one vote."[22]

Yet analysts have divided countries into many different categories. For years we simply had the First World (the industrialized Western democracies), the Second World (the communist bloc of Eastern Europe), and the Third World (all the rest);

---

[20] See Robert H. Jackson, *Quasi-states: Sovereignty, International Relations and the Third World* (Cam-bridge: Cambridge University Press, 1990).

[21] Bruce Russett, *Power and Community in World Politics* (New York: Freeman, 1974), chap. 7.

[22] Paul Gore-Booth, *With Great Truth and Respect* (London: Constable, 1974), pp. 133–134.

today these terms are of no use to us. Currently the World Bank uses three basic categories of country groups based on economic development as measured by gross national product (GNP): low-income economies (countries with a 1996 GNP per capita of $785 or less), middle-income economies (GNP per capita between $785 and $9,636), and high-income economies (GNP per capita over $9,636). Roughly 40 percent of all states, with more than 55 percent of the world's population, fall into the low-income category. Contrast this to the high-income category consisting of approximately 15 percent of all states and the same small share of world population. High-income countries come predominantly from Organization for Economic Cooperation and Development (OECD), also known as "the rich man's club." Some of the characteristics of the income-based groups are presented in Table 3.1.

Additionally, the microstates are the very smallest of contemporary states. There is no agreement on how small a state must be to be called a microstate, but most observers would include the several dozen countries with less than a quarter of a million people and/or areas of only a few hundred square miles. Despite formal sovereignty, these states are most vulnerable to external penetration or intervention; they cannot exercise even substantial control over their boundaries, territory, or population. Nonetheless, they survive. Several scholars have proposed that there has been a growing observance of international norms that outlaw war, especially war waged by the strong against the weak, which in earlier eras would have led to the disappearance of such states as sovereign entities.[23] The defense of Kuwait in the Gulf War can be seen as an affirmation of the principle of sovereignty and a rejection of the use of violence to absorb another state. This was the key normative principle on which virtually all governments of weak states could unite (and that the UN, as an organization of states

TABLE 3.1   World Bank's Classification of States, 1996

Classification	Total Population (millions)	Average GNP/Capita (dollars)	Life Expectancy (years)	Adult Illiteracy (percent)
Low Income	3,236	490	63	35
Middle Income	1,599	2,590	68	18
High Income	919	25,870	78	< 5

Source: World Bank, *World Development Indicators 1998* (New York: Oxford University Press, 1998).

[23] See Jackson, *Quasi-states*; see also John Mueller, *Retreat from Doomsday: The Obsolescence of Major War* (New York: Basic Books, 1989), and James L. Ray, "The Abolition of Slavery and the End of International War," *International Organization* 43 (1989): pp. 405–439.

rather than peoples, itself embodies). Small states in the post–World War II period were unusually free from blatant military coercion by larger states. Thus protected, they have proliferated because the potential ruling elites seek the status and prestige of statehood and the chance to have a country of their own to govern.

Nonstate Actors in the Contemporary System

A variety of other, nonstate actors are increasingly involved in the crucial issues of world politics. These actors form an important part of the global environment, affecting the possibilities and probabilities of state actions. In viewing world politics, the global system can be seen as a chessboard and the actors as the pieces that move about it. Alternately, as did Shakespeare, we can consider the world as a stage; those groups, organizations, and individuals who interact on it are the actors. This is a useful image for several reasons. First, the word *actor* conveys a broad spectrum of interacting entities; it is large enough to encompass all the entities we wish to study. Second, our emphasis is on *behavior,* and the word helps convey the idea of an entity that behaves or performs an action. In relation to nonstate actors, the term also helps to convey the idea that different actors have different roles — that some occupy center stage and are stars while others are bit players in the chorus. Yet they all interact in creating the finished production.

A variety of nonstate actors exist in the interdependent global system. James Rosenau has even suggested that currently a complex set of relations is developing that is largely independent of relations between states — a *multicentric* set of relations alongside traditional state-centric relations.[24] However, the state is still the dominant international actor on most important issues in world politics. Thus, one way to identify a significant nonstate actor is to ask whether it is taken into account in the calculations and strategies of the leaders of states and whether its continuing functions have an impact on states and other actors on the world stage.

Any organized unit that commands the identification, interests, and loyalty of individuals and affects interstate relations becomes a major competitor of nation-states. As we survey the types of nonstate actors, think of various post–World War II conflicts between international organizations and states: between the United Nations and Iraq or Serbia; between OPEC and the industrialized West; between nonstate groups like the Palestine Liberation Organization (PLO) and Israel or the Irish Republican Army (IRA) and the United Kingdom; or between a multinational corporation and a state, as in the case of the toxic gas accident at Union Carbide's plant in Bhopal, India. In almost every case the conflict arises when the nonstate actor challenges or tries to reduce the scope of the sovereignty of a nation-state in terms of territory, population, or control over its internal or external politics. The dramatic acts of international terrorism by a wide variety of nonstate groups offer another example of this competition:

---

[24] See Rosenau, *Turbulence in World Politics.*

groups other than states employ force and violence in the global system, directly challenging the monopoly of force that international law has always granted to states.

Intergovernmental Organizations

Nonstate actors in the contemporary global system include *international organizations* (IOs), and one type of IO is the **intergovernmental organization** (IGO). IGOs are composed of states, and the individuals who are sent as delegates to such organizations represent the interests and policies of their home governments. Although IGO membership is limited to states, quite often these organizations employ permanent staffs at a permanent home base, consisting of individuals whose primary loyalty is to the organization itself, not to their home government. Thus, the permanent administrative staff of the UN, the Secretariat, is an international civil service of individuals who put the organization ahead of their states. This structure may create an atmosphere of competition between the IGO and the state for the loyalty of individuals. The total number of IGOs more than tripled from 1945 to 1985, when they hit a post–World War II high of 378; by 1997 their number had declined to 258 (IGO growth is shown graphically in Figure 3.1).

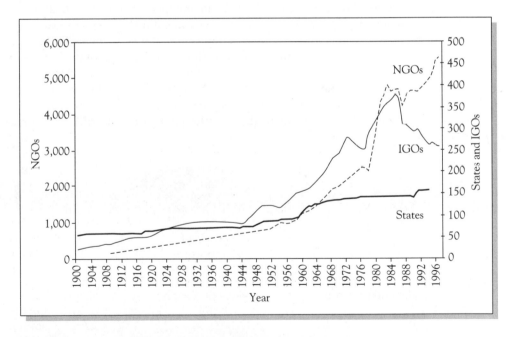

FIGURE 3.1 Growth of States, IGOs, and NGOs, 1900–1997

Note: Some data for IGOs and NGOs are interpolations.

Sources: States from the Polity Project, "Polity Data Archive III," March 31, 1998 [cited August 18, 1998]; available at <http://www.colorado.edu/IBS/GAD/spacetime/data/Polity.html>. IGOs and NGOs compiled from Union of International Associations (UIA), *Yearbook of International Organizations* (Brussels: UIA, various years).

IGOs may be usefully categorized according to the scope of their memberships and the scope of their purposes (see Table 3.2). On the one hand, we have *universal* political organizations such as the old League of Nations and the United Nations, which aim to include as wide an international membership as possible. Such organizations are also *general-purpose* organizations in that they perform political, economic, developmental, military, sociocultural, and other functions for member states. Other general-purpose organizations have more *restricted memberships:* the Organization of American States (OAS), the Organization of African Unity (OAU), and several others. Usually, limited-membership IGOs are regionally based, but not always. The Commonwealth of Nations is not regional; its membership is spread across the globe but is limited to countries with former colonial ties to the British Empire. The Group of Eight (G8) consists of the world's most advanced industrialized states from North America, Europe, and Asia.

A significantly greater number of IGOs serve *limited purposes* and are sometimes called "functional IGOs" because they perform specific functions on behalf of member states. Many of these IGOs are affiliated with the UN or related to the European Union. Those connected to the UN often have, or aim for, universal membership. Some provide various social services — for example, the World Health Organization (WHO) or the International Labor Organization (ILO) — and others, like the International Monetary Fund (IMF) and the World Bank, are involved in monetary matters and economic development. Many more have restricted membership. Some — such as NATO and the former Warsaw Pact — serve primarily military functions. Others are concerned with economic matters; among them are the various organs of the European Union and organizations like the Association of Southeast Asian Nations (ASEAN) and South America's Common Market of the South (MERCOSUR). The list becomes almost endless if we include groups with even more specific functional activities, such as the International Statistical Institute, the International Bureau of Weights and Measures,

TABLE 3.2	Classification of IGOs by Membership and Purpose	
	Universal Membership	Restricted Membership
General Purpose	League of Nations UN	OAS OAU British Commonwealth G8
Limited Purpose	IMF World Bank WHO ILO	EU ↑ NATO MERCOSUR ASEAN

the International Wool Study Group, or the Desert Locust Control Organization for East Africa.

Both the membership and purposes of IGOs evolve over time, making them difficult to classify. The Arab League, for example, was formed in 1945 with the central purpose of opposing, both politically and militarily, the formation of the Jewish state in Palestine. More recently, however, it has become more concerned with Arab economic relations and development. Similarly, NATO, the cold war military alliance of Western powers, has become active in promoting democracy and economic reform among new and aspiring members in Eastern Europe. Indeed, a more general-pupose IGO, the Euro-Atlantic Partnership Council, has been formed consisting of the sixteen member states of NATO plus another twenty-eight aspirants. The EU is probably the best example of a limited-purpose IGO that has expanded its purview — from matters of economic integration to include the partial, if halting, coordination of European foreign, and even defense, policies.

Without going into great detail on the workings of the individual IGOs, let us review them as international actors.[25] First, they have a significant and continuing impact on interstate relations. The international role of many IGOs is clearly institutionalized in that states expect them to act in certain areas. They expect the UN, say, to act in areas of conflict, as it did in 1990 to come to the aid of Kuwait after the Iraqi invasion or in 1993 to bring some semblance of order to Somalia. Regionally, both the European Union and the Organization on Security and Cooperation in Europe (OSCE) attempted to resolve the violence in Yugoslavia starting in 1991. When states find themselves in serious economic trouble, they almost automatically look to the World Bank or the IMF for various kinds of aid, as in the case of the Asian financial crisis described in Chapter 1. Developing states increasingly find that association with IGOs will help their economic performance. In addition, IGOs are actors in the sense that they continually affect the foreign policy behavior of their members, to the extent that member states join the organization and value the continuation of membership. Merely sending representatives to an organization, employing resources to maintain IGOs, or interacting with others through such organizations has an impact on the state. Perhaps most important, IGOs may be considered actors because state leaders *believe* that they behave as international actors and must be taken into account in foreign policy deliberations.

IGOs have this effect in several ways. Most clearly seen in the workings of the United Nations, but common to many other IGOs, is the function of acting as a forum in which the member states can meet and communicate. The IGO may act passively, serving only as a line of communication or a meeting place, or actively, as a mediator. IGOs perform a number of regulative functions across such areas as economics, health, communication, and transportation; examples range from the African Postal Union to the International Atomic Energy Agency. Here IGOs, with the consent of member states, set standards so that states can interact smoothly, efficiently, and with mutual

---

[25] See Harold K. Jacobson, William M. Reisinger, and Todd Mathers, "National Entanglements in International Governmental Organizations," *American Political Science Review* 80, 1 (March 1986): pp. 141–159.

benefit in a functional area of concern. This management or coordination role is essential to the orderly functioning of day-to-day global relations.

A very small number of IGOs may be termed **supranational.** Member states have granted them the authority to act independently and to make decisions that are binding on members even if some members disagree with those decisions. These IGOs indeed appear to take a degree of sovereignty away from their member states. No IGO in existence today is completely supranational, but in the evolution of the European Union, various organs of that organization, especially the European Commission, have developed extensive independent authority.[26] The mix of intergovernmentalism and supranationalism in the EU has been aptly described as "pooled sovereignty."

Nongovernmental Organizations

IGOs are not the only international organizations that have an impact on world politics, forming part of the environment of states and constraining the range of state behavior. While IGOs are organizations composed of states, **nongovernmental organizations** (NGOs) are private international actors. The important distinction regards membership: NGOs are organizations that cut across national boundaries — they are *transnational* — and are made up of individuals or national groups, not official representatives of national governments. They exist "below" the level of the state. Like the IGOs, they deal with a great variety of matters. There are religious bodies, professional organizations, sports organizations, trade union groups, and political parties. Their membership may be composed either directly of individuals (the International Political Science Association) or of various national societies that themselves are composed of individuals (like the International Red Cross, composed of the various national Red Cross organizations). International NGOs are now very numerous, having increased from fewer than 200 in 1909 to more than 800 in 1945 and to about 5,600 today (see Figure 3.1).

Most often these organizations perform rather low-level, specifically functional tasks, promoting contact across state boundaries on matters of common interest and providing nongovernmental means of communication among individuals of many nations. NGOs help knit the global society together in much the same way that private groups do within a state, although the portion of the global population with membership in NGOs is very small when compared to the portion of the national population comprising interest groups in a typical economically developed democracy. Sometimes an NGO can function as a pressure group affecting national governments or international organizations. An example is the role of the International Red Cross and the World Council of Churches in mobilizing world concern and aid for African populations facing starvation. A great many NGOs are formally consulted by the international organizations concerned with their problems (for example, health and medical organizations are consulted by the World Health Organization). Some NGOs, such as Amnesty International or the Roman Catholic Church, can exert significant influence

---

[26] See Clive Archer, *Organizing Europe: The Institutions of Integration* (London: Arnold, 1994).

on the policies of various states. The political focus of NGOs is usually on national governments, and they are effective through changing government policy rather than through direct action.

At the most micro level are individuals. While individuals are important to the operation and impact of transnational organizations and transnational linkages between and among states (in tourism, student exchange, and business and commercial links), individuals are most often powerless in international politics except when they can, through an official or unofficial role, affect the policy of a government. One analyst, however, claims that this situation is changing and that private individuals are having an ever greater impact on world affairs. Through the growing interdependence of the world system and the growing awareness of individuals of their place in the world, individual acts produce significant impacts. For example, Mathias Rust, a West German teenager acting "on behalf of world peace" landed his light plane in Red Square in 1987, exposing the vulnerabilities of Soviet air defenses and leading to the dismissal of the defense minister.[27]

Multinational Corporations

One consistent exception to the relative powerlessness of transnational actors is the **multinational corporation** (MNC). The number and importance of MNCs have grown enormously in recent years. In 1996 there were more than 44,000 firms conducting business in foreign countries — a fourfold increase since the early 1990s — with over 280,000 subsidiaries. The top one hundred MNCs (industrial, not financial) controlled more than $4 trillion in assets, had more than $4 trillion in sales, and employed more than 12 million people worldwide in 1995. And between 40 and 50 percent of their assets, sales, and employment was foreign. Most of this foreign business activity (80–90 percent) is conducted by MNCs based in the United States, Japan, and the European Union. The United States was home to thirty of the top one hundred MNCs in 1995, Japan to eighteen, and the European Union to thirty-nine (most of these British, French, or German).[28]

Clearly, giant corporations like these cannot help but affect the policies of many governments and the welfare of many people. The oil companies, for instance, would still have tremendous impact with their pricing and marketing policies even if they did not try to change the policy or personnel of national governments. The MNC has emerged in many ways as one of the major competitors to the nation-state. Whereas nonstate liberation movements and separatist groups have challenged the military and political authority of specific nation-states, the MNC is a much more broadly based and subtle competitor. This is partly because MNCs may become deeply involved in the domestic political processes of host countries — by outright bribery, by support of

---

[27] See Rosenau, *Turbulence in World Politics*, for these arguments; see p. 288 of that work for a discussion of the Rust incident.

[28] United Nations Conference on Trade and Development, *World Investment Report 1997: Transnational Corporations, Market Structure and Competition Policy* (New York: United Nations, 1997).

specific political parties or candidates, or by financing coups.[29] Examples are the actions of the United Fruit Company in the overthrow of the Arbenz government in Guatemala in 1954, the actions of British Petroleum in the removal of the Mossadegh government in Iran in 1953, and the role played by ITT in the coup against the Marxist regime of Salvador Allende of Chile in 1973.

Many multinationals predate the states that have been created since the end of World War II. MNCs also have their own spheres of influence through the division of world markets. They often engage in diplomacy and espionage, traditional tools of state interaction. Most important, MNCs have very large economic resources at their disposal, which gives them an advantage over not only many of the newer and smaller states, but also some of the established ones. For example, in 1996 Japan's Itochu Corporation had gross sales larger than the GNPs of Finland, Norway, Denmark, Greece, and Turkey (as well as all but the very largest developing countries.) Even the top one hundred MNCs that figure toward the bottom of the sales ranking have total sales exceeding the GNPs of roughly one-third of the world's nation-states. Of course, GNP and gross sales are not directly comparable accounting terms; the most accurate comparison would be between GNP and "value added" by the corporation. Nevertheless, the comparison suggests how very large some modern multinational corporations are compared with the often small, developing states with which they deal.

Nation-State versus Nonstate Loyalty

Although there are competitors to the nation-state, some very formidable in special ways, the state continues to enjoy great advantages over most other international actors. In addition to the legal status of formal sovereignty, the state generally also possesses demographic, economic, military, and geographic capabilities unmatched by other actors. Some IGOs or MNCs command the loyalty of some individuals, but the nation-state commands the loyalty of very large numbers of individuals. One clear ramification of the combination of the nation with the state (which is what actors like the PLO want) is that the state comes to embody the nation and is strengthened through the continuing process of nationalism. That is, the government of the state is seen by the people as representing and protecting cultural values as well as history and tradition. Combined with the idea of sovereignty, this relationship is a powerful force indeed — a force that can rarely be matched by nonstate actors. Before the outbreak of World War I, the socialist parties of Europe, meeting together under the aegis of the Second International, called for unity among the proletariat and a refusal by workers anywhere in Europe to take up arms against other workers in the event of war. Here was a direct clash between an NGO and the states of Europe: competition for the loyalty of the workers within the various European countries, especially Germany, France, and Britain. When the war came and choices had to be made, for a variety of reasons

---

[29] Classic studies include Raymond Vernon, *Sovereignty at Bay* (New York: Basic Books, 1971), and Richard J. Barnet and Ronald E. Müller, *Global Reach: The Power of the Multinational Corporations* (New York: Simon & Schuster, 1974); see also Volker Bornschier and Christopher Chase-Dunn, *Transnational Corporations and Underdevelopment* (New York: Praeger, 1985).

the workers rallied to the nationalist stands of their respective states, not to the Red Flag.

Two concluding, if somewhat contradictory, comments are in order. The first is that states possess, in general, a far wider range of capabilities than do nonstate actors and thus have a much larger and more varied menu. Although there has been a tremendous growth in both IGOs and NGOs and the transnational interactions among them (and between them and states), nonstate interactions clearly reflect the structure and distribution of the power of the states in the global system, and the growth of non-state activity has both mirrored and derived from the expansion of the state system itself in the postwar period. The second point, however, is simply that IGOs and NGOs do exist. And, in a world system characterized by high and growing levels of interde-pendence (which we will discuss in subsequent chapters), such actors inevitably and consistently affect the menu of constraints and possibilities of states. As components of the global environment, they must be given attention by states and by one another.

4

The World System: International Structure and Polarity

WORLD SYSTEM

RELATIONS

SOCIETY

GOVERNMENT

ROLE

INDIVIDUAL

The International Environment

Starting our analysis at the level of the international system, we have the most general picture of world politics. The international environment surrounds nation-states and their foreign policy makers; it therefore provides a crucial component to the menu from which states and decisionmakers choose their behavior. How exactly does the international environment affect the menu? How does it affect what is possible and probable in state behavior?

The Geopolitical Setting

An important aspect of world politics is **geopolitics.** Every nation-state operates within a context shaped by many other states and other international actors. Some of these entities are large and some are small; some possess great military and economic capabilities and others do not; some control important natural resources and others are resource poor. The arrangement of states includes their political-geographic arrangement as well. First, this means that we care about the physical location of states. For example, China and Russia still share over 2,000 miles of common land border, whereas the United States has a common land border with neither; Britain and Japan are islands, whereas France and Germany border many other states. Some states are distant from the centers of international activity. Australia, for example, is at the periphery of international interaction. Others — such as Egypt, Israel, and Iraq — are located along historical trade routes or paths of invasion.

The political-geographic arrangement includes not only location but also topographical features. States are concerned with their neighbors — how many there are, how close or how far, how big or how small — and they are also concerned with the features of land and sea. The menu of a particular power is different if it is an island or a continental power; lies at the end of a peninsula or at the center of a continental landmass; has long shorelines and good ports or is landlocked; has mountains, deserts, rivers, swamps, or other natural barriers as borders or has its frontiers on open, flat plains. The arrangement of these physical features will limit the possibilities and probabilities of communication and transportation of both economic goods and military capabilities.

The physical arrangement of the international environment also includes less obvious features. Useful natural resources — drinkable water and arable land, as well as forests, animal life, and mineral resources — are unevenly distributed. The definition of, for example, "useful" changes over time: states that possessed uranium prior to the advent of nuclear power did not gain by it in either wealth or influence. Finally, climate varies across the globe. As parts of the physical arrangement and environment of all states, all these factors affect opportunities for state interaction. Just as the design and structure of a chessboard (or any other game board) influence the possibilities and probabilities of movement by the pieces on the board, the international system affects the behavior of states.

Location strongly affects interaction: states tend to get into wars more often with neighbors than with others because they interact more with countries close by than with those far away. Contiguity is one factor that helps to identify "dangerous dyads," pairs of states, like India and Pakistan or Iran and Iraq, that are most inclined to engage in military conflict.[1] One view of the relationship between the closeness of states and their opportunities for interaction is that of Kenneth E. Boulding. According to Boulding, any state's power is greatest at home but then declines along a "loss of strength gradient" as the distance from home is increased. This occurs because of the increases in the time and cost of transporting one's military resources. Because of this, Boulding proposes an axiom: "the further the weaker."[2] In general, a state should be most concerned with its immediate neighbors and less concerned with those far away. The

---

[1] For evidence of this effect, see Stuart Bremer, "Dangerous Dyads: Conditions Affecting the Likelihood of Interstate War, 1816–1965," *Journal of Conflict Resolution* 36 (June 1992): pp. 309–341.
[2] Kenneth E. Boulding, *Conflict and Defense* (New York: Harper & Row, 1962), chap. 4.

exceptions, of course, are the great powers, those states with enough resources to over-come the disadvantage of distance.

The Technological Setting

Decisionmakers of a state are faced with a number of givens: geography, the arrange-ment of neighbors, and distant states. Another such given is the existing technology in the international system. As we noted when discussing opportunity in Chapter 2, tech-nology plays a major part in determining what is physically possible; in the fourth cen-tury B.C.E. Alexander the Great could not communicate instantaneously with King Darius of Persia, but Nixon could do so with Brezhnev during the crisis of the 1973 Yom Kippur War in the Middle East.

Technology is the application of human skills or techniques to accomplish human purposes. Creative genius has continually led people to develop new technologies to overcome space and time, to generate power for economic and military purposes, to communicate and transport ideas and objects. Obstacles presented by mountains, deserts, or distance are overcome by inventions — the railroad, the automobile, the air-plane. Obstacles to the spread of ideas and ideologies have been overcome by the development of radio, television, communications satellites, and the Internet. These technologies bring news from all over the world into your home as events are happen-ing. Technology also permits us to overcome obstacles posed by disease and age. Advances in medical knowledge and skills have played a large part in the explosive growth of population since World War II by lowering the rate of infant mortality and the death rate in general. New technologies also permit the extraction of resources which had been literally out of reach. The development of synthetics can expand a menu otherwise limited by the earth's resources.

In sum, the technology that exists in the international system at any time is an important factor for understanding what is possible. But technology is not static: research and development by governments, industry, universities, and individuals are continually changing the technological environment. Such change has become ever more rapid, and it has been taking less and less time for new discoveries to become operational in our world. The gap between Marconi's first radio set and commercial broadcasting was thirty-five years; but the atomic bomb went from discovery to use in six years, and the transistor made the journey in five years. The first cloned mammal was announced in February 1997; the medical and commercial applications of this technology are right around the corner.

The Global System

In the first chapter we defined a system as a set of elements, or units, interacting with each other. A set of billiard balls being broken on a pool table constitutes such a system, for the balls interact with one another. An international system, which is infinitely more complex, is a set of states and other actors interacting with each other. Sometimes it is useful to treat the international system as consisting only of states interacting like billiard balls, all with similar internal compositions and affected only by the behavior of each other. Thus we would concentrate on how the unit France interacts with other units like Italy and China. However, we said that the international system is infinitely more complex than a set of billiard balls. Why is this so?

First, other actors, both within nation-states and outside them, must be taken into account. Also, the kinds of interaction and the number of variables are much more numerous. The billiard balls act on one another only through the expenditure of energy, which can be measured on a single scale. If you know the initial location of the balls on the table, the energy-absorbing capacity of the balls and banks, the friction created by the felt, the amount of energy exerted through the cue, and the initial angles of interaction, it is possible to make a good prediction of where the balls will end up. The prediction requires quite a lot of information, some of which (such as the angles) is very hard to obtain, but the number of different variables at issue is relatively small and theoretically manageable. Furthermore, these are the only variables that matter. If you had all the information for them, the effects both of chance (an earthquake) and of ignored variables (atmospheric pressure) would be quite low. The typical billiard player does not make a lot of formal computations but does recognize certain variables as important and takes them into account based on experience and intuition. The player who "knows" the table (specific characteristics of the banks and pockets) will also have a good idea of how much force to use on the cue and the angle to try in order to get the desired distribution of the balls. Achieving the right shot may not always be possible, but the player knows how to attempt it.

The analysis of international systems requires, or at least seems to require, information about a great many more variables. We say "seems to require" because we are often not sure which variables exert a great deal of influence and which, like the atmospheric pressure in the billiards room, can be safely ignored without misleading our analyses. Any system is defined by the *attributes of its component units* (how many and of what type) and by the nature, pattern, and number of *interactions among those units*. When applying these ideas to the international system, all of the following are important:

1. The *number* of state actors is the first factor to assess.

2. The relative *size* of the various state actors: The most relevant measure of size may be population, area, wealth, economic capacity (GNP), military capabilities, some other measure, or some combination of these.

3. The numbers and types of *nonstate actors:* In addition to the intergovernmental and nongovernmental organizations mentioned in the previous chapter, we should also include a geographic or political group of states as an actor. Because of their common interests and linkages, such groupings have been called *blocs*. This is the sense in which many observers commonly used the term "Soviet bloc" during most of the post–World War II period. They assumed that the linkages among these countries were so numerous and strong that the states would often act as a unit, delegating decision-making power to an IGO (Warsaw Pact) or to one of their number (the Soviet Union). When such regional groupings, blocs, or alliances act together on a range of issues, they contribute to a serious modification of the overall arrangement of the international system. No longer does the system consist entirely of independent states relating to one another like billiard balls; now the system includes one or more clusters of billiard balls.

4. The nature of the linkages or *interactions* among states and nonactors: These include official government-to-government interactions as well as transactions across societies. The latter may take the form of trade, investment, movements of citizens (by tourism, migration, and student exchanges), communications between private citizens (via mail, telephone, fax, or the Internet), or the mass media (radio, television, print). From the viewpoint of the political analyst, any single event — a particular purchase, a single e-mail message, one student exchange — is rarely of interest; rather, it is the aggregate number of such acts that is of concern — in other words, whether the total volume of trade or communications is high or low. Alternately, there may be a certain class of events, or acts, that is of special interest. Official acts like signing a treaty, issuing a threat, or mobilizing troops convey messages to other governments and are frequently studied forms of state interaction.

5. The degree of **interdependence** existing between interacting states and nonstate actors: Very simply defined, interdependence is a relationship in which changes or events in any single part of a system will produce some reaction or have some significant consequence in other parts of the system. For example, an infected finger in the system of a human organism will affect the blood and its white cell defenses; it can cause a fever and speed up the heartbeat. Similarly, by increasing the air in the carburetor of a car, we affect the ignition within the cylinders and the speed and smoothness of the ride. The Asian financial crisis described in Chapter 1 is a good example from world politics: the economies and financial markets in Southeast Asia had become so interdependent that developments in Thailand set off an immediate chain of events throughout the region, which ultimately had implications well beyond the region.

Emergence of the Contemporary System

Interaction and interdependence make a system out of otherwise separate units. Many social, technological, economic, and political factors affect the rate and kind of interaction. Where interaction is much greater among a certain set of actors than between those actors and others outside the set, the interacting units constitute a *subsystem*. If the rate of interaction between members of the set and outsiders is extremely low or nonexistent, we may simply refer to it as a system rather than a subsystem. There has not always been an international system of global scope; regional systems existed as far back as recorded history — for example, the Chou Dynasty from 1122 to 221 B.C.E. or the Greek city-states from 800 to 322 B.C.E. — but they were relatively isolated and not part of a larger global system.

The contemporary global system did not begin to emerge until the fifteenth century C.E. European states did not interact at all with the Western Hemisphere, and they interacted in no significant way with Africa south of the Sahara or with East and Southeast Asia. Communication and transportation technologies were too primitive to permit interaction across long distances. With improvements in navigation and sailing technology, Spain, Portugal, Holland, England, and France were able to build huge colonial empires around the globe, affecting an expansion of the European system (discussed in the previous chapter). For the first time a worldwide capitalist economic system — production for a global market — emerged. Many peoples and areas were linked to this system only weakly, but many others (slaves producing sugar in the Caribbean, Indians put to work in the silver mines of South America, workers on spice plantations in Southeast Asia, consumers in Europe) found their fortunes linked to, and interdependent with, economic conditions halfway around the world. The world political system still remained fairly fragmented, however. No single state dominated the world, and for a long time it was still possible for many non-European actors to ignore Europe for most purposes. Large parts of Africa and Asia retained substantial independence until the final wave of European colonial acquisition in the second half of the nineteenth century. The United States, with its strength and relative physical isolation, was able to ignore most European political quarrels until World War I.

One indicator of the rapid integration of the global system since the height of the colonial period is the movement of people over large distances. Figure 4.1 tracks changes in transportation technology since the early nineteenth century. Beginning with sailing vessels and the earliest steamships (which moved at about five miles per hour), the curve gives the approximate maximum speed of civilian transportation over intercontinental distances. The graph rises to the speeds attained by oceangoing passenger liners at the turn of the century and then begins to advance rapidly with the development of civil aviation in the 1930s. The era of supersonic transport was inaugurated in the 1970s, and while there is certainly an upper limit for physical transportation,

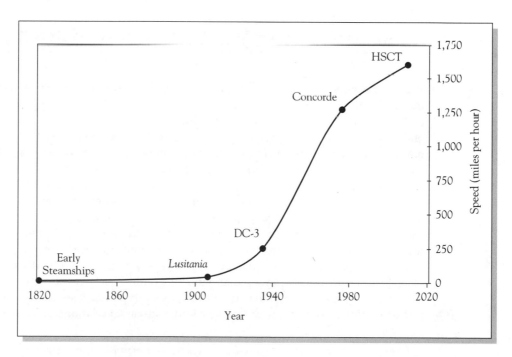

FIGURE 4.1 A Shrinking World: Maximum Speed Attainable for Intercontinental Passenger Travel

development projects underway in high-speed civilian travel (HSCT) are currently targeting speeds of mach 2.4 (about 1600 mph) by the year 2010. With these and other changes, including the explosion of Internet-based communication and commerce, the whole world has become irrevocably bound into a closely knit system.

Coupled with the enormous growth in wealth of the industrial powers over the past century, the new technology provides the means for great powers to make their influence felt virtually everywhere and for the entire global system truly to operate as an interacting system. The major powers are particularly involved in interactions with one another. During the cold war era each of the biggest powers had parts of the globe (or regional subsystems) that it dominated and within which it sharply limited the influence of other major powers. The United States was long dominant in Latin America, as was the Soviet Union in Eastern Europe. China has exercised influence in parts of East Asia, competing first with the USSR and now with Japan and Russia. Britain and France once had large spheres of influence in Africa and elsewhere but no longer have as much power, relative either to their former colonies or to the United States, to dominate these regions. At the same time, although certain major powers have clearly predominated over others in particular spheres of influence in certain time periods (for example, Latin America and Eastern Europe), most of the smaller powers within such areas usually maintain significant ties — economic, political, cultural, or military — with other powers as well. Regional subsystems are thus penetrated by the big powers' global activities.[3]

Status and Hierarchy in the International System

A system perspective focuses our attention on component units, their interactions, and the emergent whole. Both the characteristics of these units and their interactions will indicate how the units or, in our case, states and nonstate actors stand in relationship to one another. In the last chapter, we emphasized that the modern state system is, formally, an anarchy — no *legal* authority exists above the nation-state — but that states vary immensely in their resources and capabilities. Therefore, in discussing international systems it is useful to examine the degree of **hierarchy** that does in fact exist informally (that is, *extralegally*) in the international system. By hierarchy we simply mean who has the most of something (wealth, military might, prestige), who has the least, and who is positioned in the middle. Hierarchy can also indicate how states are linked together in their interactions, either essentially as equals or only through the intermediary of one or more great powers. Several writers see a feudal aspect to much of historical and contemporary international politics. They posit a world of several influence spheres, each dominated by a big power that interposes itself between small powers within its spheres (maintaining a lord-and-vassal relationship) and limits as far

[3] See Barry Buzan, *People, States, and Fear: An Agenda for International Security Studies in the Post–Cold War Era*, 2nd ed. (Boulder, Colo.: Lynne Rienner, 1991), chap. 5.

as possible the penetration of other major powers into those spheres. For instance, telephone calls between Senegal and Gabon in West Africa once had to go through Paris, and air travel in many parts of the Third World was possible only through London, Paris, or other major cities in the developed world.

When examining international politics from the perspective of the world system, we need to take into account the unequal distribution of power and influence among states as well as the principle of sovereign equality that governs their relations in the eyes of international law. The arrangement of state and nonstate actors in the international system consists of both — the principle of authority and the distribution of power — and together they constitute the **structure of the system.**[4]

Spheres of Influence

A system perspective often directs our attention to *competition* among great powers (during the cold war, the superpowers) as they move to limit each other's influence in their respective spheres of influence. But we can also examine *dominance* of the weak by the strong and the limited autonomy or independence exercised by those at the bottom of the hierarchy. The menu of policy options for smaller states is usually highly constrained by the presence of larger powers in the international system, and even more so if they sit within the sphere of influence of a major power. However, if there are two powers competing in an area, as the superpowers did in the Middle East during the cold war, each is limited by the other; each restrains its behavior in anticipation (or fear) of the other's response. The competition of two or more major powers can actually expand the menu, allowing the tails to wag the dogs. These are just some of the possible constraints imposed on states, weak and strong, by the structure of the international system.

One simple hierarchical structure is illustrated in Figure 4.2, where the lines indicate the degree of interaction that states have with one another. Thus A and B, the major powers, interact extensively with each other and with minor powers in their own spheres of influence (as indicated by the solid lines). The minor powers — u, v, w, x, y, and z — interact very little with each other (the broken lines), even though they might be in the same geographical region and have many common interests. Theories about spheres of influence tend to be concerned chiefly with relations among the great powers, or the "view from above." What goes on among the small powers at the periphery of the world system generally matters little, except that additions or losses to spheres of influence may change the distribution of power among the system's major actors, and perhaps the likelihood of war. This is the perspective of realism, which was typical of U.S. and Soviet theorizing during the cold war era. During that period, theorists in Europe and especially in the Third World saw the situation very differently. Their "views from below" were much more concerned with avoiding becoming arenas for superpower rivalry and obtaining some freedom of action for their countries. From below, great-power competition looks like great-power dominance.

---

[4] See Kenneth N. Waltz, *Theory of International Politics* (Reading, Mass.: Addison-Wesley, 1979).

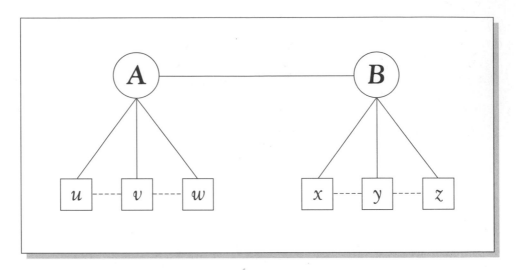

FIGURE 4.2   A Feudal International System

Superpower competition provided benefits as well as costs to some smaller countries by fostering interest by one superpower in areas that might be of importance to the other. Smaller countries found that they could play off the superpowers against each other in competition for economic and military aid. This process halted dramatically in the post–cold war era, when Soviet inability to compete in many areas also promoted American neglect. A similar phenomenon occurred during earlier periods of U.S.-Soviet détente; for example, the volume of American economic assistance to other countries declined from 0.8 percent of GNP to about 0.3 percent from 1962 to 1983, during a period when Soviet-American relations were improving (it has since dropped to 0.1 percent). The "outbreak of peace" in the late 1980s, in areas such as Angola-Namibia, Central America, and Cambodia and between Iran and Iraq, owed much to the end of the cold war and the evolution of a policy of mutual restraint between the United States and the Soviet Union. No longer would the two powers automatically support opposing factions in local disputes.

Just as theories of great-power politics look chiefly at horizontal relations among approximate equals, theories originating from small powers stress vertical relationships of dominance and exploitation. As noted, some theories characterize international politics as essentially feudal; a related theoretical perspective is concerned with the *dependence* of small, developing states on large, industrialized ones. Non-Western and European theorists have examined the effects of big powers' economic, political, and cultural penetration on small powers. The effects at issue in such theories are usually different from those emphasized by great-power theories — they are less concerned with war and international political alignments and more concerned with patterns of economic and political development in the global south.

Alliances

Alliances tell us much about the political and military structure of the international system: about the geopolitical relationships among states, about the distribution of friendship and enmity, about the distribution of military capability. Like technology, alliances can be used to overcome distance and geographic obstacles, creating new opportunities as well as risks for the states involved. Alliances, through their impact on the distribution of power, can be central to system structure, and thus to the menu of policy options presented by the international system.

Alliances combine elements of cooperation and conflict. They involve interstate cooperation (between allied states), while addressing an existing or potential conflict with one or more other states.[5] Generally speaking, cooperative behavior can be both formal and informal. Informally, two states are *aligned* if they act in a similar way toward some third international actor. Their common policies toward other actors may be a coincidence, but alignment usually means that they act cooperatively, in some sense coordinating their behavior toward other actors and their positions on issues, but without a formal agreement. They behave as a *coalition*. The United States and Israel are aligned; the two countries have been part of the same coalition in many international fora, especially at deliberations of the United Nations. **Alliances** involve more than this: coalitions are *formalized* in written treaties, and these involve agreements to cooperate specifically on matters of *military security*. The agreements specify the rights and obligations (the benefits and costs) of the alliance membership, generally for limited periods of time.

Alliances provide both opportunities and constraints. They permit the combining of capabilities, thus adding elements of flexibility to state policy and making more complicated the calculation of relative power among states. Supplementing military capabilities with those of allies can afford states a better defense against external threats, and at less cost, than having to devote additional resources of their own. Alliances also serve as conduits by which the conflicts of one or more alliance partners become the conflicts of others. For the primary parties to the conflict, alliances provide opportunities to pursue bolder courses of action than might otherwise be the case if they were acting in isolation. For their allies, however, policy options become constrained to those consistent with the terms of the alliance, which often means participating in armed hostilities initiated or provoked by alliance partners. Thus alliances have been found to be factors in the spread, or *diffusion*, of war.[6]

Alliances have been used by large nations to control and dominate smaller alliance partners and by smaller allies to manipulate larger alliance partners. An alliance leader may use alliances to create an orderly international environment in which the alliance leader is safe, secure, and, indeed, a leader. Order requires organizing relations among

---

[5] A useful overview of alliance studies is Michael D. Ward, *Research Gaps in Alliance Dynamics*, vol. 19 of *Monograph Series in World Affairs* (Denver: University of Denver, 1982); and a review of alliance theory is Glenn H. Snyder, "Alliance Theory: A Neorealist First Cut," *Journal of International Affairs* 44 (1990): pp. 103–123.

[6] See Randolph M. Siverson and Harvey Starr, *The Diffusion of War: A Study of Opportunity and Willingness* (Ann Arbor: University of Michigan Press, 1991).

the leader's allies — controlling or restraining their behavior. In the post–World War II period both the United States and the Soviet Union used their alliances in this way, particularly in Europe. NATO was officially founded in 1949 as a means to protect Western Europe from Soviet invasion. The Warsaw Pact (formally, the Warsaw Treaty Organization) was established in 1955 as a response to West Germany's entry into NATO; German militarism was still in recent memory among the Soviets and East Europeans. Their respective alliances served the security interests of the United States and the Soviet Union. However, both alliances also served to keep the lesser allies — especially the two German states — in line. Lord Ismay, the first secretary-general of NATO, once said that the purpose of that alliance was "to keep the Russians out, the Americans in, and the Germans down."

One danger of alliances is abandonment through allies reneging on alliance commitments. A different danger for the leading member of an alliance is entrapment, being dragged into conflicts by reckless smaller allies. It has been said that commitment is a seamless web: if a state does not honor its commitments to protect others, similar commitments become much less credible in the future. Small allies have often engaged their larger partners in war by painting them into a corner whereby the larger partners have little choice but to fight if they expect to be taken seriously (by friends or enemies) in subsequent confrontations. Austria-Hungary's aggressive behavior toward Serbia and Russia before World War I illustrates this relationship. Germany became a belligerent supporter of Austria-Hungary because backing down before Russia would surely mark the end of the Austro-German alliance. Nor are such relationships limited to formal alliances. According to former President Nixon and former Secretary of State Kissinger, one of the most dangerous moments in U.S.-Soviet relations occurred in 1973, when the Soviet Union threatened to intervene in the October war to prevent Egypt from being defeated. This would have forced the United States to intervene on behalf of Israel.

Nonalignment

States may also try to go it alone, avoiding alliances by some sort of neutral policy or by attempting to withdraw from the system of states as much as possible. Of course, a state's geopolitical position and the structure of the international system are important in selecting a strategy for security and survival. In the past a strategy of isolation was more useful for large countries that were self-sufficient and could retreat inside themselves to develop. Japan was able to do this until the nineteenth century, as was the Soviet Union, to some degree, during the 1920s. However, in the contemporary system, large countries with many economic and political ties and a network of economic, monetary, and resource interdependencies find it difficult to withdraw from the international system. It has chiefly been smaller countries on the geographic peripheries of international activity that attempt this strategy. The best examples are Albania and Burma; possibly another is Cambodia after the communist victory in 1975.

Because of economic and political needs, many small states in the contemporary system have opted for a nonaligned foreign policy. The expression "Third World" was originally coined to characterize all the less-developed countries that avoided alliance with the First World of the industrialized West or the Second World of the communist East. Choices of alliance or **nonalignment** have been strongly affected by the structure of the post–World War II international system. Many states chose — or were forced — to ally either with the Western bloc in some form or with the Soviet Union. However, the traditional reasons for allying with great powers have been security, stability, and status, whereas in the cold war system, allying with one of the great powers often brought just the opposite: fear of threat from the other superpower, internal instability resulting from the clash of Western- and Eastern-oriented political factions, and a decline in autonomy for states that became mere satellites or dependents of one or the other superpower. What about allying with other small powers? Any military combination would have been helpless to challenge either superpower or its military alliance. The Arab League was formed in 1945 and is the only example of a postwar small-power (non-European) military alliance.

Thus, although alliance has been a possibility, the international situation since World War II made a nonaligned strategy attractive to small powers for several reasons. For states that had recently achieved independence from a colonial status, it permitted at least the appearance of an independent foreign policy stance. Nonalignment in the form developed by India and Yugoslavia starting in the 1950s — not simply the refusal to join the Eastern or Western coalitions, but an active and assertive policy directed toward independence, world peace, and justice — also gave smaller states a purposeful policy and a positive diplomatic identity. The Nonaligned Movement (NAM), a coalition in its own right, has since grown to include a large number of otherwise diverse states. During the cold war it often acted as a third force in world affairs, but since then its role has diminished significantly.

Polarity in the International System

One is one and all alone; "two's company, three's a crowd." In any social system, however small or simple, the number of participants makes a difference. Patterns of behavior differ greatly in different-sized groups. Thucydides of ancient Greece, many nineteenth-century European statesmen, and former U.S. Secretary of State Henry Kissinger would all agree that the number of participants in the international system makes a great difference in the way the participants can and must behave, affecting the likelihood of war among them and even their very survival as independent actors. The concern with nation-states, and primarily with the relative strength of the biggest states as actors in the pursuit of power, is typical of realist analysis.

To characterize an international system, we need to know the structure of the system — the opportunities or possibilities it presents — and how the menu provided by the structure affects the international relations within the system. To understand the structure of the system, we need knowledge about the number of state actors, their relative sizes, and the existence of such nonstate actors as alliances built by various bonds or linkages between two or more states.

Perhaps the most important theoretical concept for classifying international systems concerns the *number of major actors,* or **poles,** in the system. Each acts with significant independence from other major actors; it is its own master, with a wide selection of possible behaviors. A major actor may be either a single nation-state — a major power — or a tight and cohesive *alliance* of one or more major powers with other large or small allied powers. Thus, the number of poles in a system may or may not be the same as the number of major powers.[7] States may behave quite differently in a system composed of two alliances, each including several major powers, than in a system with two major powers unallied with other states. The various states in an alliance usually retain substantial independence, at least potentially; much negotiation and bargaining may be required for members of an alliance to act together and may result in less than unanimity. The possibility that in important ways the alliance will not behave like a unified actor introduces special instabilities and uncertainties.

At one extreme is the system with only a single major actor, usually a single state, that dominates all the smaller states. There has never been such a **unipolar** global system, though a world empire would probably take such a form. The period immediately after World War II, when the European powers, including the Soviet Union, lay exhausted and the United States had a monopoly on nuclear weapons may be a partial exception, if a short-lived one. Dominated, or *hegemonic,* systems of less than global extent have been known in the past; the region of China and the Far East of several centuries ago is a good example. In the sense that a major power may be called a "pole" if it possesses a combination of significant military, economic, and political power, some observers have characterized the post–cold war period as unipolar. The United States is seen as the "unchallenged" dominant actor, the "only country with the military, diplomatic, political and economic assets to be a decisive player in any conflict in whatever part of the world it chooses to involve itself."[8] Certainly the global menu changed considerably with end of the cold war and the demise of the Soviet Union as an opposing superpower. The apparent problems of American foreign policy under both Bush and Clinton derived in part from the difficulties of adjusting to the drastically different set of opportunities and constraints that accompanied this structural change in the international system.

Multipolar systems, those with multiple power centers, have existed often in the past. During much of the eighteenth to the early twentieth centuries, a precarious mul-

---

[7] Some writers prefer to define polarity only in terms of the number of major states — for example, Kenneth Waltz, *Theory of International Politics* (Boston: Addison-Wesley, 1979) — or the distribution of power among those states, ignoring alliance patterns — for example, Jack S. Levy, "The Polarity of the System and International Stability: An Empirical Analysis," in Alan Ned Sabrosky, ed., *Polarity and War: The Changing Structure of International Conflict* (Boulder, Colo.: Westview, 1985), pp. 41–66. To ignore alliance patterns or the formation of cohesive blocs, however, would be to characterize the international system as multipolar throughout the period from 1700 to 1945 and to ignore, for instance, the way the two opposing alliance systems became solidified and hostile before World War I.

[8] This rather extreme statement of contemporary unipolarity is from Charles Krauthammer, "The Unipolar Moment," *Foreign Affairs* 70, 1 (1991): pp. 23–33, who argues that the United States can support and sustain its unipolar status; quote from p. 24. For a more recent and more cautious view, see Samuel P. Huntington, "The Lonely Superpower," *Foreign Affairs* 78, 2 (March/April 1999): pp. 35–49.

tipolar system of many great powers existed in Europe. Occasionally it broke down through the dynamic and aggressive growth of one member (for example, Napoleon's France) or because of rigidities introduced by very close alliances or longstanding, and often ideologically based, antagonisms. When two or more alliances form among a larger number of major powers, we say that the system has become **polarized,** much as metal filings cluster around the two poles of a magnet. In almost all the international systems we can identify, polarization is a phenomenon whereby a multipolar system becomes transformed by alliance formation into a **bipolar** system, one with exactly two power centers. Generally speaking, polarization refers to "the tendency for actors to cluster around the system's most powerful states."[9] The more closely they cluster, the more polarized, or "tight," the system has become.

The distinction between major powers as relatively independent actors on the one hand, and alliances as actors on the other, is often important. Around 1900 there were several states of similar size and resources: Britain, France, Russia, Germany, Italy, and Austria-Hungary. Because the alliances that existed among them were neither very tight nor permanent, the Europe of the time could be thought of as a multipolar system, one not very polarized. But just before World War I, in 1914, the great powers became so committed to rival alliance groupings — the Triple Alliance (Germany, Austria-Hungary, and Italy) and the Triple Entente (Britain, France, and Russia) — that the system became polarized to the degree that it was now accurate to speak of a *tight bipolar* system in Europe. Tight bipolar systems are relatively common in world history. A famous one, in ancient Greece, consisted of Athens and Sparta, with their respective allies; another was the United States and the Soviet Union, each with its allies, during a period immediately after World War II. The possibility that two rival alliances will form, with more than one major power on one or both sides, is common in world politics and serves as an extremely serious source of instability in multipolar systems.

After World War I the basis for a multipolar system was temporarily weakened. The victorious states — Britain, France, Italy, and the United States, along with their allies — dominated the system. Austria-Hungary was fragmented into several small countries (Austria, Hungary, Czechoslovakia, and parts of Poland, Yugoslavia, and Romania); Germany was defeated and disarmed; Russia was shattered by defeat and civil war. Nevertheless, the winning alliance quickly broke up. The United States and Japan emerged as major independent powers, and by the 1930s both Germany and Russia had substantially recovered. This worldwide major power system was composed of several states of similar power potential. However, by the outbreak of World War II in 1939, it too had become much more polarized, as in 1914. Germany, Italy, and Japan (the Axis powers) allied themselves against France and Britain. Both the United States and Russia remained somewhat aloof from the others until they became drawn into the war on the side of Britain and France (the Allied powers). The world was again divided along bipolar lines.

---

[9] David R. Rapkin and William R. Thompson, with Jon A. Christopherson, "Bipolarity and Bipolarization in the Cold War Era: Conceptualization, Measurement, and Validation," *Journal of Conflict Resolution* 23, 2 (1979): p. 263.

Polarization and the Cold War

When World War II was over, the basis for a multipolar system had been destroyed. Germany, Italy, and Japan were totally defeated. Though France was officially a victor, it too was greatly weakened by its initial defeat and the German occupation in 1940. Britain was clearly a victor politically but was drained economically and was soon to lose its major colonies. China was poor and in the midst of civil war between the nationalists and the communists: its status as a great power was only nominal. The United States and the Soviet Union were clearly the most powerful states in the world (though the United States was certainly the more powerful of the two). Their superiority was reinforced and dramatized by the fact that for most of the period they were the only two powers with large numbers of hydrogen bombs and the big, sophisticated missile systems necessary to deliver these weapons against a technologically advanced defender. Even today, the United States and Russia still have a very great nuclear advantage over any other state.

The two superpowers quickly formed opposing alliances. Many states in Western Europe and elsewhere sought protection, in alliance with the United States, against the possibility of Soviet expansion. The United States then brought other countries — notably the Federal Republic of Germany (West Germany, the largest part of divided Germany) — into NATO or into its other alliances, like the Rio Pact among Latin American states and the Southeast Asia Treaty Organization (SEATO). After installing communist governments in most Eastern European countries, the Soviet Union then incorporated those states into its new alliance, the Warsaw Pact, and formed an alliance with the new communist government of China. Thus, the bipolar system became increasingly polarized; not only were the two superpowers much stronger than anyone else, but each now was additionally strengthened by important allies.

The polarization was never complete, however, because quite a number of Asian and African nations, as well as a few European ones, stayed nonaligned, remaining apart from the rival alliance groupings. Polarization is limited to the extent that states with significant bases of power stay apart from the two contending blocs or else switch alignment from one bloc to the other. A combination of processes during the 1970s and 1980s loosened this tight bipolar structure. Alliance ties weakened as a result of disagreements over security policy; the Sino-Soviet split was the most significant. The distribution of economic strength became more diffuse with the recovery and growth of China, Germany, and Japan and the development and growth of the European Union. The direct U.S.-Soviet confrontation also softened, partly the result of increased familiarity (and fatigue) after decades of intense interaction.

Then, at the end of the 1980s, changes came in a flood. Popular revolutions in all the Warsaw Pact nations replaced their governments, mostly with anticommunist leaders. The new leaders demanded that Soviet troops leave their territories, and the Warsaw Pact collapsed. In 1990 East Germany joined West Germany, and the newly unified country inherited West Germany's membership in NATO and the European Union. Hungary, Poland, Czechoslovakia, and longtime neutrals like Austria and Sweden sought admission to the EU. Barriers to trade, travel, and other exchanges tumbled. Many Soviet/Russian citizens, especially Jews, emigrated. The economically distraught countries of Eastern Europe repudiated central planning, moving toward a capitalist market economy. They, and Russia, and the rest of the states of the former Soviet Union (FSU) sought massive inflows of private investment capital and loans from Western governments and international agencies. The Eastern pole dissolved, losing much of its discreteness along with its formal structure. All the defining economic and institutional bonds were gone, beyond reconstruction, and the bipolar confrontation came to an end.

Of course, in reality international systems never fit abstract models perfectly; for example, the U.S.-Soviet bipolar system was never one of two perfectly matched rivals. The United States and its partners were more powerful economically than the Soviet bloc. For example, in 1960 the American economy, when measured by gross domestic product (GDP), was three times as large as that of the USSR, and the wealth of the Western alliance of NATO plus Japan exceeded that of all the communist states by four to five times. Table 4.1 illustrates the differences between the blocs' major actors, both in 1960, at the height of tight bipolarity, and in 1989, when the loose bipolar system was on the verge of complete collapse with the end of the cold war. Military expenditures provide a very rough indicator of military capabilities. International comparisons are distorted by changing foreign-exchange rates, and Soviet and Chinese military spending was (and is) always very difficult to measure. With these cautions in mind, the data give a useful approximation of capabilities.

By the time the cold war ended the Soviet Union approached equality with the United States on only one dimension — military capabilities — and even here many questioned the notion of superpower parity in light of American technological superiority. That superiority was never so great, however, that the American leadership saw fit to use it directly against the Soviets. Though the United States between 1945 and the late 1960s could almost surely have inflicted more damage than it received in a general war, the likely damage to itself posed prohibitive risks. Except for the most serious threats to national survival, which fortunately never materialized, the United States would not resort to direct military conflict with the USSR. Also, at virtually all times during the cold war the Soviets had the ability to destroy America's Western European allies; knowledge of that fact doubtless helped restrain American leaders from using their military superiority casually.

Limits to Bipolarity

A difficult analytical problem always arises when we try to move from the idealized abstractions of theory to an analysis of real-world conditions. How much of a departure from the theoretical norm of equal size can be tolerated without losing whatever may be the essential characteristics of a bipolar or multipolar system? How much preponderance is required for unipolarity? And what are the relevant dimensions of equality or preponderance — population, wealth, military forces or nuclear and thermonuclear weapons only? In regard to weapons capable of mass destruction, during the cold war only the United States and the Soviet Union could credibly threaten the other or threaten to obliterate any middle-range power. However, as it became clear that the nuclear weapons of a superpower were unusable in a quarrel between that state and a smaller one — either from moral restraint or out of fear that such use would

TABLE 4.1   Relative Strength of Major Powers and Their Coalitions, 1960 and 1989

State or Coalition	GDP (billions $U.S.)	Share of Total (percent)	Military Expenditures (billions $U.S.)	Share of Total (percent)
1960				
United States	1,787	45.3	186.5	52.7
Soviet Union	514	13.0	89.5	25.3
Britain	359	9.1	21.2	6.0
France	266	6.7	21.1	6.0
West Germany	364	9.2	19.6	5.5
Japan	278	7.0	3.6	1.0
China	378	9.6	12.6	3.6
West + Japan	3,055	77.4	251.9	71.2
USSR + China	892	22.6	102.1	28.8
1989				
United States	4,492	36.5	319.1	37.5
Soviet Union	2,227	18.1	317.9	37.3
Britain	758	6.2	37.2	4.4
France	770	6.3	45.2	5.3
West Germany	858	7.0	46.6	5.5
Japan	1,687	13.7	39.5	4.6
China	1,512	12.3	45.8	5.4
West + Japan	8,656	69.6	487.6	57.3
USSR	2,227	18.1	317.9	37.3
China	1,512	12.3	45.9	5.4

Sources: Gross domestic product (GDP) data are an updated version of those in Robert Summers and Alan Heston "The Penn World Table (Mark 5): An Expanded Set of International Comparisons, 1950–1988," *Quarterly Journal of Economics* 106, 9 (1991) [cited June 3, 1998]; available at <http://pwt.econ.upenn.edu/>. Military expenditures for 1960 are from Stockholm International Peace Research Institute (SIPRI), *SIPRI Yearbook 1980: World Armaments and Disarmament* (London: Taylor & Francis, 1981); for 1989, U.S. Arms Control and Disarmament Agency (ACDA), *World Military Expenditures and Arms Transfers 1996* (Washington, D.C.: U.S. Arms Control and Disarmament Agency, 1997). The 1960 military expenditure figure for China is extrapolated based on ACDA's 1963 figure and the average growth rate from 1963 through 1966. Dollar figures are for base year 1985.

only bring in the other superpower on the opposing side — superpower leaders had to think carefully about whether they could subdue distant, small states with conventional weapons only. Distances from the great powers' bases, plus the logistical and morale advantages of fighting close to home, nullified many of the superpowers' advantages and contributed to a degree of multipolarity below the level of nuclear force even during the height of East-West confrontation. Additionally, there were many circumstances in which military might was not easily used or threatened — in UN deliberations, in trade negotiations, in disputes over access to raw materials. Such political processes often looked as if they were taking place in the context of a multipolar system.

If one or more of the world's nonaligned states should develop great resources to the point where it could, while remaining nonaligned, rival the United States as the one remaining superpower (or Russia as a "partial" superpower), then the balance would clearly be moving in the direction of a multipolar system. The current international system, however, is well below that point. Even though China has some nuclear weapons and a much larger population than any other nation (more that 1.2 billion people, as compared with 950 million in India, the second largest), it is still in the process of economic development, lacking the industrial base even to challenge Russia militarily. China could defend its own territory against virtually any assault, but its army is ill equipped compared with that of the United States when it comes to offensive action.

In the 1970s the United States tried to sustain Chinese independence from the Soviet Union (thus weakening the Soviet-led pole) without concluding a full alliance with China (which might have provoked a too-vigorous Soviet response). This policy left China without the power base or allies necessary to become a really strong actor in the system. A power composed of the fifteen members of the newly expanded European Union, with a combined population of 375 million and a total GDP of $6 trillion, might be a more convincing rival; but a fully integrated political unit in Europe, with a common defense policy, does not yet exist and is not likely in the near future. Japan has avoided building nuclear weapons or a capacity for military action far from its shores, despite its powerful economy and growing defense expenditures.

The contemporary world cannot be well characterized as bipolar. Strictly in nuclear terms, the United States and Russia remain the only really big powers. But with the Warsaw Pact disbanded and Russian abandonment of many former client states in the Third World, Russia no longer leads a bloc or coalition. It has reduced its own conventional military capabilities and is economically incapable of supporting substantial military activities beyond its borders. Except for its nuclear weapons, Russia is in many respects a less formidable power than Germany or Japan. Thus one might characterize the current system as a situation of U.S. hegemony. The United States is now the only country capable of exerting great military power at great distance, as it did against Iraq in 1991. But its economy is not strong enough to sustain a large-scale global reach. The United States, like Russia, has made some efforts to reduce the costs of its military effort or sought to share those costs with allies; Germany, Japan, Saudi Arabia, and Kuwait paid virtually all of the financial costs of the war against Iraq. It is an exaggeration, then, to characterize the United States as a hegemon capable of enforcing its will; it cannot fully play the role of a single dominating power in a unipolar system. If it tried, other states would be very fearful and would have incentives to coalesce and align themselves against it.[10] The reality is complex.

It is theoretically possible that there may someday be a large number of states in the world, none of which is especially more powerful than any of the others, and that no widespread or long-term alliances will form. Economists describe this sort of a market structure as one of perfect or near-perfect competition, in which no single buyer or seller is big enough to affect the market price of other buyers or sellers. However, such a condition has not existed in any of the international political systems or subsystems of recent history, and it is only a possibility about which to speculate.

Polarity and International Stability

Since different systems provide different menus for states, both large and small, we suspect (although little has been proved) that different systems are characterized by different patterns of state behavior. Are there any reasons to prefer one type of system to another, aside from the consideration that most people would probably prefer to live in a powerful and secure country rather than a weak and vulnerable one? Is there anything about one type of system that makes it preferable — for large states, for small states, or for most of the world's population, regardless of where they live? These questions have become increasingly significant as the world has found itself moving away from bipolarity toward unipolarity in military affairs and toward multipolarity in the economic and political realms.

One widely preferred characteristic of an international system is **stability.** In one sense, stability means *not being prone to war.* This, however, is a very ambiguous criterion; it might mean simply that wars are infrequent. But if the wars that did occur dragged on for many years, the advantages of infrequency might pale. Thus, the duration of wars is clearly important. So is severity: one can easily imagine systems where wars are rare but, when they do occur, savage; include most members of the system; and are fought to the point of unconditional surrender. If "frequency" is the number of wars fought by a given number of states in a particular period and "duration" is the number of months or years each war lasts, an index of "severity" might be based on the number of people who are killed.

These are not merely sterile academic distinctions among variables that are closely related in the real world. On the contrary, a survey of all wars between major powers over the past five centuries shows that the correlation between the number of wars begun within various twenty-five-year periods and the number of casualties is moderately negative; in other words, periods with more wars tended to have fewer casualties.[11] Wars may be frequent or severe, depending on other characteristics of the

---

[10] On why other states have not "ganged up" on the United States despite its near-hegemonic status, see Josef Joffe, "How America Does It," *Foreign Affairs* 76, 5 (1997): pp. 13–27.

[11] Jack S. Levy and T. Clifton Morgan, "The Frequency and Seriousness of War: An Inverse Relationship?" *Journal of Conflict Resolution* 28, 4 (1984): pp. 731–749.

international system. Bipolar systems, for instance, are marked by the continuing confrontation of two major powers. Many bloody wars would drain the two antagonists of their wealth and resources, either reducing them both to a level so near the second-rank powers that the system would become multipolar, or destroying the weaker one and leaving the way open for a unipolar empire. If a system is to persist, its wars — at least among the major powers — must be either infrequent or not very severe.

The bipolar system that obtained after World War II produced many crises and confrontations. Confrontations, however, do not necessarily produce violent conflicts and military fatalities; on the contrary, in the postwar period there were no acknowledged, direct, violent conflicts between the two superpowers. (Probably some American fliers and Soviet antiaircraft crews killed each other during the Vietnam War, but neither state discussed this publicly.) Both sides feared that, should any such direct conflict begin, it would be very hard to contain it at a low level of intensity and escalation would carry the risk of enormous damage to both sides. Nor were there violent conflicts between any of the major powers, save for a border skirmish between China and the Soviet Union in 1969.

The battlegrounds for almost all the violent conflicts that occurred from the end of World War II until the end of the cold war were in the less developed countries, although there has been an increase in European-based conflict — in the Balkans — since 1989.[12] Many of the quarrels involved a superpower and a small state. At least thirteen of these conflicts arose between 1945 and 1991, with ten involving the United States (North Korea and China from 1950 to 1953, Lebanon in 1958 and 1983, Cuba in 1962, Indochina from 1961 to 1973, the Dominican Republic in 1965, Grenada in 1983, Libya in 1986, Panama in 1989, and Iraq in 1991) and three involving the Soviet Union (Hungary in 1956, Czechoslovakia in 1968, and Afghanistan beginning in 1979). Most of these episodes were quite limited and did not result in heavy casualties. (The Korean, Indochinese, Afghanistan, and Iraqi cases are exceptions: the first three were of long duration, and all four were intense actions involving tens or hundreds of thousands of casualties.) The superpowers, however, proved very successful in restraining conflicts among their own allies. With only a few exceptions — one or two in Central America, between Turkey and Greece over Cyprus, and between Britain and Argentina over the Falkland Islands (known to the Argentines as the Islas Malvinas) — wars between the allies of one superpower were prevented.

Another definition of stability is *continuity in the fundamental pattern of interactions* in the international system. Changes in the number or identity of major actors affect stability only insofar as they affect that pattern. A unipolar system would be marked by a pattern of interaction involving dominance and submission to the will of the hegemon. A bipolar system is characterized by competition and conflict between two actors — a pattern of interactions very different from that of the unipolar system. A system with three major actors is marked by shifting patterns of conflict and cooperation, both of which are found on all three sides of the triangle. If an alliance between

---

[12] On the location and frequency of post–cold war conflicts, see Peter Wallensteen and Margareta Sollenberg, "Armed Conflicts and Regional Conflict Complexes, 1989–97," *Journal of Peace Research* 35, 5 (September 1998): pp. 621–634.

two of the actors becomes tight and permanent, then it is no longer a three-actor system but a bipolar one, with substantial cooperation between the two formerly autonomous actors, both of which are in conflict with the third.[13] It may be that in politics, as in love, three-actor systems are almost always unstable, falling too easily into two-against-one alliances that end in the destruction of one of the original parties. Both the Soviet Union and the United States often feared that an alliance between the other and China might be cemented. The addition of a fourth actor to that three-actor system might have made for a more reliable pattern of shifting conflict and cooperation. However, there is always the possibility that the growth of many formal and informal linkages will create a bloc among two or more actors that formerly moved independently. What was once a multipolar system could become a bipolar one; there would still be several major powers, but they would be combined into two opposing alliances.

A system that always had four or more major actors within it might be stable even if the identity of the powers changed frequently because of wars, growth, or internal dissension in some states. When the number or identity of major actors (whether national actors or alliance blocs) changes, we say that the system has been transformed to a new system only if the changes seem to produce fundamentally different patterns of interaction. In cases where there are more than four major actors it is hard to know whether the addition of yet another actor would fundamentally change interactions. The difference between a multipolar system with four actors and one with five might be substantial. Beyond that point, as conditions approached those of perfect competition, the pattern of interactions might again be different.

Balances and Imbalances of Power

Both aspects of stability have been examined by political scientists and historians wanting to assess the advantages and disadvantages of different distributions of power. The proneness of international systems toward war is a topic we address in some detail in Chapter 8, but here we want to note briefly two common views, both associated with the realist perspective. The first is that international stability is most likely when there is a **balance of power.** A balance exists when no single state or coalition of states dominates the international system; it operates in multipolar or bipolar systems, but not in unipolar systems. According to balance-of-power theory, the development of imbalances among the system's major powers is especially dangerous and threatens to engulf the system in destructive warfare. The nineteenth-century Concert of Europe worked well because the Continent's major powers were roughly equal in military strength. Stability was reinforced by Great Britain's tendency to throw its weight behind the lesser state or coalition when the balance was threatened by the rise of a would-be hegemon. Britain had long performed this role of "balancer" — for example, during the repeated contests between France and the Hapsburg dynasty and during the Napoleonic Wars — but these dynamics have become so closely associated

---

[13] For an analysis of tripolar relationships in the postwar system among the United States, the Soviet Union, and China, see Joshua S. Goldstein and John R. Freeman, *Three Way Street: Strategic Reciprocity in World Politics* (Chicago: University of Chicago Press, 1990).

with the relative stability of nineteenth century great-power politics that we sometimes speak of this multipolar period as *the* Balance-of-Power system.[14]

Another, seemingly contary, view is that the *preponderance of power* associated with hegemony is most conducive to international stability. Although the terms *hegemony* and *unipolarity* are often used interchangeably, the theory of **hegemonic stability** emphasizes a single state's ability to establish and enforce the international "rules of the game." The hegemon's dominance rests on its disproportionate share of military and economic resources, but the theory does not equate this with a unipolar distribution of power: the nineteenth century, a multipolar period, was a time of British hegemony; the post–World War II system, a bipolar one, was a period of American hegemony. British power in the nineteenth century and American power in the twentieth were such that no other state or coalition of states dared challenge them militarily. In addition, their economic might allowed them to break down, whether through coercion or beneficence, the barriers to free trade that were often the source of conflict between the major powers. These periods are thus referred to as *Pax Britannica* and *Pax Americana* — the British Peace and the American Peace.[15]

Was the relative stability of nineteenth-century Europe the result of the mulipolar balance of power or British hegemony? Was the stability following World War II, what one historian has called the "long peace," attributable more to the bipolarity of the cold war or to American hegemony?[16] Opinions differ, and so do definitions — definitions of stability, but also the meaning of power and influence. In the next chapter we discuss the latter.

---

[14] See Edward Gulick, *Europe's Classical Balance of Power: A Case History of the Theory and Practice of One of the Great Concepts of European Statecraft* (New York: Norton, 1967). Other analyses emphasize the shared norms, as opposed to brute power balancing, that operated during the period of the Concert. See Robert Jervis, "From Balance to Concert: A Study of International Security Cooperation," *World Politics* 38, 1 (1985): pp. 58–79; Paul Schroeder, "The 19th-Century International System: Changes in the Structure," *World Politics* 39, 1 (1986): pp. 1–26. Henry Kissinger, in *A World Restored: Metternich, Castlereagh, and the Problems of Peace, 1812–22* (Boston: Houghton Mifflin, 1973), credits both.

[15] For recent inquiries into this debate, see Robert Powell, "Stability and the Distribution of Power," *World Politics* 48 (January 1996): pp. 239–267; and Jacek Kugler and Douglas Lemke, eds., *Parity and War: Evaluations and Extensions of* The War Ledger (Ann Arbor: University of Michigan Press, 1996).

[16] See John Lewis Gaddis, *The Long Peace: Inquiries into the History of the Cold War* (New York: Oxford University Press, 1987). Gaddis is not satisfied with either explanation, or with any others offerred by political scientists; see chap. 10.

5

Relations between States: Power and Influence

WORLD SYSTEM

RELATIONS

SOCIETY

GOVERNMENT

ROLE

INDIVIDUAL

Two Aspects of Power

Power can be thought of as a relationship. It takes on meaning only as it affects a state's behavior toward another state or international actor. The menu of any state, then, is constrained or affected not only by its own capabilities, goals, policies, and actions, but also by those of the other entity with which it interacts — by the state's attempts to influence others and by the attempts of others to influence it. Relationships between states can be seen in two ways, both of which will be described in our discussion of power. First, we can look at how two states compare on a set of national attributes or characteristics. Second, we can look at the actual set of interactions between pairs of states.

We will be concerned with both power as a set of national attributes or *capabilities* and power as a process of exercising *influence.* Capability and influence become meaningful only when compared with the capabilities of others and their own attempts to influence outcomes. In looking at the U.S. decision to drop the atomic bomb, the key elements were the actual existence of the weapon (a military capability, derived from skill, knowledge, and resources that created the bomb) and the arguments about how the bomb could be used to influence the behavior of Japan. Remember also that comparison implies measurement: a key question in international relations is how much power an actor has. In looking at power both as a set of capabilities and as influence, we shall highlight problems of creating indicators to measure power.

Power and Influence

In an era of growing interdependence, power may simply mean the ability to have an impact on the behavior of other actors — to affect the menu of others, even if you are a small and relatively weak actor. Some people see power as the ability to reduce uncertainty in the environment, and for some it is a means to an end. For others power has come to mean causality, because explaining who has power explains why things happen. Other people say that power is like money in the sense that it can be saved and spent. Another view is that power is primarily a psychological phenomenon, which people have if others think they do. The list could go on and on.[1]

As we noted in Chapter 2, realism is a view of international politics that sees people seeking power and desiring to dominate others. Hans Morgenthau, the most widely read exponent of this approach, stated the matter succinctly in his classic textbook, *Politics Among Nations.* The section titled "International Politics as a Struggle for Power" opens with the following words: "International politics, like all politics, is a struggle for power. Whatever the ultimate aims of international politics, power is always the immediate aim."[2] This view of power is centered on struggle among sovereign states within the anarchic international system and is characterized by the use and manipulation of military resources.

Other observers, however, object to the realists' emphasis on constant struggle and their highly conflictual, coercive, and military interpretation of the concept of power. They argue that although power is central to international politics, it takes many forms. Stressing the military aspects of conflict and struggle distorts how states actually behave and attempt to reach their objectives in international politics; power is not exercised only in situations of armed conflict or potential armed conflict. More important, what does power mean and how is it to be measured among highly interdependent actors who share a common view of the world, have similar economies, and have excluded military options from their interactions? The realist view's emphasis on

---

[1] For two overviews of various perspectives on the concept of power, see David A. Baldwin, *Paradoxes of Power* (Oxford: Blackwell, 1989), and Karl W. Deutsch, *The Analysis of International Relations*, 3rd ed. (Englewood Cliffs, N.J.: Prentice-Hall, 1988), chaps. 3, 4.

[2] Hans J. Morganthau, *Politics Among Nations: The Struggle for Power and Peace,* 6th ed. (New York: Knopf, 1985), p. 31.

power does not appear applicable to just such a group of West European, North American, and other Western industrialized countries (including Japan, Australia, and New Zealand). The weaknesses of the realist view will only be magnified in a post–cold war system in which the military dimension will play a much diminished role in Europe and between the United States and Russia.

So, in our discussion, what will we mean by "power"? Let us start with a very broad definition and then break the concept down into more manageable sections. **Power** is *the ability to overcome obstacles and influence outcomes.* This is a useful formulation because it indicates that power is the ability to get what you want and to achieve a desired outcome through control of your environment, both human and nonhuman.

In most areas of social interaction, including international interaction, to influence outcomes does not mean prevailing in conflict involving violence or the threat of violence. States, like people, come into conflict with others every day on a wide variety of issues; they continually find themselves in situations where there is some form of incompatibility or *conflict of interest.* In negotiating with Japan over trade imbalances, in getting permission for military aircraft to fly over French territory, or in dealing with Canada on the effects of acid rain, to name just a few examples, the interests and objectives of the United States are incompatible in some way with the interests and objectives of the other state. As long as there are any incompatibilities between these sets of interests and objectives, conflict will arise. However, the manner in which these conflicts are resolved and the manner in which the United States attempts to prevail may have little resemblance to the realist concept of power struggle and certainly will not involve military coercion. It will, however, involve some form of *influence.*

Exercising influence is a method by which people and states get their way. If one state has gotten its way, the implication is that another state has not. This relational aspect of power is captured in Robert Dahl's classic definition: *A*'s ability to get *B* to do something that *B* would not otherwise do.[3] Influence takes many forms. One involves actually changing the existing policy of another actor: switching voting positions in the United Nations, leaving one alliance and joining another, dropping restrictions on the importation of foreign automobiles. Because influence has been used to change the behavior of another state, this is sometimes called "behavioral power."[4] It means influencing another country to stop an action it is already pursuing in order to compel a result — a policy known in political science as **compellence.** Using the atomic bomb against Japan was aimed at compelling the Japanese to surrender; the Gulf War was directed at compelling Iraq to withdraw from Kuwait. Less successful examples include the U.S. attempts, from the early 1960s to 1975, through military, diplomatic, and even economic means, to compel the North Vietnamese to withdraw from South Vietnam or, in 1979, to get Iran to release the American hostages. Because it seeks to reverse an established policy, compellence can be very difficult to achieve.

In contrast to compellence, **deterrence** aims to influence another actor *not* to do something it would otherwise do. In the contemporary system, nuclear deterrence (which we discuss in Part II) meant that during the cold war the United States influ-

---

[3] Robert A. Dahl, "The Concept of Power," *Behavioral Science* 2 (1957): pp. 201–205.
[4] See Michael Don Ward and Lewis House, "A Theory of the Behavioral Power of Nations," *Journal of Conflict Resolution* 32 (March 1988): pp. 3–36.

enced the Soviet Union not to attack it or its allies with nuclear weapons (through fear of retaliation), and vice versa. There are many theories and speculations about deterrence, and in practice it is hard to measure the concept satisfactorily. It is easier to recognize the actions that one state has influenced another state to perform than those actions that the state has been influenced not to perform. For example, did NATO's strength truly deter a Soviet attack on Western Europe, or did the USSR never intend to attack in the first place? An action that apparently was deterred might not have happened anyway, in which case a policy of deterrence is really not responsible for the outcome. Analyzing actions that did not occur, whether as causes or effects of other actions, is a difficult task for the social scientist because it involves "counterfactual" reasoning.[5]

Similarly hard to measure, but still very important for understanding world politics, is *potential influence.* Influence is a partly psychological phenomenon, based on the perceptions of the capabilities and intentions of other states. Potential influence is based on other policymakers' perceptions of the influence that one may have in specific situations. If a state has potential influence, other states will not even attempt certain activities because they know that such activities will fail or be very costly. As with deterrence, it is very difficult to measure state *A*'s successful influence in a case where state *B* never seriously considers a policy option because the costs involved are so high as to make an action inconceivable. How many times in the 1920s and 1930s might Panama have wanted to demand that the United States leave the Canal Zone? We have no idea because we cannot measure how many times the desire occurred and then was suppressed out of fear of American reaction.

When we look for the exercise of power in world politics, therefore, we cannot limit our attention to cases in which one state has directly influenced the behavior — action or inaction — of another state. In some situations, states may never have had the opportunity to behave in a certain way, to pursue policies in their interests. Powerful states can influence more than the choices of other states; they also influence other states' menus. This has been called "structural power" because it involves the ability of state *A* to influence the context or environment surrounding state *B*'s decisions — that is, the structure of the situation in which *B* finds itself.[6]

One important way in which states exercise structural power is by influencing the agenda of issues under discussion. Often this takes the form of keeping certain things *off* the international agenda. During the periods of British and American hegemony, for example, the idea that anything other than the free market should govern the flow of goods and capital across state boundaries was rarely a matter for discussion. Instead, international deliberations concentrated on how best to achieve this liberal economic order. It was not until the influence of British and American hegemony waned that

---

[5] For guidance on how to engage in counterfactual reasoning, along with some careful applications, consult Philip E. Tetlock and Aaron Belkin, eds., *Counterfactual Thought Experiments in World Politics: Logical, Methodological, and Psychological Perspectives* (Princeton, N.J.: Princeton University Press, 1996); see also David Sylvan and Stephen Majeski, "A Methodology for the Study of Historical Counterfactuals," *International Studies Quarterly* 42, 1 (1998): pp. 79–108.

[6] See Susan Strange, "What About International Relations?" in Susan Strange, ed., *Paths to International Political Economy* (London: Allen & Unwin, 1984), p. 191; and Baldwin, *Paradoxes of Power*, p. 107.

alternatives to the free market got a place on the international agenda. Thus, the increased influence of the Organization of Oil Exporting Countries (OPEC) in the 1970s stimulated discussions in the UN about how nonmarket mechanisms might be used to stabilize commodity prices and curtail some of the more exploitative practices of multinational corporations.

Foreign policymakers know well the importance of controlling the agenda; human rights violations and other nondemocratic practices are usually declared to be internal affairs (matters of national sovereignty) by states subjected to international criticism. That the issue of human rights is in fact increasingly discussed by states gives some indication of the structural power exercised by the United States and other western democracies in world politics. By concentrating exclusively on whether and to what extent states like China or Iraq actually change their behavior in response to U.S. policy, we might miss this more subtle exercise of power.

Another, even more subtle, form of structural power — one sometimes termed "soft power" — is influence over the values held by other states, and therefore what they have taken to be *their* interests, *their* goals, and *their* desired outcomes. Compared to influencing the behavior of others by getting them to do things they would not otherwise do, "there is a much bigger payoff in getting others to want what you want, and that has to do with the attraction of one's ideas."[7] A state, like the United States, with soft power is in a position where its influence over outcomes does not always require changing the behavior of other states or seizing control of the agenda at international conferences. When the state's culture, ideology, and institutions enjoy widespread appeal — for instance, American-style democracy and free-market capitalism — other explicit and more mundane exercises of power are unnecessary. "Indeed, is it not the supreme exercise of power to get another or others to have the desires you want them to have ... to secure their compliance by controlling their thoughts and desires?"[8] Of course, this type of power can appear quite insidious depending on one's perspective, which is why soft power is interpreted by many as "cultural imperialism."

Power and Capability

National attributes or capabilities greatly influence the menu of activity available to states. What is possible or probable relates to the means at one's disposal. This is especially important in gauging the actions and reactions of specific states in specific situations. Capabilities include any physical object, talent, or quality that can be used to affect the behavior (or desires) of others. Capabilities are important because they affect others' perceptions, including what one is able to do and what one is willing to do.

Threats and promises are common instruments of influence, but they have to be *credible*. Capabilities are crucial to two different aspects of a state's credibility. First, for a threat or promise to be credible, the targeted party has to believe that the other party

---

[7] Josef Joffe, "How America Does It," *Foreign Affairs* 76, 5 (1997): p. 24. On America's soft power, see especially Joseph S. Nye, *Bound to Lead: The Changing Nature of American Power* (New York: Basic Books, 1990).

[8] Steven Lukes, *Power: A Radical View* (London: Macmillan, 1974), p. 23. This study has become the classic treatment of this dimension of power.

is *able* to carry it out. One debate over using the atomic bomb against Japan concerned demonstrating the capability — the bomb — to the Japanese so that they would believe in a threat to use more weapons if they did not surrender. Today the menu of the United States makes it possible for it to threaten to destroy any other state — an option available to few other countries. Credibility, of course, also implies a perceived willingness to carry out such a threat; destruction of another country is a serious step. In 1979, during the Camp David negotiations, the American promise to deliver economic aid to Egypt and oil to Israel if they would negotiate a peace treaty was credible because the United States had both the wealth and the oil to deliver on its promises. Most other countries could not make such a promise credible because they lacked the capabilities to carry it out.

If threats and promises do not work, often punishments (political, economic, or military) are carried out. States require capabilities in order to impose the costs or the pain necessary to coerce others to behave as they wish. By doing so, and by doing so effectively, a state also enhances its credibility by showing that it is *willing* to carry out threats in a way that gets results. If this occurs, then at some point in the future threats may not have to be carried out; the mere hint of punishment will bring about the desired action. Thus, reputation is central to compellence and deterrence.[9] The actual use of military force in foreign affairs, while a major element of power, may also be seen as a *failure of influence.* The use of military force means that a state has failed to persuade another state to do something; it has had to resort to armed coercion.

The ability to get others to do one's bidding will differ with the object of one's influence. Capability is relative: what Iraq could do to Kuwait, it could not do to the United States; what the United States could do to Iraq, it cannot do to China. Knowing a state's capabilities and nothing else is of no use to our analysis of world politics; they must be studied within the context of the *influence situation.* Capabilities of states take on meaning only when they are viewed in relation to the objectives of the state and to the capabilities and objectives of others. For example, in 1998 when India was criticized by the international community for testing nuclear weapons even in the context of its conventional superiority vis-à-vis Pakistan, India responded that its nuclear program was directed not toward Pakistan, but toward China. According to Indian leaders, the country's capabilities were adequate in one context but not the other.

National Capabilities: Tangible Elements

Those who study international power and influence usually develop a set of attributes on which a state's power is based, consisting of some sort of power inventory or power potential.[10] It is not really important which specific term or scheme is used. What is important is that the analyst of international politics has some such system for

---

[9] See Jonathan Mercer, *Reputation and International Politics* (Ithaca, N.Y.: Cornell University Press, 1996).
[10] See, for example, the studies in Richard J. Stoll and Michael D. Ward, eds., *Power in World Politics* (Boulder, Colo.: Rienner, 1989).

representing the variety of possible power bases; without a systematic and explicit checklist, the analyst is likely to pay far too much attention to certain bases and forget about others completely. For example, people pay a great deal of attention to the military and economic bases of power but often neglect the moral stature of international actors. This is, in part, a legacy of the realist view of international politics. When informed that the pope was critical of his policies, Josef Stalin was reported to have asked, rhetorically, "How many divisions does the pope have?" A realist, Stalin would have been surprised at the impact of Pope John Paul II's visits to Poland in 1979 and Cuba in 1998. State leaders like Mohandas Gandhi of India and Nelson Mandela of South Africa have also been able to exercise influence on behalf of their nations due to their moral authority. We shall try, in this chapter, to touch on these neglected bases of state power.

Geography and Demography

States are constantly assessed in terms of size — we speak of superpowers, medium powers, small states, microstates. The national attributes of land mass and population are central elements of a state's base of power; they are also among the more tangible and readily measurable set of capabilities we associate with powerful states. Although sheer land area or population by themselves are not sufficient to make a state a great power, a large area often comes with a generous natural resource endowment and, along with a large population, can support a sizable agricultural and industrial base.

A large land mass makes a state difficult to conquer, as both Napoleon and Hitler learned when they marched their armies toward Moscow. Small countries are much more vulnerable to being overwhelmed by a sudden military attack: the Benelux countries (Belgium, the Netherlands, and Luxembourg) could do little to prevent invasion by German armies on their way to France during both world wars; Kuwait was helpless in the face of the Iraqi onslaught in 1990. However, a large land mass is also difficult to defend: during periods of hostility, the Soviet Union and China expended large amounts of resources policing their shared 2,000-mile long border. Topography — the physical features of the land, especially on a state's borders — is another geographic factor in national defense. Mountainous terrain, like Switzerland's, provides a natural barrier to military conquest; plains and deserts are much easier to traverse. The Golan Heights is dear to Israel because it is one of very few spots in an otherwise flat terrain that is readily defensible. Physical location (like America's, straddling two oceans), political location (like Poland's, between sometimes hostile great powers), and climate (like Russia's extremely cold winters) are other physical elements that may contribute to, or detract from, a state's ability to defend itself militarily.

Like large physical size, a large population may be either an asset or a liability, although it seems difficult to be a major power or superpower without one. As well as numbers, we also must look at the age, sex, and spatial distribution of a population and the quality of human resources — the degree to which a people's capabilities have been developed by education or good health care so that they can contribute to the state's economic, military, and cultural bases of power. For example, to understand Israel's military success in the Middle East, we must note the advantages a state gains over its neighbors by having a skilled and healthy population of men *and* women.

An important dimension of a state's human resources is what Harold Lasswell and Abraham Kaplan called "enlightenment": the extent of higher education and the access to specialized knowledge in science, engineering, and the professions.[11] Obviously, a state's military strength depends in large part on access to scientific knowledge; building modern weapons requires a body of scientific expertise that is unavailable to small, poor countries and is not uniformly available to big, rich ones. More broadly, a state needs physicians, engineers, architects, social scientists, educators, administrators, and many others with advanced training and ability. Many possible measures of this capability can be found, among them the number of students in higher education, the number of trained scientists and engineers, and the number of scientific and technical journals published.

Many aspects of enlightenment are related to wealth and material development: it is expensive to train and equip scientists. The same is somewhat true for a more basic level of knowledge that Lasswell and Kaplan labeled "skill." Skill is what it takes to get along in modern life even at a rather low level of sophistication; it may be literacy, familiarity with machinery or computers, or a primary and secondary education. Literacy is especially important because it is required to learn so many other skills and to take advantage of other kinds of enlightenment; widespread literacy is both a resource base for a government and a means whereby it can communicate information or propaganda quickly to its people. But universal education, even only to produce literacy, is costly and difficult for a poor state to provide. The argument can thus be turned around: perhaps only a literate and educated state can become rich.

Another aspect of a state's human resources involves the health and well-being of the population. What access do they have to good medical care? How long do they typically live? How free is the country from various contagious diseases that are now, in principle, preventable? Does the state possess first-class centers of medical treatment where the latest knowledge is available? How evenly distributed is good health throughout the population? Are there substantial minorities whose health facilities are markedly poorer than the average? The health of a state's population is an important base of influence. Since both industrial and military power depend in part on having a healthy population of young people, access to good medical facilities must be available to the entire population, regardless of income. One good indicator of a population's health, which measures both the quality and availability of health care, is the infant mortality rate. The infant mortality rate (per 1,000 births) in 1996 for high-income countries was 6; for middle-income countries, 37; and for low-income countries, 68.[12]

Economic and Military Resources

A state's economy is vital to its ability to wield influence in world politics, as we shall see. People have tried to measure economic size and performance by calculating gross national product (GNP). The wealth and economic growth of a state are also related to

---

[11] Harold D. Lasswell and Abraham Kaplan, *Power and Society* (New Haven, Conn.: Yale University Press, 1950).

[12] World Bank, *World Development Indicators 1998* (New York: Oxford University Press, 1998).

the availability of natural resources. Energy sources, such as petroleum, coal, and natural gas, and resources critical to industrial capacity, such as uranium for power and cobalt and chromium for making steel, are particularly important. Not only do abundant natural resources give states the ability to develop and to gain wealth from others through trade, they may also provide a state with a greater degree of *autarky,* or self-sufficiency. The more self-sufficient a state, the less vulnerable it is to the leverage attempts of other international actors. For example, for much of the post-1945 period, the Soviet Union, China, and the United States were more self-sufficient than most countries, but each steadily became less so (especially Russia from the mid-1990s).

Economic production relative to population — GNP per capita — is a good indicator of economic development, which shows how well a state has mobilized and used its natural and human resources. Economic performance, both per capita and as total GNP, provides a clue to the state's ability to turn its resources into military capabilities and its ability to exploit its menu in general. At one extreme we find the United States, with a 1996 GNP of $7.4 trillion. By itself, the United States accounts for more than one-fifth of all the goods and services produced on the earth. Current analyses indicate that the size of the Soviet economy had been overestimated for many years, and substantial steady *declines* in GNP — due partly to the breakaway of economically productive territories like the Baltic states — have dropped present-day Russia from the second position held by the USSR during most of the cold war. World Bank figures for 1996 estimate Russian GNP at about $620 billion, less than that of Mexico and Indonesia.

Military capability, of course, is a crucial element of state power and, to most realists, the central indicator. China, Russia, and the United States have millions of their populations under arms, whereas Iceland, Costa Rica, and Mauritius have no armies at all. One might also wish to count specific items in the arsenals of states, such as nuclear delivery systems, bombers, supersonic fighters, and tanks. The sophistication of weapons technology has become increasingly important. The performance of America's high-tech arms during the 1991 Gulf War caused a number of states to reevaluate their entire military establishments — from strategy, to research and development (R&D) and procurement. Major debates occurred within the Russian and Chinese defense establishments in the aftermath of the Gulf War.

A useful summary measure that takes into account many of these elements of military capability is military expenditure. Again, during the cold war, the Soviet Union and the United States far outdistanced the rest of the world; by 1989 each was spending about $320 billion on its military establishment. Their closest competitors (France, Germany, and China) spent only about 15 percent of that. There are problems when comparing defense expenditures in different national currencies, in obtaining reasonably accurate data, and in determining whether the same kinds of expenditures are counted in each case. Russian defense spending has always been difficult to calculate — in the Soviet era, due to government secrecy; in the post-Soviet era, due to instability in the value of the rouble. In general, however, if employed carefully, this rough measure of military capability is useful for evaluating most countries.

Since 1945 a key element of military capabilities has been a state's nuclear arsenal. How many warheads (bombs) does a state have? What types of delivery systems does it have, and in what numbers? How much megatonnage can a state deliver against an opponent? How vulnerable or invulnerable is a state to a first strike? Here, too, the superpower status of the United States and Russia is still evident. In September 1990, before the Strategic Arms Reduction Treaty (START) was signed, the United States had over 12,500 deliverable strategic warheads; the Soviet Union had over 10,000. START I reduced the U.S. arsenal to 8,500; the target for Russia is 6,500, but there have been delays in destroying existing systems due to a lack of funding (Russia still had an estimated 7,200 weapons in 1998). By 2003, the START II agreement will drop each country's total to 3,500 deliverable weapons. In 1998 the other major-power members of the nuclear club — Britain, France, and China — had less than 900 weapons *combined*, and the arsenals of India, Pakistan, and Israel would add probably fewer than 200 to that total.[13]

All elements of tangible military capabilities have intangible factors as well: the morale and training of officers and troops, the quality of weapons, and the decline in the effectiveness of military power over distance (the "loss-of-strength gradient"). Moreover, even with nuclear weapons there are questions of accuracy, dependability, the state of computer technology, and the quality of command and control.

Comparing Capabilities: Indexes of Power

Many people have recognized that power and influence are multifaceted and depend on a combination of capabilities. Attempts have been made to devise indexes based on two or more indicators of national capabilities. We need to take a look at how the various capabilities may be related to one another and at the possible results of using different combinations of indicators.

Table 5.1 is illustrative, showing how states rank on different indicators of capability and how these indicators relate to each other. (Further comparisons can be made by consulting Appendix B at the end of the book.) The upper half of Table 5.1 lists the top ten states based on each of several measures. Area and population, measures of geographic size, give some sense of the basic endowments with which states begin. Russia still figures at the top of the area ranking, despite having lost much territory with the breakup of the Soviet Union (including Kazakhstan, itself in the top ten). In terms of population, some developing countries make the list; in the case of Bangladesh, however, its population is surely more a burden than a strength, given its limited resources in so many other areas.

The United States and China rank at the top in economic and military strength, although the raw numbers show that the United States is way ahead on GNP and military expenditures. Russia is a formidable military power, but maintaining this position is exceedingly difficult due to its weak economy. Large developing countries — India, Brazil, and Mexico — now outstrip Russia in total economic output. Japan is not generally considered a military power, but its economy is so large that even the relatively small percentage of GNP devoted to the military (less than 2 percent) puts it among the top military spenders. When it comes to the size of the armed forces, it is not surprising that five of the top ten also rank as those with the largest populations.

[13] These figures are from the Center for Defense Information, "Current World Nuclear Arsenals," January 2, 1997 [cited June 7, 1998]; available at <http://www.cdi.org/issues/nukef&f/database/>.

TABLE 5.1 State Capabilities: Rankings and Correlations, 1995–1996

	Geography		Economic and Military Stength			Quality of Life		
Rank	Area	Population	GNP (PPP)	Military Expenditures	Armed Forces	GNP (PPP) per Capita	Energy per Capita	Infant Mortality
1	Russian Federation	China	United States	United States	China	Luxembourg	United Arab Emir.	Sweden
2	China	India	China	Russian Federation	United States	United States	Kuwait	Finland
3	Canada	United States	Japan	China	Russian Federation	Singapore	United States	Singapore
4	United States	Indonesia	Germany	Japan	India	Switzerland	Canada	Japan
5	Brazil	Brazil	India	France	North Korea	Japan	Singapore	Norway
6	Australia	Russian Federation	France	Germany	Turkey	Norway	Sweden	Spain
7	India	Pakistan	United Kingdom	United Kingdom	South Korea	Belgium	Finland	Slovenia
8	Argentina	Japan	Italy	Italy	Pakistan	Denmark	Norway	France
9	Kazakhstan	Bangladesh	Brazil	Saudi Arabia	Vietnam	Iceland	Trinidad and Tobago	Austria
10	Algeria	Nigeria	Mexico	South Korea	France	Austria	Australia	Netherlands

Correlations

	Population	GNP (PPP)	Military Expenditures	Armed Forces	GNP (PPP) per Capita	Energy per Capita	Infant Mortality
Geography							
Area	**.47**	.51	.54	.60	.09	.22	.07
Population		.59	.34	.82	−.03	−.03	.01
Economic and Military Strength							
GNP			**.92**	**.73**	.34	.32	.20
Military Expenditure				**.60**	.33	.35	.18
Armed Forces					.08	.11	.11
Quality of Life							
GNP per Capita						.79	**.64**
Energy per Capita							**.59**

Sources: Rankings for geographic, economic, and quality-of-life indicators are based on data from the World Bank, *World Development Indicators 1998* (New York: Oxford University Press, 1998); for military indicators, rankings are based on data from the U.S. Arms Control and Disarmament Agency (ACDA), *World Military Expenditures and Arms Transfers 1996* (Washington, D.C.: U.S. ACDA, 1997). Gross national product (GNP) is expressed in international dollars, based on purchasing power parity (PPP). Correlations are computed from 1995 or 1996 data for all countries. The correlations shown for infant mortality omit the minus signs.

Other indicators of capability reflect the quality of life enjoyed by the population. States without huge economies — Luxembourg, Singapore, Belgium, and Denmark — may still be quite wealthy due to their small populations. GNP per capita gives some sense of this. High commercial energy consumption per capita is another indication that individuals in society enjoy a variety of modern amenities. Other measures, like literacy and the percentage of the population completing secondary education, are so high among advanced industrialized countries as to make the nations indistinguishable from one another. The same is true for some measures of the health of society: life expectancy, for example, ranged only between seventy-seven and eighty years for the top twenty countries in 1996. Another measure, infant mortality, also shows a fairly narrow range among the most healthy societies. Here, in the last column of the table, European countries dominate the list. Of the several measures of capability, this is the only one where the United States is not ranked among the top ten (it ranks twenty-fifth, between Portugal and Cuba, which is a reflection of the large number of poor people in the United States without access to good health care).

It is helpful to know how these measures of capability relate to one another. We have seen that the United States ranks among the top ten for all but one measure; states like China and Russia are leaders when it comes to both size and military capability. More generally, do states that rank high on some measure also rank high on others, and vice versa? The bottom half of Table 5.1 shows how closely pairs of indicators are correlated. (Correlations closer to 1.00 tell us that having substantial capabilities in one area typically means having substantial capabilities in another; correlations closer to zero mean that there is less of a relationship.) The highest correlation (.92) is between GNP and military expenditures. This reinforces the observation that a strong economic base is required for a strong military establishment. It is generally the case that indicators within each category (geography, economic and military strength, and quality of life) are more highly correlated than are pairs of indicators from different categories. While the high within-category correlations (shown in bold) suggest that the alternative measures within each grouping are tapping similar state capabilities, the low between-category correlations suggest that there are indeed different aspects of state capability that need to be taken into account. Examining economic strength may also give a reasonable indication of potential military strength, but it will not tell us much about the population's quality of life.

Different analysts have tried to produce composite indexes of national power that combine various elements. Because most of the individual components of any such index are only moderately correlated with one another, the summary ranking will differ with different components, and there is no perfect all-purpose indicator. One study compared eight different indexes of power, which include anywhere from two to twenty variables combined in very different ways. Roughly, the various indexes include some way of measuring demographic capabilities, industrial capabilities, and military capabilities; many include some indicator of area or territory. The study compared the rank orderings of states produced by these various indexes and found "no appreciable change in outcome."[14] The lesson is twofold: (1) accurate measure-

---

[14] See Richard L. Merritt and Dina A. Zinnes, "Alternative Indexes of National Power," in Stoll and Ward, eds., *Power in World Politics;* quote from p. 26.

ment requires a clear conceptual understanding of the phenomenon one is trying to measure (in this case, state capability), and (2) when using such a conceptual underpinning, composite indicators of power capability will give us a generally similar picture.

National Capabilities: Intangible Elements

Any state requires more than the mere existence of the resources that make up capabilities. It must also maintain those political, social, and economic structures that will permit it to *mobilize* for governmental use of the resources that exist within its borders and to *convert* those resources into instruments of foreign policy influence. When looking at the political system of any state, we must ask whether that system efficiently administers the nation-state's resources. What is the quality of political leadership at all levels, especially the highest? Can the leaders motivate the people to support the government's policies and to sacrifice so that the state's resources can be devoted to military capabilities or heavy industry rather than to consumer goods? Can the leadership achieve and maintain the support of the people and their continued loyalty to the state? In other words, can the resources be converted into capabilities, and the capabilities into influence?

Such intangibles can be crucial. In sports, a weak team will sometimes beat one much higher up in the rankings. The weaker side does not always lose a war, and the stronger does not always win — as the French learned in Indochina and later in Algeria, and as the Americans learned in Vietnam. Intangibles such as leadership, belief in a cause, and especially the cohesion resulting from a threat to survival are important assets for smaller states in unequal, or asymmetric, conflicts. The weaker state, being willing to fight for survival against a larger adversary, increases its war power through its willingness to persevere and to suffer not only the enemy's direct threat, but also the sacrifices required by higher levels of resource extraction. The larger state, although possessing greater tangible capabilities, often is far from the conflict, is not threatened by the smaller opponent, and is less willing to suffer the costs of war.[15]

For example, much of the debate before the 1991 Gulf War revolved around the level of casualties that would be acceptable to the American people. Willingness to suffer as a dimension of power is particularly acute in democracies, as we have seen in the post-1945 colonial struggles for independence. The notion that the people in democracies do not wish to bear the costs of war was advanced long ago by the philosopher Immanuel Kant; contemporary leaders like Vo Nguyen Giap (North Vietnamese strategist and defense minister) and Saddam Hussein have echoed this sentiment. Because the citizenry ultimately bears the costs of war, and because it also ultimately determines its leaders, democratic states are wary of becoming embroiled in long, drawn-out

---

[15] In short-term confrontations, recklessness and will on the part of the initiator can be more important than physical capabilities. See Zeev Maoz, "Resolve, Capabilities, and Outcomes of Interstate Disputes," *Journal of Conflict Resolution* 27 (1983): pp. 195–229.

struggles over anything that is not of the utmost importance to national security. Thus, Saddam Hussein doubted that the American people would have the "stomach" for a prolonged military engagement far from home. He probably was not wrong about that; Iraq simply lacked the military capability to prolong the conflict. The structure of the political system of a state is thus one aspect of the mobilization of resources.

Other intangibles involve a government's skill in manipulating its resources to influence other states in diplomatic negotiation and bargaining (to be discussed shortly). We must also look at the skill and efficiency of the state's administrative organs: the size of the bureaucracy; how politicized it is, or how protected from political influences; how it is organized and directed; and the quality of its employees in terms of education, training, expertise, and dedication to service (or to corruption).

Finally, we return to the notion of credibility. The effect of attempts at influence based on promises or threats depends to a large extent not only on a government's ability to carry out the action, but also on the perception of its willingness to do so. One major intangible, then, is the reputation that a government acquires in its international dealings. Our general conclusion about political intangibles is a simple one. If a government — that is, its leadership, its bureaucracy, and the political system within which both work — is so inadequate or inefficient that it cannot bring the state's capabilities to bear in a particular international situation, those capabilities will remain latent. Capabilities that are not mobilized cannot be used to exercise influence in the international arena.

Similar questions can be asked about the economic and social systems of a state. Does the economic system reduce waste and loss? Is it efficient in the use of the state's resources? Does the social system (its values and its cultural practices) promote a unified national effort, or are there major groups that feel alienated from the national society? Is the social system oriented more toward principles of fairness and respect for human rights or toward a system of privilege? The answers to all these questions will affect how thoroughly, rapidly, and efficiently a society will be able to mobilize resources and how unified a society is in supporting its government's foreign policies. Here we might speak of national morale, a somewhat elusive notion concerning the "state of mind" of a nation.

Shifts in national morale occurred in both France and the United States during their involvements in Indochina. In each country, as the war wore on, support for military involvement decreased and general governmental policy was increasingly challenged. Vo Nguyen Giap stated bluntly that the Western powers would lose, that he could make the war go on long enough for their people to tire of the war and its costs. The outcome of the war — in Vietnam, but also in France and the United States — as well as scholarly research have proved him right.[16]

---

[16] John Mueller investigated the failure of American policy to drive the North Vietnamese to a breaking point. His findings indicate not so much an American military failure as an unprecedented willingness of the North Vietnamese to accept losses much higher than those of previous wars (for instance, battle deaths as a percentage of the prewar population were twice as high as those the Japanese suffered in World War II). See John Mueller, "The Search for the 'Breaking Point' in Vietnam: The Statistics of a Deadly Quarrel," *International Studies Quarterly* 24 (1980): pp. 497–519.

Intelligence

A very different aspect of a state's intangible capabilities of power and influence is its ability to collect and analyze information — that is, the quality of its **intelligence**. In *The Nerves of Government,* Karl Deutsch observes that "it might be profitable to look upon government somewhat less as a problem of power and somewhat more as a problem of *steering*."[17] That is, in the uncertainty of the anarchic international system, any government that knows how to get to where it wants to go has an advantage. Any government that can reduce the uncertainty of the international environment through knowledge has an advantage. Any government that can reduce the number of times it is surprised — that can provide itself with the time for planning, preparation, and pre-emption of the actions of other states — has an advantage.

Power may indeed be the ability to steer. To know how to act, how to respond, and whether to continue one's policies or to correct them, a government needs information. To know how to influence states or other international actors, a government needs information about them. The information that governments seek falls into three broad categories. Earlier in this chapter we noted that in order to use their capabilities for influence, decisionmakers have to take into account their own goals and capabilities for influence and the goals and capabilities of others. The first type of information, then, deals with the goals, plans, and intentions of other international actors. States can steer more carefully through the international environment with foreknowledge of the impending behavior of other states. The many books about the Allies' acquisition of secret intelligence during World War II indicate that advance warnings of German moves had great payoffs. It is the *failure* of intelligence-gathering organizations to provide warnings that shows the importance of such warnings.[18] Examples include American surprise at the Japanese attack on Pearl Harbor in 1941; American surprise at the North Korean attack on South Korea in June 1950; Japanese surprise at the Nixon administration's devaluation of the U.S. dollar in 1971; the failure of Israeli intelligence in the 1973 Yom Kippur war; the inability of U.S. intelligence to estimate accurately the conditions that brought down the shah of Iran in early 1979; Saddam Hussein's invasion of Kuwait in 1990; and the CIA's failure to anticipate India's nuclear weapons tests in 1998. We cannot know how best to use our tools of influence if we do not know the plans and intentions of others or if we must continuously react to surprising situations.

The same is true if we do not know the capabilities — and vulnerabilities — of others. Thus, the second kind of information is knowledge of others' military and economic strength, internal political situation, and domestic unrest. The largest portion of intelligence work is of this sort: the collection of a great deal of information about other

---

[17] See Karl W. Deutsch, *The Nerves of Government* (New York: Free Press, 1963), p. xxvii (emphasis added).

[18] Two insightful analyses of intelligence failures are Richard K. Betts, "Analysis, War, and Decision: Why Intelligence Failures Are Inevitable," *World Politics* 30, 1 (1978): pp. 61–89; and Betts, "Surprise Despite Warning: Why Sudden Attacks Succeed," *Political Science Quarterly* 95, 4 (1980–81): pp. 551–572.

states, using readily available sources of information and standard research techniques. The third type of information is *feedback*. Governments seek information about the effects of their own decisions and actions on the international environment, and steer accordingly. Feedback helps a government determine whether to continue its policies or to alter them in some way. U.S. policy in Indochina during the 1960s can be seen as a classic case of the failure of information-gathering and -processing activities, as well as the failure of U.S. leaders like President Lyndon Johnson to analyze feedback information correctly.

Intelligence involves the collection, analysis, interpretation, and storage of information, as well as the transmission of information to top-level foreign policy decisionmakers. One reason why we consider intelligence capabilities as an intangible is the unreliability of the process. As we shall see, information may be lost or distorted within the government, it may be misunderstood or disbelieved by policymakers, or it may never be collected at all. Nonetheless, governments keep up their efforts. During the cold war the United States and the Soviet Union spent vast sums on intelligence activities, as do present-day countries with immediate and pressing security problems, such as Israel. Israeli intelligence, despite its failure to anticipate the 1973 war, has often been touted as the best in the world.

Before states can attempt to influence others, then, they must obtain certain information about the world. How well a state collects and handles information will affect the utility of all its other capabilities. How well a state collects and handles information will also affect the goals and objectives of the state and how it seeks to achieve them. Once a set of objectives or goals exists, the foreign policy decisionmakers of nation-states must try to translate their capabilities into the influence required to achieve their objectives; they must implement their foreign policy decisions. They have a wide range of tools, techniques, and methods with which to deal with other states. Now we shall look further at some of the methods through which states exercise influence.

Diplomatic Influence

A British diplomat once said, "Foreign policy is what you do; diplomacy is how you do it."[19] Although this distinction is a good place to start, it is also incomplete — there are a wide variety of techniques for the implementation of foreign policy, not all of them diplomatic. **Diplomacy** involves direct, government-to-government interactions, acting upon the officials in other governments who are able to do the things we want states to do. Thus, diplomacy can be considered the central technique of foreign policy implementation, and the only truly direct technique. Other techniques are often combined with diplomatic instruments in order to more effectively influence other states. For example, after a major military victory, it is usually through diplomatic interaction that the defeated party indicates whether it will surrender or modify previously held

---

[19] Paul Gore-Booth, *With Great Truth and Respect* (London: Constable, 1974), p. 15.

peace conditions. The military instrument has had an effect on another state, but that effect can be exploited and enhanced only through diplomacy. The same may be said for economic activities, such as embargoes and other sanctions that deprive a state of needed commodities.

The central feature of diplomacy is communication. The basis for creating permanent diplomatic missions in the fifteenth century was the desire of kings and princes to have representatives in other courts to carry out continuous and systematic communication with other monarchs. Most of the legal trappings of diplomacy were established to maintain and facilitate communication and to reduce misunderstanding and distortion in interstate communication. The rules of *protocol* were established to reduce conflicts over rank and status among diplomats; *diplomatic immunity* prevents host governments from interfering with the diplomatic representatives of other states; norms of *noninterference* prevent diplomats from interfering in the domestic politics of their hosts. These practices permit representatives to get on with the business of diplomacy, and they constitute a pillar of international law.

Diplomacy has five substantive functions: (1) *conflict management*; (2) *solution of problems* facing two or more governments; (3) the increase and facilitation of cross-cultural *communication* on a wide range of issues; (4) *negotiation and bargaining* on specific issues, treaties, and agreements; and (5) general *program management* of the foreign policy decisions of one country in regard to another.[20] Procedurally, these activities result foremost in communicating the views of one's government and in exchanging information. After such negotiation, additional diplomacy is often required to implement the agreements reached; lengthy and important talks may be held on exactly how agreements are to be executed. For example, after the Arab-Israeli cease-fire was achieved in 1973, some very hard bargaining was required to separate Egyptian and Israeli forces on the Sinai Peninsula. The resulting Israeli-Egyptian talks on the "Kilometer 101" disengagements of 1973 and the implementation of the less-than-precise peace treaty of 1979 are good examples of the importance of postagreement diplomacy.

So far we have discussed diplomacy as a means by which one state directly influences another. But any discussion of the various functions of diplomacy cannot neglect another major function, which is aimed not primarily at the other party, but at third parties observing the diplomatic activities at hand. In this case diplomacy is used less to reach an agreement with the opposing party than to influence other parties through propaganda, undermining the position of the opponent, revealing the opponent's bargaining positions and other confidential information, or taking stances calculated to impress, frighten, or reassure third-party observers. Many of the U.S.-Soviet negotiations over the years were aimed at their various allies, at Third World states, and perhaps especially at China.

Disagreement over how much diplomatic communication should be open and how much secret has been a major issue in the twentieth century. After World War I, there was a reaction to the old diplomacy of the great European powers. In addition to

[20] Leon P. Poullada, "Diplomacy: The Missing Link in the Study of International Politics," in D. S. McLellan, W. C. Olson, and F. A. Sondermann, eds., *The Theory and Practice of International Relations*, 4th ed. (Englewood Cliffs, N.J.: Prentice-Hall, 1974), pp. 194–202.

a general feeling that diplomacy was a devious and dishonest business, many people felt that the secret treaties that characterized the pre–World War I period were responsible for the outbreak of the war. Idealists like President Woodrow Wilson attacked the immorality of secret treaties that offered territory if states would help others in military offensives. Wilson called for "open covenants . . . openly arrived at" (the first of his Fourteen Points). The League of Nations promoted the idea of open treaties by publishing their texts after they were negotiated. Article 102 of the UN Charter provides for the compulsory registration of treaties with the UN. If a treaty has not been so registered, it cannot be invoked within the UN system.

Openness has undermined some of the previous utility of diplomacy, since public statements are often infused with propaganda. Various speeches made in the UN General Assembly and Security Council exemplify how the propaganda function, as opposed to problem solving or conflict resolution, can prevail. After World War II, a hybrid form of diplomacy became prevalent. It combined private negotiations between diplomats with public declarations of what had been achieved — in press conferences, in joint statements, or by the publication of agreements (usually by the UN). Former Secretary of State Henry Kissinger was a master of the private conversation and the public spectacle. His techniques were a return to traditional diplomacy: hard bargaining in private; secret trips and agreements (revealed to the public only after their completion); and a style that combined the use of force with the use of words to bring about an agreement with which every side could live, but one that required every side to make concessions and compromises.

In the past the bulk of routine diplomatic communication, as well as most important talks and conferences, took place between the regular diplomatic representatives of the foreign services of states. Both day-to-day activity and major talks were handled by the diplomatic personnel of the embassies located in each state's capital. Today much of this activity, especially for smaller and less developed countries, occurs in multilateral forums such as the UN. Called *parliamentary diplomacy*, this form of diplomacy includes both the regular meetings of the international body to which permanent representatives are assigned and informal discussions that occur in a single location, where a state's diplomats can meet with representatives of many other states. The larger powers, taking advantage of instantaneous communication facilities between governmental leaders, faster transportation, and the willingness to mount summit meetings, have tended to skip over embassy personnel and ambassadors and conduct more and more of their business through the use of high-level officials like foreign ministers or secretaries of state.[21] These activities range from the bilateral cold-war "summits" of U.S. and Soviet leaders to multilateral meetings such as the regular gatherings of the Group of Eight — heads of government of the seven major Western industrial countries (the United States, Japan, Germany, France, Italy, Britain, and Canada) plus Russia.

The modern U.S. secretary of state has regularly engaged in "shuttle diplomacy" of some sort, flying between the capitals of states in conflict to facilitate communication

---

[21] See Henry Kissinger's memoirs, *White House Years* (Boston: Little, Brown, 1979), *Years of Upheaval* (Boston: Little, Brown, 1982), and *Years of Renewal* (New York: Simon & Schuster, 1999) for details of his high-level negotiations and an understanding of how such a process works.

between opposing parties who usually will not sit down together. Kissinger popularized this activity in his work in the Middle East in 1973; Reagan's secretary of state, Alexander Haig, pursued it in trying to settle the Falklands/Malvinas dispute between Britain and Argentina in 1982; James Baker, Bush's secretary of state, engaged in similar travels in 1991 as he attempted to revive a Middle East peace process following the Gulf War. Lesser representatives, or *envoys,* have also been active in American diplomatic efforts in recent years. During the Clinton administration, special envoys achieved considerable success in resolving issues between conflicting parties in Bosnia and Northern Ireland.

Negotiation and Bargaining

Diplomatic persuasion occurs in world politics more often than we think. Realists stress the threat or use of force as the way to achieve influence in a violence-prone world. However, this crude form of influence is fairly rare in the vast web of daily international interactions. More important for achieving influence, particularly in a world of growing interdependence among states, is **bargaining.** The bargaining process can be tacit, whereby intentions are demonstrated through behavior rather than direct communication, or it can occur through explicit negotiations.

The first stage of negotiation is based on the commitment to deal *in good faith.* This means that both parties are negotiating for the purpose of reaching an agreement. Each party must calculate that the benefits of reaching agreement outweigh the sacrifices that may be necessary. Often this stage requires one party to convince the other that an agreement of some sort would be in the interest of both sides (as was often crucial in Soviet-U.S. arms-control negotiations). States do not always negotiate in good faith. A state may negotiate to gather information about the capabilities, aims, and problems of the other side, or it may negotiate in order to give the opponent misleading information about its own intentions and capabilities. States sometimes choose to negotiate simply to maintain contact with the other side, even if chances of an agreement are slim in hopes that as long as both sides are talking neither will resort to armed conflict. This may have been an objective of the U.S.-Japanese talks that were in progress before Pearl Harbor.

Once the intention to deal in good faith has been communicated, the parties move on to discuss preliminary issues, which often seem as important to both sides as the agreement itself. The *location* of the negotiations must be fixed. States prefer a neutral site when bargaining with an adversary; Paris was the site of the U.S.-North Vietnamese peace talks, and Vienna, Helsinki, and Geneva were used for the U.S.-Soviet Strategic Arms Limitation Talks (SALT). Naming the *parties* to be represented can present a problem, because participation defines who has a legitimate standing in the issue. In this era of nonstate actors trying to obtain territory, and ultimately sovereignty, simply recognizing their existence is a major substantive concession. Thus, by agreeing to their participation in negotiations, a state has made more than a procedural concession. This was a sticky point for the United States in Paris regarding the Viet Cong and was continually a central issue in the protracted conflicts in Northern Ireland and between Israel and the Arabs. Until the dramatic breakthrough with Egypt in 1977, no Arab state recognized Israel's existence. Israel, in turn, refused to recognize the

Palestine Liberation Organization. The historic agreements of 1993 negotiated in Norway between Israel and the PLO (leading to the Nobel Peace Prize for Yitzak Rabin, Shimon Peres, and Yassir Arafat) could come about only after an array of such non-recognition barriers fell.

The second stage of negotiation is the bargaining over the actual *terms of the agreement,* that is, defining solutions and working out accords.[22] Because each side has different or conflicting objectives and interests, there is something over which to bargain. Much of the interaction involves attempts to find solutions to common problems. Other bargaining interactions are straightforward attempts to influence relationships. The objective is to get the opponent to agree with you as much as possible in achieving a solution to the problem. Each side wishes to minimize the costs to itself.

Bargaining takes on features of a *debate,* where "opponents direct their arguments at each other" and "the objective is to convince your opponent, to make him see things as you see them." It also resembles a *game,* where each party must take into account "the potentialities and evaluations of alternative outcomes; the object in a game is to outwit the opponent."[23] Thus, persuasion as well as threats and promises are employed in bargaining, as each side presents its conditions and demands and attempts to convince or coerce the other side to accept as many of these as possible. Threats and promises must be credible. Each side must try to figure out how far to push demands and how far to push the opponent — when to make concessions and when to dig in and say, "I have nothing more to give." In doing so, states employ specific threats and promises as well as deliberately vague threats and warnings — "we will not stand idly by . . ." or "you must bear the responsibility if . . ." A state's *bargaining reputation* includes its reputation for bluffing, standing fast, telling the truth, and honoring commitments (or not).

Bargaining involves the complex interactions of mutual influence and expectations, with each party both anticipating and reacting to the other. A feeling for the complexity of the bargaining process is given by Thomas Schelling, one of the pioneers in the study of international strategy and bargaining:

> Each party's strategy is guided mainly by what he expects the other to accept or insist on; yet each knows that the other is guided by reciprocal thoughts. The final outcome must be a point from which neither expects the other to retreat; yet the main ingredient of this expectation is what one thinks the other expects the first to expect, and so on. Somehow, out of this fluid and indeterminate situation that seemingly provides no logical reason for anybody to expect anything except what he expects to be expected to expect, a decision is reached. These infinitely reflexive expectations must somehow converge on a single point, at which each expects the other not to expect to be expected to retreat.[24]

---

[22] For a good overview of the processes, nature, and theory of negotiation, see I. William Zartman and Maureen R. Berman, *The Practical Negotiator* (New Haven, Conn.: Yale University Press, 1982); Howard Raiffa, *The Art and Science of Negotiation* (Cambridge, Mass: Harvard University Press, 1982); and Dean Pruitt and Peter Carnevale, *Negotiation in Social Conflict* (Belmont, Calif.: Brooks/Cole, 1993). See also T. Clifton Morgan, *Untying the Knot of War: A Bargaining Theory of International Crises* (Ann Arbor: University of Michigan Press, 1994).

[23] See Anatol Rapoport, *Fights, Games, and Debates* (Ann Arbor: University of Michigan Press, 1960).

[24] Thomas Schelling, *The Strategy of Conflict* (New York: Oxford University Press, 1963), p. 70.

Conflict Resolution

A conflict can be resolved in many ways. The use or threat of force — through conquest, forcible submission, or deterrence — is one method. But conflicts are also resolved through diplomacy: negotiated compromise, third-party mediation or arbitration, or adjudication of some other sort (by international courts, multilateral conferences, or international organizations).

For successful conflict resolution, the parties involved must be willing to confront the issues in dispute in a rational atmosphere of some mutual respect and open communication. Each side must try to identify the genuine differences between them and avoid taking positions merely to establish favorable conditions for the bargaining process. John Burton has even argued that bargaining situations should be avoided. His view is that conflicts are based on misunderstandings and that the important thing is to get people to sit down face-to-face. The largest issues may be set out in the presence of a mediator, who will help the parties see where misunderstandings exist. Burton argues that once favorable conditions exist for analyzing the misunderstanding that underlies the conflict, the process of conflict resolution is well on its way.[25]

Burton's view that most conflicts are based merely on misunderstandings is extreme, but his emphasis on the need to have the first stage of negotiations carefully approached and worked out is valuable. Our view is that many, if not most, conflicts are indeed concrete. Incompatibilities do exist in the global arena: the desire to occupy the same territory, to control the same governmental machinery, or to fish the same waters; disagreement over the manner in which certain groups of people (say, coreligionists or people of the same ethnic or linguistic background living within the borders of other states) should be treated. Although most conflicts do have an objective basis, the process of conflict resolution is highly subjective because of the complex nature of bargaining. Even Roger Fisher, the best-known proponent of this view of conflict bargaining, advocates taking the game element out of conflict resolution bargaining and stressing the debate element.[26] Fisher stresses trying to understand the opponent's view of the situation and then attempting to figure out what can be done to make the opponent change that view. He specifically notes that "making threats is not enough." How, then, does one try to influence the opponent? First, Fisher argues that one state must be very clear about what it wants the opponent to do. Then, always keep in mind how the opponent sees the world; put yourself in their shoes. The focus should be on *points of choice*; the choices offered the opponent should be made attractive and acceptable. Fisher's concern is that a bargainer's offers and positions appear sensible and legitimate in the eyes of the opponent. This is a hallmark of the debate. He further argues that if making threats is the best a state can do and if punishment must be resorted to, then bargaining has failed. Coercion is seen to be a failure to influence.

In bargaining to resolve conflicts, the least coercive forms of influence are often the most useful, at least initially. Promises of rewards, persuasion, reliance on the

[25] John W. Burton, *Conflict: Resolution and Prevention* (New York: St. Martin's, 1990).

[26] For presentations of Roger Fisher's general framework for bargaining, see *Getting to Yes: Negotiating Agreement Without Giving In*, 2nd ed. (New York: Penguin, 1991), written with William Ury, and *Beyond Machiavelli: Tools for Coping with Conflict* (Cambridge, Mass.: Harvard University Press, 1994), written with Elizabeth Kopelman and Andrea Kupfer Schneider.

legitimacy of claims, and sensitivity to the opponents' position seem to be better methods of influence than are threats of force. Emphasizing the legitimacy of one's own position so as to appeal to values held by the opponent is especially helpful. Fisher argues that states should be concerned with precedent and reciprocity in order to make their demands legitimate in the eyes of the opponents — to appear to act in a way consistent with their principles.

A way to do this is to use international law and international organizations. On the whole, no organization was very successful in managing conflicts between members of different cold war blocs. The United Nations was always reasonably effective in non–cold war disputes, however, doing best in the area of resource conflicts (see Chapter 10). Regional organizations do well in managing conflicts not involving force, whereas the United Nations did reasonably well with high-intensity conflicts.[27] When the cold war wound down at the end of the 1980s, the United Nations was able to do things that previously would have been impossible. With the United States and Russia cooperating, the Security Council and the secretary-general helped to end a number of civil and international wars (including ones in Namibia and Cambodia). The United Nations also played a key role in bringing the international community together against Iraq after its invasion of Kuwait. And in 1998, when the United States was preparing a military response to the Iraqi government's refusal to grant free access to UN weapons inspectors, it was Secretary-General Kofi Annan who brought about a peaceful settlement. At the outset of a dispute, the legitimacy of an international organization like the UN may be the only thing on which states can agree.

Military Influence

We have noted several times that influence may be achieved through the application of force. Throughout history rulers have used war and violence to prevail in conflict and to overcome obstacles. There is no doubt that the use of military capabilities is generally a coercive or punishment-oriented means of influence. It is also possible, however, to use these capabilities for *rewarding* others. The most obvious rewarding activity is the use of military aid. States, particularly the larger states, may thereby attempt to influence commitment to an alliance, UN voting, or general political orientation. Powers such as the United States, Russia, Britain, and France have the technology, expertise, and capability to produce the kind of advanced weaponry that most of the world's countries cannot. Other countries like Brazil, Israel, and the two Koreas have also become important suppliers of arms to developing countries, but the variety and sophistication of their exports tend to be more limited; plus, they are more inclined to be seeking economic benefits than political influence.

---

[27] See Ernst B. Haas, *Why We Still Need the United Nations: The Collective Management of International Conflict, 1945–1984*, Policy Papers in International Affairs, no. 26 (Berkeley: University of California Institute of International Studies, 1986).

Influence gained through providing weapons may be only temporary. Egypt illustrated how a recipient state can turn on its arms supplier when Sadat ejected Soviet military advisers and other personnel from the country in 1971. Although spare parts and maintenance linkages provide supplier states with their primary leverage over recipients, the exchange of aid for influence is far from an automatic equation. U.S. influence on many Israeli policies has been quite variable — from none to some. None of Iraq's arms suppliers, including the Soviet Union, was able to influence Iraqi policy in the six months before the Gulf War broke out. Indeed, in the aftermath of the war, major arms suppliers were forced to recognize the limited influence that arms trade provided, along with the harm that such weapons could inflict within various regions.

Another way to reward states with military capabilities is to promise alliance — adding one's capabilities to theirs. However, a formal treaty is not necessary for state A to aid state B by either threatening B's enemy or actually using its military forces against B's enemy. The American deterrent umbrella, whether for its allies or for other states that knew they would be protected even without a formal alliance (for example, Austria, Sweden, and Israel), exemplified this form of influence through reward.

Most instances involving the military tool of foreign policy, however, are based on exploiting the use of force or the threat thereof. Force is coercive; it is the ability to destroy or kill or take away, to occupy and control through violence. Force directly affects the distribution of security, political control, territory, and wealth in the international system. Force is used because decisionmakers *expect to benefit* from the new distributions that are anticipated after it has been used. States are influenced by the threat of force because they fear what they will lose if others use it. The military technique of influence should be seen as another means to various political ends, not as an end in itself. The objective of using force is the same as that of using any other technique: to influence outcomes.

This view of force was most powerfully argued and popularized by the Prussian officer and military historian Karl von Clausewitz, who wrote the classic *On War* following his military service against Napoleon. Clausewitz clearly saw the military instrument as a way to influence the opponent: "War therefore is an act of violence intended to compel our opponent to fulfil our will." Clausewitz also argued that war is a means to an end, that it cannot be separated from the political goals of states and indeed must be subordinated to those goals. His famous dictum reads: "War is a mere continuation of policy by other means[;] . . . not merely a political act, but also a real political instrument, a continuation of political commerce, a carrying out of the same by other means."[28]

The use of force can be a means to completely destroy an opponent. Brute force overcomes an obstacle by annihilating it, as the Romans overcame Carthage in the Third Punic War (149–146 B.C.E.). Rome did not employ force to influence Carthage to engage in desired behavior: there was nothing Rome wanted Carthage to do. Rome simply wanted to wipe its enemy from the face of the earth. When the use of force is aimed at the destruction of an opponent, influence is not the object. In most situations

---

[28] Carl von Clausewitz, *On War*, edited and with an introduction by Anatol Rapoport (New York: Penguin, 1968), pp. 101, 119.

where force is used, however, influence is the aim. The use of force is usually meant to hurt the opponent until the latter's will to resist further is broken.

Alternatively, one can merely *threaten* to use force, exploiting an opponent's knowledge of one's ability to hurt and inflict costs. Military capabilities are exploited explicitly through diplomatic channels, especially when the aim is deterrence; the deterrer must make clear to the opponent just what actions are forbidden and what will happen to the opponent if those actions are taken. Beyond the threat of force, other techniques exist for the use of military capabilities without actually resorting to violence. The aim is to convey to others the military capabilities one possesses in order to influence their view of the world and their menu. States often want to be perceived as being militarily powerful, willing to use their capabilities and thus not to be challenged or thwarted. Such a demonstration may be implicit, or it may be made explicitly through the display of military capabilities — to impress others with one's military strength and to achieve status and prestige as a powerful state. In today's system, nuclear weapons are the most obvious element of military capabilities used for prestige or status. India's nuclear explosions in 1974 and again in 1998 were motivated in large part by its quest to rival the status and prestige of China, both in Asia and in the eyes of Third World countries around the globe.

Stationing one's forces abroad may serve to influence others in any or all of the ways we have discussed: to reward allies or to threaten opponents, to support deterrence, or to project power and status. Although the end of the cold war brought about a substantial reduction in foreign-based troops, as recently as 1986 almost 2 million military personnel from twenty-eight different countries were stationed in ninety-one foreign countries on almost 3,000 military bases or installations. More symbolically, states may display their military capabilities to outside observers through a variety of activities: nuclear explosions, war games, military maneuvers, military parades like the May Day parade in Red Square, and a demonstrated willingness to send fleets around the world, as the British did during the Falklands war. Mobilizing forces or putting them on high-readiness alerts, as Nixon did during the 1973 Middle East war, can also be used to communicate to an opponent the seriousness of a situation. Here a state is less interested in demonstrating its capabilities than its willingness to use them in a critical situation.

In Chapter 8 we discuss at length military instruments of influence, specifically the causes and consequences of war, more limited uses of armed force, and the threat of force.

Economic Influence

States rely on each other for resources and commodities that enable them to develop and sustain their economies and the well-being of their peoples. Economic resources can be manipulated by those who possess them to influence those who do not. As we stressed earlier, nothing in the international system is equally distributed. This, of course, applies to economic resources as well as to the economic requirements of various states: states that possess a surplus (or a monopoly) of resources may achieve greater economic influence; states that lack the resources and commodities they require are more vulnerable to economic influence. The economic resources of states can be used across the whole range of influence mechanisms.[29] In comparison to diplomacy, however, economic means of influence may be considered indirect. Rather than direct interaction with governmental leaders, the objective is to affect some aspect of the state's society — its wealth, production, or well-being. The effect is then taken into account by the state's leaders and thus influences their behavior (just as the defeat of an army on the battlefield is taken into account and influences future behavior).

The manipulation of economic resources takes many forms. States can use trade, monetary policy, or international organizations to acquire more economic resources or to deny them to their adversaries. These resources can then be used to generate additional economic and military resources. The wealth from Iraq's oilfields enabled Saddam Hussein to amass the impressive arsenal that he used first to fight Iran and then to seize Kuwait and defy the United Nations. One argument for the use of force against Iraq was that with the wealth generated from Kuwaiti oil, Iraq could buy even more weapons, including sophisticated delivery systems for chemical-biological weapons (and possibly nuclear ones as well). Similarly, from the 1973 Arab-Israeli war until his ouster in early 1979, the shah of Iran continuously pressed for higher oil prices in order to generate the wealth he desired for both his armed forces and his ambitious economic schemes.

As with other types of influence, economic influence may be achieved through the use of rewards (the "carrot") or punishments (the "stick"). For either to work, the target state must be economically *vulnerable*. Few states can even attempt a policy of autarky because, in one way or another, all states have economic needs that they cannot satisfy. Thus, they are vulnerable to the influence of states who have leverage of some kind — who have what they need. In the past, states like Bangladesh, the Soviet Union, or many African countries have often required more food, especially grain, than they could produce. Most states require petroleum, which is produced on a large scale in only a handful of countries; in this regard Japan and the states of Western Europe are particularly vulnerable. In the 1970s, Henry Kissinger tried to use détente as a way of enmeshing the Soviet Union within a web of world trade in order to make the USSR need more from other states and thereby *become more vulnerable* within the international system. He hoped that the Soviets would thus be "more responsible" world citizens than they would be if they became totally self-sufficient. An autarkic state needs no one to help fill its needs and therefore has a much more open menu; consequently, it is less constrained by its own self-interests.

There are many possible ways to threaten or apply economic punishment. A developed country may withhold foreign aid from a poor one; a less-developed state may nationalize the corporate investments of industrialized states or increase the price of its

---

[29] For a detailed discussion of resource dependence — what it means and how it can be measured and applied to interstate relations — see Bruce Russett, "Dimensions of Resource Dependence: Some Elements of Rigor in Concept and Policy Analysis," *International Organization* 37 (Summer 1984): pp. 481–499. For a general overview of economic foreign policy tools, see David A. Baldwin, *Economic Statecraft* (Princeton, N.J.: Princeton University Press, 1985).

natural resources; trade relations may be reduced or cut off entirely; and so on. Notice that in many cases the punishment or threat of punishment consists of withdrawing an economic resource that previously had been available; but interference with normal channels of economic interaction with another country means that both sides in the pair are deprived of possible future instruments of influence over each other's policies. Throughout the 1990s there was a debate in the United States about how best to respond to the Chinese government's violation of human rights. While many argued that the United States had no business doing business with the communist government of China — one that had massacred thousands of pro-democracy students in Tiananmen Square in June 1989 — others responded that cutting economic ties to China would eliminate one of the few instruments of U.S. influence over Chinese policy. Both the Bush and Clinton administrations were ultimately persuaded by the advocates of continued "engagement."

States have often sought to wield influence through the use of *economic sanctions*. One state may take away, threaten to cut off, or fail to provide another with some economic resource, commodity, or service. The United States used such tactics against the Soviet Union in 1980 after the USSR invaded Afghanistan. The Carter administration renewed a grain embargo to attempt to influence the Soviets. In fact, however, it is rare for some economic good or service to be cut off completely. More often, punishment involves curtailing the *level* of the good or service being provided or increasing its *price*. As we have seen in the industrialized West since the first OPEC embargo in 1973, the manipulation of the supply or price of oil can bring clear-cut benefits or costs to the Western states. The Arab states have used this means to affect Western voting patterns in the United Nations, Western treatment of Israel, and Western trade agreements. Economic sanctions are frequently employed as a political-economic tool of foreign policy, and we discuss their use and effectiveness at greater length in Chapter 12.

In contrast to the various methods of applying the economic stick, foreign aid is a major carrot technique. It involves the transfer of economic goods or services from the donor to the recipient. These might include any resource or commodity, money, service, or technical advice. In economically developing countries, the needs for development capital (money and goods) and for the technical and technological skills to build a modern economy are particularly high. Aid is therefore very useful in dealing with most of the states in the international system today. Giving or withholding aid, attempting to create dependencies through its use, and attempting to substitute aid from one state for aid from another are all common strategies for influence (or escape from influence).

Aid may be used for economic development or relief. The aid may come as outright grants, loans, sales, or technical assistance. In the 1950s and 1960s, grants were the preferred form of aid. More recently, technical assistance and loans have assumed a greater role. Bilateral aid, which is provided by one state directly to another, is particularly susceptible to manipulation. Dependence relationships can be created, and aid may go to states where the donor country wants to strengthen its trading interests or to establish new investments. Donor countries often provide bilateral aid with strings: "tied aid" means that the recipient may be required to buy or trade for goods it does not want or need if it is to receive the aid that it desires. Much of bilateral economic aid goes to countries where the donor expects to gain some clear benefit for its foreign and national security policy. About half of all U.S. bilateral economic assistance, for example, goes to just two countries, Egypt and Israel. That assistance is provided for obvious political purposes. U.S. aid to Egypt displaced Soviet influence. It was also meant to compensate the Egyptians for the loss of Arab economic aid as a result of the Israeli-Egyptian peace treaty in 1979. Israel has been an important U.S. strategic ally.

In this chapter we have reviewed some of the basic techniques states use to interact and exert influence over one another. We have taken only a brief look at the major diplomatic, military, and economic methods for exercising influence; we will return to these at various points in Parts II and III. Other topics, like psychological means of influence, have been touched upon only in passing. The ideological overlay of the cold war prompted heavy use of this indirect technique, whereby states attempt to influence the values, attitudes, and behavior of the people (or specific groups of people) in other countries. Radio and television (such as Voice of America and Radio Free Europe), films, and cultural materials are aimed at the populations of opponents, allies, and neutrals alike. Propaganda is an important tool in attempting to increase other people's respect or improve their images of your rectitude.

A state's menu depends in large part on the array of techniques it possesses to influence other international actors. Its menu is also constrained by the attempts of other actors to influence that state. The tools for influence that a state possesses very much depend on its capabilities and how those capabilities stand in relation to the capabilities of others. In the next chapter we shall move within the domestic system of each state and look at the characteristics of the society and government. We have already provided a very general idea of how these domestic factors might influence the foreign policy menu of decisionmakers, and now we shall study these topics in depth.

6

Domestic Sources of Foreign Policy: Society and Polity

WORLD SYSTEM

RELATIONS

SOCIETY

GOVERNMENT

ROLE

INDIVIDUAL

Foreign Policy: What It Is and How We Study It

In the last two chapters we discussed elements of constraint and opportunity that originate outside the nation-state. In this chapter we shall look at major aspects of the nation-state itself that constrain the possibilities and probabilities open to foreign policy decisionmakers. According to Henry Kissinger, statespersons are constrained by two sets of influences: politics, power, and actions of other states; and domestic constraints, ranging from public opinion to the attitudes of the government and bureaucracy. The ideal statesperson must be able to take both sets into account, deal with them, and master them. Commenting on all the statespersons whom observers claimed (incorrectly) he was trying to emulate, Kissinger said that they had in some way failed to take into account or deal with one of these sets of constraints. A foreign policymaker must understand these constraints, master them, and transcend them, bending them to his or her own will.[1]

One way to approach the concept of foreign policy is to break it down into its component parts. We can think of a *policy* as a program that serves as a guide to behavior intended to realize the goals an organization has set for itself. The notion of sovereignty helps us distinguish domestic from *foreign*. Sovereignty means control over territory delimited by internationally recognized boundaries. Anything beyond those legal boundaries, in areas where the state has no legal authority, is foreign. **Foreign policy** is thus a guide to actions taken beyond the boundaries of the state to further the goals of the state.

The intention of foreign policy is to affect the behavior of other actors, even if only in general terms. Because nothing is distributed equally in the global system, every state requires resources, economic goods, military capabilities, political and strategic support, and cooperation and coordination with other actors. Foreign policy thus concerns behavior toward some other actor for some reason. Whether the actual behavior of a state matches its intentions is another matter. Much of foreign policy analysis is directed toward this question of the links between the intentions of behavior and its consequences. Realist and radical views of foreign policy, which stress the role of power in world politics, claim that foreign policy is based on the idea of continually trying to influence or control other actors, to get them to behave in ways beneficial to one's own state. There are, as we have seen, however, many kinds of goals and many kinds of influence.

We need to study foreign policy — both formulation and implementation — comparatively, looking for patterns of behavior associated with different types of states under different conditions and within different contexts. One key question then becomes *what* to compare. What exactly are we trying to explain (what is the dependent variable)? What is the explanation (what is the independent variable)? That is, in trying to explain foreign policy — the policy-making process, the content of the policies, or resulting state behavior — what factors, influences, and characteristics should be investigated? Another question is *how* to compare foreign policies. Should one try to compare many states at one point in time, one state over many time periods, or a large number of units over different time periods? Do we compare foreign policies in terms of evaluating their success or failure or in terms of normative issues such as whether the foreign policy produces "good" or "bad" outcomes? The answers depend to a great extent on just what research problem we are confronting.

It makes sense to study foreign policy comparatively because regular patterns of variation can be identified and explained. In a classic work on the comparative study of foreign policy, James Rosenau presented a "pretheory" of foreign policy. He argued that all influences on foreign policy (independent variables) could be categorized according to levels of analysis, and that we need to determine the relative importance

---

[1] Kissinger expressed these sentiments in "Domestic Structure and Foreign Policy," *Daedalus* 95 (1966): pp. 503–529, and in *A World Restored: Metternich, Castlereagh, and the Problems of Peace, 1812–22* (Boston: Houghton Mifflin, 1973).

of variables from each of the different levels of analysis (individual, role, societal, etc.) in affecting the foreign policy of states. Rosenau also recognized that there were significant differences among states, so he specified three critical dimensions: size (large or small), economic development (developed or underdeveloped), and the nature of the political system ("open" or "closed"). He then proposed which variables should have what effects on different types of states.[2]

Most current efforts in the comparative analysis of foreign policy focus on describing and modeling the foreign policy process: identifying the important decision-making units, looking at how individuals and groups perceive foreign policy problems and solutions, and describing the dynamics of interaction between groups of decisionmakers (either within the same government or across state boundaries). This approach to

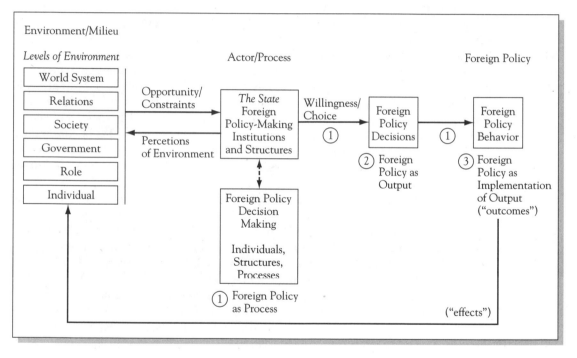

FIGURE 6.1   An Environmental Model for Foreign Policy Analysis

Source: Maria Papadakis and Harvey Starr, "Opportunity, Willingness, and Small States: The Relationship between Environment and Foreign Policy," in Charles F. Hermann, Charles W. Kegley, and James N. Rosenau, eds., *New Directions in the Study of Foreign Policy* (Boston: Allen & Unwin, 1987), p. 417.

---

[2] James N. Rosenau, "Pre-Theories and Theories of Foreign Policy," in R. Barry Farrell, ed., *Approaches to Comparative and International Politics* (Evanston, Ill.: Northwestern University Press, 1966), pp. 27–92. For a classic statement of the comparative method, see Adam Przeworski and Henry Teune, *The Logic of Comparative Social Inquiry* (New York: Wiley, 1970); for a more recent overview, see David Collier, "The Comparative Method," in Ada W. Finifter, ed., *Political Science: The State of the Discipline II* (Washington, D.C.: American Political Science Association, 1993), pp. 105–119.

foreign policy analysis can be translated into a question: Which parts of the environment, or the menu, will be most closely considered by the decisionmakers of a particular state, under what conditions, and at what stage of the foreign policy–making process? This process begins with the formulation of foreign policy goals and continues as policymakers attempt to adapt these goals to domestic and international environments. This environmental model, presented in Figure 6.1, looks at foreign policy as *process, output, outcomes,* and *effects,* taking into account both domestic and external factors.

Goals and Objectives of Foreign Policy

Foreign policy objectives are those things that leaders of states pursue. Objectives evolve and there is debate over how they should be best pursued; rarely is there national agreement or consensus on what the goals of foreign policy should be. Foreign policy decision making "involves the discovery of goals as much as it involves using decisions to achieve particular outcomes."[3]

We may think of a foreign policy objective as an "'image' of a future state of affairs and future conditions that governments through individual policy makers aspire to bring about by wielding influence abroad and by changing or sustaining the behavior of other states."[4] Objectives may be very concrete: Iraq sought territory in Iran that would give it control over the Shatt al-Arab waterway (and thus precipitated the Iran-Iraq war). Objectives may be much less concrete: creating images or promoting a specific set of values, such as "making the world safe for democracy." Some objectives, often geopolitical ones, remain constant over long periods of time, like the Russian desire for warm-water ports or the British desire for command of the seas. Others are transitory, perhaps changing from month to month; what currency exchange rate to target is an example from foreign economic policy. Some objectives have consequences that affect the whole state, like the deterrence of nuclear attack. Still others involve the interests of only a small portion of society, perhaps the wealthiest or the most politically influential citizens.

Governments often pursue objectives that are incompatible with other foreign or domestic policy objectives. Such was the case when the United States sold huge quantities of wheat to the Soviet Union in 1971 and 1972. The deal would help improve relations with the Soviet Union and might ultimately help the Nixon administration disengage from the American involvement in Vietnam; on the other hand, the administration also wanted to control inflation by keeping food prices down, an objective that thus became much harder to achieve. Israel's policy of encouraging Jewish immigration to Palestine (Zionism) has often conflicted with another Israeli foreign policy objective, the Arab states' recognition of Israel's right to exist.

In sum, leaders of states seek a wide range of public, and sometimes private, objectives, some concrete, some quite abstract, and very often in conflict. One factor distinguishing the realist, liberal, and radical perspectives is the types of objectives that they

---

[3] Paul A. Anderson, "What Do Decision Makers Do When They Make a Foreign Policy Decision?" in Charles F. Hermann, Charles W. Kegley, and James N. Rosenau, eds., *New Directions in the Study of Foreign Policy* (Boston: Allen & Unwin, 1987), p. 290.

[4] K. J. Holsti, *International Politics: A Framework for Analysis,* 5th ed. (Englewood Cliffs, N.J.: Prentice-Hall, 1988), p. 119.

believe are central in the foreign policies of states. Realists stress the immediate military/security objectives of states and downplay economic ones. For liberals, key foreign policy objectives involve the longer-term economic and social welfare of society. Radicals also highlight the economic objectives of states but argue that foreign policy is designed to promote the interests of particular classes in society, not society as a whole.

National Interests and Priorities

Hans Morgenthau emphasized that interest "defined in terms of power" determines the behavior of states. All governments, whether democratic or authoritarian, pursue such interests in the anarchy of world politics, a realm described by English political philosopher Thomas Hobbes as "every man, against every man." Realists tend to look at states as *unitary actors,* entities guided by a single set of values, preferences, and objectives, which speak with one voice (consistent with *the* national interest). Foreign policy objectives are designed to maximize the state's power, or at least to maintain it so as to secure the state's position in the global power hierarchy. One difficulty with such statements is that they can easily become mere tautologies, statements that are true by definition and hence impossible to refute. That is, one can readily construct arguments to show that nearly any action — whether initiating a war or keeping the peace, whether in accordance with international law or blatant disregard of it — is intended to enhance or preserve the power, and thus the interest, of the nation-state.

Even when this kind of argument is avoided, the fact that different countries have different histories, cultures, and socioeconomic and political structures means that foreign policy preferences, objectives, and ultimately strategies derive in large part from domestic society, and not simply from the state's place in the structure of the international system. Nor can we ignore the fact that within any given nation-state, different individuals, groups, and classes have different interests. Workers share some interests with factory owners (for instance, in seeing that their products can be sold), but they differ sharply on others (such as who should gain more from the production of those goods and whether it is better to manufacture goods with high-priced domestic labor or inexpensive foreign labor). Some manufacturers are interested in selling consumer goods in a peaceful world; others want to sell armaments that have a market only in a world where states are at war or threatened by war. It then becomes essential to ask: Whose particular interest is reflected in any particular governmental policy or act? Which individuals, groups, or classes are most influential in determining government policy? Does this change from time to time or under different international or domestic conditions? Are there some issues on which one group or class has a dominant influence and others on which some other group is dominant? These questions are absolutely unavoidable in any political system where there are several individuals or groups and where each has different wishes or interests. Contrary to the realist assumption, states are not unitary actors with a single purpose. Unless we know how different interests are reconciled into a single decision, we cannot know what particular policy will result. Without more attention to this reality, our previous discussion of state goals and objectives is necessarily incomplete.

A simple example will illustrate the importance of taking into account the foreign policy preferences of different groups within states. After Iraq invaded Kuwait in 1990 there was a debate in the United States about the appropriate response. Suppose there were only three possible courses of action: war (W), economic sanctions (S), or do nothing (N). Suppose also that there were only three groups in American society with strongly held preferences, each of roughly equal size: the militants preferred war to sanctions, but they preferred sanctions to doing nothing (W>S>N); the pacifists thought that war should be avoided at all costs, but they preferred sanctions to doing nothing (S>N>W); the humanitarians most wanted to do nothing but preferred war to sanctions because the costs of sanctions would be borne primarily by the civilian population (N>W>S).

How could these individual preferences be aggregated into a "social choice"? If society was asked to vote between war and sanctions, society would prefer war (both militants and humanitarians prefer war to sanctions). If the choice was between sanctions and doing nothing, society would prefer sanctions (militants and pacifists prefer sanctions to doing nothing). Finally, if the choice was between war and doing nothing, society would choose to do nothing (the preference of pacifists and humanitarians). Society, therefore, prefers war to sanctions and sanctions to doing nothing, but at the same time it prefers doing nothing to going to war (W>S>N>W). That is, there is an inconsistency in society's preference ordering (it is "intransitive"). Kenneth Arrow showed that in a situation such as this there is no way to generate a social preference ordering that is both transitive and fair to all groups — a problem known as *Arrow's paradox.*[5]

What was *the* national interest that prompted the United States to go to war with Iraq? It is possible that a majority of those Americans who had an opinion did in fact prefer war when compared to any single alternative course of action; not all social choices are confounded by Arrow's paradox. However, the important point is that we should not assume that war was preferred by society just because that was the *chosen* course of action. If group preferences resembled those in our illustration, then the U.S. response to the Kuwait invasion may have been an artifact of the way U.S. options were presented to the American public. If doing nothing was not considered a serious option (which is how the militants might pose the problem), then indeed war may have been preferred by most people. It is important to know which groups were vocal in making their preferences known, but we also need to know which groups were able to seize the agenda of political debate.

Agenda setting is but one of several ways in which intransitive social preferences become social choices. By rejecting the realist assumption of the state as a unitary actor — by understanding who gets involved in foreign policy making, who is in charge, how compromises are reached, and how these policy-making procedures differ in different times and circumstances — we begin to understand *whose* interests become the national interests, and how. That is why it is vital to know about the state's *structure of government* and the *societal influences* on it. Whose particular interests will the government serve at any particular time? Does the structure of the economy give particular groups or classes (such as finance capitalists, the managers of state-owned enterprises, or members of certain tribes, castes, or ethnic groups) particular clout on a particular

---

[5] Kenneth Arrow, *Social Choice and Individual Values,* 2nd ed. (New York: Wiley, 1963).

issue? Do cultural practices or shared experiences incline certain societies, or groups within them, to adopt particular outlooks on world affairs? The realist concept of a national interest may indicate certain core values or goals that most citizens share to some degree (for example, peace, prosperity, and security), but until we break away from the notion of a unitary state — that is, until we know how different groups' interests are aggregated — we really know very little about national *priorities* or how they will be pursued in international politics.

Societal Influences on Foreign Policy

Decisionmakers act in the names of their states. As we have seen, countries differ in size, income level, and other characteristics that affect their capabilities and foreign policy goals. They also differ in their histories as nations, in the ways their societies and economies are organized, and the structure of their governments. Contemporary analysts increasingly stress the linkages between domestic and international politics. In conducting foreign policy, government leaders also confront domestic pressures and must create domestic political coalitions. In effect, they must play a "two-level game," adjusting their preferences and strategies in response to simultaneous developments at the international and domestic levels.[6] President Bill Clinton's visit to China in summer 1998, for example, was like a walk on a tight rope. He had to neutralize domestic opposition to his visit by publicly criticizing China's human rights record while at the same time not offending his Chinese hosts to the point of scuttling U.S.-Chinese trade and investment opportunities. The Chinese government's willingness to engage Clinton in a discussion of human rights and other matters previously considered off-limits — which, to the surprise of many, included a live television broadcast of his condemnation of the 1989 suppression of prodemocracy activists in Tiananmen Square — seemed to suggest that the Chinese were aware of their visitor's domestic political predicament.

The ability of a government to control society and the ability of specific interests therein to communicate their needs and demands to government are both related to the openness of government. **Openness** is the extent to which a government is subject to influences from society. This means that a government is accountable: it must satisfy the people of its society or it can be removed from office by regular, agreed-on procedures that are fair by some criterion. Being open means that opposition groups in soci-

---

[6] See Robert D. Putnam, "Diplomacy and Domestic Politics: The Logic of Two-Level Games," *International Organization* 42, 3 (1988): pp. 427–462. For a recent application of this concept, see Peter F. Trumbore, "Public Opinion as a Domestic Constraint in International Negotiations: Two-Level Games in the Anglo-Irish Peace Process," *International Studies Quarterly* 42 (September 1998): pp. 545–565. See also George Tsebelis, *Nested Games: Rational Choice in Comparative Politics* (Berkeley: University of California Press, 1990).

ety can contest groups in government for the right to control the government through some type of electoral procedures. Being open means that such opposition groups can present their positions to the public through a free press and other media, and no group is systematically prevented from acting as an opposition. In the contemporary era, "democracy" denotes a country in which nearly everyone can vote, elections are freely contested, the chief executive is chosen by popular vote or by an elected parliament, and civil rights and civil liberties are substantially guaranteed.[7]

People in government have their own interests: to keep or increase their political positions and political power, their wealth and economic position, and their position or status within society, as well as to promote their ideological values, beliefs, and ideals. These and other interests lead political leaders to seek societal support — that is, the approval of public opinion — in order to gain control of government, remain in office, and then implement their policies. To do this, governments must hear and respond to the demands and needs of society. By meeting societal demands and needs (fixing high tariffs for the protection of certain industries, sending in the Marines to protect foreign investments, or establishing hard-line policies toward Iraqi or Haitian dictators to protect freedom and encourage the spread of democratic government), governmental leaders are just as constrained as they are by the state's capabilities.

We can also examine how societal interests support specific foreign policy positions of the government. Just as society's resources give decisionmakers the opportunity to act, societal support enhances their willingness to act. As noted before, neither human power and resources nor economic and military capabilities count for much if a government cannot mobilize them. Governments do not just passively respond to societal needs and demands; they also try to shape and control them. If a government cannot persuade a people to get behind its policies and use those capabilities to support its policies, the capabilities are useless. If the people are not willing to act militarily, for example, perhaps fearing a hopeless, draining involvement, the government itself may be reluctant. Officials in the Reagan administration tried to evade a congressional prohibition of aid to the Nicaraguan rebels in the 1980s with disastrous results. In 1990, President Bush very carefully built up popular, congressional, and international support before going to war with Iraq. Congress may reflect general public unwillingness to get involved and may refuse to support military intervention, as during the war in Bosnia. The governments of Germany and Japan in the 1990s, when asked for military commitments that match their economic status in situations such as the Gulf War, have said that they cannot do so because of popular opposition to military instruments of foreign policy.

---

[7] Freedom House, in their *Freedom in the World : The Annual Survey of Political Rights and Civil Liberties, 1997–1998* (New York: Freedom House, 1998), characterizes states as free, partly free, or not free on the basis of whether free, honest, and competitive elections are held; whether civil liberties (free speech, free assembly, and assurance of a fair trial) are present; and whether political terrorism is largely absent. According to their criteria, eighty-two of 192 countries (42.7 percent) could be coded as free in 1996; free and partly free countries accounted for 74.5 percent of the international system. We include these codings in Appendix B, along with data on population, area, GNP, and other societal characteristics of nation-states.

Political and Strategic Culture

The common experiences of citizens — and the selective memories they have of their parents' experiences — help provide the basic structure of belief and ideology through which these citizens view their place in the world, and hence the appropriate roles and actions of their governments. It is therefore important to understand culture, cultural differences, and the impact of culture in the formation and implementation of foreign policy. Analysts have examined states' geopolitical environments, their historical experiences, and political cultures in an effort to account for "national styles" in the conduct of foreign policy; this is sometimes referred to as *strategic culture*.[8] Compare, for example, the United States and Russia.

The United States is a country founded largely by immigrants who came to develop a vast and sparsely populated land and to construct a society in a wilderness. Most people came to the new land to realize hopes that were constrained in their home countries — hopes for political or religious expression or for economic well-being. Their experience in America often offered opportunity and rewarded individual initiative. Especially important for foreign policy, the new land was largely safe from external enemies. Once independence had been won from Britain, the limited transportation technology of the time insulated America from Europe's national wars and provided a security that prevailed for a century and a half.

Russia, by contrast, is inhabited by people who have traditionally lived in insecurity, typified by the wooden stockade fortresses that once dotted the harsh Eurasian plains. Russia was periodically conquered or invaded by Mongols, Poles, Swedes, and Germans, among others. It was ruled by autocratic leaders whose chief virtue was their ability to provide a measure of national unity and strength to ward off attackers. In time the Russian state expanded, ruling its neighbors instead of being threatened by them. As a multinational empire, czarist Russia, and later the Soviet Union, governed or repressed many subordinate nations, whose total population approached that of Russia alone. Economically, czarist Russia was a relatively primitive society, following well behind Europe in the development of industry and the accumulation of capital. When the communists took power in 1917, their ideology seemed a threat to the entire capitalist world as they proclaimed the virtues of world revolution. From 1918 to 1920, European, American, and Japanese forces intervened indecisively on the side of the czarist counterrevolutionaries. The communists ultimately consolidated their power, but only by confirming and deepening the Russian autocratic tradition. They built a modern, centralized, industrial state, one finally capable of providing security from invasion; at the same time, they became a constant threat to their neighbors.

Thus, Americans live with a tradition of security that allows them periodic forays into world politics but protects them from basic threats to national survival. Russians, by contrast, live with a tradition of insecurity and mutually threatening relations with others. Americans live with an economy developed by individual enterprise, which provides an unusual measure of opportunity for many (economic development is thought to proceed best when it is least fettered by state interference). Today's Russians

---

[8] A good review of the literature on strategic culture can be found in Alastair Iain Johnston, "Thinking about Strategic Culture," *International Security* 19, 4 (1995): pp. 32–64.

live in an economy in which capitalist development began late and was cut short and in which, under the communists, development was controlled and directed by the state bureaucracy. Americans live in a state where the government provided the religious and political liberty so many of its immigrants sought, as well as the freedom for capitalist development. Russians live in a state where people welcomed state control; without control, there could be no unity, no security, and little prosperity.[9]

Individuals, groups, and classes dominant within societies use their power to perpetuate belief systems that will reinforce their power. Americans are taught an ideology that praises freedom and extols capitalism as the engine of prosperity. Russians were taught an ideology that praised the state as the provider of individual and collective security. Though something of a caricature, we might say that in America the form of the economy shaped the kind of state that emerged: an economy of relatively decentralized, plural centers of power whose interest was best served by limiting state control. By contrast, in Russia, the strength of the state determined the kind of economy that emerged; state ownership of the means of industrial production, collectivization of agriculture, and centralized planning during the Soviet era were consistent with Russian political culture. In many respects, the conditions under which both nation-states developed no longer apply. The United States is no longer isolated in the world, the continent is no longer undeveloped, and the challenges it faces stem largely from the military, economic, and environmental interdependence between Americans and others. The Soviet Union achieved an unprecedented degree of military security; but the state bureaucracy became a burden on individual and national development, directly leading to the predicaments facing present-day Russia.

How much difference do these contrasting histories make for foreign policy? In an analysis that would become the cornerstone of America's cold-war strategy of containment, George Kennan wrote of caution and flexibility in Soviet foreign policy:

> Again, these precepts are fortified by the lessons of Russian history: of centuries of obscure battles between nomadic forces over the stretches of a vast unfortified plain. Here caution, circumspection, flexibility and deception are the valuable qualities. . . . Its political action is a fluid stream which moves constantly, wherever it is permitted to move, toward a given goal. Its main concern is to make sure that it has filled every nook and cranny available to it in the basin of world power.[10]

Kennan and many others characterized Soviet foreign policy as essentially opportunistic — not bent on world domination, but never shying away from opportunities to enhance Soviet power and influence. By contrast, many saw (and continue to see) in America's foreign policy a crusading spirit. Inverting Woodrow Wilson's wartime goal, "to make the world safe for democracy," they wonder instead how to make American democracy safe for the world. Kennan himself saw this dangerous tendency in U.S. foreign policy, which derived from American pride in its history and

---

[9] See, for example, Colin Gray, "National Styles in Strategy: The American Example," *International Security* 6, 2 (1981): pp 21–47; David R. Jones, "Soviet Strategic Culture," in Carl G. Jacobsen, ed., *Strategic Power: USA/USSR* (London: St. Martin's Press, 1990), pp. 35–49.

[10] George F. Kennan [X, pseud.], "The Sources of Soviet Conduct," *Foreign Affairs* 25, 4 (1947): p. 575.

institutions: "it behooves us Americans, in this connection, to repress, and if possible to extinguish once and for all, our inveterate tendency to judge others by the extent to which they contrive to be like ourselves."[11]

Power Elite or Pluralism?

Questions about national style or strategic culture raise further questions about how exactly the foreign policy–making process is influenced by the attitudes and opinions held by members of society. Although we cannot give any hard-and-fast answers, we can provide some guidance by further considering the content of public opinion and by asking how public opinion is expressed or shaped within different governmental forms. For example, in what way does it make sense to say that the foreign policy decisions of a democracy represent the wishes of the public? How can public opinion place constraints on the leadership, and what opportunities do the leaders have to shape public opinion? We shall look especially at ideas and information about the United States, both because a wealth of information is available and because, in such a major democracy, we would expect public attitudes to have a relatively significant effect.

A radical perspective starts with the proposition that interests among the leadership groups in American society converge. In this view, a "power elite" drawn from the highest echelons of society (government, business, the military) determines the nation's goals. Attitudes among most of the public are thus not even relevant. In the words of C. Wright Mills, the most famous proponent of this view,

> The conception of the power elite and of its unity rests upon the corresponding development and the coincidence of interests among economic, political, and military organizations. It also rests upon the similarity of origins and outlook and the social and personal intermingling of top circles from each of these dominant hierarchies.[12]

In this view, those who occupy the leading positions of power in American society basically agree on the fundamental principles by which the society is organized. Although they may disagree about details or the implementation of particular policies, their commitment to the principles of a market economy, regulated yet also protected by the ruling political structures, provides a basic common denominator. These like-minded individuals are held together by common upper-class origins, educational experience, and social and professional mingling.

The contrasting "pluralist" view of American society is held by most liberals and is typified in this comment:

> A substantial part of the government in the United States has come under the influence and control of narrowly based and largely autonomous elites. But these elites do not act cohesively with each other on many issues. They do not "rule" in the sense of commanding the entire nation. Quite the contrary, they tend to pursue a policy of

---

[11]George F. Kennan, *American Diplomacy 1900–1950* (Chicago: University of Chicago Press, 1951), p. 127.
[12] C. Wright Mills, *The Power Elite* (New York: Oxford University Press, 1956), p. 292.

non-involvement in the large issues, save where such issues touch their own particular concerns.[13]

Proponents of this view argue that there is no single power elite, but rather a *plurality* of elite groupings. Different elites tend to wield influence over different issues (in defense, education, health, and so on); they fight and win different political battles. While there may be some overlap in the membership of these elite groups, power in American society is not nearly as concentrated as radicals would have us believe. Pluralists emphasize the diversity of opinion and the unpredictability of particular political outcomes rather than any fundamental consensus on the form of political and economic order.

In a real sense, the conflict between these two perspectives is irreconcilable. One stresses that diversity, unpredictability, and the clash of opinion surely are real. (Will the defense budget be increased? Will military bases be closed? Will the North American Free Trade Agreement be supported?) The other dismisses this diversity as trivial and stresses the fact that certain values — liberal democracy, free enterprise, and the support of free enterprise by the government — are common denominators for most people in elite positions in America (or, for that matter, in Japan or Western Europe). Advocacy of alternative forms of economic or political order (socialism or fascism) is clearly outside the mainstream, being undertaken only by a small minority and without the sound perspectives essential for those considered fit for high positions of public trust.

Both views actually are correct. There are important differences within and between elite groups. At the same time, by long-term historic or global standards, the spectrum of "respectable" opinion on major public policy issues in America is not especially wide. There has, however, been some periodic widening of that spectrum. Before World War II, isolationism was widespread; until the Japanese attack on Pearl Harbor, that view had many adherents from both the right and the left. By the 1950s the number of proponents of this view had shrunk to a small minority, which was held in ill repute by the elite. There was instead a substantial consensus on an internationalist policy of military alliances, a strong defense, some foreign aid (at least to pro-American and procapitalist states), and a generally active involvement by the United States in world affairs. This policy consensus began to break down during the Vietnam War years, as opposition to American military involvement in foreign countries grew. After the Vietnam War was over and the United States seemed to suffer a series of policy reversals with respect to the Soviet Union and its allies in the Third World, opposition to an active American foreign policy again became less common and less respectable. The cycle has reversed once again with the end of the cold war, and there are renewed calls from some circles for American retrenchment from the world scene, and especially that the United States should avoid the role of world police force.

---

[13] Grant McConnell, *Private Power and American Democracy* (New York: Knopf, 1966), p. 339. The best known proponent of the pluralist view is undoubtedly Robert A. Dahl; see especially his *Who Governs? Democracy and Power in an American City* (New Haven, Conn.: Yale University Press, 1961).

Elite Opinion and Foreign Policy

In considering public opinion in general and the opinions of leaders in particular, it is important to distinguish carefully among various segments of the population. About 20 percent of the American public, for instance, has little or no interest in or information about foreign affairs, or even about politics in general. This group is typically unaware of most international events. For example, in June 1986 only 67 percent of the American people professed to have heard of SALT II, the treaty central to regulating the Soviet-American nuclear arms race.[14]

Above the 20 percent who are nonpolitical is a "middle mass" of perhaps 75 percent of the populace, whose attention moves in and out of politics, depending on the issue and on events. The attentiveness and knowledge of this group usually are not deep. For example, in the June 1986 survey reported here, of the 67 percent that had heard of SALT II, less than half knew that the United States had not ratified the treaty. In other surveys barely more were aware of the antiballistic missile (ABM) treaty, and only one-third could define "NATO." That proportion is no less than that for many other political issues, however. About the same fraction (though not necessarily the same people) could define "welfare state" and "electoral college."

About 25 percent of American adults — the "attentive public" — are somewhat knowledgeable about foreign affairs, say they follow news about other countries, and have attitudes that are fairly stable over time. Some of these people talk about foreign affairs with others and discuss their own positions. But only about 5 percent of the population can be considered politically active. Because of their interest and, to a lesser degree, their social roles (as, for example, teachers, clergy, and active participants in civic affairs), these people are often considered to be opinion leaders. Within this group is a small segment of the population that gives money or time to political activities and communicates opinions beyond personal acquaintances. These people, sometimes called "mobilizables" or "elites" (in a weaker sense than in power elite theory), typically write, speak in public, or otherwise reach an extended audience.[15] Constituting no more than 1 or 2 percent of the populace, this group primarily includes party politicians, business and labor union executives, senior civil servants, leaders in the mass media, and leaders of economic, ethnic, religious, professional, or other interest groups involved in political activities.

The Content of Elite Opinion

Not surprisingly, membership in the segment of opinion leaders or mobilizables is closely correlated with education, income, and professional status. People who have a lot of information and are politically active tend to have reasonably consistent atti-

---

[14] See Thomas W. Graham, "The Pattern and Importance of Public Knowledge in the Nuclear Age," *Journal of Conflict Resolution* 32, 2 (June 1988): pp. 319–334, esp. the appendix.

[15] These categories are taken from Barry Hughes, *The Domestic Context of American Foreign Policy* (San Francisco: Freeman, 1978), pp. 23–24; and W. Russell Neuman, *The Paradox of Mass Politics: Knowledge and Opinion in the American Electorate* (Cambridge, Mass.: Harvard University Press, 1986).

tudes that form a relatively cohesive ideology. Those who have a sizable amount of accurate information and a high degree of interest will relate various facts and principles to produce a coherent set of beliefs.[16]

Americans of higher social and economic status have tended to support official policy even more strongly than the average American, whatever that policy has happened to be. In the 1950s and early 1960s, when an active foreign policy and a strong defense were popular, highly educated, professional, upper-income Americans were more prodefense and more supportive of foreign aid and the Vietnam War than were people of lower status. When a withdrawal from some overseas commitments and a smaller defense establishment became popular later in the Vietnam period, high-status Americans held those views even more than did the total population. When, in June 1979, SALT II was still fairly popular nationwide and it looked as though it would be ratified by the Senate, higher-status people especially favored it. In the 1980s and 1990s American elites tended to favor foreign aid programs, both economic and military, and were generally more inclined than the average American to favor sending troops or military assistance to U.S. allies if they should be attacked.[17] In Western Europe, college-educated people were much more likely to favor their countries' continued membership in NATO than were their less educated or younger fellow citizens, who often endorsed a policy of neutrality toward the two superpowers.

The general tendency of elite opinion to be more supportive of official policy does not mean that American elites are of one mind on such matters. One study has shown that the foreign policy opinions of elites correspond closely to their domestic ideological orientations, which differ greatly. Those who adopt conservative views on such domestic issues as school prayer, environmental regulation, homosexuality, and welfare also tend to adopt a hard-line attitude toward the Soviet Union and were more inclined to advocate militant foreign policies generally (the quest for military superiority, destabilization of hostile regimes, and so on). Interestingly, this link between domestic and foreign policy orientation made foreign policy attitudes resistant to change even after the end of the cold war. Domestic conservatives continued to be more wary of the "new world order," and although they revised their assessment of the now-Russian threat, they seemed to retain a measure of suspicion regarding Russian intentions.[18] Table 6.1 shows some of the striking differences between conservative and liberal elites on various post–cold war foreign policy issues and how earlier views on domestic policy (in 1988) continued to be reflected in foreign policy attitudes four years later — despite the end of the cold war.

---

[16] Norman Nie, Sidney Verba, and J. R. Petrocik, *The Changing American Voter* (Cambridge, Mass.: Harvard University Press, 1979).

[17] A comparison of elite and general-public opinion on various foreign policy issues in the 1990s can be found in John E. Rielly, "The Public Mood at Mid-Decade," *Foreign Policy* 98 (Spring 1995): pp. 76–93.

[18] See Shoon Kathleen Murray, *Anchors against Change: American Opinion Leaders' Beliefs after the Cold War* (Ann Arbor: University of Michigan Press, 1996), chaps. 4, 5. Similar link between domestic cleavages and foreign policy opinion have been reported for France and, to a lesser extent, Germany; see Thomas Risse-Kappen, "Public Opinion, Domestic Structure, and Foreign Policy in Liberal Democracies," *World Politics* 43, 4 (1991): pp. 479–512.

	Domestic Orientation in 1988		
Issue in 1992	Conservatives	Liberals	Difference
The United States needs to keep ahead of Russia in strategic nuclear weapons.	79	40	39
The United States needs to develop the Strategic Defense Initiative (SDI) to protect against accidental and limited nuclear attacks.	81	19	62
It is necessary to use military force to stop aggression; economic sanctions are not enough.	78	37	41
The collapse of the Soviet Union does not mean that the United States can let down its guard; there will always be powerful, aggressive nations in the world.	94	57	37
The United States may have to support dictators because they are friendly toward us.	59	22	37

TABLE 6.1 Foreign Policy Attitudes of American Elites after the Cold War, Percent Approving or Agreeing

Source: Select data from Shoon Kathleen Murray, *Anchors against Change: American Opinion Leaders' Beliefs after the Cold War* (Ann Arbor: University of Michigan Press, 1996), Table 5.24.

Many scholars believe that the general support for official American foreign policy among American opinion leaders has unraveled. One major project has periodically surveyed top-level American leaders since 1976. The first of these surveys found a fragmentation of opinion among those leaders, which the investigators attributed primarily to the impact of the Vietnam War. About one-sixth of the leaders reported that they wanted to seek a complete military victory both at the beginning and at the end of U.S. involvement in Vietnam. Another one-sixth tended to favor a complete withdrawal from Vietnam, not only at the end, but also when the war first became a political issue. Even when surveyed again in the 1980s, these two extreme groups remained large and opposed each other on a wide range of foreign policy beliefs and attitudes. Within the two-thirds of the leaders who fell in between these two extremes or who changed their positions in the course of the war, very different conclusions have been drawn about the war and very different preferences for policy are held today. Although these nonextremists in some sense make up the center of opinion, they show little unity of opinion. They have been divided on arms control and security issues, on whether the United States should intervene militarily abroad, and on policy toward human rights and economic development in less-developed countries.[19]

These data suggest that there is no longer any elite consensus on the means by which foreign policy should be pursued or even on which ends (peace or power, for instance) are most important. It should hardly be surprising, therefore, that similar divisions exist among the general public and that broad shifts in policy usually occur whenever a new group of political leaders takes charge of the government after an election.

The Impact of Mass Public Opinion

Mass public opinion is no more fixed than elite opinion. Fluctuation in Americans' attitudes regarding foreign threats is illustrated by a public opinion survey question that has been asked repeatedly for more than fifty years. Although the wording of the question has varied slightly, its basic form has been quite stable: "Do you think we are spending too much, too little, or about the right amount for national defense and military purposes?" Figure 6.2 shows the pattern over time. The graph shows substantial fluctuation in the early years of the cold war, before a popular and elite consensus was established. After the Korean War a period of stability ensued, during which more people preferred increasing rather than reducing defense spending, but the majority of the population was content with the existing level. This consensus was shattered by the antipathy toward the military generated by the Vietnam War; since then, opinions on this matter have proved very changeable. The antimilitary mood of the early 1970s faded and was then abruptly reversed by worsening relations with the Soviets, the Iranian seizure of American diplomats as hostages in 1979, and then the Soviet invasion of Afghanistan. But by the mid-1980s that mood, too, had passed, leaving almost half the population feeling that the Reagan defense buildup had gone far enough. The Gulf War, as reflected in figures for early 1991, showed a dramatic decline in support for more defense cuts; however, this blip was clearly gone by fall 1991.

Throughout the cold war, U.S. national security policy, and the public attitudes that supported it, seemed anchored in the great ideological and power rivalry with the Soviet Union. A basic component of that policy, the ups and downs of American military spending, was largely predictable by looking at changes in the level of Soviet military spending and at public preferences, as expressed in opinion surveys, for increases

---

[19] Ole R. Holsti and James N. Rosenau, *American Leadership in World Affairs: Vietnam and the Breakdown of Consensus* (Boston: Allen & Unwin, 1984); Holsti and Rosenau, "Domestic and Foreign Policy Belief Systems Among American Leaders," *Journal of Conflict Resolution* 32, 2 (June 1988): pp. 248–294.

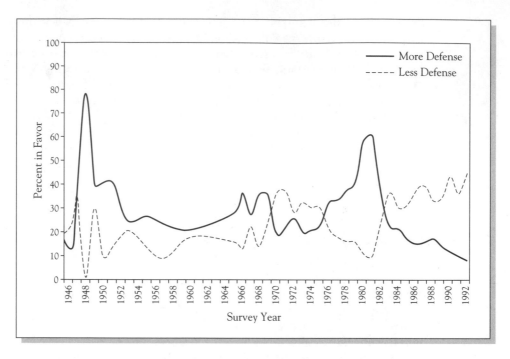

FIGURE 6.2　American Public Opinion on Defense Spending, 1946–1992

Sources: Percentages are annual averages from various surveys. 1946–1964 data computed from Bruce Russett, "The Revolt of the Masses: Public Opinion on Military Expenditures," in Bruce Russett, ed., *Peace, War, and Numbers* (Beverly Hills, Calif.: Sage, 1972), pp. 301–306; 1965–1990 data from Thomas Hartley and Bruce Russett, "Public Opinion and the Common Defense: Who Governs Military Spending in the United States?" *American Political Science Review* 86, 4 (1992): pp. 905–915; 1991–1992 data from Jonathan M. Feldman, "Public Choice, Foreign Policy Crises, and Military Spending," in Lloyd J. Dumas, ed., *The Socio-Economics of Conversion from War to Peace* (Armonk, NY: Sharpe, 1995), pp. 233–264.

or decreases in American spending.[20] The end of the cold war brought remarkable changes in both policy and attitudes. Rationales for U.S. military spending, for the use of military force abroad, and for international cooperation have likewise changed. As people revised their beliefs about the Soviet Union between 1987 and 1988, attitudes toward some specific policies — such as defense spending — also moved in a dovish direction. Public opinion is the most substantively important influence on the budget that remains after the end of the cold war. In the past it exerted a greater influence on

---

[20] For evidence that the largest influence on U.S. defense spending was Soviet military spending, see Charles W. Ostrom and Robin F. Marra, "U.S. Defense Spending and the Soviet Estimate," *American Political Science Review* 80 (September 1986): pp. 819–842, and Thomas Hartley and Bruce Russett, "Public Opinion and the Common Defense: Who Governs Military Spending in the United States?" *American Political Science Review* 86, 4 (1992): pp. 905–915.

U.S. military spending than did the deficit, and it is likely to continue to play at least as important a role with the end of the Soviet threat.[21]

The public, of course, does not speak with a single voice, and many of the divisions we see in elite foreign policy attitudes also hold for the populace at large. Those with conservative opinions on domestic issues tend to be "hawkish" on issues pertaining to foreign affairs; domestic liberals tend to be "dovish." Moreover, what separates American opinion leaders from the masses helps to account for differences within mass public opinion. Generally speaking, those with higher incomes and higher levels of education have been somewhat more likely to support arms control — according to Gallup polls, the gap can vary from 5 to 10 percent — reductions in defense spending, lower tariffs, and fewer restrictions on immigration. But higher education and income does not always translate into dovish foreign policy attitudes. These groups were more likely to support U.S. air strikes against the Serbs during the Bosnia conflict, as well as the dispatch of U.S. troops to keep the peace. They are also more inclined to approve retrospectively of the U.S. atomic bombing of Japan in 1945. Table 6.2 shows relationships between education and income patterns and American public opinion on various foreign policy issues.

The Gender Gap

Women at all education and income levels are generally more dovish on foreign policy than men — this is the so-called **gender gap.** In a January 1991 Gallup poll 78 percent of men approved of the decision to send U.S. troops to the Persian Gulf, compared with only 54 percent of women. Men and women also differed on the outcome of the Persian Gulf War, with men more inclined to say that it represented a "great victory" and that it increased American influence with other nations. Women felt more strongly that money was spent on the war that should have been spent at home and that too many Iraqis were killed.[22] Women were less likely to approve of U.S. air strikes on Bosnian Serb positions (29 percent compared to 48 percent of men, according to a Harris poll), but they did not differ significantly from men when it came to sending U.S. peacekeepers to Bosnia. In addition their retrospection on the atomic bombings of Hiroshima and Nagasaki tends to be much more critical than men's: only 45 percent now approve of that decision, compared to 74 percent of men.

The precise explanation for the gender gap is a subject of debate among feminist scholars. One view, derived from "radical" or "standpoint" feminism, suggests that aggression and violence are masculine characteristics and that women are more forgiving and peace loving. Although an extreme version of this sort of explanation would

---

[21] See Bruce Russett, Thomas Hartley, and Shoon Murray, "The End of the Cold War, Attitude Change, and the Politics of Defense Spending," *Political Science and Politics* 27, 1 (1994): pp. 17–21. They also note a similar sea change in perceptions of Russian motivations between 1988 and 1992 among American elites. Fully 80 percent of those who had agreed in 1988 that the Soviet Union was generally expansionist in its foreign policy goals did not think the same about Russia by 1992. Likewise, by 1992 an overwhelming majority agreed that defense spending should be cut.

[22] See Ole R. Holsti, *Public Opinion and American Foreign Policy* (Ann Arbor: University of Michigan Press, 1996), p. 175. Assessments of the Gulf War are those of opinion leaders, but we suspect that they apply more broadly.

TABLE 6.2	Foreign Policy Attitudes of the American Public, Percent Approving or Agreeing by Education and Income								
Issue (date of survey)	College Education				Income (thousands)				
	None	Some	Grad.	Post-grad.	<20	20–30	30–50	50–70	>70
U.S. Troops to Bosnia to Keep the Peace (1995)	50	48	51	50	46	44	56	53	54
U.S. Atomic Bombing of Japan in 1945 (1995)	55	59	68	74	51	55	59	68	69
NAFTA Will Decrease Jobs in United States (1993)	70	69	60	56	70	68	69	61	57
Too Much Immigration to United States (1993)	62	55	54	51	58	66	56	56	

Note: Figures for immigration are averages regarding Arab, Latin American, Asian, and African immigration; the last figure is for income of $50,000 or more.

Source: All data are from opinion polls conducted by the Gallup Organization, as reported in *The Gallup Poll* (Wilmington, Del.: Scholarly Resources, various years), or *Index to International Public Opinion* (Westport, Conn.: Greenwood Press, various issues).

trace these differences to the very biological essences of man and woman (an "essentialist" view), most of these scholars emphasize the differences between masculine and feminine roles as they have emerged from social practice.[23] Above all, women in American society, and most others, fulfil a nurturing role. Because their identities have become so closely tied to childbearing and child rearing, women are inclined to oppose foreign policy actions that present a threat to human life. Society's gender roles explain women's support for foreign policies that bring about peace and, more generally, improve the quality of life.

---

[23] A recent discussion sympathetic to this essentialist view is Francis Fukuyama, "Women and the Evolution of World Politics," *Foreign Affairs* 77, 5 (September/October 1998): pp. 24–40; see also the reactions in "Fukuyama's Follies: So What if Women Ruled the World," *Foreign Affairs* 78, 1 (January/February 1999): pp. 118–129.

Another view, derived from "liberal" feminism, disputes any natural inclination of women to differ from men in their attitudes about world politics, whether based on biological essence or socially constructed gender roles. This view suggests that at least some of the observed differences between men and women really boil down to differences in education and income. If women enjoyed the same socioeconomic opportunities as men, the so-called gender gap would vanish. Liberal feminists frequently point to women leaders, who have broken through society's "glass ceiling" — such as Margaret Thatcher (Britain), Indira Gandhi (India), and Golda Meir (Israel) — as evidence that women behave no differently from men in the conduct of foreign policy. Nor have women holding high positions in the American foreign policy establishment, like Madeleine Albright and Jeanne Kirkpatrick, championed more dovish postures than their male counterparts.[24]

Public Approval of State Leaders

The chief of state — the president, prime minister, or monarch — embodies the national interest. He or she is at the top of the political pyramid and is responsible for bringing together all the separate individual and group interests. Personality, character, experience, and leadership style surely matter in determining what choices a leader makes. Also relevant is the relationship he or she has with advisers and subordinates, the people who provide information, help make decisions, and are responsible for implementation. We shall look at individual characteristics and role relationships in the next chapter; here we want to ask another kind of question: How constrained is the top leader by mass and elite opinion in the society? Does public opinion matter to the chief? If so, when and how?

According to one view, mass opinions set limits on the range of actions that a political leader may safely take. One version of this view stresses the constraint that ideological anticommunism among the masses imposed on the freedom of action of leaders in the United States. American policymakers in the 1960s, for example, feared a backlash of militant anticommunism by the general populace in reaction to major foreign policy reverses. They remembered the domestic political costs incurred by the Truman administration resulting from the trauma of "losing China" and the witch-hunting of the McCarthy era. In the words of former Senator Sam Ervin, "You can't believe the terror that man [Senator Joseph McCarthy] spread among politicians." Thus, politicians feared the unleashing of a popular anticommunism that would punish them for foreign policy defeats and were therefore constrained by such beliefs even though they themselves were too sophisticated to accept the premises behind them.

Consequently, believing that the American people would not tolerate the "loss" of Vietnam, senior officials in Washington resolved that Vietnam would not be lost — at

---

[24] For an overview of women's involvement in state leadership and foreign policy, see Jane S. Jaquatte, "Women in Power: From Tokenism to Critical Mass," *Foreign Policy* 108 (Fall 1997): pp. 23–37. There are many categories of feminism in the literature, some overlapping with others on points relevant to world politics in general and the gender gap in particular. Our categories of "liberal" and "radical" (and "standpoint") feminism come from V. Spike Peterson and Anne Sisson Runyan, *Global Gender Issues* (Boulder, Colo.: Westview, 1993), chap. 5; and Christine Sylvester, *Feminist Theory and International Relations in a Postmodern Era* (Cambridge: Cambridge University Press, 1994), chap. 1.

least, not during their terms in office. They would hang on and escalate when necessary to avoid defeat, even though they knew that the long-term prospects for holding
the country were poor. They could hope to postpone the day of reckoning until a time
when they themselves would not be held responsible, perhaps even hoping against all
available evidence that events would break favorably so that the ultimate outcome
would not be disastrous. According to some analysts, this kind of thinking could be
found in every administration from Truman to Nixon.[25]

A very different point of view, however, maintains that the leader has great potential support among the populace for virtually any kind of foreign policy initiative. A
leader can take either hawkish or dovish initiatives and, with the authority and respect
he or she commands, still be backed by a substantial portion of the population. For example, the possibilities for leadership even on such a hotly disputed issue as "peace for
land" in Israel are shown by responses to a question that asked whether people would
"support a peace agreement that involves giving up most of the territories." At first, 45
percent said yes. But when the qualification, "if the government supports it" was
added, the proportion of those who would agree rose to 54 percent. Symmetrically, the
phrase "if the government is against it" dropped support to 36 percent. In two surveys
made in early 1989, the percentage of the Israeli population willing to allow Palestinians to hold local elections jumped by 17 points after the usually hawkish Prime Minister Yitzhak Shamir endorsed a similar plan. An extreme example appeared in answer
to the question, "Do you believe it is essential, or not, to support a government during
a security crisis, like war, even when one does not agree with what it is doing?" Eighty-
eight percent said yes.[26]

The ability of a nation's leader to gather popular support for foreign policy initiatives, especially during an international crisis (and provided the leader is perceived as
doing something about it), has been termed the **rally-'round-the-flag** phenomenon.[27]
This phenomenon can be seen in the experience of almost all recent U.S. presidents.
Figure 6.3 illustrates the pattern of responses to a standard Gallup survey question
asked about twice every month: "Do you approve or disapprove of the way [name] is
handling his job as president?" Both the trend and the fluctuations are the result of
many influences, including domestic events and the state of the economy as well as
foreign policy and international events. Every president begins with a "honeymoon"
jump in popularity immediately after taking office, and nearly all presidents experience some decline in their popularity over their term in office, as they carry out policies
that displease various groups in the population. George Bush had that experience, and

---

[25] This is basically the interpretation of Daniel Ellsberg, "The Quagmire Myth and the Stalemate
Machine," *Public Policy* 19, 2 (Spring 1971): pp. 217–274. See also Leslie Gelb and Richard Betts, *Vietnam: The System Worked* (Washington, D.C.: Brookings Institution, 1979). To an important degree, popular anticommunism was built up by policymakers themselves. In 1947, for example, Senator Arthur
Vandenberg advised Harry Truman to use the threat of communism to "scare the hell out of the country" as a means of getting Congress to approve aid to Greece. However, once this force was unleashed,
policymakers felt more constrained by it than they wished to be.
[26] See Asher Arian, *National Security Public Opinion in Israel* (Boulder, Colo.: Westview, 1988); and Bruce
Russett, *Controlling the Sword: The Democratic Governance of National Security* (Cambridge, Mass.: Harvard University Press, 1990), chap. 2.
[27] The phrase, from a Civil War song, is used in this sense in John E. Mueller, *War, Presidents, and Public
Opinion* (New York: Wiley, 1973).

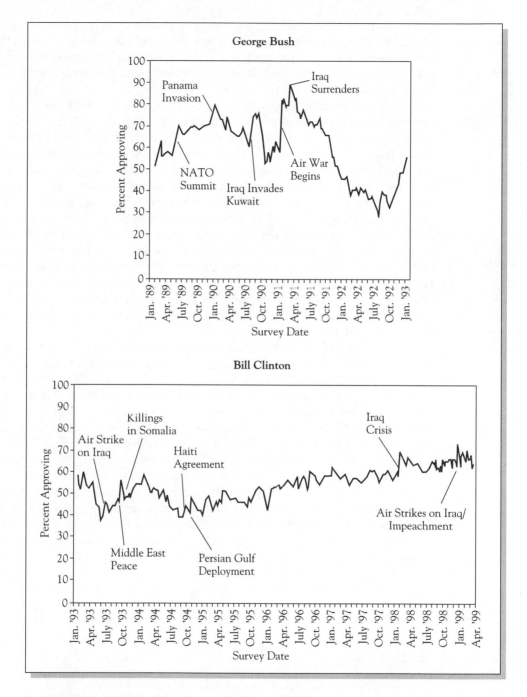

FIGURE 6.3   Presidential Job Approval, 1989–1999

Sources: The Gallup Poll Monthly, various editions; The Gallup Organization, "Clinton Job Approval," May 1999 [cited May 5, 1999]; available at <http://www.gallup.com/polltrends/jobapp.htm>.

in his case the long-term decline was magnified by his sharp, but temporary, bursts of popularity associated with major initiatives in the field of national security. (Bill Clinton seems to have defied this tendency, at least through the middle of his second term, perhaps because his initial popularity was rather modest compared to that of many other U.S. presidents.)

When, in December 1989, he ordered U.S. troops to invade Panama to depose the government of Manuel Noriega, President Bush's popularity rating rose by 9 percentage points. But it then fell fairly sharply until Iraq's invasion of Kuwait in August 1990, which triggered Bush's quick decision to impose an economic embargo and send American troops to defend Saudi Arabia against a possible Iraqi attack. That rally, however, was very short-lived, as people began to fear war with Iraq and the country was deeply divided about the wisdom of war. In the beginning of 1991, by which time Bush had carefully cultivated national and international support, negotiations with Iraq failed. Bush's support rose by an extraordinary amount — about 19 percentage points — with the beginning of the air war, went down for a while, and then rose again by 9 points with the short and successful land campaign of Operation Desert Storm. However, we see from the figure that all these rallies were extremely brief. They usually waned within two or three months, and they did not prevent a long-term decline in Bush's popularity, which, by mid-1992, brought his ratings nearly as low as Jimmy Carter's had been at his least popular.

With the end of the cold war and the absence of anything that could be depicted as an immediate threat to vital American interests, President Clinton gained very little benefit from rally effects. As Figure 6.3 shows, he got a short blip of popularity (7 points) in June 1993 by ordering an air strike against Iraq in retaliation for a plot to assassinate Bush. A somewhat larger increase (10 points) followed in September when Yitzak Rabin and Yassir Arafat traveled to Washington for the historic Declaration of Principles by Israel and the PLO (and a historic hand-shake), but that gain was short-lived since many blamed Clinton for the October 1993 deaths of American peacekeepers in Somalia. Clinton got a 10-point boost in late September 1994 when he announced that former President Jimmy Carter had reached an agreement with the Haitian dictatorship for a peaceful turnover of power (after American troops went ashore). Half that gain, however, was gone within a week![28] The only real popularity winner was Carter; 80 percent of the population approved of the job he had been doing as a foreign policy negotiator. Clinton's approval rating edged up in October 1994 (7 points) with the dispatch of American troops to the Persian Gulf, a response to Iraqi troop movements near the Kuwaiti border. Most popularity changes associated with any Clinton foreign policy action were very small and may have been nothing more than chance variations.[29] International economic achievements have not generated substantial praise

---

[28] The gain was effectively missed by Gallup, which did not survey until mid-October. See "Troop Dispatch Boosts Clinton Polls," *Christian Science Monitor,* October 13, 1994, p. 1.

[29] Each survey records opinions from a random sample of Americans for purposes of measuring the attitudes of *all* Americans. Survey researchers are generally confident that they have correctly measured those attitudes to within plus-or-minus 3 percentage points. Therefore, year-to-year variations that fall within that fairly narrow range might be due to "sampling error" rather than real changes in public approval.

from the American public; there were no jumps accompanying the passage of the North American Free Trade Agreement (NAFTA) in November 1993 or the General Agreement on Tariffs and Trade (GATT) world trade agreement in December 1994, and none accompanying U.S. efforts in February 1995 to stem the fall of the Mexican peso or, in January 1998, to contain the East Asian financial crisis.

The rally-'round-the-flag effect is not only a preoccupation of survey researchers and presidential advisors. Indeed, it caught the imagination of Hollywood with the release of the 1997 film *Wag the Dog,* a fictional account of an American president who, accused of molesting a Girl Scout, conspires to concoct an international crisis requiring U.S. military action in the hope that the president's approval rating will recover in time for his reelection. In an uncanny case of life imitating art, the film was playing in theaters when President Clinton's alleged involvement with a White House intern was made public in January 1998, right in the midst of a mounting confrontation with Iraq over UN weapons inspections. As the U.S. military prepared for an armed response to Iraqi intransigence, Clinton was accused by many, including the Iraqis themselves, of using the confrontation to deflect public criticism of the alleged affair (his approval rating went up 10 points during the last week of January). The rally-'round-the-flag effect had by then become such common knowledge that the Clinton administration went to great pains in an effort to reassure critics that the president was not trying to take advantage of it. Future American presidents may have to do the same.

Leaders of other countries may also try to take advantage of a rally-'round-the-flag effect. In spring 1982 British Prime Minister Margaret Thatcher gained great personal popularity by her tough response to the Argentine seizure of what Britain calls the Falkland Islands, and she won the next election handily. The Argentine military government also hoped to benefit from a rally. It chose a time when it was politically unpopular, and when the Argentine economy was stagnating, to rekindle the long-standing dispute with Britain and invade the islands. However, the effort to make itself popular backfired when it lost the war, and the army government was then overthrown.

A chief of state cannot do whatever he or she wants and expect general public support. There is some evidence that threatening or using force against foreign adversaries is initially more popular than are conciliatory or cooperative acts: the former seem to produce a rise of 4 or 5 percentage points in the president's popularity; the latter, only a 1- or 2-point change, often downward. But people's reaction depends partly on their images of the president. They fear extremes. Presidents perceived by the public as doves, as Carter was, tend to be most approved when they talk or act tough, as Carter did to the Soviet Union when it invaded Afghanistan. President Reagan, who was generally seen as a hawk, gained especially from more dovish acts. While the public approved his military action in Grenada in 1983, they also approved when he withdrew the marines from Lebanon.[30] In 1987, to the consternation of some of his military and hard-line political advisers, Reagan signed an agreement with the Soviets on

---

[30] Charles W. Ostrom and Dennis Simon, "Promise and Performance: A Dynamic Model of Presidential Popularity," *American Political Science Review* 79, 2 (June 1985): pp. 334–358; Miroslav Nincic, "America's Soviet Policy and the Politics of Opposites," *World Politics* 35, 4 (July 1988): pp. 452–475.

nuclear arms control in Europe. One motivation may have been to restore some of his flagging popularity.

The ability of a leader to shape public opinion and thus to generate support in a crisis usually holds for the short term only. The life of a burst of popular support is four or five months at the most, and more often it is only about two. By the end of that time, support usually returns to its previous, lower level. The reason is related to the reason for the rally in the first place. In the first week or two after a sudden military action or major diplomatic event, criticism of the president, even by opposition political leaders, is usually muted. The president has the most information about foreign policy and security affairs, especially in fast-breaking crises. Opposition leaders who criticize the president risk being exposed as poorly informed. The absence of criticism looks like bipartisan support to much of the public, and so ordinary people are also reluctant to criticize. In time, however, as the chief of state's policy begins to falter or less favorable information about the circumstances becomes available, opposition political leaders become bolder, and their renewed criticism is picked up by the media and then by the general public. The rally effect then decays.[31]

Do Wars Win Elections?

The shorter the decision time available to a leader — and it may be quite short during an international crisis — the less constrained by public opinion he or she is likely to be. The short-term rally effect helps powerfully. This is especially strong in national security affairs because people tend to feel that the commander in chief has secret information and special competence. We saw this effect after the war with Iraq began in 1991. However, if a crisis drags on, dissenting voices become more widely heard and constraints built into the democratic system of governance become more effective. Bush was careful to make clear to American critics of his policy that the United States had many allies and UN approval for his action against Iraq. Even so, American strategy was geared to a short war with few American deaths, so as to end the conflict before domestic opposition could build.

An American president who wishes to respond militarily to a foreign adversary can mount an action with existing military forces and without prior approval from Congress. A majority of the public will probably support the action, and if it is successful, it may be widely applauded. The year-in, year-out maintenance of military action abroad, however, requires congressional approval and the appropriation of funds in circumstances in which the trade-offs with domestic welfare become much more apparent and politically salient. Domestic constraints may therefore limit the president's menu of choice in a crisis by favoring those forms of military action (bombing,

---

[31] Richard A. Brody, *Assessing the President: The Media, Elite Opinion, and Public Support* (Stanford, Calif.: Stanford University Press, 1991). On Britain, see David Sanders, Hugh Ward, and David March, "Government Popularity and the Falklands War: A Reassessment," *British Journal of Political Science* 17 (March 1987): pp. 281–314. A useful review is Philip J. Powlick and Andrew Z. Katz, "Defining the American Public Opinion/Foreign Policy Nexus," *Mershon International Studies Review* 42 (May 1998): pp. 29–61.

overwhelming force in an invasion, possibly even nuclear weapons) that bring quick results, rather than protracted warfare with heavy American casualties.

In the long run, wars are almost always harmful to the political health of those who conduct them. The popularity of Truman, Johnson, and Nixon was damaged by war. After a brief spurt of national unity, wars typically produce a loss of social cohesion and low popular morale, manifested in higher rates of strikes, crime, and violent political protest. Least healthy for a leader is, of course, to lose a major war; every great-power government that lost a major war in the past century was overthrown from within, if not by its external enemies. But even leaders, and their parties, who conduct and win costly wars are likely to be punished by the voters.[32] Winston Churchill, the popular British World War II leader, lost the 1945 election to the Labour party by a landslide. Governments lose popularity directly in proportion to the length and cost (in blood and money) of the war. All of America's wars of the past century have shown this pattern, with the president who was in office when the war began and/or his party faring poorly in subsequent elections.[33]

Political leaders, especially in a democracy, live a precarious life in which the demands made on them always exceed the leaders' capacity to satisfy. They are expected to solve many — and often contradictory — social problems, to provide employment and prosperity without inflation, and, of course, to maintain peace with strength. They know that they will be rewarded or punished at the polls in proportion to the healthiness of the economy. Knowing this, they try to stimulate the economy so as to raise the necessary popular support. However, modern economies are complicated systems, often beyond ready control, and government taxing and spending policies will help some people and hurt others. Thus, leaders may be unable to buy electoral popularity by filling their constituents' pocketbooks. If they cannot control the economy, they may then turn to foreign policy in order to increase their support.

Here is where the rally-'round-the-flag effect may be especially useful. According to one study, a U.S. president is more likely to use or escalate military force if he is seeking reelection during a developing or ongoing war — the proverbial "October surprise" — because he knows that voters will be more concerned than usual about foreign affairs and therefore more likely to hold it against him if the war goes badly. He is also more likely to win congressional approval on even unrelated international issues in the month following a use of force. Another study showed that over the past century, U.S. presidents have been more likely to use, or threaten to use, military force internationally in years when the economy was doing badly or when there was a national election. As an authority on the U.S. presidency says: "The desperate search is no longer for the good life but for the effective presentation of appearances. This is a

---

[32] See Bruce Bueno de Mesquita, Randolph Siverson, and Gary Woller, "War and the Fate of Regimes: A Comparative Analysis," *American Political Science Review* 86 (September 1992): pp. 638–657.

[33] Sometimes they won the elections, but by a smaller margin than would be predicted from the prosperous state of the economy. See Arthur Stein and Bruce Russett, "Evaluating War: Outcomes and Consequences," in Ted Robert Gurr, ed., *Handbook of Political Conflict: Theory and Research* (New York: Free Press, 1980); and Timothy Cotton, "War and American Democracy: Voting Trends in the Last Five American Wars," *Journal of Conflict Resolution* 30, 4 (December 1986): pp. 616–635.

pathology because it escalates the rhetoric at home, ratcheting expectations upward notch by notch, and fuels adventurism abroad."[34]

Leaders of other democratic governments show similar behavior. A study of Israeli decisions to use force found that the Israeli government was more likely to respond militarily in periods before a national election or when the economy was doing poorly. An example was the raid on the Iraqi nuclear reactor on June 7, 1981. That was just three weeks before Menachem Begin, the incumbent prime minister, was to face voters in a general election. However substantial the military justification for the strike, it could have been postponed for a few months with little harm to Israeli security. As it was, Begin's party benefited greatly from an outpouring of public approval despite severe economic difficulties from inflation. In states without obvious military enemies the rally effect can be dramatic, even in the event of a policy conflict with their allies. For example, support for a ban on nuclear weapons entering New Zealand almost doubled (from 40 to 76 percent) after the government adopted such a ban and the United States responded with a confrontational policy.[35] If countries are more likely to engage in international military disputes when periods of domestic political turmoil coincide with opportunities abroad, this does not mean that leaders deliberately involve their countries in war solely to boost their own electoral chances. Sometimes they may actually be taking dramatic steps for peace or arms control or, more often, they may be tempted to talk tough, make threats, or indulge in small-scale uses of military force to impress the voters or divert voter attentions from their economic troubles. The risk is that sometimes these acts can get tragically out of hand.

The evidence that leaders often do try to divert attention from domestic problems with foreign adventures is nevertheless mixed. Some studies have not found any such pattern. Perhaps most democratic leaders are less cynical that we might imagine. Alternately, the leaders of foreign countries may anticipate their reactions: expecting democratic leaders to be tempted to undertake foreign diversions near elections or when the economy is doing badly, potential antagonists may be especially careful not to provoke democracies at those times. By behaving cautiously, they would be behaving strategically, thinking ahead in the continuing "What will they do if I do this?" game of international politics.[36]

Presidents do worry about their popularity with the public. It affects not only their own or their party's prospects for reelection, but also their ability to get support in Congress for their legislative program. Presidents try to preserve and build their popularity by choosing policies and policy instruments that will be popular. Franklin Roosevelt was the first president to use scientific opinion polling extensively; he closely watched public opinion before Pearl Harbor to determine his tactics to move the

---

[34] Richard J. Stoll, *U.S. National Security Policy and the Soviet Union* (Columbia: University of South Carolina Press, 1990), chap. 3; Charles W. Ostrom and Brian L. Job, "The President and the Political Use of Force," *American Political Science Review* 80, 2 (June 1986): pp. 541–566. The quotation is from Theodore Lowi, *The Personal President* (Ithaca, N.Y.: Cornell University Press, 1985), p. 20.

[35] James W. LeMare, "International Conflict: ANZUS and New Zealand," *Journal of Conflict Resolution* 31, 3 (September 1987): pp. 420–437.

[36] Brett Ashley Leeds and David R. Davis, "Domestic Political Vulnerability and International Disputes," *Journal of Conflict Resolution* 41, 4 (December 1997): pp. 814–834; Alastair Smith, "Diversionary Foreign Policy in Democratic Systems," *International Studies Quarterly* 40, 1 (March 1996): pp. 133–153.

United States into World War II. He first chose greater military spending and lend-lease — not the draft or direct intervention — because those instruments offered the greatest potential for domestic approval. President Reagan developed an extensive organization to monitor public opinion and used its information in making decisions. President Clinton has even been accused of "governing by public opinion poll." Leaders thus, in some sense, both respond to and manipulate public opinion. They respond to it by doing what will be popular in the short run when domestic economic and political conditions encourage them to maximize votes. They also may manipulate it by trying to increase their popularity without correcting the underlying causes of mass discontent that endangered their popularity in the first place.

Who Governs? Public Opinion Matters

The U.S. Congress is said to be especially sensitive to the needs and demands of particular, narrow interests. More precisely, members of Congress are likely to be especially sensitive to the needs of major interests in their constituencies or other interests that provide them with support at election time. Defense industry executives can expect a favorable hearing from the U.S. representatives in whose districts they employ many workers. Representatives from Iowa will care about foreign grain sales. The representative who chairs the House Merchant Marine Committee is likely to be solicitous of shipowners, shipbuilders, and merchant sailors, wherever those interests are located. They can provide (or withhold) financial and other support at election time.

Yet international and security issues are remote for most people, even those of the upper socioeconomic classes. Only a small proportion of the population directly benefits from military spending; in any given year relatively few travel very far abroad and even fewer obtain much information relevant for evaluating complex foreign policy issues. Foreign policy is thus a prime candidate for what has been termed "symbolic politics," situated as it is well beyond most people's day-to-day lives and not affecting their immediate welfare.[37] People do have opinions about foreign policy, sometimes strong ones, but not necessarily because the implementation of foreign policy imposes costs or benefits on their material existence (like their pocketbooks).

People may support a policy for any of three reasons: (1) because, on the basis of available information, they perceive the policy as consistent with their interests, (2) because implementing the policy is consistent with their beliefs or satisfies psychological needs, and (3) because the segment of their social environment most meaningful to them reaffirms support. Elites seem more likely than others to support official policy. They are no more or less likely than others to be personally affected by foreign policy, nor do they have distinct beliefs or psychological needs. But they are more likely to live in a social environment in which international affairs are considered

---

[37] David O. Sears, Richard R. Lau, Tom R. Tyler, and Harris M. Allen, Jr. "Self-Interest vs. Symbolic Politics in Policy Attitudes and Presidential Voting," *American Political Science Review* 74, 3 (September 1980): pp. 670–685.

important. When cues in their environment change, they are more likely to change their opinions for two reasons. First, new information indicating that a given foreign policy is inconsistent with personal beliefs and interests is more likely to reach elites, who are better informed than the mass public, thus prompting them to reassess their beliefs. Second, because such a reassessment is more common among higher-status groups as a whole, support from their social environment for the old beliefs will diminish and support for new beliefs and corresponding foreign policy will be reaffirmed.

One example is security policy in Western Europe during the cold war. Support for official NATO defense policy was always strongest among the elites there. The mass public was often less committed to NATO and to specific policies concerning nuclear weapons. During the Reagan administration, nuclear strategy underwent a change (to be discussed further in Chapter 9), and the revised strategy entailed the deployment of new intermediate-range missiles in Europe during 1983. Despite near-solid support among European governments (and elites), the general public was very skeptical. Official NATO policy was always that NATO would never start a war, but that it reserved the right of enacting a "flexible response" to a Soviet attack, including the option of using nuclear weapons. The new deployment of nuclear missiles in Europe seemed to increase that likelihood in the minds of most ordinary Europeans, who were extremely worried about the consequences of using nuclear weapons in that densely populated region of the world. Fewer than 20 percent of them in the major countries (Britain, France, Italy, and West Germany) said that they approved of a first-use policy.[38] This longstanding tension between elite and mass attitudes in Europe posed problems for Western security policy and the unity of NATO. It required the pursuit of double-track negotiations: deploying new nuclear forces while simultaneously trying to negotiate — ultimately successfully — a mutual disarmament pact with the Soviet Union.

Sometimes leaders are able to implement defense or foreign policy measures even when public opinion opposes them, as suggested by NATO's deployment of missiles in the face of widespread public protest in Europe. Similarly, in 1978, President Carter urged senators to do the "statesmanlike" thing and support the Panama Canal treaties, despite the sentiment against the treaties, which was evident in most opinion polls. Two-thirds of the Senate did support the treaties, which were ratified. The next year, however, Carter met with failure. SALT II was favored by more people than opposed it, but many either had no opinion or had never heard of the treaty. With such lukewarm approval in the mass public and a worsening international atmosphere, a majority of the Senate remained unconvinced. SALT II was dropped by the Reagan administration when it took office.

A major review of public opinion and government policy changes between 1935 and 1979 found that in two-thirds of all cases (including foreign policy issues) where there was a shift in public opinion and a subsequent change in public policy, the policy change was in the same direction as the public opinion change. Moreover, the government was more likely to shift in the direction of public preferences than against them.

---

[38] Russett, *Controlling the Sword,* chap. 4. For a postmodern analysis of NATO, including the deployment of intermediate-range missiles, with special emphasis on the tension between internal dissent and maintenance of the alliance's unified front, see Bradley S. Klein, "How the West Was One: Representational Politics of NATO," *International Studies Quarterly* 34, 3 (1990): pp. 311–325.

Studies of the interaction between attitudes toward defense spending and congressional decisions to increase or cut the president's military spending proposals have found a strong relationship between opinion and subsequent policy. Public preferences for higher or lower defense spending are very good predictors of whether actual defense spending will go up or down in the next year. The degree to which their constituencies favored higher defense spending — as measured by public opinion polls — made a great difference in whether individual members of Congress voted for the military expansion during the Reagan years.[39]

This evidence seems to indicate that the American democratic form of government is fairly responsive to the will of the general public. We must nonetheless be cautious with this interpretation because we do not know why public opinion changes. It may well be that public opinion changes because opinion leaders and elites — including government officials — first express a preference and then persuade both the attentive public and the mass public to voice that preference. Then Congress, including some of the very people who helped change public opinion, can "respond" to that public change. Certainly this possibility often seems more plausible than the simple notion of Congress merely being obedient to the "voice of the people."

Overall, our view of the importance of public opinion and the interaction between opinion change and policy change is complex. The impact of public opinion depends very much on the kind of issue, the circumstances, the level of government at which the decision is made, and other specific features of the political context. Certainly there is no immediate, automatic connection, even in a democracy, between public opinion and foreign policy. Political decisionmakers are skilled leaders of opinion, with ready access to television, newspapers, and other media; they shape opinion as well as respond to it. Always we are bedeviled by the problems of making inferences about power and of differentiating between the activity of people or pressure groups and their influence. It is clear, however, that public opinion does matter — whether as an immediate determinant of national willingness or a constraint on leaders' search for approval of particular policies and the rhetoric they use to justify their actions. What Robert Dahl said about New Haven, Connecticut, applies to the United States as a whole and to many other countries, even on matters of foreign policy: "If we ask 'Who Governs?' the answer is not the mass nor its leaders but both together."[40] Realist theories that ignore this observation miss something very important.

---

[39] The major review is Benjamin Page and Robert Shapiro, *The Rational Public: Fifty Years of Trends in Americans' Policy Preferences* (Chicago: University of Chicago Press, 1992). The findings on defense spending are in Hartley and Russett, "Public Opinion and the Common Defense," and Larry Bartels, "Constituency Opinion and Congressional Policy Making: The Reagan Defense Buildup," *American Political Science Review* 85, 2 (June 1991): pp. 457–474.
[40] Dahl, *Who Governs?* p. 7.

7

Individuals and World Politics: Roles, Perceptions, and Decision Making

WORLD SYSTEM

RELATIONS

SOCIETY

GOVERNMENT

ROLE

INDIVIDUAL

Rational Decision Making

Foreign policy decisions are made by people, either as individuals or as part of a group. The individual foreign policy decisionmaker is surrounded by several layers of environment, external and domestic, which constrain and limit in a number of ways what the decisionmaker is able or is likely to do. Each layer blends into others, which sandwich it. There are connections between systemic and societal factors, between societal and governmental factors, and between governmental and role factors. In this chapter, we shall investigate the individual in world politics as affected by role and personal idiosyncracies. These impinge directly on the individual decisionmaker who plays a part in the development and execution of foreign policy.

By looking at individuals, we have moved from the broadest context, the world system, to the narrowest, the foreign policymaker. The foreign policies of states are constantly in motion. At the center of a state's foreign policy are individuals engaged in **decision making** — the process of evaluating and choosing among alternative courses of action. When we study foreign policy decision making, we examine not only the chosen courses of action (the *content* of foreign policy), but also the factors that influence how and why decisions are made (the foreign policy *process*). Many of the factors that affect the foreign policy menu of states derive from the perceptions and images of individuals in government. If a restaurant menu is illegible; if the diner misinterprets the menu, thinking, for example, that wine is served free of charge (when clearly it is not); or if an individual feels pressured, say, to order an appetizer just because others in the party are doing so — then choice has been affected in some way. Our concern in this chapter is with those things that affect how individuals perceive world politics and how they make foreign policy decisions. That is, our concern is with willingness rather than opportunity.

Foreign policy analysis often involves making judgments regarding good and bad decisions. Many discussions stress the idea that the best decision is the most "rational" one. However, **rationality** is a very complex concept, which carries different connotations for different analysts, and there are ongoing debates about exactly what the term means. In the simplest formulation, rational behavior is purposive behavior, so rationality is an ability to relate means to ends. Exactly how closely means and ends are related, with what certainty they are related, and how closely the actual consequences of behavior match the consequences that are desired all depend on an understanding of the decision-making process. We can identify two basic views on these questions. One view of rationality assumes that decisionmakers possess all relevant information, which is used to determine the course of action that maximizes benefits relative to costs. The other view points to the difficulties encountered by humans (and organizations) when they try to digest large amounts of information, especially in an effort to calculate the costs and benefits associated with all possible courses of action. This view agrees that rationality involves purposive behavior, but also recognizes the limits imposed by human and organizational capability.

The first view is an "ideal" picture of decision making, a checklist of "perfect" conditions that would permit "perfect" decisions. No one claims that these conditions can be achieved by foreign policymakers; in fact, much scholarly work focuses on why they cannot be achieved. However, policymakers do attempt to approximate this ideal, with varying degrees of success. Graham Allison identified the four essential elements of this **rational actor model:** Faced with a given problem, the rational decisionmaker first clarifies his or her *goals and objectives* and determines which of these should take priority over others. Next, the decisionmaker identifies all of the *alternatives* or *options* available for achieving these goals and objectives. The decisionmaker then evaluates the *consequences* of these alternative courses of action. Since alternative courses of action and their consequences involve both benefits and costs, they are ordered from most to least preferred on that basis. Finally, the decisionmaker *chooses* the course of action that ranks highest in this preference ordering.[1]

---

[1] See Graham T. Allison, *Essence of Decision: Explaining the Cuban Missile Crisis* (Boston: Little, Brown, 1971), chap. 1.

A good analogy for the rational actor model is an individual playing a game, such as chess. In chess, the goal is to trap the opponent's king. There may be other intermediate objectives, like capturing the opponent's queen and protecting one's own, but the ultimate goal is checkmate. At each turn, the player considers his or her alternatives and the consequences of possible moves. What are the costs and benefits of each move? Will it position the pieces for checkmate? Will it result in the loss of a pawn, a bishop, the queen? Based on this assessment, the player chooses a move. Whether the decision turns out to be a good one or a bad one depends largely on how thorough and accurate the player was in considering the alternative moves and assessing the risks of each.

When the rational actor model is a reasonable approximation of the foreign policy-making process, analysts often treat actors (typically states) as players engaged in this sort of a game. Alternative courses of action available to each player are seen as possible "moves" and the combination of moves made by all players leads to an "outcome." Each outcome has a "payoff" or "utility" for each player equal to the sum of all the benefits derived from that outcome minus the costs. By using available information about outcomes and their utilities, a player will make the move that **maximizes utility.** Because outcomes are not always certain — they depend on one's own moves but also on the moves of other players, with perhaps an element of chance as well — players also need to estimate the probability of achieving a given outcome. When they take into account both the utilities associated with different outcomes and the probabilities of achieving them, they maximize their "expected utility."

Models of foreign policy that represent the decision-making process in this way are called *rational choice* or *formal* models. If a strategic situation involving two or more actors is set up in this way — with players, moves, outcomes, and utilities (or at least preference orderings) specified — then *game theory* can be used to predict players' moves and the most likely outcome of their interaction (an arms race, a trade agreement, a war, or some other event). Game theory is a mathematical technique used extensively in economics and increasingly in political science, and has also been very helpful in the study of world politics, as we shall see in the chapters ahead. However, there is a significant challenge involved in setting up a foreign policy problem as a game in the first place, and much controversy surrounds the appropriateness of the rational actor model of decision making that lies at the core of rational choice approaches to world politics.[2]

The notion of perfectly rational decision making was questioned many years ago by Nobel prize–winning economist Herbert Simon. He pointed out in a famous formulation that the decisionmaker does not maximize utility but rather **satisfices.** This means that the rational decisionmaker searches for an *acceptable* choice, one that satisfies a minimal set of requirements. Instead of reviewing *all* possible alternatives, the

---

[2] For good reviews of the rational choice approach in international relations, see Michael Nicholson, *Rationality and the Analysis of International Conflict* (Cambridge: Cambridge University Press, 1992), and Nicholson, *Formal Theories in International Relations* (Cambridge: Cambridge University Press, 1989). For instruction on the use of game theory, see James D. Morrow, *Game Theory for Political Scientists* (Princeton, N.J.: Princeton University Press, 1995). One application is Bruce Bueno de Mesquita and David Lalman, *War and Reason: Domestic and International Imperatives* (New Haven, Conn.: Yale University Press, 1992).

"satisficer" will usually pick the *first* alternative that meets this minimal set of require-ments. Simon argued that people attempt to act rationally but that rationality is "bounded" — limited by the capacity to process information and the tendency to adopt a simplified conception of the world.[3]

Other refinements of the rational actor model focus on the concept of utility. Ana-tol Rapoport notes that payoff or utility is defined very generally in game theory as "the psychological worth of the associated outcomes to the player in question." He also points out that "the task of determining these psychologically meaningful payoffs is the task of the psychologist, not of the game theoretician."[4] We have indicated that in determining utility, the rational decisionmaker engages in a cost-benefit analysis, but that begs the question of what goes into such a calculation. Decisionmakers may wish to maximize gains or to minimize losses; considering a range of possibilities, they may want to maximize their minimum gains (a "maximin" strategy in game-theoretic terms) or, alternatively, to minimize their maximum losses (a "minimax" strategy).

Such matters have indeed been a central concern of psychologists, and one body of work known as **prospect theory,** has found that individuals do, in fact, treat gains and losses differently. Decisionmakers seem to fear losses more than they covet gains, which translates into a willingness to take greater risks to protect what they have and fewer risks to acquire what they want. The status quo — for example, a state's current territorial possessions — often becomes a *reference point*, which helps to predict "risk-averse" or "risk-seeking" behavior. But the status quo is not always the reference point, and knowing a decisionmaker's actual reference point is important. Generally, we would expect states to take fewer risks to acquire territory than to prevent the loss of territory. This may be part of the reason why in 1990 the United States and other coun-tries dismissed early signals that Iraq would invade Kuwait. The fact that Saddam Hussein considered Kuwait to be Iraq's rightful territorial possession — part of the Basrah province of ancient Mesopotamia, which was his reference point — should have indicated to observers that they should take seriously the possibility that he would engage in risky behavior (military invasion) to repossess Kuwaiti territory.[5]

None of these challenges to the rational actor model imply that decisionmakers are irrational, only that actual decision making departs from the ideal model in various and significant ways. Nor do they suggest that rational choice approaches to the study of world politics are doomed to failure because of these imperfections. Game theory and its application to international relations are constantly undergoing innovation to

---

[3] Herbert Simon's classic formulation can be found in his *Models of Man* (New York: Wiley, 1957); see also his *Models of Bounded Rationality* (Cambridge, Mass.: MIT Press, 1982).

[4] Anatol Rapoport, *Two-Person Game Theory: The Essential Ideas* (Ann Arbor: University of Michigan Press, 1966), p. 24.

[5] Prospect theory is most often associated with the work of psychologists Daniel Kahneman and Amos Tversky; see their *Judgment under Uncertainty: Heuristics and Biases* (New York: Cambridge University Press, 1982), edited with Paul Slovic. A useful review, including the implications for world poli-tics, is Jack S. Levy, "Prospect Theory, Rational Choice, and International Relations," *International Studies Quarterly* 41, 1 (March 1997): pp. 87–112. For an application, see Rose McDermott, *Risk-Taking in International Politics: Prospect Theory in American Foreign Policy* (Ann Arbor: University of Michigan Press, 1998).

take into account decisionmakers' attitudes toward risk, the availability of limited information, and other insights into the decision-making process.[6] Like any approach, its usefulness rests on its ability to explain behavior in the real world.

Governmental Decision Making

Governments differ in many ways. Most of these differences involve the acquisition, processing, and movement of information. Governments differ in the types and numbers of organizations and institutions of which they consist, the distribution of influence among them, the numbers and types of personnel in the organizations and institutions, and the societal interests they represent. Some governments are large, made up of many organizations and staffed by hundreds of thousands of people; some are small, with few people to staff the few organizations involved. Some governments centralize powers in one institution or group; others distribute governmental power among a number of institutions. Some have strong executives who make most foreign policy; some have weak executives or executives restricted by other groups. Governments also have different forms of executives. In the United States a president shares foreign policy powers with Congress; Britain's system is a parliamentary system run by a cabinet and a prime minister. In France there is both a president and a prime minister, who are sometimes from different parties. Other systems are ruled by single parties or single individuals, as in communist governments or military dictatorships.

Some observers argue that closed, centralized governments can act more quickly and efficiently with less public input into the process. Others maintain that more open systems can get the most out of their societies and that although democratic governments work more slowly and less single-mindedly, they produce better foreign policy because they get more diverse and accurate information from society about its capabilities and about the constraints in both the domestic and foreign environments. Open and closed systems also differ in the quality of their information processing. Analyzing how well information is collected and employed may be the most useful way we have for comparing governmental structures as producers of effective foreign policies, including how well they "learn" and adapt to the world.[7] In this section and the next, we shall also look at information processing in smaller units than whole governments — at how information is handled by individuals and variously sized groups in making decisions.

---

[6] See Jonathan Bendor and Thomas H. Hammond, "Rethinking Allison's Models," *American Political Science Review* 86, 2 (1992): 301–322; see also David A. Welch, "The Organizational Process and Bureaucratic Politics Paradigms: Retrospect and Prospect, *International Security* 17, 2 (1992): pp. 112–146.

[7] See, for example, Lloyd Etheredge, *Can Governments Learn? American Foreign Policy and Central American Revolutions* (New York: Pergamon, 1985), and Dan Reiter, *Crucible of Beliefs: Learning, Alliances, and World Wars* (Ithaca, N.Y.: Cornell University Press, 1996).

Who Makes What Decisions?

How any individual affects a foreign policy decision and its implementation depends on governmental role factors as well as individual factors. Where each person stands in the government, within which organization, how close to the central decisionmaker, and the nature of the decision unit all must be taken into account. The decision unit is particularly important. One group of scholars has defined the "ultimate decision unit" as a group of actors who have both the ability to commit resources and the power and authority to do so. They also identify three broad types of decision units: a predominant leader, a single group, and multiple autonomous groups. There are many examples of predominant leaders (especially in authoritarian systems), among them Hitler, Stalin, and Saddam Hussein. Single groups would include the Soviet and Chinese politburos and the British cabinet. In the conduct of American foreign policy, a single group constitutes the ultimate decision unit under certain circumstances; on matters of war and peace, this is usually the National Security Council. During the Cuban missile crisis in 1962, when the Kennedy administration discovered that the Soviet Union had secretly placed medium-range missiles in Cuba despite assurances that they would not do so, it was Kennedy's Executive Committee that dealt with the situation.[8]

How many and what types of people are involved in foreign policy decisions will influence the impact of an individual's role and personality. The size and composition of the decision unit will affect how the decision processes work. We would not expect that the entire State Department was involved in the Cuban missile crisis decision, nor do we expect the president and his or her top advisers to be concerned with day-to-day decisions regarding the running of embassies.

The decision unit will change depending on the type of decision being made. A standard typology distinguishes among crisis decisions, general foreign policy decisions, and administrative decisions. *Crisis decisions* generally involve a few, very high-level decisionmakers. A crisis consists of a perceived threat to the decisionmakers and their state and a finite time period within which to make a decision (usually very short). Some analysts also add the element of surprise to the characteristics of crisis. *General foreign policy decisions* set out future foreign policy, looking at the present and into the near future (and often beyond). The positions of the states of the European Union on potential membership for former Eastern bloc countries, the Japanese stance toward tariffs and trade policy, or the Carter administration's decision to make a commitment to human rights a part of U.S. foreign policy are all examples of general foreign policy decisions. *Administrative decisions* are concerned with very specific situations; they are usually handled by a specific part of the foreign policy bureaucracy. They involve routine situations calling for the application of the expertise and standard operating procedures of foreign policy organizations.

Crises are defined by their position along three dimensions: threat (high), decision time (short), and awareness (surprise). These dimensions can be used to construct a

---

[8] See Margaret Hermann and Charles Hermann, "Who Makes Foreign Policy Decisions and How: An Empirical Inquiry," *International Studies Quarterly* 33 (1989): pp. 361–387.

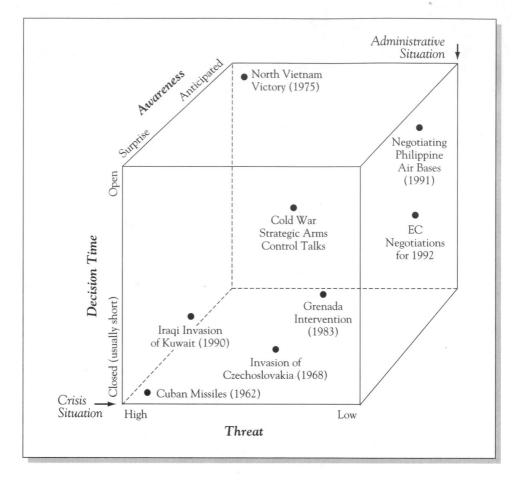

FIGURE 7.1 A Decision Cube (American perspective)

Source: Modified from Charles F. Hermann, "International Crisis as a Situational Variable,"
in James N. Rosenau, ed., *International Politics and Foreign Policy* (New York: Free Press,
1969), Figure 1.

"decision cube" like the one depicted in Figure 7.1. Crisis decisions are located toward
the front lower-left corner of the cube, and especially intense crises, like the Cuban missile crisis (highest threat, shortest decision time, and greatest surprise), are located closest to that crisis corner. Administrative decisions involve little threat and can usually
be anticipated well in advance of the time when a decision must be made; they are
located toward the back upper-right corner of the cube. General foreign policy decisions generally fall somewhere between these two extremes, with their exact positions
determined by the particular characteristics of the policy situation.[9]

---

[9] The three-dimensional definition of crisis — short time, high threat, and surprise — is most closely
identified with the work of Charles Hermann and his associates; see, for example, Charles F. Hermann,

The participants in a crisis decision are of the highest level and relatively few in number. General foreign policy decisions usually involve a large number of medium-level officials interacting with one or two of the high-level foreign policy players. Administrative decisions usually involve low-level officials. This is why different observers come up with different descriptions of how people make decisions. A variety of decision processes can be identified, generally involving different groups of decisionmakers (or different decision units) as well as different types of foreign policy situations. In fact, the problem becomes even more complicated if we look at the distinct stages of any particular decision. Decisions may be broken down into a predecisional stage, a formulation stage, and an implementation stage. The *predecisional* stage involves the collection of information and views and the scanning of the foreign policy horizon for possible problems and issues. The *formulation* stage involves the actual selection of an alternative after evaluating the possibilities. In the *implementation* stage, the decision has been translated into some form of action or foreign policy behavior.

Information: Searching, Screening, Processing

We can think of organizations, individuals, or any self-controlling system as having to react to the environment — to *steer* through it by learning. Steering requires *feedback,* the receipt of information from the environment about the consequences of existing policies. Positive feedback amplifies or reinforces our behavior, encouraging us to continue our current policy. Negative feedback indicates that we are moving away from our goal or missing it by ever greater distances and that our policy must be changed to bring it back toward the target. Karl Deutsch has pointed out that managing this steering process is the real problem of government.[10] How information gets back to us and how it is processed along the way (by governmental organizations or by individuals) will affect our image of the world and how to behave in it. In the early 1960s, when the United States was becoming involved in Vietnam, in what direction should the nation have steered? Should it have continued involvement, or should it have changed course and disengaged? Similar questions concerning steering — of taking small steps that ultimately lead away from one's goals — have been raised about U.S. and NATO policy toward the violence in the former Yugoslavia.

In the case of Vietnam, one important influence on the decisionmakers in Washington was the information they received about the effectiveness of the American effort. Military and intelligence organizations had an interest in continuing and expanding that effort and so sent back information supporting a continued increase in military involvement. Individuals with a strong anticommunist ideology and other beliefs that made such involvement seem beneficial also sent back positive feedback. More importantly, information that opposed increasing involvement — negative feedback — was suppressed or eliminated.[11] Such information was screened out at various bureaucratic

ed., *International Crises: Insights from Behavioral Research* (New York: Free Press, 1972). Michael Brecher and Jonathan Wilkenfeld have modified the time and surprise elements and added hostilities; see, for example, Michael Brecher, *Crisis in World Politics: Theory and Reality* (New York: Pergamon, 1993).

[10] See Karl Deutsch's classic, *The Nerves of Government,* 2nd ed. (New York: Free Press, 1966).

[11] See David Halberstam's account of the Kennedy administration and the Vietnam War, *The Best and the Brightest* (New York: Random House, 1969).

and individual points. Even when it was received, the information was ignored by individuals who did not want to believe it. This example demonstrates why information and images are so important; it is only through feedback that decisionmakers can steer their states through the troubled waters of the international system.

Information is a vast, ongoing wave of signals, facts, and noise. The rational actor model of decision making tends to assume "perfect information" — a very stringent requirement, which is extraordinarily costly in terms of time, energy, and money. Individuals, especially those occupying high-level positions in government, cannot process and understand all the information available to them. They must screen out some of it. Some information is simply ignored; some is altered so as not to upset existing views or beliefs; some is looked at quickly and then discarded. Both individual mental processes and collective organizational processes serve this **screening** function. The decisionmaker's ideology or worldview (such as communism or anti- communism) makes some things look more important and others less so. An individual's role in an organization — one's "job" — may involve a decisionmaker in some things and not others, thereby biasing the flow of information he or she receives. The line between organizational and psychological screening is sometimes very fine.

Decisionmakers are not *faced* with problems; they must look out into the world and *identify* or *perceive* problems. How decisionmakers see some set of present circumstances depends on what happened previously — "where the players are is strongly influenced by where they have been." Even the most obvious "problems," in retrospect, may have been seen differently at the time. Winston Churchill perceived Hitler as a danger soon after the latter came to power in 1933, but Neville Chamberlain came to that conclusion only in early 1939.[12] Similarly, at the time of the Cuban missile crisis in 1962, some members of Kennedy's Executive Committee did not think that the placement of Soviet missiles in Cuba was strategically important. Different people in different parts of government or different people occupying the same position — the same role — in government at different times, may not all see the same situation as a problem. Individual, role, ideological, and political factors will all combine to make a person see a problem. Since these factors vary across individuals, not all people, and especially not all relevant foreign policy people, will see the same problem in the same way at the same time.

In a government broken up into various organizations, each organization will often deliberately pass along only information that is beneficial to itself and not all the information that might be relevant to the situation. In the Bay of Pigs fiasco in 1961, the CIA gave President Kennedy incorrect information on the probability of success in overthrowing Castro's government. Because of individual psychological screens as well as organizational screens, decisionmakers do not have perfect information but only a collection of selected data. The psychological screens are interesting because along with presenting problems in processing information, they may lead decisionmakers to ignore or fail to grasp the significance of important information that they do

---

[12] The quotation is from Robert Jervis, "Realism, Game Theory and Cooperation," *World Politics* 40 (April 1988): p. 320; the example is from Jervis, *Perception and Misperception in International Politics* (Princeton, N.J.: Princeton University Press, 1976), chap. 1.

have. A study investigating reasons why the U.S. forces at Pearl Harbor were surprised by the Japanese attack in 1941 shows that all the important information needed to indicate an attack was coming was actually in the hands of American decisionmakers. However, because there was so much "noise" — unimportant or irrelevant pieces of data — the true signals were missed. Those signals that did get through to decisionmakers, especially those stationed at Pearl Harbor, were dismissed through the working of psychological screens.[13]

Noise is one symptom of information overload. Overload forces us to choose what to consider (a major form of screening), obscuring true signals by hiding them in noise. In World War II the Allies' strategy for locating the D day landings consciously took advantage of information overload by deluging the Germans with information, much of it false. Under this onslaught of intelligence, it was hoped, the Germans would miscalculate the invasion site — and that was exactly what happened.

The requirements of the rational decision-making model lead to a paradox. The requirement for perfect information (or at least very large quantities of information, even for minimally complex decisions) conflicts with the fact that as a decisionmaker is bombarded by more and more information, more and more screens, both bureaucratic and psychological, are used to eliminate information overload. Decisionmakers must reduce the amount of information received so that they can function. Around 190 states in the global system, hundreds of IGOs, and thousands of NGOs each send out information through words and deeds, and hundreds of diplomats as well as intelligence-gathering agencies report on this activity. Decisionmakers in the contemporary system can be overwhelmed with information. Overload forces decisionmakers to decide what to decide. Paying attention to one issue, situation, or crisis forces them to ignore others. Thus arises the paradox: in order to function, decisionmakers must distort their perceptions of the real world. The issue then becomes what degree of distortion is acceptable and how we can recognize and deal with it.

Organizations and Bureaucracies

Governments, including those portions involved in the foreign policy process, are made up of many parts — both individuals and organizations. Therefore, decisions are the products of the interaction, adjustment, and politics of people and organizations: they are *quasi-mechanical* and social processes.

Decisions are often made in a quasi-mechanical way, by reference to past decisions, precedence, or routines — the "standard operating procedures" of organizations. Organizations within governments all have a catalogue of past behavior on which to draw. Bureaucrats tend to be conservative, reluctant to trying anything new; they are happy with incremental changes based on past decisions and behavior. One way to reduce the complexity of the world and thus reduce uncertainty is to act as one has acted before. Organizations tend to have rule books, guides, and manuals that indicate how things should be done there. Anyone who has requested special treatment at

---

[13] Roberta Wohlstetter, "Cuba and Pearl Harbor: Hindsight and Foresight," *Foreign Affairs* 43 (July 1965): pp. 691–707.

a department of motor vehicles or university registrar knows how difficult it can be get a clerk to deviate from standard operating procedures.

Allison's second model of decision making contrasts sharply with the model of rational decision making. This **organizational process model** suggests that what will happen in the future (time $t + 1$) is best explained by looking at what happens today (time t). This is a neat summary of the cautious and remedial incremental approach to decision making. The model may be summarized by three main points: (1) "the actor is not a monolithic 'nation' or 'government' but rather a constellation of loosely allied organizations on top of which government leaders sit"; (2) "the preeminent feature of organizational activity is its programmed character"; and (3) "activity according to standard operating procedures and programs does not constitute far-sighted, flexible adaptation to 'the issue'."[14] Foreign policy is an "outcome" of this quasi-mechanical process, which affects both the decision that is made and its implementation.

The organizational process model highlights the importance of role factors in decision making. Role is important because it affects the way an individual *thinks* he or she should act. It has been defined as those aspects of an actor deriving from his or her policy-making responsibilities, aspects that are expected to characterize *any* person filling the same position. We can think of a role as the interaction between the individual and the political system, with the expectations of that system working on the individual. In most cases an individual in a governmental position is in a situation where precedents exist in the behavior of previous individuals who held that office. A strong personality, unafraid to innovate, shock, or take political risks, may overcome the constraints of precedent. Others may find it comfortable to tread a well-worn path. In Chapter 1 we noted that during his first six months as president, Harry Truman appeared inexperienced, unsure of himself, and strongly bound by the precedents set by Franklin Roosevelt (who had been president from 1933 until his death in April 1945).

The individual who performs a specific role is often expected to follow the needs and requirements of organizational setting rather than personal convictions. Before World War I, Winston Churchill deplored the naval arms race between Germany and Britain, recognizing that both states were spending large sums of money and raising international tensions in a competition to build more and better battleships. He also recognized that when the process was over, both sides would be in approximately the same relationship as before, and thus all of the effort would have been futile. However, as first lord of the admiralty he went before Parliament and requested more funds for naval construction. When Caspar Weinberger served as director of the Office of Management and Budget in the Nixon administration, he was known as "Cap the Knife" for his propensity to slash the budget requests of government departments and agencies. However, as secretary of defense in the Reagan administration he continually asked Congress for more money and oversaw the largest surge in peacetime defense spending in the country's history. When Samuel Hoare was the British secretary of state for air in the 1920s, he fought against naval control of the air forces within the Fleet Air Arm, yet ten years later, when he became first lord of the admiralty, he argued exactly the opposite position.

---

[14] Allison, *Essence of Decision,* pp. 79–80, 81, 89.

In addition to the quasi-mechanical dimension to decision making in large organizations, there is a social element. In a *social process*, several decisionmakers interact and the result of that social interaction is a decision. Policy making is politics. Foreign policy emerges from a normal political process, including bargaining, compromise, adjustment, arm twisting, favor trading, and the like. This is the heart of Allison's third model of decision making, the **governmental politics model.** Its image of foreign policy decision making starts with the organizational process model, but it goes further to integrate the social element. Foreign policy decisions are not merely the outcomes of organizations following standard operating procedures; they are "resultants" of various "bargaining games" among "players" in the government. Each player — president, prime minister, first secretary, adviser, senator, foreign minister, general, cabinet member — tries to set goals, assess alternatives, and makes choices, as we would expect of a rational actor. Given the limitations on information processing and other imperfections in the decision-making process, each individual player falls short of this ideal. However, because others are involved in the process, each with his or her own goals and information about alternative courses of action and their consequences, most of what should be considered will be.

Members of different organizations see different sides of a situation, depending on how that situation affects (and perhaps threatens) their organization. As Allison summarizes the situation, "where you stand depends on where you sit." An individual's priorities and self-interests are seen to derive in large measure from his or her organization's self-interests. As opposed to a realist's notion that there exists some single "national interest," there is an array of organizations and interests. Of course, each organization (or subgroup) argues that its interests are similar to, or necessary ingredients of, the national interest. In reality there are many separate interests and those interests must be reconciled in the process of foreign policy making.

Organizational process and governmental politics can be seen as two sides of the same coin. The parochial nature of organizations is one of the core concepts of Allison's organizational process model. Each organization within a government has a narrow range of interests and priorities. The mission of an organization requires capabilities — money and people — which is where bureaucratic "pulling and hauling" comes in. To acquire the necessary resources, an organization needs influence within the government, especially on budget decisions and decisions that distribute new programs and responsibilities to government organizations. Members define the reason for their organization's existence in terms of its essence: what missions an organization should have. They are deeply concerned with "organizational health," the protection (and often an expansion of the scope) of essence, as measured by budget and staffing allocations. The essence of the U.S. Army is a ground combat capability. The U.S. Navy sees its essence as maintaining combat ships to control the seas; the only problem is that people in submarines think this goal should be achieved by subs, air-power proponents support the use of aircraft carriers, and sea-power advocates stress surface combat ships.[15]

---

[15] For a useful application of organizational process models to the study of war, see Jack Levy, "Organizational Routines and the Causes of War," *International Studies Quarterly* 30 (1986): pp. 193–222; see also Yaacov Vertzberger, *The World in Their Minds: Information Processing, Cognition, and Perception in Foreign Policy Decisionmaking* (Stanford, Calif.: Stanford University Press, 1990).

Organizational health can also be protected by demonstrating how successful the organization is (or, more commonly, by demonstrating its lack of mistakes). One reason why organizations follow standard operating procedures is to cut down on uncertainty and risk. Organizations behave incrementally for the same reason. However — and this is crucial to the policy-making process — the protection of the organization also entails providing information to top-level decisionmakers that shows the organization in the best light. This involves withholding information that would embarrass the organization and implementing top-level decisions in a way that meets its best interests, and not necessarily in the spirit of the decision handed down to the organization for implementation.

Many anecdotes tell of presidents giving up in despair as they tried to get various sections of the bureaucracy to do what was wanted. John Kennedy called the U.S. State Department a bowl of jelly; Franklin Roosevelt likened the navy to a feather pillow — no matter how hard or long one punched it, it always came out the same. The strength of bureaucratic politics is seen in the way the air force reported bombing results in Vietnam, often using highly unreliable pilots' reports, which exaggerated bomb damage, rather than satellite or reconnaissance photographs; the withholding of crucial information by the CIA in the Bay of Pigs operation; and the near breakdown in U.S.-British relations over the Skybolt missile during the Kennedy administration because of intergovernmental miscommunication between bureaucracies.[16] Using Allison's analysis (as well as critiques of his work and new studies), the most closely examined case study of the impact of organizational process has been the Cuban missile crisis. It was only during a reunion of the members of the Executive Committee (ExComm) in 1987, however, that the following powerful example emerged. During the missile crisis (which Russians call the Caribbean crisis), Kennedy ordered the Strategic Air Command (SAC) to go on full alert. SAC was brought to Defense Condition 2 for the first time ever, involving high-alert status for U.S. missiles and increased numbers of strategic bombers on airborne alert.

> Most of this activity would have been observed in due course by various means of Soviet information collection. But in this case there was a unique difference: the SAC full-alert process was reported "in the clear" rather than in normal encoded messages. Soviet communications interception personnel must have been shocked suddenly to hear the SAC commander-in-chief address all his senior commanders in an unprecedented message in the clear stressing the seriousness of the situation faced by the nation and assuring them that SAC plans were well prepared and being executed smoothly. Soviet political and military leaders must have been puzzled and alarmed at this flaunting of the American strategic superiority . . . .
>
> Equally extraordinary, and not known in Moscow, was that this remarkable display of American power was unauthorized by and unknown to the president, the secretary of defense, the chairman of the Joint Chiefs, and the ExComm as they so carefully calibrated and controlled action. . . . The decision for bold action was taken by

---

[16] See, for example, Morton Halperin and Arnold Kanter, eds., *Readings in American Foreign Policy: A Bureaucratic Perspective* (Boston: Little, Brown, 1973).

General Thomas Power, commander-in-chief of SAC, on his own initiative. He had been ordered to go on full alert, and he did so. No one had told him how to do it, and he decided to "rub it in."[17]

When this story was told at the 1987 conference, the former ExComm members were startled. An observer noted that former Secretary of Defense "McNamara's eyes roll[ed] toward the ceiling in mock exasperation at this military insubordination."[18] This is a good example of the dangers of assuming that governmental decisions flow from a unitary actor or that important events have important causes (in the sense of coming from a considered decision of the top-level decision unit). This example highlights the importance of implementation and the organizations that control it.[19]

Organizations thus provide individuals with roles and the expectations attached to them. The longer a specific role exists, the more precedents are set and the more widely held are the expectations of other government members for people assuming the role. Thus, as an institution becomes older and more complex, it is more difficult for an individual to shape a role in that institution. New positions in government provide much more leeway for an individual to shape a role rather than be constrained by it. In addition, the higher the role position is in the governmental hierarchy, the less the role will constrain the individual. The higher one goes, the fewer superiors one has and the more likely one is to be confronted with new or unexpected situations. Such situations are also more open to individual influences than those of a role.

Whether an individual can modify or shape a role, then, depends on the degree of precedent, the organizational context, and how long the role has existed. The impact of a role also depends on the individual's personal characteristics and especially on his or her political skills. The bureaucratic politics model considers the power and skill of individual players to be important. Much of the power derives from an individual's position in government, or role, but this power can be expanded or reduced, depending on the personality and skill of the players involved. Although William Rogers was secretary of state for most of the Nixon years, Henry Kissinger was the unquestioned primary adviser to the president on foreign policy and national security matters. In Kennedy's administration the secretary of defense, Robert McNamara, played a more central part in foreign affairs than did Secretary of State Dean Rusk. Although the office of the secretary of state has not undergone any real role alteration, the strength and skill of its holders has varied, as have their individual relations with the presidents they advised.

---

[17] Raymond Garthoff, *Reflections on the Cuban Missile Crisis,* rev. ed. (Washington, D.C.: Brookings Institution, 1989), pp. 61–62.

[18] J. Anthony Lukas, "Class Reunion: Kennedy's Men Relive the Cuban Missile Crisis," *New York Times Magazine,* August 10, 1987, p. 51.

[19] This is not solely an American phenomenon but can be seen in many governments. The diaries of the British Labour cabinet minister Richard Crossman describe how ministers are trapped, manipulated, ignored, and infuriated by bureaucrats who presume to know what is best for the ministry, and hence the government and the country. See Anthony Howard, ed., *The Crossman Diaries, 1965–1970* (London: Methuen, 1979).

Small Group Interaction

How an individual behaves within the constraints of his or her role is also affected by the immediate environment of the decision unit. People studying organizations and social psychologists studying small-group behavior have found that being a member of a small group can affect both the perceptions and the behavior of the individual very strongly. More specifically, there are pressures on the individual to conform to the view of the group and not to challenge it. In this process, the perceptions of the individual about both situation and role may be altered to fit the collective views within the group. Here is an example not only of social decision processes (mostly through pressure on members to come to a consensus of some kind), but also of a failure of those processes. One advantage of social decision processes noted earlier was that although each individual has limited information, perceived alternatives, and so on, when that individual interacts with others, a wide range of information and alternatives is considered. We shall see that this need not be the case.

Laboratory experiments by psychologists demonstrate the pressures to conform that a small group can exert on its members. In one, a group of six to eight people compared visual images — the length of two lines, for example. However, only one member of the group was actually being observed each time this experiment was performed; the others (unknown to the single subject) had been instructed to give false answers. The subject, then, heard the other members of this small group say that the shorter line was longer, the smaller cube was larger, and so forth. At first, subjects acted puzzled and upset. Then they began to conform and to describe the objects as the others did.[20]

A version of the individual's conformity to small-group views has been studied by Irving Janis — a phenomenon he calls **groupthink.** In his study, Janis looked at a number of American foreign policy decisions, such as the Bay of Pigs invasion in 1961, the response to the North Korean invasion of South Korea in 1950, the decision to set up the Marshall Plan, the decisions to escalate the war in Vietnam, the decision making about Pearl Harbor before the Japanese attack, and the Cuban missile crisis of 1962. Janis sums up his central theme as follows: "The more amiability and esprit de corps among the members of a policy-making in-group, the greater is the danger that independent critical thinking will be replaced with groupthink, which is likely to result in irrational and dehumanizing actions directed against out-groups."[21] Groupthink is one important process that generates symptoms of defective decision making, helping analysts identify "low-quality" and "high-quality" decision making.

---

[20] See for example, S. E. Asch, "Effects of Group Pressure upon Modification and Distortion of Judgment," in D. Cartwright and A. Zander, eds., *Group Dynamics, Research and Theory* (Evanston, Ill.: Row, Peterson, 1953), pp. 189–200.

[21] Irving L. Janis, *Groupthink,* 2nd ed. (Boston: Houghton Mifflin, 1982), p. 13; see also his *Crucial Decisions: Leadership in Policymaking and Crisis Management* (New York: Free Press, 1989), and, with Leon Mann, *Decision Making: A Psychological Analysis of Conflict, Choice, and Commitment* (New York: Free Press, 1977).

Two symptoms of groupthink involve the group's self-image. A close and friendly group will produce an *illusion of invulnerability.* This feeling is associated with excessive optimism that the courses of action considered by the group will succeed in achieving their foreign policy goals, and thereby encourages risk taking. Other research has identified the phenomenon of the "risky shift." By themselves, individuals respond to real and hypothetical situations in a more conservative way than when they are in a group; the same individuals will be willing to take much riskier positions when asked about the same situations in a group setting.[22] Similarly, the group tends to have an *unquestioned belief in its own morality.* The group setting leads the individual members to feel that this group of decent people could not be anything but good. This symptom fosters group screening by leading the group members to ignore the ethical or moral consequences of their decisions; the assumption is that the group is moral and that, therefore, its decisions also will be moral. A third symptom is a *stereotyped view of the opponent's leadership* as too evil to engage in good-faith negotiation or too stupid to counter the policies considered by the group.

The groupthink process leads to a *shared illusion of unanimity* that often overcomes role influences. Efforts are made to *rationalize the group's decisions,* to justify them no matter what they might be, screening out warnings or contrary information that might lead the group to reconsider its decisions. Groupthink also leads to *direct pressure* on any individual who argues against the stereotypes the group produces, as well as to *self-censorship* of doubts and arguments that deviate from the emerging group consensus (as in the perception experiment just described). The conditions that promote groupthink derive from group cohesiveness: how well knit the group is, how well it sticks together. This cohesion is fostered when the group is isolated from outsiders and outside views, and especially when one or more members behave as *mindguards* by filtering out information that might challenge the predominant images held by the group.[23]

The appearance of a group leader who promotes a preferred solution is another major influence on the creation of groupthink. For this effect to take place, it is not necessary that the others in the group be toadies. A person becomes a leader because of a number of personal and role characteristics; others in the group will go along with him or her because of shared values or because of the leader's control of promotion decisions. A good example is the U.S. decision in 1950 to send military aid immediately to South Korea after the administration was informed of the North Korean attack. President Truman walked into the meeting of his advisers and approved the plan presented by Secretary of State Dean Acheson. The rest of the discussion was based on Acheson's view rather than on any other. On the other hand, one of the reasons groupthink was less apparent during the Cuban missile crisis was because John Kennedy consciously removed himself from a number of the sessions of the Executive Committee so that his presence would not inhibit the broadest possible review of options. Groupthink appears to have been minimized in the Cuban decision because each participant acted

---

[22] See David G. Myers and Helmut Lamm, "The Polarizing Effect of Group Discussion," in Irving L. Janis, ed., *Current Trends in Psychology: Readings from the American Scientist* (Los Altos, Calif.: Kaufmann, 1977).

[23] The eight symptoms of groupthink are summarized in Janis, *Groupthink,* pp. 174–175.

as a generalist (not as a representative of a particular role) and was also supposed to be as skeptical and challenging as possible, in an informal atmosphere without a formal agenda or rules of protocol.

A variety of possible remedies for groupthink have been suggested by scholars, from "devil's advocacy" — assigning someone the role of challenging major assumptions and decisions — to multiple advocacy. In the latter, chief executives are advised to ensure that individuals with a range of views are encouraged to participate in group deliberations and advocate those views; executives are to make sure that all views can be heard.[24] Phenomena like groupthink probably cannot be eliminated, but they can be reduced and decisionmakers can be alerted to their existence and their potential effects on decisions and actions.

Individual Perceptions and Beliefs

We now turn to individuals — their needs, desires, and perceptions — and the impact these have on their foreign policy decisions. To quote a study of the way enemies are perceived in politics:

> In a striking section of *The Hero in History,* Sidney Hook tries to imagine "A World without Lenin" in order to demonstrate the historical importance of what he calls the "event-making man." In political science, no less than history, we must also confront the problem with which Hook wrestles. Stated more formally, we are concerned with the impact of *personal* as well as institutional, cultural, social, and economic factors on the conduct of foreign policy.[25]

Decisionmakers hold images of the world; these images are not necessarily accurate representations of the "real" world. The study of the images held by foreign policy decisionmakers — the psychological environment of foreign policy leaders — involves studying their belief systems and how their images of other peoples, states, leaders, and situations affect their decisions and behavior.

The psychological environment affects the way the menu is perceived, just as the other environments do. This requires a few assumptions. The first is that foreign policy is made and implemented by people; we do not see states as monolithic, impersonal creatures that somehow behave on their own. The second assumption, the point Hook was making, is that individuals can make a difference in the foreign policy process of a given state, that the governmental structure, as well as the processes of policy making, permits individuals to have an impact on foreign policy. Presidents, secretaries of state, prime ministers, foreign ministers, revolutionary leaders, and dictators can strongly

---

[24] See, for example, Alexander L. George, "The Case for Multiple Advocacy in Making Foreign Policy," *American Political Science Review* 66 (1972): pp. 751–785.

[25] David J. Finlay, Ole R. Holsti, and Richard R. Fagen, *Enemies in Politics* (Chicago: Rand McNally, 1967), p. 233.

influence the foreign policy processes of their own states and of others. Although he never admitted that he could be analyzed either psychologically or psychoanalytically, Henry Kissinger was a firm believer in the importance of the individual statesperson in history. As a practicing diplomat, he felt that he had to know and understand the psychological makeup of foreign diplomats and decisionmakers. In addition to this view (which prompted him to have U.S. intelligence services draw up psychological profiles of the foreign leaders with whom he negotiated), he saw individuals as important to the outcomes of diplomacy and history: "But when you see [history] in practice, you see the differences that the personalities make. The overtures to China would not have worked without Chou En-lai. There would have been no settlement in the Middle East without Sadat and Golda Meir or Dayan."[26] Anyone doubting the impact that single individuals can have on the workings of foreign policy, relations among states, or even the structure of the international system need only examine the consequences of the policies pursued by Mikhail Gorbachev after his accession to power in 1985.[27]

The third assumption derives from the first two. Given that foreign policy is made by people and that individuals can have an impact, we assume that the way these people see the world is important. What affects their perception? The unique characteristics that affect an individual's decision making and behavior include a number of things that are relatively easy to study and some that are quite difficult. An individual's **idiosyncrasies** are made up of values, personality, political style, intellect, and past experience. They work together, creating a set of images about the world.

Before a situation — a problem — exists for the foreign policy decisionmaker, several things have to occur. First, there has to be a *stimulus* from the environment — a trigger event. Then *perception* of the stimulus must take place; this is a process by which an individual selects, organizes, and evaluates incoming information about the surrounding world. Finally, there must be an *interpretation* of the perceived stimulus. Both perception and interpretation depend heavily on the images that already exist in the mind of the individual decisionmaker. In applying social psychology to history, we want to ask: To what information are decisionmakers exposed? How do they interpret it? How does it affect their beliefs? All this goes back to the differences between how people see the world and how it really is. An individual's response to a stimulus will be based on his or her perception of that stimulus, not necessarily on the objective nature of the stimulus itself. Decisionmakers, like other human beings, are subject to all the psychological processes that affect perception — defense mechanisms, reduction of anxiety, rationalization, displacement, and repression — as well as to other characteristics that make up individual personalities.[28]

---

[26] Quoted in Hugh Sidey, "An International Natural Resource," *Time*, February 4, 1974, p. 24.

[27] See, for example, Gordon A. Craig and Alexander L. George, *Force and Statecraft*, 2nd ed. (New York: Oxford University Press, 1990), chap. 11.

[28] For a classic statement of the nature and impact of images, see Kenneth Boulding, *The Image* (Ann Arbor: University of Michigan Press, 1956). There is a wide variety of psychological approaches and theories about human behavior. Although we have drawn from a range of these approaches, we have not highlighted the debates among them, such as the one between personality theories and cognitive theories. See Deborah W. Larson, *Origins of Containment: A Psychological Explanation* (Princeton, N.J.: Princeton University Press, 1985), chap. 1. A useful review is Michael D. Young and Mark Schafer, "Is There a Method in Our Madness? Ways of Assessing Cognition in International Relations," *Mershon International Studies Review* 42, 1 (May 1998): pp. 63–96.

Selective Perception and Misperception

Our images affect our perceptions in many ways. Initially, a person's values and beliefs help determine the focus of his or her attention — what is selected as a stimulus and what is actually looked at and attended to. Then, on the basis of previous attitudes and images, the stimulus is interpreted. In an *open image,* new information, contradictory information, or modifying information is incorporated into existing images, changing them to fit newly perceived reality. A *closed image* is one that, for various psychological reasons, resists change, ignoring or reshaping contradictory information or selecting only the bits and pieces that might be used to support the image already held. Whether open or closed, images are screens. Each of us is attentive to only part of the world around us, and each of us has a different set of images for interpreting incoming information.

Even if we could obtain perfect information about alternatives and consequences, problems of perception make meaningless the notion of an ideal, or perfectly rational, choice among alternatives. From all that information, only some of it will be perceived or selected. The interpretation of the information will depend on the individual decisionmaker's belief system and images. **Misperception** means that, for any number of reasons, the behavior of one state or its decisionmakers is seen to diverge from what has actually taken place or diverges from the meaning of the act intended by the state or decisionmakers taking that action. In misperception, images screen out important signals — ignoring them completely, interpreting them incorrectly, or changing the information to fit existing images.

Images can act as intervening variables, mediating between the incoming information and the behavior based on that information. There are a number of psychological processes and mechanisms by which decisionmakers process information and select it on the basis of held images. These are cognitive distortions, the difficulties that any "careful and logical" individual will have in processing information under conditions of uncertainty.[29] Like all of us, decisionmakers perceive the world selectively for different reasons and in different ways. People try to achieve **cognitive consistency:** they want the images they hold not to clash with or contradict each other. Sometimes new information forces an image to change so that it becomes incompatible with other held images (*cognitive dissonance*); this often happens when information contradicts a stereotype of a group of people or an enemy. Rather than change one image and cause a reappraisal of others, a person may simply ignore or reshape the new information.

The use of often imperfect *historical analogies* also leads to selective perception, which involves noticing those details of a present episode that look like a past one while ignoring important differences. One of the most famous examples of this mechanism is the Munich syndrome. Decisionmakers in the United States and Britain who had been active during the 1930s, when the Western democracies attempted to appease Hitler (the symbol of which was the Munich agreement), tended to use this traumatic

---

[29] Another distortion is *affective distortion,* distortion resulting from personal emotions like hostility or insecurity, which is addressed later in the chapter. For a review of studies on misperception and distortion, see Robert Mandel, "Psychological Approaches to International Relations," in Margaret G. Hermann, ed., *Political Psychology* (San Francisco: Jossey-Bass, 1986), p. 253. Perhaps the most inclusive work in the area of misperception is Robert Jervis's classic, *Perception and Misperception in International Politics* (Princeton, N.J.: Princeton University Press, 1976).

event as an analogue for postwar events that only partially resembled it. The use of historical analogies may have been more important than ideology in the development of the American containment policy after World War II. For the British, the Suez crisis of 1956 was generated in part by the selective perceptions of Prime Minister Anthony Eden, who saw Egypt's Nasser as another Hitler, and thus as someone who could not be appeased. A study of the effect of Reagan's belief system on his dealings with the Soviet Union suggests that he was greatly affected by the Cuban missile crisis, which, until the rise of Gorbachev, served as Reagan's main historical analogy.[30] A related process affecting perception is *wishful thinking*, the influence of desires on perception. Leaders who strongly wanted to see peace thought they saw it in 1938 when Prime Minister Chamberlain returned to Britain from Munich after the carving up of Czechoslovakia, and they exulted that there was "peace in our time."

Some common misconceptions recur in foreign policy. First, foreign policy decisionmakers often underestimate how unclear a message, speech, or other communication may be to someone else (in spite of the sender's best efforts). Second, decisionmakers often do not realize that their behavior may not convey what they intend to communicate. They assume that others will understand their actions and behavior much more easily than is the case. These two observations are directly related to the more substantive misconceptions that are common in foreign policy. An important one is the tendency for decisionmakers to see other states, particularly adversaries or competitors, as more hostile than they are. Here misperception involves selecting the information that supports hostility or to interpret behavior as being hostile. Social-psychological research shows that the characteristics and effects of behavior generate similar characteristics and effects. A "malignant process" of hostile interaction ensues because

> the evaluation of an act is affected by the evaluation of its source — and the source is part of the context of behavior. For example, research has shown that American students [were] likely to rate more favorably an action of the United States directed toward the Soviet Union than the same action directed by the Soviet Union toward the United States. We [were] likely to view American espionage activities in the Soviet Union as more benevolent than similar activities by Soviet agents in the United States. If each side in a conflict tends to perceive its own motives and behavior as more benevolent and legitimate than those of the other side, it is evident that the conflict will spiral upward in intensity.[31]

The Image of the Enemy

Because others are seen as more hostile, individuals construct a particular *image of the enemy*. This image leads one to see the behavior of other states as not only hostile, but also more centralized and coordinated than it really is. When looking at the behavior of

---

[30] See Larson, *Origins of Containment;* Larson, "The Role of Belief Systems and Schemas in Foreign Policy Decision Making," *Political Psychology* 15 (March 1994): pp. 17–33; and Russell Leng, "Reagan and the Russians: Crisis Bargaining Beliefs and the Historical Record," *American Political Science Review* 78 (June 1984): pp. 338–355. See also Richard E. Neustadt and Ernest R. May, *Thinking in Time: The Uses of History for Decision Makers* (New York: Free Press, 1986).

[31] Morton Deutsch, *The Resolution of Conflict: Constructive and Destructive Processes* (New Haven, Conn.: Yale University Press, 1973) p. 354.

other states, one ignores or underestimates the role of chance, mistakes, and particularly the influence of bureaucratic politics. This result derives from the use of the rational actor model, which assumes that the other state is monolithic, acting in a rational, single-minded way, and that every event has a good reason for occurring. When others act in the way you want, the tendency is to overestimate the influence you had on the opponent's behavior; on the other hand, when the adversary does something undesired, the tendency is to find internal forces in the opposing state to explain the behavior. Seeing others as opponents or enemies has a powerful influence on the perceptions and behavior of the leaders of states.

The image of the enemy derives partly from psychological **defense mechanisms.** These act to protect the individual from things that would otherwise make him or her uncomfortable and anxious. One defense mechanism is *projection* onto others of feelings, characteristics, and desires that we cannot admit exist in ourselves. A major factor in projection is the creation of a *scapegoat*. An enemy serves as a scapegoat when it is accused of bringing about an outcome that was actually perpetrated by another, often oneself. The accusation is used to justify one's own behavior, which is similar to that foisted on the opponent. In foreign relations an enemy is usually seen as aggressive, seeking dominance and conquest, and capable of evil and brutality. Being able to crusade against such an enemy brings great psychological satisfaction. One can ignore one's own behavior and preserve one's self-image because no matter how badly one is behaving, the object of that behavior is an enemy that is even more evil. Much of this sort of behavior was observed in the United States during the Vietnam War, when some Americans failed to question various U.S. tactics such as napalm bombing, the torture of prisoners, or the killing of civilians.

Having an enemy allows one the satisfaction of recognizing one's own moral superiority, of having a cause and being needed by that cause to oppose and defeat that enemy; one has as well the satisfaction of being able to hate and kill without being bothered by one's conscience. Having an enemy permits one to see the world in clear-cut distinctions of good and evil, precluding anxiety. A nasty "they" helps to define the "we." During World War II, the Japanese and Americans each held strong images of their own racial superiority and the other's barbarism; these images then excused the commission of terrible atrocities by both sides. On the American side, there were pronounced differences in the way the German and Japanese enemies were portrayed in wartime propaganda, which John Dower attributes to racism. While Germany (usually Hitler and his military leadership) was portrayed as evil and bent on world domination, images of the Japanese (usually *all* Japanese) were typically subhuman — monkeys, rodents, insects. Such subhuman caricatures of the enemy encouraged a view of war fighting as extermination. As Dower writes, "it was in this atmosphere that precision bombing of Japanese military targets was abandoned by the United States and the 'madmen' and 'yellow vermin' of the homeland became primary targets."[32]

A study of the two world wars and the Vietnam War delineated what has been called a "black-white diabolical enemy image." Included in this is a view of one's coun-

---

[32] John W. Dower, *War without Mercy: Race and Power in the Pacific War* (New York: Pantheon, 1986), p. 300.

try as "virile" and "moral" — a positive self-image contributing to an unquestioned "pro-us" feeling, with no shades of gray. The image of the enemy distorts one's view: seeing the opponent as something evil, one lacks empathy and cannot see an opponent's desire for peace, an opponent's fear, or an opponent's anger; one is unable to see the world as the opponent might see it. This inability makes for only a very incomplete view of a situation, and a dangerous one at that: one cannot see how one's "virtuous" behavior may appear to the other party and is unaware of how one's action may worsen a situation. In addition, by seeing another party as an enemy, one often screens out any conciliatory, cooperative, or tension-reducing behavior by the opponent, thus losing possibilities for constructive conflict resolution. Ignoring such overtures, one may miss chances to avert a war or to end a war already begun.[33] Before the outbreak of World War I, the decisionmakers of each state perceived, correctly or not, threats of hostile behavior from states in the other alliance; these perceptions led to hostile behavior toward those opposing states. The process fed on itself and the resulting *conflict spiral* escalated a minor incident (the assassination of an Austrian archduke) into a world war.

Some writers hope that the analysis of such selective perception or misperception may sensitize decisionmakers to the dangers that exist and make them more thoughtful about how they communicate to others and interpret others' behavior and how their own behavior appears to an opponent. Decisionmakers should be made aware that they do not make unbiased analyses but are influenced by the images they hold. Because such images are held, they should be made as explicit as possible so that decisionmakers and others understand the basis for decisions and actions. Other advice to decisionmakers has included the suggestion of trying to put oneself in the place of the opponent and see what the situation looks like from the other side — "seeing with the eyes of the other."[34] A related attempt, trying to understand how things work on the other side and trying to go beyond the rational actor model, could help one evaluate decisions from a framework outside one's own images and beliefs or those of a small group of people. Such advice is similar to the suggestions for avoiding the negative consequences of groupthink.

The following excerpt, describing how American decisionmakers viewed the United States and the Soviet Union during the cold war, is a good description of the pitfalls described above:

> I have heard it argued: "Oh, well, they [the Soviets] know we [the United States] have no aggressive intentions. They know we have no idea of using these arms for an attack on them." To this there are two things to be said. When one attempts to explain to

---

[33] See Ralph K. White, *Nobody Wanted War: Misperception in Vietnam and Other Wars* (New York: Doubleday, 1970); and Dean G. Pruitt, "Aggressive Behavior in Interpersonal and International Relations," in Paul C. Stern, Robert Axelrod, Robert Jervis, and Roy Radner, eds., *Perspectives on Deterrence* (New York: Oxford University Press, 1989). See also Arthur E. Gladstone, "The Concept of the Enemy," *Journal of Conflict Resolution* 3 (1959): pp. 132–137. Much of this discussion is based on observations by Gladstone and White.

[34] This advice is from Joseph DeRivera, *The Psychological Dimension of Foreign Policy* (Columbus, Ohio: Merrill, 1968), a pioneering work connecting social psychology to the analysis of foreign policy. See also Janis, *Crucial Decisions.*

people in the Pentagon and to likeminded civilians that perhaps the Russians are not really eager to attack the West — that they have very good reasons for not planning or wishing to do anything of that sort, one is met with the reply: "Ah, yes, but look at the size of their armaments, and concede that in matters of this sort we cannot be bothered to take into account their intentions — intentions are too uncertain and too hard to determine; we can take into account only capabilities; we must assume the Russians to be desirous, that is, of doing anything bad to us that their capabilities would permit them to do." Now is it our view that [we] should take account only of *their capabilities,* disregarding *their intentions,* but we should expect them to take account only of *our supposed intentions,* disregarding *our capabilities?* . . . If we are going to disregard everything but their capabilities, we cannot simultaneously expect them to disregard everything but our intentions.[35]

Ideologies and Belief Systems

A **belief system** is the collection of beliefs, images, or models of the world that any individual holds: "The belief system is composed of a more or less integrated set of images which make up the entire relevant universe for the individual. They encompass past, present, and expectations of future reality, and value preferences of 'what ought to be.'"[36] The belief system performs some very important functions for the individual. It helps orient the individual to the environment, organizes perceptions as a guide to behavior, helps establish goals, and acts as a filter to select relevant information in any given situation. A coherent and organized belief system — often referred to as an *ideology* — helps a person to make sense of new pieces of information or to adopt an opinion on a new problem. All of us hold ideologies of some sort so that we do not have to deal with each issue on a purely ad hoc, isolated basis. Not all belief systems are coherent; some foreign policy decisionmakers do not begin with clear or coherent belief systems. In addition, while belief systems influence political behavior, behavior in office also helps to shape policymakers' belief systems.

In the last chapter we noted that the foreign and domestic policy beliefs of American elites share a common structure. The belief dimensions underpinning foreign policy attitudes are not separate from the dimensions that underpin attitudes about domestic politics. Both sets of beliefs are derived from common core values. For example, the never-ending debate on the redistribution of wealth and whether to help the needy runs through both domestic and foreign policy. In international affairs, it appears in attitudes about combating world hunger or giving aid to less developed countries; domestically, it appears in attitudes about the redistribution of income from the wealthy to the poor through taxation and welfare payments. Another example is beliefs about the utility and desirability of violence and its use as a deterrent: in foreign policy, this arises on matters of military intervention, covert operations, and civil-

---

[35] George Kennan, *The Cloud of Danger* (Boston: Little, Brown, 1978), pp. 87–88 (emphasis added).
[36] Ole R. Holsti, "The Belief System and National Images: A Case Study," *Journal of Conflict Resolution* 6 (1962): pp. 244–252.

military relations; domestically, we see it in regard to crime fighting and the death penalty. The joining of liberal to dovish views and conservative to hawkish views has been found repeatedly in research on opinions in the United States — for example, in surveys of the general public, in studies of voting in the U.S. Senate and House of Representatives in the 1960s and 1970s, and more recently in research analyzing the pre– and post–cold war attitudes of American foreign policy elites.[37]

The belief systems of foreign policy decisionmakers generate more specific **operational codes** (sometimes called "schemata" or "cognitive maps") — mental constructs that help to organize knowledge about an other actors or situations. In the early 1950s, Nathan Leites reviewed Russian literature and the writings of the Bolsheviks in order to reconstruct the operational code of the Russian Communist leaders. Ole Holsti used a similar approach to analyze the views of John Foster Dulles, Eisenhower's secretary of state from 1953 to 1959. He found that two of Dulles's instrumental beliefs about the conduct of foreign policy were: when one's opponent is strong, one should avoid conflict; when one's opponent is weak, one should be willing to run risks. In a good example of projecting one's beliefs onto others, Dulles held an "inherent bad faith" image of the Soviet Union, believing that it could not be trusted and would only act in a friendly way when weak or afraid. Psychologists have found that an individual's operational code may include "scripts," which detail familiar sequences of events one expects to encounter in particular situations.[38]

Personality and Physiology

There have been many psychological, psychoanalytical, and personality studies of individual foreign policy decisionmakers, as well as studies of leaders compared on the basis of personality characteristics. One of the classic studies of this type argued that Woodrow Wilson's approach to a number of issues involving power and control over others, including his unwillingness to compromise with political opponents — manifest in his handling of the Treaty of Versailles, which the U.S. Senate refused to ratify thereby killing Wilson's dream of American participation in the League of Nations — were rooted in his childhood. Wilson's need to dominate others stemmed from his competition with and aggression toward his father: "political power was for him a compensatory value, a means of restoring the self-esteem damaged in

---

[37] See Shoon Kathleen Murray, *Anchors against Change: American Opinion Leaders' Beliefs After the Cold War* (Ann Arbor: University of Michigan Press, 1996).

[38] Nathan Leites, *A Study of Bolshevism* (Glencoe, Ill.: Free Press, 1953); Holsti, "The Belief System and National Images." See also Alexander George, "The Operational Code: A Neglected Approach to the Study of Political Decision Making," *International Studies Quarterly* 13 (1969): pp. 190–222. For an effort to reconstruct scripts used by American and Russian foreign policymakers, see Richard K. Herrmann and Michael P. Fischerkeller, "Beyond the Enemy Image and Spiral Model: Cognitive-Strategic Research after the Cold War," *International Organization* 49, 3 (1995): pp. 415–450.

childhood." Kaiser Wilhelm, the German monarch in 1914, had an analogous insecurity complex of massive proportions.[39]

Studies of Hitler and Stalin also reveal basic personality disturbances. Stalin's paranoia was matched in the early cold war period in the United States by that of James Forrestal, the first secretary of defense, who committed suicide. Extreme personality disturbances are relatively rare among leaders of large bureaucratized organizations like nation-states, especially under normal conditions, where a potential leader has to work his or her way up through the organization over a long time. People who think or act very peculiarly will be weeded out of positions of leadership or will fail to be promoted. A person with a severe personality disturbance is likely to spend so much energy coping with psychological problems that he or she will be unable to perform at the level required for high achievement in a large organization.

During times of great social and political upheaval, however, a person with very unusual personality characteristics may achieve power in situations where normal people are unable to cope with social problems. Hitler, for instance, came to power in a period of terrible inflation and unemployment in Germany; Stalin, during the upheaval following a revolution and civil war. Moreover, the behavior of such a leader — especially one entrenched for many years in an authoritarian system — may become much more abnormal over time. Both Hitler and Stalin became even more aberrant after the first decade in power.

When the accession to power is more routine, the range of personality types found in office will be substantially narrower. Even so, there is enough variation to warrant the use of psychoanalytic techniques to study foreign policy decisionmakers, sometimes through the use of a categorization system. The most famous of these is a typology created for the study of American "presidential character." The character and style of any president, it is argued, are rooted firmly in his political experiences very early in his career. The experience and style of the individual are molded in the "first independent political success" and go far in determining whether the individual is "active" or "passive" (how much energy is given to the job) and whether the individual is "positive" or "negative" (whether the individual actually enjoys the job). An active and confident president who enjoys the job — an active-positive — would be one like Franklin Roosevelt or John Kennedy. Bill Clinton is also of this type. The opposite, a president with little liking for the office and low activity and self-confidence, is a passive-negative: Calvin Coolidge, for example. Some of our recent presidents have been active-negatives: almost compulsively active in office but not deriving much pleasure from the job because of low self-esteem and confidence; examples are Lyndon Johnson and Richard Nixon. Reagan has been categorized as a "passive-positive" — receptive and compliant, with superficial optimism and a strong need for affection.[40]

---

[39] See Alexander George and Juliet George, *Woodrow Wilson and Colonel House: A Personality Study* (New York: Dover, 1964), p. 320. For a review of three decades of commentary and debate on the Georges' work, see William Friedman, "Woodrow Wilson and Colonel House and Political Psychology," *Political Psychology* 15 (March 1994): pp. 35–59. On Kaiser Wilhelm (and Hitler), see Robert G. L. Waite, "Leadership Pathologies: The Kaiser and the Führer and the Decisions for War in 1914 and 1939," in Betty Glad, ed., *Psychological Dimensions of War* (Newbury Park, Calif.: Sage, 1990), pp. 143–168.

[40] James D. Barber, *The Presidential Character,* 3rd ed. (Englewood Cliffs, N.J.: Prentice-Hall, 1985).

Psychobiographical analyses of Henry Kissinger have attempted to link his past experience to his personality and style, which in turn affected his behavior in the foreign policy arena. One observer sees the trauma of Kissinger's boyhood world crumbling about him in Nazi Germany as the main influence. The "inner chaos" that resulted motivated his search for external order, his search for the "strong individual" — even if it is an opponent. Another psychohistorian sees Kissinger's quest for order as the basis for his quest for power. The picture that emerges is of an active-negative, a man of incredible energy and drive who never succeeded in dispelling unease over the chaos that might recur at any time. Perhaps it is not unusual that two active-negatives like Nixon and Kissinger were able to work well as a foreign policy team. Studies of Ronald Reagan indicate that from boyhood he found success through an "energetic attack on obstacles in his path and the avoidance of emotional and intellectual ambiguities." His turn to the political right in the late 1940s "was an adaptation to a personal and political crisis. Anti-communism served certain ego defensive and social adjustment needs for him at a time when his personal and private life had bottomed out."[41]

If we are concerned with the range and variety of personality types that hold office, and how early life experiences can affect both character and style, we cannot overlook the possible impact of gender on decisionmakers. A number of recent writers argue that investigation of gender roles is necessary for understanding how different gender socialization affects perceptions of power, order, and progress. Recent research on post–World War II America, for example, has shown that this gender explanation accounts for differences between American men and women — women have been more opposed to war and less militaristic than men; men are also much more partisan than women. The research indicates that women "learn to put off the use of violence until later in the course of a conflict than do men, to escalate its use more slowly, and to be more emotionally upset by it."[42] Some psychoanalytic accounts trace gender-based attitudes toward autonomy (masculine) and obligation (feminine) to early childhood experiences. Becoming male involves a recognition that one's mother is not like oneself, and thus separate, whereas becoming female involves recognizing mother-daughter sameness and connectedness. Some of the patterns we observe among decisionmakers may derive partly from the predominance of men in the foreign policy process, since for them "self is established defensively against others who threaten to revive their submerged longings for original connections."[43]

[41] See Dan Caldwell, ed., *Henry Kissinger: His Personality and Policies* (Durham, N.C.: Duke University Press, 1983), especially the chapter by Dana Ward; Harvey Starr, *Henry Kissinger: Perceptions of International Politics* (Lexington: University Press of Kentucky, 1984); Betty Glad, "Reagan's Midlife Crisis and the Turn to the Right," *Political Psychology* 10 (1989): pp. 593–624; and the set of psychobiographical studies in Barber, *The Presidential Character.*

[42] Pamela Johnston Conover and Virginia Sapiro, "Gender, Feminist Consciousness, and War," *American Journal of Political Science* 37 (November 1993): p. 1096. See also Jean Bethke Elshtain, *Women and War*, 2nd ed. (Chicago: University of Chicago Press, 1995), for a critical examination of gender stereotypes regarding war and peace.

[43] Christine Sylvester, *Feminist Theory and International Relations in a Postmodern Era* (Cambridge: Cambridge University Press, 1994), p. 40; see also her "Feminists and Realists View Autonomy and Obligation in International Relations," in V. Spike Peterson, ed., *Gendered States: Feminist (Re)Visions of International Relations Theory* (Boulder, Colo.: Lynne Rienner, 1992), pp. 155–177. Sylvester applies to world politics some more general observations made by Nancy J. Hirschmann in "Freedom, Recognition, and Obligation: A Feminist Approach to Political Theory," *American Political Science Review* 83, 4 (1989): pp. 1227–1244.

Private Motives and Public Objects

These various examples of psychological-, personality-, and individual-oriented research all hark back to the classic formulation of Harold Lasswell — that there is a displacement of *private* motives onto *public* objects. Just as all people take out their emotions, frustrations, and personality quirks on the world around them (kicking the dog when you are angry with your spouse), decisionmakers will also displace their private (idiosyncratic) personality drives onto the world around them. In their case, however, private drives can have wide-ranging influence, for the outside world is also the world of diplomacy and foreign policy decision making.

One way to study private motives and public objects is to match indicators of various types of personalities to the behavior most likely to be associated with that personality. For example, scholars have been concerned with the personality attributes associated with the willingness to take risks, to cooperate, or to go to war. Some of these studies have used content analysis of decisionmakers' statements to isolate personality characteristics such as the need for power, conceptual complexity, trust or distrust of others, need for affiliation, belief in control over events, and nationalism. Such studies have shown that the greater the need for power exhibited by the decisionmaker, the more aggressive his or her government will tend to be. Leaders who are more **cognitively complex,** who have the ability to see various sides to issues rather than viewing them in simple terms of black and white, tend to be more cooperative.

One creative study looked at the cognitive complexity — sometimes called "integrative complexity" — of leaders during crisis. Characteristics such as flexibility, empathy, and the ability to recognize alternatives were considered. The analysis of speeches and other public words showed what we would expect: compared to precrisis measures, the cognitive complexity of foreign policy decisionmakers *dropped* during the stress and pressure of a crisis. There was one exception. Of the sixteen individuals studied, only Andrei Gromyko evidenced an increase of integrative complexity during crisis. Perhaps Gromyko's ability to keep his head while those around him were losing theirs was one reason for his amazing longevity in office. Until his death in 1989 he had served with every Soviet leader except Lenin and dealt with every American administration since Franklin Roosevelt's. Applying the same analysis to successful nineteenth-century foreign policy leaders, similar results emerged for individuals such as Bismarck and Wellington. Even more interesting, such increases in integrative complexity were not a mere function of time in office, but were a function of personality.[44]

Similar studies have also been done on people at lower levels in the foreign policy bureaucracy, such as foreign policy specialists in the U.S. State Department. One found a relationship between personality factors and the willingness to use force. Those who were mistrustful, who had low self-esteem, who liked to compete with others, and who were active and ambitious were more likely than other personality types to advocate the use of force by the United States. Interestingly, however, if people combined ambition with high self-esteem, they were also more likely to advocate the use of force.[45]

---

[44] Michael D. Wallace and Peter Suedfeld, "Leadership Performance in Crisis: The Longevity-Complexity Link," *International Studies Quarterly* 32 (December 1988): pp. 439–451.
[45] Lloyd Etheredge, *A World of Men: The Private Sources of American Foreign Policy* (Cambridge, Mass.: MIT Press, 1978).

The Stress and Strain of Foreign Policy

If we look at foreign policy and foreign policy decisions as the product of human behavior, it would be foolish to overlook the fact that decisionmakers are physical beings, influenced by their physiology and possibly by their genetic heritage. On a very simple level, whether information is received and the degree to which it is understood and interpreted depend on the physical ability of the individual. Thus, the physical as well as the mental health of decisionmakers can affect foreign policy and the decision-making process. The strain of high public office is great: look at before-and-after photographs of almost any U.S. president since World War II. The effect of this strain often breaks down the health of the leader. This is even more important when we remember that many political leaders, particularly the heads of governments and senior ministers, are older individuals and thus even more susceptible to the strains of office. Some remain in office to an advanced age, like Mao Zedong (age 84), Charles de Gaulle (79), Ronald Reagan (77), and Leonid Brezhnev (75). The former communist countries seemed particularly susceptible to groups of aged leaders. The average age of the Eastern European leaders in 1989, when communism fell, was 76. None of the Chinese communist leaders who were responsible for the Tiananmen Square attack, also in 1989, were under 75.

People today are basically the same physical creatures that evolved as plains hunters tens of thousands of years ago. Human physiology operates so that in a situation provoking fear, anger, or anxiety, the body gears up for "fight or flight." Physiological reactions — increased heartbeat, the release of adrenaline, the movement of blood to the muscles — prepare the body for physical combat or for running away as fast as possible. The stress that builds up in the body is released by one or the other of these physical actions. The body chemistry of today's foreign policy decisionmaker still works that way, but "fight or flight" is only a metaphor. The modern official does not run screaming down the White House lawn but sits in conference or talks on the telephone or broods alone in an office. The internalized stress is not released as intended, and the health of the decisionmaker is impaired. The stress imposed by a crisis negatively affects performance in information handling and clarity of thought.

A study of the medical histories of twentieth-century political and military leaders indicates an extremely high rate of medical disabilities. These ailments and the drugs and other treatments taken for them have a number of purely physiological effects on the individual that could affect his or her perception of the world and decision-making procedures. Even common psychoactive drugs like alcohol, caffeine, tranquilizers, and sedatives can affect perceptions and mood without an individual's knowing it. For example, alcohol can increase risk taking and recklessness (what effects might Boris Yeltsin's reputed alcohol problem have had on his decision to attack Chechnya?); tranquilizers can increase hostility; and cocaine can induce feelings of euphoria and increased strength.[46]

Perhaps the best example of these effects is the behavior of British Prime Minister Anthony Eden during the Suez crisis of 1956. From a variety of sources, it was clear

---

[46] See Hugh L'Etang, *The Pathology of Leadership* (New York: Hawthorn, 1970); and Roy Lubit and Bruce Russett, "The Effects of Drugs on Decision Making," *Journal of Conflict Resolution* 28 (1984): pp. 85–102.

that Eden was ill, suffering from hypertension and nervous disorders. Reports claim that he was also taking benzedrine, which imparts a feeling of control and confidence. We know that Eden's decision-making behaviors at that time differed markedly from those he had displayed in other cases. He was much more secretive and consulted only a very small group of colleagues. He suffered a physical breakdown right after the crisis. We have already noted that stress can lead to suicide, as in the case of Forrestal or the attempted suicide of Presidential National Security Adviser Robert McFarlane during the Iran-Contra affair in 1986.

Many American presidents and high-level decisionmakers have suffered from major physiological problems. Critics of Franklin Roosevelt claim that he was too ill from high blood pressure during the 1945 Yalta Conference to negotiate effectively with Stalin, that he delayed decisions and gave in on issues to speed the conclusion of grueling bargaining sessions so that he could rest.[47] Woodrow Wilson had a stroke during his stressful and unsuccessful campaign for the League of Nations. Some analysts blame the stroke, rather than lifelong psychological problems, for his stubborn, uncompromising, and counterproductive behavior thereafter. Eisenhower's heart attacks weakened his control over policy; his turning over the government to Vice President Nixon partly prompted the adoption in 1967 of the Twenty-fifth Amendment to the Constitution on presidential disability and succession. Many have suggested that Ronald Reagan's failing memory allowed the activities that culminated in the Iran-Contra scandal to go unchecked (he was diagnosed with Alzheimer's disease after he left office). The death of top decisionmakers or their inability to function can bring the decision-making processes of government to a halt or cause great disruption. The ill health of Brezhnev, Andropov, and Chernenko in the early to mid-1980s brought great instability and uncertainty to the analysis — and conduct — of Soviet foreign policy.

Conclusion to Part I

In Part I we have looked at a series of environments and contexts within which states and nonstates interact, as well as sources of influence and constraint on the foreign policy-making process itself. We began with the world system and concluded with a look at the individual and his or her psychological environment. Processes operate at various levels to exert an impact on the opportunities facing decisionmakers and their willingness to act — their menus and their choices. One way to review these processes, at various levels of analysis, is to consider the extent to which they change over time, as we do in Table 7.1.

Notice the general pattern regarding change. Factors that operate at more aggregated levels of analysis (world system, international relations) tend to change rather slowly compared to those operating at lower levels (role, individual). Anarchy, the

---

[47] Robert H. Ferrell, *The Dying President: Franklin D. Roosevelt, 1944–1945* (Columbia: University of Missouri Press, 1998), says he was "in no condition to govern the Republic" (p. 4).

TABLE 7.1	Factors Affecting Foreign Policy and Their Susceptibility to Change		

Level of Analysis	Factor Affecting Foreign Policy		
	Slow Change	Moderate Change	Rapid Change
World System	Anarchy	Polarity	
		Spheres of Influence	
		Technology	
Relations	Geography	Military Capability	
	Demography	Economic Capability	
		Diplomatic Practices	
Society	History	Social Structure	
	Political Culture	Public Opinion	
		National Interests	
Government		Governmental Structure	
		Openness	
Role		Decision Unit	Information Flow
		Organizational Process	
Individual	Human Physiology		Misperceptions
			Beliefs
			Personalities

Source: Adapted from James N. Rosenau, "The Study of Foreign Policy," in James N. Rosenau, Kenneth Thompson, and Gavin Boyd, eds., *World Politics* (New York: Free Press, 1976), p. 18.

principle of authority underlying sovereignty in the international system since the seventeenth century, has obviously been quite resistant to change. States' natural endowments change very little unless their borders change; historical legacies and political cultures also endure. Most of the factors we have discussed fall within an intermediate category of change. In some instances, when change does occur it is an event of great moment — as with the end of the cold war and the resulting change in system polarity and spheres of influence, as well as governmental structure and openness in the case of Russia. Other factors affecting foreign policy undergo moderate change because shifts tend to be gradual; states' military and economic capabilties are examples, as are changes in social structure and public mood. The organizational and bureaucratic processes described earlier in this chapter are also noteworthy for their incremental nature.

Aside from the physiological elements discussed in the previous section, which apply generally to the human race, the processes operating on individual decision-makers tend to provide for relatively rapid change in foreign policy. It is not that the perceptions and belief systems of individual policymakers change so readily — indeed, we have repeatedly emphasized their resistance to change in the face of new information — and most do not possess multiple personalities. Rather, these factors tend to reside in the minds of individuals; they accompany foreign policymakers when they ascend and descend from positions of influence. The constant circulation of individuals through the corridors of power, along with their peculiar images of the world and personal idiosyncracies, is the predominant source of unpredictibility in world politics.

INTERNATIONAL CONFLICT AND COOPERATION

Yet in all times, kings and persons of sovereign authority, because of their independency, are in continual jealousies, and in the state and posture of gladiators.
— THOMAS HOBBES

Against uncertain fears, protection must be sought in divine providence and innocent precaution, and not in the exercise of our strength.
— HUGO GROTIUS

8

Military Conflict: Why States and Other Actors Resort to Force

Violent Conflict in World Politics

Many believe that in the nuclear age, military power has become obsolete. The use of nuclear weapons against another nuclear-armed state would seem to provide no political utility at all: either the state that used them would also be destroyed by a retaliatory attack, or the devastation would be so great that no territory, wealth, or population would be gained after their use. The costs of a nuclear war would be unprecedented. Given the complex and vital interdependencies of modern society because of the importance of cities and their vulnerability to disruption, nuclear weapons would bring a society to a standstill within a few hours. Distance and time, elements that once protected states in war, would do so no longer. Moreover, nuclear weapons have been of no use against guerrilla operations or terrorists, nor can they be used to seize territory or control of a government. The main value of nuclear weapons, once they were created, has rested in their nonuse: in deterring their use by other nuclear powers.

There has also been the feeling that any use of force is dangerous because of the risk of escalation — that a war could spread to the nuclear powers. This led some people to proclaim that all war was obsolete. The use of force by Saddam Hussein to take Kuwait and the United Nations response (led by the United States) indicate that this is not the case. The actual use or threat of use of conventional military force against nonnuclear powers, particularly those not located in Europe, and for separatist or revolutionary purposes, has retained value. War has been ubiquitous throughout history, and the use of war as a foreign policy tool continues to the present day.

The legitimacy of force or the threat of force is maintained in several ways. The UN Charter permits states, either individually or collectively in alliances, to use force for self-defense. The collective security function of the UN itself is based on the threat to use the collective force of its membership against transgressors of international law, as exercised against the North Koreans in 1950 and Iraq in 1991. Such staunch neutrals as Switzerland and Sweden have based their neutrality on strong military establishments. Their military strength is a form of display to deter any would-be aggressor; because of the impression they made, they would argue, they avoided being attacked by Nazi Germany during World War II. Other states have used force when it was convenient or necessary. Even India, whose first leaders had been the most outspoken in opposition to violence, has turned to armed force on several occasions since independence (in 1961 against Portugal in a dispute over Goa, in 1962 in a border war with China, and in 1947, 1965, and 1971 against Pakistan).

John Mueller argues that norms against the use of force were on the rise even before World War I but were spurred on by that conflict and by World War II.[1] There are, in fact, indications that this is happening. As will be discussed later in this chapter and again in Chapter 11, democracies only rarely fight each other. In addition, there are broader patterns. According to data from the Correlates of War Project, about 15 percent of all "militarized disputes" escalated to war in the period from the Napoleonic Wars to World War II, while only about 3 percent have done so since then.[2] During the cold war the nuclear superpowers, with their adversarial relationship, deterred each other from using nuclear weapons against the other superpower or against any other states. They and their allies in Europe refrained from the direct use of force (conventional and nuclear) in Europe. However, they often employed military force elsewhere, as did other states in the system. A look at which states are engaging in conflict, in which parts of the world, suggests that any argument about the obsolescence of the military tool has applied mostly to the superpowers, to East-West relations in Europe, and among the group of advanced industrial democracies.

A central object of violent struggle has been the control of the state. Since World War II almost 150 governments have been created. Because of the multiethnic or multitribal populations of many of these states and the worldwide ideological clash between Western-oriented parties and communist parties, governments have been under constant siege. Force has been used as a principal tool by nonstate actors to chal-

---

[1] John Mueller, *Retreat from Doomsday: The Obsolescence of Major War* (New York: Basic Books, 1989).
[2] See J. David Singer, "Peace in the Global System: Displacement, Interregnum, or Transformation?" in Charles W. Kegley, Jr., ed., *The Long Postwar Peace* (New York: HarperCollins, 1991).

lenge established governments for control of a state or a region that hopes to become a state of its own. The use of force by nonstate actors is one of a number of challenges to the nation-state in the contemporary system. As noted, state sovereignty is the legal status that gives the state a monopoly on the internal and external use of force. This monopoly has been and continues to be severely contested, the largest proportion of the post-1945 conflicts being some form of civil war or internationalized civil war.

Human Aggression

Of all the forms of international interaction, war is the most studied. In an influential analysis of war Kenneth Waltz located various theoretical explanations at three different levels of analysis — what he called "images." The *first image* focuses on human nature and the psychological needs and deficiencies we all supposedly possess by virtue of our genetic make-up. It corresponds to the individual level of analysis introduced in Chapter 1 and presented more fully in Chapter 7:

> According to the first image of international relations, the locus of the causes of war is found in the nature and behavior of man. Wars result from selfishness, from misdirected aggressive impulses, from stupidity. Other causes are secondary and have to be interpreted in the light of these factors. If these are the primary causes of war, then the elimination of war must come through uplifting and enlightening men or securing their psychic-social readjustment.[3]

People have always been concerned about human nature, wondering if there is a built-in human instinct for violence, aggression, and domination. The debate over "nature versus nurture" is an old one. What accounts for human actions: innate genetic characteristics or the cultural environment? A form of the debate continues between ethology (the study of animal behavior) and anthropology. The most extreme ethologists say that there is a strong biological basis for human behavior and that biological influences on behavior are very powerful.[4] More moderate exponents claim that ethology simply provides us with analogies between mechanisms found in animals and similar mechanisms found in human cultures. Opponents of the *sociobiological perspective* claim that the genetic or biological impact on social interaction is either extremely small or nonexistent.

For animals higher on the evolutionary ladder, the influence of the environment is greater. Each animal has a "biogram," a program, or template, built into its genes. For the oldest and least complicated forms of life, much if not all behavior is guided by such a program. However, more of the behavior of a higher animal depends on stimuli from its environment — hearing its parents sing the proper bird song or watching a mother lion hunt. Human beings have by far the most open and flexible biogram of all. Group

---

[3] Kenneth Waltz, *Man, the State and War: A Theoretical Analysis* (New York: Columbia University Press, 1959), p. 16.

[4] Classic statements of this view include Konrad Lorenz, *On Aggression* (New York: Harcourt, Brace, and World, 1966), and Desmond Morris, *The Naked Ape* (New York: Dell, 1967) and *The Human Zoo* (New York: McGraw-Hill, 1969).

life itself may be a biological necessity, built into human genes, along with language, but what group one lives with, what culture one is surrounded by, and what language one speaks are all completely undetermined. Anthropologists have demonstrated that just about any conceivable type of behavior, in almost every conceivable combination, can be found in the groups of men and women that live and have lived on earth.

Contrary to the sociobiological view, war, violence, and aggression may not be built into humanity and thus may be prevented. The famous anthropologist Margaret Mead argued that war was simply another human invention; John Mueller maintains a similar view that war, like slavery and dueling, can be "unlearned." One review, by a psychologist, of the available arguments concludes that humans are not inherently violent.[5] Although ethology provides us with some interesting analogies and explanations for human behavior, it cannot explain decisions to go to war or to act cooperatively in international relations. We cannot fall back on "human nature" to explain foreign policy behavior. We are all human, and thus we share the same human nature — but some societies are much more peaceful than others. The people of modern Scandinavia are widely regarded as peaceful and antiwar; Sweden, for instance, has not fought a war since its conflict with Russia ended in 1809. Their ancestors, however, were the fierce Vikings who pillaged and looted all around Europe during the Middle Ages. From Hagar the Horrible to Dag Hammarskjöld.

Under the auspices of the Spanish National Commission of the United Nations Educational, Scientific, and Cultural Organization (UNESCO), a group of leading biologists and social scientists from twelve countries (and five continents) formulated the Seville Statement on Violence in 1986. The statement, adopted by numerous academic and professional organizations in many disciplines and countries, specifically rejects the proposition that armament and war are inevitable because of the inherent influences of human nature (see Table 8.1). Instead, we should do much better to look at how certain types of situations affect an individual's perceptions and feelings, and ultimately individual and group decision making.

Relative Deprivation and Aggression

Theories about status and feelings of deprivation are common in psychology, sociology, and political science. The most important versions assert that aggressive behavior stems from frustration arising out of a feeling of **relative deprivation.** People may act violently or aggressively not because they are poor or deprived in some absolute sense but because they feel deprived relative to others or to their expectations of what they should have.[6] Perhaps the best example is pre–World War I Germany's demand for its "place in the sun"; this was a desire for recognition as a great power, especially in comparison to Britain, exacerbated by Kaiser Wilhelm's personal insecurities and jeal-

---

[5] See Leonard Berkowitz, "Biological Roots: Are Humans Inherently Violent?" in Betty Glad, ed., *Psychological Dimensions of War* (Newbury Park, Calif.: Sage, 1990), pp. 24–40.

[6] This concept was developed in Ted Robert Gurr's study of internal war, *Why Men Rebel* (Princeton, N.J.: Princeton University Press, 1970), but it also applies well to interstate war.

TABLE 8.1	The Seville Statement on Violence, May 16, 1986

- IT IS SCIENTIFICALLY INCORRECT to say that we have inherited a tendency to make war from our animal ancestors. . . . Warfare is a peculiarly human phenomenon and does not occur in other animals.

- IT IS SCIENTIFICALLY INCORRECT to say that war or any other violent behavior is genetically programmed into our human nature. While genes are involved at all levels of nervous system function, they provide development potential that can be actualized only in conjunction with the ecological and social environment.

- IT IS SCIENTIFICALLY INCORRECT to say that in the course of human evolution there has been a selection for aggressive behavior more than for other kinds of behavior. . . . Violence is neither in our evolutionary legacy nor in our genes.

- IT IS SCIENTIFICALLY INCORRECT to say that humans have a "violent brain." While we do have the neural apparatus to act violently, it is not automatically activated by internal or external stimuli. . . . There is nothing in our neurophysiology that compels us to react violently.

- IT IS SCIENTIFICALLY INCORRECT to say that war is caused by instinct or any single motivation.

ousies. Similarly, before the Seven Weeks' War in 1866 between Prussia and Austria, Prussia's grievances with Austria had been related to "pride of place" — a demand for equal status with Austria in the German Diet.

Feelings of relative deprivation can arise by comparing one's past, present, and expected future condition. Images of this condition are strongly affected by where one (or one's country) sits within the hierarchy of various global or regional systems based on status, prestige, military power, wealth, and so on. Feelings of relative deprivation are likely to arise when a formerly prosperous individual experiences a severe economic setback. Such feelings are widespread during recessions and depressions and often result in severe political unrest. Karl Marx thought that revolutions would occur as the result of the increasing poverty of the working class. Prolonged, severe depression in Germany in the 1930s played a key part in preparing Hitler's rise to power. Some observers fear the parallels between the experience of Weimar Germany and growth of an intensely nationalistic, fascist-like movement in the economically troubled atmosphere of post–cold war Russia.

On the other hand, in some cases an improvement in people's material conditions can release unrest. Alexis de Tocqueville described the situation before the French Revolution in these terms:

Thus, it was precisely in those parts of Europe where there had been most improvement that popular discontent was highest. . . . Patiently endured so long as it seemed beyond redress, a grievance comes to appear intolerable once the possibility of removing it crosses men's minds.[7]

A more complicated hypothesis combines these two views and asserts that the most dangerous time for social unrest, or for challenges to the status quo in any sort of system, is when a sustained period of improving conditions is followed by a sudden, sharp setback. The period of improvement may lead people to expect continuing improvement; thus, when the setback occurs, it causes more distress than if it had followed a period of unchanged conditions.[8]

Another perspective emphasizes the importance of people's comparisons with one another: "I may be satisfied, even with a bad lot, providing that you do no better. But to the degree that I find my situation relatively poor compared to yours, then I am likely to be dissatisfied." Here it is necessary to specify what group or individual is relevant for comparison. For the landless peasant in a traditional society, the condition of the rich landlord may be beyond the peasant's dreams, but the modest prosperity of the middle peasant (the kulak in Russia after the 1917 revolution, for example) may arouse acute feelings of relative deprivation. Generally, such feelings seem more severe for comparisons among people in close contact than for widely separated social groups or strata. Hence, poor whites may feel angrier and more threatened by the gains of blacks than they do about the privileges of rich whites, even though poor whites as well as blacks may be better off than their parents were. Importantly, the revolution in communications technology has fostered this phenomenon across continents, cultures, and economic classes.

These two perspectives, emphasizing comparisons across time and across groups, can be usefully combined. The first suggests when serious discontent may arise; the second suggests where in the social system it will be most manifest. Theories of relative deprivation have received a good deal of attention. Part of the reason is that the present day seems to be a period of substantial change in people's status or in their consciousness of differences in status. Feelings of relative deprivation may also arise among those who are excluded from the benefits of improved economic conditions. Many people in the slums and barrios of the developing countries, for instance, may sometimes be better off economically than they had been, but transistor radios, television by satellite, and the Internet (if they can gain access) have made them more aware of how well off people in other countries and elites in their own countries really are. This is what is sometimes called the problem of "rising expectations."

---

[7] Alexis de Tocqueville, *The Old Regime and the French Revolution* (Garden City, N.Y.: Doubleday, 1955), pp. 176–177.

[8] A classic statement of this hypothesis is James C. Davies, "The J-Curve of Rising and Declining Satisfaction as a Cause of Some Great Revolutions and a Contained Rebellion," in Hugh Davis Graham and Ted Robert Gurr, eds., *Violence in America: Historical and Comparative Perspectives* (Washington, D.C.: National Commission on the Causes and Prevention of Violence, 1969). See also James C. Davies, ed., *When Men Revolt and Why* (New Brunswick, N.J.: Transaction, 1997).

Conflict between States

Military conflict between states has varied widely both in terms of severity (the extent of death and destruction involved) and scope (the number of participants involved). The most severe form of interstate conflict is, of course, called **war;** those that have involved numerous participants, including multiple great powers, are called "global wars" or "systemic wars." Table 8.2 lists these global wars beginning with the Thirty Years' War, which inaugurated the contemporary state system. The Thirty Years' War was the longest global war and was especially destructive by the standards of the time

TABLE 8.2   Global War in the Contemporary State System

War	Dates	Great Power Involvement	Battle Deaths
Thirty Years' War	1618–1648	Britain, France, Hapsburgs/Austria, Netherlands, Spain, Sweden	2,071,000
Dutch War of Louis XIV	1672–1678	Britain, France, Hapsburgs/Austria, Netherlands, Spain, Sweden	342,000
War of the League of Augsburg	1688–1697	Britain, France, Hapsburgs/Austria, Netherlands, Spain	680,000
War of the Spanish Succession	1701–1713	Britain, France, Hapsburgs/Austria, Netherlands, Spain	1,251,000
War of the Austrian Succession	1739–1748	Britain, France, Hapsburgs/Austria, Prussia, Russia, Spain	359,000
Seven Years' War	1755–1763	Britain, France, Hapsburgs/Austria, Prussia, Russia, Spain	992,000
French Revolutionary/ Napoleonic Wars	1792–1815	Britain, France, Hapsburgs/Austria, Prussia, Russia, Spain	2,532,000
World War I	1914–1918	Austria-Hungary, Britain, France, Germany, Italy, Japan, Russia, United States	7,734,300
World War II	1939–1945	Britain, France, Germany, Italy, Japan, Russia, United States	12,948,300

Source: Jack S. Levy, *War in the Modern Great Power System, 1495–1975* (Lexington: University of Kentucky Press, 1983), and Jack S. Levy, "Theories of General War," *World Politics* 37, 3 (1985): pp. 344–374.

(over 2 million battle-related fatalities), giving urgency to the clarification of sovereign rights at Westphalia in 1648. It was not until the wars of the French Revolution and Napoleon's bid for European supremacy that war would result in a greater loss of life. The two world wars of the twentieth century saw the advances of the industrial revolution put to use on the battlefield; the toll was an exponential increase in destructiveness, especially considering the relatively short duration of these conflicts compared to previous global wars.

States have fought over many things. In a study of the range of issues that have led states into conflict, Kalevi Holsti identified 177 wars and major armed interventions as having occurred between 1648 and 1989. Four armed conflicts occurring since 1989 can be added to that list: the U.S. invasion of Panama in 1989, the Iraqi invasion of Kuwait in 1990, the subsequent war against Iraq by a U.S.-led coalition of states in 1991, and the conflict between Azerbaijan and Armenia over Nagorno-Karabakh in 1992 and 1993. Table 8.3 summarizes what Holsti found to be the issues most often leading to warfare.[9] Disputes over possession of territory are by far the most common, constituting at least one of the issues in contention in almost half (46 percent) of the 181 major armed conflicts in the 350 years since the Peace of Westphalia. And these disputes over territory don't even include struggles for control of strategically important pieces of land or waterways; they are counted separately as issues of "strategic territory" and have figured in 20 percent of all wars and major armed interventions. Some of the most intractable issues dividing Israel and its Arab neighbors are of this type, most notably Israel's occupation of the Golan Heights and, until recently, a strip of land in southern Lebanon.

If we examine the history of the contemporary international system, we find that territorial disputes were the most common issues contributing to war in the 1648–1714, 1715–1814, and 1918–1941 periods. During the nineteenth century and since the end of World War II the most common conflict-producing issue has been "nation-state creation," which includes disputes resulting from national liberation and unification movements as well as secession. The importance of this issue during the nineteenth century reflected the rise of national independence movements accompanying the wave of European colonization that began in the 1870s. The wave of decolonization following World War II — the ultimate success of these movements — accounts for the importance of this issue as a source of international conflict in the second half of the twentieth century. Most of these conflicts were not really *interstate* wars but rather wars waged by European states in their own colonial territories. Such colonial conflicts were fought by the Netherlands in Indonesia (1945–49); by France in Vietnam (1946–54), Tunisia (1952–56), Morocco (1953–56), and Algeria (1954–62); by Britain in Palestine (1946–48), the Malay Archipelago (1948–60), and Cyprus (1955–60); and by Portugal in Guinea (1962–74), Mozambique (1965–75), and Angola (1968–1974). Decolonization was not a peaceful transition.

---

[9] See Kalevi J. Holsti, *Peace and War: Armed Conflicts and International Order, 1648–1989* (Cambridge: Cambridge University Press, 1991), especially chap. 12, on the grouping of conflict-producing issues. For a listing of recent conflicts and the issues involved, see Peter Wallensteen and Maragreta Sollenberg, "Armed Conflict and Regional Conflict Complexes, 1989–97," *Journal of Peace Research* 35, 5 (September 1998): pp. 621– 634.

TABLE 8.3 Issues in War and Major Armed Intervention, 1648–1998

1648–1998	
Issue	Percent of Wars
Territory	46
State Creation	30
Economics	28
Ideology	25
Survival/Predation	22
Strategic Territory	20
Human Sympathy	18
Number of Wars	*181*

1648–1714	
Issue	Percent of Wars
Territory	55
Economics	41
Survival/Predation	23
Strategic Territory	23
Human Sympathy	14
State Creation	5
Ideology	0
Number of Wars	*22*

1715–1814	
Issue	Percent of Wars
Territory	67
Economics	42
Survival/Predation	17
Strategic Territory	17
Ideology	14
Human Sympathy	11
State Creation	8
Number of Wars	*36*

1815–1914	
Issue	Percent of Wars
State Creation	55
Territory	42
Ideology	23
Human Sympathy	23
Economics	19
Strategic Territory	13
Survival/Predation	7
Number of Wars	*31*

1918–1941	
Issue	Percent of Wars
Territory	47
Survival/Predation	37
Strategic Territory	30
Ideology	27
Human Sympathy	23
Economics	23
State Creation	13
Number of Wars	*30*

1945–1998	
Issue	Percent of Wars
State Creation	47
Ideology	42
Territory	32
Survival/Predation	24
Economics	23
Strategic Territory	21
Human Sympathy	19
Number of Wars	*62*

Source: Compiled from Kalevi J. Holsti, *Peace and War: Armed Conflicts and International Order, 1648–1989* (Cambridge: Cambridge University Press, 1991), Tables 3.1, 5.1, 7.1, 9.1, 11.1; updated by the authors.

Other patterns in Table 8.3 are noteworthy. Economic issues — those involving commercial navigation, access to resources, colonial competition, and protection of commercial interests — were much more likely to figure prominently in wars during the seventeenth and eighteenth centuries than during later periods. The first round of European colonization that began in the fifteenth century had as its primary motive the acquisition of foreign territory and control of trade routes designed to enhance states' wealth and power. Frequent wars were fought as the European powers confronted one another in their imperial quests. The First Anglo-Dutch War (1652–54), for example, grew out of an attempt by Britain to challenge Holland's predominance in commercial shipping in the Baltic Sea. The Second Anglo-Dutch War (1665–67) had similar roots, this time Britain's interference in the Dutch slave trade out of western Africa and its seizure of New Amsterdam (New York). Czar Peter the Great, in seeking to open up Russian trade routes to western Europe, presented a challenge to Swedish hegemony, thereby precipitating the Great Northern War (1700–1721). These sorts of wars became rare by the nineteenth century, but economic issues have nonetheless been a factor in almost one-fourth (23 percent) of the wars fought since 1945. Access to disputed oil reserves was a major issue in Iraq's invasion of Kuwait in 1990, and some of the more cynical observers of the Gulf War suggested that the U.S.-led liberation of Kuwait was primarily intended to ensure that oil prices remained low.

The role of ideology in generating international conflict has increased over time and has been most prominent since World War II. We have witnessed a shift away from disputes over concrete issues like territory and commerce toward conflicts over ideas about proper forms of political, economic, and social interaction. The cold war, in which the forces of capitalism were pitted against the forces of communism, provided a conducive atmosphere for this type of conflict. Related to conflicts over ideology are conflicts over religion and ethnicity, and states have often gone to war in order to protect their religious or ethnic brethren or to support them in their "irredentist" efforts to unite with their own kind in adjacent states. The most recent example of this sort of conflict ("human sympathy") was the one between the former Soviet republics of Armenia and Azerbaijan over the treatment of Armenians in Azerbaijan's Nagorno-Karabakh region. Accompanying these and other issues is often predation — the desire to completely eliminate another state as a sovereign entity — in which case the target state is fighting for its very survival. Predation has been ever-present in the contemporary international system but was at its height in the period between the two world wars, the best example being the 1939 conquest of Poland by Nazi Germany from the west and Soviet Russia from the east. In the post–World War II period, Israel's right to exist was an issue in the Arab-Israeli wars of 1948, 1967, and 1973.

Identifying the issues that bring states into war is sometimes difficult, and distinguishing between primary and secondary issues of contention can be more difficult still. Empirical research is complicated further because there is often little agreement about what exactly constitutes a "war," especially in the post–World War II international system. With the disappearance of legal trappings such as formal declarations of war, different scholars have used different criteria to determine which events should be included in their lists of wars and which should be counted as lesser military disputes. The Correlates of War Project reports 943 militarized interstate disputes involving the use of force between 1946 and 1992, including blockades, occupations, clashes, and raids. Of these, 25 are considered interstate wars because they resulted in more than 1,000 battle-related deaths (not all were accompanied by formal declarations of war). In another study, Herbert Tillema defines an overt military intervention as "combatant or combat-ready military operations conducted upon a foreign territory by units of a state's regular military forces" and identifies 690 cases of intervention, comprising a total of 285 international armed conflicts, from 1945 through 1991. During this period, 106 states undertook military interventions, 80 of them (75 percent) Third World states. Almost all interventions (95 percent) occurred in the Third World, and most of the 2.4 million fatalities resulting from military intervention (92 percent) were sustained by Third World states.[10] Whatever the precise definition of war or military intervention and whatever the exact count of such disputes, it is clear that policymakers still perceive utility in the use of force.

Domestic Economic Structure and War

According to *second image* explanations, to return to Waltz's classification, "the internal organization of states is the key to understanding war and peace."[11] One dimension of a state's internal organization is its form of governance. We have mentioned that many researchers and policymakers contend that democratically governed countries are less warlike, at least toward other democracies, than authoritarian countries; this "democratic peace" is explored at greater length in Chapter 11. Another dimension of internal organization is the state's economic structure and the relationship between economic organization and war has been studied extensively.

Realist theories of world politics assume that it does not matter much how different countries' economic systems are organized: equally rich and powerful countries will have about the same goals, whether they have capitalist or socialist economies. Liberal theories, however, say that it does make a difference. Some liberal theorists have believed that capitalists' interests in free trade and prosperous foreign markets would promote world peace: as poor countries developed along capitalist lines, they too would contribute to building a more peaceful world order. But other liberals, and especially Marxists and other radicals, have long claimed that capitalist countries are likely to have particularly aggressive foreign policies. This aggression is not limited to acts of war. Capitalism is sometimes considered the cause of a variety of imperialist acts, loosely defined as efforts to exert political or economic control over smaller or weaker states. Political and military interventions in less developed countries are of special interest. Other foci of attention include military spending, "militarism," and arms races.

The theories differ substantially as to which particular aspects of capitalism cause imperialism or war. Some radicals cite the alleged needs of the entire capitalist economy, claiming that the capitalist system as a whole (or at least the capitalist economy of

---

[10] Correlates of War Project, "Militarized Interstate Disputes," April 1998 (cited August 3, 1998); available at <http://pss.la.psu.edu/ mid_data.htm>. The Overt Military Intervention dataset is described in Herbert K. Tillema, *Overt Military Intervention in the Cold War Era* (Columbia: University of South Carolina Press, forthcoming); regional figures are reported in chap. 2.
[11] Waltz, *Man, the State and War,* p. 81.

any major nation-state) is dependent on military spending or on continued access to foreign markets for goods or investment opportunities. Others point to the interests and power of particular groups or classes. Foreign investors, the military-industrial complex, or other economically defined groups may have an interest in an aggressive or expansionist foreign policy that can potentially yield great gains for them, even though many other members of the system — capitalists as well as workers — suffer net losses from such a policy. A minority of economic interests, therefore, may successfully maintain a policy that benefits them even though it may be detrimental to the capitalist economy as a whole. Finally, some theories are addressed less to readily definable material interests than to the value structure, that is, the ideology of capitalist systems. According to these theories, this value structure, concerned as much with the desire to preserve the capitalist system as to extend it, produces behavior that is excessively responsive to economic growth and the incentive of material rewards. The resulting foreign policy is thus expansionist and hostile to socialist states with different value structures, whose adoption by major segments within the capitalist system would undermine the privileged place of the capitalists themselves. Contradicting these theories are others that stress the relative unimportance of economic motivations in influencing foreign policy; instead, they emphasize political and cultural ends and other kinds of ideological motivations.

Most of the classical economic interpretations attribute imperialism to demands arising from the organization of production in capitalist economies. The liberal English economist J. A. Hobson argued that the very unequal distribution of income and wealth in capitalist countries, especially England, left the poor unable to consume much. "Underconsumption" in the domestic market in turn forced capitalists to invest their capital abroad and to compete with others to control foreign markets. The capitalist system of the time was to blame, but according to his theory imperialism was not inherent in capitalism.[12]

Many Marxist writers of the early twentieth century developed extremely influential theories of imperialism. Most famous is the work of V. I. Lenin. Like Hobson, Lenin observed that underconsumption led to the accumulation of surplus capital, a process that became especially pronounced with the emergence of monopoly production. Because industrial and banking interests combine to gain effective control of the state, the drive to export surplus capital became a competition among countries rather than simply a competition among corporations, ultimately leading to war among the capitalist powers. Imperialism was therefore the "highest stage" of capitalism, and imperialist wars — and he considered World War I, which was ongoing at the time he was writing, just such a war — were the predictable outcomes.[13] Later Marxist writers drew similar conclusions from capitalist countries' need for market outlets for their products as well as their capital, and their continual need for new sources of raw materials.

All these theories came from an effort to explain European colonialism, which divided up the world into competing empires in the decades preceding World War I. These theories, however, have been the subject of intensive criticism, with a number of

---

[12] J. A. Hobson, *Imperialism: A Study* (London: Allen & Unwin, 1902).
[13] V. I. Lenin, *Imperialism: The Highest Stage of Capitalism* (New York: International Publishers, 1939).

studies pointing out empirical evidence that contradicts them. For example, most British foreign investment did not go to the African and Asian colonies or other less-developed countries; instead, more than three-fourths went to the United States, to the predominantly white-settled countries of the British Empire, and to other advanced capitalist countries, which should have been plagued by surplus capital conditions supposedly existing in Britain.

Realist theorists have offered primarily political or strategic explanations for imperialism, taking account of economic factors but arguing that the typical situation was one of investments in the service of diplomacy, not vice versa:

> Private investments have usually, in actual practice, been subordinated by governments to factors of general political or military strategy which have a more direct bearing on power. Thus, it is that private investors have received strong, even outrageously exaggerated governmental backing where they have been tools and agents of power and prestige politics, while other investors whose projects seemed to run counter to the government's line of political endeavor have experienced official indifference or even active opposition.[14]

Other writers, carefully examining British actions in Africa, also declared that British objectives were political and strategic, not economic. Karl Polanyi concluded that "business and finance were responsible for many colonial wars, but also for the fact that a general conflagration was avoided. . . . For every one interest that was furthered by war, there were a dozen that could be adversely affected. . . . Every war, almost, was organized by the financiers; but peace also was organized by them."[15]

Joseph Schumpeter is the best known theorist to stress noneconomic influences. Although he acknowledged that some monopolists have an interest in the conquest of lands producing raw materials and foodstuffs, he regarded it as a "basic fallacy to describe imperialism as a necessary phase of capitalism, or even to speak of the development of capitalism into imperialism."[16] Some capitalists may gain, but only a small minority. The gains from war for capitalists as a class are more than offset by their losses and burdens. Imperialism is primarily an affair of politicians and military personnel. Basically, imperialism stems from attitudes and behavior patterns among the militarists, a group that evolved historically, in the precapitalist era, to defend the state and establish its security.

In part stimulated by these theories, Nazli Choucri and Robert North examined the great powers' colonial expansionism as a primary cause of World War I. Colonial expansion — especially once the Southern Hemisphere had been almost entirely carved up among the imperialist states — led to increasing clashes over colonial

---

[14] Eugene Staley, *War and the Private Investor* (Garden City, N.Y.: Doubleday, 1935), pp. 361–362.

[15] Karl Polanyi, *The Great Transformation* (Boston: Beacon, 1957), p. 16. On British actions in Africa, see R. E. Robinson and John Gallagher, *Africa and the Victorians* (New York: St. Martin's, 1961). Strategic interests arose for Britain *because* of its existing imperial holdings in India, the jewel in Britain's imperial crown, which leaves open the possibility that the basic motivation was to protect the economic interests there.

[16] Joseph Schumpeter, *Imperialism and Social Classes* (New York: Meridian, 1955), p. 84.

borders and spheres of influence. The colonial conflicts increased the incentives of the great powers to maintain large armies and navies so that they could hold and defend their colonies. Moreover, these conflicts, together with the arms races they stimulated, led to increasingly violent relations among the great powers, creating repeated crises of which the last, in August 1914, resulted in World War I. Choucri and North, in examining changes in each country's colonial holdings, military expenditures, and so forth, found substantial evidence for each of the links in this chain. Furthermore, they found that economic pressures, stemming from rising income, population, and trade, produced pressures to obtain foreign markets and raw materials that led to the acquisition of colonies.[17]

This evidence is compatible with many liberal and Marxist theories which assert that imperialism, and ultimately war among imperial powers, had important economic roots. However, this evidence is also fully compatible with the view that individual capitalists did not want large-scale war. A quite different study, for example, has shown a very high correlation between leaders' perceptions of hostility and the outflow of gold from London in the 1914 crisis. Prices on the security markets of all the major powers collapsed at the same time, because financiers were horrified by the impending war.[18] Choucri and North look at the population, technological, and economic forces that drive a national economy to expand by gaining access to markets and resources — something they call "lateral pressure." This expansion may generate conflict with other nations' interests. If war then looms, no one may want it, yet decision-makers may find their menu in the crisis so constrained that they must take actions they would prefer to avoid.

System Polarity and War

In addition to first and second image explanations of war, there is a *third image.* "The requirements of state action are, in this view, imposed by the circumstances in which all states exist"; war, that is to say, can be explained by the characteristics of the international system, especially the distribution of power.[19] One common theory argues that bipolar systems will be most successful in avoiding major war, despite the fears and hostilities likely to be built up between the two principal antagonists. In a bipolar system the two major powers are rather evenly matched and neither has a good chance of easy victory. War would be long and costly, and the risks of losing, even for the side that may initially seem stronger, would be substantial.[20]

Consequently, there is always the risk that if a war does break out between the two great antagonists it will be terribly severe; even a low probability of conflict may, in the face of tremendous potential damage, seem unacceptably high. Thus, the result is a great emphasis on crisis management and efforts to avoid direct confrontation

---

[17] Nazli Choucri and Robert C. North, *Nations in Conflict: National Growth and International Violence* (San Francisco: Freeman, 1975).

[18] Ole R. Holsti, *Crisis, Escalation, War* (Montreal: McGill–Queen's University Press, 1972), chap. 3.

[19] Waltz, *Man, the State and War,* p. 160.

[20] The best known case for the stability of bipolar systems is that made by Waltz in his *Theory of International Politics* (Reading, Mass.: Addison-Wesley, 1979).

between the two major antagonists themselves, leaving their local or regional proxies to fight. Even wars that begin only as internal conflicts somewhere on the fringes of a power sphere may potentially be transformed into struggles between blocs and the bloc leaders. After coexisting in the same system for a long time, the leaders of the two sides will have learned what kinds of acts are likely to provoke dangerous reactions from the opponent. This is perhaps especially true for the nuclear bipolar system, but it may also have been true of other pairs in the past.[21]

Some analysts stress that in the post–World War II bipolar system the leaders of each of the two big alliance blocs were very much stronger than any other member of its bloc. The two superpowers, enforcing the order and discipline of hierarchy within each alliance, could reduce the likelihood that their small allies would drag them and others into wars. Opposing bloc members therefore did not face too much uncertainty about possible serious shifts in alliance memberships and the overall power balance. This type of situation was very different from that in 1914, when the inability of great powers to control either their big or small allies contributed greatly to the onset of World War I. Somewhat related is the view that the U.S. and Soviet blocs could be considered "empires" during much of the cold war and that evidence on historical empires indicates that the core states of competing empires avoid war.[22]

At the end of the cold war, people began to ask more insistently why there had been such a long peace — forty-five years without war between major powers, amounting to an almost unprecedented situation. Bipolarity is one possible explanation. Realists, who think that the structure of the international system very much affects the likelihood of great-power war, began to predict that with the end of the bipolar cold war system we would be entering a period of great uncertainty and risk.

On the other hand, nuclear weapons may have been an equally important influence, given the particular caution that the mutual vulnerability of the United States and the Soviet Union fostered. Nuclear weapons made any major-power war seem impossibly costly. Yet World War II, which was fought with only conventional, nonnuclear weapons until the very end, was also hideously costly in both lives and economic destruction, demonstrating to many people that sustained war between developed industrialized states would always be a losing proposition. By this argument, all the chief antagonists of World War II learned that lesson and would have avoided war with each other again, even if nuclear weapons had not been a factor and regardless of whether the postwar distribution of power was bipolar or multipolar.[23]

---

[21] See Joseph S. Nye, Jr., "Nuclear Learning and U.S.-Soviet Security Regimes," *International Organization* 41, 3 (1987): pp. 371–402, and Roger E. Kanet and Edward A. Kolodziej, eds., *The Cold War as Cooperation: Superpower Cooperation in Regional Conflict Management* (Baltimore: Johns Hopkins University Press, 1991).

[22] Manus Midlarsky, "International Structure and the Learning of Cooperation: The Postwar Experience," in Charles W. Kegley, ed., *The Long Postwar Peace: Contending Explanation and Projections* (New York: HarperCollins, 1991), pp. 105–122. See also Morris Blachman and Donald Puchala, "When Empires Meet: The Long Peace in Long-Term Perspective," pp. 177–201 in the same volume.

[23] Kenneth Waltz, in *The Spread of Nuclear Weapons: More May Be Better*, Adelphi Papers, no. 171 (London: International Institute for Strategic Studies, 1981), says that nuclear weapons, as well as bipolarity, contribute to stability. On the excessive cost even of conventional war between developed states, see John Mueller, *Retreat from Doomsday: The Obsolescence of Major War* (New York: Basic Books, 1989).

In general, pessimistic analyses of the future of the world system, based on the demise of bipolarity, must be treated with caution; it is important to consider alternative explanations for the long post–World War II peace.[24] The absence of all-out war during the cold war era may indeed be attributable to the bipolar international system — or it may just be a coincidence that the system was bipolar and there was no big war. Other factors can, in theory, explain the absence of war, and we cannot rule out any of them by looking only at the single case of the cold war.

At the other extreme from unipolar and bipolar systems is a system with quite a different menu — many independent centers of power, none of which is strong enough to dominate the others. Perhaps such a system would both be quite stable, maintaining the same pattern of interactions, and have little war. In a system with many states and no permanent polarities, the leaders of one country must maintain proper relations with most of the others. Alignments are likely to shift frequently, as an opponent on one issue today might be needed as an ally on another issue tomorrow. To protect the possibility of future cooperation, a state must not let any temporary antagonisms get out of hand and embitter overall relations. Multiple and cross-cutting ties of this sort are common in stable democratic politics within states and are important factors in promoting peaceful problem solving. The larger the system, the more numerous the possibilities for coalition forming, and the better the chances for this mechanism to work smoothly. Over a long period, however, there might be wars in which many defeated states would be eliminated; if so, there would be a gradual decrease in the number of actors over time.

Such a many-poled system is hardly in prospect. A more relevant model shows a balance of power among several, but not many, states or groups of states. A balance-of-power system is characterized by a special pattern of state behavior: if several major powers are competing with one another, they will usually group together to prevent any one power or group from becoming dominant. Roughly equivalent capabilities among groups — and especially a willingness to shift alliances or even go to war to keep any one actor from upsetting the balance of power — form the heart of this system. Thus, the balance-of-power process is based on deterring potentially dominant states or alliances, along with the willingness to go to war if such deterrence fails.

With this kind of system, it is likely that rather frequent wars among the major powers could be tolerated without producing major changes in the system. Many such systems may have depended on frequent trials of strength, limited in duration and intensity, to test the balance of power among their members and ensure that no state should grow disproportionately. The virtues of this system are supposedly in the relative restraint with which wars are fought and the stability of the system itself. The frequency of wars nevertheless means that a price is being exacted for the stability. The human and material cost of the total amount of warfare in the system is not necessarily less than in bipolar systems, which presumably have fewer, but more intense, wars.

---

[24] For a statement of the pessimistic view, see John Mearsheimer, "Back to the Future: Instability in Europe after the Cold War," *International Security* 15, 1 (1990): pp. 5–56. Rebuttals to Mearsheimer's argument appear in the "Correspondence" section of the next two issues of *International Security*. For a more general discussion of the impact of polarity, see Charles W. Kegley and Gregory A. Raymond, *A Multipolar Peace? Great Power Politics in the Twenty-First Century* (New York: St. Martin's, 1994).

System Transformation and War

Another source of instability arises from change in the international system. Scholars concerned with the rise and decline of system leaders and their challengers have focused on the differential growth rates among the great powers. Especially rapid economic growth can increase a state's capabilities even without a conscious decision by its leaders to increase the state's power in the international system. Technological innovation may occur faster in one state than in another — affecting production, creating new means of exploiting resources, or producing a potent new weapon. Slowdowns in the growth of state power can come from "imperial overstretch," to use Paul Kennedy's term, or from a variety of domestic political and economic conditions. High levels of civil conflict, or even revolution, can seriously weaken a state, as can economic stagnation. Thus, economic and military capabilities may shift significantly, sometimes in relatively short periods of time. A variety of economic, technological, or sociocultural changes may lead to the breakdown of one system and the emergence of another.[25]

The threat to international stability stems directly from both the differential growth of power and the frequent trials of strength that test new power relationships. Such conflicts are an integral part of the balance-of-power system. If wars do occur, sometimes a major power may be eliminated or fatally weakened because of a miscalculation, bitter hatreds among citizens of the victor toward the vanquished, or the lack of internal cohesiveness of the loser. For instance, at the beginning of World War I none of the major enemies of Austria-Hungary expected that empire to break up and utterly disappear from the ranks of major powers. When a major power is eliminated, it may be very hard to find another state capable of filling the gap. Some big states will continue to grow bigger despite the efforts of others to restrain them. Thus, there are certain elements in any system that tend to eliminate some major powers and to strengthen others, making precarious the maintenance of the sensitive balance required in the long run.

The importance of changes in systems as a cause of war is clear from a careful look at pre–World War I Europe. Between 1900 and 1914 Europe was increasingly polarized, most notably by the addition of previously unallied England to the entente of France and Russia, by increases in the tightness of the opposing alliance, and by a growing shift in military capabilities in favor of the new Triple Entente. States that are the furthest apart on measures of power are the least likely to fight each other. Both sides can easily calculate who would win in a military showdown, and the weaker is likely to give in to all but the most extreme demands. Of course, the weaker side does not always give in, as was apparent in the confrontation between the United States and Iraq. Nor does the stronger state always win a war. The United States easily defeated Iraq, but two decades earlier it lost heavily to North Vietnam.

Why is change so threatening to international peace and stability? In a classic statement, A. F. K. Organski argued that "nations are reluctant to fight unless they

---

[25] For discussions of the differential growth of power, power transition, and system change, see Robert Gilpin, *War and Change in World Politics* (Cambridge: Cambridge University Press, 1981); Paul Kennedy, *The Rise and Fall of the Great Powers* (New York: Random House, 1988); and Jacek Kugler and A. F. K. Organski, "The Power Transition: A Retrospective and Prospective Evaluation," in Manus Midlarsky, ed., *Handbook of War Studies* (Boston: Unwin Hyman, 1989), pp. 171–194.

believe they have a good chance of winning, but this is true for both sides only when the two are fairly evenly matched, or at least they believe they are."[26] Organski focuses on the period of "power transition," when a rising challenger approximates the power of the dominant state: "If great change occurs within a single lifetime, both challenger and dominant nation may find it difficult to estimate their relative power correctly, and may stumble into a war that would never have been fought if both sides had foreseen where the victory would lie." It is the condition of change that affects calculations of relative power. The challenger may start a war because it thinks that now, for the first time, it has a good chance to win, or the dominant power may foresee its own strength declining and thus calculate that it is better to fight now, while it still has some advantages, than to risk waiting until its position may be significantly worse. Change makes calculations of power and war outcomes difficult because the evidence is ambiguous (even though the decisionmakers may not see the ambiguity). Decisionmakers may miscalculate; miscalculations may then lead to the escalation of small wars, creating a period when major wars are especially likely.

Organski also suggests that "a rapid rise in power . . . produces dissatisfaction in itself," based perhaps in the perceptions of relative deprivation, status, and hierarchy discussed in earlier in this chapter. This means that the newly powerful state has not yet acquired respect or status as an equal power, so its leaders seek ways to gain respect. Under these changing conditions they may be more willing to risk going to war. Earlier we noted Germany's feeling of deprivation when its rapid economic and military growth was not matched by a "place in the sun" with the other great powers. This attitude played a part in Germany's uncritical support of its ally Austria-Hungary, whose attack on Serbia alarmed Russia and brought on the First World War.

Other analysts associate system change with international instability, but go further to suggest that these transformations, and the global wars that go with them, occur at fairly regular intervals. George Modelski, for example, has identified "long cycles" in global politics, each lasting approximately a hundred years. Modelski says that global wars, fought by major powers, result in the establishment of a dominant world power and thus a high concentration of political, military, and economic capabilities. This concentration cannot last forever. Dominant states lose their economic dynamism; they overextend themselves militarily; they may lose their will to dominate. As dominance wanes over a century-long period and new challengers rise, the conditions for the next global war are created. More recent work finds global cycles of shorter duration, with periods of economic expansion making it possible for the major powers to sustain big wars.[27]

---

[26] This and the following quotations are from A. F. K. Organski, *World Politics*, 2nd ed. (New York: Knopf, 1968), pp. 294, 480, 361. Work on the likelihood of changes in relative power leading to war includes: A. F. K. Organski and Jacek Kugler, *The War Ledger* (Chicago: University of Chicago Press, 1981), and Jacek Kugler and Douglas Lemke, eds., *Parity and War: Evaluations and Extensions of* The War Ledger (Ann Arbor: University of Michigan Press, 1996).

[27] George Modelski, ed., *Exploring Long Cycles* (Boulder, Colo.: Rienner, 1987). For a review of long-cycle and similar theories of global war, see William. R. Thompson, *On Global War: Historical-Structural Approaches to World Politics* (Columbia: University of South Carolina Press, 1988). Joshua S. Goldstein, in *Long Cycles in War and Economic Growth* (New Haven, Conn.: Yale University Press, 1988), finds a relationship between economic cycles and cycles of war and peace.

What might third-image explanations tell us about the current international system and the prospects for stability and peace? The essentially bipolar structure of the cold war is gone. The changes in the relative strength of the poles came first from differing internal rates of economic growth (the failure of Soviet-style command economies compared with market ones) and then from the Soviet Union's loss of allies. The end of the cold war involved no power transition, nor was a power transition even approached. Systemic change occurred, but without general war. In this case, the challenger simply faded back. If we were to take seriously the arguments about why bipolar systems are more stable than multipolar ones, we might fear that the new configuration would become more prone to war — especially if we considered the new system closer to a multipolar one than to a unipolar one. A rapid change in the relative power of the leading states could be grounds for concern. What if the current Russian leadership is unable to reform and stimulate the Russian economy, or if a rapidly growing China and a new, anti-Western government in Russia were to ally with each other? Alternatively, the problem of a new power transition, with China surpassing the United States, may present itself.[28]

Most third image theories in international relations do not allow us to predict war and peace into the future unless we can also predict, independently, the conditions that make war or peace more likely. Whether the international system will be peaceful in, say, 2050 depends on whether the distribution of power is bipolar, multipolar, or in transition — and in the year 2000 we have no way of knowing which of those conditions, or any others, will exist. But here theories of long cycles stand out as an exception. These theories differ on the exact duration of the long cycle, but they agree that global war is associated with decline of hegemonic power and that the current hegemon is the United States. Predictions for the next phase of hegemonic decline, the most dangerous phase of the long cycle, vary from circa 2020 to 2050, depending on the analyst. Such scenarios for the outbreak of global war are not pleasant to contemplate, and we can only hope that other developments in world politics will invalidate long cycle theory for the twenty-first century and beyond.

War and Rational Choice

The international system — its distribution of power, whether static or in the process of transformation — provides a context within which conflict between states is more or less likely. Of course, the international contexts that are most conducive to conflict versus stability depend on what theories we find most persuasive in light of the evidence. Whatever our conclusion, however, third-image explanations tell us little about the actual calculations and decisions that bring states into war with one another or keep them in peace. Historians and political scientists have examined in great detail the sequence of events, and the decisions preceding them, that erupted in specific wars like World War I, as well as those that stopped short of war like the Cuban Missile Crisis. The wealth of historical detail available to students of war and peace makes constructing general models of decision making difficult indeed.

---

[28] Bruce Russett and Allan C. Stam, "Courting Disaster: An Expanded NATO vs. Russia and China," *Political Science Quarterly* 113, 3 (1998): pp. 361–82.

As we suggested at the beginning of Chapter 7, many adopt a rational choice approach to the study of international conflict, which often involves the application of game theory. We can illustrate this approach through the use of a "decision tree," as depicted in Figure 8.1. The figure sketches the interaction of two states, *A* and *B*. At each node in the diagram (the circles), either state *A* or state *B* must make a decision. That decision will then require decision by the other state, and the interaction continues until some outcome is achieved (as indicated by the squares). At each node, we assume that the state chooses the course of action that will lead to the best outcome for that state. Consider the bottom-most node on the right-hand side of the tree, where state *A* must decide whether to use force or not. The situation has gotten to that point because *A* made a demand of *B* and *B* in turn made a demand of *A*. If war is expected to yield a better outcome for *A* than a negotiated settlement, then *A* will choose to use force.

Now consider the third node down the left side of the tree, where *A* must decide whether or not to make a counterdemand. This situation has resulted because, although *A* made no demand of *B*, *B* did, in turn, make a demand of *A*. State *A* must now contemplate three possible outcomes of its decision: *A*'s acquiescence to *B*'s demand, *B*'s use of force in response to *A*'s counterdemand, or a negotiated settlement. In deciding whether or not to make a counter demand, *A* must therefore consider the utility of each of these outcomes, as well as the probability that each will occur. Of course, state *A* knows with certainty that electing not to make a counter demand will

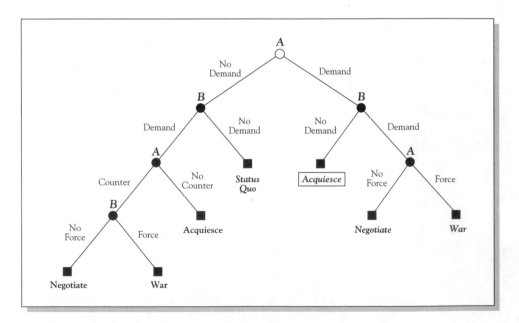

FIGURE 8.1   Decision Tree Depicting an International Interaction Game

Source: Adapted from Bruce Bueno de Mesquita and David Lalman, *War and Reason: Domestic and International Imperatives* (New Haven, Conn.: Yale University Press, 1992), p. 30.

mean its acquiescence; but if A is to make a counter demand, the outcome will depend on B's decision to respond with force or to seek a negotiated settlement. Even if A prefers a negotiated settlement to acquiescence, it is not in A's interest to make a counterdemand of B if B is likely to respond with force.

It may be that many real-world interactions between states can be located somewhere on this sort of a decision tree. To predict actual outcomes, we must have information about the relative value of each outcome to the states involved and their own estimates of the likelihood of each outcome. The recurring confrontations between the United States and Iraq over UN weapons inspections will serve as an illustration. In January and February 1998, and again in November of that year, the United States was on the verge of mounting a military action against Iraq for its refusal to give UN weapons inspectors unfettered access to suspected weapons sites, in accordance with the terms of surrender that concluded the Gulf War. On both occasions when Iraq refused to grant access to the inspectors, the United States had a choice to make: to demand compliance with the UN inspection regime, or not. If the United States made no demand, there was no reason to expect that Iraq would, out of the blue, make its own demand of the United States. That is, in Figure 8.1, with the United States represented as A and Iraq as B, the left branch of the decision tree after the second node is not applicable to this particular case. There were only four possible outcomes (indicated in italics): UN weapons inspections remain suspended (status quo); Iraq grants unconditional access (B's acquiescence); Iraq grants conditional access, say, in return for an easing of the economic embargo (negotiate); or the U.S. employs military force against Iraq to enforce the inspection regime (war).

How did the two sides value these alternative outcomes? The Iraqis most preferred the status quo of suspended inspections and least preferred an American use of force. If they did have to permit inspections, they preferred that this be accompanied by an easing of the embargo (thus, status quo > negotiate > acquiescence > war). The United States most wanted to see an unconditional resumption to UN weapons inspections. The status quo was the worst alternative for the United States, and even compromise was unacceptable. Iraq had repeatedly flouted the UN inspections and the United States was determined to see them continue unimpeded (so, for the United States, acquiescence > war > negotiate > status quo). On both occasions, knowing that a failure to demand the resumption of inspections would mean a continuation of the status quo, the United States insisted on full Iraqi compliance, and backed this up with a military buildup in the Gulf. The Iraqis, for their part, knew that pressing their own demands for the easing of economic sanctions would result in American military action, so unconditional compliance with the inspection regime was their best option. In both February and November 1998, inspections were allowed to resume and military action was averted. The actual story, of course, is more complicated than this, but here we probably have the essence of the strategic interaction between the United States and Iraq during these two crises.

But U.S. military action was not averted during the subsequent crisis in December 1998 and the months to follow. What happened? One possibility is that Saddam Hussein misjudged the Clinton administration's preferences, and thus its resolve. *If* the administration had actually preferred a negotiated settlement to the use of military force, then an Iraqi refusal to acquiesce in the face of the U.S. demand to resume inspections would have resulted in a negotiated settlement. Such a miscalculation on the part of Saddam Hussein could account for the "war" outcome. Another possibility is that Iraq itself actually preferred the war outcome to acquiescence. Several observers suggested that Iraq really had nothing left to lose by provoking U.S. military strikes, and possibly something to gain if those strikes served to split the permanent members of the UN Security Council, whose unanimity seemed central to a continuation of both the inspection regime and the economic embargo. Indeed, Russia and China strongly opposed the use of American (and British) military force against Iraq, and France signaled its displeasure by criticizing both sides for escalating the crisis.

In this game-theoretic model of the crisis (or crises) each side tries to anticipate future sequences of events and then eliminates present courses of action that may result in the least favorable outcomes. This way of "solving" the game is referred to as *backward induction* and is a powerful tool for predicting outcomes when information about the actors' preferences is known. It is important to keep in mind that successful predictions depend fundamentally on getting each side's preferences right, and that is the hard part. However, even in the absence of definitive estimates of the actors' preference orderings, these very simple models can still be useful for understanding the ways in which crisis situations and calculations (or miscalculations) of the actors involved may lead to deadly outcomes.

One study found that a model only slightly more complicated than the one shown in Figure 8.1 helped to explain the outcomes of 469 disputes between European states between 1815 and 1970. It also helped to account for another 238 nondisputatious interactions drawn at random. The hardest part of this or any such study is judging the preferences held by state leaders, the degree of certainty or uncertainty in their expectations, and certain psychological factors important in decision making like the tendency to take or avoid risks. Sometimes this information can be estimated based on available historical data; at other times, specialists on certain areas of the world and certain time periods can be consulted and their judgments used in the analysis.[29] In its various forms, game theory has emerged as a promising approach to the study of conflict between states.

Conflict within States

The main forms of contemporary nonstate violence have been guerrilla warfare and terrorism. Both are revolutionary activities, challenging the rule and authority of governments. Some observers have called these "new" forms of international violence, but

---

[29] See Bruce Bueno de Mesquita and David Lalman, *War and Reason: Domestic and International Imperatives* (New Haven, Conn.: Yale University Press, 1992). For a review of this and similar work, see Bruce Russett, "Processes of Dyadic Choice for War and Peace," *World Politics* 47, 2 (January 1995): pp. 268–282. An analysis that makes use of information provided by area specialists is Bruce Bueno de Mesquita, David Newman, and Alvin Rabushka, *Red Flag over Hong Kong* (Chatham, N.J.: Chatham House, 1996). This is not a study of international conflict per se, but rather an effort to forecast developments in Hong Kong after the transition to Chinese rule.

in fact each has a long history. What is new is their prominence in the changing patterns of international conflict. According to some data, 80 percent of the wars between 1900 and 1941 were of the traditional sort, waged by the armed forces of two or more states. Since 1945 about 80 percent of violent conflict has occurred on the territory of only one state and has been internally oriented.[30]

Ethnopolitics, Rebellion, and Civil War

Many conflicts in contemporary international politics arise from threats (or perceived threats) to group identification and loyalty. One problem is that states and nations may not coincide on the same territory. The separate nationalisms of different ethnic groups may threaten to tear a state apart, as in the former Yugoslavia. Different national identities within a state may tempt another state to intervene on behalf of a minority. Sometimes a feeling of nationality may spill over many states, calling into question the legitimacy of separate states (as in the case of pan-Arab nationalism). States may therefore suppress minority rights (Bulgaria long prohibited public use of the Turkish language by its Turkish minority); they may force minorities to emigrate (as Vietnam forced the ethnic Chinese boat people to flee) or may even kill them (as Nazi Germany systematically killed Jews). Although we commonly refer to entities in the international system as nation-states, there are in fact many multinational states and multistate nations. The mismatch of state and nation has been the cause of much conflict in world politics.[31]

In the post–World War II system, states with no logic beyond the arbitrary boundary lines drawn on maps by colonial powers are split by diverse tribal, religious, ethnic, and racial groups and are struggling to forge group loyalty from this diversity. Kazakhstan is representative of the potential problems confronting some former Soviet states — less than 45 percent of the population are Kazakhs, over one-third are ethnic Russians, and about 100 other ethnic groups exist in a country that is about four times the size of Texas. While no one factor appears to be sufficient to account for group loyalty, it may be that a cleavage along any of these lines is sufficient to bring about **ethnopolitical** or **communal conflict.** The pressures toward separatism or fragmentation in the world system are powerful and widespread. Most modern states are mosaics of distinct peoples, and their security and aspirations often are not respected by those in control of the central government.[32]

States have fought intense civil wars over unity or separation. The Ibo rebellion and the attempt to establish Biafra was defeated by the Nigerian government in a war

---

[30] Two classic studies of the causes of internal conflict are Harry Eckstein, "On the Etiology of Internal Wars," *History and Theory* 4, 2 (1965): pp. 133–163; and Gurr, *Why Men Rebel.* Recent discussions include Michael Brown, ed., *The International Dimensions of Internal Conflict* (Cambridge, Mass.: MIT Press, 1996); and Steven R. David, "Internal War: Causes and Cures," *World Politics* 49, 4 (July 1997): pp. 552–576.

[31] See Walker Conner, *Ethnonationalism: The Quest for Understanding* (Princeton, N.J.: Princeton University Press, 1994).

[32] Donald Horowitz, *Ethnic Groups in Conflict* (Berkeley: University of California Press, 1985); Chaim Kaufmann, "Possible and Impossible Solutions to Ethnic Civil War," *International Security* 20, 4 (Spring 1996): pp. 136–175.

that lasted from May 1967 to January 1970. In contrast, the Bengali secession from Pakistan was successful. The Bengali population of East Pakistan rose in riots and instituted a general strike in March 1971 after being denied victory at the polls. Though sharing a common religion, East and West Pakistan differed in ethnicity, language, and economic factors and were separated by approximately 1,000 miles of Indian territory. West Pakistani armed attacks on the East Pakistanis led to the December 1971 war between India and Pakistan. The Indian victory permitted the Bengalis to declare their own independent state, Bangladesh. India, a large and diverse country, has itself been wracked by conflict among different linguistic, regional, racial, and religious groups. Violence involving the Sikh religious minority in the Punjab was responsible for the assassination of Prime Minister Indira Gandhi in 1984. Her son, Prime Minister Rajiv Gandhi, was assassinated in 1991 by a Tamil group who blamed him for India's abandonment of the Tamil separatist movement in Sri Lanka. The 1990s also saw the intensification of a Muslim drive for an independent Kashmir and insurgent separatism in the northeast state of Assam. Such communal conflict was intensified by a revival of Hindu nationalism and the rise to power of the Bharatiya Janata Party (BJP).

Fears of a breakdown in nationalism, however, are not confined to the less developed states or only to those states formed since World War II. Loyalty is based on group interaction. If some part of a group feels it is being exploited or not treated fairly, or that there no longer exists mutual benefit from association with the larger group, the loyalty and we-feeling will disintegrate. The *process* of national integration is a continuous one, and unless tended to, it is always susceptible to disintegration. The most graphic instance of disintegration is seen in the violent aftermath of the breakup of Yugoslavia. We can also see its effects in the rapid dissolution of the Soviet Union — and in Russia after that, where the government fought a bloody war against Chechnyan rebels from December 1994 until August 1996.

While many new developing countries must worry about diverse ethnic groups that lack strong feelings of national unity, even the older states of Europe must continually work to make ethnic minorities *feel* a nationalist connection to the nation-state as a whole. There are more or less well-organized nationalist movements among the Bretons and Corsicans who are governed by France, the Basques in Spain, and the Welsh and Scots in Britain. In Canada, French speakers in the province of Quebec have a long tradition of separatist politics. Canada's handling of this problem is a good example of how an established and developed state risks being broken apart and of the dilemmas that a democracy faces in such a situation. Attempts at nation building included the institutionalization of bilingualism, special constitutional arrangements, and the creation of specifically Canadian images for the national flag and national anthem (the previous flag had incorporated the British Union Jack and the anthem had been "God Save the Queen"). That political crises continue to occur in Canada over the proper constitutional arrangements required to deal with the separatist movement in Quebec and yet satisfy the western provinces indicates the difficulties of building and maintaining a state.

The Minorities at Risk Project reports that during the 1990–1995 period, 115 countries (or about two-thirds) were home to substantial ethnic groups that were politically active. In 40 percent of these states, ethnic groups constituted more than one-quarter of the total population. As we can see from Table 8.4, a total of 268 groups were active during this period, and 112 of these were engaged in active rebellion against the central government: political banditry, campaigns of terrorism, guerilla activity, or civil war. There were 33 groups in 23 countries that were involved in large-scale guerilla or protracted civil war against the government. Many groups are also engaged in *intercommunal* conflict; 105 groups participated in sporadic violent attacks against other groups or anti-group demonstrations, with more than half these taking part in more severe communal rioting or warfare. The human costs of ethnopolitical conflict are immense. In 1993 to 1994 alone, they caused nearly 4 million deaths and the displacement of almost 27 million refugees; more than 60 percent of these deaths and displacements occurred in Africa, many as the result of the intense communal conflict between the Hutus and Tutsis in Rwanda and Burundi.[33]

TABLE 8.4 Ethnopolitical Groups: Rebellion and War, 1990–1995				

Region	States with Active Groups	Number of Active Groups	Groups in Active Rebellion	Groups Fighting Wars
Western Democracies and Japan	13	30	11	0
East Europe and former USSR	25	59	16	8
Asia	19	57	32	7
North Africa and Middle East	11	26	11	6
Sub-Saharan Africa	30	66	32	11
Latin America and Caribbean	17	30	10	1
Total	*115*	*268*	*112*	*33*

Note: The last column includes groups engaged in large-scale guerilla activity or protracted civil wars.

Source: Compiled from data released by the Minorities at Risk Project, "Tracking the Status and Condition of Ethnopolitical Groups Around the Globe," March 22, 1998, [cited August 4, 1998]; available at <http://www.bsos.umd. edu/cidcm/mar/>.

---

[33] Figures for deaths and displacements come from Ted Robert Gurr, "Peoples against States: Ethnopolitical Conflict and the Changing World System," *International Studies Quarterly* 38 (1994): pp. 347–377. Other figures are compiled from data released by the Minorities at Risk Project, "Tracking the Status and Condition of Ethnopolitical Groups Around the Globe," March 22, 1998 [cited August 4, 1998]; available at <http://www.bsos.umd.edu/cidcm/mar/>. A recent report from the Minorities at Risk Project is Ted Robert Gurr and Will H. Moore, "Ethnopolitical Rebellion: A Cross-Sectional Analysis of the 1980s with Risk Assessments for the 1990s," *American Journal of Political Science* 41, 4 (October 1997): pp. 1079–1103.

Internal armed conflict is much more prevalent than interstate conflict. The Uppsala Conflict Data Project reports that during 1997 there were thirty-three separate armed conflicts in progress in twenty-six states (see Table 8.5). Only one of these, the latest in the long-running series of clashes between India and Pakistan over the Kashmir, was an interstate conflict. All the rest were internal: conflicts over the composition of government or the type of political system ("government"), or conflicts over secession or territorial autonomy ("territory"). Three of these conflicts — in Congo, Sierra Leone, and Zaire — did involve some kind of foreign intervention, but the vast majority were purely internal affairs. Africa and Asia remain the most conflict-ridden regions of the globe, as they were throughout the cold war.[34]

Unconventional Conflict

The labels "unconventional" and "irregular" are often used to describe conflicts that do not take the form of mass armies engaging one another on the battlefield, or the traditional air- and sea-based military operations in support of such engagements. Guerrilla warfare — operations conducted by paramilitary forces in enemy-held territory — has been labeled as such, but guerrilla tactics have become so widespread since World War II, especially since the wars of decolonization, that it hardly seems correct to call them unconventional.[35] In any event, the kind of conflicts we have in mind are those in which combatants on one or more sides in a dispute avoid pitched military battles with the enemy. In the case of guerrilla warfare, combatants stage raids, ambushes, and sabotage from remote and inaccessible bases in mountains, forests, jungles, or the territory of neighboring states. Virtually all conflicts within states have at one time or another involved guerrilla warfare, and most have witnessed some form of terrorism.

Although governments and other actors usually intend to morally condemn unconventional tactics when they refer to "guerrillas" or "terrorists" — as opposed to "freedom fighters" — groups usually resort to such tactics out of necessity. They typically command few resources and must pursue cost-effective methods of military combat and political disruption. In the modern era, given to great disparities in the capacity of different groups to muster political, economic, and military power, it is perhaps not surprising that more and more of the disadvantaged have turned to unconventional means. They do have a long history, however. In the first century C.E., the Jewish Zealots employed these tactics in their attempt to dislodge Roman forces occupying what is now Israel, and culminating in the storied siege of Masada by the Roman Tenth Legion. Although they were not all terrorists, many in the nineteenth-century anarchist movement in western Europe and Russia advocated such tactics, especially

---

[34] Wallensteen and Sollenberg, "Armed Conflict and Regional Conflict Complexes, 1989–1997."
[35] For an overview of the changing character of warfare, see Martin van Creveld, *The Transformation of War* (New York: Free Press, 1991).

TABLE 8.5 Armed Conflicts in 1997

Location	Issue	Severity
Middle East (3)		
Egypt	Government	Minor
Israel	Territory (Palestine)	Intermediate
Turkey	Territory (Kurdistan)	War
Asia (14)		
Afghanistan	Government	War
Cambodia	Government	Intermediate
India		
Kashmir	Territory	Intermediate
Assam	Territory	Intermediate
Manipur	Territory	Minor
Nagaland/Manipur	Territory	Minor
Tripura	Territory	Minor
Andhra Pradesh, etc.	Government	Minor
India-Pakistan	Territory (Kashmir)	Intermediate
Indonesia	Territory (East Timor)	Intermediate
Myanmar		
Karen	Territory	Intermediate
Shan	Territory	Intermediate
Philippines	Territory (Mindanao)	Minor
Sri Lanka	Territory (Tamil)	War

continued

TABLE 8.5   Armed Conflicts in 1997 *(continued)*

Location	Issue	Severity
Africa (14)		
Algeria	Government	War
Angola	Territory (Cabinda)	Minor
Burundi	Government	Intermediate
Chad	Government	Minor
Comoros	Territory (Anjouan)	Minor
Congo	Government	War
Ethiopia	Territory (Somali)	Minor
Niger		
Air and Azawad	Territory	Minor
Toubou	Territory	Minor
Senegal	Territory (Casamance)	Intermediate
Sierre Leone	Government	Intermediate
Sudan	Government/Territory	War
Uganda	Government	Intermediate
Zaire	Government	War
Americas (2)		
Columbia	Government	Intermediate
Peru	Government	Intermediate

Note: A Minor conflict is one involving fewer than 1,000 battle-related deaths since its inception. An Intermediate conflict is one involving more than 1,000 deaths since its inception, but fewer than 1,000 during 1997. A war involves more than 1,000 deaths during 1997.

Source: Data compiled by the Uppsala Conflict Data Project, Department of Peace and Conflict Research, Uppsala University, and published in Peter Wallensteen and Margareta Sollenberg, "Armed Conflict and Regional Conflict Complexes," *Journal of Peace Research* 35, 5 (September 1998): 621–634.

political assassination; Italian King Humbert I, U.S. President William McKinley, Greek King George I, and French President Marie François Sadi Carnot were all victims of anarchist assassination.

Terrorism

The principal purpose of **terrorism** is not the actual destruction produced but its dramatic and psychological effects on populations and governments. Brian Jenkins has said that "terrorism is theater." The objectives of terrorism are to frighten target audiences through the use of dramatic and shocking acts, which include bombings, assassinations, kidnappings, the taking of hostages, and hijackings.[36] Although guerrilla groups sometimes employ such tactics, terrorism is not the same as guerrilla warfare. Terrorist acts are not directed toward enemy combatants; their targets are civilians, government workers, or noncombatant military personnel. It involves the systematic use of violence for political ends, an ongoing series of acts intended to produce fear that will change attitudes and behavior toward governments.

Nonstate actors at various points in time have sought to undermine governments by making them appear weak, ineffectual, and unable to protect the population. Terrorists wish to gain publicity and attention and to convince the people and government that they are an important political force. Terrorism also weakens governmental support when the government responds indiscriminately with its police and military forces to terrorist acts, "retaliating" on sectors of the population not connected with the terrorists. Thus, a government may actually help the antigovernment group by alienating ordinary citizens. Because governments find it so hard to punish those responsible, terrorism can be a frustratingly effective weapon. Some of the most prominent terrorist groups in recent years include Aum Shinrikyo in Japan, the Basques (ETA) in Spain, the Islamic Resistance Movement (HAMAS) in Israel, the Irish Republican Army (IRA), the Tamil Tigers in Sri Lanka, the Kurdistan Workers' Party (PKK) in Turkey, and the Shining Path (Sendero Luminoso) in Peru. The twin bombings of the American embassies in Kenya and Tanzania in 1998, attributed to Osama bin Laden and his Al Qaeda movement, sparked talk of a new kind of transnational terrorist — one without commitment to any particular territory (and without territorial aspirations), and one skilled in the use of transnational communications and financial networks as a means of coordinating the activities of his dispersed followers.

It is important to distinguish dissident terrorism from establishment terrorism, or **state terrorism.** States also use terror against their own populations to gain or increase control through fear. Tactics include expulsion or exile, failure to protect some citizens from the crimes of others (as in state-tolerated vigilante groups), arbitrary arrest, beatings, kidnappings ("disappearances"), torture, and murder. This use of terror also has a long history. Two famous historical examples of the systematic use of terror by

---

[36] Brian M. Jenkins, *International Terrorism: The Other World War* (Santa Monica, Calif.: Rand, 1985). For more recent discussions, see Walter Laqueur, "Postmodern Terrorosm," *Foreign Affairs* 75, 5 (September/October 1996): pp. 24–36; and Bruce Hoffman, *Inside Terrorism* (New York: Columbia University Press, 1998).

governments against internal opposition are France during the Terror of 1793–1794 and the Soviet Union under Stalin during the "purges" of the 1930s. One scholar has chronicled "democide" — genocide and mass murder — during the twentieth century. From 1900 to 1987 almost 170 million people have been killed by their own governments, far more people than killed in wars. The major "megamurderers" during this period were the most authoritarian states — the Soviet Union, the People's Republic of China, Germany (from 1933 to 1945), and Nationalist China (from 1928 to 1949); the least murderous countries were democracies. One conclusion drawn by the author is that, "Power kills, absolute power kills absolutely."[37]

Another form of terrorism is **state-sponsored terrorism** — international terrorist activity conducted by states or, more often, the support of terrorist groups through the provision of arms, training, safehaven, or financial backing. In sponsoring terrorism against other governments, a state pursues the same objective mentioned above: weakening the control of governments of other states by hurting and embarrassing them. In this sense states are using the actions of terrorist groups in surrogate warfare. As of 1998 the U.S. government designated seven states as sponsors of terrorism, but Iran and Libya stand out as especially active (the others include Cuba, Iraq, North Korea, Sudan, and Syria).[38] Iran is accused of supporting the Hezbollah in Lebanon, the Palestine Islamic Jihad, HAMAS, the PKK, and other groups. Libya has been implicated in the bombings of a Berlin discotheque in 1986, Pan Am Flight 103 over Scotland in 1988, and UTA Flight 772 over Niger in 1989.

Figure 8.2 shows the trend in international terrorism over the last thirty years. From 1968 the number of terrorist incidents rose steadily to its peak of 666 incidents in 1987; since then the number of terrorist acts has been declining. Terrorism-related casualties (deaths plus injuries) have shown no clear trend over the years. The huge increase in casualties during 1995 reflects the sarin gas attack on the Tokyo subway system by Aum Shinrikyo, which killed eleven and injured thousands.[39]

We can see from Table 8.6 (page 210) where international terrorist incidents take place. According to U.S. State Department statistics, of the 2,721 international terrorist incidents between 1991 and 1997, the areas with the greatest number of incidents were Europe (37.9 percent) and Latin America (30.5 percent). Recall from Table 8.4 that both Western Europe and Latin America had the *fewest* internal "conventional" conflicts. Africa, with its large number of internal armed conflicts, accounted for less than 3 percent of terrorist incidents and fewer than 2 percent of total casualties — although these shares were drastically different in 1998 due to the two American embassy bombings,

---

[37] See Rudolph J. Rummel, *Death by Government: Genocide and Mass Murder since 1900* (New Brunswick, N.J.: Transaction, 1994).

[38] U.S. Department of State, "Patterns of Global Terrorism: 1997," April 1998 [cited August 5, 1998]; available at <http://www.state.gov/www/ global/terrorism/gt_index.html>. For an overview of state-sponsored terrorism, see Michael Stohl and George A. Lopez, eds., *Terrible beyond Endurance? The Foreign Policy of State Terrorism* (Westport, Conn.: Greenwood, 1988).

[39] For an empirical analysis of trends in international terrorism during and after the cold war, see Walter Enders and Todd Sandler, "Transnational Terrorism in the Post–Cold War Era," *International Studies Quarterly* 43 (March 1999): pp. 145–167. They conclude that, contrary to the impression given by the media, there has been a reduction in terrorism since the end of the cold war.

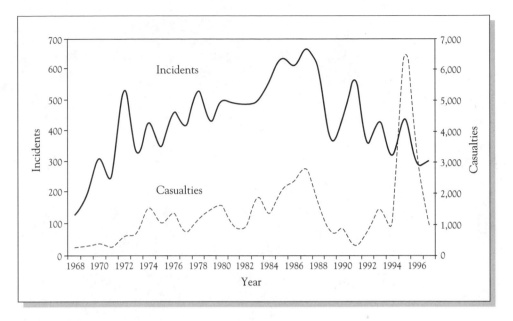

FIGURE 8.2   International Terrorism, 1968–1997

Note: Casualties include killed and wounded.

Sources: U.S. Department of State, *Patterns of Global Terrorism,* 1996 and 1997 reports [cited August 5, 1998]; available at <http://www.state.gov/www/global terrorism/gt_index.html>; 1981 and 1984 reports reprinted in Robert A. Friedlander, ed., *Terrorism: Documents of International and Local Control,* vols. 4, 6 (New York: Oceana, 1984, 1992).

which killed more than 250 and wounded nearly 5,000. Contrasting figures on internal war and terrorism indicate that terrorism is indeed the weapon of groups that are relatively weak — in comparison to their goals and their opponents — and is used in areas where such groups cannot mount some form of organized military challenge to the government. As with guerrilla war, the instruments of terrorism are constantly and consciously directed toward political influence and political ends.

Information Warfare

Access to information has long been an important element in warfighting. In the fourth century B.C.E. the philosopher-general Sun Tzu wrote: "Though the enemy be stronger in numbers, we may prevent him from fighting. Scheme so as to discover his plans and the likelihood of their success. Rouse him, and learn the principle of his activity and inactivity." In making one's own plans, he continued, "the highest pitch you can attain is to conceal them; conceal your dispositions." The success of the Golden Horde against numerically superior forces in Russia and eastern Europe during the thirteenth century rested on continuously updated information about the enemy's whereabouts and formation. Scouts and messengers (the "arrow riders") were able to apprise Batu

TABLE 8.6   International Terrorism by Region, 1991–1997

Region	Percent of Incidents	Percent of Casualties
Africa	2.8	1.5
Asia	6.2	55.7
Eurasia	3.5	1.7
Europe	37.9	8.3
Latin America	30.5	6.5
Middle East	18.4	19.3
North America	0.7	7.2
Total Number	*2,721*	*14,137*

Source: Compiled from U.S. Department of State, "Patterns of Global Terrorism," 1996 and 1997 reports, [cited August 5, 1998]; available at <http://www.state.gov/www/global/terrorism/gt_index.html>.

Khan of developments within four or five days, which during this period was the closest thing to "real-time" intelligence. At the same time, Mongol advantages in mobility and deception enabled them to keep their own location secret. Armed with superior information, the Horde could strike at the enemy's communications causing disarray and undermining any numerical advantage. When the Mongols advanced into Syria and Egypt, however, they met their match in the Mamelukes who, among other displays of military prowess, made use of carrier pigeons.[40]

Information warfare involves the manipulation, corruption, or denial of information. It can include many things, from disruption of an opponent's ability to command and control its military forces (à la Golden Horde) to psychological tactics, like the broadcasts of Tokyo Rose during World War II or the rock-and-roll music blasted by U.S. Marines in Panama in their attempt to drive dictator Manuel Noriega out of the Vatican embassy. Other forms still inhabit the realm of speculation, especially those tactics that are often referred to as "cyberwar" or "hacker war." Although we have not yet witnessed this sort of information warfare, imagining the form that it might take

---

[40] See Sun Tzu, *The Art of War*, edited by James Clavell (New York: Delacorte, 1983), p. 28. The contemporary relevance of the Mongol way of warfare is discussed in John Arquilla and David Ronfeldt, "Cyberwar Is Coming!" *Comparative Strategy* 12, 2 (Spring 1993): pp. 141–165.

and protecting against it has become a preoccupation of the defense establishments of the United States and many other industrialized countries.

Technological advances in communication and computation have been integrated into the modern military as part of the so-called "revolution in military affairs" (RMA). Many aspects of information warfare, therefore, represent advances in the conduct of conventional conflicts between states or between states and nonstate actors. The precision-guided munitions ("smart bombs") launched by American forces against Iraq's communications network during the Gulf War was the application of new technology to an otherwise old objective in warfare. The psychological operations conducted by the U.S. Army prior to the 1994 invasion of Haiti, in which pro-Aristide leaflets were tailored to specific segments of the population based on market-research techniques, was simply a sophisticated use of wartime propaganda.

Other techniques of information warfare, as yet untried, may become tools for waging unconventional conflict. Such "info-terrorism" might take the form of inserting a computer virus into telephone-switching software thereby disrupting the phone system, or planting a "logic bomb" set to go off at a specified time to wreak havoc on the electronic routers controlling a commuter rail line. Air and ground transportation, financial and stock markets, telecommunications networks, electric power grids, and many other aspects of modern civil society rely on computer programs for their smooth functioning and, hypothetically at least, could be subject to hacker attacks. The effort required to attend to the so-called year 2000 (Y2K) problem — the need to reprogram systems that could not distinguish between the year 2000 and year 1900 because both were stored as "00" — gave some indication of the prevalence of computers and computer software in the management of our daily lives. Since terrorists cannot muster the resources necessary to engage the enemy militarily, a laptop and modem would seem ideally suited to their needs.[41]

There may also be a tendency to overstate the importance of information warfare for future conflict between and within states. As we have said, targeting an opponent's command and communications facilities and engaging in psychological operations have long been elements in military conflict. The information revolution has enhanced such capacities, in the case of modern militaries, but did not invent them. Info-terrorism targeted at the civilian population — sometimes called "netwar" because it aims at the networks connecting society — would constitute more of a break with the past. Still, it is somewhat ironic that the very developments that seem to usher in the possibility of information warfare also suggest limits to its effectiveness. For every accomplished hacker there is an equally accomplished computer security specialist. Moreover, networks, including computer and communications networks, are webs with multiple pathways between any two points. Although that may provide the info-terrorist many more points from which to hack into crucial systems, for every way in there is a way around. Well-designed backup systems take advantage of network

---

[41] The implications of the information revolution for both conventional and unconventional conflict were brought to popular attention by futurists Alvin Toffler and Heidi Toffler in their *War and Anti-War: Survival at the Dawn of the Twenty-first Century* (Boston: Little, Brown, 1993). See also John Arquilla and David Ronfeldt, eds., *In Athena's Camp: Preparing for Conflict in the Information Age* (Santa Monica, Calif.: Rand, 1997).

redundancy, allowing the stream of information to seek out alternative channels in the event of disruption. As we exit the era of mainframe computers and continue to move in the direction of distributed computing, this sort of redundancy will only increase.

It is perhaps a sad commentary on human evolution that advances in technology are almost immediately integrated into our methods of destruction. Indeed, as we will see in Chapter 12, the quest for improved military capability has often been the driving force behind technological progress. The Internet itself emerged from an effort by the U.S. defense establishment to create a robust communications infrastructure that would not collapse during a nuclear war. The relationship between technology, weaponry, and conflict is complex one, which we continue to explore in the next chapter.

9

The Security Dilemma: Armament and Disarmament

Armed Forces

The armed forces play an important role in politics within and between states. The need to support and supply mass armies was a central driving force in the evolution of the institutional apparatus of the modern state in fifteenth- and sixteenth-century Europe. Even today the armed forces are at the forefront of state building and modernization in many countries, often in relatively young states that were formerly part of colonial empires. The conduct of foreign relations throughout history has been so infused with the acquisition, display, and use of military power that the study of international relations is sometimes, but erroneously, equated with the study of military affairs — or simply "bombs and rockets." Although no student of world politics, having gotten this far in the book, would make such a mistake, this chapter is in fact about bombs and rockets, and about the politics and policies that surround their deployment, management, and, in the case of arms control, their decommissioning.

The military as an institution can trace its roots at least as far back as ancient Mesopotamia's standing armies equipped with bows and spears. Since then, armies and their means of conducting warfare have gone through many transformations, the most significant ones being linked to the evolution of technology. The horse-drawn chariot gave birth to the cavalry, gunpowder made possible explosive munitions, and the industrial revolution led to the development of mechanized fighting forces. Armies took to the air with advent of air travel, while the exploration of space permitted the intercontinental delivery of bombs by self-propelled ballistic missiles. Of course, the most profound and threatening of these many military-technological advances was the development of the atomic bomb. The deployment and proliferation of nuclear weapons prompted not only fundamental shifts in military strategy but also a widespread desire for progress in the area of arms control and disarmament.[1]

In Chapter 12 we will explore the political economy of defense and disarmament, which includes topics relating to military technology and the role of the state in promoting technological advancement in the pursuit of national security. In this chapter we focus more generally on arms acquisition by states, the dynamics of arms races, and the mixed historical record of arms control.

Arms Acquisition

Why do countries arm? One straightforward explanation — sometimes called the "action-reaction" hypothesis — is that states acquire arms in response to the arms acquisitions of their adversaries. Lewis F. Richardson, the most influential theorist of the arms acquisition process, pointed to the "very strong motive of fear, which moves each group to increase its armaments because of the existence of those of the opposing group."[2] When both sides are ensnared in this action-reaction process, we have the makings of an **arms race.** In the early cold-war years, it seemed to many Americans that the action-reaction phenomenon was all one way, that the United States was reacting to Soviet militarization (and other forms of aggressive behavior). However, when the period of isolation under Stalin drew to a close and Soviet and U.S. scientists began to make contact with each other, it became apparent that Soviet citizens typically held the mirror image of the American perspective: they saw the Soviet Union as simply reacting to American threats. From this exchange, people developed a more general understanding that in some real sense each side was reacting to the other and that it was extraordinarily difficult to sort out particular causes, especially once the action-reaction process was underway.

We can see from Figure 9.1 that Soviet and American military expenditures were more or less constant from the end of the Korean War until the early 1960s when they begin a clear move upward. An arms race need not imply an ever-escalating spiral. A race does imply competition, but if two long-distance runners maintain a steady pace,

[1] For broad historical overviews of developments in military technology and war fighting, see John Keegan, *A History of Warfare* (New York: Vintage, 1993); Martin Van Creveld, *Technology and War: From 2000 B.C. to the Present* (New York: Free Press, 1991); and Robert L. O'Connell, *Of Arms and Men: A History of War, Weapons, and Aggression* (New York: Oxford University Press, 1989).
[2] Lewis F. Richardson, *Arms and Insecurity: A Mathematical Study of the Causes and Origins of War* (Pittsburgh: Boxwood Press, 1960), p. 13.

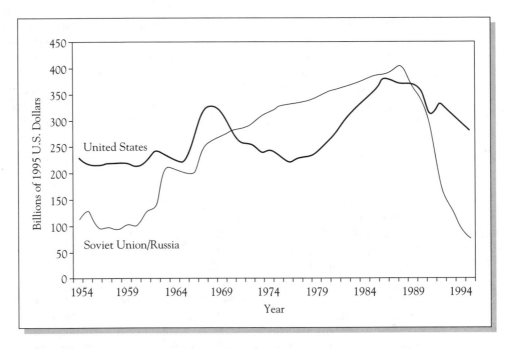

FIGURE 9.1 American and Soviet/Russian Military Expenditures, 1954–1995

Sources: For 1954–1962, Stockholm International Peace Research Institute, *World Armaments and Disarmament,* various years (Oxford: Oxford University Press). For 1963–1995, U.S. Arms Control and Disarmament Agency, *World Military Expenditures and Arms Transfers,* various years (Washington, D.C.: U.S. Government Printing Office). Soviet figures are based on estimates made by the U.S. intelligence community.

the race is progressing just as much as if their speeds were continually increasing. It is this element of competition, or *interaction*, that characterizes an arms race. Such interaction seemed to be present in Soviet and U.S. behavior throughout the cold war. It was not always a mechanical process of action and reaction, but moved in fits and starts in response to particular decisions that seemed especially provocative.[3] The notion of a race surely does not explain every element of superpower relations. It may tell us about interaction in arms spending at a general level but not about the presence or absence of competition in the acquisition of specific weapons systems. Moreover, the idea of interaction does not explain what happened in the 1970s. The action-reaction hypothesis suggests that the Soviet Union would have moderated its military spending once the Americans slowed down theirs after Vietnam. No such moderation took place, as we can see from Figure 9.1. Something other than a straightforward action-reaction process was driving Soviet military spending during these years.

---

[3] David Kinsella and Sam-man Chung, "The Long and the Short of an Arms Race," in Murray Wolfson, ed., *The Political Economy of War and Peace* (Boston: Kluwer, 1998), pp. 223–246.

Other explanations for arms acquisitions focus on domestic influences. One hypothesis refers to bureaucratic pressures or "inertia" within the government. As we saw earlier (in discussions of the organizational process model in Chapter 7), the leaders of large organizations are typically concerned with the well-being of their organizations, especially in maintaining or increasing their budgets. Moreover, a leader's own power in the government and in society at large depends heavily on the size of the organization. Just about the best predictor of the size of any organization's current budget is the size of its last budget. Military organizations are by no means exceptions to this observation.[4] Usually, when a major weapons system becomes outmoded or obsolete, the military organization will provide a ready interest group to press either to modernize the weapons or to replace them with something else that will do a similar job and keep the same people and resources employed. For example, as the B-52 bomber became more nearly obsolete, air force generals looked around for a new bomber, and the B-1 was developed to replace it. And because of the air force's organizational interests, air force evaluations of the merits of a proposed new strategic bomber were unlikely to be entirely objective.

This argument does not imply that military leaders are corrupt or that their advice to maintain or acquire a weapons system is necessarily mistaken. Their evaluation of the national interest and that of most objective observers might well coincide. But it does imply that decisions to reallocate resources within a government will be strongly resisted by those organizations, including the military, that are faced with budget reductions or the elimination of programs. In short, this year's military budget is a good predictor of next year's military budget. Another hypothesis suggests that many elements of society — labor unions, defense contractors, politicians, as well as government bureaucrats — have a stake in maintaining a high level of military spending. Together they constitute a **military-industrial complex,** and according to the radical perspective their influence is especially strong in capitalist states. A more balanced version of the argument recognizes the undo influence of an analogous military-industrial complex in socialist states.

Arms acquisitions are also caused, or at least facilitated by an expanding economy. In a growing economy more resources can be devoted to military purposes without reducing anyone's share of the expanding pie. By the same token, a stagnating economy may force leaders either to squeeze civilian needs or to cut back their military expansion. Part of Gorbachev's interest in ending the cold war and in arms control stemmed from the snowballing collapse of the Soviet economy from the accumulated strain of decades of military buildup.[5] Indeed, economic troubles for

---

[4] The most important early work on this topic was Otto Davis, M. A. H. Dempster, and Aaron Wildavsky, "A Theory of the Budgetary Process," *American Political Science Review* 60, 3 (September 1966): pp. 529–547; see also Aaron Wildavsky, *The New Politics of the Budgetary Process* (Boston: Scott, Foresman, 1988). For applications to the U.S. Department of Defense, see Arnold Kanter, *Defense Politics: A Budgetary Perspective* (Chicago: University of Chicago Press, 1979), and Stephen J. Majeski, "Dynamic Properties of the U.S. Military Expenditure Decision-Making Process," *Conflict Management and Peace Science* 7, 1 (Fall 1983): pp. 65–86.

[5] The Soviet economic collapse seems not to have been precipitated by pressures from the Reagan defense buildup but rather had begun earlier. See Fred Chernoff, "Ending the Cold War: The Soviet Retreat and the U.S. Military Buildup," *International Affairs* 67, 1 (1991): pp. 111–126.

both superpowers may well have been the most important force working to end the arms race.

Together, all the domestic influences seem so strong that some analysts have maintained that military-industrial complexes are essentially autistic actors that, like autistic children, shut themselves off almost completely from outside social stimuli and respond only to their own internal psyches. By this characterization, the arms race is not really a race at all, if by race we mean that the runners really care about each other's positions. The governmental and societal leaders in an autistic system maintain a level of military capability almost solely as a result of demands and pressures from within their own countries, not as a result of international incidents or military gains by the other "racer." By this explanation, states race against themselves; international events are irrelevant except as they provide an excuse for societal elites to demand sacrifices for military purposes. The enemy's actions thus become useful domestic propaganda to support policies that leaders desire on other grounds. Such an explanation certainly does not rule out some collusion between the leadership groups of two ostensibly competing countries, each acting aggressively to permit the other to justify its own buildup.

Which influences are most important? It is one thing to list the various things that may drive arms acquisition and quite another to assess the truth of the assertions or their relative importance. Most of the explanations seem plausible, and there is some evidence for each. Nazli Choucri and Robert North report that for most of the major powers in the years before World War I a host of factors contributed to increases in military expenditures, including those we have just discussed. In general they conclude that domestic factors were more powerful than international ones:

> The primary importance of domestic factors . . . does not preclude the reality of arms competition. Two countries whose military establishments are expanding largely for domestic reasons can, and indeed almost certainly will, become acutely aware of each other's spending. Thereafter, although spending may continue to be powerfully influenced by domestic factors, deliberate military competition may increase and even take the form of an arms race (although the race may be over specific military features and may be a very small portion of total military spending).[6]

Other research efforts have concentrated on the U.S.-Soviet and NATO–Warsaw Pact arms competition. Results often do not point unequivocally to the dominance of either domestic or international influences. Rather, it is clear that both matter under conditions that vary at different times and for different participants.

Many difficulties arise in analyzing arms races. Establishing an action-reaction process requires that we study the behavior of competing states over a period of time, and even the lengthy cold war rivalry between the United States and Soviet Union provides only sketchy information. The data available on arms acquisitions tend to be highly aggregated; usually we must deal with total military spending rather than, say, spending for strategic arms, which might be the most relevant figure to an arms-race

---

[6] Nazli Choucri and Robert North, *Nations in Conflict: National Growth and International Violence* (New York: Freeman, 1975), p. 218.

hypothesis. The quality of the data on Soviet military spending is very poor and subject to rather wide differences in interpretation. Time lags in the budgetary process, whereby weapons systems are funded over the course of several years, add further complications. As a result, any analysis is bound to include a substantial degree of uncertainty. Moreover, both the organizational process and action-reaction explanations lead us to expect very similar behavior — namely, steady or gradually increasing expenditures by both sides. Given these and other difficulties, it can be very hard to separate different causes and to document those differences in a convincing way.[7] With the present state of our art and science, we can say only that both domestic and international influences operate and that these influences, from different levels of analysis, often reinforce each other.

Global Military Presence

In 1987, all nations together spent a record $1.4 trillion on their militaries (in 1995 dollars). Since then global military spending has dropped over 40 percent and in 1997 was less than $800 billion — a level not seen since the mid-1960s. In 1987 military expenditures represented 5.2 percent of the value of world production; in 1996 the military accounted for just 2.8 percent, a 46 percent decline. In the eyes of many $800 billion continues to represent too high a sum to be devoted to national defense, but the decline in world military spending since the end of the cold war is still rather impressive.

The dramatic downsizing of military establishments in the last decade — the total number of active duty personnel has also dropped by about 20 percent — as well as the resources at their command highlights the impact of the cold war on the perceived requirements of national security. Developing states, including those recently freed from colonial rule, looked to the major powers in the international system for cues when building their own defense establishments. Often they did not need to look far. In 1991, the United States had more than 425,000 troops stationed in 23 foreign countries or territories; the Soviet Union deployed nearly 400,000 troops abroad in more than 20 countries. France and Britain also stationed substantial numbers of armed forces abroad. By 1997 this global military presence had diminished, with the demise of the superpower competition, but remained quite substantial, as we see from Table 9.1.

Maintaining a large military is expensive, especially when large numbers of forces are stationed overseas. Since the end of the cold war the number of American active duty personnel has fallen by almost 30 percent, and the number deployed overseas is about half of what it was in 1991. Still, the United States seeks to maintain the capacity to prevail in two "nearly simultaneous" regional conflicts, and is really the only country with truly global military reach. The dissolution of the Soviet Union and the subsequent downsizing of the Russian military has left it with about one-third the number of

---

[7] For an extensive review of the arms-race literature, see Craig Etcheson, *Arms Race Theory: Strategy and Structure of Behavior* (New York: Greenwood, 1989). See also Bruce Russett, "International Interactions and Processes: The Internal vs. External Debate Revisited," in Ada Finifter, ed., *Political Science: The State of the Discipline* (Washington, D.C.: American Political Science Association, 1983); and Walter Isard, *Arms Races, Arms Control, and Conflict Analysis* (Cambridge: Cambridge University Press, 1988), chap. 2 (written with Charles H. Anderton).

TABLE 9.1   Global Military Presence, 1997

Country	Defense Expenditures	Armed Forces	Ready Reserves	Foreign Deployment
United States	$267 billion	1,447,600	1,433,000	Australia, Azores (Portugal), Belgium, Bermuda, Diego Garcia, Germany, Greece, Guam, Guantanamo (Cuba), Honduras, Iceland, Italy, Japan, Kuwait, Netherlands, Norway, Panama, Portugal, Qatar, Saudi Arabia, Singapore, South Korea, Spain, Turkey, United Kingdom
				Total: 205,240
Russia	$71 billion	1,240,000	2,400,000	Abkhazia (Georgia), Africa, Armenia, Cuba, Georgia, Moldova, South Ossetia (Georgia), Syria, Tajikistan, Transdniestr (Moldova), Ukraine, Vietnam
				Total: 73,595
France	$37 billion	380,820	292,500	Antilles, CAR, Chad, Djibouti, French Guiana, Gabon, Germany, Ivory Coast, New Caledonia, Polynesia, Senegal
				Total: 39,010
Germany	$27 billion	347,100	315,000	United States, United Kingdom
				Total: 720
United Kingdom	$36 billion	213,800	315,800	Antarctica, Ascension Island, Brunei, Canada, Cyprus, Falkland Islands, Germany, Gibraltar, Nepal, West Indies
				Total: 34,915
China	$38 billion	2,840,000	1,200,000	None
Japan	$43 billion	235,600	235,600	None

Note: Foreign deployment does not include off-shore deployments or deployments for UN peacekeeping missions.

Source: Compiled from International Institute for Strategic Studies, *The Military Balance 1997–1998* (London: Oxford University Press, 1997).

troops marshaled by the Soviet military in 1991. Russian forces abroad in 1997 were a mere 20 percent of Soviet forces abroad in 1991.[8] China has a very large military — in terms of personnel, twice that of the United States — but a limited capacity to project power much beyond the East Asian theater.

Weapons of Mass Destruction

The destructive potential of modern weapons needs little emphasis. The largest conventional bombs detonated during World War II (the so-called "blockbusters") could seriously damage buildings within one-tenth of a mile. The atomic bomb dropped on Hiroshima at the end of that war had a yield of approximately 15,000 tons of TNT and destroyed most buildings within a mile and a half of the blast. Later scientific developments raised this figure substantially, to about eighteen miles for big 25–megaton hydrogen bombs (the destructive equivalent of 25 *million* tons of TNT). In contrast to conventional weapons, **nuclear weapons** use the massive amounts of energy released by atomic nuclei when they split (fission) or combine (fusion).

Before World War II, military aircraft had a combat radius of only a few hundred miles and could carry only a ton or so of high-explosive bombs. Today, bombers and missiles are able to reach halfway around the globe, carrying payloads with explosive power nearly 100 million times that of a pre–World War II bomber. Indeed, one Trident submarine can carry weapons equal in firepower to three times that used in all of World War II. Studies of possible full-scale nuclear exchanges between the United States and the Soviet Union during the cold war (using thousands of warheads on urban and industrial targets) indicated the devastating results to both societies. For example, estimates of American deaths within thirty days of such an exchange ranged from one-third to two-thirds of the total American population. Such studies also demonstrated the vulnerability of modern, urban, and technologically based societies. Well over half the American population (as well as over 70 percent of its doctors) lives in its seventy-one largest urban areas. Gas pipelines, oil pipelines, and electricity grids would be fragmented. Without fuel, the entire transportation system would be crippled. Railroad lines would be chopped up. Water supply and sewage facilities would break down everywhere, creating epidemics and further straining the already impossibly overburdened medical facilities. If food were still available in agricultural areas (and not contaminated), it could not be processed and shipped, since those facilities are generally in metropolitan areas. No possible level of preparation or civil defense could significantly ease this disaster.

We have not even mentioned long-term ecological results, such as depletion of the ozone layer, the selective destruction of some plants and animals and survival of the hardier forms, cancer from radioactive fallout, and so on. Worse yet, a major scientific

---

[8] Based on figures reported by the International Institute for Strategic Studies in *The Military Balance, 1991–1992* (London: Brassey's, 1991), and *The Military Balance, 1997–1998* (London: Oxford University Press, 1997).

report in 1983 raised the possibility of "nuclear winter" and global climatic catastrophe. Dust and especially soot from fires following nuclear explosions might bring on a period of darkness — making it much too dark to see, even at midday, for a week — and a temperature drop of 36 degrees Fahrenheit in the Northern Hemisphere; the temperature, even in summer, would remain below freezing for three months. An entire growing season for crops might be lost.[9]

Nuclear weapons, along with chemical and biological weapons (to be discussed later), are aptly referred to as **weapons of mass destruction** (WMD). These weapons are, of course, immensely destructive. But they also are, at least in most cases, designed to distribute their effects over large areas, therefore not discriminating between military and non-military targets. Fortunately, weapons of mass destruction have been used on only a few occasions, but the human suffering associated with even these rare events — like the American bombings of Hiroshima and Nagasaki or the Iraqi gas attacks against the Kurds — has left an indelible mark on the conscience of the international community. That is the reason why the vast majority of the effort devoted to arms control and disarmament has concentrated on weapons of mass destruction, despite our relative inexperience with their effects.[10]

A Brief History of the Nuclear Arms Race

Let us now examine the evolution of the nuclear arms race between the United States and the Soviet Union during the cold war. First, we shall outline a brief history of the strategic arms race, using four broad historical periods, and then analyze the interactions, attempting to understand how the world entered, endured, and survived the era of nuclear confrontation. The deployment of nuclear weapons by the two superpowers during these historical periods is illustrated by Figure 9.2, which plots the growth, and post–cold war decline, of strategic offensive nuclear stockpiles.

The Period of U.S. Nuclear Monopoly: 1945–1950   After World War II, the United States and to a lesser degree the Soviet Union both disarmed from the high levels of global war. The atomic bomb was the central element in America's policy of deterrence. Although the Soviet Union retained large land forces (which could have threatened Western Europe), for all practical purposes the Soviets had no atomic weapons. They exploded their first bomb in 1949, but it was several years before they built up a stockpile adequate for fighting a war, and, in any case, they lacked intercontinental bombers capable of reaching the United States. The Americans could have bombed the Soviet Union, inflicting substantial damage, though the number of American bombs was not large (probably only about 300, even at the end of this period), and they were

---

[9] See Arthur M. Katz, *Life after Nuclear War* (Cambridge, Mass.: Ballinger, 1982); Carl Sagan, "Nuclear War and Climatic Catastrophe: Some Policy Implications," *Foreign Affairs* 62 (Winter 1983/84): pp. 256–292; and Stanley Thompson and Stephen Schneider, "Nuclear Winter Reappraised," *Foreign Affairs* 64 (Summer 1986): pp. 981–1005.

[10] Even the fairly technical exercises designed to compute the likely effects of different types of nuclear blasts under various climatic conditions can prove rather gut-wrenching. See, for example, Samuel Glasstone and Philip J. Dolan, eds., *The Effects of Nuclear Weapons* (Washington, D.C.: U.S. Department of Defense and U.S. Department of Energy, 1977).

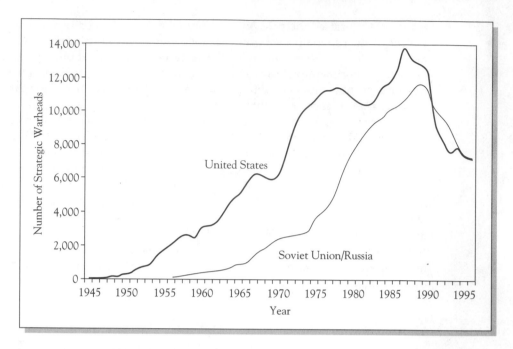

FIGURE 9.2   The Rise and Decline in Superpower Offensive Nuclear Forces, 1945–1996

Note: Totals include warheads carried by bombers, intercontinental missiles, and submarines; they exclude warheads deployed as theater forces (even when capable of striking U.S. or Soviet/Russian territory).

Source: National Resource Defense Council Nuclear Program, "U.S. and USSR/Russian Strategic Offensive Nuclear Forces, 1945–1996," January 1997 [cited September 16, 1998]; available at <http://www.nrdc.org/nrdcpro/nudb/dainx.html>.

fission (atomic) weapons rather than the much more devastating *fusion* (thermonuclear, or hydrogen) weapons that followed.

The Period of U.S. Nuclear Dominance: 1951–1957   As the culmination of a series of threatening incidents in the emerging cold war — the communist takeover of Czechoslovakia and the Berlin blockade in 1948, a communist victory in China, and the Soviet atomic bomb explosion in 1949 — the Korean War (which began in June 1950) initiated a great American program of rearmament, during which annual U.S. defense expenditures nearly tripled. U.S. Secretary of State John Foster Dulles declared that the United States would respond to any further communist attack on "free world" nations "in a manner and at a place of our own choosing." In other words, in the face of any such "proxy war" the United States would feel free to strike not at the small communist ally but directly at the Soviet Union, in "massive retaliation" with nuclear weapons. Such a threat was credible because the United States had by then built up a very large stockpile of nuclear weapons and an intercontinental bombing force to deliver them, including the hydrogen bomb (first tested by the United States in 1952 and by the Soviets in

1953). The ability to inflict damage was so greatly imbalanced in favor of the United States (which also maintained bases in Europe and Asia quite near the USSR) that we can speak of this era as the period of American strategic dominance. In response the Soviet leaders pursued a very cautious and generally unprovocative foreign policy — and a major rearmament effort.

The Period of U.S. Preponderance: 1958–1966   American dominance over the Soviet Union decreased from 1958 to 1966, and the new term we use to describe American superiority is simply *preponderance*. Still, it was a period when the United States could at least consider the option of attacking the Soviet Union with nuclear weapons in response to a proxy war started by a Soviet ally. The United States still had something of a **first-strike capability** in that it could hit the Soviet Union first and greatly reduce the Soviet ability to retaliate. Any American temptation to relax was eliminated by the shock of *Sputnik:* in 1957 the USSR became the first country to put a satellite into orbit around the earth, indicating that the USSR had perfected very large rockets that could also be used as intercontinental ballistic missiles (ICBMs) — the delivery vehicles for nuclear and thermonuclear bombs. Behind in this technology, the United States feared a Soviet first-strike capability — that the Soviet Union would build so many ICBMs that they could attack and destroy the bombers on which the United States relied for its deterrent. This led to a new crash program of development and deployment of American land- and sea-based ICBMs (though the "missile gap" never actually materialized). American preponderance was maintained, although the Soviet Union was increasingly developing a capability to do much damage to the United States, in retaliation if not in a first strike. Partly to remedy this imbalance, in 1962 the Soviets put a variety of nuclear-armed missiles and bombers into Cuba, precipitating the Cuban missile crisis of October 1962. During the ten-day crisis, President Kennedy made it clear that the United States was prepared to launch a nuclear first strike against the forces in Cuba and perhaps against the Soviet Union if those forces were not removed. Because the United States had such overall nuclear predominance (as well as local nonnuclear superiority in the Caribbean, an area of vital importance to it), the Soviet leaders believed the American counter threat and withdrew their missiles and aircraft. However, in reaction to this very public demonstration of their weakness, the Soviet leaders began a new program of strategic armament, revealed in steadily expanding stockpiles of nuclear warheads and rising levels of military expenditure after 1965 (see Figures 9.1 and 9.2 p. 215 and p. 222).

The Period of Essential Equivalence: 1967 to the End of the Cold War   From 1966 until 1975, the United States was deeply involved in another long, painful, and costly land war in Asia, this time in Vietnam, during which American military expenditures climbed to new heights. By 1973, in reaction to the war, American military expenditures dropped below the pre-Vietnam level and remained there until 1977, then resumed a slow climb. Meanwhile, the Soviet Union maintained its military buildup in conventional as well as nuclear arms. By the 1970s it was spending more than the United States on its military, was keeping up with the United States in the expansion of strategic nuclear warheads (though remaining behind in absolute numbers), and now possessed more nuclear launchers. Most observers characterize this period as one of essential equivalence when all elements of strategic weapons are taken into account. Through the mid-1960s the United States maintained a clear quantitative (and qualitative) superiority in all classes of strategic delivery vehicles: ICBMs (land-based missiles, like the Minuteman), SLBMs (submarine-launched ballistic missiles, like the Trident), and long-range bombers, like the B-52. By the 1970s, however, the Soviet Union had developed very large rockets and warheads and surpassed the United States in numbers of ICBMs; the United States retained advantages in bombers and deliverable warheads from SLBMs.

The result was a situation in which neither side could attack the other without suffering enormous damage from the opponent's retaliation. This gave the United States and the Soviet Union the capability of **mutual assured destruction,** sometimes abbreviated MAD. In other words, each side possessed a **second-strike capability:** the capacity to absorb an enemy attack and have enough weapons remaining to retaliate and inflict unacceptable damage on the opponent. Thus, no matter how the size of nuclear arsenals was measured, for all intents and purposes neither side could win a nuclear war. The logic of the strategic relationship was quite simple. A country with first-strike capability might be tempted to attack by the *belief* that the opponent could not retaliate (and therefore had no effective deterrent threat). In a situation where *both* sides had achieved second-strike capabilities and both were able to retaliate, the deterrent threats of each were believable, and neither was tempted to strike. The situation was thus "stable" — neither country had an incentive to launch an attack and start a war.

With the end of the cold war and the dissolution of the USSR, the strategic rivalry basically collapsed. As the result of arms control agreements (discussed in a later section), the United States and Russia are very near strategic nuclear parity, both in terms of warheads and delivery vehicles. Table 9.2 summarizes this strategic nuclear balance

TABLE 9.2	American and Russian Strategic Nuclear Forces, 1998			
	Bombers	ICBMs	SLBMs	Total
United States				
Delivery Vehicles	92	575	432	1,099
Warheads	1,800	2,000	3,456	7,256
Russia				
Delivery Vehicles	70	751	384	1,205
Warheads	806	3,610	1,824	6,240

Source: William M. Arkin, Robert S. Norris, and Joshua Handler, *Taking Stock: Worldwide Nuclear Deployments 1998* (Washington, D.C.: National Resources Defense Council, 1998), pp. 14, 27.

as of 1998. But the nuclear balance is but one aspect of the overall military balance. The United States currently channels far more resources to its military (see Figure 9.1) and has achieved a level of military-technological development that Russia will not rival in the near future. That, combined with uncertainties regarding the preparedness of Russian military forces, has left the United States as the "only remaining superpower," a position of military preponderance not experienced since the early 1960s.

Proliferation

Weapons **proliferation** refers to the increase in the number of states (and potentially nonstate actors) that possess a certain class of weaponry. The proliferation of nuclear weapons involves a number of dangers. One concern is the acquisition by governments of the material and know-how needed to make nuclear bombs. New nuclear powers, which would likely include a number of aggressive authoritarian states, will lack the experience of existing nuclear powers in controlling the use of such weapons and will lack the resources to manage the elaborate command and control capabilities required; this is especially true of the less-developed countries. Also, many of these governments will be involved in serious local conflicts, a situation that increases pressures to use such weapons in warfare. Since both India and Pakistan conducted a series of nuclear weapons tests in 1998, fear has been expressed in many quarters that their long-running conflict over the Kashmir might become the spark that ignites the world's first nuclear war. Such factors as these convince us that a world of many nuclear powers would be a perilous one indeed, despite some arguments that a system in which *everyone* possessed nuclear weapons would be quite stable — due to a mega-balance of terror of all against all.[11] Just because the "long peace" during the cold war may in some measure have been the result of mutual U.S.-Soviet deterrence does not provide a basis for arguing that proliferating nuclear weapons in the present system would have peacekeeping value.

A second danger is the opportunity it provides for terrorists to gain control of nuclear materials (which may have been acquired by governments for peaceful purposes) or finished weapons. Perpetrators of "nuclear terrorism" may be based within the countries they wish to harm, or far away, simply taking advantage of opportunities to acquire nuclear materials from governments that are unable to take sufficient security precautions. Such concerns have increased since the end of the cold war: many have doubts about the degree of control exercised over Russia's nuclear materials and technology since the slashing of resources available to the military, scientific, and industrial community.[12]

[11] Kenneth Waltz has advanced this argument, which is vigorously rebutted by Scott Sagan. See Sagan and Waltz, *The Spread of Nuclear Weapons: A Debate* (New York: Norton, 1995). John Mearsheimer has presented arguments similar to Waltz's with regard to the creation of a strong Ukrainian nuclear force; "The Case for a Ukrainian Nuclear Deterrent," *Foreign Affairs* 72 (Summer 1993): pp. 50–66. In the same issue, Steven E. Miller rebuts Mearsheimer in "The Case against a Ukrainian Nuclear Deterrent," pp. 67–80.

[12] See, for example, Graham T. Allison, Owen R. Coté, Jr., Richard A. Falkenrath, and Steven E. Miller, *Avoiding Nuclear Anarchy: Containing the Threat of Loose Russian Nuclear Weapons and Fissile Material* (Cambridge, Mass.: MIT Press, 1996).

To meet the threat of nuclear proliferation, several different kinds of incentives for proliferation must be recognized. For some countries, the problem of security against present nuclear powers may be paramount. Pakistan's nuclear program is directed toward perceived security threats from India, which had first demonstrated its nuclear potential in 1974. India's program is directed, at least in part, toward China. More often, however, security is sought against local powers that are not yet nuclear. Israel has been motivated by security threats from the Arab countries, while South Korea is concerned about North Korea. For still other states, military security may not be a primary concern; rather, they may wish to obtain big-power prestige or the technological advances that can be obtained from the development of nuclear capabilities (as was possibly the case in past Argentine efforts). For still others — India, for example — perhaps all three kinds of incentives are involved.

Stemming the proliferation of **chemical weapons** presents a major challenge because some can be assembled with widely available chemical agents and commercial equipment. Easily produced and potentially very destructive, they have been called the poor man's atomic bomb. Chemical agents, like tear gas, are commonly used in riot control, but those used in chemical warfare are more nefarious, attacking the body's nervous system, blood, skin, or lungs. Chlorine and mustard gas were first used in the trench warfare of World War I. Napalm was used in flamethrowers during World War II, and was made infamous by American forces in Vietnam who used it (along with the herbicide known as Agent Orange) as a jungle defoliant. Iraq used mustard gas and nerve agents to defend against Iran's "human wave" attacks during the Iran-Iraq war, and against Iraqi Kurds after that war. In 1995, the Japanese group Aum Shinrikyo released sarin gas in the Tokyo subway system, killing eleven and injuring more than 5,000, highlighting the danger of chemical proliferation to nonstate actors engaging in terrorism.

Perhaps even more than chemical weapons, **biological weapons** have acquired a sinister reputation for capacity to produce potentially frightening effects on the cheap.[13] Biological agents consist of living organisms (bacteria, fungi) and viruses, as well as the toxins derived from them, that cause disease and death to humans, livestock, or agricultural crops. The use of biological weapons during warfare has been less frequent, or at least less blatant, than the use of chemical weapons, although the early history of human warfare includes accounts of biological agents introduced into drinking water and food supplies. When the plague struck Tatar forces laying siege to Kaffa (in the Crimea) during the fourteenth century, corpses were hurled over the city walls spreading disease among the city's inhabitants, eventually forcing their surrender. Japan's notorious Unit 731 is now reported to have conducted biological warfare experiments on Chinese prisoners of war during the Japanese occupation of Manchuria in the 1930s, culminating in the actual use of bacteriological (bubonic plague) bombs against Chinese cities beginning in 1940.[14] More recently, fungal toxins (in the form of "yellow rain") were used by Vietnam in Kampuchea and by the Soviet Union in Afghanistan.

---

[13] John D. Steinbruner, "Biological Weapons: A Plague upon All Houses," *Foreign Policy* 109 (Winter 1997–98): pp. 85–96.
[14] Nicholas D. Kristof, "Japan Confronting Gruesome War Atrocity," *New York Times,* March 17, 1995. See also Sheldon H. Harris, *Factories of Death: Japanese Biological Warfare 1932–45 and the American Cover-up* (New York: Routledge, 1994), on the reported cover-up by U.S. officials in exchange for data from the Japanese experiments.

It is nearly impossible to stem the proliferation of chemical and biological weapons by restricting access to the substances and technologies necessary for their production. Punitive measures, like the 1998 American bombing of a Sudanese chemical plant suspected of producing elements of the chemical agent VX, may only be marginally more effective.[15] It might be that reversing the trend in chemical and biological proliferation must rest on moral persuasion, or simply the fear conjured up by images of the uncontrolled stockpiling of these weapons of mass destruction — and their increasingly probable use.

The Security Dilemma

The very principle underlying contemporary international relations — sovereignty — helps to explain driving forces behind arms acquisition and arms races, as well as the difficulties associated with arms control. Sovereignty means that states exist in a formally anarchic environment. No legitimate or legal authority is empowered to control, direct, or watch over the behavior of sovereign states (as, for example, the federal government of the United States does over the fifty states of the union). One consequence of such a system of sovereign states is that each state must in the end look out for its own security, protection, and survival.

If there is no legitimate, legal authority to enforce order and punish rule-breakers, then there is no legal or formal recourse if allies or friends fail to assist a state — you cannot sue them to fulfill their alliance contracts! Thus, self-help in the international system means that each state must take measures to provide for its own defense. A tragic flaw of the formally anarchic state system is that the requirement for self-help often leads to what has become known as the **security dilemma:**

> Wherever such anarchic society has existed — and it has existed in most periods of known history on some level — there has arisen what may be called the "security dilemma" of men, or groups, or their leaders. Groups or individuals living in such a constellation must be, and usually are, concerned about their security from being attacked, subjected, dominated or annihilated by other groups and individuals. Striving to attain security from such attack, they are driven to acquire more and more power in order to escape the power of others. This, in turn, renders the others more insecure and compels them to prepare for the worst. Since none can ever feel entirely secure in such a world of competing units, power competition ensues, and the vicious circle of security and power accumulation is on.[16]

---

[15] Some analysts believe that the best protection against weapons of mass destruction would be for the United States to withdraw from many of its overseas involvements, combined with implementation of a rigorous program of civil defense. See, for example, Richard K. Betts, "The New Threat of Mass Destruction," *Foreign Affairs* 77, 1 (January/February 1998): pp. 26–41.

[16] John Herz, "Idealist Internationalism and the Security Dilemma," *World Politics* 2 (1950), 157. See also Robert Jervis, "Cooperation under the Security Dilemma," *World Politics* 30 (1978): pp. 167–214; and Charles L. Glaser, "The Security Dilemma Revisited," *World Politics* 50 (1997): pp. 171–201.

Thus, one state's security may be seen and defined as another state's *insecurity*. The means by which one state prepares to defend its territory and people may be threatening to others — and is thus perceived as offensive, rather than defensive, behavior (what did Israeli activity look like to the Arab countries during most of the post-1948 period?). States may never feel secure because they never know how much is "enough" for their security. This is particularly so when their own efforts at security spur on the efforts of others.

The formally anarchic system of sovereign states promotes a realist vision of struggle in world politics, through the security dilemma and the concomitant stress on threat, military power, and self-help. The need for military power, and for constant alertness as to its accumulation and use by others, stems directly from the structure of a system of sovereign states and — if we subscribe to realist assumptions — the power-seeking dimensions of human nature. The security dilemma is central to many aspects of interstate relations besides arms racing, and analogous forms of competitive state behavior appear in international political economy as well, as we shall see in later chapters. How states cope with these conditions creates some degree of order out of anarchy.

The Prisoner's Dilemma

The continuing and parallel increases in superpower military spending (Figure 9.1) and the deployment of nuclear forces (Figure 9.2) are two manifestations of an arms race. Game theory, introduced in the last chapter as an approach for analyzing the outbreak of war, stresses the interdependence of each side's choices and the combination of conflict and cooperation found in many social situations. As an approach to the study of world politics, game theory is comprised of many different "games" that have been constructed by analysts for purposes of examining situations commonly encountered in relations between states (and nonstate actors as well). One game, called the **prisoner's dilemma**, illustrates how people — including the leaders of states — can become trapped by self-defeating acts.[17]

In the basic story of the prisoner's dilemma, two people are arrested. Each is held incommunicado in a police station after being arrested for an armed robbery. Each prisoner is presented with a pair of unattractive options, and each is questioned separately and given a choice by the district attorney (DA): "I'm pretty sure that you two were responsible for the robbery, but I don't have quite enough evidence to prove it. If you will confess and testify against your partner, I will see to it that you are set free without any penalty, and your accomplice will be sentenced to ten years in prison. You should be aware that I am making the same proposal to your buddy, and if he accepts my offer, you will be the one locked up for ten years; he will go free. If you both confess, then my prosecution need not hinge on your testimony alone, or his alone. We will have a little mercy, but you'll both go away for seven years. If you both keep quiet, we won't have the evidence to convict you of armed robbery, but we can convict you on

---

[17] For a nontechnical account of the role and evolution of game theory, including the prisoner's dilemma game, in U.S. strategic thinking, see William Poundstone, *Prisoner's Dilemma: John von Neumann, Game Theory, and the Puzzle of the Bomb* (New York: Doubleday, 1992).

concealed weapon charges, which carry sentences of one year in prison. If you want to take a chance that your fellow prisoner will keep quiet, go ahead. But if he doesn't — and you know the sort of guy he is — you will do very badly. Think it over."

What will the prisoners do in this situation? To help predict the outcome we could construct a decision tree similar to the one presented in the last chapter (see Figure 8.1). However, since each prisoner must make a decision without knowledge of the decision made by the other, we can use a matrix like the one in Figure 9.3. The two prisoners, labeled *Blue* and *Red*, each have to decide between two options, confess or keep quiet. The uncertainty for each prisoner is whether there exists "honor among thieves," so we use the label *cooperate* for keeping quiet (upholding honor among thieves) and the label *defect* for confessing to the DA (squealing among thieves). With two players, each with two options, there are four possible outcomes in the prisoner's dilemma. If Red confesses (defects) and Blue keeps quiet (cooperates), Red goes free and Blue gets ten years. That is the best of the four possible outcomes for Red (we assign it a value of 4) but the least attractive outcome for Blue (a value of 1), and it is represented by the bottom-left cell in the matrix. The exact opposite outcome results if Blue confesses and Red keeps quiet, as shown in the upper-right cell. If both confess, they both get seven years, which is bad, but not the worst, for both (a value of 2), as shown in the lower-right cell. The upper-left cell is the outcome when both keep quiet — not the best for both, but still a relatively short time in prison (a value of 3).

If Blue is rational, that prisoner would reason as follows: "Let me first assume that Red cooperates. In that case I should defect, since going free [4 in the bottom-left cell] is better than a year in jail [3, top-left cell]. Next let me assume that Red defects. Again I should defect; seven years in prison is not good [2, bottom-right cell], but it's better than ten years [1, top-right cell]. Looks like either way, I should confess." In other words, Blue has a *dominant strategy:* to make the same choice (defect) no matter what

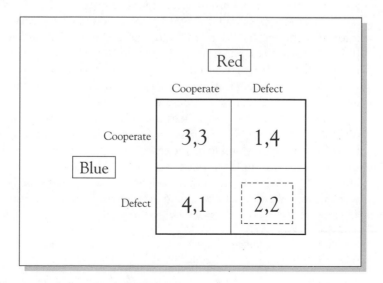

FIGURE 9.3 The Prisoner's Dilemma

Red does. Unfortunately for Blue, Red also has a dominant strategy, to defect. The outcome is predictable: each prisoner, rationally looking out for his own self interest, squeals on the other and both end up spending seven year in prison. Had they only been able to cooperate in upholding honor among thieves, they *both* would have been better off. That is the dilemma.

In game theory, an outcome like the defect-defect outcome in the prisoner's dilemma is called an **equilibrium.** This is the outcome where neither player has an incentive to choose differently if acting alone. The bottom-right cell in Figure 9.3 represents an equilibrium outcome because neither Blue nor Red has an incentive to switch unilaterally from defect to cooperate: doing so would increase the sentence to ten years for the one cooperating.[18] An outcome like cooperate-cooperate in the prisoner's dilemma is sometimes called the *socially optimal* outcome because both players together cannot do any better. The other cells in Figure 9.3 represent outcomes in which one or both prisoners do worse than one year in prison. The dilemma in a prisoner's dilemma is that the equilibrium outcome is not the socially optimal outcome. Sadly, many situations in international relations have this feature.

Consider the U.S. and Soviet arms acquisitions during the cold war. Now we move from a situation of easily specified choices (confess, keep quiet) and easily measured outcomes (years in prison) to one with choices and outcomes that are much harder to measure. We must simplify the situation while at the same time capturing the essence of strategic situation. Assume that each superpower had but two options, to arm (defect) or to restrain from arming (cooperate). Given these options, it seems that each side's preference ordering among the four possible outcomes was analogous to that of each prisoner in the prisoner's dilemma: unilateral armament (4) was preferred to mutual restraint, since the superior power could use its military advantage as leverage; mutual restraint (3) was preferred to mutual armament, since a military balance could be struck without diverting resources from domestic needs; and mutual armament (2) was preferred to unilateral disarmament (1), since preventing manipulation by a militarily superior opponent was worth the diversion of resources. Because the strategic interaction between the United States and the Soviet Union had the same structure as the prisoner's dilemma game, the outcome was similarly predictable: an arms race, as represented by the defect-defect outcome. Unfortunately for the superpowers, both would have been better off had they maintained a military balance without becoming embroiled in an arms race (cooperate-cooperate).[19]

Given each side's preferences in a prisoner's dilemma, are two countries in an arms race condemned to the risk and waste of a never-ending, costly arms competition? In 1950 that seemed to be the case. President Truman's scientific advisers told him that they could build a powerful new thermonuclear weapon — the hydrogen bomb — hundreds of times more powerful than the atomic bomb. Some Americans would have liked best to be sole owner of the new bomb (unilateral armament) but

---

[18] In the last chapter, the game depicted by the decision tree in Figure 8.1 also has an equilibrium outcome, which is the one we arrived at through backward induction.

[19] For an application of prisoner's dilemma and other game theoretic concepts to superpower relations, see Steven J. Brams, *Superpower Games: Applying Game Theory to Superpower Conflict* (New Haven, Conn.: Yale University Press, 1985).

would have settled for a situation in which no country had it (mutual restraint). However, the Soviets had pretty much the same scientific knowledge that the Americans had, and neither power would consider allowing the other to have such a fearsome weapon unless it also had one. It seemed better to go ahead and build the hydrogen bomb if the Soviets were going to build it also (mutual armament). Even though building a hydrogen bomb would leave both countries exposed to its dangers, it seemed better than being at the mercy of the Soviets without a counter weapon (unilateral restraint). Lacking any prospect of an enforceable agreement that neither would build hydrogen bombs, each side felt forced to build a weapon that it wished did not exist.[20] This is the essence of the security dilemma: one may lose greatly by failing to trust the other, but one risks losing even more if the trust proves misplaced.

Obviously the superpower arms race did end, contrary to what the prisoner's dilemma leads us to expect. Does that mean that game theory is unhelpful for understanding major changes in interstate relations like the end of the cold war? No, it only means that the prisoner's dilemma game no longer captured the essence of American and Soviet preferences toward the end of the cold war period. How might we use game theory to account for this transition?

The prisoner's dilemma assumes that the best outcome for oneself is military superiority. But imagine instead that the United States decided that the alleged advantages of superiority, especially strategic nuclear superiority, are overrated. (In the famous words of Henry Kissinger, "What in the name of God is strategic superiority? . . . What can you do with it?") When both sides have large and secure nuclear retaliatory forces (MAD), the side that happens to have more nuclear weapons than the other may not be able to derive much military or political advantage from its edge. While the United States might have preferred to have more weapons than the Soviet Union, at some point it grew tired of the arms race and preferred mutual restraint, even mutual disarmament. At the same time, the United States wanted to avoid disarming while the Soviet Union continued to arm. In short, what was once the most preferred outcome for the United States is now only the second-most preferred outcome; the two least preferred outcomes remain unchanged. If we assume that all Soviet preferences remain the same as in the prisoner's dilemma, the situation resembles Part A of Figure 9.4 — a one-sided prisoner's dilemma.

Unlike in the prisoners' dilemma, where defecting was a dominant strategy for the United States, now its best choice depends on what the Soviets do. If the United States thinks the Soviets will cooperate, then it should cooperate and achieve its most preferred outcome of mutual restraint; if the Soviets will defect, then so should the United States. While it may appear that there is a way out of the arms race, there is not. The American side will easily discern that the Soviets still have a dominant strategy to defect, in which case they must do the same. This calculus was in fact quite common in American cold war rhetoric. It was easy to believe that the Soviets had more malign intentions than our own. We knew that we wanted to avoid an arms race but nevertheless found ourselves in one, and it was convenient to assume that the Soviets were to blame. Since it was hard to see what the Soviet Union was actually doing, and we had

---

[20] See Richard Rhodes, *Dark Sun: The Making of the Hydrogen Bomb* (New York: Simon & Schuster, 1995).

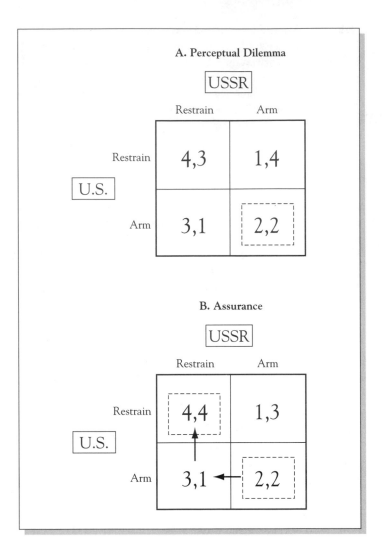

FIGURE 9.4   Ending the Arms Race: Perceptual Dilemma and Assurance

little chance to judge their intentions first hand, we readily attributed hostile intentions to them (recall, from Chapter 7, the "image of the enemy"). If we had reasons to doubt their intentions, or were suspicious merely because of inadequate contact, then the safest line of action was to continue defecting. While the great opportunity for mutual disarmament will be lost, the risk of being in a militarily inferior position was avoided. The equilibrium in a one-sided prisoner's dilemma is still defect-defect and thus an arms race.

It is disheartening to note that defection on the American side may have been driven not by Soviet preferences, but by *perceived* Soviet preferences. If the Soviets too preferred mutual restraint to their own strategic superiority, there was no escaping the security dilemma unless and until the Americans understood that — and vice versa. Because the one-sided prisoner's dilemma captures well the importance of what each side thinks about the other's preferences, it has been called the "perceptual dilemma." Indeed, there is survey evidence suggesting that *both* American and Soviet leaders judged their own most preferred outcome to be mutual restraint while believing that their counterparts still sought superiority.[21] How much earlier might the cold war have ended had our perceptions been more accurate?

Overcoming the Dilemma

In looking at the winding down of the arms race at the end of cold war, there is an implication that the superpowers' preferences did change. They may have changed because it became impossible to achieve a meaningful superiority, because each power decided that military superiority could not bring any politically useful results, or because high levels of arms on both sides associated with the effort to gain superiority became too threatening. In the real world people do change their preferences about what they want, what they may be capable of achieving, and what they are willing to try to achieve. The superpowers revised preference orderings, and increasing mutual understanding regarding the preferences held by the other produced a situation resembling Part B of Figure 9.4.

There are two equilibria in this game: mutual defection, as in the prisoner's (and perceptual) dilemma, and mutual cooperation. Because Soviet and American leaders in the 1980s inherited a history of suspicion and cold war, they found themselves in the defect-defect cell, continuing the arms race even though both sides preferred the socially optimal outcome of mutual cooperation. One side had to take a risk. If one side cooperated instead of defecting it would find itself in a disadvantageous position (the top-right cell or bottom-left cell, depending on which side decided to cooperate). However, that disadvantage would be short lived since even the side with the advantage would have an incentive to cooperate in order to achieve its most desired outcome of mutual cooperation. Since that outcome would also be a stable equilibrium, there would be no more incentive to defect and the arms race would end. Since one side must make a short-term sacrifice in order to assure the other of its good intentions, this has been called the **assurance game.**[22]

While it is doubtful that he consulted game theory, Gorbachev seems to have been guided by precisely this calculus when embarking on the Soviet foreign policy known as "new thinking." As Jack Snyder wrote in 1987, "Gorbachev and his circle see

---

[21] See S. Plous, "Perceptual Illusions and Military Realities: The Nuclear Arms Race," *Journal of Conflict Resolution* 29, 3 (September 1985): pp. 363–388.

[22] For a more elaborate discussion of the willingness of players to make short-term sacrifices in order to bring about even better outcomes, see Steven J. Brams, *Theory of Moves* (Cambridge: Cambridge University Press, 1994). The assurance game is also known as the "stag hunt," based on a situation described by Jean-Jacques Rousseau in his discussion of the state of nature. Two (or more) hunters must cooperate to capture a stag, and the success of the hunt (mutual cooperation) rests on each trusting that the other will not defect from the hunting party to chase down a hare, which would satisfy the individual's hunger but not the group's. Without that trust (or assurance), each individual will defect to chase the same hare, although it would have been better for all of them had they trapped the stag.

America as innately hostile, but they believe that America's aggressiveness can be defused through Soviet self-restraint and concessions."[23] Among many other concessions, Gorbachev accepted the Reagan administration's "zero option" for intermediate nuclear force reductions, requiring a greater Soviet sacrifice, and agreed to disproportionately deep cuts in Soviet (and Warsaw Pact) conventional forces in Europe, which also assumed a decidedly defensive force posture. Fortunately, after considerable hesitation in some quarters of its foreign policy establishment, the United States reciprocated, setting the arms race (and the cold war generally) on its downward spiral.

None of the games we have considered are **zero-sum games,** in which one side's gain equals the other side's loss. In most of the games we play for sport, such as chess or tennis, winning or losing is not everything. Even when we lose the match, we presumably gain from the exercise and the pleasure of the competition. In international relations, too, it is a fundamental mistake to think of most conflict as zero-sum situations. When the rational pursuit of individual gain results in an outcome neither side wants, it may still be possible to resolve these conflicts of interest by appealing to the prospect of mutual benefit, or to the fear of mutual demise. An undesirable equilibrium outcome is only partly the result of each side's preference ordering. It also results from other aspects of the strategic interaction, like the information each possesses about the other.

Confrontations between the same parties occur repeatedly in international politics. In these circumstances, a country's actions at a particular time have consequences not only for that interaction, but in subsequent confrontations as well if those actions reveal information about its interests or strategy. It is a logical next step, then, to consider what happens when players interact in what they think will be a repeating series of games (sometimes called "iterated games"). Many experimental psychologists and other experts, including Anatol Rapoport and his colleagues, have examined situations like this under laboratory conditions. Their studies now include thousands of players, each making fifty to several hundred plays.[24] There is a typical sequence that many players adopt. At the beginning, participants often play cooperatively, with rewards to each partner. After a short while, however, one partner becomes tempted to defect. The victim will usually retaliate after being betrayed once or twice, so both take the punishment outcome. At this point each may try to reestablish cooperation, but without means for overt communication that is difficult to do. Would-be cooperators often find themselves at their least preferred outcome, interpret this as betrayal, and so return to defection.

In international politics, too, it may be very hard to change to cooperative behavior. The first initiatives may not be seen as cooperation at all, or if perceived as such they may be interpreted as weakness and thus be exploited. Many Americans were wary of Gorbachev's new thinking. Soviet reforms, they suspected, were merely designed to give the Soviet military some breathing space. Once the economy was

---

[23] Jack Snyder, "The Gorbachev Revolution: A Waning of Soviet Expansionism?" *International Security* 12, 3 (Winter 1987/88): p. 118.

[24] Experimental results discussed in this section have been regularly reported in several journals, including *Behavioral Science; Journal of Conflict Resolution; Simulation and Gaming;* and *International Journal of Game Theory.*

streamlined, we would witness a new infusion of resources into the military and the Soviet Union would resume its offensive military posture. And all this just as the United States had been lulled into complacency. Others thought that Soviet concessions were a sign of vulnerability, a vulnerability to be exploited in order to force a complete collapse of the Soviet economy and substantial military retrenchment. Indeed, the Soviet Union itself dissolved and the Russian military is a shadow of its former self, although there remains considerable debate regarding America's role in pushing its opponent to that point.[25]

In experiments, after a good deal of trial and error, many players do, in fact, succeed in cooperating consistently again, but it may be a long, painful time before this favorable pattern is established. Under these conditions, each play is eventually seen not as an end in itself, but as a means of communicating one's hope of promoting joint cooperation in later plays. In this way the game resembles the ongoing politics among states, where cooperation breeds expectations of cooperation and defection breeds expectations of defection. Ultimately, over many plays, it becomes possible to develop trust as the players become increasingly confident that each knows how the other will behave.

Competitive strategies are more common where there are no means of communication between the players. Many kinds of information need to be communicated: knowledge of activities, reasons for those activities, intentions, and preferences matter in varying degrees. Formal government-to-government communication facilities are a key element, and so are trade and various person-to-person contacts, such as tourism and cultural exchange. When players do communicate, it is essential that the communication be honest. If one player uses the opportunity to deceive the other, the result is often a longer run of mutual defection and double-crossing than happens when no communication is permitted. For example, President Carter decided to impose economic sanctions on the Soviet Union after its invasion of Afghanistan partly because he was angry that Brezhnev had lied to him. Brezhnev had told Carter that Afghanistan leader Hafizullah Amin had "requested the assistance" of Soviet troops — troops who then supervised Amin's deposition and assassination.

Players are more likely to cooperate if they expect to play many more times. This is because players develop reputations. A player who usually defects may develop a reputation for defecting, and when other players meet that player, they are also likely to defect immediately. The player with the reputation for defecting will often be punished with responses in kind. Any advantage he or she may get from finding an occasional sucker could be wiped out, overall, by defections on the part of other vigilant players. But a player who develops a reputation for cooperating may get others to cooperate right away when next they meet. If so, having been taken advantage of by a few regular defectors may be more than compensated by the favorable outcomes of meeting other cooperators.

---

[25] See, for example, Archie Brown, *The Gorbachev Factor* (New York: Oxford University Press, 1996), and Philip Zelikow and Condoleeza Rice, *Germany Unified and Europe Transformed: A Study in Statecraft* (Cambridge, Mass.: Harvard University Press, 1995), as well as William C. Wohlforth's review of this and other literature in "Reality Check: Revising Theories of International Politics in Response to the End of the Cold War," *World Politics* 50, 4 (July 1998): pp. 650–680.

Robert Axelrod has done some of the most interesting work on how rational people learn to cooperate in conflictual situations. In one experiment he conducted a computer tournament among thirteen social scientists to see whose programmed strategy for playing repeated prisoner's dilemma games would be most successful. Because the measure of success was the total number of points accumulated in all match-ups, it turned out that players who defected too often fared poorly overall even though they often bested their opponents. Defecting brought short-term gains, but it also brought reciprocal defections and bad outcomes for both players. Of all the strategies played, Axelrod found that **tit for tat** (cooperating after the opponent cooperated, defecting after a defection) was most successful, especially when coupled with *optimism* (opening with a cooperative move) and being somewhat *forgiving* (punishing once, then trying again to cooperate). Interestingly, in any paired match-up, the tit-for-tat player can at best tie an opponent; tit for tat never wins an individual match. However, because the strategy elicits cooperative behavior from others, bringing socially optimal outcomes, the overall performance of tit for tat was better than other strategies less adept at bringing out the best in their opponents. What allows for this evolution of cooperation is the expectation that players will encounter one another again — a sufficiently long "shadow of the future."[26]

It makes a difference how the experimenter describes the purpose of the game to the players before they begin. The object may be presented as (1) each player doing his or her best, regardless of what happens to the other player, (2) each player doing better than the other, or (3) both players doing well. Not surprisingly, people cooperate least often when the experimenter emphasizes doing better than the other; the game description becomes a self-fulfilling prophecy. Similarly, it may matter very much what preconceptions people bring to the analysis of international politics. People can be taught to think about joint rewards and to care about others. Those who have been taught, informally or in school, to think in stark realist terms (that it's a dog-eat-dog world) will be less ready to cooperate when they choose policies. When we believe that the overriding goal is to maximize our own interests over all others, non-zero-sum situations may be interpreted as zero sum, and the outcome of our interactions becomes mutual misery.

Thinking back to the prisoners in the police station, imagine how different their situation would have been if one or both of them had subscribed to the principle of honor among thieves and possessed a prickly conscience that made it painful to betray the other. Suppose that both were in fact innocent — and moral, at that. Each might well prefer to accept a long prison term rather than unjustly condemn the other to an even longer term. The utility of each outcome would not coincide merely with jail terms. In these circumstances, where the pangs of conscience associated with squealing now make unilateral defection a distasteful outcome, the prisoners would actually get what would be for them the best possible outcome: both would refuse to defect and thus

---

[26] Robert Axelrod, *The Evolution of Cooperation* (New York: Basic Books, 1984). The tit-for-tat strategy was submitted by Anatol Rapoport. See also Axelrod's *The Complexity of Cooperation: Agent-Based Models of Competition and Collaboration* (Princeton, N.J.: Princeton University Press, 1997), especially chaps. 1, 2.

would receive the very short jail sentence. In international politics it is often easy to dismiss the effect of moral conscience, but such considerations should not be ignored.

Even though the détente of the early 1970s itself did not last, many of its elements (scientific and cultural exchanges, the Helsinki accords, certain arms-control agreements) survived and provided the basis for the dramatic East-West thaw that began in the 1980s. Both sides learned from past mistakes of both misguided trust and excessive suspicion. We must always remember that world politics requires both conflict and cooperation. This is a fundamental argument against excessively realist strategic thinking about international problems. The idealism of one side alone cannot make all conflicts go away; yet if we insist on seeing the world as a constant struggle, we indeed make it more so.

Deterrence

With the dissolution of both the Warsaw Pact and the Soviet Union in 1991, and with Russia entering the Partnership for Peace with NATO in 1994, the cold war ended *without* escalating into a hot, nuclear war. How was this achieved? If one of the costs of arms races was the steady increase in destructive potential, how is this process reversed before that destructive potential is put to use?

In the cold-war confrontation between the United States and Soviet Union, crisis stability (that is, no sudden escalation to nuclear war) and the relative stability of the arms race (that is, few very sharp increases in spending) both depended on the fact that neither side possessed a first-strike capability. Because of existing technology, *neither* side's nuclear retaliatory forces became highly vulnerable. If *one* side had been vulnerable, the situation would have been quite different. It also would have been different if *both* sides' forces had been vulnerable, since striking first would have made a significant difference in the outcome of a war and each side might have been tempted to beat the other to the punch. This sort of vulnerability would have been highly dangerous in a crisis situation, and it was this understanding that fueled the arms race.

The difference between first- and second-strike capability is crucial to understanding the arms race and nuclear deterrence. As we mentioned, first-strike capability means that one can attack and destroy the other's retaliatory capability while suffering "acceptable" damage. It can thus become very tempting to make the attack. Under conditions of stable deterrence, each side has only a second-strike capability — the capacity to absorb a first strike and still retaliate causing unacceptable damage — not a first-strike force. Each has an assured capability to inflict enormous destruction on an attacker; thus neither is tempted to attack the other. To protect their second-strike capabilities, both sides spent many billions of dollars on the research, development, and procurement of advanced weapons. The arms strategies they followed included:

1. Producing *large numbers* of delivery vehicles so that an attacker would not be able to destroy all of them.

2. *Dispersing* delivery vehicles widely, again to multiply the number of targets an attacker would have to hit, and making it impossible for one attacking warhead to wipe out more than one delivery vehicle. For that reason bombers were widely dispersed among many airfields and ICBM silos were separated.

3. *Hardening* the launching sites of delivery vehicles. For example, American missile silos were built to be enclosed in enough steel and concrete to withstand the blast of a near miss.

4. Making the delivery vehicles *mobile,* since a moving target is hard to track and hit; submarines for launching missiles take advantage of this feature.

5. *Concealment* of missile launching sites. Again, submarines, operating hundreds of feet below the surface of the ocean, are well concealed, making the submarines for launching SLBMs the most dependable and secure strategic second-strike force.

6. The *active defense* of retaliatory forces, including systems which would intercept bombers and (it was also hoped) missiles.

7. A policy of *launch under attack.* This meant that land-based ICBMs that were vulnerable to a first strike would be launched before they could be struck by incoming missiles. This would have been a desirable policy only if we could be confident of avoiding false alarms (and it might not have been desirable even then).

All these ways to protect nuclear retaliatory forces required intensive and costly efforts to provide secure means of command, control, communication, and intelligence — known in government as C^3I — from headquarters to the numerous, dispersed, mobile, and well-concealed launching sites. Civilian leaders must be confident that they have secure command and control facilities from which to deal with the military chiefs and that the military will operate only on orders from the civilian commander in chief or those to whom authority has been delegated.

Neither side depended solely on one type of weapons system in its strategic forces. Each side possessed land-based intercontinental missiles, large numbers of bombers capable of attacking the other's home territory (intercontinental bombers and, in the case of the United States, bombers stationed in Europe or on aircraft carriers), and, most important, many SLBMs on submarines. Together, aircraft, land-based missiles, and submarine-based missiles formed a **nuclear triad,** with each leg having different capabilities and each protected in different ways. This formed the core of the strategic planning of both sides. Even though one or even two parts of the triad might become vulnerable through technological change, the other element(s) would still be secure. Without major breakthroughs in antisubmarine warfare, the SLBMs were depended upon for retaliation. With them, neither side could have had a secure first-strike capability, and deterrence remained stable.

Crisis Instability

We must now step back from the details of military hardware to consider the theory of deterrence and how it may work in a crisis. The normal, noncrisis mode of nuclear deterrence is the "balance of terror," and resembles an assurance game (recall Part B of Figure 9.4). The best outcome for both sides is restraint, the mutually optimal equilibrium outcome. A decision to attack (like a decision to arm) would prompt a similar defection by the opponent, thereby shifting the situation to the suboptimal (indeed, devastating) equilibrium outcome of a nuclear exchange. But under normal conditions the balance of terror prevents this from occurring and nuclear deterrence works.

A policy of restraint was acceptable only so long as neither side had a first-strike capability and so long as each was confident that the other was not bent on acquiring that capability. This stability could have been undermined by several possible developments. A great technological breakthrough for one side, such as an extremely effective ABM (antiballistic missile) and air defense system and very accurate MIRVs (multiple independently targeted reentry vehicles), would have raised the gains from a first strike by reducing the damage expected from the opponent's retaliation. Even the perception — correct or mistaken — that the adversary was about to achieve such a breakthrough might suddenly have changed the estimates of the country receiving such information. If the adversary seemed about to gain the ability to attack you, a preemptive attack might have seemed the rational thing to do.

Most kinds of technological change by themselves were unlikely to shake the foundation of stable deterrence so long as both superpowers maintained heavy research and development programs and maintained their nuclear triads. A plausible set of events that could have upset the stability of nuclear deterrence might have occurred during a crisis — perhaps one something like the Cuban missile crisis of 1962. According to Henry Kissinger:

> If crisis management requires cold and even brutal measures to show determination, it also imposes the need to show opponents a way out. Grandstanding is good for the ego but bad for foreign policy. Many wars have started because no line of retreat was left open. Superpowers have a special obligation not to humiliate each other.[27]

As it happened, in 1962 President Kennedy was careful to give Khrushchev an opportunity to withdraw the Soviet missiles with some dignity. Kennedy termed the outcome a victory for peace, not a victory for the United States.

Suppose that Kennedy had dramatized the outcome of missile crisis as an American victory and a great loss of prestige for the Soviets, claiming that it proved they were unable to deter any serious American pressure against the communist world. Then suppose Kennedy had followed up with efforts to overthrow the Castro government. In these circumstances, the value of mutual restraint to the Soviets — and especially to the humiliated Khrushchev, who would have faced immediate ouster — might have taken second place to nuclear attack as long as there was a possibility that the damage imposed by the American retaliation would fall short of annihilation. At the same time, Khrushchev might have interpreted Kennedy's actions as indicating that the Americans had much greater confidence in their own first-strike capability than he had previously thought. That might have led the Soviets to raise substantially their estimates of the damage the United States could inflict and a suspicion that the Americans too might be preparing to initiate an attack. Thus, even though a Soviet first strike would still have resulted in a bad outcome for them — defection would no doubt be

---

[27] Henry Kissinger, *Years of Upheaval* (Boston: Little, Brown, 1982), p. 595.

mutual, the second worse outcome for the Soviets (and Americans) — using even a moderate first-strike capability might have looked better to the Soviet Union than restraint under continuing conditions of humiliation and manipulation by the Americans. In short, the situation would have *become* a prisoner's dilemma.

Brinkmanship

Many international crises do not resemble the prisoner's dilemma so much as they do the adolescent game of **chicken,** which was popularized during the 1950s. Two youths would line up their cars facing each other on a deserted stretch of road. Each car would have its left wheels on the center line, and they would drive toward each other at high speed. Friends might be riding in the cars; others would stand on the sidelines, cheering on the contestants. If neither car swerved, they would collide, and the occupants would be badly injured or killed. That, of course, was the worst outcome. But the next worst was to be the driver who swerved first, the humiliated "chicken." An acceptable, if not especially satisfying, outcome was to swerve at exactly the same moment as the adversary. The best outcome was for the *other* driver to swerve: this produced immense satisfaction, and praise, derived from making a chicken out of one's opponent. (Sometimes the stakes were much higher, requiring the chicken to forfeit the title of his automobile.) The usual result was that one driver would swerve; less often, both players would pull away simultaneously. No one really intended to kill or be killed. But occasionally there was the sobering result (and a little sobering was in order) when both players miscalculated and neither swerved in time.

Figure 9.5 shows the chicken game in matrix form. Notice that there are two equilibria in this game: Blue stands firm while Red gives in and swerves, or vice versa. One common tactic employed in chicken was for a driver to take his hands off the steering

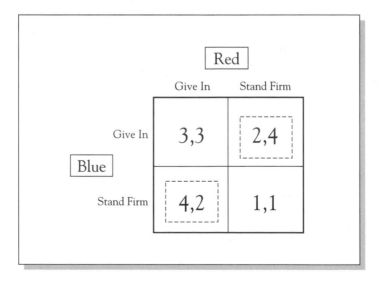

FIGURE 9.5   International Crisis as a Game of Chicken

wheel, thereby communicating to the other driver that he no longer controlled his vehicle and their mutual fate was no longer in his hands. The other driver, being rational, would have no choice but to swerve. As contestants became wise to such tactics, more desperate measures were called for in order to demonstrate the lack of control, like jumping into the passenger seat.

International crises often resemble games of **brinkmanship** like chicken, contests of nerve to see who will be first to give in. Plausibly the Cuban missile crisis was such an instance, in that nuclear war would be the worst result for both countries: there would be no meaningful winner and both would be left worse off than if one had capitulated. The goal was to make the adversary swerve or, if absolutely necessary, be able to swerve oneself at just the last minute before someone (possibly an unauthorized lower-level commander) began using nuclear weapons deliberately or by accident. Of course, it was Khrushchev who swerved in this case, and the chicken game suggests that it was the rational thing to do. However, Soviet leaders swore they would build up their forces so that the United States could never threaten them that way again. Chicken is a dangerous game. In nuclear diplomacy, it assumes that both sides will be able to control their forces well enough that war will not occur accidentally and that at least one party will be fearful (or sensible) enough to swerve in time. A player who was once humiliated may be unwilling to swerve in a subsequent crisis.

Deterring a nuclear "bolt from the blue" was not the central problem for American and Soviet strategists during the cold war because that sort of surprise attack did not present a credible threat in an era of MAD. The problem, especially for U.S. policymakers, was how to credibly threaten nuclear response to lesser forms of aggression, like a Soviet invasion of Western Europe, when nuclear retaliation would surely follow. Jonathan Schell summed it up nicely when he said that each superpower's nuclear arsenal was "like a gun with two barrels, of which one points ahead and the other points back at the gun's holder. If a burglar should enter your house, it might make sense to threaten him with this gun, but it could never make sense to fire it."[28]

One solution adopted by the United States was not unlike the tactic used by the bold drivers in the game of chicken. An important feature of nuclear command and control is that the authority to launch nuclear weapons devolves during times of crisis. If sole authority remained with the high-level military commanders (including the president, as commander-in-chief), U.S. retaliatory capacity might be neutralized by a "decapitating" Soviet first strike. In reality, as a crisis escalates more and more authority passes to local military commanders to use the nuclear weapons in their possession. If the Soviets attacked Western Europe with all their conventional military might, there was not much that U.S. forces in Europe could have done to repel the invasion. But the Soviets had to consider the prospect that local U.S. commanders, their forces overrun (and their families in danger), had nuclear weapons at their disposal. From the perspective of American nuclear strategists, that was like taking your hands off the steering wheel: "Look, we are no longer in full control of our nuclear response, so it's up to you to swerve." It is what Thomas Schelling called "the threat that leaves something to chance."[29]

---

[28] Jonathan Schell, *The Abolition* (New York: Knopf, 1984), p. 54.
[29] See Thomas Schelling, *The Strategy of Conflict* (Cambridge, Mass.: Harvard University Press, 1960), chap. 8.

Strategists may have devised a way to enhance the credibility of nuclear retaliation, but this solution was rather frightening to the rest of us. (Who wants to ride with a driver willing to let go of the steering wheel?) Scenarios for nuclear attack may seem improbable, but in fact they were not. Kennedy said at the time of the Cuban missile crisis that he thought the chances of nuclear war were about one in three. Perhaps he was mistaken, but even if the odds were lower such a belief can become a self-fulfilling prophecy. Thinking that war is near can bring it near through pressures for preemption, just as thinking war is near can bring greater efforts to avoid disaster. The problem with brinkmanship is that human leaders are fallible; they can easily misunderstand each other's intentions, especially under the enormous pressures of a nuclear crisis. We might be inclined to rest a little easier since the cold war has ended. Severe crisis is less likely as conflicts over spheres of influence abate, with good political relations defusing much of the danger posed by strategic technology. But there is huge destructive capacity harnessed in the nuclear weapons that the United States and Russia still deploy, not to mentioned those deployed by the other nuclear states. With India and Pakistan, the two most recent members of the nuclear club, glaring at each other across contested Kashmir, it is clear that the dangers of crisis instability and nuclear escalation remain very real. Nuclear proliferation also poses the risk that a future nuclear crisis would be multilateral; we can imagine that China may well become involved in a Indo-Pakistani conflict. Such crises — and the brinkmanship they might encourage — would be much harder to control than the bilateral crises of the past.

Arms Control and Disarmament

The nuclear balance of terror and the fear of accidental or uncontrolled nuclear launches highlighted for both world leaders and the general public the need to restrain the U.S.-Soviet arms race and the proliferation of weapons of mass destruction.[30] When reviewing the history of arms control, especially the bilateral agreements signed by the United States and the Soviet Union, it is important to remember that arms control is not necessarily disarmament. **Arms control** is a process that produces agreements on the production, management, and use of weapons — their types, characteristics, conditions of deployment (to prevent accidents), and so forth. Many arms control agreements are concerned with the creation of stability in the sense that neither side is tempted to use weapons first. The aim of **disarmament** is to reduce the numbers of weapons. Thus, arms control may be seen as a distraction from the quest for disarma-

---

[30] See, for example, Scott D. Sagan, *The Limits of Safety: Organizations, Accidents, and Nuclear Weapons* (Princeton, N.J.: Princeton University Press, 1993). For a sometimes disturbing account of the procedures for managing U.S. nuclear forces during a crisis, see Paul Bracken, *The Command and Control of Nuclear Forces* (New Haven, Conn.: Yale University Press, 1983). On Russia's nuclear command and control system and the dangers posed by Russian domestic turmoil, see Bruce G. Blair, *The Logic of Accidental Nuclear War* (Washington, D.C.: Brookings, 1993).

ment. Alternatively, some kinds of disarmament could work against the stability sought through arms control (for instance, by reducing second-strike capabilities).

Generally, multilateral treaties aim to prevent the spread of weapons of mass destruction to areas and countries where they have not already been deployed. Thus, treaties regarding the Antarctic, outer space, the seabed, and environmental modification all provide that signatories will continue to refrain from doing something they have not yet done. Biological and chemical weapons agreements have called for destroying stocks of weapons, but most analysts of modern warfare agree that both biological and chemical weapons are generally inferior to nuclear ones as weapons of mass destruction. If a state already has large stocks of nuclear weapons, chemical and especially biological weapons are largely superfluous except for small encounters. Thus, the most important targets of biological and chemical weapons agreements are the nonnuclear states, who seek to acquire them as substitutes for nuclear weapons (perhaps while they conduct nuclear weapons research). The danger becomes much greater as more and more countries are able to build or buy medium-range ballistic missiles, which provide the means of delivering these weapons.

Nuclear Arms Control

In May of 1994 the United States and Russia officially announced that they had stopped targeting each other's territory with missiles. While perhaps considered unremarkable in the post–cold war atmosphere, such an event was the result of a long process of arms control, both between the two superpowers and in multilateral agreements over various forms of weapons of mass destruction. The major arms-control agreements since World War II — both bilateral agreements between the United State and the Soviet Union (or Russia) and multilateral agreements — are listed in Tables 9.3 and 9.4. For multilateral agreements, the final column indicates the number of countries that either signed the original agreement (whether or not they have formally ratified it) or acceded to the agreement since it entered into force.

The limitations on weapons types, characteristics, and deployment that enhance stability can be broken down into several basic categories. Some arms control agreements *create nuclear free zones* in an effort to exclude arms races from certain areas by forbidding the deployment of nuclear weapons there. Some of these have been created in frontier areas, such as the Antarctic, outer space, and the seabed. Other treaties declare the intention of signatories not to see weapons introduced into their own region; states are forbidden from either acquiring nuclear weapons themselves or allowing external powers to station nuclear forces on their territories. Such agreements, like those signed by countries in Latin American, the South Pacific, and Africa, also include promises by the nuclear powers to respect these prohibitions.

Arms control may be aimed at *minimizing risks of accidental nuclear attacks*, especially those that might derive from miscommunication. In the first bilateral agreement signed by the United States and Soviet Union, which followed the Cuban missile crisis, the superpowers agreed to install a "hot line" providing for emergency communication between their heads of state. Emergency communication between their foreign policy and defense officials has been facilitated more recently by the creation of a

TABLE 9.3   U.S.-Soviet and U.S.-Russian Arms Control Agreements

Signed	Agreement	Provisions
1963	Hot Line Agreement	Establishes direct teletype communications between heads of state for use in emergency. Updated in 1971 and 1974.
1971	Accidents Measures Agreement	Institutes various measures to reduce risk of accidental nuclear war.
1972	Incidents at Sea Agreement	Provides for measures to help prevent dangerous incidents on or over the high seas involving ships and aircraft.
1972	Anti-Ballistic Missile Treaty (SALT I)	Limits development, testing, and deployment of anti-ballistic missile systems to two sites in each country — reduced to one site by 1974 protocol.
1972	Interim Agreement on Offensive Arms (SALT I)	Five-year freeze on total number of fixed, land-based ICBMs and on SLBMs. Later extended to 1980.
1973	Prevention of Nuclear War Agreement	Institutes various measures to help avert outbreak of nuclear war in crisis situations.
1974	Threshold Test Ban Treaty	Prohibits underground tests of nuclear weapons with explosive yields greater than 150 kilotons. (Ratified in 1990.)
1976	Peaceful Nuclear Explosions Treaty	Bars explosions greater than 150 kilotons for peaceful purposes, such as excavation or mining. (Ratified in 1990.)
1979	Offensive Arms Agreement (SALT II)	Limits numbers and types of strategic nuclear delivery vehicles. (Not ratified.)
1987	Intermediate-range Nuclear Forces Treaty	Eliminates all ground-launched ballistic and cruise missiles with ranges between 500 and 5,500 kilometers.
1987	Nuclear Risk Reduction Centers Agreement	Establishes communication centers capable of high-speed facsimile communications between foreign- and defense-policy officials.
1988	Ballistic Missile Launch Notification Agreement	Provides for advance notification of date and area of any ICBM or SLBM missile launches.
1991	Strategic Arms Reduction Treaty (START I)	Reduces number of strategic warheads by about one-third. In Lisbon Protocol (1992), Russia, Belarus, Ukraine, and Kazakhstan agree to former USSR treaty obligations.
1993	Strategic Arms Reduction Treaty II (START II)	Reduces number of deployed strategic nuclear warheads to between 3,000 and 3,500 by 2003 and bans multiple-warhead ICBMs.

Source: U.S. Arms Control and Disarmament Agency, "Treaties and Agreements," n.d. [cited September 29, 1998]; available at <http://www.acda.gov/treaties.htm>.

TABLE 9.4	Multilateral Arms Control Agreements since 1959		
Signed	Agreement	Provisions	Signatories
1959	Antarctic Treaty	Prohibits all military activity in the Antarctic area.	37
1963	Limited Test Ban Treaty	Prohibits nuclear explosions in the atmosphere, outer space, and underwater.	131
1967	Outer Space Treaty	Prohibits all military activity in outer space, including the moon and other celestial bodies.	127
1967	Latin America Nuclear-Free Zone Treaty	Prohibits Latin American countries from acquiring, manufacturing, testing, using, or stationing nuclear weapons.	31
1968	Non-proliferation Treaty	Prohibits acquisition of nuclear weapons by nonnuclear nations.	185
1971	Seabed Arms Control Treaty	Prohibits emplacement of nuclear weapons and other weapons of mass destruction on the ocean floor or its subsoil.	117
1972	Biological Weapons Convention	Prohibits development, production, and stockpiling of biological agents and toxins intended for hostile use and requires destruction of existing stocks.	157
1977	Environmental Modification Convention	Prohibits manipulation of the dynamics, composition, or structure of the earth, including its atmosphere, and of outer space for military or other hostile purposes.	85
1980	Nuclear Material Convention	Establishes guidelines for international transport of nuclear material and the protection, recovery, and return of stolen nuclear material.	50
1985	South Pacific Nuclear-Free Zone Treaty	Prohibits countries and territories of the South Pacific from acquiring, manufacturing, testing, using, or stationing nuclear weapons.	18
1986	Confidence- and Security-Building Measures in Europe	Stockholm Document requires advance notification of large-scale military activities in Europe. Updated provisions contained in the Vienna Document of 1994.	54
1987	Missile Technology Control Regime	Seeks to restrict the export of ballistic missiles, space launch vehicles, unmanned air vehicles, and related technologies.	29

continued

TABLE 9.4   Multilateral Arms Control Agreements since 1959 *(continued)*

Signed	Agreement	Provisions	Signatories
1990	Conventional Armed Forces in Europe Treaty	Reduces NATO and Warsaw Pact forces in the Atlantic-to-Urals region. Former Soviet states agree to USSR obligations in 1992 Tashkent Agreement.	30
1992	Open Skies Treaty	Parties allow a quota of overflights of their Territory for purposes of observing military activities.	27
1993	Chemical Weapons Convention	Prohibits development, production, and stockpiling of toxic chemicals intended for hostile use, and requires destruction of existing stocks by 2007.	169
1996	Wassenaar Arrangement on Export Controls	Seeks to restrict the export of conventional weapons, dual-use equipment, and their production technologies.	33
1996	Comprehensive Test Ban Treaty	Prohibits all nuclear explosions, including those intended for peaceful purposes.	150
1996	African Nuclear Weapon Free Zone Treaty	Prohibits African countries from acquiring, manufacturing, testing, using, or stationing nuclear weapons.	54
1997	Anti-personnel Mine Convention	Prohibits production, stockpiling and use of anti-personnel mines, and requires destruction of existing stocks.	132

Note: Signatories are the number of states that signed (but have not necessarily ratified) or have acceded to the agreement.

Sources: U.S. Arms Control and Disarmament Agency, "Treaties and Agreements," n.d., [cited September 29, 1998]; available at <http://www.acda.gov/treaties.htm>. Anti-personnel Mine Convention information from "International Campaign to Ban Landmines," 1998 [cited October 3, 1998]; available at <http://www.icbl.org/>.

"nuclear risk reduction center" in each country. These and other treaties — for example, the agreement dealing with incidents at sea — have sought to make it easier to control crises that may escalate to the nuclear level.

Arms control has long sought to *set limits on the characteristics of weapons*, both nuclear and non-nuclear, especially their capacity for inflicting human suffering. In the twelfth century, the second Lateran Council under Pope Innocent II disallowed the use of crossbows against Christians (though not against non-Christians). The Hague

Agreements of 1899 and 1907 outlawed the use of exploding and expanding ("dum-dum") bullets because they caused unnecessary human suffering. Following on the Hague Agreements, which also banned the use of projectiles armed with poison gases, the Geneva Protocol of 1925 recognized that "the use in war of asphyxiating, poisonous or other gases, and of all analogous liquids, materials or devices, has been justly condemned by the general opinion of the civilized world" and sought to extend the ban to include bacteriological methods of warfare. These agreements provide the basis for the 1972 Biological Weapons Convention and the 1993 Chemical Weapons Convention, both of which prohibit not only the use of these weapons, but also their development, production, and stockpiling.

Some weapons characteristics are considered especially destabilizing. As a result of the Strategic Arms Limitation Talks (SALT), the two superpowers agreed in 1972 to limit their deployment of anti-ballistic missile systems because they undermined the second-strike capabilities that provided the foundation for mutual deterrence. Thus, the Reagan administration's Strategic Defense Initiative — since scaled back and reconstituted as the Ballistic Missile Defense (BMD) Program — was criticized for being both destabilizing and a violation of the ABM Treaty. The 1974 Threshold Test Ban Treaty was designed to inhibit the creation of a destabilizing first-strike capability by prohibiting nuclear test explosions with yields in excess of 150 kilotons. Since high-yield nuclear testing might be accomplished under the guise of explosions for "peaceful purposes," like excavation or mining, those were also banned in 1976. Neither test ban was ratified until 1990, but both countries are presumed to have adhered to their provisions after signing.

Other bilateral arms control agreements between the United States and the Soviet Union, and later Russia, have set limits on the number of nuclear weapons that can be deployed. SALT was the first forum for their efforts and succeeded in slowing the growth of the superpowers' nuclear arsenals. The 1987 Treaty on Intermediate Nuclear Forces (INF) represents a milestone in arms control, for two reasons. Although the treaty only covered about four percent of the superpowers' nuclear forces, it was the first arms control agreement that actually reduced the number of nuclear weapons. The SALT agreements had only established ceilings that could not be exceeded by future deployments. INF provided for on-site inspections and other verification procedures that had been insurmountable hurdles in previous talks. Verifying the elimination of an entire class of nuclear weapons would prove far easier, and less intrusive, than verifying whether some numerical limit had been exceeded.

The agreement and its successful implementation, even while almost insignificant from a military point of view, proved to have a substantial impact on political relations between the superpowers, and that is the second reason it became a milestone in the history of arms control. Arms control treaties, in almost any form, build confidence and trust among the parties to the agreement. The INF Treaty had that effect, setting into motion a process that has culminated in the very deep cuts required by the two Strategic Arms Reduction Treaties (START I and START II), cuts that are graphically displayed in Figure 9.2 (p. 222). Even SALT II, which was never ratified by the U.S. Senate as a result of the Soviet invasion of Afghanistan six months after its signing, built confidence and trust between the superpowers for as long as they continued to adhere voluntarily to the limits set by the treaty.

Most observers agree that *stemming the proliferation of weapons of mass destruction* will continue to be the central issue of arms control as we move into the twenty-first century. In signing the Non-proliferation Treaty (NPT) of 1968, states that did not already have nuclear weapons promised not to acquire them, and states that did have nuclear weapons promised not to transfer them to non-nuclear states. The bargain between the nuclear powers and non- nuclear states in the NPT was that this "horizontal" proliferation of nuclear capability would be restricted in return for real reductions in the nuclear powers' existing arsenals — that is, an end to "vertical" proliferation. As an effort to dampen the upwardly spiraling arms race, SALT was welcome; but it is only with the START agreements that the United States and Russia began to live up to promises long overdue. Real disarmament is now occurring. Meeting in New York in May 1995, parties to the NPT agreed to extend the original treaty permanently into the future. By 1998 there were 185 signatories, making it the most widely adhered to treaty in the history of arms control.

Despite widespread adherence to the NPT, the spread of nuclear materials and technology remains an issue. By the 1980s Israel, India, and South Africa — none having signed the original NPT — had crossed the threshold to actual possession of a nuclear capability. Until 1998, there was some uncertainty about Pakistan's nuclear capability, but that was put to rest when it engaged in dueling nuclear tests with India in May of that year. Other non-NPT states such as Argentina and Brazil were moving in the same direction during the 1980s and early 1990s, as were NPT states like South Korea and Taiwan. But since 1992, with the U.S.-Russian arms reduction agreements and the accession of France and China to the NPT, these sub-threshold states had canceled their nuclear weapons programs. South Africa destroyed all seven of the bombs it had built, and signed the NPT in 1991; Argentina signed in 1995. A worrisome development, however, is the emergence of a new group of "renegade" states: parties to the NPT who continue to attempt to acquire nuclear weapons, including Iraq, Iran, Algeria (and possibly Libya and Syria). The renegade state attracting perhaps the most attention has been North Korea, with its ever-changing policies towards the NPT, on-site inspection of its nuclear facilities, and negotiations over its compliance to the treaty.[31]

Although they also help to control proliferation, some arms control efforts to curb nuclear testing have had as a central purpose *limiting environmental damage*. One of the first arms-control agreements of the cold war was the Limited Test Ban Treaty, signed in 1963, which banned nuclear test explosions everywhere but underground — explosions that might cause "radioactive debris to be present outside the territorial limits of the State under whose jurisdiction or control such explosion is conducted." The 1996 Comprehensive Test Ban Treaty (CTBT) closes off two avenues left open for nuclear testing by the Limited Test Ban Treaty: neither underground testing nor testing for

---

[31] For a discussion of both threshold and renegade states, as well as a detailed review of current non-proliferation activities, see John Simpson, "The Nuclear Non-proliferation Regime after the NPT Review and Extension Conference," in Stockholm International Peace Research Institute (SIPRI), *SIPRI Yearbook 1996: Armaments, Disarmament and International Security* (New York: Oxford University Press, 1996). See also Michael Klare, *Rogue States and Nuclear Outlaws: America's Search for a New Foreign Policy* (New York: Hill and Wang, 1995), and David J. Karl, "Proliferation Pessimism and Emerging Nuclear Powers," *International Security* 21, 3 (Winter 1996/97): pp. 87–119.

"peaceful purposes" is excluded from the prohibition. The CTBT has been signed by 150 nations (within months of their May 1998 nuclear tests, both India and Pakistan expressed their intention to accede to the treaty as well) and places serious constraints on nuclear weapons development and qualitative improvement.

Controlling Conventional Weapons and Technology

Most arms control agreements target weapons of mass destruction, but there have been some noteworthy efforts to address the proliferation of conventional weapons, as well as advanced weapons technology. Following on fifteen years of Mutual and Balanced Force Reduction (MBFR) talks, NATO and Warsaw Pact countries began negotiations on Conventional Armed Forces in Europe (CFE) and in 1990 concluded a treaty requiring substantial cuts in the number of tanks, armored vehicles, artillery, combat helicopters, and aircraft deployed in the European theater. The most celebrated recent accomplishment in conventional arms control is the Anti-personnel Mine Convention outlawing the production and use of landmines, which entered into force in 1999. The movement to ban landmines was a truly grassroots effort spearheaded by the International Campaign to Ban Landmines, for which the NGO and its coordinator Jody Williams received the 1997 Nobel Peace Prize.

The U.S.-led war against Iraq and its aftermath heightened interest in the acquisition of advanced-technology weaponry throughout the world, including missile delivery systems. Such interest in turn raised concern among the five permanent members of the UN Security Council: the United States, Russia, China, Britain, and France — the countries responsible for about 80 percent of the global trade in conventional weapons. Earlier, in 1987, the Missile Technology Control Regime (MTCR) had been established as a voluntary association of countries committed to establishing guidelines for the export of missiles (and missile-production knowhow) that might be used to deliver weapons of mass destruction. A more concerted effort seemed to be required, so meetings were held in 1991–92. These efforts were only partially successful, but ended in late 1992 when China walked out in protest over U.S. sales of jet fighters to Taiwan. The effort to replace the cold war–era Coordinating Committee for Multilateral Export Control (CoCom) — mainly NATO members cooperating to restrict the transfer of military technology to the Warsaw Pact — was more successful. In 1996, the Wassenaar Arrangement was announced, whereby member states (this time including former Warsaw Pact countries) agreed to begin putting in place restrictions on the export of conventional weapons and advanced weapons technology.[32]

Many people — government leaders, citizens, and scholars — have devoted their energies to reducing the prospects of war and reducing the number and destructiveness of weapons with which wars might be fought. Our review of arms-control and disarmament efforts since World War II leaves us with a mixed picture. There has been progress. The world has not blown up; no nuclear weapon has been exploded in war since 1945. By historical standards, that is a long time without a global war. Despite the

---

[32] A good overview of the post–cold war arms trade and efforts to control it is Paul Cornish, *Controlling the Arms Trade: The West versus the Rest* (London: Bowerdean, 1996).

common fears voiced in each decade, there has not been a steady proliferation of nuclear weapons. Beyond the United States, Russia, Britain, France, and China, only India and Pakistan have exploded nuclear devices — though Israel and perhaps a few other states could and might. As we have seen, there have been international agreements to ban nuclear weapons from many environments and to prohibit nuclear testing and proliferation. Chemical and biological weapons of mass destruction are being controlled, while international public opinion has turned sharply against states willing to deploy inhumane weapons like landmines. Such progress should not give way to complacency, however. There are still a lot of nuclear weapons in the world, and there are nagging uncertainties about the ability of some states to control them during times of crisis. Not all states have signed the most comprehensive arms control treaties, and not all those who have can be depended upon to abide by their terms. It may not be a realist dog-eat-dog world out there, but neither is it an idealist utopia.

10

International Law and Organization

Ethics and War

Our discussion in the last two chapters concentrated on several dimensions of military conflict and arms acquisition: the historical record, analytical perspectives that illuminate our understanding, and empirical evidence supporting (or not supporting) hypotheses about causes and consequences. There are also ethical dimensions. Occasionally we have alluded to moral and ethical considerations as possible restraints on both conflict and armament, but that has been the extent of our discussion of ethics. We have not considered such issues as what kinds of actions are moral or ethical or what ethical principles *should* guide our behavior and the behavior of our leaders in war and in peace. Nor have we considered the ethical principles and laws that *do* guide behavior in world politics, or the ways states have organized themselves in order to encourage ethical behavior. These are the kinds of issues we will now take up.

Moral or ethical propositions concern how people ought to behave rather than how people do behave. This is the stuff of **normative theory.** Ethical reasoning is essentially *deductive* reasoning. One starts with a few basic principles — such as, "all humans are created equal" — and deduces from them a set of propositions that provide further guidance for identifying behavior consistent with those principles. Just because the subject matter is often morality and peace does not mean that normative theories are, or need be, "warm and fuzzy" or "politically correct" theories. The deductive reasoning used to construct normative theories about world politics is often as rigorous as game theory or other forms of mathematical reasoning.

Many social scientists are reluctant to engage in ethical discussions because of the great difficulty we have, in modern industrial societies, establishing a common frame of reference. Few people live in cultures where a single value system is dominant. Although modern values are heavily influenced by Greek and Judeo-Christian traditions, there is no commonly accepted authority, and only a few propositions are shared across most contemporary religions and other ethical systems. Humanists, Marxists, agnostics, and atheists share some common ground with religious believers, but that ground is not very extensive. Even within many of the major traditions, authority is repudiated and a wide variety of opinions are tolerated.

We cannot, however, completely ignore such issues in a discussion of deterrence and war. Are there circumstances in which nuclear weapons should not be used, or even deployed? According to widely accepted ethical precepts, are there targets that should not be attacked, whether by nuclear or conventional weapons? Our purpose here is not to insist on answers, but to offer a number of considerations essential to an informed discussion of the issues.

Realism and Pacifism

At one end of the spectrum of ethical thought about warfare are views associated with realism: (1) that any act in war is justifiable if it seems to serve the national interest, and (2) that rightness depends solely on the ends sought rather than on the methods used to obtain those ends. The first view implies that if the populace as a whole is thought to desire something, leaders should seek to obtain it with whatever means are available. This version of realism takes a very pessimistic view of human nature and the human condition. It holds that regardless of the moral restraints that bind our interpersonal behavior, international politics is so anarchic — a war of each against all — that mere self-preservation requires the abandonment of moral inhibitions. For those who hold to the second view, there are legitimate and illegitimate goals in world politics; but if your goals or ends are just, any means may be employed to reach them. Both views involve *utilitarian* reasoning: behavior is ethical if it brings the greatest good to the greatest number. According to the more restrictive first view, however, the "greatest number" is judged only in reference to a state's own population.

Although many people may express their adherence to such principles, it is not clear how many really believe that they alone are guides to action. Most adults come to believe that the law is important; it should be obeyed most of the time; and, if it is disobeyed, it should not be disobeyed lightly. Civil disobedience, for example, is considered permissible only if undertaken for some higher moral purpose. International law is generally regarded as one of the least authoritative and least effective forms of law, but, as we shall see, even it is given some respect and observance, and not solely out of self-interest. When occupying the Vietnam village of My Lai, Lieutenant William Calley ordered, supervised, and participated in the killing of hundreds of civilians. He defended his action on the grounds that it was necessary to safeguard his troops from Vietcong guerrillas, some of whom may have been disguised as civilians, and thus he claimed to be acting in accordance with the first view expressed above. Nevertheless, his act did violate U.S. Army regulations and most Americans' moral sense of what was right and wrong. Calley was tried and convicted by a military court of justice.

Similarly, after World War II many German and Japanese wartime leaders were tried by Allied military tribunals at Nuremberg and Tokyo. They were charged with the deliberate killing of civilians and prisoners of war and with "waging aggressive war." Some of these acts, such as killing prisoners, were clearly forbidden by instruments of international law, such as the Geneva Convention. Others, like waging aggressive war, were less clearly outlawed. Yet it was widely agreed that the enemy leaders had committed acts that were morally if not legally outrageous, and many of the leaders were convicted and executed. Despite the frequency with which we hear the old adages "war is hell" and "all's fair in [love and] war," most people act as though they believe that some legal and ethical restraints are relevant to international behavior — even war.

Pacifism is very different from a realist "all's fair" position. A completely pacifist position may result from a philosophical and moral predilection for nonviolence, a rejection in principle of the use of force as an instrument of national policy, a belief in the spiritually regenerative effect of a nonviolent response to violence, or an overriding concern for the preservation of human life. Like other normative theories, pacifist arguments are often based on rigorous deduction from first principles, despite the fact that many associate pacifism only with certain forms of social activism like "draft dodging."[1]

Pacifism has deep roots in a number of secular and religious traditions. It seems to have been the dominant view in the early Christian church before the Roman emperor Constantine converted to Christianity. The Roman Empire was pagan and often persecuted Christians; no Christian could in good conscience serve in the army of such a power. Pacifism is not the dominant tradition in contemporary Christianity, but it is still a common and respected view in many Christian churches. It is a central principle of the Society of Friends (the Quakers) and was practiced by Martin Luther King, Jr., in his program of civil disobedience against racial segregation. Mohandas Gandhi blended part of this Christian pacifist tradition with Hinduism in his resistance to British rule in India, and his example has had great influence worldwide. Plans for nonviolent resistance — a war without weapons against a would-be conqueror — are commonly discussed and sometimes practiced.[2]

---

[1] See, for example, Robert L. Holmes, *On War and Morality* (Princeton, N.J.: Princeton University Press, 1989).

[2] Gene Sharp, *Civilian-Based Defense: A Post-Military Weapons System* (Princeton, N.J.: Princeton University Press, 1990).

Just Wars

Between the realist "all's fair" position and the pacifist "all's unfair" position are a variety of intermediate views. For those who accept the use of force as a legitimate instrument of state policy in some but not all circumstances, there are two sets of ethical principles to consider when judging the morality of war. "War is always judged twice, first with reference to the reasons states have for fighting, secondly with reference to the means they adopt."[3] The first judgment applies to the justice *of* war, or *jus ad bellum,* and the second to justice *in* war, or *jus in bello.*

The set of principles that concentrate on what conditions justify an initial resort to military force are typically less concerned with how the conflict is conducted once it is begun. In the American philosophical tradition, the only just war is one undertaken in self-defense. In this context self-defense includes (1) defense of one's allies in keeping with a formal commitment, (2) assistance to a small power under the principle of collective security when authorized by an international organization, such as the United Nations, even if there is no treaty commitment, or (3) assistance to another government in response to its request for aid. Furthermore, the "self" to be defended is generally defined broadly to include not only the physical territory but also the values and way of life believed to characterize the nation. No other grievances, however severe, would justify the initiation of war; grievances should always be addressed only through negotiation or arbitration, or they should be endured in the hope that they will become more tolerable as circumstances evolve.

This position can become a very conservative one politically and is rejected by those who declare that oppression and exploitation must be resisted by force if necessary. The most common Marxist view holds that a war need not be undertaken in self-defense to be justifiable; war-making is blameless if its purpose is to redress class oppression or national subjugation. In this respect the Marxist approach differs widely from the classical American doctrine. Even for the Marxist, however, a just war must not have a reactionary effect. For example, a nuclear war that would devastate both capitalist and socialist civilizations, thereby undermining the progress made by socialist revolutions, would be unjust according to this view.

Quite a different position, embodied in the **just war tradition,** stems from Christian moralists. Just war theory has its origins in ancient Greek and Roman thought, was developed in the Middle Ages and later refined, and now is the predominant Christian view. It was at the core of a pastoral letter from Roman Catholic bishops in the United States that attracted much attention in 1983. It also provides a foundation for very similar positions taken by some non-Christian thinkers today.[4]

---

[3] Michael Walzer, *Just and Unjust Wars: A Moral Argument with Historical Illustrations,* 2nd ed. (New York: Basic Books, 1992), p. 21.

[4] For an introduction to the just war tradition, see Paul Christopher, *The Ethics of War and Peace: An Introduction to Legal and Moral Issues* (Englewood Cliffs, N.J.: Prentice Hall, 1994). See also National Conference of Catholic Bishops, *The Challenge of Peace: God's Promise and Our Response* (Washington, D.C.: U.S. Catholic Conference, 1983), and Kenneth Wald, "Religious Elites and Public Opinion: The Impact of the Bishops' Peace Pastoral," *Review of Politics* 54 (Winter 1992): pp. 112–143. Similar statements, though less prominent and comprehensive, have been made by other religious groups. For an earlier, Protestant statement, see Paul Ramsey, *The Just War: Force and Political Responsibility* (New York: Scribners, 1968).

The just war tradition — both *jus ad bellum* and *jus in bello* — has evolved over the centuries, but the first comprehensive and systematic statement of the so-called "laws of war" is often traced to Hugo Grotius, the seventeenth century jurist, in his *The Law of War and Peace*. Grotius identified several conditions that must be met if the resort to war is to be considered legitimate in light of prevailing international norms. Two of them, that there be just cause and that war be a last resort, also find expression in the UN Charter. For Grotius, *just cause* refers primarily to the right of self-defense, as it does in the UN Charter, which identifies "the inherent right of . . . self-defense if an armed attack occurs" (Article 51). However, in addition to self-defense, Grotius and others writing in the just war tradition (but not the UN) argue that just cause includes punishing (not only repelling) an aggressor, as well as preventing egregious humanitarian abuses. The principle of *last resort* suggests that states should exhaust all peaceful means of resolving disputes before resorting to military force, a condition that is easily met when a state has been attacked and is merely engaging in self-defense. This principle is also expressed in Article 33 of the UN Charter, which calls on states to "first of all, seek a solution by negotiation, enquiry, mediation, conciliation, arbitration" and other nonviolent means.[5]

The just war tradition also requires that war be declared by a *legitimate authority*, and that it be *declared publicly*. These *ad bellum* principles were once meant to exclude private wars, terrorism, and vigilante actions. Now it means that the basic constitutional rules of the state must be followed. In the United States, the president is commander in chief, but Congress must declare war. In the contemporary post–cold war world, certain rules about the use of military force seem to be emerging. As the United States and Russia become able to agree in the UN Security Council (where they, China, Britain, and France have individual veto power), it becomes expected that they should agree and that collective security operations against an aggressor should have UN approval. This expectation of joint response restrains any one big powerful state from unilaterally deciding that it has a just cause in defending someone else. In effect, some powers of legitimate authority are shifting from a national to an international level.

The most commonly professed principle governing the actual conduct of war is **discrimination,** or the requirement that combatants respect the immunity of noncombatants. The requirement of discrimination forbids direct, deliberate attacks on civilians. In their pastoral letter, the U.S. bishops wrote, "Under no circumstances may nuclear weapons or other instruments of mass slaughter be used for the purpose of destroying population centers or other predominantly civilian targets. . . . No Christian can rightfully carry out orders or policies deliberately aimed at killing noncombatants." This is a strong statement. It implicitly condemns the bombing of Dresden, a German city with no military significance; the firebombing of hundreds of thousands of Japanese civilians in World War II; and the atomic bombing of Hiroshima and Nagasaki, cities that were chosen as civilian, not military, targets. According to this principle, the fact that these bombings may have hastened the end of the war and even may have reduced the total number of civilian casualties from what they might otherwise

---

[5] A good reference source is W. Michael Reisman and Chris T. Antoniou, eds., *The Laws of War: A Comprehensive Collection of Primary Documents on International Laws Governing Armed Conflict* (New York: Vintage, 1994).

have been is not sufficient justification. By this principle, the direct killing of civilians as a means to achieving some end, however good, is never morally permissible.[6]

Noncombatants are usually easy to identify: children, the elderly, hospital patients, and farmers, for example. There are gray areas, however, such as civilians working in munitions factories or otherwise engaged in war-related production. One principle used to distinguish innocent civilians from civilians who may be subject to attack is that the latter are those supplying soldiers with the tools of combat, as opposed to the means of sustenance. That would allow the bombing of weapons factories, and perhaps even facilities that produce military uniforms, but would forbid attacking civilians working in food processing plants.

The principle of discrimination directly opposes policies adopted by the nuclear powers. Until 1973 American *declaratory* policy always emphasized "countercity" deterrence; that is, the ability to destroy a large fraction of any enemy's industry and to kill a large fraction of the enemy's population in retaliation for any attack on the United States or its allies. American *operational* policy (what in fact was in the war plans) never concentrated on civilian targets, despite the declaratory policy. A war plan from 1948 (actually known as "Broiler"), for example, called for the use of thirty-four bombs against targets in twenty-six cities. The targets of these plans included military sites, "military-related industry," transportation centers, and electricity-producing facilities. Most of these targets were in major population centers, and bombing them would have resulted in a large number of civilian deaths. Some decisionmakers saw these deaths as unintended but unavoidable; to others they were "bonus effects" that strengthened deterrence.[7]

Another principle applies both when states resort to war and while they fight. As an *ad bellum* principle, **proportionality** is met when the legitimate aims sought by a state resorting to war outweigh the harm that will result from the prosecution of the war. Proportionality recognizes that in almost any war, some civilians will unavoidably be killed if military targets are hit, and it accepts some number of civilian deaths as a by-product of striking a military target. But civilians are not to be killed without limit, even unintentionally. Massive civilian casualties would surely occur in any nuclear war, even one consisting of nuclear launches directed only at military targets. The bishops' letter is filled with references to the interspersing of military facilities and civilian living and working areas, resulting in a "horrendous" number of civilians who would necessarily be killed coincidentally with the hitting of military targets. Under these circumstances, the good sought by a nuclear war is not likely to outweigh the harm done, thereby violating the norm of proportionality.

The notion that in war the good sought and the harm done must be proportionate suggests that discrimination alone — not *targeting* innocent civilians — is not enough

---

[6] Americans have had great difficulty coming to terms with this judgment in regard to the atomic bombings of Japan, as was brought out in bold relief by the fiftieth-anniversary remembrances. See Gar Alperovitz, *The Decision to Use the Atomic Bomb, and the Architecture of an American Myth* (New York: Knopf, 1995), especially bk. 2; Robert Jay Lifton and Greg Mitchell, *Hiroshima in America: Fifty Years of Denial* (New York: Grosset/Putnam, 1995); and Barton J. Bernstein, "The Atomic Bombings Reconsidered," *Foreign Affairs* 74, 1 (January/February 1995): pp. 135–152.

[7] David Alan Rosenberg, "The Origins of Overkill: Nuclear Weapons and American Strategy," *International Security* 7, 4 (Spring 1983): p. 371.

to make a military action morally acceptable. The *in bello* version of proportionality is sometimes referred to as *double effect*. The idea here is that, like wars as a whole, the individual military actions undertaken during wartime have both good and bad effects. In order for those actions to be just, the good effect must outweigh the bad. Double effect requires that noncombatant immunity be observed — that the bad effect be unintended — but also requires that this unintended bad effect be proportional to the legitimate objective of the military action. The use of toxic defoliants by the United States in Vietnam probably violated the principle of double effect. The aim was legitimate: to reveal enemy forces, allowing them to be targeted by aerial bombardment. But the use of defoliants like Agent Orange caused long-term environmental damage and contamination. These bad effects were unintended, but we should ask whether destroying the enemy's cover was worth the adverse and foreseeable consequences for the civilian population.

Was the Gulf War a Just War?

In August 1990, after Kuwait refused to acquiesce to a series of Iraqi demands, and without physical provocation, Iraqi forces invaded and occupied the country. Within a week, Kuwait was annexed. A UN coalition of forces, led by the United States, claimed to have *just cause* in repelling the Iraqi invasion and restoring Kuwait's independence. In the just war tradition, self-defense warrants the resort to force, and in the UN Charter (which Iraq signed in 1945), *collective* self-defense is called for when necessary to reverse aggression by a stronger state against a weaker one. Even with the Kuwaiti government's less-than-sterling record on human rights, that nation had a right to resist occupation, and other nations had a right to help it. The liberation of Kuwait was authorized by UN Resolution 678, and thus the war against Iraq was *declared publicly* by a *legitimate authority*.

While there is some debate on this issue, a plausible case can be made that Operation Desert Storm was a *last resort*, launched only after diplomacy and negotiation had failed. Diplomacy had narrowed the gap between the coalition and Iraq, but serious differences were not settled. Economic sanctions were tried, but President Bush declared that they had failed and that force was ultimately needed to get Iraq out of Kuwait. Reasonable people do still disagree — among them, General Colin Powell, then Chairman of the Joint Chiefs of Staff. He thought sanctions should have been given more time. We will never know whether sanctions would have been sufficient to effect an Iraqi withdrawal, but it is certainly the case that war was not a first resort, that other nonviolent means were tried before turning to military force.[8]

Another principle governing the resort to war that we have not yet mentioned is that there be a *reasonable chance of success*. When resistence is futile, and especially when

---

[8] For a behind-the-scenes account of the high-level discussions and debates preceding the Bush administration's decision to go forward with Operation Desert Storm, see Bob Woodward, *The Commanders* (New York: Simon & Schuster, 1991). Walzer generally considers the Gulf War a just war, even if it was not always conducted justly; see his Preface to the second edition of *Just and Unjust Wars*. For other views, see Jean Bethke Elshtain et al., *But Was It Just? Reflections on the Morality of the Persian Gulf War* (New York: Doubleday, 1992).

it would be suicidal, the just war tradition enjoins states to refrain from war even in self-defense. However, with the overwhelming military force that could be arrayed against Iraq by the UN coalition, there was no question that this criterion for just war was met. All told, then, and with perhaps a few reservations about last resort, it seems that Operation Desert Storm was consistent with the principles of *jus ad bellum*.

How about *jus in bello?* In conducting their military operations, the United States and its allies attempted to observe the principle of *discrimination* by the use of "smart bombs" that made it possible to precisely target Iraqi military facilities, even in civilian areas, with relatively few civilian deaths. There were some targeting intelligence errors, however. For example, American aircraft hit a bomb shelter in Baghdad, causing several hundred noncombatant deaths.

Some of the most morally questionable operations conducted during the Gulf War were in fact directed at Iraqi military forces. Laws governing warfare, like those contained in the Hague and Geneva Conventions, prohibit inhumane killing and the mistreatment of prisoners of war (including, of course, killing them). In the process of breaching Iraqi defense lines, American ground forces bulldozed trenches and buried Iraqi soldiers alive. Although these assaults were conducted so as to maximize the speed and decisiveness of the initial penetration of Iraq's forward defenses, they raise serious concerns about the morality, if not the legality, of U.S. military conduct. In another incident, Iraqi forces were retreating from Kuwait City to Basra along the Jahra road when American air attacks stopped the lead units while coalition armored divisions sealed off their escape routes. Trapped Iraqi forces were then attacked by various air units, including many that had seen only limited action in the war, in what many would later call a "turkey shoot." (The Jahra road was subsequently known as the "highway to hell.") These Iraqi forces were not prisoners of war, but we might reasonably ask whether they were given any real opportunity to surrender.

The biggest questions from a just war viewpoint turn on the issue of *proportionality* and *double effect.* Was the just cause of liberating Kuwait worth killing as many as 100,000 Iraqis during the war itself?[9] Were the unintended effects of the coalition's bombing campaign proportional to the legitimate military objective of destroying Iraq's military infrastructure? Allied air forces targeted power stations, hydroelectric plants, oil refineries, and transportation facilities in order to undermine the Iraqi military's ability to sustain the fight. But many civilian deaths resulted from disease due to the destruction of water, sewage, and health facilities, the devastation of agricultural capacity, and the loss of essential transportation and electricity. Although estimates of civilian deaths during the war itself range from 2,000 to 10,000, the bad effects of the air campaign continued long after the Iraqi surrender. Answers to questions of proportionality are inevitably subjective.[10] Nevertheless, maybe it is a good thing that they

---

[9] This is a high-end estimate, but this number of casualties could have been anticipated from the outset of the conflict. For one such forecast, see Claudio Cioffi-Revilla, "On the Likely Magnitude, Extent, and Duration of an Iraq-UN War," *Journal of Conflict Resolution* 35, 3 (September 1991): pp. 387–411. Most estimates of actual Iraqi fatalities range between 25,000 and 40,000.

[10] In a national survey in February 1991, most Americans described Operation Desert Storm as a just war. When asked to evaluate it by each of the just-war principles, the greatest reservations (but still with large majority support) concerned discrimination and proportionality. See *The Gallup Poll Monthly,* February 1991, p. 120.

were asked explicitly in the public debate. The debate affected the way the war was conducted and will affect decisions about whether and how to fight in the future.

Humanitarian Intervention

Armed intervention is the use of military force to interfere in the domestic affairs of an independent state without the consent of that state's government. An armed **humanitarian intervention** is one in which the main purpose is to relieve human suffering. We have indicated that just cause for the resort to military force is interpreted rather narrowly in international law. The principle of sovereignty seems to sanction defense against aggression and little else, including intervention on behalf of the oppressed. Yet states have intervened militarily in the affairs of others, and have often couched these interventions in terms of humanitarian obligation, if not international law. That may be convenient for states looking to justify what is in fact a crude use of force in pursuit of national interests. However, there have been times when such moral considerations do appear plausible, even if in these cases military intervention furthered political interests as well. Thus, in 1971 India intervened to rescue the Bengalis in East Pakistan from massacre at the hands of the Pakistani army. India's military intervention saved a lot of innocent people (and stemmed a massive refugee exodus), but it also created an independent Bangladesh, thereby dismembering India's longtime military rival. In 1979 Vietnam invaded Cambodia (then known as Kampuchea), overthrowing Pol Pot and putting an end to a forced collectivization campaign that cost more than one million lives, and in the process installing a friendly regime.

The UN Charter, and various aspects of international law, are providing greater room for maneuver on the matter of intervention. The Charter specifies not only an "act of aggression" as grounds for the collective use of force, but also a "threat to the peace." Still, during the cold war it was exceedingly hard for the UN Security Council to agree on cases of aggression, let alone *threats* to peace. Just-war theorists have been more forthright in arguing in favor of military intervention "when a government turns savagely upon its own people."[11] International law, too, condemns such savage acts as genocide — the UN General Assembly approved the Convention on the Prevention and Punishment of the Crime of Genocide in 1948 — but the emphasis has been on punishment of war criminals rather than prevention through military intervention. Nevertheless, with the end of the cold war has come a gradual erosion of the norm against intervention when the lives of civilians are threatened on a large scale. After the Gulf War, the UN Security Council established safe havens in northern Iraq for Kurds who had fled Iraqi repression. This was a first for the UN, even if its significance is somewhat diminished by the fact that Iraq had just been defeated in a UN-sanctioned war. At the end of 1992 the Security Council acted again, sanctioning a U.S.-led military intervention in Somalia where warring clans were impeding humanitarian relief efforts.

By the time a new round of "ethnic cleansing" was underway in the Balkans in March 1999, now by the Serbs in Kosovo, the Security Council was once again

---

[11] Walzer, *Just and Unjust Wars,* p. 101; see also Michael J. Smith, "Humanitarian Intervention: An Overview of the Ethical Issues," *Ethics and International Affairs* 12 (1998): pp. 63–79.

immobilized by internal disagreement. Although the Council had three years before sanctioned NATO air strikes against Bosnian Serb positions to relieve pressure on besieged Muslim enclaves, when the Kosovo crisis erupted NATO acted without UN approval. Although Russian opposition to the NATO action can be understood in political terms — the Milosevic regime being a Russian ally, even if a dubious one — the intervention did represent a greater departure from the norm of noninterference than did other post–cold war interventions. In the case of Bosnia, NATO assistance was invited by an internationally recognized sovereign government, while in Somalia there was no sovereign government. NATO member states justified the Kosovo action on both humanitarian grounds and as a means of checking a Serbian threat to regional peace and security. The Kosovo Liberation Army (KLA) welcomed the intervention, of course, but NATO did not claim that the KLA was the rightful government of an independent Kosovo. That is, no pretense was made that this was anything other than an armed intervention into the domestic affairs of a sovereign state. Regardless of how the outcomes of these humanitarian interventions are judged, sovereignty appears increasingly violable in the eyes of the international community when egregious human rights abuses are being perpetrated.[12]

The Ethics of Deterrence

Many strategists have maintained that advances in nuclear weaponry are movements in the direction of greater moral acceptability. Some say that improvements in accuracy, coupled with the elimination of the very large warheads placed on older missiles, means that the damage caused by a nuclear exchange could be limited. On first encounter, it seems hard to argue against smaller weapons with greater accuracy. A reduction in unintended civilian deaths would be consistent with traditional moral principles. On examination, however, the problems are immense. As mentioned in the last chapter, any large-scale nuclear exchange, even of discriminating weapons, could result in tens of millions of civilian casualties. The combination of immediate casualties from blast and radiation with longer-term casualties from fallout, disruption of the medical, sanitation, transportation, communication, and economic systems, ecological devastation, climatic effects, and so forth would be very great, even if attacks were limited to strictly military targets. The effect would hardly be different than if population centers had been specifically targeted. There are not many causes to which such death and destruction would be proportionate.

One problem is therefore the illusion that any large-scale nuclear exchange could in any real sense be limited in its consequences. The other problem is the expectation that nuclear war could be fought in some precise fashion of strike and counterstrike, that in any major nuclear exchange the war could be restricted to a limited number of

---

[12] See Thomas G. Weiss and Jarat Chopra, "Sovereignty under Siege: From Intervention to Humanitarian Space," and Jack Donnelly, "State Sovereignty and International Intervention: The Case of Human Rights," both in Gene M. Lyons and Michael Mastanduno, eds., *Beyond Westphalia? State Sovereignty and International Intervention* (Baltimore: Johns Hopkins University Press, 1995), pp. 87–114, 115–146. These two essays come to somewhat different conclusions about the persistence of sovereignty as an impediment to humanitarian intervention.

strictly military targets. There were (and are) people who imagine that such a war could be waged with acceptable consequences. The majority of analysts, however, have considered the likelihood of such limitation, under wartime conditions of anger, confusion, ignorance, and loss of control, to be extremely small. John Steinbruner, commenting on such scenarios in the early 1980s, suggested instead that "the result would not be a finely controlled strategic campaign. The more likely result would be the collapse of U.S. forces into isolated units undertaking retaliation on their own initiative against a wide variety of targets at unpredictable moments."[13] Moreover, discrimination is not the only just war principle at issue. The idea of "winning" or "prevailing" in a nuclear war seems fanciful to most, and thus violates the norm requiring that war have a *reasonable chance of success.*

So much for what could — or could not — be done in war: Is deterrence, as contrasted to what one actually does in war, different? After all, the purpose of deterrence is to prevent war. The trouble is that, whatever our good intentions, deterrence can fail. If we make plans — build weapons, set up strategic programs, proclaim doctrines, instruct commanders — on the basis of principles that we are not willing to act upon, we may be called to act upon them anyway. Many things happen almost automatically. In the 1914 crisis the great powers' competitive mobilization plans worked in lockstep, making World War I almost unavoidable once mobilization was underway. Plans we adopt in the name of deterrence could be activated, whatever our desires, when a crisis occurs. If war should come as the result of some uncontrollable crisis or a physical or human accident, plans calling for morally unacceptable acts in the name of deterrence would very likely be implemented — as morally unacceptable acts.

One of the nagging ethical questions of the nuclear age is: If it would be immoral to launch a nuclear strike, is it not also immoral to threaten one? An often-quoted statement by Paul Ramsey offers a simplistic, but still troublesome, analogy:

> Suppose that one Labor Day weekend no one was killed or maimed on the highways; and that the reason for the remarkable restraint placed on the recklessness of automobile drivers was that suddenly everyone of them discovered he was driving with a baby tied to his front bumper! That would be no way to regulate traffic *even if it succeeds* in regulating it perfectly, since such a system makes innocent human lives the *direct object* of attack and uses them as mere means for restraining the drivers of automobiles.[14]

The success of nuclear deterrence is a dubious criterion by which to judge its morality, yet in the end that is the only justification we can grasp. We can take some solace in the fact that most of us living in the shadow of the nuclear cloud can and do go about our lives with few of the restraints experienced by Ramsey's tethered babies. But that might not always be the case, and in times of nuclear crisis — which seem less and less impossible as nuclear proliferation continues — that unpleasant analogy may not be altogether inappropriate.[15]

---

[13] John Steinbruner, "Nuclear Decapitation," *Foreign Policy* 45 (Winter 1981–82): p. 23.
[14] Ramsey, *The Just War,* p. 171.
[15] On the continuing relevance of nuclear ethics, see Charles W. Kegley, Jr., and Kenneth L. Schwab, eds., *After the Cold War: Questioning the Morality of Nuclear Deterrence* (Boulder, Colo.: Westview, 1991).

International Law

In earlier chapters, especially Chapter 5, we discussed how states carry on regularized relations with one another. The practice of diplomacy is a good example. However, traditional practices of diplomacy must be augmented by other mechanisms to maintain and increase regular, smooth interactions of states. International law is such a mechanism. Our perspective on international law falls somewhere between two extreme views: that international law has no impact on the activities of states, and that international law can solve all our global problems. Following the approach of political scientist Stanley Hoffman, we will look at international law as a magnifying mirror that "faithfully and cruelly" reflects the realities of world politics. International law must be seen within a political context, within the historical context of the Westphalian state system that created international law in its modern form, and within contemporary international politics. But this is a reciprocal interaction. Politics creates law, but law also shapes the form of future politics by serving as part of the menu from which states select actions (or inaction) as they conduct their foreign relations.

Naturalism, Positivism, and Realism

International law is closely related to international norms and ethics. We can identify three major philosophical perspectives on law and ethics; they go by different names, but we will refer to them as naturalism, positivism, and realism.[16] From the perspective of **natural law,** there exists a community of humankind, and members of this community share certain rights and responsibilities irrespective of their status as citizens of states. The subjects of international law, those whom the law protects, are individuals. Early versions of naturalism were rooted in Christian theology, which meant that non-Christians often did not have the same rights as Christians in the eyes of international law. However, other proponents of this view, like eighteenth-century German philosopher Immanuel Kant, insisted on the universal application of international law and ethics. Instead of deriving from God's law, the ultimate source of law is human nature and no one can rightfully be excluded from its protection. It is for this reason that Kant's perspective is often called "universalism."

The polar opposite perspective is that of **realism.** Realists have little use for international law. They do not deny that laws exist or even that states seem to behave in accordance with them much of the time. What they do deny is that international law has any impact on the behavior of states or, more properly, the behavior of those individuals acting on behalf of states. To the extent that states appear to be acting according to the dictates of international law, realists prefer to draw our attention to national

---

[16] For extended discussions of major schools of thought, see Hedley Bull, *The Anarchical Society: A Study of Order in World Politics,* 2nd ed. (New York: Columbia University Press, 1995); Chris Brown, *International Relations Theory: New Normative Approaches* (New York: Columbia University Press, 1992); and Terry Nardin and David R. Mapel, eds., *Traditions of International Ethics* (Cambridge: Cambridge University Press, 1992).

interests as the true explanation. At most, the invocation of international law to justify state behavior is a figleaf concealing the otherwise crude exercise of power. When the niceties of law conflict with the national interest, there should be no doubt about which will trump the other.

In between naturalism and realism is the **positivist view.** Like realists, most positivists are reluctant to identify universal ethics or laws that apply to the entire human community. For them, international law consists of the customs, agreements, and treaties that states actually make, and nothing more than that. The positivist view acknowledges that states act in accordance with law when it serves their interests; but unlike realism, positivism emphasizes consent, and especially the obligations that follow once consent is given. States usually do feel bound by the agreements they make — *pacta sunt servanda,* pacts must be observed — even though that may clash with the national interest on occasion. Positivism has been the predominant approach to the study of international law since the nineteenth century, and its roots are often located in the work of Hugo Grotius (though natural law figured prominently in Grotius's writings).

A popular international law text defines international law simply as "the system of law which governs relations between states." Other definitions stress the notion that international law is a body of rules that nation-states (and recently, other international actors) take into account, accept, and consider binding upon them in relations with other states. One international legal scholar has summed it up well: "It is probably the case that *almost all nations observe almost all principles of international law and almost all of their obligations almost all of the time."*[17] In many ways, then, international law serves the same purpose as domestic law; it provides a set of rules that constrains behavior and brings order to society — the society of states.

But is international law really "law"? Domestic law consists of a set of rules that have typically been *legislated* by a legitimate, centralized political authority capable of *enforcing* them. In the international arena, no legitimate central authority exists with both legislative and enforcement powers. Nevertheless, institutions and practices do exist that *make, interpret, and execute* rules. These include IGOs, as well as the official diplomatic interactions of states. The sources and the functions of international law thus have both formal and informal features. International law has many functions, including coordinating and facilitating functions similar to those of domestic law, and some of those functions are served by less-than-formal international practices and procedures. "International law should be regarded as true but imperfect law."[18] Compared with domestic law, it is relatively decentralized, but if we recognize that law is more than formal command backed up by force, then international law really can be regarded as "law."

States pay great attention to international law (for example, the legal adviser's staff at the U.S. state department reviews most of the department's work). However, if

---

[17] Louis Henkin, *How Nations Behave: Law and Foreign Policy, 2nd ed.* (New York: Columbia University Press, 1979), p. 47. The international law text is Michael Akehurst, *A Modern Introduction to International Law,* 6th ed. (London: Routledge, 1996); see p. 1.
[18] Gerhard von Glahn, *Law among Nations,* 4th ed. (New York: Macmillan, 1981), p. 4.

the fear of enforcement by armed agents of a central authority is not the cause of states' conforming to rules, what is? Again, remember that nothing is distributed evenly in the international system. States need all sorts of things possessed by other states and international actors. The great bulk of world politics and transnational interaction consists of the exchange of goods, services, people, and information. All states benefit from this regular and routine flow of people (including diplomats), goods, and information. Thus, states see it as in their own self-interest to constrain their behavior according to the rules of international law, most of which eases and routinizes such interaction.

Sources, Functions, and Subjects of International Law

Article 38 of the Statute of the International Court of Justice identifies three major sources of international law. These are (1) international conventions or treaties, (2) custom, and (3) the general principles of law recognized by civilized nations. Two secondary sources are the judicial decisions of international courts and the writings of "qualified publicists," or legal scholars. The primary source of international law is a formal one, deriving from conventions and treaties. Custom, or the evolution of patterns of behavior that states accept and give consent to, is the next most important source. This reinforces the positivist view of international law and shows how states shape international law and how international law can change and evolve. The importance of interstate treaties and interstate customs also points to the state-centric bias in contemporary international law, which has been built up around the principle of sovereignty. With rather few exceptions, states, not individuals, are the subjects of international law

The rules of international law serve a number of functions in helping states create and preserve order. One basic function is to act as a means or language of communication that conveys some sense that an authoritative set of rules does indeed operate in international relations. This communication is needed to educate states and their leaders and to socialize them in the political culture of the international system. By letting international actors know what their rights and duties are, international law thus *clarifies expectations* and adds some precision to relations. All this helps promote predictability and order in world politics. In this way, international law also serves management and coordination functions. That is, international law is used less to command behavior or to enforce conflict resolution than to help *coordinate behavior* (like traffic laws do in domestic society). This function is very important because the problems of coordination are common in world politics.

Some international law has sought to command behavior, especially on matters related to international armed conflict. As we indicated in the first part of this chapter, a centuries-old preoccupation with norms and laws governing just conduct during wartime has resulted in what some have called "the war convention."[19] This is one area where states have gone to great effort to actually codify in formal treaties the types of restraint that should be exercised during this most primitive and violent form of interstate interaction. The first major accomplishments in this regard were The Hague Con-

---

[19] See, for example, Walzer, *Just and Unjust Wars*, esp. part 3.

ventions of 1899 and 1907, which clarified and extended the basic rules of warfare, including the treatment of civilians and prisoners, as well as issues relating to neutrality and military occupation (see Table 10.1). In light of violations of The Hague Conventions during World War I, the Geneva Convention of 1929 took up many of the same issues. Violations were less flagrant during World War II, but there were still enough to prompt another round of conferences at Geneva. The 1949 Geneva Conventions (there are four) further codify proper conduct during war, and with more than 170 signatories there seems to be widespread agreement about what proper conduct means.

The Geneva Conventions coincided with the formation of the UN, perhaps obviating the need to address the laws of war in the UN Charter. As we mentioned, the charter does take up the conditions under which the resort to war is permissible, but goes no further than that. It has been left to the UN General Assembly (the plenary body) to grapple with such things as the definition of aggression. The General Assembly has not

TABLE 10.1   Formal Declarations on the Laws of War

Subject	The Hague Conventions	Geneva Conventions	Nuremberg Judgment	UN Charter	UN General Assembly
Resort to Military Force				•	•
Use of Military Force					
Land Warfare	•	•			
Sea Warfare	•				
Aerial Warfare	•				
Weapons of Mass Destruction	•	•			•
Treatment of Civilians	•	•			
Treatment of Prisoners	•	•			
Prosecution of War Crimes		•	•		•
Neutrality	•				
Military Occupation	•	•			
Terrorism					•

Source: Compiled from W. Michael Reisman and Chris T. Antoniou, eds., *The Laws of War: A Comprehensive Collection of Primary Documents on International Laws Governing Armed Conflict* (New York: Vintage, 1994).

sought to further elaborate on the laws of war aside from calling on its nuclear-armed members not to use their weapons. However, that body has addressed itself to the prosecution and punishment of war crimes and, more recently, to the issue of international terrorism.

International law, in the form of treaties and conventions, applies to a wide array of state behavior in world politics. It deals with questions of territory and nationality: which territory and people belong to which state, what states are allowed to do on their own territory and on the territory of others. Because states are the parties to these international contracts, the state-centric bias of international law is plain to see. The most obvious exception concerns the matter of war crimes. After emerging victorious from World War II, the Allies established international military tribunals at Nuremberg and Tokyo to render judgments about the wartime conduct of the vanquished. These were obviously one-sided affairs, but they established certain precedents regarding *personal accountability* for conduct during war. The Nuremberg Judgment established the principle that neither government officials nor soldiers following orders from their superiors are relieved of responsibility for war crimes. "Crimes against international law are committed by men, not by abstract entities, and only by punishing individuals who commit such crimes can the provisions of international law be enforced." So widely accepted had this principle become that in July 1998 a permanent International Criminal Court was created to try cases involving war crimes, crimes against humanity (including rape and other forms of sexual violence), and genocide.

There is a flip side to individual responsibility, and that is individual rights. Recent activity on issues relating to **human rights** — rights possessed by individuals because they are human, not because they are citizens of one or another state — represents an expansion of the domain of international law and a real erosion of state sovereignty. Concepts of universal human rights, embodied in international declarations and treaties, deny states the prerogative to withhold those rights from their own citizens; individuals are considered to be legal entities separate from their state of national origin. Individuals are thus removed from important areas of state control. Human-rights norms have increasingly become the basis for intrusion by IGOs and NGOs into the domestic affairs of states — striking at the relation of the state to its citizens, and thus at the fundamental principles of legitimacy and sovereignty. Monitoring and publicizing human-rights violations by NGOs such as Amnesty International or Human Rights Watch may be the best mechanism for deterring or restraining violators.[20]

Enforcing International Law

We have pointed out that international law exists in various forms and that most states obey it most of the time, but why do they obey it? Realists argue that state behavior that accords with international law is merely coincidental with the pursuit of national

---

[20] A good general introduction to the issue of human rights is Jack Donnelly, *International Human Rights* (Boulder, Colo.: Westview, 1993). See also Michael Perry, *The Idea of Human Rights: Four Inquiries* (New York: Oxford University Press, 1998); Henry J. Steiner and Philip Alston, *International Human Rights in Context: Law, Politics, Morals* (Oxford: Clarendon, 1996); and R. J. Vincent, *Human Rights and International Relations* (Cambridge: Cambridge University Press, 1986).

interest. The positivist view has to acknowledge that self-interest has a lot to do with law-abiding behavior by states. If each state violated international law whenever it wanted, order would soon yield to chaos; the future would be unpredictable and dangerous. Clearly, when the stakes are high and when states are in very conflictual situations, then treaties, agreements, UN resolutions, and all the rest stand a good chance of being disregarded. But most of the time such conditions do not prevail. Order seems to be an outcome that states rank high in their preference orderings. Chaos — a truly anything-goes system, all the time and on all issues — would be costly for all states.

For example, one traditional area of international law concerns the rules of immunity extended to diplomatic personnel. These rules were established so that diplomats could engage in intergovernmental communication without interference. Without them, the processes of bargaining and negotiation would soon give way either to more violent forms of interaction or to no interaction at all. A good deal of the very strong reaction against the Iranian government's involvement in taking U.S. diplomats hostage in 1979 derived from this fear. If all governments condoned such behavior, based on justifications like the Iranians' grievances against the deposed shah, then international diplomacy would become impossible.

States restrain themselves because they do not want to set a precedent for certain types of behavior. There are striking examples of the effects of international law on state behavior, based on principles that reflect the shared interests of states. One is international law on the acquisition of territory. By "intertemporal law," territorial ownership is legal if the means used to acquire territory were legal at the time of acquisition — law cannot be applied retroactively. That is, not all that long ago it was legal to acquire territory through war and force. Even though the UN Charter states that territory cannot now be acquired by conquest, a 1970 UN resolution states that this should "not be construed as affecting titles to territory created prior to the Charter regime and valid under international law."[21] Thus, Iraq had no legal claim to Kuwaiti territory (no matter how the territory was lost), and few other states supported such a claim. The reaction to Argentina's claim to the Falklands/Malvinas was similar. Although many Third World states had supported Argentina's anticolonial rhetoric, only a very few supported its military action to acquire the territory by force.[22] The legal principle of intertemporal law reflects the interests of states; almost every state is composed of territory once claimed by some other state or group. To recognize this as an excuse for military action threatens every state — especially less-developed countries (LDCs) — as well as international order. States reacted to Argentina and Iraq through fear of the precedent of using force to retake lands based on historical claims.

Related to fear of disorder and chaos is the fear of reprisal. By breaking some rule, such as taking diplomatic hostages or using military force to acquire territory, a state may be inviting a similar reaction from the state experiencing the transgression. The term *reprisal* has a specific meaning in international law. It denotes an action, normally illegal but under existing circumstances permissible, that is taken in response to

---

[21] See Akehurst, *A Modern Introduction to International Law*, pp. 152–153.
[22] For a case study of the Argentine situation, see Thomas M. Franck, "The Strategic Role of Legal Principles," in Bruce Russett, Harvey Starr, and Richard Stoll, eds., *Choices in World Politics: Sovereignty and Interdependence* (New York: Freeman, 1989), pp. 295–304.

another illegal act. The fear of reprisal also includes the possibility that states other than those immediately affected will punish a lawbreaker in some way, not necessarily by similar actions. In international law the term *retorsion* is used to describe lawful retaliation of any kind. Thus, the first concrete response by member states of the UN to Iraq's military invasion of Kuwait was to impose economic sanctions. If international solidarity among an offending state's adversaries is high, states that fail to apply sanctions against that offending state may themselves be punished. For example, punitive actions were taken against states, such as Jordan, that appeared to be disregarding the trade sanctions against Iraq, which had been approved almost unanimously by the UN.

Fear of disorder and fear of reprisal are two reasons why states obey international law. There is another reason, which can be illustrated with an analogy from domestic law. The vehicle code includes the rule that drivers must obey traffic signals. Not all do, but most drivers obey most traffic signals most of the time. Why do they obey? First, there is the concern for safety: ignoring a traffic signal may result in collision and injury or death. This is not unlike states' fears of the dangers of a disorderly world system devoid of rules and norms of international conduct. Second, there is the possibility that disobeying a traffic signal will result in traffic citation and a fine, in the event that the offending driver is spotted by a traffic cop. Such mechanisms of enforcement do not exist for international law, but this sort of consideration resembles in many ways states' fears of punishment in the form of reprisal.

Now suppose you are the driver. It is very late at night, the library has just closed, and you are driving home. The traffic light ahead has just turned red; there are no other motorists in sight, and no police cruisers. Do you stop? You probably do. And you probably wait for the light to turn green before proceeding, which can take frustratingly long considering the fact that there really is no traffic to regulate at that hour. You do not stop and wait because you are afraid of collision, nor do you fear punishment. You stop and wait because you have been trained as a good driver and socialized as a good citizen. It's the right thing to do. There may be occasions when you yield to temptation and run the light, but mostly you obey the law, as do most others — and for no other reason than: it's the law.

We should not neglect similar motives for obeying international law. Most states want to be good citizens of international society, and often appear willing to forego certain advantages to demonstrate their good citizenship.[23] Even if a state intends to violate international law when the national interest dictates, the very act of signing a treaty entails costs since that state has taken on the extra burden of having to defend apparent hypocrisies. Leaders justify their behavior in terms of international law and in questionable cases try to indicate that their behavior conforms to international law. The Reagan administration, which was accused of disregarding international law in

---

[23] The idea that states are socialized through their interactions with other states in the international community is explored in Alexander Wendt, "Anarchy Is What States Make of It: The Social Construction of Power Politics," *International Organization* 46, 2 (Spring 1992): pp. 391–425; see also Ian Hurd, "Legitimacy and Authority in International Politics," *International Organization* 53, 2 (Spring 1999): pp. 399–408.

invading Grenada, in mining Nicaraguan harbors, and in bombing Libya, nevertheless made a great effort to contend that those particular actions were permitted within the rules of international law. The Bush administration acted similarly during its military intervention in Panama. It justified its action by arguing that it protected U.S. citizens, protected the Canal, restored democracy to Panama, and was needed in order to arrest dictator Manuel Noriega on drug charges. This action was code named "Operation Just Cause" in an attempt, however transparent, to appeal to the laws of just war.

There is, of course, a self-interest side to all of this. States value their *appearance* as law-abiding citizens of the international community. A reputation as a state that others can depend upon and trust enhances the state's influence in many ways. At minimum, there is the expectation that something like a golden rule operates in world politics: if a state behaves properly, it can expect proper behavior from others. The lack of support for Iran in its war against Iraq, which was initiated by Iraq, was due in part to Iran's clear disregard for the norms of international law regarding diplomats, internal interference, and shipping rights, among other offenses. As a "renegade state," Iran elicited little sympathy for its own plight from an international community it had itself so often offended. While realists might be quick to point out that a golden rule operates in international relations only because states have found it to be in their self-interests, the positivist would respond that that is self-interested behavior with which we can all live.

International Organization

Scholars have generally approached the study of **international institutions** broadly, defining them as both the formal and the informal practices that constitute appropriate behavior in world politics. Although we often think of institutions as formal organizations housed in buildings (like the Smithsonian Institution), it is important to remember that institutions do indeed involve common *practices* (like the institution of marriage).[24] International law, again broadly speaking, can therefore be seen as the formal and informal rules that define these practices (as in "to love, honor, and obey"). Law does not necessarily come before practice; as we have indicated, even formal international law often codifies long-standing customs of states — practices that have already become "institutionalized." It is, however, sometimes useful to distinguish conceptually the rules that prescribe behavior (law) from the behavior itself.

---

[24] For a thorough examination of differing conceptions of international institutions, see Robert O. Keohane, *International Institutions and State Power: Essays in International Relations Theory* (Boulder, Colo.: Westview, 1989), esp. chap. 7. On less formal norms, including a thorough review of the literature, see Gregory A. Raymond, "Problems and Prospects in the Study of International Norms," *Mershon International Studies Review* 41, 2 (November 1997): pp. 205–245. For an illuminating study of the evolution and stability of international norms based on computer simulation, see Robert Axelrod, *The Complexity of Cooperation: Agent-Based Models of Competition and Collaboration* (Princeton, N.J.: Princeton University Press, 1997).

International organization refers to the ways states arrange themselves for purposes of promoting cooperative and collaborative practices in world politics, and the result of this process of arrangement is the creation of international organizations (IOs). States sign treaties, which add considerably to the body of international law. Many of these treaties also create international organizations, usually intergovernmental ones; such IGOs are a *product* of international law. However, the growing number of IGOs is also one of the primary *sources* of international law in the contemporary system. The charters of these organizations — their rules, agreements, and resolutions — constitute many of the bylaws of everyday international interaction. Some IGOs, such as the UN (through the International Law Commission), have helped to codify, collect, and apply international law derived not only from IGOs but from treaties, custom, and the work of international courts. IGOs have been useful in applying international law, in helping to coordinate states' compliance, in organizing states around their common interests, and in pointing out the benefits of cooperation. Large regional organizations, such as the European Union (which we discuss in Chapter 14), have worked extensively to promote economic cooperation. Others, such as the Organization of American States and the Organization of African Unity, have worked to control and manage conflict in their regions.

Realists usually see international organizations as of little importance, the same way they view international law. Again, IGOs obviously exist and states conduct much of their business in forums provided by such organizations. But for realists, IGOs are "epiphenomena" — mere reflections of states' simultaneous pursuit of national interests. As John Mearsheimer puts it, international organizations "are basically a reflection of the distribution of power in the world. They are based on the self-interested calculations of the great powers, and they have no independent effect on state behavior." Liberals, most of whom adopt the positivist view of international law, see international organizations as more important. Even among those liberals who may share some skepticism about the performance of existing international organizations, there is the hope that they might become more useful in the future.[25]

Roles for International Organizations

In thinking about IGOs in relation to international order, we need to stress their *formal* nature: they are created by two or more states (and possibly other IGOs) by a formal constitution or instrument that establishes some form of continuous administrative structure. This formal structure then seeks to pursue the common interests of the members.

First, and very important, an IGO provides a forum where states can interact with each other diplomatically at an established site. In this way it aids cooperation by

---

[25] See John J. Mearsheimer, "The False Promise of International Institutions," *International Security* 19, 3 (Winter 1994/95): p. 7, and the replies to his critique, which appeared in *International Security* 20, 1 (Summer 1995). The debate was about international institutions broadly conceived, but many points apply specifically to international organizations.

providing a permanent mechanism for addressing policy issues. States also expect the IGO to help with certain problems — for example, the World Health Organization with disease control, or UNESCO with education. An IGO often collects and makes available a great deal of information on specific problems and on its member states. UN publications, for instance, provide voluminous data on a wide variety of economic, demographic, social, cultural, and political matters (some of which is used in this book). This information may be crucial in complex coordination or problem-solving situations. Finally, IGOs also perform regulative and distributive functions. IGOs make and administer rules on how states should behave in certain areas — from the IMF in monetary policy to the UN in regard to the use of force to the EU on almost every area of economic interaction of its members. IGOs can distribute things, such as billions of dollars in loans from the World Bank or judgments from the International Court of Justice.

As realists rightly point out, states also use IGOs, along with international law, as *instruments* to further their own foreign policy interests. IGOs can legitimize the behavior of states otherwise undertaken based solely on calculations of self-interest. The United States operated through the Organization of American States in order to justify U.S. intervention in the Dominican Republic in 1965. Most people suspect that the U.S. would have gone to war with Iraq to liberate Kuwait even if force had not been authorized by the UN Security Council; but UN support gave Operation Desert Storm a legitimacy that would never have characterized a unilateral American intervention. During the repeated crises erupting over Iraq's refusal to grant free access to UN weapons inspectors in 1997 and 1998, the Clinton administration sought UN approval for potential military action. As it became clear that the Security Council was not of one mind on the matter, Secretary of State Madeleine Albright was quick to remind the members that UN approval was not needed anyway.

Although it is sometimes easy to criticize ineffectiveness and inefficiency on the part of IGOs, especially the United Nations, we need to remember that their members are nation-states. International organizations are only as successful as their member states allow them to be. Furthermore, they are only as successful as the international community perceives them to be. With the end of the cold war, states seem to be increasingly turning to the UN and other IGOs for help in solving both international and domestic problems. As with obedience to international law, a process of socialization goes on here. IGOs may become more effective in world politics not because they have the authority to impose solutions on uncooperative members — generally, they don't — but because states have become accustomed to turning to them first.[26] It is true that states sometimes turn to organizations like the UN only to provide cover for the pursuit of their national interests, but that alone is evidence that state leaders know this is considered the right thing to do.

---

[26] For a speculative essay on this process and the possibility that states will surrender substantial portions of their sovereignty, see Alexander Wendt, "Collective Identity Formation and the International State," *American Political Science Review* 88, 2 (June 1994): pp. 384–396.

The United Nations System

Besides being a major source of international law and the most extensive system of international organization in the contemporary world — in both the extent of its membership and the broad scope of its aims and activities — the UN has faithfully reflected the nature of world politics throughout the period of its existence.

In the aftermath of World War II, the UN reflected the desire of the victorious states to maintain world peace and to attack the conditions that appeared to foster war: colonialism, poverty, inequality, and ignorance. The UN Charter, drawn up and signed by fifty-one states in San Francisco in 1945, was largely the product of American, British, and Soviet negotiations. Those negotiations began well before the end of the war and in the early phases concentrated on maintaining unity in the fight against the Axis powers, but as Allied victory neared, broader objectives relating to global peace and security came to dominate the discussions. Much of the bargaining over the goals and structure of the new international organization was conducted during the Dumbarton Oaks Conference, held in Washington, D.C., in 1944.

The founders of the United Nations learned much from the failures of its predecessor, the League of Nations, and from the realist critique of the idealism that clouded the vision of the League's founders. They recognized that the organization was to be composed of sovereign states; they did not see the UN as a device to take away or undercut their sovereignty, although some later observers have felt that this *should* be the UN role. Since the international system lacked a central authority, one strategy for promoting international cooperation was the creation of an IGO that all states, or almost all states, would be willing to join. Thus, their realism was tempered by enough idealist vision to seek new international institutions and procedures to promote common interests and manage conflict, even while maintaining state sovereignty. Mechanisms to coordinate behavior and promote political and economic cooperation would become even more crucial as international interdependencies multiplied and created new sources of potential conflict. Perhaps one reason for the remarkable survival of the UN has been its usefulness in an era when environmental, economic, and ethical issues have joined peace and security as central matters of concern for the international community. With many new international actors, most with vulnerabilities associated with global interdependence, the Westphalian state system seems ready for a semipermanent fixture like the United Nations.

Structure and Politics

The Security Council, the General Assembly, the Secretariat, the International Court of Justice, the Trusteeship Council, and the Economic and Social Council constitute the six agencies identified in the charter as the principal organs of the UN, as depicted in Figure 10.1. Today's UN system of some thirty multilateral institutions has been built incrementally over the years to promote cooperation in response to new international

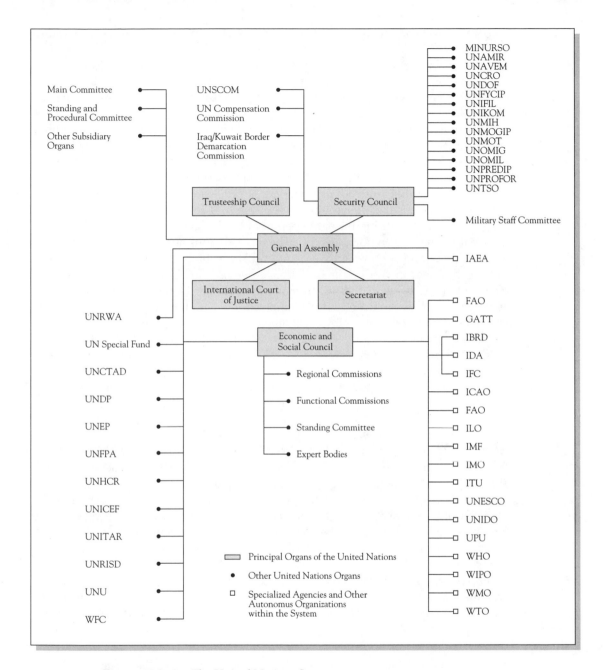

FIGURE 10.1 The United Nations System

Source: U.S. Central Intelligence Agency, *The World Factbook 1998* (Washington, D.C.: U.S. Government Printing Office, 1998), Appendix B; available at <http://www.odci.gov/cia/publications/factbook/appb.html>.

problems.[27] Its headquarters are in New York City, but in an eighteen-acre international zone not considered to be territory of the United States.

This UN structure reflects the system within which it was created. The Security Council is the primary organ of action, and as such it reflects the unequal distribution of power in the system — at least as it existed when the charter was signed at the end of World War II. The five major-power victors (the United States, Britain, France, the Soviet Union/Russia, and China) became permanent members of the Security Council (the "P5"), while ten other seats on the council rotate among other members of the UN. In addition to their permanent seats, each of the P5 has the right to veto actions considered by the council. These two features of the Security Council give its permanent members substantial influence over matters of peace and security coming before the UN. In this way, the charter sought to save the UN from a major weakness of the League of Nations: during the entire period of the League's existence, at least one of the great powers was a not a member. The most obvious absences from the P5 given *today's* distribution of power are Germany and Japan. Both have completely recovered from their defeat in World War II and have demonstrated their good citizenship as members of the society of states, so many believe that Germany and Japan should assume roles in the Security Council commensurate with their current standing in the international community.[28] However, any change in the Security Council would require an amendment to the UN Charter, which would have to be ratified by two-thirds of all member states, including the P5. No agreement on expansion of the council seems able to meet this test.

The Security Council reflects the special role that the great powers must play in the world body. The veto permits each power to protect its interests by remaining in the organization. The heavy use of the Soviet veto during the early years of the UN (114 times from 1945 to 1975) was an attempt to compensate for disproportionate U.S. influence in the General Assembly, which is the UN's plenary body. Figure 10.2 shows that in 1946 states from the Americas and Western Europe dominated the General Assembly with over 60 percent of the membership. Although the General Assembly had been set up as a world parliament on the basis of one-state/one-vote sovereign equality (Article 2 of the charter), it too was dominated by the great powers in the early days of the UN. When the structure of the international system was tightly bipolar, but imbalanced in favor of the West, the cleavages in the General Assembly were predictable. Not only did East-West issues dominate the agenda (with about 30 percent of the membership coming from Europe), but the United States could and did exercise a great deal of influence over members' votes in the General Assembly. Even as a measure of East-West balance was introduced, for a long period many small and nonaligned countries

---

[27] These institutions include some organizations that predate the UN itself — such as the International Labor Organization and the Universal Postal Union. See Roger A. Coate, "Increasing the Effectiveness of the UN System," in Roger A. Coate, ed., *U.S. Policy and the Future of the United Nations* (New York: Twentieth Century Fund, 1994), p. 44.

[28] For an analysis of likely dynamics in an enlarged UN Security Council, see Barry O'Neill, "Power and Satisfaction in the Security Council," in Bruce Russett, ed., *The Once and Future Security Council* (New York: St. Martin's, 1997), pp. 59–82.

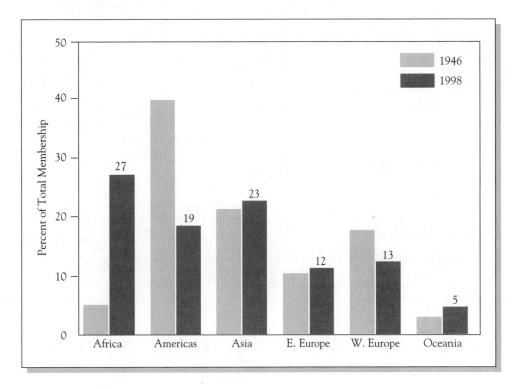

FIGURE 10.2   UN Membership by Region, 1946 and 1998

were dissatisfied with the UN system because of its dominance by the great powers and their problems.

During the 1970s and 1980s the group most dissatisfied with the United Nations was the industrialized North. The UN, by welcoming all states, has grown through the addition of non-Western states created by the process of decolonization. Figure 10.2 shows the dramatic increase in African and Asian membership from 1946 to 1998. With this change, which began in earnest in 1960, came a shift in emphasis from East-West to North-South issues (which we discuss in Chapter 15). Economic issues, and particularly issues of development and equity, have come to dominate many areas of the UN. The UN membership has powerfully affected the objectives, processes, and success of the organization, especially as they have organized into "groups" whose purpose is to foster the common interests of the members. These groups, and how they overlap in membership, are shown in Figure 10.3. The anticolonial stance of the newer members was often supported by the anti-Western communist states. After 1970 the United States found itself unable to command a majority in the General Assembly (as reflected in 60 vetoes the United States exercised in the Security Council between 1976 and 1990, compared to only 7 by the Soviet Union). This state of affairs was strikingly evident

1

3
Albania	Kyrgyzstan
Armenia	Latvia
Azerbaijan	Lithuania
Bosnia and	Moldova
Herzegovina	Poland
Belarus	Russian
Bulgaria	Federation
Croatia	Slovak Republic
Czech Republic	Slovenia
Estonia	Tajikistan
Georgia	Turkmenistan
Hungary	Ukraine
Kazakhstan	Uzbekistan

Romania

2
Antiqua and Barbuda	Haiti
Argentina	Honduras
Brazil	Mexico
Costa Rica	Paraguay
Dominica	St. Kitts and
Dominican	Nevis
Republic	St. Vincent
El Salvador	Uruguay

4 Yugoslavia

Bahamas	Ecuador	St. Lucia
Barbados	Grenada	Suriname
Belize	Guatemala	Trinidad and
Bolivia	Guyana	Tobago
Chile	Jamaica	Venezuela
Colombia	Nicaragua	
Cuba	Panama	
	Peru	

Key to Group Numbering

1. Group of 77
2. Latin America and
   Caribbean Group
*3. Eastern European Group
4. Nonaligned Movement
5. African Group
6. Islamic Conference
7. Arab Group
8. Asian Group
9. Western Europe
   and Other States
10. European
    Community
11. Nordic Group

5
Angola	Cote d'Ivoire	Madagascar	Seychelles
Benin	Equatorial	Malawi	Swaziland
Botswana	Guinea	Mauritius	Tanzania
Burundi	Ethiopia	Mozambique	Togo
Cape Verde	Ghana	Namibia	Zaire
Central African	Kenya	Nigeria	Zambia
Republic	Lesotho	Rwanda	Zimbabwe
Congo	Liberia	Sao Tome	

6
Burkina Faso	Guinea Bissau
Cameroon	Mali
Chad	Niger
Comoros	Senegal
Gabon	Sierra Leone
Gambia	Uganda
Guinea	

7
Algeria	Morocco
Djibouti	Somalia
Egypt	Sudan
Libya	Tunisia
Mauritania	

8 China Japan

Bangladesh	Malaysia
Brunei	Maldives
Indonesia	Pakistan
Iran	

Bahrain	Qatar
Iraq	Saudi Arabia
Jordan	Syria
Kuwait	United Arab
Lebanon	Emirates
Oman	Yemen

Fiji
Korea,
 Republic of
Marshall
 Islands
Myanmar
Philippines
Samoa
Solomons
Thailand

9
Australia
Austria
Canada
Liechtenstein
New Zealand
San Marino

Turkey

Afghanistan	Mongolia
Bhutan	Nepal
Cambodia	Papua New Guinea
Cyprus	Singapore
India	Sri Lanka
Korea, D.R.	Vanuatu
Laos	Viet Nam

Malta

10
Belgium	Netherlands
France	Luxembourg
Germany	Portugal
Greece	Spain
Ireland	United Kingdom
Italy	

11 Denmark

Finland
Iceland
Norway
Sweden

Member of No Group:
 Israel
 South Africa
 United States

* As of January 1993, all of the former Soviet Republics
  were technically still members of the Eastern European
  group, although several of them are in Asia.
  A possible realignment of regional groups was
  under consideration.

◄   **FIGURE 10.3** UN Groups and Their Overlapping Memberships

Source: Robert E. Riggs and Jack C. Plano, *The United Nations: International Organization and World Politics,* 2nd ed. (Belmont, Calif.: Wadsworth, 1994), p. 62.

when, despite strenuous U.S. opposition, the People's Republic of China was admitted to membership in 1971 and Nationalist China — Taiwan — was expelled.[29]

One of the most contentious issues in the United Nations has been the allocation of the organization's scarce resources. In 1997, the UN's regular budget was $1.25 billion, with another $1.3 billion going to support peacekeeping operations. Member states make contributions to the UN budget based on their relative wealth, so that the eight richest states contribute roughly 70 percent of both the regular and peace-keeping budgets. The U.S. assessment alone is 25 percent of the regular budget and 30 percent for peacekeeping. The budgetary process has become an issue of contention because although the secretary-general assembles UN budgets, these must be approved, and are often revised, by the General Assembly where all members have an equal voice irrespective of their financial contributions. Those states that contribute 70 percent of the UN's resources cast fewer than 5 percent of the votes that determine the way those resources are allocated. Some states have expressed their dissatisfaction with the budgetary politics in the UN by withholding portions of their assessed contributions. The United States is the UN's largest debtor; in 1998 it owed the organization $1.6 billion for past and current assessments (about $600 million for the regular budget and $1 billion for peacekeeping). That was almost two-thirds of the $2.5 billion owed to the UN by all member states. To add some perspective to these figures, consider that the U.S. defense budget for 1998 was $260 billion — 100 times what the UN spent on regular operations and on peacekeeping and 100 times what the organization is owed.

The changing nature of the UN has been influenced not only by the number of new members, but also by the circumstances under which they became sovereign states. Many of these newer UN members are independent in part because of the work of the Trusteeship Council, which was established to bring an end to colonialism and to guide the former colonial areas to independent statehood as soon and as peacefully as possible. Most observers agree that the Trusteeship Council fulfilled its purpose well — so well, in fact, that with the independence of its last trust territory, Palau, in 1994, the council suspended its regular operations. It may be called on in the future to help reconstitute "failed states" where the central institutions of government have collapsed (in the mid-1990s Somalia was sometimes mentioned as a candidate), but so far that has not happened.

The Economic and Social Council is assigned the task of dealing with international economic, social, educational, and health matters. It is supposed to improve the world's living standards by attacking poverty, ignorance, and inequality as causes of war. Many health matters have been successfully dealt with; many educational and cultural dissemination programs have also had positive results. The Economic and

[29] An analysis of more recent voting patterns in the UN General Assembly can be found in Soo Yeon Kim and Bruce Russett, "The New Politics of Voting Alignments in the General Assembly," in Russett, *The Once and Future Security Council,* pp. 29–57.

Social Council overseas a number of programs that have received a great deal of attention, often praise, in their own right: for example, the UN Conference on Trade and Development (UNCTAD), the Office of the High Commissioner for Refugees (UNHCR), the UN Children's Fund (UNICEF), and the UN Environment Program (UNEP). Other UN agencies, like the World Bank (IBRD, for International Bank for Reconstruction and Development), the IMF, and the World Trade Organization (WTO) technically report to the Economic and Social Council but have a great deal of autonomy as IGOs.

The UN acts as a forum for diplomacy and facilitates communication among member states. Activities directly related to the settlement of disputes are listed in Article 33 of the charter and include negotiations, inquiry, mediation, and arbitration. The UN can facilitate each of these. States make use of the UN's "good offices" — a place for formal negotiations or, as is often the case, a forum that eases communication between parties who might want to launch formal negotiations at a later date. Through it agencies and staff, the UN can also serve as a neutral investigating body that provides unbiased information relevant to a dispute and its resolution. Similarly, the UN can act as a third-party mediator, an active participant in negotiations to help states in conflict arrive at acceptable solutions. Arbitration, wherein conflicting parties agree to be bound by solutions arrived at by third parties, is another approach to conflict resolution. In 1998, Peru and Ecuador agreed to submit their border dispute to binding arbitration by the United States, Brazil, Argentina, and Chile. It is rare for states to surrender sovereignty in this way when it comes to matters of national security (Peru and Ecuador fought briefly in 1995 over this fifty-mile stretch of territory), but it may be a sign of things to come. The UN seems well suited to this role, if not now, then certainly in the future as states gain more confidence in the organization's independence and fairness.

Another mechanism mentioned in Article 33 is adjudication, or judicial settlement, in which a dispute is brought before an international court. The International Court of Justice (ICJ, sometimes called the World Court) is the judicial organ of the UN. Although the record is quite mixed, the ICJ has proven useful in a number of cases. The ICJ has judged cases involving issues ranging from fisheries to frontier disputes to nuclear testing. A number of cases are submitted to the Court but then removed from the ICJ by the parties. Some are settled out of court; the rest are removed because one party refuses to accept the ICJ's jurisdiction in the dispute. Indeed, distrust of the ICJ and unwillingness to let an outside party determine a state's interests are the main reasons that many issues are not brought before the Court. States use the ICJ when they feel it would be a useful tool of their foreign policy. The United States, for instance, went to the ICJ after Iranian students seized American diplomats in 1979, but refused to accept the ICJ's jurisdiction in the case brought by Nicaragua regarding the covert U.S. mining of its harbors.

The secretary-general of the United Nations (currently Kofi Annan of Ghana) heads the Secretariat, which is organization's executive and primary administrative body. While members of the Security Council and General Assembly are states — delegates represent the interests of their home governments, and not (necessarily) those of the UN — the loyalties of secretary-general and the Secretariat staff are to the organization. Article 100 of the charter states: "In the performance of their duties the secretary-general and the staff shall not seek or receive instructions from any government or from any other authority external to the Organization. They [are] responsible only to the Organization." The administrative tasks of the Secretariat are immense, requiring a staff of 25,000 international civil servants, and the size of this bureaucracy is often seized upon by critics of the world body.[30] Perhaps the most important duty of the Secretariat has been to administer peace-keeping operations, which emerged during the cold war as a practical substitute for the collective security arrangements envisioned by the UN's founders.

Collective Security and Peacekeeping

The UN Charter identifies international peace and security as the organization's first goal, and the UN's founders wanted the organization to play a central role in collective security. Recall that **collective security** means that all members agree to oppose together a threat to the security of any one of them, an arrangement that realists dismiss as idealistic.[31] Chapter VII, Articles 39–46 of the UN Charter call on all members to make available to the Security Council, by special agreements, armed forces and facilities "for the purposes of maintaining international peace and security." These forces were to provide the basis for UN-authorized military actions against aggressor states. Almost immediately, however, the cold war began. Soviet-American hostility made it impossible for the permanent members of the Security Council to concur on the terms for a UN military force, and no agreements with individual states were ever reached. In its first forty-five years the UN only once designated a state as an aggressor; that was North Korea, in 1950, and the designation was made while the Soviet representative was boycotting the Security Council for its refusal to recognize China's new communist government as the rightful occupant of China's seat at the UN. The subsequent war with North Korea, while authorized by the UN and conducted with troops from fifteen states, was nonetheless dominated by American military planning and personnel.

Not until 1990, after the Iraqi occupation of Kuwait, was collective security again invoked. Then the United States and the Soviet Union were in substantial agreement, and careful negotiations between them, and with other major powers, made possible the UN-authorized military actions against Iraq. There was, of course, no standing UN military force for those operations either. Rather, a multinational coalition was assembled on an ad hoc basis. In this operation, too, the United States dominated the coalition and substantially controlled military and political strategy; the UN exercised only very general supervision. It remains to be seen whether that experience will serve as a precedent for similar peace-enforcement operations in the future, or even serve to

---

[30] See, for example, Jesse Helms, "Saving the U.N.: A Challenge to the Next Secretary General," *Foreign Affairs* 75, 5 (September/October 1996): pp. 2–7. For more sympathetic reform proposals, see Paul Kennedy and Bruce Russett, "Reforming the United Nations," *Foreign Affairs* 74, 5 (September/October 1995): pp. 56–71.

[31] For a defense of collective security in light of realist criticisms, see Charles A. Kupchan and Clifford A. Kupchan, "The Promise of Collective Security," *International Security* 20, 1 (Summer 1995): pp. 52–61. For a balanced assessment of UN efforts at establishing collective security, see Adam Roberts, "The United Nations: Variants of Collective Security," in Ngaire Woods, ed., *Explaining International Relations since 1945* (Oxford: Oxford University Press, 1996), pp. 309–336.

stimulate creation of some sort of permanent UN military capability that might also act as a deterrent to aggression. In the years since Operation Desert Storm, there have been no repeats, and by 1998 the Security Council was divided on whether collective military intervention was appropriate even as a means of enforcing the terms of Iraq's surrender (namely, allowing UN weapons inspections).

The other kind of operation in which the UN can employ military force is **peacekeeping.** Peacekeeping is very different from military enforcement: its purpose is conflict management or settlement, and it does not involve assigning guilt or identifying an aggressor. Rather, it involves recognition that a violent conflict or threat to peace is at hand. Here the role of the UN is to stop fighting already under way, separate the warring parties, and create conditions for them to negotiate instead of fight. During the cold war the UN had little success with conflicts involving both superpowers because each could veto any proposed UN action. It was often more successful, however, in dealing with medium and minor powers in situations where the superpowers were not strongly involved on opposite sides. Beginning with the Suez crisis in 1956, it has dispatched lightly armed peacekeeping forces of varying magnitudes to many trouble spots (earlier missions consisted of observers only). More than thirty peacekeeping missions have been concluded since then and there were seventeen in place in 1998 (see Table 10.2). To date, the largest peacekeeping operation by far was the force deployed in former Yugoslavia from 1992 to 1995. That operation involved about 38,000 military personnel and cost $4.6 billion. Nearly 1,600 peacekeepers (including observers) have been killed in the line of duty since 1948.

Peace-keeping operations are almost always carried out only with the consent of the conflicting parties; when the UN takes sides in a civil war, as in Somalia, it is less successful.[32] The key to many operations has been the use of UN forces to separate the armies of the warring parties and to maintain a cease-fire. The importance of such activities was made painfully clear in 1967, when Secretary-General U Thant acceded to the request by Egypt's President Nasser to remove the UN forces that had been stationed on the Sinai border between Israel and Egypt (but in Egyptian territory) since the Suez war. Israel's decision to launch the "preemptive" strike of the 1967 Six-Day War was strongly influenced by the absence of a UN barrier to a possible Egyptian attack, which the Israelis believed to be imminent. The UN's original peacekeeping role — standing between hostile forces — has been expanded to *peacebuilding* activities such as maintaining security or stability within a wide area (as in southern Lebanon), providing humanitarian assistance (Cyprus), disarming insurgents (Nicaragua), and monitoring elections (Namibia, Nicaragua, and Haiti). Gradually, therefore, the UN has become important in managing conflicts within a single country rather than purely between countries and has taken on a role in helping to secure peaceful transitions of government. It is increasingly helpful in aiding the establishment of democratic governments when the parties involved want such

---

[32] The difficulties encountered during the multifaceted peacekeeping operation in Somalia are described in William J. Durch, "Introduction to Anarchy: Humanitarian Intervention and 'State-Building' in Somalia," in William J. Durch, ed., *Peacekeeping, American Policy, and the Uncivil Wars of the 1990s* (New York: St. Martin's, 1996), pp. 311–365. A good overview of UN peacekeeping efforts can be found in Paul F. Diehl, *International Peacekeeping* (Baltimore: Johns Hopkins University Press, 1994).

TABLE 10.2 UN Peacekeeping Missions, 1998

Location	Mission	Start	Troops	Police	Observers	Deaths
Africa						
Angola	MONUA	1997	635	388	93	13
Central African Republic	MINURCA	1998	1,345	20	0	1
Sierra Leone	UNOMSIL	1998	15	3	38	0
Western Sahara	MINURSO	1991	243	79	199	8
Americas						
Haiti	MIPONUH	1997	0	282	0	0
Asia						
India/Pakistan	UNMOGIP	1949	0	0	45	9
Tajikistan	UNMOT	1994	0	2	70	8
Europe						
Bosnia and Herzegovina	UNMIBH	1995	3	1,955	0	6
Croatia	UNMOP	1996	0	0	28	0
Croatia	UNCPSG	1998	31	150	0	0
Cyprus	UNFICYP	1964	1,233	35	0	168
Macedonia	UNPREDEP	1995	655	26	35	4
Georgia	UNOMIG	1993	0	0	96	3
Middle East						
Golan Heights	UNDOF	1974	1,042	0	0	39
Iraq/Kuwait	UNIKOM	1991	905	0	194	13
Lebanon	UNIFIL	1978	4,455	0	0	228
Middle East	UNTSO	1948	0	0	153	38
Totals			*10,562*	*2,940*	*951*	*538*

Source: United Nations, "UN Peacekeeping Operations," 1998 [cited October 14, 1998]; available at <http://www.un.org/Depts/dpko/>.

help (sometimes in collaboration with regional IGOs like the Organization of American States).[33]

The "Three United Nations"

For all its failures and limitations, the UN has become a powerful instrument for achieving **human security** in its broadest sense. Its founders established it with a broad vision of peace and security, and the UN continues to evolve within a changing global context. While it has not satisfied all high hopes at the end of the cold war, it has accomplished far more than its detractors recognize — and more than many of its member governments. The UN consists of organs devoted to three broad, different purposes — but organs that, as in a human body, complement each other and cannot be effective alone.

The most obvious UN is the UN of security against violence. This is the UN of the Security Council, with its powers of peacekeeping, applying economic sanctions, and carrying out collective security operations against blatant aggressors like Iraq. This UN also includes the secretary-general, who has powers to promote the peaceful settlement of disputes through good offices, negotiation, and mediation.

The second UN — the UN of economic security and the provision of basic human needs — is less obvious. This is the UN of the specialized agencies and much of the Secretariat. It includes emergency humanitarian assistance, the Food and Agriculture Organization (FAO), the World Health Organization (WHO), and the United Nations Development Programme (UNDP). It is also the UN of the IMF and the World Bank, affiliated organizations disposing of enormous capital resources in an effort to provide international economic stability and well-being.

Often the least visible, but equally important, is the UN of security of human rights. This is the UN that oversaw the treatment and ultimately the transition of trusteeships like Namibia. It includes the International Court of Justice, the Electoral Assistance Unit of the Secretariat, the Commissioner of Human Rights, and the High Commissioner for Refugees. It is the UN of the Universal Declaration of Human Rights and numerous other statements on self-determination, discrimination, the rights of women and children, servitude and forced labor, and the administration of justice. Moreover, it is the UN that, in 1998, succeeded in establishing a permanent International Criminal Court to prosecute genocide and other crimes against humanity.[34]

In all three of its aspects, the UN has achieved successes as well as failures. Against the tragedy of Bosnia are substantial peacekeeping and peace-building successes, in places such as Cambodia, El Salvador, and Namibia. WHO eradicated smallpox world-

---

[33] Important discussions of the UN role in peacekeeping and democratization can be found in two reports by former Secretary General Boutros Boutros-Ghali: *An Agenda for Peace: Preventive Diplomacy, Peacemaking and Peace-keeping* (New York: United Nations, 1992), and *Agenda for Democratization* (New York: United Nations, 1995), both available at <http://www.library.yale.edu/un/un3d.htm>. For discussions of the broadened concept of peacekeeping since the end of the cold war, see Alvaro de Soto and Graciana del Castillo, "Obstacles to Peacebuilding," *Foreign Policy* 94 (Spring 1994): pp. 69–83; and Roland Paris, "Peacebuilding and the Limits of Liberal Internationalism," *International Security* 22, 2 (Fall 1997): pp. 54–89.

[34] See Human Rights Internet, "UN Information: Treaties, Conventions & Agreements," n.d. [cited October 14, 1998]; available at <http://www.hri.ca/uninfo/treaties/>.

wide. Many underdeveloped economies have benefited from UN development assistance. The Electoral Assistance Unit has helped conduct democratic elections in more than forty countries. UN rhetoric on human rights, while often ignored, has become embodied in international conventions and declarations that now take the form of domestic law in many states, binding governments to observe their normative principles.

The UN in its varied guises has attempted to deal with serious environmental, economic, and political problems, which may ultimately be the most crucial the world faces because of the interdependencies of the current world system. The UN has held special conferences in all these areas to bring states together to air their differences, to propose various policies, and to work out agreements. The three UNs have a synergy; they reinforce and build on each other. There can be little economic security if there is no security against violence, within countries as well as between them. Peace building, in the wake of conflict, requires reestablishing economic security and protection of human rights for the vanquished, for minorities, and for majorities that govern democratically. These are the sort of successes that explain the relative longevity of the UN as an international organization and lead most observers to believe that it will remain a force in world politics for the foreseeable future.

11

Causes of Peace and Nonviolent Transformation

The Zone of Peace

Many of the achievements of the past five decades in the rich industrialized countries of the world are very impressive indeed. Despite occasional bouts of recession and/or inflation, these countries have seen a period of economic well-being unrivaled in history. Despite serious inequalities and remaining pockets of real poverty within many industrialized countries, for the first time in history prosperity has been widespread. In contrast to the prosperity experienced by most of the great empires of the past, economic well-being in the industrialized world today is enjoyed by far more than just the ruling classes.

All this has happened in spite of the enormous loss of life and physical destruction caused by World War II, at the end of which the economies of Japan, Germany, and many other states were in ruin. Moreover, all states — but especially the industrialized countries — are now tightly linked by a network of trade, investment, communications, and travel to a degree also unprecedented. Most citizens of Europe and North

America could probably afford an intercontinental trip, and the plane journey is a matter of hours. The prospering national economies are tightly interdependent: growth, inflation, and recession are readily transmitted from one country to another with little control. However, they have *managed* their interdependence to produce positive results for all involved.

Equally important but not noticed so often as the achievement of prosperity is the achievement of peace. Among the developed market economies of the Organization for Economic Cooperation and Development (OECD) — the countries of Western Europe, the United States, Canada, Japan, Australia, and New Zealand — there has been no war or other violent conflict since 1945. Not only has there been no war among them in more than fifty years, but there has been no expectation of, or preparation for, war among them.[1] The enduring hostility between France and Germany since the nineteenth century appears well buried since the 1960s. Individual German and French citizens may not love one another, but neither do they expect the other's state to attack or wish to mount an attack. Europeans, Americans, and Japanese may still fear security threats from outside the OECD; they may continue to use or threaten to use military force against small or poor states to retain their spheres of influence. But among countries within the OECD area, peace and the confident expectation of peace is the norm. When the U.S. government wanted the British and French to withdraw from Suez in 1956, it coerced them with economic sanctions, not with military force. Despite periodic and sometimes shrill trade disagreements between the United States and Japan, there has been no hint of armed violence.[2]

Among the most industrialized countries of the world, there exists what many call a **zone of peace.** This is an extraordinary achievement by the standards of recent history. Until 1945, war or the expectation of war among most of these countries was the norm. (There were some localized exceptions — for example, among Canada, the United States, and Britain, and among the countries of Scandinavia.) Future OECD countries were the instigators and major combatants of both world wars, which resulted in the deaths of tens of millions of people. The preceding century saw many major wars among these same countries, beginning with the extended Napoleonic Wars among all the major states of Europe (and provoking the War of 1812 between Britain and the United States) and including several wars leading to the unification of Germany in 1870. Even in periods of peace, it was recognized that peace was precarious and depended upon states being ready, willing, and able to fight — it required the maintenance of a balance of power. Crises and war scares were common; several conflicts threatened to provoke a general European war before one finally did in August 1914.

---

[1] A marginal exception is the brief, limited conflict between Greece and Turkey over the control of Cyprus in 1974. However, Greece and Turkey are the least wealthy and least industrialized countries of the OECD, and Greece was led by a nondemocratic military government (important factors, as we shall see).

[2] For a pessimistic view of the future of U.S.-Japanese relations, see George Friedman and Meredith Lebard, *The Coming War with Japan* (New York: St. Martin's, 1991). So contrary to the conventional wisdom is their view that the authors acknowledge in the preface that their conclusions might appear "preposterous."

The vast majority of international wars since 1945, however, have been fought in less-developed countries (LDCs), and mostly among LDCs (perhaps with outsiders supplying one or both sides). The global incidence of violent conflict has been so lop-sided that Max Singer and Aaron Wildavsky contrasted the zone of peace in the indus-trialized world with "zones of turmoil" in the developing world.[3] No war has been fought on the territory of an OECD country. This may have been partly due to NATO's deterrence of a Soviet and East European attack on Western Europe, as well as the secu-rity guarantees extended to other OECD countries. But there is still the total lack of war *between* OECD countries that is not so easily explained. The significance of the zone of peace is reinforced if we consider that almost all of the civil wars fought since World War II have taken place within LDCs (again, often with outside intervention).

Peace among the OECD countries is also an extraordinary achievement by the standards of world history. The countries involved contain a total population of over 800 million, spread over a geographic area equal to nearly half the land of the Northern Hemisphere. By both measures it is a larger zone of peace than has ever existed before. These are simple facts, but facts that cry out for explanation — particularly given the expectations of realists and radicals. If we could understand why such a large set of peoples, who only recently fought bitterly and bloodily, now live at peace with one another, we would know something very important.

We have talked often about possible causes of war. Applying the levels-of-analysis scheme, we have discussed power rivalries in the context of different kinds of interna-tional systems, threats and bargaining in the relations between states, economic sys-tems as the source of societal pressures for expansion, bureaucratic politics as a source of policies unsuited to the "national interest," and fear and misperception by individ-ual decisionmakers. But the question "What are the causes of peace?" is not simply the opposite side of the question "What are the causes of war?" Reversing the various social and international developments that have contributed to warfare is often not possible. It may be that other countervailing processes must operate in parallel in order to diminish the likelihood of war and bring about lasting peace. If we could find the causes of peace among the OECD countries, we might have a key to expanding this zone of peace over a wider area, even the entire globe.

Peace: Salaam or Sulah?

To some, peace is simply the absence of war, the absence of organized violent conflict. For most of us, however, that is not enough. The kind of peace we want is not a world in which every individual or group who could conceivably resort to violent conflict is simply destroyed — that would leave no one but the extreme pacifists. Ideally, we wish to achieve a stable peace, which can be defined as *the absence of preparation for war or the serious expectation of war.* A stronger view of stable peace is that the alternative of

---

[3] Max Singer and Aaron Wildavsky, *The Real World Order: Zones of Peace/Zones of Turmoil* (Chatham, N.J.: Chatham House, 1993). See also James M. Goldgeier and Michael McFaul, "A Tale of Two Worlds: Core and Periphery in the Post–Cold War Era," *International Organization* 46, 2 (Spring 1992): pp. 467–491.

war is never even considered. Kenneth Boulding called stable peace "a situation in which the probability of war is so small that it does not really enter into the calculations of any of the people involved."[4] If we prepare for or expect violent conflict — or if we repress violent conflict by force — we have what Boulding called "unstable peace." Others have called this "negative peace." An unstable or negative peace can be enforced by deterrence, the fear of violent retribution, but we may continually fear the breakdown of peace in the event that deterrence fails.

If there is no balance — if deterrence is merely a one-way rather than a mutual relationship between two hostile parties — then we talk of repression. For some people, especially the most privileged, the absence of violent conflict even if achieved by repression and coercion may be better than the outbreak of violent conflict, but it is hardly anyone's ideal. Repression and coercion can be found in the relationships between powerful and weak states as well as between powerful and weak groups within states. People may be deprived of political liberties, made materially poor, or allowed to die from sickness or starvation without direct physical violence. Some analysts thus refer to "structural violence" — deprivations enforced, often subtly, by coercive social and political systems — in contrast to the direct or physical violence of war or imprisonment.[5]

The central distinction between stable peace under conditions that are generally acceptable to both sides and a situation of negative peace maintained only by threats (whether unilateral or mutual) is clear enough. The notion of stable peace can be pushed further to describe not only the absence of any expectation of war, but also the elimination of deprivation and structural violence — a condition sometimes called "positive peace." These different conceptions of peace correspond roughly to the Arabic terms *suluum*, which means an enduring peaceful relationship based on mutual respect and well-being, and *sulah*, which means only the end of hostilities or a truce.

Stable peace exists within the OECD area, and there is movement toward positive peace. Conditions of injustice, coercion, and repression have not completely disappeared, but the accomplishments of the OECD are substantial compared with most other parts of the world. The most pronounced accomplishments are evident in relations between countries; the greatest hurdles remaining for the achievement of positive peace exist in social relations within countries. The most significant cases of violent political deaths in the last decade or so have been within the United Kingdom (the conflict in Northern Ireland) and Spain (violence by Basque separatists). In both of these cases the violent acts have involved people who do not wish to be subject to their present government and seek either independence (the Basques) or inclusion in another country (the Republic of Ireland). Today, the conflict in Northern Ireland is well on its way toward resolution, but it is still the case that in the OECD violence directed at existing governmental institutions by separatists is more of a threat than is violence between governments. This is a point to which we shall return.

---

[4] Kenneth Boulding, *Stable Peace* (Austin: University of Texas Press, 1979), p. 13.
[5] See Johan Galtung, "Violence, Peace and Peace Research," *Journal of Peace Research* 6, 3 (1969): pp. 167–191.

The Democratic Peace

In a controversial article published in 1989, Francis Fukuyama argued that the dismal record of Soviet-style socialism had demonstrated once and for all that there can be no serious competitor to Western liberalism — free-market capitalism plus political democracy — as an organizing principle for modern society. Taking cues from the work of German political philosopher Georg Hegel, Fukuyama suggested that:

> What we may be witnessing is not just the end of the Cold War, or the passing of a particular period of postwar history, but the end of history as such: that is, the end point of mankind's ideological evolution and the universalization of Western liberal democracy as the final form of human government.[6]

Fukuyama surmised that the triumph of Western liberalism — the "end of history" — would be accompanied by increasingly peaceful interstate relations. But he did not go so far as to predict the complete and total end of international conflict. Rather, when conflict does erupt, it is more likely to involve states that have not (yet) embraced Western liberalism. Conflict between nonliberal states (those "still in history") is distinctly possible, as is conflict between them and liberal states. What is unlikely is conflict between liberal states. This view is widespread, even among those who do not fully subscribe to Fukuyama's other views on the triumph of the West, and the phenomenon has become known as the **democratic peace.**

Social science research points to an irrefutable observation: stable democracies are unlikely to engage in militarized disputes with each other, or to let any such disputes escalate into war. This is true even when taking into account the other factors that also affect the frequency with which countries have conflicts with one another — geographic distance, alliance membership, economic interdependence, and wealth being among the most important. The more democratic each state is, the more peaceful their relations are likely to be. Democracies tend to reciprocate each other's cooperative behavior, to accept third-party mediation or good offices in settling disputes, and generally to resolve conflicts peacefully. Notice that this is a "dyadic" phenomenon: the most widely accepted empirical finding is the high probability of peace between pairs of democratic states. However, there is an emerging body of research suggesting that democratic states may be more peaceful generally, whether in their relations with other democracies or with nondemocracies — a "monadic" finding.[7]

---

[6] Francis Fukuyama, "The End of History?" *The National Interest* 16 (Summer 1989): p. 4. See also his *The End of History and the Last Man* (New York: Free Press, 1992).

[7] The empirical literature on the democratic peace is now vast. Thorough and insightful reviews include Steve Chan, "In Search of Democratic Peace: Problems and Promise," *Mershon International Studies Review* 41, 1 (May 1997): pp. 59–91; and James Lee Ray, "Does Democracy Cause Peace?" *Annual Review of Political Science* 1 (1998): 27–46. For arguments and research in support of the monadic variant of the democratic peace, see especially R. J. Rummel, *Power Kills: Democracy as a Method of Non-Violence* (New Brunswick, N.J.: Transaction, 1997).

It is the democratic form of government that seems to matter. If similarity of form of government alone were enough, then we would expect to have seen peace between the Soviet Union and China, between the Soviet Union and its Eastern European neighbors, and between China and Vietnam. Despite important differences in political values and organization among the communist countries, they were much more like one another, especially in values or ideology, than like the democracies or even like right-wing dictatorships. Yet war or the threat of war between these countries was commonplace. The relations between democracies seem to be qualitatively different. Woodrow Wilson expressed this conviction in his 1917 war message to Congress when he asserted that "a steadfast concert of peace can never be maintained except by a partnership of democratic nations." Bill Clinton echoed this belief in his 1994 State of the Union message when he said, simply, "Democracies don't attack each other."

There is, then, good reason to believe that a zone of peace exists in the industrialized world largely because it is also a zone of democracy. Since the restoration of democracy in Greece, Portugal, and Spain in the early 1970s, all OECD countries have had democratic forms of government. Their governments are, by worldwide standards, relatively nonrepressive — certainly less repressive than many governments in the less developed world or the former communist regimes of Eastern Europe. In this respect the present OECD governments also differ markedly from many of their governments in the late 1930s, when Germany, Italy, Japan, Spain, and Portugal were all ruled by fascist dictatorships.

Cultural and Structural Explanations

Two main explanations have been offered for the democratic peace.[8] One emphasizes perceptions of individual rights, expectations of limited government, shifting coalitions, and toleration of dissent by a presumably loyal opposition. By this *cultural explanation,* the perceptions and practices that permit the peaceful resolution of conflicts of interest without the threat of violence within democracies come to apply across national boundaries toward other democratic countries. In short, people within a democracy perceive themselves as autonomous, self-governing people who share norms of live-and-let-live and who respect the rights of others to self-determination — *if* those others are also perceived as self-governing, and hence not easily led into aggressive foreign policies by a self-serving elite. The openness of society and free flow of information that characterize democracies facilitate these perceptions. They also help prevent the development of demonic enemy images, which are often created by elites as necessary to justify war against another people. The same cultural restraints that are assumed to limit our aggression, both internally and externally, may also be expected to limit similarly governed people in other states. Even though all these

---

[8] These are presented in Bruce Russett, *Grasping the Democratic Peace: Principles for a Post–Cold War World* (Princeton, N.J.: Princeton University Press, 1993), chap. 2. Other explanations for peace in the OECD, not focusing directly on democratic governance, are also considered. A similar account, and one that attempts to integrate the two explanations, can be found in John M. Owen, "How Liberalism Produces Democratic Peace," *International Security* 19, 2 (Fall 1994): pp. 87–125.

images may involve a significant degree of myth as well as reality, they still operate as powerful restraints on violence between democratic systems.

By contrast, these restraints do not apply when the two countries are governed according to very different norms and at least one of them is not democratic. The leaders of the nondemocratic state are seen as being in a permanent state of aggression against their own people, and thus also against foreigners. For example, the essence of U.S. cold war ideology was always that the United States had no quarrel with the Russian people, but only with the communist elites who repressed them. Such a vision of the other people as not in self-governing control of their own destiny justified a hostile U.S. foreign policy toward the Soviet Union.

An alternative, *structural explanation* suggests that institutional constraints — regular elections, division of powers within government, checks and balances — make it harder for democratic leaders to move their countries toward war. Leaders must, to varying degrees, persuade the legislature, the government bureaucracy, and even private interest groups that the resort to military force is in the national interest. They must mobilize public opinion. In a democracy, support for war can be built by rhetoric and exhortation, but it cannot be readily compelled. The complexity of this process requires time as leaders of various institutions are convinced and formal approval is obtained; but this time also allows for negotiation and other forms of peaceful conflict resolution. Perceptions matter here, too. In a crisis between democracies, each leadership anticipates that the other will have to engage in a difficult and lengthy process before military force can be used. They expect to have an opportunity to reach a peaceful settlement; they will not fear surprise attack by the other democracy and are therefore less likely to cut short the negotiating process in order to preempt one.

Leaders of nondemocratic states may also anticipate that institutional constraints will make a democracy slow to go to war. If the nondemocracy has aggressive intentions, its leaders may be more likely to threaten or bully a democracy to make concessions. A democratic leadership is aware of the strategic disadvantages that accompany an open political process. Preparation for war can be a very public process — there for all to see, including one's foreign adversaries — and may increase a democracy's sense of vulnerability to manipulation by authoritarian states facing fewer institutional constraints. In the United States, the framers of the constitution had to balance democratic principles of governance, like the separation of powers, with the realization that failing to concentrate war powers in the executive branch would leave the republic with less flexibility in its foreign relations compared to nondemocracies. Most observers would conclude that U.S. military history did not bear out such fears, but that may be just the point. Acutely aware of their vulnerabilities, democracies are extra vigilant in their dealings with nondemocratic states and seem to be more easily provoked. This logic is consistent with some of the research driving earlier phases of the democratic peace debate, namely, that democracies are not especially peaceful when it comes to their relations with nondemocratic states.[9] Ongoing social science research on the monadic effect of democracy may yet lead to a revision of that particular conclusion, but the

---

[9] See, for example, Melvin Small and J. David Singer, "The War-Proneness of Democratic Regimes," *Jerusalem Journal of International Relations 1 (1976): pp. 50–69.*

fact remains that when democracies *do* fight, their adversary is extremely likely to be nondemocratic.

Peace and Rational Choice

The cultural and structural constraints operating within a democracy are domestic factors affecting the state's opportunity to use force as an instrument of foreign policy. Compare these to other domestic factors, like the rally-'round-the-flag effect, which affect the state's willingness to engage in diversionary war. Various studies have integrated the cultural and structural explanations of the democratic peace by examining how both relate to the menu of options available to decisionmakers in democratic states, thereby conditioning their choices during periods of international crisis.

In one study, Bruce Bueno de Mesquita and David Lalman begin by providing some empirical support for the two main assumptions underlying cultural and structural explanations for the democratic peace: (1) that democratic states abhor violence as a means of settling differences, and (2) that leaders in democracies suffer greater domestic political costs when using violence than do leaders in nondemocracies. Both the "dovishness" of democratic states and the domestic political costs of using force mean that the calculations that leaders must make when choosing a course of action will differ from the calculations made by leaders of nondemocratic states. This can be illustrated through the use of game theory.

Recall the "international interaction game" from Chapter 8 (see Figure 8.1). In that model there was a point at which state *A*, after having made a demand *of* state *B* and having received a demand *from* state *B*, then had to decide between using force or not using force. That is the point in the interaction — called a "decision node" — where the two states entered a crisis situation. In Figure 8.1, the crisis ended in war if *A* decided to use force, and negotiation if *A* decided not to use force (see *A*'s last decision node on the right branch of that game tree). We can introduce some more detail into this part of the game, thereby making it more representative of crises in the real world. Figure 11.1 shows what Bueno de Mesquita and Lalman labeled the "crisis subgame":

> We have characterized a crisis as beginning at that moment when states *A* and *B* have each tabled demands and neither has conceded to the other. Up until the crisis stage, the use of force in the dispute has not been imminent. That is, the leaders' strategic choices have not yet involved military options. They have maneuvered back and forth, giving and taking, bargaining over the issues that separate them. A military crisis occurs when the parties are unwilling to accept the current state of affairs (or the current arrangement of policies) and have not found a mutually acceptable rearrangement without the threat of force.[10]

The crisis starts when state *A* must decide whether or not to use force in the face of *B*'s recalcitrance. If *A* does use force (the right branch), and *B* reciprocates the use of force,

---

[10] See Bruce Bueno de Mesquita and David Lalman, *War and Reason: Domestic and International Imperatives* (New Haven, Conn.: Yale University Press, 1992), p. 33.

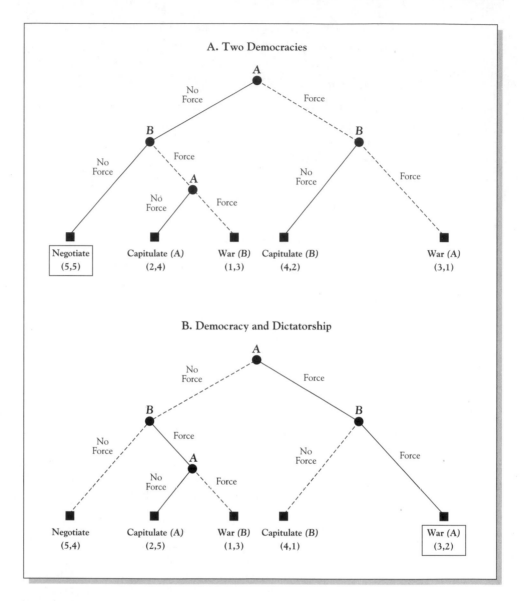

FIGURE 11.1   A Crisis Subgame: Democracies and Dictatorships

Source: Adapted from Bruce Bueno de Mesquita and David Lalman, *War and Reason: Domestic and International Imperatives* (New Haven, Conn.: Yale University Press, 1992), p. 159.

the outcome is a war initiated by A; when B does not reciprocate, the outcome is B's capitulation. If A does not use force (the left branch), then B must decide whether to initiate the use of force. If B decides not to, the outcome is a negotiated settlement. If B does use force, A must decide whether to reciprocate the use of force. If A does reciprocate, the outcome is a war initiated by B; otherwise, A capitulates.

This game tree can help us predict the outcome of a crisis if we know how each side values the five possible outcomes. Leaders in a democratic state must confront the domestic political costs of war, and are therefore inclined to rank war low in their order of preferences. If war is inevitable, they will prefer to initiate it rather than wait passively by; but if they have lost the initiative, they may well prefer to capitulate than fight. If those leaders are also dovish — not out to *forcibly* impose their will — then their opponent's capitulation will be better than either war or their own capitulation, but not as good as a negotiated settlement. Overall, then, a democratic state A's preference ordering may be as follows: negotiate > capitulation by B > war initiated by A > capitulation by A > war initiated by B. If state B is also democratic, it may have an analogous preference ordering. As we did when discussing the prisoner's dilemma and other games in Chapter 9, we can attach numbers to each of these five outcomes, indicating the preferences of each side. Thus, as shown in Part A of Figure 11.1, negotiation (5,5) is most preferred by both A and B, war initiated by B (1,3) is least preferred by A but ranked third from the bottom by B, and so on.

What is the predicted outcome of a crisis between two democracies? Using backward induction, let us start with B's decision once A has chosen to use force (the right branch). For B, reciprocating A's use of force leaves it worse off than capitulating, so B would capitulate under those circumstances. (B's decision to reciprocate the use of force is drawn as a dashed line to designate it as a course of action *not* chosen). Now A reasons that if it chooses to fight, the result will be B's capitulation, the second most preferred outcome for A. In order to compare this outcome to the one that would follow if A chooses not to use force, A must look ahead to situation in which B has been the one to initiate the use of force (down the left branch). Under those circumstances, A is better off capitulating than fighting a war initiated by B. State B can see this and therefore will expect A's capitulation if it chooses force. Still, while B's choice of force leaves it in a good position, that outcome is still not as good for B as a negotiated settlement. Therefore, B will not use force. State A, having reasoned through the likely outcome of its initial decision to not use force, can now compare negotiated settlement to the likely outcome of using force, B's capitulation. Negotiation is preferable to A, so A chooses not to use force and the crisis proceeds along the (solid) path to the negotiation outcome. That is the equilibrium outcome, and that is the outcome we predict when two democracies (with these preferences) find themselves in a crisis situation.

What happens when a democracy finds itself in a crisis situation with a nondemocratic country, say a dictatorship? First, democratic state A must consider that dictatorship B ranks the five possible outcomes differently than would another democracy. One difference is that dictatorships do not confront the same domestic political costs when they become involved in war. Therefore, fighting a war initiated by an opponent may be more desirable than capitulation for a dictatorship. Another difference is that a dictatorship may be more hawkish — preferring to bend an opponent to its will rather than negotiating. In short, a dictatorship B may have the following preference ordering: capitulation by A > negotiate > war initiated by B > war initiated by A > capitulation by B. These are shown at the base of Part B of Figure 11.1.

Now when state A contemplates the use of force (the right branch), it reasons that B will reciprocate, and therefore expects the outcome of this choice to be a war that it has initiated. In choosing not to use force (the left branch), again A has to imagine itself having to respond to B's use of force, and again A prefers capitulation to war. But B, predicting A's decision, will prefer that outcome to a negotiated settlement and so can be expected to resort to force even when A does not. Having thought the process through, leaders of state A must weigh their own capitulation against their initiation of war. Neither outcome is especially good for A, but war is better. Democratic state A therefore elects to use force, and the crisis proceeds down the path to war. When a democracy becomes embroiled in a crisis with a dictatorship, we would predict that the democracy may well initiate a conflict so as to preempt the anticipated use of force by the opponent. That is the equilibrium outcome. As Bueno de Mesquita and Lalman observe, "the high domestic political constraint faced by democracies makes them vulnerable to threats of war or exploitation and liable to launch preemptive attacks against presumed aggressors."[11]

As with other applications of game theory, we do not expect that decisionmakers have exactly these preferences under all circumstances, or that they go through exactly these calculations. But this sort of crisis subgame does seem to capture a basic logic of strategic interaction during moments of international crisis. The model could be elaborated, and has been, to take into account other factors considered by decisionmakers in democratic and nondemocratic systems, making the game more realistic. Some studies, for example, have concentrated on detailing the different domestic political costs that democratic leaders face when they employ military force, the most obvious being electoral defeat.[12]

Realists say that all states fight when it serves the national interest; the type of domestic political system makes little difference. Liberals have often claimed that democracies are inherently more peaceful than other states. And radicals have argued that democracies, most of them capitalist, are in fact more aggressive than socialist states, who are the ones most likely to live peacefully with one another. In this debate the realists seem to have had the best case. However, as we indicated, some recent social science research suggests that there is some evidence in support of the notion that democracies are more peaceful in general, especially if we restrict our attention to the twentieth century, even if the evidence is not as robust as that supporting the dyadic democratic peace.[13] One possibility is that other developments in contemporary

---

[11] Bueno de Mesquita and Lalman, *War and Reason,* p. 159.

[12] An example is Bruce Bueno de Mesquita and Randolph M. Siverson, "Nasty or Nice? Political Systems, Endogenous Norms, and the Treatment of Adversaries," *Journal of Conflict Resolution* 41, 1 (February 1997): pp. 175–199.

[13] See Kenneth Benoit, "Democracies Really Are More Pacific (in General): Reexamining Regime Type and War Involvement," *Journal of Conflict Resolution* 40, 4 (December 1996): pp. 636–657; David L. Rousseau, Christopher Gelpi, Dan Reiter, and Paul K. Huth, "Assessing the Dyadic Nature of the Democratic Peace, 1918–88," *American Political Science Review* 90, 3 (September 1996): pp. 512–532.

international relations have combined with the spread of democracy to create and potentially expand the zone of peace.

Perpetual Peace

In the last chapter, we mentioned that the writings of Immanuel Kant advocated a universalist approach to international law whereby all individuals, regardless of national citizenship, enjoy equal rights. We will return to this notion in Chapter 16 when we discuss international human rights. For now, Kant's ideas are relevant also for understanding the zone of peace. Writing in 1795, Kant presented three "definitive articles for perpetual peace among states":

1. The civil constitution of every state should be republican.
2. The law of nations shall be founded on a federation of free states.
3. The law of world citizenship shall be limited to conditions of universal hospitality.[14]

In his first article, by "republican" Kant meant a constitution that provides for individual freedom and equal status under the law, as well as a separation of executive and legislative powers within government. Interestingly, Kant was critical of democratic forms of government as despotic, since the will of the majority is imposed on the minority. However, what he had in mind was direct democracy, in which the citizenry is directly involved in both legislation and the execution of laws, and which exists more in theory than in practice. Representative democracy, the form of democratic government we see today, does correspond to Kant's conception of republicanism. Representative government is conducive to peace, according to Kant, for the same sorts of reasons highlighted by structural explanations of the democratic peace: "if the consent of the citizens is required in order to decide that war should be declared, . . . they would be very cautious in . . . decreeing for themselves all the calamities of war."

In his second article, Kant calls for international law anchored in a federation of free states. He did speak of a federation or union of states, not a world government. He also felt that each member had the right to demand that all other members have representative forms of government, making this a "pacific union." Kant expected that representative forms of government were bound to spread, and since they are "inclined toward perpetual peace" the pacific union would expand as more and more states joined in order to "secure freedom under the idea of the law of nations." In contemporary

---

[14] See Immanuel Kant, *Perpetual Peace, and Other Essays on Politics, History, and Morals,* translated and with an introduction by Ted Humphrey (Indianapolis, Ind.: Hackett, 1992). Kant's ideas and their relevance to contemporary international relations, including the democratic peace, are discussed in Michael W. Doyle, *Ways of War and Peace* (New York: Norton, 1997), chap. 8. See also Andrew Hurrell, "Kant and the Kantian Paradigm in International Relations," *Review of International Studies* 16 (1990): pp. 183–205.

international relations, the largest federation of states is, of course, the United Nations, but its membership consists of a large number of states that would not meet Kant's criteria for republicanism. Other international organizations (IOs) — most notably, the European Union, but also the less formal OECD — do consist solely of representative democracies and, given their peaceful relations, they seem to fit his idea of pacific union.

In his third definitive article, Kant refers to world citizenship and universal hospitality. He was concerned that individuals be treated fairly when guests in other lands and that as guests they should treat their hosts likewise. In particular, he lamented the treatment of indigenous peoples by European "commercial states" — that is, exploitation perpetrated "under the pretense of establishing economic undertakings." But he was also critical of the inhospitality shown by the coastal inhabitants of the Barbary Coast, who interfered with European commerce in the Mediterranean and the Atlantic. Essentially, Kant called for the free exchange of goods between peoples. What we refer to today as economic interdependence is more conducive to perpetual peace than the economic plundering that Kant thought so plainly violated principles of universal hospitality.

There are, then, three legs upon which perpetual peace stands according to Kant, each corresponding to one of his three definitive articles. Figure 11.2 illustrates this notion of perpetual peace, using both Kant's terminology and the terminology of contemporary world politics. We have already discussed the democratic ("republican") leg. We now turn to two other characteristics of the zone of peace.

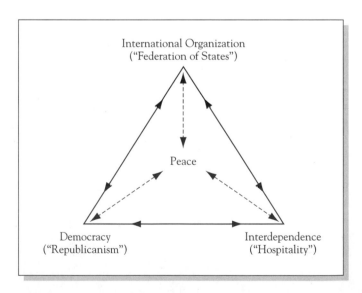

FIGURE 11.2 Kant's Prescription for Perpetual Peace

Source: Bruce Russett, "A Neo-Kantian Perspective: Democracy, Interdependence, and International Organizations in Building Security Communities," in Emanuel Adler and Michael Barnett, eds., *Security Communities* (New York: Cambridge University Press, 1998), p. 371.

Economic Interdependence and Growth

Economic interdependence gives one party a material stake in the prosperity and stability of the other's economic system. One cannot sell goods or services to others unless the others can afford to buy them. When strong economic links work both ways, each party has an important stake in the other. Trade among the OECD countries, for example, typically accounts for over 75 percent of their total international trade. The ratio of foreign trade to GNP is another useful indicator of the degree of interdependence — of the importance of foreign commerce to the overall level of economic activity. The total trade of OECD countries is about one-third of their GNP.

The relatively weak economic ties within the industrialized world during the Depression years after 1930 help explain the political tensions that culminated in World War II. Trade ties give states a strong incentive for maintaining peaceful relations. To use, or even to threaten, military violence against an important trading partner is likely to disrupt commercial exchange. Military conflict endangers importers' preferred supply of goods and services; it endangers exporters' markets. If one state's nationals have invested heavily in the economy of the other state, war could mean the destruction of the very facilities they own there. Trade and investment also serves as a medium for communication. Interests, preferences, and needs on a broad range of matters beyond immediate commercial exchange are communicated between societies in the course of regularized and stable economic relations. These communications form potentially important channels for averting militarized conflict.

Social science research largely supports the link between trade and peace, especially since World War II, although the empirical evidence has not been scrutinized as closely as the evidence linking democracy and peace. It does appear that the more any two states trade with each other, the less likely they are to experience wars or militarized disputes. Moreover, this pacifying effect of trade operates in addition to the pacifying effects of democratic governance, as well as other factors making states reluctant to fight (distance, relative power, and so on). Economically interdependent states do have disputes — witness the frequent bickering between the United States and Japan over trade practices and access to markets — but "trade wars" are not hot wars.[15]

Economic interdependence is a dyadic phenomenon, characteristic of pairs of states with extensive trade ties. There is also an economic explanation for peace that is essentially monadic. Joseph Schumpeter argued that individuals in industrialized societies are materialistic, too preoccupied with commercial production and the acquisition of wealth to be distracted by foreign conquest. Even imperial wars in pursuit of economic advantage are not worth the costs for the majority in society and really only benefit a select group. As societies become more industrialized and wealthy — and,

---

[15] On trade and peace during the post–World War II period, see John Oneal and Bruce Russett, "The Classical Liberals Were Right: Democracy, Interdependence, and Conflict, 1950–1985," *International Studies Quarterly* 41 (June 1997): pp. 267–294. For a comprehensive review of the empirical literature, see Susan M. McMillan, "Interdependence and Conflict," *Mershon International Studies Review* 41 (May 1997): pp. 33–58. To gain some historical perspective, see Richard Rosecrance, *The Rise of the Trading State: Commerce and Conquest in the Modern World* (New York: Basic Books, 1986).

Schumpeter adds, democratic — pacifism will spread, and so too will the prospects for lasting international peace.[16]

A high level of industrial activity and a high rate of economic growth are prominent features of the OECD. Virtually all the OECD countries experienced rapid economic expansion after World War II. This was especially true for the defeated states, Germany and Japan, which benefited from various forms of American assistance and by 1960 had totally recovered from their devastation. By contrast, the negative economic growth for most OECD countries during much of the 1920s and 1930s — the time of the Great Depression — was probably a major cause of World War II. Germany's economic difficulties, including rampant inflation followed by mass unemployment, led directly to Hitler's accession to power in 1933. Many of the industrialized countries, in an effort to maintain their own balance of payments, adopted various protectionist measures to restrict imports from other industrial countries. The result was a set of "beggar-thy-neighbor" policies that reduced international trade and led to a further decline in everyone's income. Conflicts over economic policies were a major cause of international tension and contributed to Japanese expansionist political and military actions. Here we have a good example of low or negative growth severely damaging the prospects for peace.

OECD countries are by far the world's richest, with an average GNP per capita of over $21,000 in 1996, when the world average was about $5,100. Of the world's twenty-five wealthiest countries (again, in terms of GNP per capita), twenty-two are OECD members. Moreover, these high living standards apply more equally among the various developed industrialized countries than they do globally. Whereas worldwide GNP per capita ranged from $80 in Mozambique to more than $45,000 in Luxembourg, the range within the OECD was narrower: from Luxembourg to Turkey's $2,800. That may still seem like a large gap within the OECD, but more than one hundred countries in the world are poorer than Turkey.[17]

Income is also distributed more equally within these countries. Figure 11.3 shows the average distribution of household income for countries in the OECD (outlined) and those outside the OECD (shaded). The biggest contrast is for the richest in society: the wealthiest 20 percent of households earn 48 percent of the income on average in countries outside the OECD, but among OECD countries the richest 20 percent earns only 39 percent of the income. At the same time, the middle classes and the poorest earn a larger share of income in the OECD than they do in other countries. Certainly there are serious inequalities even within the OECD, particularly among ethnic and racial minorities or in particular geographic regions. But the fact that these societies' considerably greater wealth is distributed more equally than is lesser wealth in other societies does represent significant social progress.

Within the OECD, however, equality is not a sufficient condition for peace. Economic inequalities, while significant, do not constitute the main grievance in Northern Ireland, where conflict has been based on religious and cultural differences. The

---

[16] See Joseph Schumpeter, *Capitalism, Socialism, and Democracy* (New York: Harper Torchbooks, 1950). For a discussion of "commercial pacifism," and specifically the views of Schumpeter and Adam Smith, see Doyle, *Ways of War and Peace*, chap. 7.

[17] World Bank, *World Development Indicators on CD-ROM*, 1998 [electronic database].

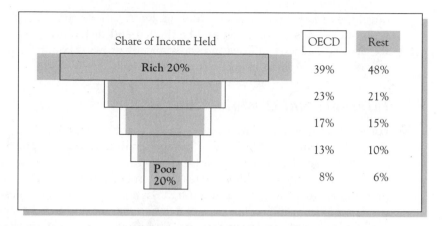

FIGURE 11.3 Income Distribution within Societies: OECD and the Rest of the World

Source: Averages are computed from income distribution data collected by the World Bank; see *World Development Report, 1998/99* (Washington, D.C.: World Bank, 1998), Table 5. Data are available for twenty-one OECD and sixty-nine other countries and generally apply to the early or mid-1990s.

Basques live in one of the most prosperous parts of Spain; again, the conflicts are over cultural and linguistic autonomy rather than economics. These few exceptions are not enough to indicate that economic equality is irrelevant to peace. It still may matter in important ways. Without equality, a "negative peace" is likely to exist simply by virtue of the dominance of the rich over the poor. Thus, the trade relations between rich and poor countries may be significant, but if they are not seen as producing equivalent rewards on both sides, they will not promote truly peaceful relations. High levels of wealth and equality do mean that all citizens would have a great deal to lose in a war. The level of destruction from a big war among industrialized countries would be far greater than the gain realized from any victory.

This suggests that perhaps a combination of economic interdependence, growth, and income equality constitutes a set of conditions for peace. This makes sense if most decisions to go to war are rational acts — that is, if war is initiated by decisionmakers who calculate, to the best of their ability, the probable costs and benefits of their acts. It is true that decisionmakers value many things besides material advantage (honor, prestige, cultural autonomy, their own political positions, and so forth). Moreover, they often calculate poorly, on the basis of incomplete or erroneous information. What may look like an act that will produce more benefits than costs may turn out to do quite the opposite. Nevertheless, decisionmakers attempt to make such calculations. In a war among OECD countries, the prospective gains would not be high (a conquered "rich" country would not be so much richer than its "poorer" conqueror). The costs of such a war, however, would likely be very high: economic growth would be interrupted, many buildings and much capital equipment would be destroyed, and existing wealth would be severely eroded. With such high prospective costs, war with another developed-market economy just does not look cost-effective at all. Any rational wars, with other kinds of countries, will be limited and distant, where the expected losses would be low. Rich countries and economically growing countries are less likely than others to have serious disputes with each other.[18]

International Organization

For Kant, a federation of free states would contribute to the maintenance of perpetual peace. Explanations of the role of international organizations and international law resemble cultural explanations for the democratic peace. Peace between democracies is based on the tendency of those states to externalize their democratic processes of conflict management and resolution. Organizations, norms, and rules are established *within* societies to reduce the costs of decision making and to enhance efficiency in the creation and implementation of policy. Democratic societies have established not only laws, but procedures for the creation, interpretation, and execution of laws. Legislatures, courts, and administrative bodies at various levels of society serve these functions. Organizations not only facilitate the use of law in conflict management, they also socialize citizens and thereby promote adherence to social norms. In general, organizations within society ease interactions between individuals — they reduce "transaction costs" — and help individuals to recognize and pursue common interests.

Leaders of democracies would expect to use international organizations and international law in the same way: to reduce international transaction costs in the pursuit of common interests. International organizations are often regarded as weak and ineffectual, as we noted in the last chapter, particularly on matters that critically affect states' security interests. It is true that in most circumstances international organizations lack the effective coercive power that national governments have over their constituencies. However, international organizations (global and regional) can and do fulfill many of the same functions *among* nation-states as domestic organizations do *within* nation-states. For example, a national government coerces all of us by requiring us to pay taxes. We may grumble, but on the whole we accept this coercion as long as it is applied reasonably equally among people. Because we want most of the benefits that a modern government provides — health care, education, defense — we are more or less willing to be coerced into paying our taxes. Most institutions to which OECD states belong lack this kind of coercive power, but they do *facilitate* mutual attention and problem solving among the members.

This leg of Kant's perpetual peace has been the subject of less social science research than either of the other two legs. One study has found that dense links of IGO membership reduced the initiation of conflict in the post–World War II period — and this is in addition to the effects of democracy, economic interdependence, and other factors inhibiting conflict between states.[19] More empirical investigation remains to be

---

[18] The theoretical argument is well presented by John Mueller, *Retreat from Doomsday* (New York: Basic Books, 1989).

[19] Bruce Russett, John R. Oneal, and David R. Davis, "The Third Leg of the Kantian Tripod for Peace: International Organizations and Militarized Disputes, 1950–1980," *International Organization* 52 (1998): pp. 441–467.

done on the connection between international organization and peace. In the meantime, there has been a resurgence of interest in some theoretical notions that laid dormant for much of the cold-war period: international integration and the emergence of security communities.

Integration and Peace

Achieving peace by integrating smaller political units into larger ones has long been a goal of political theorists and policymakers. The Roman Empire brought the *Pax Romana* — the Roman peace — to much of the world for several centuries. Although there were some revolts within the empire and continuing battles with the barbarians on its borders, the Roman Empire did preside over a remarkable era of peace as well as prosperity. Of course, it was largely a peace of domination, not the kind of stable or positive peace to which we aspire. Writing in the fourteenth century, Florentine poet Dante nevertheless looked back on the Roman Empire as being far better than the situation he knew — almost constant warfare among the Italian city-states. He argued that "in a multitude of rulers there is evil" and hoped for the emergence of a unified Italy under a single crown.

Following the devastation of World War II, the second enormously destructive war in only thirty years, some people adopted the principles of **world federalism,** the idea that permanent peace could be achieved only by establishing a world government. In Europe many leaders vowed that wars among Europeans had to cease and saw some form of European unification as the means to secure that goal. There was, for example, an attempt to create a European Defense Community (EDC). Deteriorating relations with the Soviet Union were made still more threatening by the outbreak of the Korean War in 1950. Many Europeans and Americans came to the conclusion that the military security of Western Europe could not be guaranteed unless West Germany could be rearmed. Germany had been occupied after World War II, by the United States, Britain, and France in the western zone and by the Soviet Union in the eastern zone; it had no army and no control over its foreign policy. Because of their recent Nazi experience, the Germans were still intensely distrusted. The EDC, therefore, was conceived as a way to harness German personnel and industrial strength to the common defense. It also would have controlled German militarism by uniting all the member states' armies under a single commander. The EDC would have had a directly elected European parliament and an executive that could be dismissed by the parliament, making it virtually a "United States of Europe." But plans for the EDC were shelved in 1954 after being defeated by a vote in the French Parliament.

Transnational Cooperation

For some theorists, the important aspect of domestic institutions is that they can forcibly keep the peace. They are the wielders of the only legitimate instruments of violence (the army and police), and as a result can impose order and compel obedience for the common good of society. Although the world federalists did not expect that coercive authority could be completely transferred to a world government, their visions were very ambitious — and idealistic — in this regard. Others, like David Mitrany, were more pragmatic. Mitrany felt that the proper role for international organizations was to help states solve specific problems, especially on matters that were not confined within national boundaries, like air traffic, international health and safety standards, and refugee movements. The idea was that IOs should aim to solve problems arising in specific functional areas, and should not attempt to be all things for all states. This approach to international organization was called, appropriately, **functionalism.**

Mitrany and other adherents to this view believed that this was the best path to peace. Many international problems highlighted by functionalists could be handled by cooperative efforts undertaken by specialists and technicians trained in those functional areas. Politicians, for the most part, could stay out. With the role of state leaders kept to a minimum, there would be less danger that transnational cooperation would be undermined by balance-of-power considerations or other national jealousies that seemed to preoccupy state leaders. Successful collaboration on one set of problems would encourage similar efforts in other functional areas, a process that Mitrany called "ramification"; others would later use the term "spillover." Before long a web of international institutions would be created with overlapping membership. Not only would solutions be found to problems that might otherwise contribute to interstate hostility, but the costs of armed conflict would escalate because that would threaten to disrupt the transnational networks that were working to everyone's benefit.[20]

Functionalists had more success than the world federalists in seeing their vision implemented. Jean Monnet, head of the French economic planning commission and formerly an official with the League of Nations, wanted to see Mitrany's ideas applied in the regional context of Western Europe. One problem that needed attention was the regulation of coal and steel production, an economic sector in which France and Germany were quite interdependent. Indeed, control of the mineral-rich region of Alsace-Lorraine had been a central issue of contention since France first lost it to Germany after the Franco-Prussian War of 1870–1871; possession of the territory went from Germany to France after World War I, and from France to Germany and back to France during World War II. In May 1950 Robert Schuman, foreign minister of France, announced that the French government

> proposes that Franco-German production of coal and steel as a whole be placed under a common High Authority, within the framework of an organization open to the participation of the other countries of Europe. The pooling of coal and steel production should immediately provide for the setting up of common foundations for economic development as a first step in the federation of Europe, and will change the destinies of those regions which have long been devoted to the manufacture of munitions of war, of which they have been the most constant victims. The solidarity in production thus established will make it plain that any war between France and Germany becomes not merely unthinkable, but materially impossible.[21]

---

[20] David Mitrany, *A Working Peace System* (London: Royal Institute of International Affairs, 1943).
[21] Robert Schuman, "Declaration of 9 May 1950," n.d. [cited August 10, 1998]; available at <http://www.europa.eu.int/abc/9–may/files/decl-en.htm>.

From this initiative the European Coal and Steel Community (ECSC) was born a year later, including not only France and Germany but also Belgium, Luxembourg, the Netherlands, and Italy. (Monnet was the first president of the ECSC's High Authority.) This was the first major European **supranational** institution — that is, an institution with powers to overrule the members' national governments on certain issues.

Promoting interdependence among the heavy industry sectors of the European economies seemed a good way to limit the independent war-making ability of individual states. Wider economic union could do so even more effectively. During the Nazi occupation of France, Monnet had declared:

> There will be no peace in Europe if States re-establish themselves on the basis of national sovereignty, with all that this implies by way of prestige policies and economic protectionism. . . . The countries of Europe are too small to give their peoples the prosperity that is now attainable and therefore necessary. They need wider markets. . . . To enjoy the prosperity and social progress that are essential, the States of Europe must form a federation or a "European entity" which will make them a single economic union.[22]

This kind of thinking led to the signing of the 1957 Treaties of Rome, which established the European Atomic Energy Community (Euratom) and the European Economic Community (EEC, also called the Common Market), by the same six countries that had formed the Coal and Steel Community. These separate institutions were then merged into the European Community (EC), which expanded its membership, and its functions, and was later renamed the European Union (EU). We discuss the evolution of the EU as an integrated economic bloc of nation-states at length in Chapter 14; for now, it is important to recognize the vision of peace that ultimately gave birth to the elaborate set of institutions that comprise today's EU.

For Mitrany and Monnet, peace could be achieved *despite* the conflictual inclinations of state leaders, by gradually expanding transnational cooperative networks below the highest levels of government. The process of European integration they imagined was almost automatic, and irreversible. For others, like Ernst Haas, integrating Europe required the active involvement of political elites. There was no "sneaking up" on the nation-state. An expanding web of European institutions would not materialize — nor would lasting peace — unless elites themselves *transferred their loyalties* to these new institutions and encouraged the process of spillover. French national interests and German national interests would have to be reconceived as European interests.[23]

It is certainly true that stable peace has been achieved among members of the EU. For countries now so highly interdependent, the EU institutions are essential in solving members' common problems and perhaps in preventing tensions that could endanger the peace. However, the zone of peace includes all the OECD countries, not just the EU.

---

[22] Jean Monnet, *Memoirs*, trans. by Richard Mayne (Garden City, N.Y.: Doubleday, 1978), p. 222.

[23] Ernst B. Haas, *The Uniting of Europe: Political, Social, and Economic Forces, 1950–1957* (Stanford, Calif.: Stanford University Press, 1958); see also his *Beyond the Nation State* (Stanford, Calif.: Stanford University Press, 1964). Haas's and other similar revisions of functionalist thinking are labeled "neofunctionalism."

Although there are a variety of important institutions like the Council of Europe, NATO, and the OECD itself, these are not in any significant way coercive organizations. For instance, in peacetime the NATO Supreme Headquarters does not command the troops of the constituent countries. Save for the institutions of the EU, they must work principally by negotiation and consensus among members, not by enforcement.

Transnational Communication

Some scholars of international integration and peace, most notably Karl Deutsch and his associates, describe a process of integration based on a wide array of intersocietal transactions that are of mutual benefit to the people involved. These transactions become facilities for attention to one another and for identifying one's interests with those of others. One cannot help to meet the needs of another without knowing what those needs are; that is, without a large, continuous flow of information. There is a social fabric between as well as within nations that is built from such bonds as trade, travel (migration or tourism), cultural and educational exchange, and communication (telephone, television, the Internet, and so on). These ties communicate the needs and perspectives of one group of people to others; they strengthen the sense of a collective identity within the larger community. In the tradition of sociological theory, these community bonds are part of the *Gemeinschaft* — common loyalties and values, a feeling of belonging together — in contrast to the *Gesellschaft*, which emphasizes contractual arrangements and institutions.

Transnational bonds affect not only political elites but also the attitudes and beliefs at all "politically relevant strata" of the population, which include the mass public in democracies. Deutsch describes the emerging sense of **community** as

> a matter of mutual sympathy and loyalties; of "we-feeling," trust, and mutual consideration; of partial identification in terms of self-images and interests; of mutually successful predictions of behavior . . . in short, a matter of a perpetual dynamic process of mutual attention, communication, perception of needs, and responsiveness in the process of decision making.[24]

The community-building process is based on learning — learning that such transactions provide benefits, that such benefits outweigh the costs involved, and that there are positive payoffs in continuing and expanding such transactions. As peaceful transactions increase, peoples develop greater responsiveness to one another. They develop the "we-feeling," trust, and mutual consideration upon which integrated political communities must be based.

Though they usually seem to bind nations or social groups together, trade, tourism, and migration can also serve as irritants. The most important qualification — a serious one — is that the exchanges must be mutual and on a basis of relative equality. Ties perceived as exploitative or colonial, however strong, do not seem to bring groups together. Contacts that are involuntary for one party (an extreme case being the

---

[24] Karl W. Deutsch et al., *Political Community and the North Atlantic Area: International Organization in the Light of Historical Experience* (Princeton, N.J.: Princeton University Press, 1957), p. 36.

payment of reparations) are not facilitative, nor are highly status-conscious relations, such as those between employer and employee. Contacts between very disparate cultures are also as likely to arouse conflict as to bring the cultures together. Tourists from rich countries to poor countries, for instance, may create animosities among their hosts and distress in their own minds. The nature of the contacts in each particular case must be examined before any firm conclusions about their effects are made. However, a very general observation can be made: ties between nations that are culturally similar and perhaps geographically close are more likely to be favorable.

Security Communities

The most tangible outcome of this transactional process of integration is the emergence of what Deutsch and colleagues call a **security community:**

> A security community is a group of people which has become "integrated." By *integration* we mean the attainment, within a territory, of a *"sense of community"* and of institutions and practices strong enough and widespread enough to assure . . . dependable expectations of "peaceful change" among its population. By sense of community we mean a belief . . . that common social problems must and can be resolved by processes of "peaceful change."[25]

In describing a security community as the result of a process of social integration, there is an emphasis on peaceful change, an ability and willingness to accommodate new demands and needs, not merely the maintenance of a status quo that may be unjust. It is a situation in which participants have a relationship that is reasonably equal and symmetrical and in which they frequently harmonize their interests, compromise their differences, and reap mutual rewards. There still may be some conflicts of interest, but the use or threat of force to resolve conflict is absent. This is positive peace.

Individuals' perceptions of their self-interest can be greatly broadened so that they are willing to make certain sacrifices whether or not those sacrifices are directly reciprocated. For example, members of a family will make sacrifices for their common welfare or for the welfare of one of them. The identification and affection may be so strong that on some matters a husband or a wife comes to prefer to do what the spouse wants rather than what he or she had originally desired. While observers adopting the radical perspective have been highly critical of the subtle ways in which the internalization of common values can encourage behavior that seems to contradict self interests, a community-building perspective emphasizes the positive aspects. In effect, there is a tacit agreement — tacit because if stated openly it becomes a very fragile affair — not to coerce others and to limit the scope of bargaining. One gives up certain bargaining options without having to admit it: within the OECD community, states have substantially given up the use of military force against each other (a circumstance that runs in the face of realist beliefs). As within marriage, each partner bargains. But in a reason-

---

[25] Deutsch et al., *Political Community and the North Atlantic Area*, p. 5.

ably good relationship the partners recognize their common interest in keeping the bargaining limited and share a desire to avoid coercing or breaking up the union.

Social integration need not involve the creation of a single political entity, or "amalgamated" security community; states may retain their sovereign independence, thereby forming a "pluralistic" security community, but one still based on a degree of shared identity.[26] The only serious expectation or actuality of violent conflict within the OECD area in recent years has been within a few countries, notably in Northern Ireland. It is not simply that an institution — the common government — is unable to prevent violence; rather, the fact of common government is a *cause* of the violence. The separatists want to be free of the common government. There have been many cases of civil war or secessionist revolution in history. The revolt of the thirteen American colonies and the later unsuccessful secession attempt by the Confederate states well illustrate this fact. One of the most significant contributions of Deutsch's work was to point out what should have been obvious: people may fight against a common government but then live in peace as separate states (for example, the Republic of Ireland and the United Kingdom). Common institutions are no panacea for peace; thus, neither is any simple prescription of world government. For Deutsch the goal of integration is peace; institution building at best contributes to that kind of integration but is often irrelevant or even destructive to it. A second significant contribution of Deutsch's work has been his reminder that there is always the possibility of *disintegration*. Integration must be thought of as a difficult process that needs continual attention — an "imperfect assembly line" that may fail at any number of points.[27]

Zones of Turmoil

We have discussed various explanations of the democratic peace, Kant's prescription for perpetual peace, and notions of peace through integration. Each cluster of explanations sheds light on the zone of peace in contemporary world politics.[28] We now can speculate on whether the experience of the OECD countries gives us any reason to hope that a stable peace based on something more than simply dominance or mutual

---

[26] See, for example, Thomas Risse-Kappen, "Collective Identity in a Democratic Community: The Case of NATO," in Peter Katzenstein, ed., *The Culture of National Security: Norms and Identity in World Politics* (New York: Columbia University Press, 1996).

[27] See Karl W. Deutsch, "National Integration: Some Concepts and Research Approaches," *Jerusalem Journal of International Relations* 2 (1977): pp. 1–29. Deutsch's conception of security community has begun to attract renewed interest. See, for example, Emanuel Adler and Michael Barnett, eds., *Security Communities in Comparative and Historical Perspective* (Cambridge: Cambridge University Press, 1998); and Harvey Starr, *Anarchy, Order, and Integration: How to Manage Interdependence* (Ann Arbor: University of Michigan Press, 1997).

[28] For a discussion of the relationships between these three clusters of explanation, as well as an attempt to integrate them, see Bruce Russett and Harvey Starr, "From Democratic Peace to Kantian Peace: Democracy and Conflict in the International System," in Manus Midlarsky, ed., *Handbook of War Studies,* 2nd ed. (Ann Arbor: University of Michigan Press, 1999).

deterrence can be achieved in other parts of the world. In doing so, we discard realist assumptions about the inevitability of the pursuit of power leading to violent conflict among all kinds of states. We are thinking like liberals — some might say idealists — in search for hints about what an alternative world might look like. Yet we are thinking "realistically" in that we are asking whether conditions that *already* exist in part of the world might be extended further.

One hopeful sign is that the global levels of political democracy and economic interdependence can be expected to continue their upward trends. Figure 11.4 shows the average "democracy score" for all countries in the world from 1950 to 1994. The index is constructed by the Polity Project in order to assess the degree of democratic governance in each state based on political participation, executive recruitment, and constraints of the chief executive.[29] The average level of democracy has been steadily

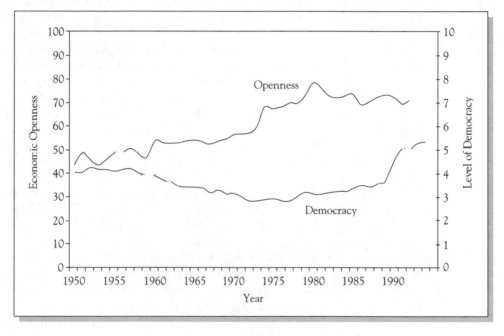

FIGURE 11.4 Political Democracy and Economic Openness in the World, 1950–1994

Source: Both trends show annual averages for all countries in the world. Level of democracy is computed from the democracy index (0–10 scale) compiled by the Polity Project; see "Polity Data Archive," 1998 [cited September 14, 1998]; available at <http://www.colorado.edu/IBS/GAD/spacetime/data/Polity.html>. Economic openness is computed from the openness index (imports and exports as a share of GDP) compiled by the Center for International Comparisons; see "Penn World Table," 1995 [cited September 14, 1998]; available at <http://pwt.econ.upenn.edu/>.

---

[29] See Keith Jaggers and Ted Robert Gurr, "Tracking Democracy's Third Wave with the Polity III Data," *Journal of Peace Research* 32, 4 (November 1995): pp. 469–482.

increasing since the mid-1970s, and rather sharply since the end of the cold war. Figure 11.4 also shows the trend in interdependence, as measured by economic openness (imports and exports as a share of GDP). Economic openness in the world was on the rise from 1950 to the early 1980s, and since then it has maintained those relatively high levels. Since political democracy and interdependence have been identified as essential components of stable peace by very many scholars, these trends do indeed encourage the hope that the peace enjoyed by the OECD can be expanded to other regions.

Many countries that had formerly been dictatorships — both communist countries and military regimes — have moved partially or almost entirely toward free democratic governments. The shift has been dramatic and almost worldwide. A key question is whether relations in all of Europe, including the former communist countries, can be those of a security community. Liberalization in the Soviet bloc began in the 1980s. By 1991 several Eastern European countries were fully democratic, and all had progressed far in that direction. That bodes well for a peaceful future in all of Europe. In none of these states, however, is democracy secure. If perceiving another state as democratic is important to peace, one aspect of that must be the perception that the other is dependably, stably democratic. That is much less certain. Few Eastern European countries have an experience of stable democratic practices and institutions (none, except for the former Czechoslovakia, had more than ten years of multiparty democracy in this century prior to 1990). They are beset by ethnic and nationalist rivalries. These forces led to the peaceful separation of the Slovak and Czech Republics, but they have been accompanied by much violence in Russia (for instance, in Chechnya) and especially in the former Yugoslavia (Bosnia and Kosovo).

Democracy does not automatically cure these ills; by relieving the dictatorial controls that previously suppressed the expression of nationalism, it may even make things worse. Previously suppressed tensions can now be openly expressed. People who long hated each other in silence now can say how much they hate each other. Minorities long held in a state against their will now can seek independence. Political mobilization can play into the hands of leaders who wish to fan ethnic hatred so as to build separatist power bases. Even minorities who might prefer to remain in a multiethnic state fear that new and imperfectly established democratic norms and institutions will provide very imperfect guarantees for the protection of minority rights. Democracy thus may seem to be part of this growing global problem.

Indeed, the process of moving, often abruptly, from authoritarian rule to democracy feeds uncertainty and brings fear as well as hope. But democracy itself, once established, is part of the solution. Although some established democracies do exhibit serious tensions among ethnic groups, they typically manage them without major lethal violence. Democracies offer institutionalized protections to minorities, and they provide peaceful procedures and expectations for containing and resolving conflicts. Killings, when they happen, are usually the work of fringe groups representing only a minority within the minority. Full-scale civil war — not uncommon in destabilized authoritarian systems — is virtually unknown in established democracies. True, ethnic conflicts and rival nationalisms may be successfully suppressed for decades by tough and effective authoritarian states. But this is negative peace, not a permanent solution.

Another related problem is the difficult economic situation in states undergoing democratic transitions. All of the East European states have experienced abrupt drops in their national incomes, as they have lost their former assured markets and supplies in other communist countries (previously joined economically in COMECON) and, especially, as they moved painfully from socialist command economies to free-market ones. The people may not indefinitely support democratic governments that cannot deliver the economic goods; we have seen the reelection of former communist leaders in several places. Some former Soviet republics such as Azerbaijan, Turkmenistan, and Uzbekistan have already been downgraded from "partially free" to "not free" by some analysts (see Appendix B). These countries are not yet dependably stable democratic regimes, and they are the ones most likely to constitute exceptions to the democratic peace.

The prospects are especially worrisome for Russia, partly because it is by far the biggest of the former communist countries and still a nuclear superpower. In addition, democratization and the creation of a market economy have further to go there than in almost any other European country. Nationalism is also an especially serious problem in Russia. Whether the country can both remain somewhat united and become fully democratic remains to be seen. One, or both, of those goals may have to yield.

What we are saying, then, is that even if stable and established democracies are generally at peace with one another, one cannot say that the *process of democratization* is necessarily a peaceful one. A brand-new democracy may be unstable and may face fierce problems of restructuring its economy and satisfying diverse interests and ethnic groups. Under these perhaps temporary circumstances, nationalism and pressures to divert attention from domestic problems to foreign antagonists may lead to conflicts with neighboring states.[30] Or authoritarian neighbors may see a new and not yet consolidated democracy as weak and a suitable target for aggression. (Transitions from democratic to authoritarian regimes are equally dangerous, however. Political instability in general, not just democratization, is the problem.)

Similarly, the requirements for economic growth and the equality of economic distribution worldwide are very demanding, given the experience of the LDCs over the past few decades. Economic stagnation has been the lot of many; although others have strong records of growth by conventional measures like GNP per capita, the record of equitable distribution within those countries is very mixed. Often economic inequality is maintained by authoritarian and coercive political institutions — a further departure from the conditions that obtain in the industrialized countries. On this basis, it is possible to imagine stable peace arising in some areas of the developing world where conditions are favorable, as seems to be occuring between Argentina, Chile, Brazil, and some other countries of South America. Still, it is much harder to imagine its achievement worldwide. There is the intriguing but daunting possibility that stable peace, economic equality, decent living conditions, and political liberties may be bound together

---

[30] This is a conclusion reached by Edward Mansfield and Jack Snyder, "Democratization and the Danger of War," *International Security* 20,1 (Summer 1995): pp. 5–38. But for a different interpretation of the evidence, see Michael D. Ward and Kristian S. Gleditsch, "Democratizing for Peace," *American Political Science Review* 92, 1 (March 1998): pp. 51–61.

in an inseparable package; thus to strive for one requires us to strive for them all. In the meantime, alongside a widening zone of peace there will still be zones of turmoil.

Conclusion to Part II

In Part II of this book we have examined major themes in international conflict and cooperation. We started by discussing the basic causes of social violence, and then considered several explanations for interstate conflict. Causes of war can be located at all of the levels of analysis we introduced in Part I, and the focus of researchers typically depends on the theoretical approach to world politics they find to be most persuasive. Thus, realists have examined causes at the systemic level, especially the distribution of power, while liberals and radicals often concentrate on domestic politics and economics. More recently, the rational choice approach, which models the strategic interaction of players in a "game," has provided key insights into the tragic logic that traps state leaders as they head down the road to war. We also considered the forces driving conflict within states, especially ethnonationalism, as well as various forms of unconventional conflict. Although the cold war has ended, internal conflicts and terrorism remain as disturbing features of contemporary world politics.

Hostility cannot become warfare unless states, and also nonstate actors, acquire the instruments with which to fight. Clearly they have, and the capacity of modern military arsenals — particularly weapons of mass destruction — to wreak havoc on the human race, not to mention other species, is truly frightening. One wonders how the major states of the world could have arrived at such a high state of militarization, considering not only the risks of mass destruction but also the substantial economic costs involved. Again, game theory illustrates well the logic that drives this security dilemma. One ray of hope has been the real progress in arms control that first accompanied, then followed the end of the cold war. Now disarmament, and not only arms control, is meeting with success in certain areas.

Of course, world politics is not all about weapons and war. In most societies violence is not the typical form of social interaction; behavior is usually guided by social norms, laws, and institutions. So, too, in the society of states. We have discussed the importance of international organization and law, including the existence and widespread (though certainly not universal) adherence to laws governing warfare, the most primitive form of state behavior. Although few mechanisms exist in world politics for the enforcement of international law — international organizations like the UN do not have the same authority in international society as national governments do in domestic society — we should not underestimate the extent to which states really do feel bound by the norms and laws that bring order to world politics. Domestic order rarely rests solely on coercion, and neither does international order.

Peace, not war, is the normal state of affairs in world politics. That is no reason for complacency, however. We can learn much from the enduring peace that has emerged among the industrialized countries of the OECD. Explanations vary, but most emphasize pacifying effects of democratic governance as well as increased social and economic transactions between states. Can the zone of peace be expanded during the twenty-first century? There are grounds for optimism. But some of the biggest impediments to both domestic and international stability — and therefore to stable peace — derive from international economic uncertainties. In Part III we turn to the nexus between politics and economics in world affairs.

INTERNATIONAL POLITICAL ECONOMY

Commerce and manufacturers gradually introduced order and good government, and with them the liberty and security of individuals.
— ADAM SMITH

Finance capital and the trusts are increasing instead of diminishing the differences in the rate of development of various parts of the world economy.
— V. I. LENIN

12

Political Economy of National Security and Defense

Approaches to Political Economy

Political economy, as the term implies, refers to the intersection of politics and economics. It is a concept used to describe individual and state behavior, as well as the outcomes of social interaction, that involve both political and economic considerations. **International political economy** (IPE), then, focuses on the combined political and economic behavior, as well as outcomes, taking place among state and nonstate international actors. It refers equally to the politics of international economics and the economics of international politics. World politics provides few examples of purely political phenomena; there are economic dimensions to most of the issues we have examined in this book, as there are political dimensions to nearly all matters examined by international economists. However, subjects usually considered to be the focus of IPE include international trade and monetary relations between states, the activities of international institutions that facilitate economic cooperation, and global economic development. We examine each of these subjects in the chapters that follow.

Other topics, like some of those discussed in this chapter, have much to do with *domestic* political economy, but are relevant to world politics because they pertain to national security and defense. The economic impact of defense spending, the local effects of military base closings, and the conversion of military-related manufacturing to civilian use are examples. These issues have taken on added significance with military downsizing in the United States, Russia, and elsewhere following the end of the cold war. But before we turn to such topics, let us reconsider the main theoretical approaches to world politics and their perspectives on international political economy.

Realism, Liberalism, and Radicalism

In Chapter 2 we introduced three alternative views of international relations, and throughout the book we have highlighted the ways in which these perspectives differ on various issues in world politics, especially international conflict and cooperation. These same alternative views — realism, liberalism, and radicalism — can be found when we shift our discussion to topics in international political economy.

The realist perspective emphasizes the role of the state in global economic affairs, in much the same way that the state occupies center stage in global political affairs. The realist approach to the study of international political economy — relatively new in the long history of realist thought, which has tended to neglect the economic dimensions of world politics — is often called "neorealism." Realists are the intellectual descendants of **mercantilists.** Mercantilism was the economic doctrine pursued by the major states of Europe during the sixteenth and seventeenth centuries. Monarchs believed that the best way to maximize the wealth and power of their states was to actively encourage exports while discouraging imports, thereby adding to their stocks of gold and silver (the currency of international trade at that time). The surplus could then be used to build the bureaucratic infrastructure of the state and to support national armies.

Realism is not the same as mercantilism, but the emphasis on the state's ability and willingness to intervene in the market in the pursuit of national interests is reminiscent of mercantilist doctrine. Indeed, the realist approach to international political economy is sometimes called "neomercantilism." Consistent with their focus on the state as the guarantor of economic power, realists are skeptical that nonstate actors can have much of an independent impact on global political-economic relations. When IGOs and NGOs, including multinational corporations (MNCs), seem to be most effective in world affairs, it is because their activities promote the national interests of the most powerful states in the international system, not because they wield much influence by themselves.

Liberals, on the other hand, are less confident that the state occupies such an exalted position in the international political economy. To be sure, states are important actors — perhaps the *most* important actors — but when it comes to the global economy, the state shares the stage with some very significant others. International organizations and MNCs may not have the resources available to major states in the international system (including, of course, national armies), but traditional forms of state power are not always effective in contemporary economic affairs. Liberals therefore tend to focus on the limits of state power and the tendency of states to redefine their national interests in the context of changing international economic conditions.

Where the realist view sees potential conflict the liberal view sees potential harmony. If, as realists suggest, foreign economic policy is designed to maximize a state's wealth and power in world affairs, then states will be wary of policies and agreements that diminish their position in the global pecking order. In other words, states are interested in maximizing their **relative gains.** But liberals argue that states pursue **absolute gains;** arrangements that improve the welfare of society are really what motivate a state's foreign economic policy, even when those arrangements may be of greater benefit to others. Because it is easier to satisfy parties seeking absolute gains than those who are also jockeying for a better position relative to others, liberals are more inclined than realists to see potential for international cooperation on global economic matters. For realists, when states seem to be cooperating, it is probably because this "cooperation" has somehow been coerced (or perhaps purchased) by the most powerful states.

Liberals also tend to have abiding faith in the individual and in the market. In contrast to realists, they view human nature with considerable optimism. Social harmony is possible, both domestically and internationally, and it is better achieved by deferring to the "invisible hand" of the free market than by resorting to the heavy hand of state intervention. This argument was first developed in the eighteenth century by Scottish philosopher Adam Smith — in his now-famous *The Wealth of Nations* — as a reaction to the mercantilist beliefs driving the foreign policies of European states during his time.[1] As we shall see in the next chapter, these competing perspectives lead to very different conclusions regarding the benefits of free trade, the costs of interdependence, and the possibility of international cooperation.

The third perspective we introduced in Chapter 2 was radicalism, or Marxism as it is often called. Actually, Karl Marx wrote relatively little about *international* political economy; the task of adapting Marxist thought to international relations was taken up by V. I. Lenin, among others.[2] In contrast to liberals, radicals do not expect that social harmony can be achieved among individuals of different classes. Like realists, they are suspicious of what may appear on the surface to be cooperative economic arrangements between states, especially states at different stages of economic development. Economic relations between the developed countries of the North and developing countries of the South are fundamentally unequal. But while realists believe that international cooperation is undertaken for the benefit of the most powerful *states* in the international system, radicals argue that it is the international capitalist *class* that benefits. Capitalists in the advanced industrialized countries obviously gain from international trade and from foreign investment by their MNCs, but even capitalists in less developed countries profit from unequal economic relationships. Workers are the losers all around, particularly those in less-developed countries. According to the radical view, by treating states as if they were unitary actors pursuing wealth and power,

---

[1] See Adam Smith, *An Inquiry into the Nature and Causes of the Wealth of Nations,* edited by Kathryn Sutherland (Oxford: Oxford University Press, 1993).

[2] See especially V. I. Lenin, *Imperialism: The Highest Stage of Capitalism* (New York: International Publishers, 1939).

realists overlook important class-based conflicts of interests in the international political economy.

These competing perspectives on the political-economic dimensions of international relations are evident in many of the issues we address in Part III. No single view dominates the study of international political economy. On some matters, realism, liberalism, and radicalism offer alternative and plausible interpretations of the same thing — international trade, economic development, globalization, and so on — but it may be more accurate to say that these viewpoints illuminate different aspects of IPE, as we shall see.

Economics and Statecraft

In Chapter 5 we discussed briefly the economic instruments used by states to influence other states. The use of economic techniques for international influence is designed to exploit the vulnerability of other states in order to persuade them to do something they would not otherwise do. Few states can completely isolate themselves economically, because other states have at least some of what they need. Thus, most states are subject to attempted influence through the manipulation of these economic dependencies. Whether the manipulation of economic ties is effective as a means of influence is another question, and has been the subject of debate among scholars and policymakers for a long time.

Economic Coercion

Economic statecraft is defined broadly to include any economic means of influencing the behavior of another state. That encompasses both positive and negative sanctions. Negative economic sanctions are forms of **economic coercion,** and these can vary greatly in terms of severity. The use of tariffs, quotas, and other restrictions on free trade usually fall toward the less-severe end of the spectrum, and we discuss these policy instruments in the next chapter. For the moment, we want to focus on more severe forms of economic coercion. The most extreme form of economic coercion is *economic warfare,* which involves "a major use of economic force to change the behavior of or to extract an advantage from an adversary, normally accompanied by the use of political force and sometimes by the use of military force."[3]

One comprehensive study of economic sanctions reported that of the 115 sanctions imposed on states by other states from World War I until 1990, a little more than 40 percent sought to bring about only modest policy changes on the part of the target.[4] That

---

[3] John C. Scharfen, *The Dismal Battlefield: Mobilizing for Economic Conflict* (Annapolis, Md.: Naval Institute Press, 1995), p. 13. For another careful discussion of the many concepts associated with economic statecraft, see David A. Baldwin, *Economic Statecraft* (Princeton, N.J.: Princeton University Press, 1985).

[4] Gary Clyde Hufbauer, Jeffrey J. Schott, and Kimberly Ann Elliot, *Economic Sanctions Reconsidered: History and Current Policy,* 2nd ed. (Washington, D.C.: Institute for International Economics, 1990).

economic sanctions need not mean economic warfare is also evident from the list of countries experiencing U.S. sanctions at the end of 1998, which includes Canada and Japan — U.S. allies and close trading partners whose specific trade or investment practices had at some point raised the ire of the U.S. Congress. The Helms-Burton Act, for example, passed in 1996, sought to punish foreign companies that invest in Cuban assets formerly owned by Americans but nationalized by the Castro regime. Such punishments differ markedly from the much more coercive sanctions regime imposed on Cuba itself.

Sanctions can have more ambitious aims, like destabilizing an unfriendly government or impairing a target's military activities. Prior to the mid-1970s, such goals were about as common as attempts to bring about modest policy changes, but since the 1970s they have represented a much smaller share of the total; the increased use of economic sanctions has been associated with the pursuit of mostly modest goals. On the other hand, there does seem to be a greater willingness on the part of the international community to turn to sanctions as a means of punishing states seen to be in violation of fundamental international norms. During the cold war, the UN Security Council imposed sanctions only twice — against Rhodesia and South Africa — in both instances for the white minority regime's systematic violation of the black majority's human rights. UN-mandated sanctions have been much more common since the end of the cold war, as is clear from Table 12.1 . They have been imposed on Iraq for its invasion of Kuwait, on Yugoslavia for the use of force against its former republics, on Libya for its support of terrorism, as well as on Somalia, Liberia, Rwanda, Haiti, and Sierra Leone for various forms of domestic repression. The UN has even targeted a domestic faction *within* a state: in 1993 the Security Council embargoed petroleum and petroleum products going to UNITA guerrillas fighting in Angola (in addition to arms and other forms of military assistance).

The success of economic coercion depends on how vulnerable the target is to being cut off from a particular foreign good or service (an embargo), or from a particular foreign market for its own goods and services (a boycott). The key issue here is substitutability. If the target state can find substitutes for the items covered by the sanction regime, and can do so at acceptable costs, then economic sanctions will fail to change the target state's behavior. At minimum, this would seem to require that prior to the imposition of sanctions the state being punished should have important economic ties with the punishing state. For example, the countries of Western Europe, faced with the 1973 oil embargo and price increases by Arab members of OPEC, were strongly affected because they had based their energy policies on the assumption of a continued flow of low-priced oil from the OPEC states, which provided an overwhelming proportion of their supply

The state being punished must also be unable to find a substitute for the sanctioned item, in terms either of goods or of markets. When the United States under President Dwight Eisenhower attempted to punish Cuba by cutting the U.S. quota of Cuban sugar, Cuba was able to substitute markets by getting the Soviet Union to purchase the newly available sugar. Similarly, when the United States and Western companies cut off Cuba's oil supplies, Castro was able to substitute Soviet oil. On the other hand, when the Arab oil suppliers decided to embargo oil to the United States, Western Europe, and Japan in 1973, there was some short-term acquiescence by European

TABLE 12.1 UN-Mandated Sanctions, 1965–1998

Target	Resolution	Sanction	Duration
Rhodesia	217	Arms and Oil Embargo	1965–1979
	232	Suspension of Economic Relations	
	460	Sanctions Lifted	
South Africa	418	Arms Embargo	1977–1994
	919	Sanctions Lifted	
Iraq	661	Comprehensive Trade Sanctions	1990–
	670	Flight Ban	
	712	Oil-for Food Provisions	
	986	Oil-for-Food Provisions	
	1137	Diplomatic Sanctions	
	1158	Oil-for-Food Provisions	
Yugoslavia (Serbia and Montenegro)	713	Arms Embargo	1991–
	757	Comprehensive Trade Sanctions, Flight Ban, Cultural Boycott	
	820	Sanctions Strengthened	
	942	Sanctions Imposed on Bosnian Serbs	
	943	Sanctions Eased	
	1022	Sanctions Partially Suspended (also resolutions 988, 1003, and 1015)	
	1074	Sanctions Lifted	
	1160	Arms Embargo	
Somalia	733	Arms Embargo	1992–

TABLE 12.1   UN-Mandated Sanctions, 1965–1998 *(continued)*

Target	Resolution	Sanction	Duration
Libya	748	Arms Embargo, Flight Ban, Diplomatic Sanctions	1992–1998
	883	Government Funds Frozen, Oil Equipment Ban	
	1192	Sanctions Suspended	
Liberia	788	Arms Embargo	1992–
Haiti	841	Arms and Oil Embargo, Foreign Assets Frozen	1993–1994
	861	Arms and Oil Embargo Suspended	
	873	Arms and Oil Embargo Reinstated	
	917	Trade Sanctions	
	944	Sanctions Lifted	
Angola (UNITA)	864	Arms and Oil Embargo	1993–
	1127	Flight Ban, Diplomatic Sanctions	
	1173	Trade Sanctions, Foreign Assets Frozen	
Rwanda	918	Arms Embargo	1994–
	1011	Sanctions on Government Lifted, Sanctions on Nongovernmental Forces Remain	
Sudan	1054	Diplomatic Sanctions	1996–
	1070	Flight Ban	
Sierra Leone	1132	Arms and Oil Embargo	1997–
	1156	Sanctions Lifted	
	1171	Arms Embargo	

Note: Sanctions with no termination year were still in effect at the end of 1998.

Source: UN Office for the Coordination of Humanitarian Affairs, "Toward More Humane and Effective Sanctions Management: Enhancing the Capacity of the United Nations System," October 1997 [cited April 13, 1999], Table 1; available at <http://www.reliefweb.int/ocha_ol/pub/misc/index.html>; updated by the authors.

countries and Japan to Arab demands. The Arab states controlled such a large proportion of the oil supply that most of the target countries found substitution difficult. Nevertheless, one country singled out by the Arabs as "unfriendly" — the Netherlands —
soon found that it could meet its oil needs by indirect routes. The chief economic effects
were produced by the huge oil price increases rather than by targeting specific countries for embargo. Even then, the effects were largely shifts in target countries' rhetoric
(moderated public statements, nearly meaningless votes in the UN), not more substantive shifts. Probably the most important change was simply to increase the prominence
of the Arab-Israeli conflict on the agenda of world leaders (especially the United
States).[5]

The punishing state, too, must be able to substitute or be able to afford the cutbacks in supply or purchases. If the oil producers had desperately needed every
petrodollar garnered from oil sales, then the embargo would not have worked. But
there were plenty of other states in the world willing to purchase their oil, and most oil-
producing states could easily accept a reduction in oil revenues. In other words, the
state doing the punishing must not be as vulnerable to the threatened disruption as the
state being punished. Critics of the increased use of economic sanctions in U.S. foreign
policy highlight the consequences for U.S. economic performance, especially lost jobs.
A study by the Institute for International Economics estimated that in 1995 U.S. economic sanctions meant a loss of $15 to $19 billion in exports to twenty-six countries and
as many as 200,000 jobs in the export sector. For many, such costs are too high given the
spotty success rate of economic sanctions as a foreign policy tool.[6]

Changing the behavior of a target state through economic coercion can be very difficult. A major debate over the necessity of resorting to military force against Iraq in
1991 involved whether or not UN-mandated economic sanctions alone would have
compelled Iraq to withdraw from Kuwait. It is clear that sanctions weakened the country considerably and made living conditions far more difficult. It is not clear, however,
whether such effects would have moved Saddam Hussein to comply with the UN resolutions. The continued use of sanctions after the Gulf War has not ousted Hussein
from power, but it has prevented Iraq from rebuilding its military forces. A similar
debate on the effectiveness of sanctions surrounded the moves by the South African
government to dismantle the apartheid system in 1991 and the consequent lifting of
sanctions by the United States. These cases do show that the greater the number of
states complying with sanctions, and the more complete that compliance (more so with
Iraq than with South Africa), the greater the impact sanctions will have.[7] They also

---

[5] Roy Licklider, *Political Power and the Arab Oil Weapon* (Berkeley: University of California Press, 1988).
[6] Gary Clyde Hufbauer, Kimberly Ann Elliot, Tess Cyrus, and Elizabeth Winston, "U.S. Economic
Sanctions: Their Impact on Trade, Jobs, and Wages," Institute for International Economics Working
Paper, April 1997 [cited April 15, 1999]; available at <http://www.iie.com/catalog/wp/1977/sanc-
tion/sanctnwp.htm>. For an analysis of the effects of domestic politics on the effectiveness of economic sanctions, see T. Clifton Morgan and Valerie L. Schwebach, "Economic Sanctions as an
Instrument of Foreign Policy: The Role of Domestic Politics," *International Interactions* 21, 3 (January
1996): pp. 247–263.
[7] For a study of the conditions leading to widespread compliance with multilateral sanctions, see Lisa
L. Martin, *Coercive Cooperation: Explaining Multilateral Economic Sanctions* (Princeton, N.J.: Princeton
University Press, 1992).

raise the issue of the indirect nature of economic techniques and which segments of the population are actually punished. The argument can be made that the poorest people bear the heaviest costs of sanctions; sanctions affect the governing elites last and least. One study estimated that 90,000 Iraqis die annually from disease and malnutrition caused by sanctions.[8] For sanctions to have an effect on leaders, either the leaders must care about the domestic conditions within their countries, or those deteriorating conditions must actually threaten their grip on political power.

The success of economic sanctions needs to be measured in terms of the objectives sought through sanctions: compliance, subversion, deterrence, international symbolism, or domestic symbolism. Sanctions often do not bring about compliance with major demands. They may be effective in subverting the government of another state, but only if the state is small and its government already shaky. A study of twentieth-century applications of economic sanctions determined that, overall, sanctions succeeded to a significant degree about one-third of the time; when the objective was only modest policy changes, the success rate was somewhat higher. Sanctions are also of limited use as a deterrent. However, they can be used as international and domestic symbols of political support, opposition, or ideology. Not so risky or provocative as the use of military force, they can still provide the public image of "doing something."[9]

There are ways to fight back against economic sanctions, to reduce the costs they impose. The Nixon administration's energy policy for counteracting the Arab oil "weapon" is illustrative. Nixon announced that the American aim had to be energy self-sufficiency by 1980. Until self-sufficiency could be reached, he said, people should learn to sacrifice and even learn to like it. One of the first suggestions the Nixon administration made was that thermostats be turned down in homes, adding that cooler temperatures were healthier. The speed limit on American highways was cut to 55 miles per hour, and it was argued that in addition to saving fuel, this speed was also safer. The United States also took the lead in organizing oil-consuming states into the International Energy Agency as a means of coordinating energy policies, stockpiling supplies, and providing mutual aid if another embargo occurred. The Nixon strategy also included plans for increased mining of coal, expanded oil exploration, and a greater emphasis on nuclear-generated electricity. All of these measures were designed to diminish U.S. vulnerability to future oil shocks by securing substitutes for Arab oil.

Geo-economics?

Economic warfare is often an outgrowth of a general state of war between states; rarely, if ever, have states engaged in normal economic relations while their militaries fought on the battlefield. Economic warfare has also been used by states to attempt to disrupt military campaigns against third parties. Thus, after the Japanese invasion of Manchuria in 1937 the United States began blocking the sale of oil and steel to Japan,

---

[8] John Mueller and Karl Mueller, "Sanctions of Mass Destruction," *Foreign Affairs* 78, 3 (May/June 1999): pp. 43–53.

[9] James M. Lindsay, "Trade and Economic Sanctions as Policy Instruments: A Reexamination," *International Studies Quarterly* 30 (June 1986): pp. 153–173; Huffbauer, Schott, and Elliot, *Economic Sanctions Reconsidered.*

and by 1941 the U.S. had imposed a full trade embargo. But economic competition can also be a cause of war. Although U.S. actions were ostensibly a response to Japan's military activities in China and Southeast Asia, some historians suggest that this should be seen as part of a larger U.S.-Japanese struggle for resources, one that precipitated the attack on Pearl Harbor and full-scale war in the Pacific. Foreign trade and investment are essential to contemporary industrial capitalism, and the attempt to secure foreign markets or commodities has led to clashes over spheres of influence.

In Chapter 8 we discussed various explanations for interstate war, and we referred to a study by Nazli Choucri and Robert North of the underlying causes of World War I. They trace many forms of geopolitical competition — arms races, alliance formation, and ultimately violent conflict — to forces originating within societies:

> In a growing population there will be an increasing demand for basic resources. . . . When demands are unmet and existing capabilities are insufficient to satisfy them, new capabilities may have to be developed. But a society can develop particular capabilities (including resources) only if it has the necessary existing capabilities to do so. Moreover, if national capabilities cannot be attained at reasonable cost within national boundaries, they may be sought beyond.[10]

These internal forces exert *lateral pressure,* which pushes states to expand their activities beyond their borders. The resources that states require are often sought by peaceful means (typically foreign trade and investment), but sometimes, as during the period before World War I, states find themselves clashing with one another over what they mutually desire. Thus, German and French imperial interests collided in northern Africa, culminating in the Moroccan crises of 1905–06 and 1911. Austro-Hungarian territorial expansion frustrated Serb aspirations for a Greater Serbia, resulting in the Bosnia crisis of 1908, and this recurring clash would ignite a continental war six years later.

Internal pressures to expand the state's activities beyond its borders have not subsided in the contemporary world; if anything, they have increased. However, many analysts suggest that the costs of great-power war, along with changing international norms regarding the resort to force, make violent conflict over economic resources and practices less likely, especially among the world's major powers. As Edward Luttwak puts it, there has been a shift from geopolitics to *geo-economics:* "If commercial quarrels do lead to political clashes, as they are now much more likely to do with the waning of the imperatives of geopolitics, those political clashes must be fought out with the weapons of commerce."[11] The prefix *geo-* implies more than routine economic competition among states. It suggests that the realist "logic of conflict" still motivates the global struggle for power, even though the most effective instruments for that struggle are to be found in the economic arena.

---

[10] Nazli Choucri and Robert C. North, *Nations in Conflict: National Growth and International Violence* (San Francisco: Freeman, 1975), pp. 5, 16.
[11] Edward N. Luttwak, "From Geopolitics to Geo-Economics: Logic of Conflict, Grammar of Commerce," *The National Interest* 20 (Summer 1990): p. 21.

OPEC's use of the "oil weapon" in the 1970s and its subsequent rise to prominence as an international actor — all without firing a shot — seems to have foreshadowed the geo-economic era that Luttwak and others describe. At the same time, the Gulf War — both the Iraq-Kuwait phase and the U.S.-Iraq phase — serves as a reminder that states will go to war at least partly over economic resources, especially over control of such vital resources as oil. Oil wealth is now driving a transformation of the Caspian region into what may become a new locale for great-power competition. The newly independent states of Azerbaijan, Kazakhstan, and Turkmenistan are well positioned to profit economically and politically from the vast oil and natural gas reserves beneath the Caspian Sea. The region is landlocked, so pipelines must be built to transport the oil to the sea before it can make its way to world markets. The proposed routes have important geo-economic (and geopolitical) implications, since neighboring states hosting the pipelines could manipulate the flow of oil. Possible routes from Baku, Azerbaijan, for example, might go through Russian or Georgian territory to the Black Sea, through Georgia and Turkey to the Mediterranean, or through Iran to the Persian Gulf. Given the state of U.S.-Iranian relations and volatility in the U.S.-Russian relationship, the United States clearly preferred the route to the Mediterranean, but had difficulty persuading oil companies to take on such a costly project.

Political Economy of Defense

In the West and elsewhere, the end of the cold war brought renewed debate about the future of the **defense-industrial base** — a state's capacity to develop and manufacture the implements of national defense. Does the risk of a renewed threat from Russia, China, or emerging nuclear states require continued expenditure on expensive strategic nuclear weapons? Do ever-present regional conflicts require continued expenditure on conventional forces that can be employed for global reach? If the military and its arsenal is going to be significantly downsized, what factories and military bases, at home and abroad, should be closed? How much of the defense-industrial base should be retained in case rearmament is needed? Important economic issues are involved in such decisions, and they highlight the different interests, objectives, and strategies of various groups within society.[12]

The Military-Industrial Complex

In his last public address as president, General Dwight Eisenhower warned about the political influence of a newly powerful **military-industrial complex.**

---

[12] A good introduction to these issues is Ethan Barnaby Kapstein, *The Political Economy of National Security: A Global Perspective* (New York: McGraw-Hill, 1992). For an overview of defense-industrial issues in the United States, see Jacques S. Gansler, *Affording Defense* (Cambridge, Mass.: MIT Press, 1989). The more technical literature is usefully summarized in Todd Sandler and Keith Hartley, *The Economics of Defense* (Cambridge: Cambridge University Press, 1995).

We have been compelled to create a permanent armaments industry of vast proportions. Added to this, three-and-a-half million men and women are directly engaged in the defense establishment. We annually spend on military security alone more than the net income of all United States corporations.

Now this conjunction of an immense military establishment and a large arms industry is new in the American experience. The total influence — economic, political, even spiritual — is felt in every city, every statehouse, every office of the federal government. . . . In councils of government we must guard against the acquisition of unwarranted influence, whether sought or unsought, by the military-industrial complex. The potential for the disastrous rise of misplaced power exists and will persist.

The phrase "military-industrial complex" is now a common expression. In addition to defense industries and the professional military, the military-industrial complex can be interpreted broadly to include politicians whose districts benefit directly from military spending and even labor unions whose memberships are employed disproportionately in the defense sector. The expression often carries negative connotations, as it did for Eisenhower. Whether or not society as a whole benefits from aggressive foreign policy and high levels of military preparedness, certain groups and sectors of the economy clearly do benefit. Its harshest critics suggest that the military-industrial complex exerts pressure on the central government to maintain its military posture at high levels even when foreign threats diminish and without regard to the potential economic costs imposed on other sectors of the national economy.

In Chapter 6 we discussed the radical view that states are essentially governed by a power elite comprised of individuals from the highest echelons of society — politics, business, the military — whose professional paths cross regularly. One manifestation of elite interaction, according to radicals like C. Wright Mills, is overlapping membership on corporate boards, which create a pattern of "interlocking directorates." Although he did not focus specifically on boards of directors, Gordon Adams attempted to identify overall levels of personnel transfer between the U.S. Department of Defense (DoD) and defense contractors in the private sector in the 1970s. This "revolving door" allows defense corporations to improve their products by making use of the scientific and technical expertise of former military officers and civilian employees of DoD. More importantly, perhaps, defense contractors can gain information about future research areas deemed important by U.S. military planners, as well as insights into the workings of the procurement process on the government side.[13] We can see from Table 12.2 that although the revolving door serves both DoD and military contractors, there is a much larger personnel flow from government to private industry than vice versa.

Several studies have examined military procurement in the United States to see if there is empirical evidence to support hypotheses related to the military-industrial complex. In general, radicals and other critics argue that the cozy relationship between politicians, the military, and defense contractors — what Adams calls the "iron triangle" — perverts free-market competition for military contracts. Almost any *pattern* in military procurement is suspect, since it suggests that non-market considerations

---

[13] See Gordon Adams. *The Iron Triangle: The Politics of Defense Contracting* (New York: Council on Economic Priorities, 1981), esp. chap. 6.

TABLE 12.2	The Resolving Door: Personnel Flows between the Defense Department and Major Military Contractors, 1970–1979

| | | Flow to Company | | |
Company	Total Flow	DoD Military	DoD Civilian	Flow to DoD
Boeing	388	316	35	37
General Dynamics	238	189	17	32
Grumman	88	67	5	16
Lockheed	304	240	30	34
McDonnell-Douglas	200	159	12	29
Northrop	360	284	50	16
Rockwell	233	150	26	47
United Technologies	73	50	11	12
Total	*1,874*	*1,455*	*186*	*233*

Source: Adapted from Gordon Adams, *The Iron Triangle: The Politics of Defense Contracting* (New York: Council on Economic Priorities, 1981), p. 84.

have come into play. One analyst, for example, has identified a "follow-on imperative," whereby a contract for a new weapon system (or major component) is awarded to a company as its production of a similar older weapon is winding down. This enables the company to keep its production line open — a good thing for the contractor, but it does not necessarily mean that the contract has been awarded to the most competitive bidder. Sixteen of twenty major aerospace contracts awarded between 1960 and 1988 may be explained in part by the follow-on imperative, including the F-111 bomber as a follow-on to the B-58 (General Dynamics) and the C-5A transport as follow-on to the C-141 (Lockheed).[14]

Other procurement practices may be designed to benefit politicians. One study showed that U.S. defense contracts accelerated right before election time, giving a boost to the economy and allowing incumbents to take some credit for improved economic conditions. Prime contractors also tend to distribute their subcontracts among

---

[14] James R. Kurth, "The Military-Industrial Complex Revisited," in Joseph Kruzel, ed., *American Defense Annual, 1989–1990* (Lexington, Mass.: Lexington Books, 1989).

companies located in a number of congressional districts, presumably to ingratiate themselves with as many legislators as possible. Another study found that while pork-barrel politics do not account for congressional voting on major nuclear weapons projects like the B-1 bomber or the MX missile, legislators do have their constituents in mind when they vote on matters related to military bases.[15] Such procurement decisions may improve politicians' chances for reelection, but they are not necessarily the best ones from a strict national-security point of view. Although these various findings do not lend unequivocal support to the more radical portraits of the military-industrial complex in the United States, they do point to a closer than arms-length relationship between politicians, the military, and defense contractors, and to the fact that considerations other than cost effectiveness and national security often enter into decisions regarding military procurement.

Some argue that in the United States, where free-market principles hold great sway and where government intervention in the economy is practically taboo, large defense budgets constitute a "covert industrial policy." An **industrial policy** is a set of arrangements whereby the central government assists certain industries, often called "national champions," deemed to be crucial to the nation's economic strength. These arrangements might include strategically targeted government purchases, capital for plants and equipment, subsidies for research and development, and the promotion of exports. The United States has generally frowned on industrial policies adopted by some of its major trading partners in Europe and Japan as contrary to the spirit of free trade. One response to American criticism has been that the United States accomplishes much the same thing under the guise of national defense. The U.S. government has sponsored large-scale projects in the interest of military readiness that have also generated "spin-offs" for civilian industry. The computer, for example, had its origins in code-breaking during World War II, and by 1950 the government was providing up to $20 million a year to support computer R&D. Research and development on computer networking, including the internet, and integrated circuitry has also been supported by the U.S. defense budget. As one student of the computer industry has pointed out, "government support for applied research and development would be acceptable only if aimed at a noneconomic objective, like national security."[16]

Although many radical scholars link the development of a military-industrial complex to capitalism, a similar constellation of interests was evident in the Soviet Union. State industrial managers had incentives to promote the growth, power, prosperity, and technological preeminence of the arms-manufacturing plants they controlled. They, too, shared interests with their clients in the Red Army and the Strategic Rocket Forces, along with hawkish ideologues in the Communist party. A cold war —

---

[15] See Kenneth R. Mayer, *The Political Economy of Defense Contracting* (New Haven, Conn.: Yale University Press, 1991), and James M. Lindsay, *Congress and Nuclear Weapons* (Baltimore: Johns Hopkins University Press, 1991). On the role of domestic political and economic interests in the early evolution of America's postwar foreign policy, see Benjamin O. Fordham, *Building the Cold War Consensus: The Political Economy of U.S. National Security Policy, 1949–51* (Ann Arbor: University of Michigan Press, 1998).
[16] Kenneth Flamm, *Creating the Computer: Government, Industry, and High Technology* (Washington, D.C: Brookings Institution, 1988), esp. chap. 3; quote from p. 78. See also Glenn R. Fong, "The Political Economy of Pentagon-Industry Collaboration in Technology Development," in Andrew L. Ross, ed., *The Political Economy of Defense: Issues and Perspectives* (New York: Greenwood, 1991).

though not necessarily a hot one — helped to maintain their privileges and central roles in Soviet society. On both sides of the cold-war divide, therefore, entrenched economic and political interests maintained the momentum of established hard-line policies. In a perverse way, the military-industrial complex in each country helped the other. Each embodied the foreign threat that its counterpart needed to justify its own activities.[17]

Guns versus Butter

Prosecuting a war can put enormous strains on a state's economic resources. Transforming a peacetime economy into a wartime economy requires a mobilization of industrial and human resources as well as centralized planning in order to prioritize the war effort over other economic activities. When there is a wealth of unused resources — that is, when there is idle industrial capacity and high levels of unemployment — wartime economic mobilization can pull a national economy out of its doldrums. For example, industrial mobilization for World War II is credited for finally ending the Great Depression in the United States. However, when there are few slack resources in a society, wartime mobilization can cause severe economic strains. Even if economic resources are not scarce when the war begins, scarcities can quickly set in as the war drags on and it may not be long before price controls and other forms of centralized economic planning become necessary to deal with shortages and bottlenecks. During World War II the U.S. War Production Board resisted many such economic controls as "socialistic," but its restraint may have hampered the country's war effort.

The relationship between military preparedness and economic performance during peacetime is hotly debated, and the expression **"guns versus butter"** is used by many to summarize the essential trade-offs involved. There are actually two related issues here. First, is there a connection between peacetime military activities, especially defense spending, and the health of the national economy? Second, does production by the military-industrial complex (guns) absorb resources that might otherwise go to social programs (butter) designed to improve the lot of society's poor and dispossessed?

Radical scholars and others have suggested that politicians use peacetime defense spending to stimulate the national economy during periods of slow growth. In the 1930s, British economist John Maynard Keynes argued that persistent unemployment was due to a deficiency in demand for goods and services and that government spending could be used to compensate for downturns in the business cycle. In Britain and the United States, this Keynesian logic motivated spending on large public works projects — fiscal policy — designed to help lift these economies out of the Depression. As a component of government spending, military spending itself might be used in this way, as a *countercyclical tool*. Such a policy has been called "military Keynesianism," and some radicals associate this with an advanced stage of capitalism in which industrial production, including defense production, is concentrated in relatively few hands. There is a tendency in this stage of capitalism for monopolistic firms to produce more

[17] On the evolution of the Soviet military-industrial complex, see, for example, Ulrich Albrecht, *The Soviet Armaments Industry* (Char, U.K.: Harwood Academic Press, 1993).

than what the market demands. Radicals argue that this surplus production is absorbed through government spending in order to prevent the collapse of the capitalist system. Some social spending is acceptable, especially if necessary to pacify anti-capitalist forces, but that alone cannot sustain the economy. Military spending is a preferred solution to this "underconsumption problem" because monopoly capital continues to reap profits from production. It has the added benefit of appealing to many outside the military-industrial complex who do not gain economically but who approve of high levels of defense spending out of a sense of patriotism.[18]

It is hard to test this "underconsumption thesis" satisfactorily. The defense establishment does represent a large component of many national economies, in both the industrialized and developing world. In the United States, the Department of Defense employed 725,000 civilians in 1999, with a total payroll of $41 billion, while another 2.2 billion were employed in defense-related industries. Taken together, that was over 3 percent of the total civilian workforce. In 1999 the U.S. government spent $277 billion on national defense (including defense-related energy and space expenditures), which amounted to 3. 1 percent of all goods and services produced in the U.S. economy. No other country spends as much on defense, but the U.S. military burden is only a little higher than the worldwide average (2.8 percent of GNP in 1995), and many other countries' military expenditures represent a considerably larger portion of the national economy. For example, Russia, Kuwait, Saudi Arabia, and Oman each spend more than 10 percent of GNP on national defense, according to the U.S. Arms Control and Disarmament Agency, while North Korean defense spending represents almost 30 percent of its GNP.[19] The military-industrial complex clearly is an important economic actor in many societies today.

Does military spending have an impact on economic performance? Whether or not politicians use military spending as a fiscal stimulus, as radicals suggest, many liberals believe that the overall effect of large defense budgets is to *sap the nation's economic health.* Many point to the impressive postwar economic growth rates in countries like Germany and Japan (until recently), which were achieved in the context of small defense burdens. But an extensive body of research into the relationship between defense spending and aggregate economic performance in many countries during different times periods has turned up contradictory evidence, much of it suggesting that defense spending has no overall effect — positive or negative — on the national economy. As one scholar familiar with this vast literature concluded, "defense spending may not be the fiscal tail that wags the economic dog. Whether and how much it does so will depend in part on a country's economic structure, in part on its political institutions and culture, and in part on the incentives that motivate its officials." Even in a country like the United States, with its huge defense establishment, there are a variety

---

[18] The classic study is Paul A. Baran and Paul M. Sweezy, *Monopoly Capital: An Essay on the American Economic and Social Order* (New York: Monthly Review Press, 1966); see especially chaps. 6, 7.

[19] U.S. figures are from U.S. Department of Defense, *National Defense Budget Estimates for FY 2000* (Washington, D.C.: U.S. Department of Defense, 1999). Other figures are from U.S. Arms Control and Disarmament Agency, *World Military Expenditures and Arms Transfers 1996* (Washington, D.C.: U.S. Government Printing Office, 1997).

of factors responsible for economic ups and downs, and military-related economic activities may not stand out as especially influential.[20]

This is not to say that peacetime military preparedness has no economic effects. Defense plants and military bases can have profound *effects on a local economy*. U.S. Department of Defense outlays for payroll (civilian and military) and for military contracts in the states of Alaska, Missouri, Mississippi, Maryland, and Maine accounted for more than 5 percent of gross state product in 1996; in Virginia and Hawaii the figures were roughly 10 percent. At the local level, the cancelation of a major weapons program, or worse, the closing of an entire plant or military base, can mean laying off a large share of the workforce, which reverberates as shopkeepers and others who serve that community see the demand for their goods and services decline or evaporate altogether. Critics of America's "permanent war economy" sympathize with the plight of local communities in such predicaments, but point to the larger problem of structural dependencies in the U.S. economy that link the fate of local economies to the vagaries of weapons procurement and military planning.[21]

Critics point to other distortions that may not be apparent at the aggregate level of national economic performance (growth rates, unemployment rates, inflation, and so on). These generally have to do with *opportunity costs* — the benefits foregone by investing in the military as opposed to more economically productive or socially redeeming pursuits. Because workers in the defense industry are drawn disproportionately from the higher skilled occupations (like the scientific and engineering community), money spent on defense could employ a lot more people if invested elsewhere. Furthermore, money withdrawn from weapons procurement would go farther even if it remained in the high-technology sector of the economy, say critics, because military contractors worry little about cost overruns when the central government is picking up the tab, which encourages "gold plating," waste, even fraud and abuse. Customers in the civilian sector of the economy are more attentive to costs, increasing the incentives for productive efficiency. The $436 hammer and the $640 toilet seat are now legendary in the United States, and although many of these headline-catching "abuses" can be explained by government accounting practices — like allocating indirect costs equally among all the parts used in production — there is a widespread perception that the government is not getting its money's worth.

Related to this question of opportunity costs is the question of *defense-welfare trade-offs*. Many view central government expenditures as a pie of relatively fixed size; a larger military slice means a smaller slice for social programs like education, health, and welfare. It is important to keep in mind that the dynamics at issue here are

---

[20] For a review of the literature, see Steve Chan, "Grasping the Peace Dividend: Some Propositions on the Conversion of Swords into Plowshares," *Mershon International Studies Review* 39, 1 (August 1995): pp. 53–95; quote from p. 68. A study of U.S. defense spending that comes to this general conclusion is David Kinsella, "Defence Spending and Economic Performance in the United States: A Causal Analysis," *Defence Economics* 1, 4 (August 1990): pp. 295–309.

[21] See, for example, Seymour Melman, *The Permanent War Economy: American Capitalism in Decline*, rev. ed. (New York: Simon & Schuster, 1985), and Ann Markusen and Joel Yudken, *Dismantling the Cold War Economy* (New York: Basic Books, 1992). State-level figures are based on U.S. Census Bureau, *Statistical Abstract of the United States 1998* (Washington, D.C.: U.S. Census Bureau, 1998), tables 573, 719.

essentially political, not economic. Although there may be some dispute about whether defense spending is more economically productive than social spending — which type of spending employs more people, and which adds more to the GDP — the real debate concerns social obligation and role of government in society. Research on the defense-welfare tradeoff generally has not supported the hypothesis that politicians take money from social coffers to increase military spending. In fact, trends in government spending on such things as education and health are relatively smooth in most industrialized societies, while military spending is more volatile, responding to international crises and commitments. Figure 12.1 shows these spending trends for the United States (in constant 1999 dollars). One apparent exception to the general absence of a defense-welfare trade-off is spending during the Reagan administration. In the 1980s the trend in federal spending on education and health did indeed dip in the context of increases in the defense budget. But that had very much to do with Reagan's conservative social agenda combined with his anticommunist national security policy, not a pervasive tendency of politicians to trade butter for guns.[22]

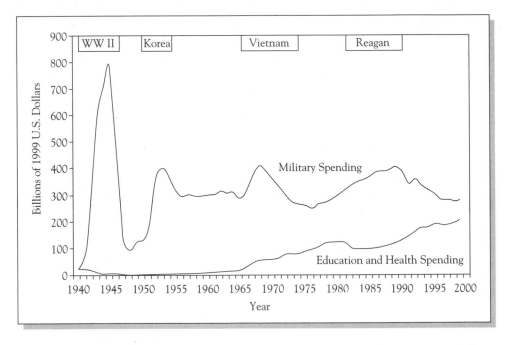

FIGURE 12.1   Military Spending and Social Spending in the United States, 1940–1999

Source: U.S. Office of Management and the Budget, *Historical Tables: Budget of the United States Government, Fiscal Year 2000* (Washington, D.C.: U.S. Government Printing Office, 1999).

---

[22] See, for example, Alex Mintz and Chi Huang, "'Guns' vs. 'Butter': The Indirect Link," *American Journal of Political Science* 35 (1991): pp. 738–757; and Jin Whyu Mok and Robert D. Duval, "Guns, Butter, and Debt: Balancing Spending Tradeoffs between Defense, Social Programs, and Budget Deficits," in Alex Mintz, ed., *The Political Economy of Military Spending in the United States* (London: Routledge, 1992), pp. 192–216.

A Peace Dividend?

Many arguments linking excessive military spending to economic ills are compelling. Although it is often difficult to observe any clear relationship between defense expenditures and economic growth, unemployment rates, inflation, debt, or other measures of national economic performance in the short term, many scholars believe that an economy devoting a substantial share of its material and human resources to military production — because it is continuously engaged in, or preparing for, war — diverts valuable energies away from other more economically productive pursuits, and in the long run will have settled for a level of prosperity well below its potential. After a sweeping historical survey of the economic forces propelling states to great-power status, and those that brought them down, Paul Kennedy highlighted "the conundrum which has exercised strategists and economists and political leaders from classical times onward":

> To be a Great Power — by definition, a state capable of holding its own against any other nation — demands a flourishing economic base. . . . Yet by going to war, or by devoting a large share of the nation's "manufacturing power" to expenditures upon "unproductive" armaments, one runs the risk of eroding the national economic base, especially vis-à-vis states which are concentrating a greater share of their income upon productive investment for long-term growth.[23]

Thus, the end of the cold war was welcome not only because it dissipated the looming threat of nuclear Armageddon. It also seemed to promise a **"peace dividend"** — an economic windfall now that so many resources have been freed up in this new peaceful chapter in U.S.-Russian relations.

The military buildup during the Reagan administration may have been partly to blame for the economic slowdown in the United States during the early post–cold war period. Large and sustained defense-spending increases in the context of tax cuts fed ballooning budget deficits. Government borrowing kept interest rates high throughout the 1980s, eventually choking off economic activity and thereby contributing to the recession of the early 1990s. But by the end of the decade the United States had downsized its military substantially. Compared to a decade earlier, military manpower — whether measured as active duty personnel, civilian employees of the Defense Department, or defense-industrial workers — had declined by one-third. Defense spending was down by almost the same amount, and that portion used for weapons procurement had dropped by 55 percent. Military infrastructure had been reduced by about 20 percent, including the closure of almost one hundred major military bases and hundreds of smaller facilities. Although hopes were high for a post-cold war peace dividend, the immediate effects of military downsizing probably aggravated the economic problems of the early 1990s.

Because many still believe that it makes good economic sense to shrink the defense-industrial base, efforts have focused on lessening the pain of transition. The

---

[23] Paul Kennedy, *The Rise and Fall of the Great Powers: Economic Change and Military Conflict from 1500 to 2000* (New York Random House, 1987), p. 539.

process of dismantling the U.S. cold-war economy is an instance of **defense conversion**, which can include any or all of the following:

1. diversification and conversion of defense-industrial plants to nondefense production

2. transferring defense technology to nondefense firms

3. reorienting defense research and development toward dual-use technologies

4. integrating isolated defense industries into a civil/military industrial base

5. retraining laid-off defense workers

6. helping communities adjust to the economic effects of defense cutbacks and downsizing[24]

The post–cold war adjustments and dislocations that still confront some U.S. firms and communities are substantial, but overall they pale in comparison to the demobilization and conversion that followed World War II. Yet the post–World War II transition was remarkably smooth, given the enormity of the wartime mobilization, and that was because during the war itself the Roosevelt administration had been planning for it. The cold-war "mobilization," on the other hand, was more gradual and lacked the finiteness of a hot-war mobilization. Although the argument can and has been overstated, in certain respects the United States really did have a permanent war economy. Dismantling the local and regional economic dependencies that evolved over more than forty years of cold war has not been an easy task.

Defense conversion in the Russian economy has been even more difficult. From 1992 to 1994, 1.6 million workers left defense-industrial production jobs, along with 800,000 who exited defense-related scientific institutes. One researcher has found this mass exodus — highlighted by most Western observers as evidence of successful market restructuring — less interesting than the fact that roughly the same number of personnel *stayed* in these Soviet-era defense enterprises, despite dismal working conditions, low pay, and an uncertain future. And although the enterprise managers do fare better than their workers, they don't do particularly well; yet many have held tightly to their jobs despite opportunities to strike out as independent entrepreneurs in the Russian free market. The endurance of the Soviet-era military-industrial complex, however shrunken, can be explained partly by "cultural notions of what it means to preserve the enterprise."[25] Such notions are powerful indeed in an industry that occupied such an exalted position in cold-war Soviet society.

---

[24] Jacques S. Gansler, *Defense Conversion: Transforming the Arsenal of Democracy* (Cambridge, Mass.: MIT Press, 1995), pp. 40–41.

[25] Kimberly Marten Zisk, *Weapons, Culture, and Self-Interest: Soviet Defense Managers in the New Russia* (New York: Columbia University Press, 1997), p. 59; employment figures based on those reported on pp. 32–33. See also Michael McFaul and Tova Perlmutter, eds., *Privatization, Conversion, and Enterprise Reform in Russia* (Stanford, Calif.: Center for International Security and Arms Control, 1994). On defense conversion in Eastern Europe, see Yudit Kiss, *The Defence Industry in East-Central Europe: Restructuring and Conversion* (New York: Oxford University Press, 1997).

The International Arms Market

In 1934, H. C. Englebrecht and F. C. Hanighen put forth *Merchants of Death,* a polemical account of the *international* activities of armament makers. They pointed to the existence of small coteries of politically influential arms merchants operating in all of the world's major capitals, and suggested that their interests were virtually identical. Although they themselves did not consider the international arms trade to be the root cause of the "war system," they had some sympathy for the increasingly widespread view that this was a corrupt and dangerously irresponsible business:

> They picture a group of unscrupulous villains who are using every device to profit from human suffering and death. They conjure up a picture of a well-organized, ruthless conspiracy to block world peace and to promote war. Theirs is an ethical reaction easily understood. For the business of placing all our vaunted science and engineering in the service of Mars and marketing armaments by the most unrestricted methods of modern salesmanship is indeed a thoroughly anti-social occupation.[26]

Merchants of Death became an instant bestseller, fueling the flames of American isolationism that culminated in the Neutrality Acts of 1931–1939. The book's message, in essence, was that American neutrality was compromised during the World War by arms merchants with both national- and foreign-government connections, whose profit motive and strict adherence to commercial principles in peddling their wares left them little incentive to ponder either the moral dimensions of their profession or the national interest. The arms business is exactly that — a business — and business is good when nations are at war, or when they fear it.

Today the international arms trade is not strictly business. Prior to the passage of the Neutrality Acts and the formation of the Munitions Control Board, the export of weaponry by American merchants was effectively unregulated. By the outbreak of World War II in Europe, the U.S. government had established controls over private arms sales, and thus what was for the arms merchants a means of profit became for the government an instrument of foreign policy. Governmental supervision over arms exports was established during the 1930s in most European nations with significant production capabilities as well, though with typically less fanfare than in the United States. This new role for arms transfers was inaugurated in the U.S. with the signing of the Lend-Lease Act of 1941, which authorized the president "to sell, transfer title to, exchange, lease, lend, or otherwise dispose of . . . any defense article" to any country whose defense was deemed essential to U.S. national security. The hope was that direct American involvement in the European war could be avoided, but at minimum the United States would have to commit itself as the "great *arsenal* of democracy."

---

[26] H. C. Englebrecht and F. C. Hanighen, *Merchants of Death: A Study of the International Armament Industry* (New York: Dodd, Mead, 1934), p. 6.

Arms transfers are an important instrument of influence in world politics, as we pointed out in Chapter 5, and for this reason state leaders must be attentive to the economic viability of the nation's arms producers. When domestic demand for armaments is insufficient to make arms production a profitable enterprise, defense firms search out export opportunities in order to maintain acceptable unit costs of production. Without arms exports, or large subsidies from the central government, production lines may become too costly to keep open. While the central government has an interest in defense-industrial efficiency, at some point corporate downsizing may threaten to shrink the country's defense-industrial base below what is considered necessary for purposes of national security. Defense industries must be able to support military mobilization in response to unforeseen international developments. They must also continually engage in military research and development if they are to supply the state with the means of engaging in military campaigns of the future. These capacities are maintained through the production and sale of armaments, whether at home or abroad.

Of course, all of this begs some important and divisive questions. What are acceptable profit levels for defense firms? When profits (and salaries) depend on government purchases and subsidies, the answer to this question cannot rest solely with corporate executives and their stockholders, at least in a democracy. When arms transfers threaten to destabilize high-tension regions in the Third World, as many claim, or when the potential exists that exported weaponry may be used against one's own military forces in some future confrontation — a situation known as the "boomerang effect" or "blow-back" in military-strategic circles — then profits, market share, and other economic calculations are probably not the most important ones.[27]

Global Arms Transfers

The arms trade peaked during the 1980s. According to the Stockholm International Peace Research Institute, and as shown in Figure 12.2, the annual trade in major conventional weapons hovered between $45 and $50 billion worth (in constant 1997 dollars) during that period, and has dropped rather substantially since the end of the cold war.[28] The top weapons importers are shown in Table 12.3. During the cold war, the two superpowers supplied most of the world's imported weaponry. From 1980 to 1991, between them they accounted for about 65 percent of global arms transfers; the Soviet Union's share was 37 percent, the U.S. share, 28 percent. Now, the United States dominates the arms market, supplying nearly 50 percent of all weaponry from 1992 to 1997, while Russia has accounted for a mere 13 percent. From the end of World War II the two superpowers were the world's *first-tier* arms suppliers. First-tier suppliers engage

---

[27] Recent studies of the impact of arms transfers on regional conflict include David Kinsella, "Arms Transfer Dependence and Foreign Policy Conflict," *Journal of Peace Research* 35, 1 (January 1998): pp. 7–23; and Gregory S. Sanjian, "Promoting Stability or Instability? Arms Transfers and Regional Rivalries, 1950–91," *International Studies Quarterly* 43, 4 (December 1999): pp. 641–670.

[28] These and subsequent figures come from Stockholm International Peace Research Institute, "Transfers of Major Conventional Weapons: Facts and Figures," July 1998 [cited April 23, 1999]; available at <http://www.sipri.se/projects/armstrade/facts_and_figures.html>. See also Stockholm International Peace Research Institute, *SIPRI Yearbook 1998: Armaments, Disarmament and International Security* (New York: Oxford University Press, 1998).

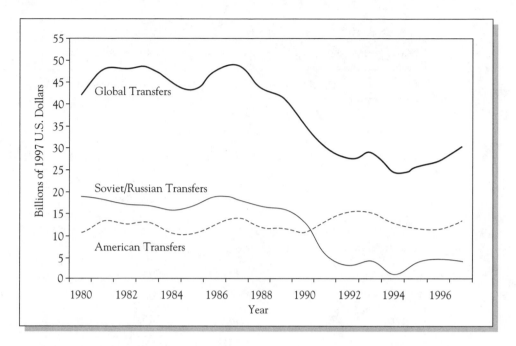

FIGURE 12.2   Global Arms Transfers, 1980–1997

Source: Stockholm International Peace Research Institute, "The 50 Leading Suppliers of Major Conventional Weapons, 1980–97," July 1998 [cited April 23, 1999]; available at <http://www.sipri.se/projects/armstrade/suppliers.html>. Data are based on estimates of the market value of major conventional-weapons transfers, not what was actually paid, and converted into 1997 dollars by the authors.

in innovations at the military-technological frontier — for example, today's "smart" and "brilliant" weapons — and they have the military-industrial capacity to produce (and export) the entire range of weaponry, from artillery to advanced fighter aircraft and missile systems.[29] The United States is currently alone at the furthest reaches of the technological frontier, but the Soviet Union was an innovator throughout the cold war and Russia retains considerable potential despite its present economic difficulties.

Like the first-tier producers, *second-tier* producers are able to manufacture much of the most advanced weaponry available, but their capacity for military-related scientific and technological innovation is more limited. Their most advanced arms production is

---

[29] See Keith Krause, *Arms and the State: Patterns of Military Production and Trade* (Cambridge: Cambridge University Press, 1992), esp. chap. 1. Krause offers a comprehensive examination of the global arms transfer and production system from the so-called Military Revolution of the sixteenth century through the end of the cold war. A still unsurpassed comparison of the interwar and post–World War II arms trade is Robert E. Harkavy, *The Arms Trade and International Systems* (Cambridge, Mass.: Ballinger, 1975). A good introduction to the arms trade and related issues is Frederic S. Pearson, *The Global Spread of Arms: Political Economy of International Security* (Boulder, Colo.: Westview, 1994).

TABLE 12.3   Leading Arms Importers, 1980–1997

Cold War		Post–Cold War	
Arms Importer	1980 to 1991 Average (millions, 1997 $U.S.)	Arms Importer	1992 to 1997 Average (millions, 1997 $U.S.)
Iraq	3,505	Saudi Arabia	2,195
India	3,304	Turkey	1,682
Saudi Arabia	2,074	Taiwan	1,681
Syria	1,904	Egypt	1,542
Japan	1,547	Greece	1,266
Egypt	1,385	China	1,246
USSR/Russia	1,344	Japan	1,232
Libya	1,245	South Korea	1,168
East Germany	1,118	India	1,138
Czechoslovakia	961	Kuwait	868

Note: Figures are annual averages for the period indicated, and are based on estimates of the market value of major conventional-weapons transfers, not what was actually paid.

Source: Stockholm International Peace Research Institute (SIPRI), "The 50 Leading Recipients of Major Conventional Weapons, 1980–97," July 1998 [cited April 23, 1999]; available at <http://www.sipri.se/projects/armstrade/recipients.html>.

often based on imported know-how, even though they may adapt it. Thus, second-tier producers like Britain, France, and Germany manufacture indigenously designed fighter aircraft, but they do not yet produce stealth fighters; when they do, these will be based on U.S. scientific and technological innovations in the 1980s and 1990s, perhaps adapted for new and specific military purposes. Innovation at the technological frontier requires a substantial devotion of resources to military research and development. Major military R&D programs are made possible by government subsidized initiatives — like the Ballistic Missile Defense (BMD) program in the United States, successor to the Reagan administration's Strategic Defense Initiative (SDI) — as well as confidence among private-industry participants that their efforts will someday be rewarded by large government purchases of newly developed weapons systems or components. Such incentives for innovation are not as strong in a second-tier country as they are in the first tier, nor is the defense-industrial base as large or diversified.

Smaller government defense budgets in second-tier countries also give an added push to arms exports as a supplement to domestic procurement. Of the total value of arms exported worldwide from 1992 through 1997, British, French, and German exports each accounted for 6 to 8 percent, up from 2 to 3 percent during the 1980s. In contrast to quantity, the quality of the military equipment supplied by these countries does not differ markedly from the equipment supplied by the United States or Russia. Indeed, the international arms market has become considerably more competitive than it was during the cold war. The unwillingness of first-tier producers to supply state-of-the-art equipment to anyone other than their own military forces has the effect of leveling the arms-export playing field.

Post–cold war military downsizing and a more competitive international arms market have given momentum to defense-industry consolidation in both first- and second-tier countries. The recent wave of defense mergers and acquisitions began in the United States, where the larger defense-industrial base could support a larger number of independent firms than in Europe. But with major cuts in domestic procurement, American companies began to consolidate in preparation for leaner times at home and more competition abroad. Lockheed and Martin Marietta merged in 1995 to form Lockheed Martin, which then bought Loral in 1996; Boeing acquired McDonnell Douglas in 1997; Raytheon bought Hughes the same year. In the span of about three years, what were once seven of the world's top ten defense companies had become three. A fourth, Northrop Grumman, remains an independent company, but not for lack of effort: Lockheed Martin tried to acquire the company, but dropped its attempt when antitrust alarms went off in both the U.S. Justice Department and the Pentagon. The world's leading defense firms are listed in Table 12.4. U.S. companies still make up seven of the top ten, and account for 75 percent of their total revenue from military sales.

The Europeans have long contemplated cross-border consolidation of defense-industrial resources, since that would allow their firms to become more competitive in military R&D and in the international arms market. That has proven difficult, but there have been a number of transnational mergers and acquisitions, and the European Union has actively sought to facilitate defense collaboration and ultimately the creation of a single European defense industry, the centerpiece of which would be the tentatively named European Aerospace and Defence Company.[30] In the meantime, consolidation has proceeded within countries. In 1999, France's Aérospatiale, which is state owned and had already acquired a large stake in Dassault, merged with Matra, while British Aerospace announced a merger with GEC. Whatever the end result of the wave of defense-industrial consolidation in the United States and Europe, it is clear that the high end of international arms market will soon be dominated by a relatively small number of defense conglomerates.

---

[30] On the defense industry in Europe, see Terrence R. Guay, *At Arm's Length: The European Union and Europe's Defence Industry* (London: Macmillan, 1998)

TABLE 12.4   Leading Global Defense Firms, 1997

Rank	Firm	Country	Defense Revenue (millions $)	Defense in Total (percent)	Sectors
1	Lockheed Martin	United States	18,500	66	A, M, SP, E, C
2	Boeing	United States	13,775	30	A, M, SP, E, H, C, O
3	British Aerospace	Britain	10,091	74	A, M, E, AR, C, O
4	Northrop Grumman	United States	8,200	89	A, M, E, C, O
5	Raytheon	United States	6,270	46	A, M, E, C
6	General Electric Co. (GEC)	Britain	5,774	31	SP, E, S, C
7	Thompson-CSF	France	4,184	65	M, SP, E, S, AR, C, O
8	TRW	United States	3,800	35	SP, E, C
9	General Dynamics	United States	3,650	90	A, E, MV, S, C, O
10	United Technologies	United States	3,311	13	SP, E, H
		Leading Non-OECD Firms			
25	Samsung	South Korea	1,160*	1	A, M, E, MV, S
31	Israeli Aircraft Industries	Israel	1,091	65	A, M, SP, E, MV, S, H, C
41	Ordnance Factories	India	620*	85	A, O
53	Rafael	Israel	504	95	M, E, MV, S, H, C, O
55	Denel	South Africa	450*	64	A, M, E, MV, AR, O
58	Hindustan Aeronautics	India	435	94	A, M, SP, E, H, C
59	Daewoo	South Korea	430*	1	E, S, O
62	Elbit Systems	Israel	415	100	E, C
64	Tadiran	Israel	401	36	E, C
65	Hyundai	South Korea	400*	2	MV, S

Note: A = aircraft; M = missiles; SP = space systems; E = electronics; MV = military vehicles; AR = artillery; S = ships; H = helicopters; C = communications; O = ordnance.

*Figures are for 1996.

Source: "Top 100 Worldwide Defense Firms," *Defense News,* July 20–26, 1998, p. 12; supplemented with data in Elisabeth Sköns, Reinhilde Weidacher, et al., "The 100 Largest Arms-Producing Companies, 1996," *SIPRI Yearbook 1998: Armaments, Disarmament, and International Security* (New York: Oxford University Press, 1998), pp. 260–266. Original *Defense News* rankings for non-OECD firms are adjusted based on information from the Stockholm International Peace Research Institute (SIPRI).

The Proliferation of Military Technology

In addition to the first- and second-tier of arms producers and exporters, there are *third-tier* producers, some of which are active in the international arms market. Third-tier arms producers rely more heavily than second-tier producers on imported technology, including weapons designs, and they are not capable of producing the same range of weaponry. When they enter the international arms market, they are typically "niche suppliers," specializing in the manufacture of specific weapons systems specially adapted for particular purposes.

The most advanced of the third-tier arms producers is China, which averaged about $2 billion worth of arms exports per year in the 1980s, but less than half that since the end of the cold war. Chinese exports represent about 3 percent of the global arms market, and it does export a wide variety of military goods. Although these facts might question the appropriateness of labeling China a third-tier supplier, China's present capacity in high-technology arms production — much based on old Soviet designs, though modified using Chinese (and Western) technology — really is not in the same league as Europe's second-tier capacity. Other important third-tier arms producers include Brazil, Israel, India, North Korea, South Africa, and South Korea. Third-tier suppliers as a group provided between 3 and 6 percent of all imported weaponry during the 1990s, which is down from the 6 to 9 percent they supplied when the global arms market peaked in the late 1980s. Table 12.4 lists some of these countries' leading defense enterprises.

There are several motivations for arms production in third-tier countries. Actual or potential threats to national security are exacerbated when states find themselves dependent on others for the implements of defense. States that have been subject to weapons embargoes, especially during wartime, bristle most at the thought of lasting arms-import dependence, and as one observer has noted, "all of the current major developing world arms producers . . . have had significant restrictions placed on their ability to acquire weapons at various points in the past."[31] Another motivation is the hope that developing an indigenous arms production capacity will help promote wider economic development, a strategy commonly referred to as "military-led industrialization." Another motivation is symbolic. Certain national characteristics and forms of state behavior are infused with symbolic significance, and the possession of a nuclear weapons capability is probably the best example. But also important to states is the possession of advanced conventional weapons, and even more so the capacity to manufacture them. When India successfully test-fired its own intermediate-range ballistic missile in April 1999, the Indian prime minister described the Agni-II as "a symbol of resurgent India" and vowed that "yes, we will stand on our own feet."[32]

---

[31] Krause, *Arms and the State*, p. 162.

[32] Quoted in "Over 2,000 Km Range Agni-II Successfully Test-fired," *Times of India*, April 12, 1999. On nuclear symbolism, see Scott D. Sagan, "Why Do States Build Nuclear Weapons: Three Models in Search of a Bomb," *International Security* 21, 3 (Winter 1996/97): pp. 54–86. On the symbolic importance of high-tech conventional weapons, see Dana P. Eyre and Mark C. Suchman, "Status, Norms, and the Proliferation of Conventional Weapons: An Institutional Theory Approach," in Peter J. Katzenstein, ed., *The Culture of National Security: Norms and Identity in World Politics* (New York: Columbia University Press, 1996), pp. 79–113.

To some extent the global diffusion of advanced military technology is inevitable. In fact, many scholars anticipate an acceleration of technological diffusion in the context of the current restructuring of the international arms market. Although Europe has not yet succeeded in creating an integrated defense industry, there are numerous collaborative defense-industrial ventures in Europe, and many trans-Atlantic programs as well. Some involve *coproduction,* in which defense firms in two or more countries jointly produce a weapons system originally developed by one of them. Others are *codevelopment* projects, whereby companies and research institutes from different countries collaborate in the development of new weapons systems from the earliest stages of the "product life cycle." Such arrangements facilitate the rapid diffusion of military technology among participating firms and countries.

These sorts of joint ventures linking first- or second-tier producers with third-tier producers are far fewer, though they are becoming increasingly common. One staple of the cold-war arms trade, *licensed production,* continues to be a source of technological diffusion to the third tier. This involves a transfer of the rights and wherewithal to produce a weapons system or component originally developed and manufactured by a supplier. Licensing the production of aging weapons designs (and sometimes rather young ones) was one means of currying favor with local elites in the superpowers' cold-war competition for friends and allies in the Third World. Today, with increasing competition among first- and second-tier suppliers for business clients, as opposed to political clients, buyers can demand this and other forms of military-technology transfer as a condition for their purchases. Although economic motivations may have replaced political motivations on the part of arms suppliers, implications for the diffusion of military technology are the same — in fact, they may be more serious.[33]

On the other hand, the globalization of arms production and the emergence of huge defense conglomerates in the United States and Europe may have the effect of squeezing all but a very few third-tier suppliers out of the international arms market. The resources necessary to participate in the much-discussed "revolution in military affairs" (RMA) for the moment seem to be available only to the United States, but Europeans and Russians can hope to be on board before too long. Countries in the developing world may come to conclude that their military preparedness in the contemporary context requires that they abandon any serious plans for military-industrial autarky in exchange for the acquisition of advanced weaponry on the international arms market.

The arms trade and the other topics we have discussed in this chapter are examples of the close relationship between national security and both national and international economics. Economic transactions create interdependencies within and between societies. When these interdependencies derive from or have implications for national security and defense, they cease being strictly economic issues governed solely by economic logic. In the next chapter we continue our discussion of economic interdependence and its importance in world politics.

---

[33]See Richard A. Bitzinger, "The Globalization of the Arms Industry: The Next Proliferation Challenge," *International Security* 19, 2 (Fall 1994): pp. 170–198.

13

Interdependence and Economic Order

Interdependence

As new states and other international actors have come into being and as new technologies and ideologies have altered the international environment, the practices of states and other international actors have adapted to these changes to maintain order within the international system. Although there is formal anarchy — the absence of a central authority with coercive power — within that system, we have seen that there is actually also much order, cooperation, coordination, and collaboration in international relations. There is, as Hedley Bull calls it, an "anarchical society." Such a society exists because there is *order.* Recurring patterns of behavior shape the expectations of the actors in the international system; behavior is often *predictable.*[1]

This is a crucial point. It means that order can exist without formal rules or with only a primitive system of rules. Order is difficult enough to obtain within societies

---

[1] See Hedley Bull, *The Anarchical Society: A Study of Order in World Politics* (New York: Columbia University Press, 1977), chap. 1.

that have central governmental authorities; the environment of world politics creates even more problems. The ability to create order and the frequency and virulence of conflicts depend largely on the relationships among international actors. One feature of systems and the relationships among the components of those systems is interdependence. Interdependence both contributes to the problems of creating order and creates the conditions necessary for attaining order. In this chapter we shall look at interdependence and its effects on order in world politics.

Sensitivity and Vulnerability

Interdependence is a quality of a system. In systems, things ramify; more effects than we imagine or expect ripple through the system because of the interdependent relationships that link actors. When there is a change in the system, we should be prepared for surprising consequences. Examples include the French Revolution of 1789, the Russian Revolution of 1917, and the October 1973 war of Israel versus Egypt and Syria, which led to the Arab use of oil as a weapon and, in turn, to worldwide economic problems and conservation efforts that changed the nature of life in advanced industrial countries — and so on. Surprise effects have a number of sources, not simply the major changes that can accompany war or revolution. The interdependent linkages among economic, ecological, political, and social phenomena in the present world system are graphically illustrated by the events of 1972. Poor weather in the winter of 1971 to 1972 destroyed one-third of the Russian winter wheat crop. However, the government bureaucracy failed to increase the spring wheat acreage. To meet wheat demands, a massive wheat sale was arranged with the United States in July 1972, doubling the price of wheat in North America and generating public anger. In addition, North American wheat was not available for India (whose food supply had been worsened by monsoon and war) or for China and Africa (both hit by drought), with Africa especially facing conditions of massive starvation. Two analysts note:

> The most outstanding lesson which can be drawn from these events is a realization of how strong the bonds among nations have become. A bureaucratic decision in one region, perhaps the action of just one individual — not to increase the spring wheat acreage — resulted in a housewives' strike against soaring food prices in another part of the world and in tragic suffering in yet another part of the world.[2]

International interdependence has two different dimensions. First, international actors are **sensitive** to the behavior of other actors or developments in parts of the system. The degree of sensitivity depends on how quickly changes in one actor bring about changes in another and how great the effects are. By "changes" we mean shifts in foreign policy or transformations of actors themselves (a new form of government, the onset of internal instability, economic collapse, and so on). States and other actors are sensitive when changes implemented or experienced by others cannot be ignored; they require some policy response or affect some other change. Second, actors who are sen-

---

[2] Mihajlo Mesarovic and Eduard Pestel, *Mankind at the Turning Point* (New York: New American Library, 1974), pp. 19–20.

sitive to external changes may also be **vulnerable** to their effects. Vulnerability is measured by the costs imposed on a state or nonstate actor by external events, costs that the actor must absorb because it cannot pursue alternative policies that might minimize those costs.[3]

The Asian financial crisis discussed in Chapter 1 illustrates both of these concepts. The interdependence of Southeast Asian financial systems was such that when the Thai currency began its freefall in summer 1997, it sparked a similar drop in the Indonesian currency, and then in the currencies of Malaysia and the Philippines. Within a few months the currencies of South Korea, Singapore, and Taiwan had also lost much of their value. Despite great efforts by central bankers in these countries to maintain the value of their currencies, they simply did not have the resources to do so. They were vulnerable, and the economic costs imposed by the crisis were substantial. Other countries were not so vulnerable, but still felt the impact of developments in the Asian financial markets. The United States, Japan, and some European countries, as well as IGOs like the IMF and the World Bank, scrambled to provide financial assistance to help prop up the value of the Asian currencies and avert economic collapse. They were sensitive; alternatives were available to them in order to prevent the financial crisis from enveloping their own economies.

Sensitivity and vulnerability are not well-defined conceptual boxes in which states and other actors can be placed when analyzing developments in the international political economy. They are better seen as two ends of a continuum. Where an actor falls on the sensitivity-vulnerability continuum depends not only the concrete circumstances, but also on the passing of time. Japan was not as vulnerable to the financial crisis as the Southeast Asian economies, but the impact was felt much harder there than in the United States. The economies of Latin America did not feel the effects of the crisis for several months, but after about a year Brazil required an international financial bailout of its own. Thus, different systems, and different actors within those systems, may be characterized by different levels of sensitivity and vulnerability. In the current system — truly global and woven together by networks of communication, transportation, commerce, and finance — we find far more sensitivities and vulnerabilities than existed in international systems of the past.

Conflict and Harmony

Interdependence is one form of constraint on states and other actors in the international system. What is on one actor's menu depends very much on how that menu is connected to the menus of other actors. How might interdependence constrain the menu? Changes by or in one actor will have some significant consequences for other actors, whether they like it or not. The images of the "global village," the "spaceship earth," and the "shrinking planet" are all derived from this idea of interdependence.

The liberal view of interdependence is essentially positive and optimistic; interdependence is conducive to more and more cooperation among states as they are brought together through various forms of interaction. The models of integration discussed in

---

[3] See Robert O. Keohane and Joseph S. Nye, *Power and Interdependence,* 2nd ed. (New York: Harper-Collins, 1989), chap. 1.

Chapter 11 were based on increasing the interdependent linkages between states through functional integration (as in the movement for European unity) or through social, economic, and political integration based on inter-societal transactions. Some integration models go so far as to predict that the outcomes of these integration processes will eventually lead to world community or a world state, although most liberals do not put a great deal of faith in such forecasts.

In contrast, the realist view points to interdependence as a constraint on states and therefore as a potentially very important source of conflict. Interdependence — especially if it is lopsided, making one party much more dependent than the other — can also generate frustration and anger, as states hopelessly wish for past times when they were not inextricably linked with others and when they had greater freedom of action. Mutual dependence need not mean mutual reward, as implied by liberal views of integration. One scholar simply notes that "the growth of interdependence increases the capacity of all relevant actors to injure each other."[4]

Interdependence and the idea of sovereignty, which carries the formal and legal assumption of autonomy and equality among states, do not mix well. Consider again the Peace of Westphalia. The statesmen and leaders who fashioned this settlement ending the Thirty Years' War were creating agreements that met the needs of their time. Very clear *trade-offs* were made between autonomy and self-control on the one hand and the lack of order inherent in an anarchic international system on the other: princes who were striving for independence of action from the control of religious or imperial authority (the pope and the Holy Roman Emperor) were willing to create a system of states that had no formal source of authority or higher order. This **Westphalian trade-off,** although sensible at the time, has fostered a set of contemporary problems arising from growth in the levels and scope of interdependence. The Peace of Westphalia stressed independence and autonomy; interdependence generates complex problems, which require solutions involving collective, not unilateral, action. The balance has been changing, especially in the decades since World War II. Increasingly, the international community has come to stress the need to reduce the formal anarchy of the system in order to solve the problems of contemporary interdependence.

International Trade

Nearly $7 trillion worth of goods and services were traded between states in 1996; that was more than 21 percent of all goods and services produced worldwide. High-income countries account for most international trade (over 70 percent), but they are not necessarily the most open economies. The United States trades far more than any other state, but its imports and its exports each represent only about 10 percent of GDP. The figures for Japan are even lower. Most countries account for tiny shares of total global trade,

---

[4] Oran Young, "International Regimes: Problems of Concept Formation," *World Politics* 32 (April 1980): pp. 331–356.

but trade is very important to many national economies. In some countries, Malaysia for example, imports and exports each represent more than 75 percent of GDP, and there are several others where the figure exceeds 50 percent.[5] Although there is considerable variability in the trading behavior of states, there can be little doubt that trade is a centerpiece of international interaction.[6]

Comparative Advantage and Free Trade

The basic principles behind international trade have been known for a long time. Adam Smith, writing in the eighteenth century, argued that states trade because some states can produce some goods more efficiently than others. Each state has an interest in concentrating its efforts on what it does best. It can then trade some of those goods for goods that other states produce more efficiently. As an illustration, imagine two states, *A* and *B*, each of which produces two goods, pizza and beer. Assume also that *A* is better at making pizza and *B* is better at brewing beer. Each week, a worker in state *A* can produce either 50 pizzas or 2 kegs of beer. A worker in state *B* can produce either 40 pizzas or 3 kegs of beer. If 200 workers in each state are split evenly between pizza making and beer brewing, then the production (and consumption) of *A* and *B* are as shown in the top half of Table 13.1. What if *A* reallocates its 100 beer brewers to pizza making and *B* reallocates its pizza makers to the brewery? *A* could then trade those 5,000 extra pizzas for the 300 extra kegs of beer that *B* now has on hand. Both states benefit: *A* gets more beer than it could produce on its own; *B* gets more pizzas.

The gains from trade are easy to see in cases like this when each states has an absolute advantage in the production of some good. David Ricardo, a British economist writing in the early nineteenth century, extended these principles to situations in which a state possessed only a **comparative advantage.** Imagine now that state *A* can produce both pizza *and* beer more efficiently than state *B* — 50 pizzas and 2.6 kegs per worker per week, compared to 40 pizzas and 2.4 kegs in state *B*. The bottom half of Table 13.1 shows what *A* and *B* would produce (and consume) when they do not trade. What if they do trade? Imagine that *A* reallocates 75 of its brewers to produce pizzas, while the remaining 25 brewers continue to produce their 65 kegs per week. Suppose that *B* reallocates 90 of its pizza makers to the brewery; the remaining 10 make their 400 pizzas. Now the 3,750 pizzas produced by *A*'s reallocated workers can be traded for 216 kegs of beer produced by *B*'s reallocated workers. Again, both states benefit: *A* gets more kegs of beer (65 + 216 = 281) than it could produce on its own; *B* gets more pizzas (400 + 3,750 = 4,150). Looked at in a different way, for every keg of beer *A* produces, it must produce about 19 fewer pizzas (50 ÷ 2.6). But for every keg that *B* brews, it produces only about 17 fewer pizzas (40 ÷ 2.4). Even though *B* is less efficient than *A* at brewing beer, beer is *B*'s *comparative* advantage.

Of course, specializing production in order to gain from trade is not without potential pitfalls. Our illustration assumed a straightforward barter — pizza for beer —

---

[5] Calculation based on data reported by the World Bank's *World Development Report 1998/99: Knowledge for Development* (Washington, D.C.: World Bank, 1998), Table 20.

[6] A good introduction to the politics of international trade is Bruce E. Moon, *Dilemmas of International Trade* (Boulder, Colo.: Westview, 1996).

TABLE 13.1   The Gains from Trade

	Absolute Advantage			
	No Trade		Trade	
	Pizzas	Kegs of Beer	Pizzas	Kegs of Beer
State A	5,000	200	5,000	300
State B	4,000	300	5,000	300
	Comparative Advantage			
	No Trade		Trade	
	Pizzas	Kegs of Beer	Pizzas	Kegs of Beer
State A	5,000	260	5,000	65 + 216
State B	4,000	240	400 + 3,750	240

when, in reality, the exchange of goods depends on their relative prices in world markets. Economies oriented toward the production of a few goods are more sensitive to the uncertainties of the international market, and price fluctuations can cause severe dislocations (declining wages, unemployment) for workers in affected industries. There are other considerations as well. Specializing in the production of agricultural goods or the extraction of natural resources (referred to as "commodities") may not be very conducive to the development of technologically advanced economy, which is a goal of virtually all states. We shall explore these and other issues relating to the so-called "international division of labor" in Chapter 15.

Protectionism

Very few states in the international system can produce everything their populations need to survive and prosper. Even for those that can, pursuing an economic policy of **autarky** — minimizing trade in favor of domestic production of all goods and services required by society — is not very cost-effective, given the principles of comparative advantage. In the past nations have sought to isolate themselves from the world economy when productive efficiency was of secondary importance to state leaders, as it was during the global depression of the 1930s. During this period the United States, Britain, France, Germany, and Japan all sought to stimulate domestic production and thereby reduce unemployment by placing restrictions on imports. Some countries, like

Iraq in the 1990s, have had little choice but to pursue autarky because their economic isolation has been imposed for military reasons. For other countries, like Albania in the 1970s and 1980s (it was communist but at odds with both the Soviet bloc and China), economic isolation was simply a part of political isolation.

Like so many other concepts, in the real world neither free trade nor autarky are absolutes; they are instead opposite ends of the spectrum of trade practices. In between are varying degrees of **protectionism.** Protectionism is a policy of restricting, but not eliminating, imports in an effort to maintain or nurture — to protect — the economic viability of domestic industries. As we pointed out in Chapter 12, governments may elect to protect industries, like silicon chip manufacturing, because domestic production of certain goods is deemed crucial for reasons of national security. More often, domestic industries are protected for political and economic reasons. Newly industrializing countries (NICs), for example, have actively protected their "infant industries" from the effects of cheap foreign imports until they have developed and are efficient enough to compete in international markets. Developed countries sometimes engage in protectionism because foreign competition threatens the well-being of industries that wield a great deal of political influence. Automobile manufacturers in the United States and farmers in France are two groups that have had the political clout to enlist from their national governments some degree of protection from foreign imports.

States use various techniques to control imports of goods and services. A state can impose **tariffs** on products entering its borders. Tariffs are taxes or duties levied on imported goods in order to raise revenue or to regulate the flow of foreign goods into a country. When tariffs are imposed, a particular imported item becomes more expensive to purchase and fewer will be sold relative to similar domestically produced goods. Tariffs protect domestic industries, but they can also be manipulated in an effort to influence trading partners. When the tariffs imposed on goods imported from one state are no higher than the tariffs imposed on those same goods from any other state, the first state is said to have *most-favored-nation* (MFN) status — a term that can be somewhat misleading since a state with MFN status is being treated the same as most other trade partners, not better. The United States, which provides a huge export market to other countries, has often sought to exert influence by promising or withdrawing MFN status. In 1975 U.S. Senator Henry Jackson and others tried to influence Soviet policy on the emigration of Jews by holding up an agreement to extend MFN treatment to the USSR. The attempt failed. A similar situation arose with China after the brutal repression of the democracy movement in 1989; there was debate in the U.S. government over whether China should be punished by withdrawing MFN status. China has not been sanctioned through the withdrawal of MFN status. American leaders have generally concluded that the Chinese economy is too large for such sanctions to be effective. Furthermore, because the United States needs China's cooperation to pursue nonproliferation and other U.S. foreign policy goals, economic coercion may have adverse side effects even if it was effective in curbing the Chinese government's repression of internal dissent.

Protectionism includes other **nontariff barriers to trade** (NTBs). *Quotas* control imports not through prices, but through the amount of goods permitted to enter a country from a specific source for a specific time period. These were used by the United States to restrict imports of Japanese automobiles in the 1980s, although the quotas were ostensibly *voluntary export restrictions* (VERs) by Japan. Other mechanisms for controlling trade include *subsidies and loans* to domestic industries, which effectively reduce the costs of domestic production. As we discussed in the last chapter, some forms of economic behavior have been used strictly to punish other states. These include the *boycott,* in which states cease to buy the goods, resources, or services of another state. Boycotts cut the target state off from its markets. Similarly, an *embargo* stops the sales of economic items to another state. An embargo cuts off the state's supply of resources and products from the outside.

Tariff and nontariff barriers to trade constitute state intervention in the market. But not all trade barriers are the result of direct action taken by national governments. Groups within society often appeal to nationalist sentiments in an effort to sustain the viability of certain domestic industries, and especially to protect jobs. In the United States, for example, labor unions and other industry groups often encourage consumers to purchase goods "Made in the USA." Even small businesses advertize that they are "American Owned and Operated." Similar campaigns have been undertaken in other countries as well. Japanese consumers have long been discouraged from purchasing imported rice, and some campaigns have gone so far as to suggest that the consumption of foreign rice is contrary to the essence of being Japanese.[7] Rarely are such appeals isolated from other more explicit forms of protectionism — for instance, government subsidies to American automakers or Japanese rice farmers — but they are unique in that they constitute a form of **economic nationalism,** as opposed to economic policy.

Trade and the Prisoner's Dilemma

Most economists and politicians extol the virtues of free trade. All states engage in some form of protectionism, but the goal for many states and IGOs (the World Trade Organization, the Group of Eight, regional trade groups, and others) has been to break down existing trade barriers and to minimize protectionist sentiments. The goal of free trade has often been elusive because there are powerful incentives to protect domestic industry, especially when external markets remain open. The situation resembles a prisoner's dilemma.

Recall from Chapter 8 that in certain situations, like arms races, the rational strategy that *each side* pursues in order to maximize its own self-interest (defect, or arm) results in a "socially suboptimal" outcome (mutual armament) — another outcome would have been better for *both sides.* Had each adopted an alternative strategy (cooperate, or disarm), they would have achieved the socially optimal outcome (mutual disarmament). Now let us consider two trading states. Each state, *A* and *B,* must choose between protectionism and free trade. If state *A* erects trade barriers, it will be protecting its domestic industry, and if state *B* does not erect trade barriers, its markets will remain open to *A*'s exports. That is the best outcome for state *A* because it is able to screen out the dangers of free trade (excessive competition) while continuing to enjoy the benefits (expanded markets). All of this occurs at the expense of state *B,* which is

---

[7] See Emiko Ohnuki-Tierney, *Rice as Self: Japanese Identities through Time* (Princeton, N.J.: Princeton University Press, 1993).

why protectionist policies are sometimes called "beggar-thy-neighbor" policies. The worst outcome for *A* is the opposite situation: *B* erects barriers to *A*'s exports while *A*'s markets remain open. The second best outcome for both states is free trade. Their markets stay open, trade increases, and they both enjoy the benefits of comparative advantage — increased consumption and industrial efficiency due to specialization. The next-to-worst outcome is mutual protectionism. Trade declines when both sides erect barriers, the benefits of comparative advantage diminish, and the potential for inefficiencies increase because firms have fewer opportunities to specialize their production. Such an ordering of the four possible outcomes makes this a prisoner's dilemma, as depicted in Figure 13.1.

As in any prisoner's dilemma, both sides have an incentive to defect (erect trade barriers), since no matter what the other side does defecting will yield a better outcome for the defector. Unfortunately, the equilibrium outcome is mutual protectionism, even though both sides are better off in a relationship of free trade.[8] But achieving free trade requires cooperation, which can be exceedingly difficult when state leaders must also contend with domestic groups seeking protection from the uncertainties of the international market. As we noted in Chapter 6, analysts have emphasized the linkages between domestic politics and international relations, looking at state leaders as playing simultaneous or "two-level games." Negotiating and gaining approval for the North American Free Trade Agreement (NAFTA) involved just such a process. The treaty was signed by the United States, Canada, and Mexico in 1992. Once signed,

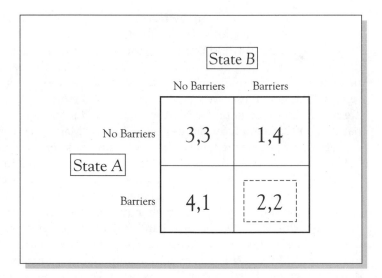

FIGURE 13.1 Trade Barriers and the Prisoner's Dilemma

---

[8] For discussions of the applicability of the prisoner's dilemma to the problem of free trade, see John A. C. Conybeare, "Public Goods, Prisoner's Dilemmas, and the International Political Economy," *International Studies Quarterly* 28 (1984): pp. 5–22, and Joanne Gowa, "Bipolarity, Multipolarity, and Free Trade," *American Political Science Review* 83, 4 (December 1989): pp. 1245–1256.

NAFTA still had to be approved, and in the U.S. this became the task of a newly elected president, Bill Clinton. The administration faced considerable domestic opposition from labor and environmental groups, and from within Clinton's own party. In an effort to assemble a pro-NAFTA coalition, U.S. representatives returned to the negotiating table to make further adjustments to the treaty, signing a series of supplemental agreements in 1993.

Collective Goods

States act to achieve their goals and interests both singly and in groups. As the world has become more tightly linked through various interdependencies, states have found themselves grouped together in international organizations and regional groupings or subsystems that are economic, political, and military in nature. States also belong to a world system. We may think of each state (as well as the other international actors) as a member of a group (or system) that includes the entire globe. Being a member of a group complicates what any individual member can achieve and how the member achieves it because of the influence of the sensitivity and vulnerability of interdependence. Clearly, interdependence affects how individual interests relate to group interests. Sometimes leaders of states think they are acting in their own interests when they are not.

How can we not act in our own best interest? First consider how individual interests relate to group interests. This relationship is clearly illustrated in *Catch-22*, Joseph Heller's novel about World War II. Yossarian, a bombardier in the U.S. Army Air Force in Italy, refuses to fly any more missions. Major Major, a superior officer, in trying to persuade Yossarian to fly, asks, "Would you like to see our country lose?" Yossarian replies, "We won't lose. We've got more men, more money and more material. There are ten million men in uniform getting killed and a lot more are making money and having fun. Let somebody else get killed." Major Major then responds, "But suppose everybody on our side felt that way." Yossarian's answer is devastatingly to the point: "Then I'd certainly be a damn fool to feel any other way. Wouldn't I?"[9]

Here is another variant of the prisoner's dilemma. If all the other fliers are willing to fly their missions — that is, to cooperate — then Yossarian would be unwise to go along. He should defect. With 10 million men in the war, his individual presence will not make a difference. On the other hand, if none of the others wishes to fly either — all are defecting — then his response, "I'd be a damned fool to feel any other way," is indeed sensible. His presence would again make no difference, so again he should defect. However, if all the other fliers were to take the same position, then the following dilemma develops: despite the fact that missions have to be flown, it is not rational for any single individual to participate. For the collective, the goal of winning the war can be achieved only through group action. However, such group action consists of the activities of individuals, and Yossarian makes it clear that it is not in the interest of any

---

[9] Joseph Heller, *Catch-22* (New York: Dell, 1961), p. 107.

single individual to perform the actions needed to achieve the group's goal. So, how do groups of supposedly rational actors ever accomplish collective goals? Why, for example, should any single state dismantle its trade barriers when it continues to enjoy access to the open markets of other states? And why, if other states do not open their markets, should any single state do otherwise?

In our discussion of international trade we have spoken of the exchange of goods — pizza, beer, automobiles, and so on. A "good" is simply the consequence or outcome of an activity. If such consequences or outcomes are tangible things that can be possessed as property or consumed by a single person, we call them **private goods.** The discipline of economics is devoted primarily to the study of private goods and the way they are allocated within or between societies. The allocation of private goods is determined by the availability of the good (supply) and how much is desired (demand). Economists study how supply and demand interact at different price levels to determine the amount of a good that will be produced and thus allocated among consumers. Under ideal conditions, the free market resolves any misallocation of goods: when something is desired but not supplied, its price rises until potential suppliers find it in their interest to make the good available to those who want it.

Suppliers of goods incur costs when producing and distributing goods to consumers, and expect to recoup those costs when the goods are sold at a particular price. But if we think of Yossarian as a potential supplier, we can immediately see certain limitations of the free market. As a bombardier, Yossarian is essentially a producer, along with many others, of a good: victory in war. However, he elects to stop producing that good because the costs to him (death, with high probability) will never be repaid. Furthermore, if others do supply the good — and he is sure they will — then he gets paid anyway, even though he is not a supplier. That is because the good itself, victory, is its own repayment and everyone on the winning side can partake of its benefits. Victory in war is a good, but it cannot be possessed or consumed exclusively by those who pay for it. It is a **public good** or **collective good.** Although collective goods are provided through the actions of individuals, once provided they belong to the group. They are not possessed by individuals and therefore cannot be exchanged in the manner of private goods. As we shall see, liberals argue that free trade is a collective good that benefits the entire international community, even those states that do not fully participate in providing the good.

Collective goods possess two special characteristics. The first is *jointness of supply.* If a good is supplied to any member of a group, then it is supplied to all members of that group. In contrast to private goods, collective goods are therefore indivisible. If new members are added to the group, the other members who are currently benefiting from (or "consuming") the good will not receive a diminished amount. An example of a collective good is network television. When a television station broadcasts its programs over the airwaves, all households within the range of transmission can view them. And the fact that more people may tune their televisions to that station at certain times does not diminish its availability to others. When a government provides deterrence for its population, that deterrence is jointly supplied. When Washington threatened Moscow with retaliation for an attack on the United States, it provided deterrence for every individual in the United States. Once one person is protected by the deterrent threat, all are protected; once California is protected, so are Montana and Delaware. An increase in population does not reduce the deterrence provided to all the rest. The addition of Alaska and Hawaii to the Union in 1959 did not diminish the deterrence already being provided to the other forty-eight states.

The second characteristic of a collective good is *nonexclusiveness.* A jointly supplied good may be either excludable or nonexcludable; that is, even though a good is jointly supplied, it can be withheld from nonmembers. Cable television is an example of a jointly supplied good that is excludable. Once the cable signal is supplied to any one cable subscriber, the addition of new subscribers does not reduce the supply of the good. However, it is excludable: those who do not pay for the service are not hooked up to the cable and thus cannot receive the service. Jointly supplied goods can be excludable, but a collective good is jointly supplied and nonexcludable. If the United States is deterring a nuclear attack on its own territory, it cannot exclude any specific group of persons — foreign diplomats or foreign tourists, prisoners, or citizens who do not pay taxes. Any people in the territory of the United States are part of the group included in nuclear deterrence and cannot be denied its benefits.

Free Riders

The characteristics of collective goods have important implications for how individuals behave in groups. Of all the regular viewers of public television, only a small number make contributions during those periodic fundraising drives. By failing to contribute, the others are not prevented from watching public TV. Victory in war has some of these same properties. If the war is won, all citizens of the victorious country will have won: some of the benefits — political freedom and ideological victory — will go to all if they go to one. It is also difficult to exclude citizens from this collective good of victory (though there may be penalties for draft dodgers and the like). Therefore, individuals must decide whether to help in achieving the good or be "free riders" on the efforts of others. This is exactly the choice that Yossarian faces, and his reluctance to fly any more missions, if shared by others, creates the dilemma identified by Major Major: if everyone wants to be a free rider, the collective good may never be achieved. Again, keep in mind that this **free-rider dilemma** is simply a collective version of the prisoner's dilemma, which exists between two individuals.

In the ideal case, where only private goods exist, an economic mechanism — the free market — allocates goods within a group or society. This mechanism does not work well for the allocation of collective goods because of their indivisibility and nonexcludability. If individuals are strictly rational in the economic sense of desiring to maximize benefits and minimize costs, a collective good may never be provided, even if all members of a group desire that good. This dilemma arises from the clash between individual interests and outcomes and group interests and outcomes. If the good is a collective good (and thus jointly supplied), the group member will receive its benefits whether that member pays for it or not (gets a free ride). The rational individual will not have to pay for a benefit that he or she will gain anyway, as long as others pay. The rational individual thus will not contribute and will wait for someone else to shoulder the burden. In addition, one does not want to be the sucker and pay for the good that others will enjoy at no cost. Yossarian did not want to be one of those getting killed while others were "making money and having fun" — not when there were 10 million other men in uniform. Economic mechanisms alone cannot overcome the temptation to free ride, and this is why "collective action" is so difficult in world politics (and in other spheres of social life).[10]

This dilemma is interesting because it shows the extreme interdependence of group members involved with collective goods. If everyone takes a free ride, an important good may not be produced. If many decide to take a free ride, a good may be only partially provided, as, for example, when some states refuse to pay dues to international organizations that for various reasons do not wish to throw nonpayers out of the organization. This has happened with the United States and France in the UN. If member states refuse to contribute their share of troops and equipment to a defense alliance, security may be underprovided since deterrence must rest on fewer military capabilities. In fact, one major area of research in international relations has focused on the extent to which deterrence can be understood as a collective good and alliance burden sharing as an effort to overcome the free-rider dilemma.[11]

In the contemporary world system, more and more objectives of states require group action because of interdependence: monetary policy, trade, alliances, or other aspects of security, such as nonproliferation of nuclear weapons. The very idea of *order* in the international system may be seen as having collective-good properties. If there is some stability, predictability, and regularity in international affairs, adding new actors may not diminish it, and it is difficult (although not impossible) to exclude actors from the benefits of international order and coordination.[12] It is possible to interpret the "new world order," much heralded after the end of the cold war, as something from which all members of the group — the world — might benefit. Part of the strong reaction to the Iraqi invasion of Kuwait stemmed from the perception that just when the disintegration of the East-West conflict was opening new opportunities for global cooperation, Iraq's behavior threatened not only Kuwait but the collective good of order for the whole system.

Many areas of international political economy have been studied using collective-goods concepts, including international common property resources like the high seas, international trade, international monetary policy, the creation of international law, and international organizations. Global environmental issues can also be understood in this context. Cleaning up an international body of water like the Rhine or the Mediterranean requires group action. Although a state might appear to be following its own interests by electing to free ride, in the long run it may be acting against them if the good desired — a clean waterway — is never achieved. Because the condition of the waterway is jointly supplied and nonexcludable, anyone using it will benefit from its cleanliness (just as all will be harmed by its pollution at the hands of one or more

---

[10] The classic statement of the collective action problem is Mancur Olson, *The Logic of Collective Action: Public Goods and the Theory of Groups* (Cambridge, Mass.: Harvard University Press, 1965). For a more recent review, see Todd Sandler, *Collective Action: Theory and Applications* (Ann Arbor: University of Michigan Press, 1992).

[11] See Todd Sandler, "The Economic Theory of Alliances," *Journal of Conflict Resolution* 37 (September 1993): pp. 446–483. The pioneering work is Mancur Olson and Richard Zeckhauser, "An Economic Theory of Alliances," *Review of Economics and Statistics* 46 (1966): pp. 266–279.

[12] See Duncan Snidal, "Coordination versus Prisoners' Dilemma: Implications for International Cooperation and Regimes," *American Political Science Review* 79 (December 1985): pp. 923–942.

countries). Here, free riding will stop the good of clean water from being achieved altogether, cause clean-up to take much longer, or cause it to be only partially achieved. We will return to the collective-goods concept when we discuss the global environment in Chapter 16.

Strategies for Achieving Collective Goods

There are ways in which states in the current system have overcome the prisoner's dilemma and the pressures to defect. There must be strategies to overcome free riding and to promote collective action. Collective goods present situations where the strictly economic forces of the marketplace cannot bring about solutions and where political and social action must be taken to achieve the desired collective good. Six broad strategies for achieving collective goods will be presented, all of which in some way increase the costs of defecting or increase the payoffs of cooperation.

One way to get individuals to cooperate is through *coercion.* Yossarian, for example, was in the army because it was against the law to refuse to be drafted. While he was in the army, the army could threaten imprisonment, even execution, if he refused to fight. Within states, tax systems are backed up by threats of punishment for nonpayment (that is, for free riding). When a union achieves a union shop, it forces all workers to join the union, eliminating the free rider who would not join but would still enjoy most of the benefits, like safe working conditions, obtained by the union from management.

This type of coercion is difficult in international relations. The power to tax is not readily given to IGOs because it is a threat to sovereignty. (Note, however, that the EU does have such authority in a number of areas.) Sometimes an individual state can coerce others to contribute to the collective good by threatening to end its own contribution. The United States, for example, attempted to coerce its cold war allies to take on a larger share of the burden in NATO by threatening to pull U.S. troops out of Europe. Coercion was also an important element in the Soviet Union's management of burden-sharing in the Warsaw Pact. If a group is small, a free-riding member is more easily identified and social pressure can be applied to encourage the member's cooperation. A government and its leaders may lose prestige if other governments feel that they are not pulling their weight or cooperating. NATO's annual review to identify and spotlight slackers has been used in this way. Such pressure was put on states that bore low costs during the Gulf War or that dragged their feet in paying their share.

In world politics, positive strategies based on *rewards* of some kind seem to be more useful than negative ones based on coercion. Members of a group are sometimes coaxed to participate in collective action by offers of private goods as "side payments." For example, states may join alliances and provide a share of the defense burden if they receive new and sophisticated weapons in return. Side payments can also be used to encourage certain behavior on the part of nonallies. In 1994, in an attempt to persuade North Korea to contribute to the collective good of nuclear nonproliferation, the United States promised to provide two light water nuclear reactors, useful for purposes of generating electricity but not for the production of weapons-grade nuclear fuel.

Another noncoercive strategy is *education* to increase individual perceptions of the self-interest to be gained from group and long-term interests. For example, Malta's representative to the General Assembly, Arvid Pardo, proposed in 1967 that the General Assembly deal with ways to extract the resources of the seabed in the interests of humanity as a whole, calling the seabed resources the "common heritage of mankind." Educational tasks have been performed by professionals acting collectively as "epistemic communities" — transnational groups "united by a belief in the truth of their model and by a commitment to translate this truth into public policy, in the conviction that human welfare will be enhanced as a result."[13] One such community, the Club of Rome, consists of academics, scientists, and IGO personnel gathered to study and educate the world about the nature and consequences of global interdependence, especially the implications for global resource depletion.

The intent behind this strategy is to force policymakers to confront the free-rider problem and to understand what the structure of the decision situation looks like. If policymakers understand that their interests are best served in the long run, they will be better able to deal with these problems. This educational strategy is also related to the process of integration that consists of shifting loyalties to new and larger political units with broader interests. But this is a slow process, and a number of our collective-goods problems require immediate attention and quick action.

A collective good can be provided if one member of the group desires that good so much that it is willing to *pay the whole cost* (or most of it) by itself and does not care that other group members also receive the good. In effect, one member offers to be the sucker. Besides valuing the good highly, this member is usually richer in resources or wealthier than other members; it can shoulder most of the burden with fewer sacrifices. Studies of some IGO budget assessments and burden-sharing in alliances such as NATO and the Warsaw Pact show that the larger members will pay proportionately more to get the things they want, even if others ride free. Evidence for this behavior has included the U.S. desire to provide deterrence for itself and its NATO allies, as well as the U.S. role in stabilizing international trade, as we shall see.

One other strategy for achieving collective goods is to create localized or regional organizations from a number of small groups of states and then to create some sort of federal structure to tie together and coordinate these groups. This approach involves *the use of IGOs* to address collective-goods problems through the creation of regimes, often following the functionalist integration model (as discussed later).

These general strategies for coping with and resolving collective-goods issues involve both formal and informal mechanisms. These mechanisms help states coordinate their activities and collaborate in a positive way. The strategies just discussed only hint at a very powerful informal process that helps to facilitate collective action. The most problematic aspect of the prisoner's dilemma is trusting the other side in a specific situation; in the free-rider dilemma, the issue of trust pertains to the rest of the group. When one or both prisoners go to jail, the question of trust becomes moot. This is a *single-play* situation. But most relationships in social life, and certainly in international relations, are *continuous*. That is, there are multiple plays in any game, and the players can learn what will happen to them if they defect, or, in collective situations, if

---

[13] Ernst B. Haas, *When Knowledge Is Power: Three Models of Change in International Organizations* (Berkeley: University of California Press, 1990), p. 41. See also Peter Haas, "Introduction: Epistemic Communities and International Policy Coordination," *International Organization* 46 (Winter 1992): pp. 1–36.

they free ride. In Chapter 9 we discussed Robert Axelrod's research showing that in experimental games players did best by following a tit-for-tat strategy: cooperating while the other player cooperates, retaliating when the other defects. If both players follow the never-defect-first principle, they avoid the dilemma.[14]

It thus may be possible to deal with the collective action problem if states realize that they are involved in a continuous relationship (as in an iterated prisoner's dilemma). All plays of an iterated game are played under the "shadow of the future." In any given iteration, players know that they are likely to find themselves in a similar situation later on. In this context, the temptation to defect or free ride diminishes. You might be able to hurt the other player, but the other player can also hurt you — if not now, then the next time around. This **reciprocity** can promote something akin to the golden rule: if the circumstances are such that states can be expected to "do unto others . . . ," then cooperation becomes the best strategy, even in a prisoner's dilemma. Mutual cooperation has thus been called the game's "nonmyopic equilibrium" because it is achieved when players take a far-sighted view. Reciprocity is even more important when we recall that there are many games being played at the same time, that states interact in many issue areas at the same time, and that these are *linked* (especially as interdependence becomes tighter). A state may defect in one game (for example, arms control), but it will have to worry about the other player's defection in another (retaliatory acts in trade, wheat sales, alliance formation, military spending). The payoff matrix of costs and benefits thus will be affected by calculations of future costs and benefits.[15]

The notion of reciprocity is central to understanding the workings of international law and the importance of formal and informal rules and expectations. It also helps explain how we can have order and a certain amount of stability and predictability in formally anarchic situations.

Regimes and International Order

If states and other international actors are to overcome the free-rider problem, how should they organize themselves? There are, as we have seen, a number of strategies for achieving collective goods. One method, in the words of one analyst, is to "bind the members of the international community to rules of conduct, to which they agree, and which will restrain each member from free riding, and allocate burdens equitably, as a matter of international legal commitment."[16]

---

[14] Robert Axelrod, *The Evolution of Cooperation* (New York: Basic Books, 1984).
[15] The concept and role of reciprocity is developed in Charles W. Kegley, "The New Global Order: The Power of Principle in a Pluralistic World," *Ethics and International Affairs* 6 (1992): pp. 21–40. Linkage among different issues on different levels is treated in George Tsebelis, *Nested Games: Rational Choice in Comparative Politics* (Berkeley: University of California Press, 1990).
[16] See Charles P. Kindleberger, "Dominance and Leadership in the International Economy: Exploitation, Public Goods, and Free Rides," *International Studies Quarterly* 25 (1981): p. 252.

International law can do this, but the rules of conduct that affect international behavior go beyond those of international law. International law does not exist by itself; neither does international organization. Some groups of states, and some forms of interaction, exhibit strong elements of international order. Scholars have used the term **regime** to identify the complete set of *rules* that govern behavior in some specified area of international relations. This concept helps us understand the full array of constraints imposed by international society. Regimes have been defined as networks of "rules, norms and procedures that regularize behavior and control its effects," and as "sets of implicit or explicit principles, norms, rules, and decision-making procedures around which actors expectations converge in a given area."[17] The regularization of behavior means the creation of patterns — patterns of procedures, patterns of compliance to norms and rules, and most especially, patterns of expectations: "What these arrangements have in common is that they are designed not to implement centralized enforcement of agreements, but to establish stable mutual expectations about others' patterns of behavior."[18]

What do these arrangements consist of and from where do these common understandings come? There are formal components and informal components; there are national components, transnational components, and international components. The set of governing arrangements consists of national rules (the domestic laws of states), international rules (international law, the charters of IGOs, and the regulations, resolutions, and practices of IGOs), and private rules (the practices of MNCs and other NGOs, their charters, and other regulations). These are the formal products of governments and international organizations. Regimes also include the norms and principles that reflect patterns of behavior not yet formally codified in law or organization. The development of international law through custom — the actual practice of states that is accepted as law — is an important example of informal norms that act as rules to constrain behavior. Norms, principles, and customary law all have a major psychological component in that the policymakers of states feel they *should* act in certain ways because they are expected to (and expect others to), whether or not a rule has been formalized by treaty.

Thus we have sets of governing arrangements relating to various issue areas in international relations. Issue areas may be functional and thus be very wide or very narrow, paralleling the structure of functional IGOs. One scholar notes, "We live in a world of international regimes." Their concerns range from monetary issues, to trade issues, to the management of natural resources, to the control of armaments, to the management of power, to the management of outer space and the seabed.[19] Regimes may also be geographic, covering problems that arise within a specific area; Antarctica

---

[17] Keohane and Nye, *Power and Interdependence,* p. 19; and Stephen D. Krasner, "Structural Causes and Regime Consequences: Regimes as Intervening Variables," in Stephen D. Krasner, ed., *International Regimes* (Ithaca, N.Y.: Cornell University Press, 1983), p. 2.

[18] Robert O. Keohane, *After Hegemony: Cooperation and Discord in the World Political Economy* (Princeton, N.J.: Princeton University Press, 1984), p. 89.

[19] See Young, "International Regimes: Problems of Concept Formation," p. 331. For an overview of the vast literature on regimes, see Andreas Hansenclever, Peter Mayer, and Volker Rittberger, "Interests, Power, Knowledge: The Study of International Regimes," *Mershon International Studies Review* 40, 2 (October 1996): pp. 177–228.

presents such an example. Just as with IGOs, some regimes have only a few members, like that overseeing North Pacific fisheries, while some are very large, such as the UN conflict-management regime.

Some of the most extensive analysis of regimes has focused on the post–World War II economic relations of the Western industrialized countries. In the postwar system, the victorious industrialized countries consciously sought to create an international economic order — or regime — that would tie the states of the world together in order to promote economic growth and peace. The 1920s and 1930s were periods when economic isolationism, protectionism, and conflict helped lead the world into war. After World War II, the United States used its Marshall Plan aid to encourage European coordination, management, and economic interdependence in areas like international monetary policy and trade. But interdependence involves vulnerability and sensitivity. In the late 1960s and 1970s, when the spectacular economic growth of the postwar era slowed, economic interdependence began to be increasingly costly as well as beneficial. The question, again, is: How to manage interdependence, build new arrangements and institutions to solve the problems posed by economic interdependence, and ensure that the collective goods of global economic stability and peace continue to be provided?

Hegemony and Regimes

At the end of World War II, the Western powers were agreed in their basic views of the international economy. The cornerstone of their vision was a liberal system, one without the sorts of economic barriers that had been set up in the 1930s. This was to be a relatively unhampered economic system based on capitalism, the free market, and minimal barriers to trade. To make the system work, states had to cooperate. Establishing this system was seen as a major step toward creating peace and order in the world, particularly within the group of OECD states. Free trade, free movement of capital, and stable monetary relations all depended on stability and order in the world, and most importantly in the North Atlantic area. Thus, there was a relationship between political-military stability and economic stability. The area had to be militarily secure from outside threats as well as internally peaceful. The same state that could provide military order — the United States — was also the only state economically strong enough to provide order in the economic system. As the one dependable locale of economic growth, the United States would be the "engine" of global economic development.

In this international system based on U.S. military and economic predominance, the United States followed a policy of leadership, or, as some observers describe it, **hegemony.** In a hegemonic system, "one state is able and willing to determine and maintain the essential rules by which relations among states are governed. The hegemonial state not only can abrogate existing rules or prevent the adoption of rules it opposes but can also play the dominant role in constructing new rules."[20] Under U.S. leadership, the major economic features of the postwar period were "rapidly expand-

---

[20] C. Fred Bergsten, Robert Keohane, and Joseph Nye, "International Economics and International Politics: A Framework for Analysis," *International Organization* 29 (1975): p. 14.

ing and generally non-discriminatory trade, large-scale and rapid movements of funds from one center to another under fixed exchange rates, and the rapid growth of huge multinational enterprises."[21]

Hegemony can be a useful, if not a necessary, mechanism for helping a group to achieve collective goods; this is one of the strategies we discussed earlier in the chapter. Mancur Olson said that a single member of a large group can constitute what he calls a "privileged" group — in this case, a group of one — whereby this member provides the collective good for the whole group. Similarly, Charles Kindleberger argued that a stable world economy needs a "stabilizer." Other scholars suggest that a large group needs an "entrepreneur" to provide the political leadership necessary to help the group achieve the collective goods it desires. In sum, these views suggest that the stability of the international political economy, including the effectiveness with which states deal with collective action problems, is affected by the presence or absence of a hegemonic power. Indeed, realists, with their emphasis on state power, have often argued that the best explanation for regime formation and change is the rise and decline of hegemonic states in the international system. At the end of Chapter 4, we alluded to this **hegemonic stability** perspective in the context of our discussion of the distribution of power.[22]

A related perspective on hegemony was provided by Karl Deutsch, who suggested that one helpful condition for a security community is a strong "core area" with "the capacity to act — a function of size, power, economic strength, and administrative efficiencies."[23] It is doubtful that the existence of a large core area is essential to the kind of security community that currently exists among OECD countries, where economic stability and peace seem more secure now, when the United States is less predominant, than just after World War II. Nevertheless, earlier U.S. predominance may have been very important in setting in motion the economic prosperity and interdependence that now underlie that peace. In this sense there is some virtue in having one big power in the international system: if it chooses, it can not only bully others but also make short-term sacrifices that will in the long run benefit all members, not just itself. The real problem in the identification and existence of a hegemon, however, has been pointed out by Kindleberger: distinguishing between leadership and domination. The utility and desirability of having a hegemon may very well depend upon where states sit in the international economic system. As we shall see, LDCs that are dependent on that hegemony and that see it as domination will have views very different from those of developed, industrialized states, which see it as leadership.

[21] Keohane and Nye, *Power and Interdependence*, p. 19.

[22] See Olson, *The Logic of Collective Action*; Kindleberger, "Dominance and Leadership," p. 252; and Norman Froelich, Joe Oppenheimer, and Oran Young, *Political Leadership and Collective Goods* (Princeton, N.J.: Princeton University Press, 1971). Sympathetic reviews of hegemonic stability theory include Joanne Gowa, "Rational Hegemons, Excludable Goods, and Small Groups: An Epitaph for Hegemonic Stability Theory?" *World Politics* 41, 3 (April 1989): pp. 307–324; and David Lake, "Leadership, Hegemony, and the International Economy: Naked Emperor or Tattered Monarch with Potential?" *International Studies Quarterly* 37, 4 (December 1993): pp. 459–489.

[23] Karl W. Deutsch et al., *Political Community and the North Atlantic Area: International Organization in the Light of Historical Experience* (Princeton, N.J.: Princeton University Press, 1957), p. 138.

Some analysts claim the problem today is that international interdependence has grown and is outpacing the ability of states to manage it. One view, more common prior to the end of the cold war than today, is that the strains of interdependence are more pronounced because of decline of the United States as the guarantor of international political and economic stability. For example, by the 1970s the United States had lost control over the international monetary system, partly because of its governmental deficits and mounting international debt. Although the demise of the Soviet Union as a political-military challenger and America's resurgent economic position at the end of the century did make predictions about the end of American hegemony appear a bit premature, it is clear that the United States no longer occupies the exalted position it once did. The United States has been constrained by its own economy in its ability to respond to the needs of the newly democratized countries in Eastern Europe, to many LDCs with debt problems, or even to the financing of the Gulf War (American diplomacy focused on raising funds from its wealthy allies and regional oil producers).

Does this mean that the United States can no longer function as a system leader? The question really is that raised in Chapter 5: How do we define power? There can be no doubt that U.S. *control over resources* has diminished steadily since the end of World War II. However, a loss of control over resources does not necessarily mean less *control over actors;* lower levels of tangible capabilities do not mean less influence. This was true even before the United States found itself the sole remaining superpower after the cold war ended. Now we must also recognize that U.S. control over resources, especially its predominance in the area of information and communications technology, has probably increased in recent years. The Gulf War, as well as the seemingly effortless punitive strikes against Iraq since then, indicates that the United States still possesses significantly more advanced military capability than any other country. The information revolution also has been more effectively harnessed by the United States than by any other country as a means to drive economic efficiency and growth. Whether a hegemon or not, the United States still occupies a preeminent position in the international system and can exercise leadership (if not domination) in global relations.

The Monetary Regime

As a result of agreement in values and outlook, a small number of industrialized states led by the United States created the basis for a liberal international economic order for the developed, noncommunist states. One aspect of this order had to do with the international monetary system.

When individuals trade goods and services, they use currency as a medium of exchange. When trade is conducted across state borders, goods and services are valued in different national currencies, and exchange rates — the value of one currency relative to another — allow traders to compare the relative prices of these goods and services. Such price comparisons are made much easier if there is a common medium of exchange (for example, gold, British pounds, or American dollars); national currencies need only be converted into this common medium, rather than into the national currency of each and every trading partner. For this kind of system to work smoothly, however, traders must be confident that the values of goods and services are relatively stable, and not subject to wild fluctuation. Because changing currency values affect the values of traded goods, independent of the quality of those goods or the real costs of producing them, individuals engaged in international trade also prefer that exchange rates not be subject to wild fluctuation. Thus, international trade rests squarely on a stable international monetary system. An international **monetary regime** is designed to help states manage their exchange rates, maintain their reserve currencies (or assets like gold) used as a common medium of exchange, and regulate the movement of international capital.

In July 1944, forty-four states met at Bretton Woods, New Hampshire, intent on creating an international monetary order that would promote economic and political stability. Specifically, they sought to institutionalize the strengths of the previous monetary system, while avoiding the weaknesses that led to its demise during the Great Depression. Prior to the Great Depression, a "gold standard" was in effect; most major national currencies could be exchanged for gold on demand. This helped to stabilize currency values, for currencies were pegged to a precious metal with intrinsic worth. But there was always the temptation to devalue the national currency by raising the price of gold in the hopes that this would encourage exports, which would then be cheaper to foreign consumers. Under normal conditions, states resisted this temptation in the interest of international financial stability, but during in the economic depression of the 1920s and 1930s, states succumbed and sought to stimulate domestic demand through currency depreciation. (The gold standard had been abandoned during World War I, but many states returned to it after the war.) There ensued a series of competitive devaluations that choked off international trade and deepened the global depression.

The monetary policies of states during the interwar period manifested a collective goods problem. Stable exchange rates were in all states' interests since they facilitated international trade and economic growth, yet each state was tempted to free ride by devaluing its currency. When the temptation became widespread during the global economic crisis, the collective good of monetary stability could not be provided. Prior to this period, in the context of stable exchange rates, trade was made that much easier because the British pound served as a common medium of exchange. Since Great Britain had been on the gold standard since the early nineteenth century, many countries also held reserves of British pounds, since they were "as good as gold." Most international economic transactions were conducted using pounds (much less cumbersome than using gold bullion), and this was possible as long as Britain could exchange gold for pounds on demand. But the British economy had weakened substantially by end of World War I. Although the pound was pegged to gold at its prewar price, its value was artificially high given the diminishing demand for British exports. Holders of British pounds preferred the gold; Britain's gold reserves were depleted, forcing it to end the currency's convertibility in 1931.[24]

In an effort to return to the financial stability of the gold-standard era, the agreement signed at Bretton Woods in 1944 fashioned a system of **fixed exchange rates.** The dollar would become the primary reserve asset (outside the communist economic

---

[24] For a classic discussion of this period, see Charles P. Kindleberger, *The World in Depression* (Berkeley: University of California Press, 1973). A useful and more detailed explanation of the international monetary system from 1870 through 1973 can be found in Paul R. Krugman and Maurice Obstfeld, *International Economics: Theory and Policy,* 4th ed. (Reading, Mass.: Addison-Wesley, 1997), chap. 18.

bloc), just as gold had been used in the nineteenth century and the British pound in combination with gold at the end of the nineteenth and beginning of the twentieth centuries. It was pegged at $35 per ounce of gold, and the firm commitment of the U.S. government to convert dollars into gold meant that now the dollar was as good as gold. The value of other currencies were fixed relative to the dollar, and states would hold reserves in the form of both gold and dollars (and other foreign currencies as well, once they too became convertible).

This fixed exchange-rate system was designed to provide the financial stability necessary to promote an expansion of international trade. It disciplined states' monetary policies. During the interwar period, inflation was rampant. Germany was the most extreme example: saddled with heavy war reparations, the German government simply printed money when it ran out, totally undermining the value of the German mark. While less profligate, other countries also printed money, particularly as a means of financing post–World War I reconstruction. However, under the Bretton Woods system, expanding the money supply to the point of undermining confidence in the national currency would encourage local investors to cash in their notes for dollars, since the dollar's value was more dependable. The state's dollar reserves would be depleted, making it difficult or impossible to maintain the fixed dollar exchange rate of its national currency, as required by the Bretton Woods agreement. (To "prop up" the national currency, the state's central bank uses its foreign exchange reserves to purchase the currency so as to contract the money supply, thereby making the currency that remains in circulation more valuable.) Nor was the U.S. central bank, the Federal Reserve, free from constraints. Expanding the U.S. money supply would diminish confidence in the dollar, leading to a depletion of U.S. gold stocks as foreign central banks cashed in their weakening dollars. Stemming the outflow of gold by raising its price was not an option for the Fed under Bretton Woods; the price of gold was fixed at $35 an ounce.

The Bretton Woods agreement established the International Monetary Fund (IMF). The IMF would help countries maintain their fixed exchange rates. The interwar experience taught observers that states would find it difficult to contract their money supplies for purposes of maintaining fixed exchange rates when doing so would have an adverse effect on economic growth and employment. The IMF, using a pool of foreign currency reserves contributed by member states, would make loans to states, allowing them to support the value of their currency during periods of economic difficulty. For states that needed a great deal of support, the IMF reserved the right to exercise some supervision over the borrower's economic policies, both monetary and fiscal — a stipulation known as **IMF conditionality.** The fixed exchange-rate regime was not overly rigid, however. Recalling Britain's experience after World War I, when the pound was overvalued relative to the global demand for British products, the architects of the IMF built in provisions whereby states facing similar circumstances could devalue their currencies to ease the adjustment process and prevent the depletion of international reserves. But, again, devaluation was not an option available to the United States under Bretton Woods. Strains on the new fixed exchange-rate system would be further eased by the creation of the International Bank for Reconstruction and Development (IBRD), or World Bank, which provided loans for postwar economic recovery, and direct U.S. assistance in the form of the Marshall Plan.

In reality, the constraints on the United States were not as limiting as those on other states under the Bretton Woods system. The United States did not need to maintain the dollar exchange rate, since all other currencies were pegged to the dollar. It only had to be willing provide foreign central banks with gold in return for dollars. But for a time, not only was the U.S. dollar as good as gold; it was better than gold. The price of gold was fixed, while the dollar (in the form of treasury bills) paid interest. Foreign central banks willingly accumulated dollars rather than cash them in with the Fed. In fact, a "Eurodollar" market emerged wherein European banks, as well as offshore branches of American banks, began lending their dollar deposits (beyond the reach of U.S. regulators). Confidence in the dollar did not last, though.

The second half of the 1960s saw a large increase U.S. government expenditures associated with Johnson administration's Great Society programs to reduce poverty and America's widening involvement in the Vietnam War. The resulting price inflation fed speculation that there needed to be a devaluation of the dollar relative to European currencies. Devaluation was not a simple matter for any country under the system of fixed exchange rates, but for the United States it was especially difficult because it required a coordinated and simultaneous *revaluation* of other currencies that were pegged to the dollar. Since revaluation would raise these countries' export prices compared to U.S. goods, cooperation was not forthcoming. Faced with continued depletion of U.S. gold stocks as confidence in the value of the dollar sunk — by now there was a "dollar glut," not enough American gold to cover the accumulation of dollars in foreign hands — the Nixon administration declared, in August 1971, that the United States would no longer exchange gold for dollars. The administration also imposed a 10 percent surcharge on import duties, to remain in effect until America's major trading partners agreed to revalue their currencies. As the result of an agreement reached at the Smithsonian Institution in Washington, D.C. in December, the surcharge was lifted and foreign currencies were revalued (by 8 percent, on average).

The Smithsonian realignment proved to be only a temporary reprise for the fixed exchange-rate system. The U.S. trade deficit continued to deteriorate and the Fed pursued an expansive monetary policy to finance U.S. government deficits. Both contributed to the feeling that the dollar was still overvalued. Massive selling of dollars in the foreign-exchange market in February 1973 brought the crisis to a head. The Nixon administration announced a unilateral 10 percent devaluation of the dollar, but that was not enough to stabilize the market. When the market opened on March 19, most European currencies and the Japanese yen were floating against the dollar. Bretton Woods had finally collapsed.[25]

The move to **floating exchange rates** in 1973 was meant as a transition to a new system of fixed rates, one that recognized the new, less lop-sided distribution of economic power within the OECD. During the October 1973 war between Israel and the Arab states, several member states of the Organization of Petroleum Exporting Countries (OPEC) showed their displeasure with American support of Israel by placing an embargo on oil exports to the United States (and the Netherlands, another supporter of

---

[25] For a detailed discussion of the events leading to the collapse of the fixed exchange-rate system, see John S. Odell, *U.S. International Monetary Policy: Markets, Power, and Ideas as Sources of Change* (Princeton, N.J.: Princeton University Press, 1982).

Israel). There was some speculation that embargo might be widened, causing the price of oil to be bid up as importing countries moved to secure future supplies. OPEC used its newfound leverage to increase oil prices further, and by the beginning of 1974 oil was selling for $12 a barrel, four times the market price just three months earlier. The oil shock helped to push industrialized economies, along with the economies of many non-oil LDCs, into recession. Global economic slowdown was brought on by across-the-board price increases driven by high energy costs. The combination of high prices and stagnating economic growth — until then, the two did not normally occur at the same time — led economists to coin a new term, "stagflation."

The oil shock sealed the fate of the fixed exchange-rate system. Dealing with domestic stagflation was a difficult task in itself; the imposition of exchange-rate targets as an additional chore for economic policy was no longer realistic. Most policymakers concluded that the process of adjusting to the oil shock was smoother in the context of floating exchange rates. The degree of stagnation and inflation was different for different countries, and their fiscal and monetary policies could be more closely tailored to their own domestic economic conditions. In addition, certain government-imposed controls on the movement of international capital, necessary to maintain exchange rates, were now lifted. This benefited LDCs by making it easier to borrow in international financial markets in order to sustain domestic spending programs and economic growth.

A system of floating exchange rates has operated since 1973. The most noteworthy exception is the European Monetary System (EMS), and of course the European Monetary Union that was set into place in January 1999 (we discuss both in the next chapter). During periods of global economic crisis, like the Asian financial meltdown of 1997, there have been calls to reconstitute what remains of the Bretton Woods system, particularly the practices of the IMF. So far, however, no multilateral arrangements have been constructed to take the place of Bretton Woods as a means of offsetting the fluctuations and uncertainties of today's international financial markets.

The Trade Regime

As with the monetary regime, the United States was the primary organizer and support behind the postwar system of liberal international trade. The view of a nondiscriminatory, multilateral, and market-based system was shared by the industrialized Western powers, in part as a reaction to the protectionism of the 1930s. Cooperation in the reduction of trade barriers, not protectionism, was the liberal view of trade.

Although the United States was willing to lead in this area also, the issues were much more complex because of the effects of trade on internal political issues. Although discussions on trade policy and arrangements began in 1943, the first element of the international trading order to take hold was the General Agreement on Tariffs and Trade (GATT) in 1947. Reflecting the liberal consensus, GATT was based on free trade and nondiscrimination, with the members agreeing to the most-favored-nation principle. Furthermore, GATT established rules aimed at reducing trade barriers and mediating trade disputes. The agreement included a plan to establish an International Trade Organization (ITO), which would help member states implement the principles of GATT much like the IMF functioned with respect to the monetary arrangement negotiated at Bretton Woods. The Truman administration considered the ITO charter too restrictive on U.S. policy and never submitted the treaty for ratification. Instead, GATT itself became institutionalized, with a secretariat, a director general, and staff to handle the work relating to trade negotiations.

GATT was the central feature of the world trade regime (outside the communist bloc), and worked very well for the developed countries as quotas and other trade barriers were removed and trade was encouraged. Much of the postwar prosperity derived from this increase in trade. Trade talks were conducted continuously under the auspices of GATT in what became referred to as trade "rounds" (summarized in Table 13.2). A high point of trade cooperation through GATT were the tariff reductions achieved during the Kennedy Round of negotiations (named after President Kennedy, during whose term the talks began), which was concluded in 1967. After this point, however, all the factors that caused strains in the monetary regime also brought trouble to trade.

Inflation and the increasing interdependence of trade relations caused political discontent in certain economic sectors within countries that were being hurt by the competition of foreign goods. Within each country there were political pressures from segments of society seeking protection from foreign competition. The problems emerging in monetary relations also became trade problems, especially as European and

TABLE 13.2   GATT Trade Rounds

Years	Primary Location	Called	Issues	Participants
1947	Geneva	Tariffs		23
1949	Annecy, France	Tariffs		13
1950–1951	Torquay, England	Tariffs		38
1956	Geneva	Tariffs		26
1960–1961	Geneva	Dillon Round	Tariffs	26
1964–1967	Geneva	Kennedy Round	Tariffs, Dumping	62
1973–1979	Geneva	Tokyo Round	Tariffs, Nontariff Barriers	102
1986–1993	Geneva	Uruguay Round	Tariffs, Nontariff Barriers, Trade in Services, Intellectual Property, Textiles, Agriculture, WTO Created	123

Source: World Trade Organization, "About the WTO," January 1998 [cited December 27, 1998]; available at <http://www.wto.org/about/facts4.htm>.

Japanese goods came to rival U.S. goods and helped lead to U.S. balance-of-trade deficits. The United States went from a trade surplus of $3.8 billion in 1967 to a deficit of $6.4 billion in 1972.[26] Some European actions in particular were highly preferential or protectionist, especially in the EC's Common Agricultural Policy. Japanese restrictions on imports of U.S. agricultural products and U.S. restrictions on imports of Japanese textiles and electronics became continuing irritants. The United States was no longer able or willing to shoulder the burden of the free trade regime.

From 1967 onward, pressures for trade protection and discrimination increased in the United States, Europe, and Japan. The loss of cheap oil as an energy source and, with wage increases, a loss of cheap labor contributed to the decline in competitiveness that fed these demands. The August 1971 "Nixon shock" included what would become a continuing American insistence on changes in European and Japanese trade practices. By 1973 it was clear that a new international trading order had to be established. In September representatives of about one hundred states convened in Tokyo to launch a new round of trade negotiations. The Tokyo Round, lasting until 1979, took up some of the complex issues of international trade not addressed in previous rounds, including the nontariff barriers like import licensing and customs valuations. The results were mixed. There were agreements to dismantle some NTBs, but in many cases only the industrialized participants promised to adhere to the arrangements (so they were called "codes" rather than agreements).

A new round of talks was launched in Punta del Este, Uruguay, in September 1986. The agenda was very ambitious, including issues left unsettled at the conclusion of the Tokyo Round, as well as new ones like trade in services, intellectual property rights, and North-South trade. The Uruguay Round concluded in 1994 with a trade accord signed in Marrakesh, Morocco. It took three and a half years longer than intended, but its achievements were substantial. First, in the area of market access, participants were aiming for a one-third reduction in tariffs on average; the final agreement reduced them by almost 40 percent. (Figure 13.2 shows the sixty-year trend in tariff reduction among industrialized countries.) GATT was extended to include agreements on textiles, agriculture, dumping, export subsidies, licensing procedures, and various technical barriers to trade. Second, while GATT had been directed mainly at the trade in goods, it was now supplemented by a General Agreement on Trade in Services (GATS) and an Agreement on Trade Related Aspects of Intellectual Property Rights (TRIPs), which covered patents, trademarks, copyright, product designs, and so on.

Finally, the Uruguay Round established the World Trade Organization (WTO) — a belated but in the end probably more effective international organization than what was envisioned for the ITO in 1948. According to the United States Information Service,

> the WTO will help to resolve the "free rider" problem in the world trading system, since membership is only available to countries which were contracting parties to the GATT, agree to adhere to the Uruguay Round Agreements, and submit schedules of

---

[26] Council of Economic Advisors, *Economic Report of the President* (Washington, D.C.: U.S. Government Printing Office, 1998), Table B-103, p. 398.

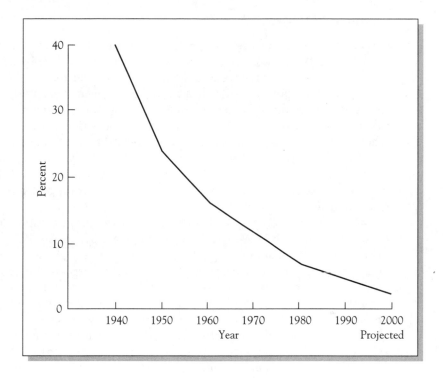

FIGURE 13.2   Average Tariffs of Industrial Countries

Source: U.S. Government Office of the U.S. Trade Representative.

market access commitments for goods and services. This eliminates the shortcomings of the GATT system in which, for example, only a handful of countries voluntarily adhered to the principles on subsidies under the 1979 Tokyo Round Agreement.[27]

The WTO is located in Geneva, and consists of a permanent staff of about 500 with a 1998 annual budget of $80 million. It is an IGO; its membership consists of over 130 nation-states that agree to abide by the terms of the WTO's charter, the Marrakesh Agreement. In a manner similar to the UN and other IGOs, the WTO provides a forum for states to come together to address issues relating to trade. It monitors compliance with the rules and procedures that emerged from the Uruguay Round of trade talks, and serves as a third party to settle trade disputes between states. In short, it institutionalized the world trade regime, which had been almost fifty years in the making since the signing of GATT in 1947.

---

[27] United States Information Service, Geneva, "The World Trade Organization," *Briefing Book on International Organizations in Geneva,* n.d. [cited December 27, 1998]; The Structure of the WTO; available at <http://www3.itu.int/missions/US/bb/wto.html>.

Order or Disorder?

Although analysts have debated the extent of America's economic decline since the end of World War II, no one disputes the fact that the United States is not the unrivaled economic powerhouse it once was. It still plays the lead role on the world economic stage, but the supporting cast, both state and nonstate actors, have much more significant roles than before. Whether the United States is still a hegemon, or whether instead the international political economy has entered a period "after hegemony," as one scholar puts it, depends on how that concept is defined.[28] Either way, hegemonic stability theory suggests that with the decline of hegemony comes an increase in international economic and monetary instability. The disorderliness of the international political economy since the mid-1970s is precisely what the realist perspective would have predicted.

The postwar monetary and trade regimes were both complicated by economic recovery and growth in Western Europe and Japan. By the late 1970s it was clear that the U.S. economy could no longer be the sole engine of worldwide economic growth. Japan and Germany, in particular, had to share in the responsibilities, and the required coordination of economic policies has often been a source of friction among the leading industrialized countries.[29] One recurring pattern has been for the United States to pressure Japan and Germany to pursue expansionary policies to stimulate economic growth, while the latter resist for fear of excessive domestic inflation. Beginning in 1979, the Fed pursued a restrictive monetary policy in order to reduce U.S. inflation, which also caused a sharp appreciation of the dollar. But the rising costs of American imports, combined with rising oil prices following the second oil shock in 1979, led to price inflation abroad, thus prompting foreign central banks to pursue restrictive monetary policies as well. (The United States was said to be "exporting" its inflation.) That led to a global economic recession from 1981 to 1983, the worst since the Great Depression of the 1930s.

Poor economic performance in the 1980s, along with the mounting U.S. trade deficits that accompanied an appreciation of the dollar (see Figure 13.3), translated into trade surpluses for America's major trading partners. Japan became America's largest creditor, and the trade disputes between the two countries have become major issues of contention that will not be solved easily or soon. It was during the 1980s that imported Japanese cars began to account for a substantial share of the North American market. Although American consumers now tend to take the prevalence of Japanese automobiles in the marketplace for granted, the initial shift in the automobile market engendered feelings of resentment among American workers, feelings frequently tinged with elements of racism. Such attitudes resurfaced when Japanese companies began

---

[28] Keohane, *After Hegemony*. See also Bruce Russett, "The Mysterious Case of Vanishing Hegemony; or, Is Mark Twain Really Dead?" *International Organization* 39 (1985): pp. 207–231; and Susan Strange, "The Persistent Myth of Lost Hegemony" *International Organization* 41 (1987): pp. 551–574.

[29] The importance of Germany and Japan in the world economy was widely recognized at the 1978 Bonn Summit. See Robert Putnam and C. Randall Henning, "The Bonn Summit of 1978: A Study in Coordination," in Richard N. Cooper et al., *Can Nations Agree? Issues in International Economic Cooperation* (Washington, D.C.: Brookings Institution, 1989).

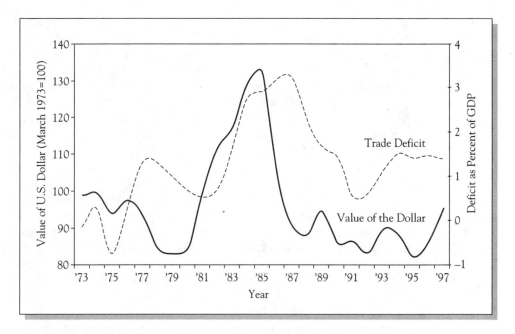

FIGURE 13.3   Value of the U.S. Dollar and the U.S. Trade Deficit, 1973–1997

Note: The graph shows the movement in the multilateral trade-weighted value of the dollar (left scale) and the trade deficit in goods and services as a share of gross domestic product (GDP) (right scale).

Source: Data are from Council of Economic Advisors, *Economic Report of the President* (Washington, D.C.: U.S. Government Printing Office, 1998), Tables B-110, B-103.

investing in American real estate and the entertainment industry. In 1989, for example, Mitsubishi acquired 80 percent of New York's Rockefeller Center; at about the same time, Sony purchased Columbia Pictures and Matsushita bought MCA/Universal — both considered icons of American popular culture. Such developments were viewed with alarm by many Americans on both sides of the political spectrum.[30]

The Japanese economic miracle was part of an economic resurgence and growth along the whole Pacific Rim, especially in the Newly Industrializing Countries (NICs) of Taiwan, South Korea, Singapore, and Hong Kong (also known as the "Asian Tigers"). During the 1980s the Pacific Rim countries replaced Western Europe as the major trading partners of the United States — and mostly with trade surpluses. The Asian NICs' currencies depreciated almost as fast as the dollar, maintaining these

---

[30] For a penetrating study of the public discourse during this period, see Gearóid Ó Tuathail, "Japan as Threat: Geo-economic Discourses on the USA-Japan Relationship in US Civil Society, 1987–91," in Colin H. Williams, ed., *The Political Geography of the New World Order* (New York: Belhaven, 1993), pp. 181–209.

countries' competitiveness and allowing them to export twice as much to the United States as they imported from it. Meanwhile, rapid increases in Japanese productivity, and continuing Japanese informal as well as official restrictions on imports of goods and services, enabled Japan to export three times as much to the United States as it imported. The Pacific Rim countries of Brunei, Indonesia, Malaysia, the Philippines, Singapore, Thailand, and now Vietnam are members of the Association of South East Asian Nations (ASEAN). ASEAN has facilitated economic cooperation among its members and represents yet another source of economic growth in the Pacific Rim.[31]

The 1980s saw an increase in protectionist sentiments in the United States. In 1988, the U.S. Congress passed the Omnibus Trade and Competitiveness Act, which included a provision known as "Super 301" requiring that the president identify states engaging in unfair trade practices and subject to possible retaliation. As of June 1998, the U.S. trade representative had initiated fifty investigations into the practices of U.S. trade partners in accordance with Super 301, about one-third of them directed at Japan or members of the European Union.[32] The bill also authorized a review of foreign direct investment in the United States for potential threats to national security. The Clinton administration has been especially assertive in its efforts to break down remaining trade and investment barriers, both in its bilateral economic policies and in multilateral forums like GATT and the WTO.

The rise of China as a major economic power has complicated matters further. Chinese controls on imports and foreign investment are far more restrictive than Japan's. In 1996, the U.S. merchandise trade deficit with China was $40 billion; when trade in services is included, the 1996 deficit exceeded the U.S. deficit with Japan. Although the United States has welcomed China's integration into the world economy, initiated in the late 1970s, China's domestic market is less accessible than any other on the Pacific Rim. In 1996 the average tariff rate applied by the eighteen Asia-Pacific Economic Cooperation (APEC) member states was 9 percent, while China's average tariff was 23 percent (though down from 40 percent in 1988).[33] Many Chinese firms have been accused of "pirating" computer software, audio recordings, and other high-tech goods protected by copyrights and patents in the West — not only reducing Chinese demand for U.S. imports of these goods, but even allowing Chinese firms to compete sharply with the original producers in Asian export markets. After very hard bargaining, in February 1995 China agreed to stop these abuses, but its record of compliance has been mixed. If China is to join the WTO, something it very much wants to do, it's trade poli-

---

[31] See Steve Chan, *East Asian Dynamism: Growth, Order, and Security in the Pacific Region,* 2nd ed. (Boulder, Colo.: Westview, 1993). The East Asian model of economic growth is touted by James Fallows in *Looking at the Sun: The Rise of the New East Asian Economic and Political System* (New York: Pantheon, 1994). The Asian economic crisis of 1997–1998 did much to deflate that economic model, but for earlier critiques see Paul Krugman, "The Myth of Asia's Miracle," *Foreign Affairs* 73, 6 (November/December 1994): pp. 62–78; and Bill Emmott, *Japanophobia: The Myth of the Invincible Japanese* (New York: Times Books, 1994).

[32] Based on a listing of investigations provided by the United States Trade Representative, "Section 301 Table of Cases," June 4, 1998 [cited January 4, 1999]; available at <http://www.ustr.gov/reports/301report/act301.htm>. Super 301 was a revision of section 301 of the 1974 Trade Act. There have been almost 120 investigation initiated since 1975.

[33] Council of Economic Advisors, *Economic Report of the President,* table 7.1, p. 232.

cies will have to be brought in line with the existing rules of the multilateral trade regime. WTO membership may also necessitate some economic restructuring, and a degree of economic "transparency" — scrutiny of its trade policies and practices — that the Chinese government has not been comfortable with heretofore.

As its predominance in the world economy has waned, the United States has looked to its major partners (the EU and Japan) to carry more of the burdens, both in maintaining the trading system and in contributing to the costs of military security (as in the Gulf War). None is willing or able to do the job alone, and it is not clear even what a "fair share" would be. The Japanese, for example, resist spending more directly on defense. They insist that by their capital investment in LDCs and their investments in the United States, in effect subsidizing the federal budget while the United States spent so much on defense, they are doing their share. If U.S. allies are to share in the effort to maintain and strengthen international monetary and trade regimes, they will do so increasingly on their own terms and in their own ways.

U.S. leadership in world economic affairs was somewhat enhanced in the latter half of the 1990s, however. The American economy was performing well and after some difficult restructuring American companies had become much more competitive in the global marketplace. At the same time, the Asian economic crisis raised doubts about the Japanese model of economic development, emulated elsewhere in East and Southeast Asia, boosting the confidence of proponents of American-style free-market capitalism. Moreover, the United States has been called upon repeatedly to help rescue countries in economic trouble. It spearheaded and contributed substantial funds to the bailouts of Mexico in 1994, as well as of South Korea, Russia, and Brazil in 1998 — a sign that American leadership, if not hegemony, is alive and well in the international political economy.

American economic resurgence notwithstanding, the United States must learn new patterns of economic diplomacy. Many countries of the Pacific Rim have pursued a model of state-centered capitalism different from that of the United States. Their domestic markets, investment efforts, and export policies are characterized by a partnership between their state bureaucracies and private corporations. Lessons learned from the recent Asian economic crisis are not likely to completely undo economic practices reinforced by three decades of often stellar economic performance. The Asian countries, as well as those of continental Western Europe, traditionally have been more comfortable with protectionism than have the British and Americans. They have often pursued policies of **strategic trade,** whereby the state promotes certain export industries by providing government subsidies or other forms of assistance.[34] While the current trend seems to be in the direction of openness, it is not clear whether the structures of international free trade can be retained or whether barriers will again emerge during periods of global economic difficulty. The possibility that the world economy may split into competing protectionist blocs (a German-led Europe, a Japanese-led Asia, and an American-led Western Hemisphere) also cannot be ignored.

Whether we see order or disorder in international political-economic relations often depends on whether we are inclined to see the glass as half-full or half-empty.

---

[34] For a thorough discussion of strategic trade policy in the OECD, see Krugman and Obstfeld, *International Economics,* chap. 11.

The decline of U.S. economic might relative to other countries was inevitable. The post–World War II economies of Europe and Japan could not remain in tatters indefinitely, and industrialization was bound to be successful in many developing countries, including the newly independent ones. The United States itself actively promoted economic reconstruction and development; its diminishing capacity to steer global economic affairs in many ways testifies to the success of U.S. policy, not failure. There is, to be sure, more uncertainty and instability in the international monetary system, and the bickering over trade practices is frequently shrill. Such developments have accompanied the decline of American hegemony, but how could it have been any different?

What most liberals find noteworthy is the extent of cooperation that has transpired in international economic relations even in the absence of a single hegemonic power. States have cooperated despite the temptations to free ride, or perhaps because free riding is no longer feasible without a hegemon to carry the load. While America's economic clout is not what it once was, wielding it has become less necessary as Europe and Japan have become more accustomed to sharing leadership responsibilities in helping to manage global economic stability. The annual economic summit meeting of the Group of Five (G5) — then the G7, and now the G8 — beginning in 1975 epitomizes the recognition that, although the United States is often treated as first among equals, leadership in the contemporary world economy is too much for one state and must be shared. The frequent meetings of the Trade Ministers' Quadrilateral (the "Quad"; the United States, Canada, Japan, and the European Union) since 1982 are another indication of an increasingly institutionalized joint leadership that has emerged "after hegemony." The collaboration and economic policy coordination required to bring an element of stability to a global economic system consisting of almost 200 trading states, 45,000 multinational corporations, and more than $1.5 trillion in currency trading per day would seem unattainable on its face. That government ministers and central bankers ever meet with success is impressive indeed.

The commitment to free trade on the part of an ever-increasing number of states, in spite of the periodic lapses into protectionism, undergirds the considerable order we find in world politics today. It gave rise to GATT after World War II and ultimately transformed GATT into the WTO, an international organization in its own right. Free trade thrives under conditions of monetary stability, and the Bretton Woods regime provided that for two and a half decades before the inevitable redistribution of economic power forced its collapse. The commitment to monetary stability remains, as does the IMF, a core Bretton Woods institution, even though the current monetary regime allows exchange rates to float. How to achieve monetary stability after Bretton Woods continues to be an issue of contention. Some Asian leaders, as well as many policy analysts in Europe, have advocated the use of capital controls to prevent the sort of speculative attacks that gave rise to the Asian financial crisis, while the United States continues to oppose restrictions on the free movement of capital. It is too early to tell whether these differences will be narrowed to the point of making possible a new, post–Bretton Woods monetary regime.[35]

---

[35] See Robert Wade and Frank Veneroso, "The Gathering World Slump and the Battle over Capital Controls," *New Left Review* 231 (September/October 1998): pp. 13–42; see also Benjamin Cohen, *The Geography of Money* (Ithaca, N.Y.: Cornell University Press, 1998).

The degree of free trade and monetary stability is uneven worldwide. States have found that chiseling away at trade barriers and stabilizing exchange rates is easier when efforts are concentrated among fewer countries at roughly similar levels of economic development; collective goods are less likely to be undermined by free riding when restricted to small groups. One of the consequences has been the formation of trade blocs, a topic we take up in the next chapter.

14

Regional Economic Integration and Globalization

The European Union

Many state leaders have concluded that larger economic entities typically fare better in the modern world economy than smaller ones. Large domestic markets provide the demand necessary to support diverse industrial and service sectors. What is more, domestic demand is a great deal more dependable and predictable than the demand for exports, which is subject to the vagaries of the international political economy, like protectionism and monetary instability. Economic self-sufficiency, or autarky, is really not an option in the contemporary international system, but large and diverse economies stand a better chance of weathering the effects of international economic crises. Large domestic markets provide no guarantees, of course; economic (and political) mismanagement can just as easily send a large economy into a tailspin as a small one. But small and specialized economies, even if well-managed, can be overwhelmed by international economic forces beyond the control of state leaders or other domestic economic actors.

There may be no better single explanation for the vitality and resilience of the U.S. economy than its large domestic markets. China has become a major economic force in world affairs because of the sheer size of its economy. Its vast population has permitted industrialization even in relative isolation from the world economy, and now with increasing openness it presents potentially huge markets for foreign imports. The stake that industrialized countries have in seeing Russia avert economic collapse — quite aside from the threat of rogue military elements — is similar: a prosperous Russian population could become a substantial source of demand for goods and services produced abroad. As we discussed in Chapter 5, natural endowments count for much when it comes to state power; large populations mean large markets, and large markets promote industrialization and economic strength.

The immediate goal of **economic integration** is the creation of a single market out of a number of separate markets previously defined by national boundaries. Multilateral economic cooperation and policy coordination is designed to enable the free movement of goods and services, labor, and capital across state borders, which will promote economic competitiveness and prosperity in the region. The most successful effort to date has been the creation of what is now called the European Union (EU). In this chapter we discuss the evolution of the EU as well as the emergence of other economic blocs like the North American Free Trade Area (NAFTA). We also consider the increasingly transnational character of economic activities, such as those of multinational firms, especially the degree to which they are transforming the nature of world politics. In such developments many observers see a substantial whittling away of state sovereignty and the beginning of the end of the Westphalian state system.

From Rome to Maastricht

Recall from our discussion in Chapter 11 that the visionaries of a united Europe thought that this was the best way to achieve peace in a region racked by two continent-wide wars in three decades. Functionalists like David Mitrany and Jean Monnet reasoned that the interdependencies that characterized Europe's present level of social and economic development gave rise to technical problems and management tasks that were best handled by specialists, not politicians. As the web of transnational problem-solving personnel and procedures grew and brought more and more benefits to European states, not only would state leaders have less to fight about, they would also think twice about trampling these transnational linkages on their way to yet another European war.

The first step along the path to European unification was the formation of the European Coal and Steel Community in 1951 to coordinate coal and steel production by France, West Germany, Belgium, Luxembourg, the Netherlands, and Italy — the "Six," or as the community expanded, the "Inner Six."[1] The Six were so encouraged by

---

[1] A good introduction to the historical evolution of the European Union and its current functions and policies is David Wood and Birol Yeşilada, *The Emerging European Union* (New York: Longman, 1996). See also Clive Archer, *Organizing Europe: The Institutions of Integration* (London: Arnold, 1994).

the success of the ECSC that they sought to deepen their collaboration. They agreed to form the European Defense Community (EDC) in 1952. Both Europeans and Americans had come to the conclusion that the military security of Western Europe could not be guaranteed unless West Germany could be rearmed. Germany at this time was still occupied, by the United States, Britain, and France in the western zone and by the Soviet Union in the eastern zone; it had no army and no control over its foreign policy. World War II was very fresh in the Europeans' memories, and most remained wary of German militarism. The EDC, therefore, was seen as a way to harness German personnel and industrial strength to the common defense. It also would have checked German militarism by uniting all the member states' armies under a single commissariat. However, the EDC Treaty, after ratified by five of the Six, was defeated by the French Assembly in 1954. It was shelved after that, along with a draft treaty establishing a European Political Community (EPC).

The designs for a defense and political community were too ambitious for Europe at this time. Not enough Europeans (especially the French) were ready to give up such sweeping powers to a supranational institution. In retrospect, this is not surprising; the functionalist notion of "spillover" suggested a piecemeal process of European unification. The **Treaties of Rome,** establishing the European Atomic Energy Community (Euratom) and the European Economic Community (EEC) and signed by the Six in 1957, were more consistent with this idea of gradualism. Still, Euratom was only modestly effective, since atomic energy was intertwined with matters of national security and Europeans (again, especially the French) were reluctant to surrender much sovereignty in this regard. The EEC was quite successful, however. The Six were to be constituted as a *customs union,* meaning that they were to first eliminate all tariffs between them and then adopt a common set of tariffs on imports from countries outside the community. The customs union was complete in 1968, and by then the ECSC, Euratom, and the EEC had been merged and would become known as the European Community (EC).

Britain viewed early moves toward European integration with considerable skepticism, and even today, as a full member of the EU, tends to remain somewhat aloof relative to continental members.[2] As the Six were negotiating what would become the Treaties of Rome, Britain was pushing for the creation of a *free trade area,* whereby tariffs within the community would be dismantled, but without common tariffs imposed on imports from outside the community as called for by a customs union. The British were partly concerned that joining the customs union would interfere in the special relationships the country had with both the United States and members of the British Commonwealth. But the Six rejected the British plan, at which point the British approached Austria, Denmark, Norway, Portugal, Sweden, and Switzerland. These seven countries formed the European Free Trade Area (EFTA) in 1960. When Britain finally did apply for EC membership its entry was vetoed in 1963 by France. Britain reapplied in 1967, along with Ireland, Denmark, and Norway, and in 1973 the EC was expanded to nine members (Norwegian membership was defeated at the polls).

---

[2] Stephen George, *An Awkward Partner: Britain in the European Community* (New York: Oxford University Press, 1990).

In the late 1970s, Greece, Spain, and Portugal applied for EU membership; Greece was admitted in 1981, Spain and Portugal in 1986. Actually, aside from expanding the size of the EC, the process of economic integration slowed during the 1970s and early 1980s. European economies were plagued by rising inflation, increasing unemployment, and slow growth — an economic malaise that would come to be called "Eurosclerosis" because many felt it was due to welfare-state legislation and market rigidities. Beyond achieving a customs union, the movement toward European unification as laid out in the Rome treaties seemed dead in the water. The treaty establishing the economic community called for a Common Agricultural Policy (CAP), and although that was in place by the late 1960s, it was a source of contention within the EC as well as between the EC and countries outside the community, particularly the United States. The CAP basically entailed protecting European farmers from external competition through subsidies and price supports while fostering economic interdependence among the Six. Within the EC, tensions arose because countries like Germany, where agricultural exports were less important to economic well-being, were subsidizing agricultural production in countries where the export of farm products was more important, like France, and later Ireland, Greece, Spain, and Portugal. The tensions between the EC and large agricultural producers like the United States arose because American farmers were less able to compete in European markets as a result of European protectionism.[3]

After signing the Treaties of Rome, the Six were often referred to as the "Common Market." This was something of a misnomer, for although the Six did intend to form a *common market* — whereby barriers to the free movement of labor and capital are removed, along with remaining nontariff barriers to trade in goods — little progress had been made even by the mid 1980s. But with the signing of the **Single European Act** (SEA) in 1986, the creation of a common market became the EC's first priority. The Europeans were increasingly of the view that in order to compete effectively with large American and Japanese firms, European industries needed to consolidate, and this was not possible as long as there were restrictions on the flow of European capital and labor within the EC. The SEA not only specified in some detail the measures that must be undertaken in order to create a single European market, it set as its target date the end of 1992 — and the project became known as *Europe 1992*. An important element of the project was a concrete plan for achieving European *monetary union*. Monetary union had long been an element in the grand plan of European unification, but the SEA now took up the question of implementation: the establishment of a central banking system and the introduction of a single European currency. We return to a discussion of monetary union later in the chapter.

The SEA breathed new life into the process of European unification; the pessimism that accompanied Eurosclerosis gave way to Euro-optimism. Member states focused their efforts on the steps required to achieve a common market in accordance with *Europe 1992*. They also began seriously negotiating the stages that the EC would have to pass through in order to enter into economic and monetary union, an especially

---

[3] Fiona Butler, "The EC's Common Agricultural Policy (CAP)," in Juliet Lodge, ed., *The European Community and the Challenge of the Future*, 2nd ed. (New York: St. Martin's, 1993), pp. 112–130.

sensitive issue since this involves surrendering sovereignty over the state's monetary policy. Monetary policy can have a significant effect on national economic performance and therefore, in European democracies, on a sitting government's prospects at election time. Also on the agenda was political union. From 1989, with the fall of the Berlin Wall, West and East Germany were moving toward reunification. Fearful that a united Germany would wield too much influence on the continent, particularly in Eastern Europe, France and Britain eventually agreed that the EC should be strengthened through institutional reforms and movement toward a common foreign policy.

In 1992, the twelve EC foreign ministers signed the far-reaching Treaty on European Union in the city of Maastricht, the Netherlands. Because national sovereignty was at stake in the agreements on both monetary union and the common foreign and defense policy, ratification of the **Maastricht treaty** proved more difficult than state leaders expected. During the negotiations, Britain had insisted on the right not to participate in certain aspects of what was now formally dubbed the Economic and Monetary Union (EMU), as well as the Social Charter, which provided for the standardization of social policy and workers' rights essential to a single European labor market. Popular opposition elsewhere in the EC was mobilized only after the Maastricht treaty was signed. Danish voters said no to the treaty in a 1992 referendum; they approved the treaty only after it was stipulated that Denmark, too, could opt out of certain provisions. The French approved the treaty by the narrowest of margins, while domestic legal haggling prevented German ratification until the end of 1993.[4] Finally, however, the Maastricht treaty went into effect and the EC officially became the EU.

With the addition of Austria, Finland, and Sweden to its ranks in 1995, the EU grew to its current size of fifteen. (Norway again applied for membership in 1992 and was again admitted to the community, but in a 1994 referendum Norwegian voters again disapproved.) Cyprus and Malta applied for membership in 1990, Hungary and Poland in 1994, and Bulgaria, Estonia, Latvia, Lithuania, Romania, and Slovakia in 1995. Turkey applied to join in 1987 and entered into a customs union with the EU in 1996. Thus, the evolution of the EU has consisted of *deepening* — tighter integration on the way to economic, monetary, and some forms of political union — as well as *widening*, in terms of expanded membership. These trends are not mutually reinforcing. Integration works best among a homogenous set of economies; the addition of new members, often poorer and less industrialized, has required extra provisions and more complex negotiations, thereby slowing somewhat the deepening process. Widening also complicates the process of political unification, as far as it goes. The EU's inability to present a truly united front in response to developments in former Yugoslavia, for example, suggests that there will be some tough hurdles to be cleared if the EU is to maintain coherent and consistent foreign policy.

Today's EU is said to be supported by three "pillars." The first, somewhat confusingly referred to as the European Community pillar, consists of all the arrangements that came before the Maastricht treaty — those established by the ECSC and Rome

---

[4] See Alan W. Cafruny and Carl Lankowski, eds., *Europe's Ambiguous Unity: Conflict and Consensus in the Post-Maastricht Era* (Boulder, Colo.: Rienner, 1997).

treaties, as amended by the SEA — plus post-Maastricht provisions regarding the common market, economic and monetary union, and institutional reform. The second pillar, the Common Foreign and Security Policy (CFSP), calls on member states to safeguard their common values and independence, to strengthen their individual and collective security, and to promote democratic governance and respect for human rights "by gradually implementing . . . joint action in the areas in which the Member States have important interests in common" and by "refrain[ing] from any action which is contrary to the interests of the Union or likely to impair its effectiveness as a cohesive force in international relations."[5] With the demise of the Soviet threat, those areas of common interests have indeed been hard to identify, at least in practice. At the same time, post–cold war instabilities in Europe and elsewhere, along with uncertainties about U.S. defense commitments, have made progress on CFSP appear even more urgent. Since Maastricht, most CFSP-related efforts have been channeled through the Western European Union (WEU), a collective defense organization formed in 1954 but otherwise overshadowed by NATO. The Amsterdam Treaty, signed in 1997, is an attempt to strengthen the CFSP pillar, including the EU's capacity to embark on joint military action. The third pillar of the European Union is Justice and Home Affairs (JHA). Asylum, immigration, antiterrorism, and drug interdiction fall into this realm of cooperation. Such matters require coordinated policies given the free movement of people within the EU, a component of the EC pillar.[6]

Institutions of the European Union

The institutional structure of European Union is composed of five main governing bodies: Council of Ministers, Commission, Parliament, Court of Justice, and Court of Auditors (see Figure 14.1). The Council of Ministers, the Commission, and, increasingly, the Parliament constitute the primary engine for policymaking in the EU, while the two courts serve judicial and oversight functions. The leaders of member states also meet periodically as the European Council. Another institution, the European Central Bank, is the EU's monetary authority and, like the central banks in each of the member states, its activities remain relatively independent from the dictates or scrutiny of EU political authorities.

The *Council of Ministers* is the EU's ultimate law-making authority. Its fifteen members come from each member state, and the ministers who comprise the Council depend on the issue under discussion. Foreign ministers come together to address the CFSP as well as more general matters, agricultural ministers address farm policy, economic and finance ministers take up monetary affairs, and so on. Member states have

---

[5] Treaty on European Union, Title V, Article J.1; available at <http://europa.eu.int/abc/obj/treaties/en/entoc01.htm>.

[6] For more thorough discussions of the second and third pillars of the EU, see David Garnham, "European Defense Cooperation," in Dale L. Smith and James Lee Ray, eds., *The 1992 Project and the Future of Integration in Europe* (New York: M. E. Sharpe, 1993), pp. 198–216; and Juliet Lodge, "Internal Security and Judicial Cooperation," in Lodge, *The European Community and the Challenge of the Future*, pp. 315–339.

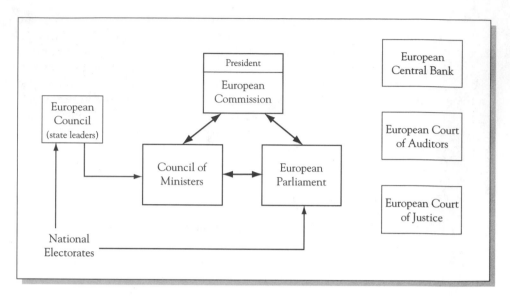

FIGURE 14.1   Major Institutions of the European Union

different numbers of votes (ranging from two for Luxembourg to ten each for France, Germany, Italy, and the UK) and most decisions in the Council require a "qualified majority" of votes (more than 70 percent of the total). Decisions on some matters, like EU membership and taxation, require unanimity. Unanimity is also required on issues relating to the CFSP, but up to five member states may "constructively abstain" from those votes. The official name for the Council of Ministers is the Council of the European Union — not to be confused with the European Council, which is comprised of state leaders along with the President of the Commission. Meetings of the European Council are essentially summit gatherings and have provided the overall direction for the EU's evolution.

The *European Commission* is the EU's main organ for policy proposal and implementation. There are twenty commissioners (two from France, Germany, Italy, the United Kingdom, and Spain, and one from each of the other member states), one of whom serves as Commission president. Unlike the Council of Ministers, the Commission's first loyalty is to the European Union itself, making this body and its staff of 15,000 a favorite target of resentment and ridicule — unresponsive, faceless "Eurocrats" residing in Brussels, far removed from the concerns of ordinary citizens. Member states agree to be bound by rulings of the Commission, which gives it some measure of *supranational* authority, and is another source of resentment among those concerned that states are unwisely abdicating their sovereign powers and responsibilities. The Commission president, a member of the European Council, can be very influential among European statesmen. For example, Jacques Delors, president from 1985 to 1995, played a central role in formulating the set of provisions that were ultimately encompassed in the Maastricht treaty, including the plan for monetary union.

The *European Parliament*, which convenes in Strasbourg, is also involved in the policymaking process. Although its powers have traditionally been quite limited, the Maastricht and Amsterdam treaties enhanced its role substantially. On many issues, the EU now uses a "co-decision" procedure whereby the Parliament may amend Commission proposals to the Council of Ministers, amend or reject positions taken by the Council, and confer with the Council and Commission in "conciliation committees" when there are lingering differences in draft legislation. A decision-making procedure that does not include Parliamentary veto power (called the "cooperation" procedure) still operates in matters relating to economic and monetary union. There are 626 members of the European Parliament, chosen in community-wide elections and serving five-year terms. Political parties and voting blocs cut across national boundaries; in the 1994–1999 Parliament, the two largest blocs of seats were held by the European Socialists (214 seats) and the European People's Party, a Christian-Democratic group (181 seats).

The *European Court of Justice* (ECJ) and the *Court of Auditors* are both located in Luxembourg. Both consist of fifteen officials, one from each EU member state. The ECJ provides authoritative interpretations of the community's treaties and ensures that they are properly applied by EU institutions and member states. Its judgments are binding, and thus in regard to member states it represents another source of supranational authority in the EU. Since 1989 the ECJ has been assisted by "The Court of First Instance," which hears complaints brought by individuals and companies against EU institutions. This is in marked contrast to UN Court of Justice, where litigants have traditionally been nation-states. The Court of Auditors is the EU's financial watchdog. It sees to it that EU expenditures are in accordance with certain budgetary rules and regulations, and its operations are intended to reassure European taxpayers.[7]

Institutionally, the EU is a complex of intergovernmental and supranational organizations — a combination that is said to involve **pooled sovereignty.** The Commission, the Court, and now the Parliament (through the co-decision procedure) can take actions that are binding on member states. However, states retain their sovereignty through the European Council, which directs the EU's evolution, and through the institutional powers of the Council of Ministers. As two scholars have pointed out, "In the EU, all bodies, whether intergovernmental or supranational, are collective actors, but the intergovernmental bodies have the upper hand."[8]

Monetary Union

For those Europeans concerned about the loss of national sovereignty, the move toward monetary union is especially ominous. The idea of monetary union had been seriously contemplated since the late 1960s. State leaders were beginning to view a united Europe as a potential counterweight to the United States on global financial issues, especially since U.S. policy was raising questions about the country's ability

---

[7] For a review of theory and research pertaining to the ECJ, see Walter Mattli and Anne-Marie Slaughter, "Revisiting the European Court of Justice," *International Organization* 52, 1 (Winter 1998): pp. 177–209.

[8] Wood and Yeşilada, *The Emerging European Union*, p. 2.

to sustain its position in the Bretton Woods regime (see Chapter 13).[9] When Bretton Woods collapsed, the rug of stability was torn out from under intra-European exchange rates, and thus threatened the stability of their trade relations as well. In an informal arrangement that became known as the "snake," several European countries continued to link their currency values to each other, while together they floated against the dollar.

The snake lasted until 1979, at which time Europe embarked on a more formal procedure for maintaining monetary stability: the European Monetary System (EMS). All member states of the EC (and later EU) were members of the EMS, but membership in the EMS had no practical effect unless the state was a party to the EMS's Exchange Rate Mechanism (ERM). The ERM operated by first constructing a "basket currency," called the European Currency Unit (ECU), defined as the average weighted value of all EC currencies. Most central banks were then required to maintain their currency exchange rates within a couple percentage points of an assigned "par value" relative to the ECU (Spain and Portugal were allowed wider bands, as were, initially, Italy and Britain). In addition to their own reserves, central banks could draw from a central resource pool when necessary to comply with the ERM. In essence, this European Monetary Cooperation Fund was the regional equivalent of the IMF under the Bretton Woods regime.

The EMS worked fairly well. European exchange rates remained rather stable and the system was flexible enough to permit periodic currency realignments. But in the early 1990s the EMS began to experience pressures not unlike those that brought down Bretton Woods. As we have indicated, the Maastricht treaty specified a timetable for achieving economic and monetary union. The first stage of the process — based on the Delors Plan, so-called because Commission President Jacques Delors played the chief role in its formulation — included the creation of a single European market, already well underway when the treaty was signed, and the maintenance of all EU currencies in the narrow bands of the ERM. The second stage was to involve increasing coordination of monetary policies, a further narrowing of the ERM bands, and the establishment of a European System of Central Banks (ESCB) comprised of all national central banks and headed by an independent European Central Bank (ECB). This phase was to commence in 1994. In the third stage of economic and monetary union, targeted for 1999, the Delors Plan called for the fixing of EU exchange rates, the introduction of a single European currency to eventually replace national currencies, and the vesting of all monetary policy-making authority in the ESCB.

Unfortunately, things got off to a bad start. One problem was German reunification. At the time of reunification in 1990 East German workers were paid far less than their counterparts in the west and their labor unions immediately demanded wage parity. At the same time, workers in the east had fewer of the skills required for modern industrial production, and that was not boding well for private investment in the region. It was therefore up to the German government to provide the capital needed in

---

[9] The relationship between U.S. policy and the push for European monetary integration is examined in C. Randall Henning, "Systemic Conflict and Regional Monetary Integration: The Case of Europe," *International Organization* 52, 3 (Summer 1998): pp. 537–573. For a detailed historical and theoretical treatment of European monetary integration, see Daniel Gros and Niels Thygesen, *European Monetary Integration,* 2nd ed. (London: Longman, 1998).

the east, which it did — but without raising taxes, thereby contributing to already rising inflation. To curb inflation, the Bundesbank raised interest rates. As the mark appreciated, other European central banks tried to maintain exchange rates by tightening their own monetary policies. They might have sought a currency realignment in the ERM, something that had been done numerous times in the past, but with the EMU clock ticking they wanted to avoid anything that would smack of monetary instability. As tight monetary policy worsened already slow economic growth elsewhere in Europe, Germany was increasingly criticized for putting its own economic health above that of the community — the same sort of complaints that were directed at the United States as the Bretton Woods regime began to unravel.

The EMS crisis came to a head in September 1992. Danish voters had already rejected the Maastricht treaty, with its provisions for monetary union, and the fight was turning out to be much closer than expected in France. These political developments fed suspicion that European central banks might have to abandon their ERM targets in the face of public disapproval. Speculative attacks finally forced Italy to devalue its currency, the first currency realignment in the ERM since 1987. When the British pound came under attack, the Bank of England was forced to spend billions defending its value; it gave up on September 16 ("Black Wednesday") and allowed the pound to float, dealing a severe blow to the EMS. Then Italy pulled out of the ERM, while Spain devalued and imposed capital controls. In the months that followed the Portuguese and Irish currencies were also devalued. A new round of intense currency speculation occurred in the summer of 1993, this time directed at the French franc. In August, after the Bank of France spent all of its reserves and the Bundesbank sold $30 billion in deutschmarks to support the franc, the ERM bands were widened — all to avoid a *formal* devaluation of the French currency.

EU leaders have persevered despite the setbacks: Europe has now entered stage three of the Delors Plan for EMU. The European Central Bank, located in Frankfurt, became operational in January 1999 and a single European currency, the euro, entered into circulation on schedule. Until 2002, the euro is serving as an accounting currency. That means, for example, that the euro is used in ECB operations and in the denomination of public debt. It also means that private citizens may open bank and credit card accounts denominated in euros. The euro does not become legal tender until 2002, at which time it will forever replace individual national currencies. But while citizens of European countries may take comfort (and some pride) in their ability to continue to use their own national currencies to conduct personal economic transactions, the establishment of "irrevocable conversion rates" means that they are now, in essence, using euros, no matter what their banknotes look like.

When stage three of monetary union commenced in January 1999 eleven of the fifteen EU members entered the euro zone. EU states agreed that certain criteria would need to be met before joining the monetary union — regarding inflation, government deficits, interest rates, and participation in the ERM — and Greece had not met any of these at the start of stage three, while Sweden had not met one (the ERM). Britain and Denmark did meet the criteria, but elected to delay entry in accordance with treaty provisions. Greece indicated that it intended to join the monetary union by 2001, but there has been considerable skepticism that it can clear the economic and financial hurdles of membership by then. Denmark and Sweden, where public hostility toward the euro was easing, may well join by 2002 when the euro becomes legal tender in Europe. Britain may hold out even longer in light of the public's coolness to the idea that the pound sterling, once the symbol of British financial greatness, would go the way of the British empire.

Politics of the Euro

This latest step in the uniting of Europe is a bold one. By entering into monetary union, a state surrenders to the ECB its monetary policy, an important tool for correcting cyclical downturns in economic growth. Although European economic performance has converged significantly over the last decade, there are regional differences, especially between northern and southern Europe, which suggests that a one-size-fits-all monetary policy may become problematic. Many assume, for example, that for the ECB and its first president, Wim Duisenberg of the Netherlands, inflation will top the list of economic ills that must guarded against in the single European market. That has traditionally been the view of the Bundesbank as well, and Euro-skeptics take this as a sign that Germany's economic priorities may come to dominate EU monetary policy.[10] On the other hand, state leaders are often tempted to manipulate monetary policy for political purposes, which is why monetary authority usually resides in a quasi-independent central bank. Locating monetary policymaking responsibility in a supranational institution like the ECB further removes the temptation, introducing monetary discipline while at the same time diminishing national politicians' accountability for the hard economic choices that could cost them votes at election time. Like Odysseus of Greek mythology, who ordered himself bound to the shipmast so he could not succumb to the enchanting song of the Sirens, EU member states may well derive some political benefit from having their hands tied.

In considering the politics of Europe's monetary integration, one scholar has identified the main fault lines that are likely to separate winners from losers in the years ahead.[11] Within Europe, the financial sector and big business stand to gain from a tight monetary policy and low inflation, and they have been strong advocates of a European central bank created in the image of the Bundesbank. Labor, however, wants a central bank willing to use monetary policy to stimulate growth and employment, and has been supportive of monetary union as a means of diminishing the influence of the Bundesbank and its preoccupation with inflation. Outside of Europe, the issue is the strength of the euro and an international currency. Europe's financial sector stands to gain from a strong euro, one that rivals the dollar as the currency of choice for international exchange and investment, since that would increase demand for European financial services. It may also make it easier for foreigners to purchase European goods, but European exporters are also mindful that a strong euro will make their goods more expensive relative to their competitors. Here, too, European labor stands to lose if cheap imports start to put pressure on domestic producers to cut wages in order to lower costs. How these competing political and economic interests play out

---

[10] See, for example, Martin Feldstein, "EMU and International Conflict," *Foreign Affairs* 76, 6 (November/December 1997): pp. 60–73.

[11] Jeffry Frieden, "The Euro: Who Wins? Who Loses?" *Foreign Policy* 112 (Fall 1998): pp. 25–40.

will be watched closely by students of world politics as the ECB and the euro come to occupy what are sure to be central roles in the international political economy.

Emerging Economic Blocs

European integration has been a long and gradual process. In many ways it has conformed to the process imagined by the early functionalists, who were looking for a way to eventually short-circuit the national rivalries that led to two devastating world wars. But contrary to some functionalists' expectations, national sovereignty is not being chiseled away by specialists and technicians behind the backs of state leaders; the EU did not sneak up on the nation-states of Europe. As Ernst Haas and other *neofunctionalists* predicted, the process of integration has required the active involvement of national politicians.[12] Indeed, if the EU has snuck up on anyone, it has been the rank-and-file citizenry of Europe, whose attitudes toward European unification have oscillated between resentment and apathy at best. State leaders have pushed the process because they see the economic benefits of large integrated markets. They are not the only ones.

The North American Free Trade Area

In 1988 the United States and Canada signed a free trade agreement, which reduced trade and investment barriers and provided guidelines for the trade in services, and in 1992 were joined by Mexico in signing the North American Free Trade Agreement (NAFTA).[13] NAFTA is not nearly as comprehensive as the treaties establishing the EU, and in contrast to European functionalists, its founders were not motivated by a grand vision of continental peace. There were political motivations, however, especially for the United States. Global trade negotiations under GATT were often less pressing for the Europeans, since they could always return home to their own regional free trade area. It is no coincidence that the arduous Uruguay Round of GATT was successfully concluded shortly after NAFTA was signed; NAFTA enhanced the U.S. bargaining position vis-à-vis the Europeans.

NAFTA creates a free trade area. There is no customs union, no coordination of economic or monetary policy, or anything remotely resembling the EMU in Europe. The economic dominance of the United States in North America and especially the vast economic gulf between Mexico and its two NAFTA partners make the differences among the EU member states look small by comparison. Instead of economic

---

[12] See especially two works by Ernst B. Haas, *The Uniting of Europe: Political, Social, and Economic Forces, 1950–1957* (Stanford, Calif.: Stanford University Press, 1958), and *Beyond the Nation State* (Stanford, Calif.: Stanford University Press, 1964).

[13] Gary Clyde Hufbauer and Jeffrey J. Schott, *NAFTA: An Assessment* (Washington, D.C.: Institute for International Economics, 1993); Delal M. Baer and Sidney Weintraub, eds., *The NAFTA Debate: Grappling with Unconventional Trade Issues* (Boulder, Colo.: Rienner, 1994).

integration, NAFTA aims at a gradual elimination of tariff and nontariff barriers to trade. There are limited provisions for the movement of capital, but these come with certain exemptions in politically sensitive areas. For instance, Mexico's national oil company, Pemex, a potent symbol of Mexican sovereignty, can still enjoy protection from foreign competition under the terms of the agreement. Similarly, Canada, ever sensitive to American cultural domination, insisted on exemptions for "cultural industries" (film, music, print media, and so on).

Extending the U.S.-Canadian free trade agreement to include Mexico was a difficult accomplishment. Trade barriers on certain products — most notably automobiles, auto parts, and textiles — have always been touchy issues in U.S.-Mexican relations. NAFTA also brought to the fore issues involving labor practices and environmental degradation. U.S. labor unions were concerned about exploitative labor practices (like sweatshops and child labor) in Mexico and elsewhere, both as a matter of principle and because such inexpensive labor was helping to lure away production facilities at the expense of American workers. Environmental groups were concerned about further environmental damage, which was already bad along the U.S.-Mexican border as a result of the proliferation of loosely regulated industries seeking the advantages of cheap Mexican labor (known as "maquiladoras"). New provisions regarding these and other issues required painstaking negotiations, but NAFTA was modified in 1993 and then ratified.

Many observers suggest that the economic benefits of NAFTA for the United States are relatively minor. Both Canada and Mexico gain better access to the huge U.S. market, a benefit they cannot quite reciprocate. Mexico also gains credibility in the eyes of foreign investors, who can take some comfort in the fact that the Mexican economy is now more formally linked to the stable U.S. and Canadian economies. The United States, for its part, does stand to gain in certain areas like financial services and intellectual property, but overall the benefits may be more political than economic. In addition to enhancing its bargaining power with the EU, NAFTA is emblematic of the general liberal principles of free trade and deregulation on which the United States has often stood in its international dealings.

Other Trading Blocs

An important trading bloc that has emerged in Latin America is the Mercado Común del Sur (Mercosur) encompassing Argentina, Brazil, Paraguay, and Uruguay. Mercosur was established in 1991 and is more ambitious than NAFTA in that it is an effort to form a common market and not merely a free trade area or customs union. Its formation and development have been pushed by the democratic governments that succeeded previous dictatorships. They see economic integration as a protector of democracy as well as an engine of growth. Other countries in South America have concluded limited trade agreements with Mercosur (Chile and Bolivia, possibly Peru), while Mercosur and the Andean Community (a free-trade area consisting of Bolivia, Columbia, Ecuador, Peru, and Venezuela) have explored the possibility of an inter-bloc trade agreement. There are also trade arrangements in effect in Central America and the Caribbean. Other agreements found in the Western Hemisphere are nonreciprocal. Through the Caribbean Basin Initiative (CBI) and the Andean Trade Preference Act (ATPA) the United States gives preferential access to its markets without requiring similar access for U.S. goods.

Lastly, an initiative that has captured the imagination of many is the Free Trade Area of the Americas (FTAA), a plan — some would say dream — to bring together *all* the countries of the Western Hemisphere (save perhaps Cuba). Whether or not the hemispheric FTAA succeeds, a web of regional trade agreements already connects virtually every country in the Americas, as we can see from Figure 14.2.[14]

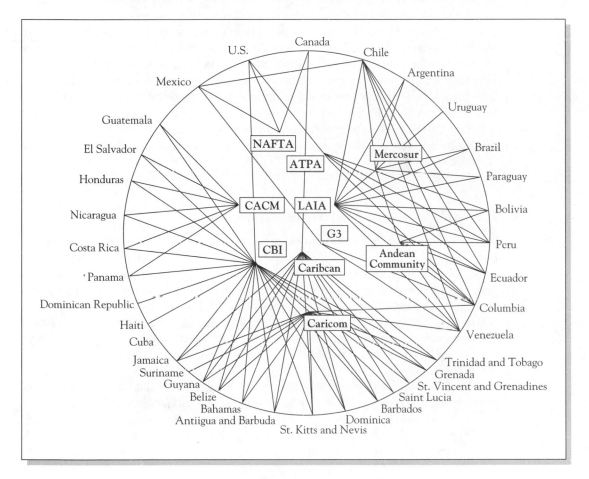

FIGURE 14.2   The Web of Trade Agreements in the Western Hemisphere

Note: CBI is the Caribbean Basin Initiative and ATPA is the Andean Trade Preference Act; both are preferential trade arrangements with the United States. Caribcan is the Caribbean-Canada preferential trade arrangement. Other agreements are listed in Table 14.1 The Free Trade Area of the Americas would include all countires except Cuba.

Source: Jeffrey A. Frankel, *Regional Trade Blocs in the World Economic System* (Washington, D.C.: Institute for International Economics, 1997), Figure 1.1, p. 10.

[14] See Gary C. Hufbauer and Jeffrey J. Schott, *Western Hemisphere Economic Integration* (Washington, D.C.: Institute for International Economics, 1994).

Significant trading blocs exist in Asia and the Pacific as well. Free trade agreements have been reached by the ASEAN countries, by Australia and New Zealand, and by the countries of South Asia. Other overlapping arrangements include some of these same countries. An increasingly watched development is the Asia Pacific Economic Cooperation (APEC) forum. APEC is an effort to establish a free trade area comprising countries along the Pacific Rim. If successful — and there are many skeptics — it would be the largest trading bloc by far, accounting for 40 percent of the world's population and more than half of global economic output. There are also several trade arrangements in effect in Africa, the Middle East, and now Central Asia. Some, like the Southern African Customs Union (SACU), are noteworthy for going beyond free trade to later stages of economic integration. However, many of these agreements have been signed by states that engage in relatively low levels of trade with one another (less than 5 percent of their total foreign trade, as can be seen in Table 14.1). Although these arrangements may bring about more intrabloc trade in the future, their economic significance may be outweighed by the politically salient fact that agreements, any agreements, require a spirit of regional cooperation, and this is probably reason enough to welcome such developments.

Regionalism and Multilateralism

The proliferation of regional trade blocs is an institutional manifestation of **regionalism,** defined by two analysts as "the disproportionate concentration of economic flows or the coordination of foreign economic policies among a group of countries in close geographic proximity to one another."[15] The term *disproportionate* seems to imply that the level of intrabloc economic activity exceeds what would be "natural" in an ideal world of perfectly free global trade. Indeed, there is much debate about whether the rise of regionalism comes at the expense of the worldwide, multilateral trading system envisioned by defenders of free trade and pursued by member states of the GATT, now the WTO.

The period prior to World War II saw a disintegration of the world trading order into competing economic blocs. In the case of the U.S.- and Japan-led blocs, these were regional; but France and especially Britain increasingly came to confine trade to their far-flung colonial possessions. Somewhat ironically, in an effort to avoid a recurrence of these beggar-thy-neighbor policies that helped push European and other major powers into world war, the founding fathers of the EU sought to replace one form of regionalism with another, this time tying the European powers together in a single economic bloc. Although few suspect that the new and emerging configuration of eco-

---

[15] Edward D. Mansfield and Helen V. Milner, "The Political Economy of Regionalism: An Overview," in Edward D. Mansfield and Helen V. Milner, eds., *The Political Economy of Regionalism* (New York: Columbia University Press, 1997), p. 3. Another good overview of regionalism is Jeffrey A. Frankel, *Regional Trading Blocs in the World Economic System* (Washington, D.C.: Institute for International Economics, 1997), chap. 1. The term *regionalism* has also been used to describe the efforts of local actors — cities, counties, or other substate geographical entities — to bypass central governments while developing ties across national boundaries. See, for example, John Newhouse, "Europe's Rising Regionalism," *Foreign Affairs* 76, 1 (January/February 1997): pp. 67–84.

nomic blocs will lead to global war between the EU and NAFTA or APEC, the criticism of regionalism remains. The concern is that agreements that reduce trade barriers within a region may be accompanied by increasing restrictions on trade with states outside the region, and that is not compatible with the global liberalization of trade (and ultimately peace).[16]

The WTO, the organization charged with promoting multilateralism in international trade, does not frown upon regionalism, provided certain criteria are met. Under the terms of GATT (and now GATS), states notify the WTO of the regional trade agreements they sign. There are over 100 such agreement currently in force and it is the job of the WTO's Committee on Regional Trade Agreements to review them. Article XXIV of the GATT requires that regional trade agreements not include provisions which raise barriers to trade with nonmembers. It also says that regional agreements should eliminate most restrictions on regional trade, and also that there should be substantial progress toward deeper economic integration. These latter requirements are intended to discourage regional arrangements designed primarily to keep trade out; the WTO applauds "open regionalism" since these agreements help clear the path toward global liberalization.[17]

Recall from the last chapter that free trade can be understood as a collective good. Collective goods are harder to provide when the number of states in the collective is larger. A single defection from the free-trade regime will seem less consequential to a potential defector, giving rise to the free-rider problem as many members of the group make the same calculation. Larger groups also tend to have less in common — deriving from different economic strengths and weaknesses, for example — making it more difficult to forge trade agreements acceptable to all. By focusing on a smaller collective, regional trade liberalization would seem to offer a better chance for success.[18] As long as regionalism does not degenerate into regional protectionism these efforts are therefore seen in a positive light.

The current momentum behind regionalism is due to relatively recent developments in the world economy. One important factor was the new life breathed into the process of European integration with signing of the SEA and then the Maastricht treaty. As it became clear that the EU was actually entering the common-market phase and that the EMU was just around the corner, proponents of regional integration

---

[16] Economists also believe that leaving unchanged the barriers to trade with nonmembers will have adverse effects as the net result will be a diversion of some interregional trade to intrabloc trade. For a critique of regionalism on these and other grounds, see Jagdish Bhagwati and Arvind Panagariya, "Preferential Trading Areas and Multilateralism: Strangers, Friends, or Foes?" in Jagdish Bhagwati and Arvind Panagariya, eds., *Free Trade Areas or Free Trade? The Economics of Preferential Trading* (Washington, D.C.: AEI Press, 1996).

[17] For a discussion of the role of GATT and the WTO in reviewing regional trade agreements, see Gary Sampson, "Regional Trading Arrangements and the Multilateral Trading System," in Till Geiger and Dennis Kennedy, eds., *Regional Trade Blocs, Multilateralism, and the GATT: Complementary Paths to Free Trade?* (London: Pinter, 1996), pp. 13–30.

[18] See, for example, Kenneth A. Oye, "Explaining Cooperation under Anarchy: Hypotheses and Strategies," in Kenneth A. Oye, ed., *Cooperation under Anarchy* (Princeton, N.J.: Princeton University Press, 1986), pp. 1–24; and Stephen Haggard, "The Political Economy of Regionalism in Asia and the Americas," in Mansfield and Milner, *The Political Economy of Regionalism*.

TABLE 14.1 Regional Trading Arrangements

Name	Members	Type	Population (millions)	Output ($billions)	Trade ($billions)	Intra-bloc Trade (%)
Europe						
European Union (EU)	Austria, Belgium, Denmark, Finland, France, Germany, Greece, Ireland, Italy, Luxembourg, Netherlands, Portugal, Spain, Sweden, United Kingdom	CM	275	7,132	3,421	64
European Free Trade Association (EFTA)	Iceland, Liechtenstein, Norway, Switzerland	FTA	12	387	221	1
European Economic Area (EEA)	EU members, Iceland, Liechtenstein, Norway	FTA	375	7,262	3,493	66
Central European Free Trade Area (CEFTA)	Czech Republic, Hungary, Poland, Romania, Slovak Republic, Slovenia	FTA	66	198	103	9
Americas						
Free Trade Area of the Americas (FTAA)	Western Hemisphere countries	FTA*	716	8,548	2,004	50
North American Free Trade Area (NAFTA)	Canada, Mexico, United States	FTA	382	7,665	1,721	43
Latin American Integration Association (LAIA)	Argentina, Bolivia, Brazil, Chile, Columbia, Cuba, Ecuador, Mexico, Paraguay, Peru, Uruguay, Venezuela	SC	407	1,487	372	16

Name	Members	Type	Population (millions)	Output ($billions)	Trade ($billions)	Intra-bloc Trade (%)
Americas *(continued)*						
Mercado Común del Sur (Mercosur)	Argentina, Brazil, Paraguay, Uruguay	CU	201	861	131	19
Andean Community	Bolivia, Columbia, Ecuador, Peru, Venezuela	FTA	99	196	70	10
Caribbean Community (Caricom)	Bahamas, Jamaica, Belize, Montserrat, St. Kitts and Nevis, Antigua and Barbuda, Dominica, St. Lucia, Barbados, St. Vincent and the Grenadines, Trinidad and Tobago, Grenada, Guyana, Suriname	CM	6	17	16	6
Central American Common Market (CACM)	Costa Rica, El Salvador, Guatemala, Honduras, Nicaragua	FTA	32	42	19	13
Group of Three (G3)	Columbia, Mexico, Venezuela	FTA	150	503	195	3
Asia and Pacific						
Asia Pacific Economic Cooperation (APEC)	Australia, Brunei, Canada, Chile, China, Indonesia, Hong Kong, Japan, Malaysia, Mexico, New Zealand, Papua New Guinea, Philippines, Singapore, South Korea, Taiwan, Thailand, United States	FTA*	2,146	14,469	3,959	74
East Asian Economic Caucus (EAEC)	Brunei, China, Indonesia, Japan, Malaysia, Philippines, Singapore, South Korea, Taiwan, Thailand	n.a.	1,725	6,372	2,092	50

continued

TABLE 14.1 Regional Trading Arrangements (*continued*)

Name	Members	Type	Population (millions)	Output ($billions)	Trade ($billions)	Intra-bloc Trade (%)
Asia and Pacific (*continued*)						
ASEAN Free Trade Area (AFTA)	Brunei, Burma, Cambodia, Indonesia, Laos, Malaysia, Philippines, Singapore, Thailand, Vietnam	FTA	410	539	530	22
South Asian Preferential Trade Arrangement (SAPTA)	Bangladesh, Bhutan, India, Maldives, Nepal, Pakistan, Sri Lanka	PTA	1,198	394	83	4
Australia-New Zealand Closer Economic Relations Trade Agreement (ANZCERTA)	Australia, New Zealand	FTA	21	375	122	9
Sub-Saharan Africa						
Southern African Customs Union (SACU)	Angola, Botswana, Lesotho, Malawi, Mauritius, Mozambique, Namibia, South Africa, Swaziland, Tanzania, Zambia, Zimbabwe	CU	136	148	52	1
African Economic Community (AEC)	African countries	n.a.	628	279	135	2

Sub-Saharan Africa (*continued*)

Name	Members	Type	Population (millions)	Output ($billions)	Trade ($billions)	Intra-bloc Trade (%)
Economic Community of West African States (ECOWAS)	Benin, Burkina Faso, Cape Verde, Cote d'Ivoire, Gambia, Ghana, Guinea, Guinea-Bissau, Liberia, Mali, Mauritania, Niger, Nigeria, Senegal, Sierra Leone, Togo	PTA	180	66	39	1
Economic Community of the Countries of the Great Lakes (CEPGL)	Burundi, Rwanda, Zaire	n.a.	57	28	3	1
Common Market for Eastern and Southern Africa (Comesa)	Angola, Burundi, Congo (Democratic Republic), Comoros, Djibouti, Egypt, Eritrea, Ethiopia, Kenya, Lesotho, Madagascar, Malawi, Mauritius, Mozambique, Namibia, Rwanda, Seychelles, Somalia, Sudan, Swaziland, Tanzania, Uganda, Zambia, Zimbabwe	PTA	255	44	24	2
Cross Border Initiative (CBI)	Burundi, Comoros, Kenya, Madagascar, Malawi, Mauritius, Namibia, Rwanda, Seychelles, Tanzania, Uganda, Zambia, Zimbabwe	FTA	135	36	16	2
Economic and Customs Union of the Central African States (UDEAC)	Cameroon, Central African Republic, Chad, Congo, Equatorial Guinea, Gabon	n.a.	26	14	8	1

continued

TABLE 14.1 Regional Trading Arrangements (*continued*)

Name	Members	Type	(millions)	($billions)	($billions)	Trade (%)
Sub-Saharan Africa (*continued*)						
West African Economic and Monetary Union (WAEMU)	Benin, Burkina Faso, Cote d'Ivoire, Mali, Mauritania, Niger, Senegal, Togo	n.a.	60	22	11	1
North Africa, Middle East, and Central Asia						
Arab Maghreb Union	Algeria, Libya, Mauritania, Morocco, Tunisia	SC	70	93	58	4
Arab Common Market	Egypt, Iraq, Jordan, Libya, Mauritania, Syria, Yemen	n.a.	117	107	47	4
Gulf Cooperation Council (GCC)	Bahrain, Kuwait, Oman, Qatar, Saudi Arabia, United Arab Emirates	FTA	24	205	151	4
Black Sea Economic Cooperation (BSEC)	Albania, Armenia, Azerbaijan, Bulgaria, Georgia, Greece, Moldova, Romania, Russia, Turkey, Ukraine	SC	327	752	n.a.	n.a.
Economic Cooperation Organization (ECO)	Afghanistan, Azerbaijan, Kazakhstan, Kirghizia, Iran, Pakistan, Tajikistan, Turkey, Turkmenistan, Uzbekistan	SC	333	305	n.a.	n.a.

Note: SC = sectoral cooperation; PTA = preferential trade arrangement; FTA = free trade area; CU = customs union; CM = common market; n.a. = not available

*In negotiation.

Source: Compiled from Jeffrey A. Frankel, *Regional Trading Blocs in the World Economic System* (Washington, D.C.: Institute for International Economics, 1997), Appendix A; updated by the authors. These arrangements involve the granting of tariff preferences beyond most-favored nation (MFN) or General System of Preferences (GSP) standards for goods. Certain bilateral and nonreciprocal agreements are excluded from the list, as are some smaller and superceded arrangements. Figures are for 1994.

elsewhere had a successful model to follow. Another factor encouraging regionalism, at least in the Americas and the Pacific Rim, has been changing attitudes among U.S. policymakers. Until the 1980s, when it came to European integration "Americans would override their instinctive aversion to regional trading arrangements by taking a dose of geopolitical medicine." With geopolitics less of an issue — the peace in Europe is stable, the Soviet threat is gone — one might expect American hostility to regionalism to resurface, but that has not happened. Instead, the United States has embraced regionalism. A liberal interpretation would emphasize that U.S. policymakers came around to the view that regional economic cooperation really can be a stepping stone to multilateralism. A realist, on the other hand, would find more significance in the U.S. *retreat* from multilateralism, emphasizing instead that the decline of American hegemony has prompted U.S. policymakers to pursue regionalism as a means of protecting American interests.[19]

Globalization

The term **globalization** has proliferated in our public discourse over the last decade. It suggests different things to different people, but by globalization we generally mean a process whereby economic, political, and socio-cultural transactions are less and less constrained by national boundaries and the sovereign authority of national governments. Two important processes are driving globalization. First, the continuing advancement of technology has made the transnational movement of goods, people, and ideas — both desirable and undesirable — increasingly easy to accomplish. Second, national governments seem to be both less able and less willing to exercise control over the goods, people, and ideas that cross their borders. This is not to say that national sovereignty is dead. Rather, due to changes in opportunities *and* willingness, governments have become more inclined to surrender some of the control over cross-border transactions they once exercised by virtue of their sovereign authority. In many cases governments have been forced to surrender; their efforts to control financial and information flows, for example, are often ineffective. In many other cases, however, national governments have chosen not to impede the process of globalization, either because they perceive globalization to be in their national interests or because they want to act in accordance with international norms.

Interdependence is at the root of globalization. Analysts focus on the extensive new webs of interdependence that are creating a truly global system for the first time. Due to the dismantling of colonial empires and the march of technology, there is much that is new since the end of World War II. Much seems new even since the end of the

---

[19] Anna Murphy, "Regionalism and Multilateralism: Keeping up with the European Union," in Geiger and Kennedy, *Regional Trade Blocs, Multilateralism, and the GATT;* Anthony Payne, "The United States and Its Enterprise for the Americas," in Andrew Gamble and Anthony Payne, eds., *Regionalism and World Order* (New York: St. Martin's, 1996); quote from Frankel, *Regional Trading Blocs in the World Economic System,* p. 5.

cold war. We need to acknowledge, however, that a lot of what is being discussed as interdependence is not at all new but is just being recognized for the first time. Thus, we can talk about both the *conditions* of interdependence (the existence of linkages that hold the system together) and the *cognitions* of interdependence (people seeing or perceiving that interdependence exists).

A "New" Interdependence?

Many of today's conditions are indeed quite new, especially in that some states are much more sensitive and vulnerable than ever before to developments originating beyond their borders. We have suggested that some states, despite their *legal* sovereignty, are so small and poor that they have very limited autonomy in world politics; these states are constantly buffeted by systemic economic, monetary, and political forces and are far more sensitive and vulnerable than most states in the past have been. Globalization and national sovereignty are not mutually exclusive; states have some degree of choice about how to distribute the costs and benefits of the market.[20] Small states, like Iceland or Singapore, may be more socially cohesive than big ones, and so better able to mobilize resources to compete for capital and markets. But almost all international actors, big and small, are more interdependent today because of the increasing opportunities for interaction that have been provided by technological advances in communication and transportation — the increasing ability to send words and things farther, faster, and at less cost (the "microelectronic revolution"). Transnational linkages have proliferated not only between the governmental elites of nation-states, but also between their societies, and at multiple levels. These inter-societal linkages have been facilitated by the activities of nongovernmental organizations (NGOs), including, of course, multinational corporations.

Technology has expanded the physical capabilities of people to interact with each other — economically, politically, socially. However, interdependence is also about people's enhanced awareness of such interactions. A major consequence of the "information revolution" is the rapid spread throughout the world of analytic capabilities to individual citizens. These capabilities come from the ability to communicate through telephone networks, electronic mail and fax facilities, and radio and television. The cost of a three-minute telephone call from New York to London fell from over $50 in 1950 to just 36 cents in 1998 (even accounting for inflation). The number of television sets worldwide rose from 55 per 1,000 people in 1965 to 211 in 1996. The explosive growth in computer usage, and especially the widespread use of the Internet to disseminate and retrieve information, has added a significant new dimension to the information revolution. Neither the personal computer nor the Internet are new inventions, but their availability to ever increasing numbers of people from most segments of most societies is a relatively recent development. In 1996 there were 50 personal computers and 3.5 Internet hosts for every 1,000 people. While these aggregate figures do mask some very real differences between richer and poorer regions of the globe (see

---

[20] Geoffrey Garrett, *Partisan Politics in the Global Economy* (Cambridge: Cambridge University Press, 1998).

TABLE 14.2 The Global Information Revolution, 1996					
Countries	Daily News-papers	Tele-visions	Mobile Phones	Personal Computers	Internet Hosts
World	98	211	28	50.0	3.48
High Income	303	611	131	224.0	20.35
Middle Income	62	252	8	12.1	0.24
Low Income	12	47	0	2.3	0.01

Note: Figures represent numbers per 1,000 people.

Source: World Bank, *World Development Report 1998/99: Knowledge for Development* (Washington, D.C.: World Bank, 1998), Table 19; available at <http://www.worldbank.org/wdr/wdr98/contents.htm>. The figure for newpapers is for 1994; for Internet hosts, 1997.

Table 14.2), the growth in access to electronic communication and information is a worldwide phenomenon.[21]

Thus the "new" interdependence is based to a large degree on new patterns of human attention. Individuals can see things that are happening in faraway places, anywhere on the planet. The democratic revolutions across Eastern Europe have been called the "television revolutions," as people in each country watched and then emulated what had just happened somewhere else in the region. When the Milosevic regime in Yugoslavia began to clamp down on the independent media as the Kosovo crisis came to a head in 1999, Serbian Radio B92 began to rely almost exclusively on the world wide web to disseminate its news reports, advertizing "banned Radio B92 still live on the web."[22] Three years before, when Radio B92 was forced off the air for its coverage of anti-government street demonstrations, it sent audio files via the Internet to the BBC, which then broadcast B92's reports back to Yugoslavia and worldwide. The system was used again during the Kosovo crisis.

The information revolution highlights the psychological dimension of interdependence. This psychological aspect means not only that people are aware that activities are taking place elsewhere, but they are aware that they are aware. They understand

---

[21] The information revolution is one of the major themes of Rosenau's sweeping look at change in the contemporary system; see his *Turbulence in World Politics* (Princeton, N.J.: Princeton University Press, 1990), esp. chaps. 12, 13. See also Manuel Castells, *End of Millennium,* vol. 3 of *The Information Age: Economy, Society, and Culture* (Malden, Mass.: Blackwell, 1998).

[22] Radio B92, "Banned Radio B92 Still Live on the Web," March 30, 1999 [cited March 30, 1999]; available at <http://www.b92.net/>.

that they belong to some sort of global village, to use Marshall McLuhan's famous term, and that they exist as part of some larger world community. Television and radio have brought foreign events into homes all around the world: "For Shakespeare it was a metaphor, but for our generation it has become a reality: the world is now literally a stage, as its actors dance across the TV screen" — and the computer screen.[23]

Interdependence increases as states become more vulnerable to penetration of various kinds. Interdependence can occur only when the hard shell of the state — its sovereignty — is cracked. Because of both increased interdependence and increased awareness of interdependence, governmental decisionmakers have to think about and take into account the effects their internal policies have on foreign relations with other states. As much as Slobodan Milosevic would have liked Serbian activities in Kosovo to remain an internal Yugoslav affair, the refugee crisis that ensued, and his regime's inability to control information leaving the country, brought about a foreign policy crisis and ultimately a military clash with NATO. The remarkable changes in South African politics, as well as the progress toward peace by Israel and its neighbors, were clearly impelled by growing interdependence during the post–cold war period. Whether or not actions, events, or policies are meant to cross state boundaries or to affect the peoples and governments of other states, they do.

Transnational Relations

National boundaries have become less and less relevant. Many scholars, writers, and even statesmen feel that continuing to view the world in terms of the traditional Westphalian logic is not very useful and may be downright harmful, given the nature of contemporary interdependencies.[24] These observers are implicitly calling for a reversal of the Westphalian trade-off; they feel that if governments continue to look at the world in terms of old images (including that of sovereign nation-states concerned with maintaining their autonomy and enhancing their power), such views will lead to wrongheaded policies that may be disastrous for humankind. This view has been most extensively expressed by liberals who see the world in terms of **transnational relations** rather than international relations.

We defined globalization as the increasingly prevalent movement of goods, information, and ideas across national boundaries *without* significant, direct participation or control by high-level governmental actors. These patterns of penetration and linkage involve heavy participation by various kinds of nonstate actors, particularly NGOs. As one scholar points out, NGOs are "changing societal norms, challenging national governments, and linking up with counterparts in powerful transnational alliances. And they are muscling their way into high politics, such as arms control, banking, and trade, that were previously dominated by the state."[25] This view, common among those who

---

[23] Rosenau, *Turbulence in World Politics*, p. 344.
[24] See, for example, Richard Rosecrance, "The Rise of the Virtual State," *Foreign Affairs* 75, 4 (July/August 1996): pp. 45–61.
[25] P.J. Simmons, "Learning to Live with NGOs," *Foreign Policy* 112 (Fall 1998): p. 84. See also Jessica Mathews, "Power Shift," *Foreign Affairs* 76, 1 (January/February 1997): pp. 50–66.

adopt a liberal perspective, begins to call into question the importance of sovereignty, of national boundaries; it challenges the realist conception of world politics as consisting primarily of the interaction of governments in an anarchic international system. Because each state has become so permeable, so open to outside influences, domestic and international politics are becoming indistinguishable. These transnational patterns can be seen more clearly in Figure 14.3, which contrasts the realists' state-centered view of international politics and the liberals' transnational view of world politics.

The main point to note is the multiplicity of interactions that bypass the governments of states and act directly on their domestic environments. In the transnational view, nonstate actors (especially NGOs) are much more important actors than previously thought, as are the interest groups or subnational actors that exist within states. We have discussed the influence of tribal, ethnic, or separatist groups within states, as well as that of economic interests, MNCs, and parts of the governmental bureaucracy. These last, acting in accordance with the organizational process model, often interact

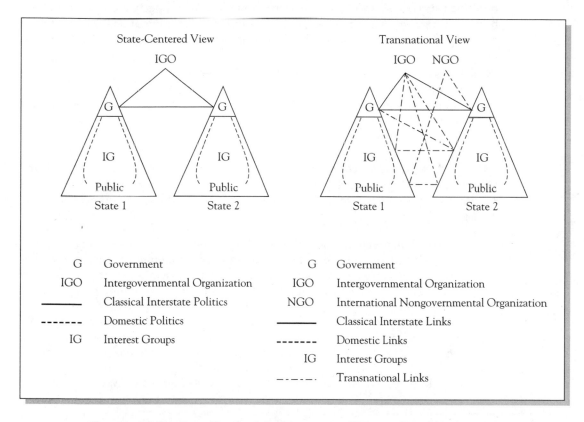

FIGURE 14.3 State-Centered and Transnational Views of World Politics

Source: Raymond Hopkins and Richard Mansbach, *Structure and Process in International Politics* (New York: Harper and Row, 1973), p. 134. Adapted from Robert O. Keohane and Joseph S. Nye, "Transnational Relations and World Politics: An Introduction," *International Organization* 25 (Summer 1971): pp. 332–334.

directly with comparable parts of other states' bureaucracies, many times without the knowledge of the top decisionmakers of the states involved. Both the NGOs and the subnational actors are distinct from state actors and can act independently from states.[26] Some observers even argue that there is no neat hierarchical pattern of influence and authority; in other words, states are not necessarily the most powerful actors, nor subnational actors the least powerful. As we already saw when discussing power in different issue areas, it is impossible to rank states above MNCs or other groups all the time in all circumstances.

These transnational actors make up Rosenau's multicentric world — the groups of many thousands of diverse actors (individuals, groups, organizations, movements) that seek autonomy of action from states. In the multicentric world, nonstate (and nonterritorial) actors confront an "autonomy dilemma" quite different from the security dilemma confronted by states. The liberals' transnational view holds that nonstate actors can significantly affect the interests and behavior of nation-states. The different needs and vulnerabilities of states, IGOs, and NGOs provide all actors with some levers of influence. This is especially important to the liberal perspective on world politics because it suggests that the issues that have been central to international interaction are changing, that military- and security-related issues are not always the primary ones, even to nation-states. Indeed, interdependence generates a new set of problems and demands on those with sovereign authority. Traditionally, the power of states has been based in large part on military capability. But military capability is not easily mustered, nor is it appropriate or even effective when dealing with the sorts of economic and social issues that preoccupy the minds of statesmen in today's interdependent world.

The realists' state-centered view focuses on power and security. Liberals, by focusing our attention on transnational relations, claim that such matters are no longer central but are replaced by economic, cultural, social, and other concerns. As with the phenomenon of regional integration, this perspective presents us with a multitude of anomalies, things that we should not expect to happen (or to be very important) if the realist view held.

> For every quintessential "realist" happening — such as the Soviet invasion of Afghanistan or the U.S. intervention in Central America — innumerable events occur for which realism has, at best, a strained and insufficient explanation. A private group, the Natural Resources Defense Council (NRDC), negotiates with the superpower governments to monitor nuclear test-ban agreements; a representative of the Church of England serves as a link between terrorists and governments in the Middle East; a variety of organizations make decisions to invest or disinvest in an effort to alter the social policies of the South African government; the IMF instructs national governments on their economic policies; . . . Poles in the United States are given the franchise in the 1989 Polish elections, and their ballots are believed to be decisive in one Warsaw district; . . .

---

[26] The seminal work on transnational relations is Robert Keohane and Joseph S. Nye, eds., *Transnational Relations and World Politics* (Cambridge, Mass.: Harvard University Press, 1972). Another early analysis, which highlights the relations between state bureaucracies, is Samuel Huntington, "Transnational Organizations and World Politics," *World Politics* 25 (1973): pp. 333–368. Transnational advocacy groups and movements are examined in Margaret Keck and Kathryn Sikkink, *Activists beyond Borders: Advocacy Networks in International Politics* (Ithaca, N.Y.: Cornell University Press, 1998).

a novel published in England leads to the withdrawal of ambassadors from Iran and to an assassination in Belgium; two poisoned grapes from Chile disrupt world markets, provoke actions by several governments, lead to labor tensions in the docks of Philadelphia, and foster disarray in Chile itself.[27]

As our discussion of the EU and other evolving regional trade blocs suggests, expanding and deepening webs of interdependence are nowhere more evident than in global economic affairs. International economist Jeffrey Sachs identifies four areas in which national economies have become increasingly interdependent. The first and perhaps most obvious area is trade; since World War II international trade has consistently outpaced global production, and almost all national economies have become more dependent on trade (measured as a share of GDP). However, in a second area, financial flows, the growth in interdependence has been even more pronounced in recent years. In 1998, $1.5 trillion worth of global currencies were traded everyday — up from less than $200 billion in 1986. Foreign direct investment has been steadily climbing since the mid-1980s, while foreign portfolio investment, much more mobile than direct investment, surged in the early 1990s (leveling off thereafter). The activities of multinational corporations (MNCs) represent a third way in which the global economy is becoming integrated. MNCs are responsible for the growth in foreign investment, and as much as one-third of the total trade in goods worldwide consists of trade between the affiliates of the same corporation. The fourth way, according to Sachs, is through the "harmonization of economic institutions." Not only are more countries adopting free-market approaches to economic development, they are also obligating themselves to this course by signing international treaties on trade, foreign investment, and currency convertibility, as well as on other matters that signal some convergence in economic thinking and practice.[28]

Transnational Actors

To the extent that military issues have moved from the center of the issue agenda, this is due in no small way to the increasing sensitivity and vulnerability of states and non-state actors in the context of contemporary economic interdependence. And, as Sachs and many others point out, one of the main instruments by which economic interdependence has grown is through the activities of multinational business. We noted in Chapter 3 that there are several ways in which MNCs rival states. The global "mega-corporation" is transforming the world political economy through its increasing control over three fundamental resources of economic life: the technology of produc-

---

[27] Rosenau, *Turbulence in World Politics*, pp. 93–94. Rosenau provides a wide variety of examples of the spiraling growth of transnational interactions — how they characterize the multicentric system as well as their impact on the state-centric system.

[28] Jeffrey Sachs, "International Economics: Unlocking the Mysteries of Globalization," *Foreign Policy* 110 (Spring 1998): 97–111. Institutional convergence — the tendency of political and economic institutions of modern nation-states to take increasingly similar forms — is a topic examined at some length by international sociologists. For a review of that literature, see Martha Finnemore, "Norms, Culture, and World Politics: Insights from Sociology's Institutionalism," *International Organization* 50, 2 (Spring 1996): pp. 325–347.

tion, finance capital, and marketing. Industry is no longer constrained by geography, since transnational production makes national boundaries irrelevant. Transnational production also makes loyalty to any one state irrelevant, and recall that loyalty is the basis of nationalism. Multinational corporate thinking is wary of nationalism; MNCs are careful not to favor any one country in which they do business over any other:

> "For business purposes," says the president of the IBM World Trade Corporation, "the boundaries that separate one nation from another are no more real than the equator. They are merely convenient demarcations of ethnic, linguistic, and cultural entities. They do not define business requirements or consumer trends. Once management understands and accepts this world economy, its view of the marketplace — and its planning — necessarily expand. The world outside the home country is no longer viewed as series of disconnected customers and prospects for its products, but as an extension of a single market."[29]

Although economic activities probably constitute the bulk of transnational relations, there are obviously many nonstate actors engaged in transnational military activity. Revolutionary nongovernmental groups move across national boundaries for sanctuary and aid in order to make violent attacks on people in power whom they identify as enemies. Terrorist groups may be factions of nationalist or separatist groups, or they may be ideological sects, such as the German Red Army faction or the Japanese United Red Army, or they may be transnational gangs that recruit from many countries. They may also collaborate with each other:

> In May 1970 three members of the Japanese United Red Army opened fire at the Lod Airport terminal near Tel Aviv, killing 27 and injuring 69. Many of the victims were Puerto Ricans visiting the Holy Land, prompting one survivor to ask, "What are Japanese doing killing Puerto Ricans in Israel?" The answer to this puzzled inquiry appears to be that the Japanese radicals were recruited for this mission by the Palestinian group Black September.[30]

Such groups produce several forms of interdependence. First, modern communications techniques make it possible for them to be aware of and then to copy the tactics of other terrorist groups. Thus, it is not uncommon to find a rash of kidnappings or airplane hijackings occurring around the world after a major successful use of the technique. Communications, especially the microelectronic revolution, are crucial to the whole concept of terrorism, as we discussed in Chapter 8. The contemporary terrorist has a global audience that can be affected in many ways by a lone act that is geographically distant in the system but that is made psychologically near through communications technology.

---

[29] Richard Barnet and Ronald E. Müller, *Global Reach: The Power of the Multinational Corporation* (New York: Simon & Schuster, 1974), pp. 14–15. See also Richard Barnet and John Cavanaugh, *Global Dreams: Imperial Corporations and the New World Order* (New York: Simon & Schuster, 1994). For a less critical view, see John Stopford, "Multinational Corporations," *Foreign Policy* 113 (Winter 1998–99): pp. 12–24.
[30] Peter C. Sederberg, *Terrorist Myths: Illusion, Rhetoric, and Reality* (Englewood Cliffs, N.J.: Prentice-Hall, 1989), p. 114.

Terrorist and guerrilla activity may also lead to governmental interactions and thus to more interdependence in the system. Governments have acted together to train antiguerrilla and antiterrorist units. Governments have also acted through IGOs, such as the United Nations or the Organization of American States, to outlaw or provide for cooperation against certain acts (for example, by treaties prohibiting offenses against diplomats). National police forces have been coordinated through Interpol to combat terrorism as well as the growing phenomenon of transnational criminal organizations. Transnational terrorism has even prompted countermeasures from purely transnational NGOs, such as the international airline pilots unions, which brought direct pressure against governments and IGOs to institute measures against hijackings. Add to all of this the activities of private military companies hired by states to provide strategic assessments, to train government troops, and occasionally to engage in direct combat against antigovernment guerrillas.[31]

Globalization and the growth of transnational interactions in the post–World War II era has presented the sovereign state with new problems and new challenges. These are highlighted in the liberal perspective's challenge to realism. This challenge, as outlined above, can be summarized using the three elements of Keohane and Nye's concept of "complex interdependence": (1) complex interdependence refutes the notion that only states count, and argues that there are numerous other consequential actors and interactions that make up world politics; (2) complex interdependence argues that there no longer exists a set hierarchy of issues dominated by the concerns of military security; and (3) complex interdependence precludes the use of military force among states whose societies are linked by a web of transnational relationships, or as a means of settling certain types of issues regardless of the extent of such relationships.[32]

The autonomy promised by sovereignty has been buffeted and challenged by advancing technology, economic transactions, information flows, and the activities of nonstate actors that regularly penetrate the state's hard shell. The late twentieth century has been a period of turbulence, characterized both by high levels of complexity and by high degrees of change. Many see this as a time of transition, when long-term patterns of behavior are in flux; Rosenau has called it a period of "postinternational politics." This is another way of indicating a shift in the Westphalian trade-off, as states seek to adapt to a changing environment. In adapting to their environments, states do display different combinations of sensitivity and vulnerability. The industrialized countries of the northern hemisphere have frequently exhibited a greater measure of sensitivity relative to vulnerability, while the opposite has more often been the case for developing states of the global south. This is a rather crude generalization to be sure, but it is at the center of the so-called North-South development gap, which is the subject of the next chapter.

---

[31] Phil Williams, "Transnational Criminal Organizations and International Security," *Survival* 36 (Spring 1994): pp. 96–113; David Shearer, "Outsourcing War," *Foreign Policy* 112 (Fall 1998): pp. 68–81.
[32] See Robert O. Keohane and Joseph S. Nye, *Power and Interdependence,* 2nd ed. (New York: Harper-Collins, 1989), pp. 24–29.

15

Development and Underdevelopment: The North-South Gap

The Development Gap

Interdependence binds units within systems, and managing interdependence is a way of dealing with present and future world problems. But interdependence has two aspects. The security dilemma, arms races, and nuclear strategy illustrate possible *negative aspects* of interdependence, from the management of interdependence based on threats to the use of military instruments of influence. The models and reality of integration demonstrate the *positive aspect* of interdependence. Looking at developed Western democracies, we have seen how the various bonds of economic transactions can be productively and positively managed through cooperation, learning how to coordinate and comply with others to the mutual benefit of all. The relationships highlighted in the discussion of the political economy of developed democracies were based on open markets and democratic forms of governance. Coercive dominance is missing from relationships based on integration.

Do these same relationships obtain between developed and developing countries? How about among less-developed countries (LDCs) themselves? We may think of some dependence relationships between developed and developing countries as *pathologies* of interdependence. Asymmetric or one-sided relationships of sensitivity and vulnerability create an incomplete set of interdependent relationships and thus produce yet another set of problems that need to be managed.

Several Developing Worlds

For large portions of the world's poor, economic development remains an ever-retreating mirage. Reality is a parched existence in the midst of physical misery. More than one-third of the people on earth (2 billion) live in low-income countries. Although the privileged classes in those countries live very well indeed, the average person must survive on a per capita GNP of about $350. Another 40 percent of the world's population (2.3 billion people) lives in lower middle-income countries with an average per capita GNP of $1,230. Compare this to the 16 percent in the high-income group, whose 926 million people have an average per capita GNP of $25,700. The richest countries (the top 20 percent) account for 86 percent of global consumption; the poorest (the bottom 20 percent), just over 1 percent. Citizens in the richest countries use almost 60 percent of the world's energy, consume over 80 percent of all paper, and drive more than 85 percent of all motor vehicles. Corresponding figures for citizens in the poorest countries range from 1 to 4 percent. Moreover, a person in a poor country does not live as long; the average life expectancy across all developing countries is 62 years (51 years in the least developed countries) compared with 74 years in the developed countries. And it is children who suffer most of all from poverty. In the developing world, almost 10 percent of newborns will die before the age of five; in the low-income countries the figure is more than 17 percent. Industrialized countries, on the other hand, have managed to get under-five mortality rates below 1.6 percent on average, and here the contrast between the developed and developing worlds seems particularly stark.[1]

It so happens that most of the globe's developing economies are located in the southern hemisphere, while industrialized economies are more often found in the north. The discrepancy in development levels, both economic and human, has thus been called the **North-South gap.** By calling this a "gap" we are forced to recognize that there is nothing natural or inevitable about the sorry conditions of the world's poor; they can do better, because others do better. *How* to do better is the subject of great debate among policymakers, academics, and humanitarians, but there can be no question about the possibility of progress in economic and human development. Figure 15.1 shows various measures of human development — life expectancy, literacy, caloric intake, and child mortality — for both the least developed countries and the developing world as a whole. These are indexed to the *actual* levels of development in the industrialized world (set equal to 100), thereby giving a sense of the North-South gap and the degree of progress that is in fact possible. Again, we see the appalling effects of poverty on children in the South, where the rate of survival to age five is a mere fraction of that in the North.

---

[1] Figures come from the UN Development Programme, *Human Development Report 1998* (New York: Oxford University Press, 1998), and refer to the years 1995, 1996, or 1997.

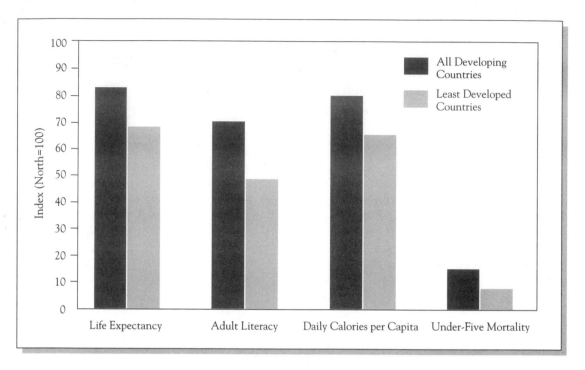

FIGURE 15.1 North-South Human Development Gap, 1995–1996

Note: The height of the bars represent performance relative to the industrialized countries of the North, so the distance between the top of the bars and the top of the graph is the North-South gap.

Source: Data are from United Nations Development Programme, *Human Development Report 1998* (New York: Oxford University Press, 1998).

Most Western social scientists, particularly North Americans, did not expect the persistence of poverty in LDCs. It was clear forty years ago that economic development in poor countries would be slow and difficult, the result of a long process of accumulating capital investments and human skills. However, most analysts did not expect the gap between the North and South, or between the rich and the poor within countries of the South, to be so great for so long. But the record of development is not uniformly dismal. Indeed, we find a mixed picture, even one that allows for cautious optimism. The last half-century has witnessed a remarkable differentiation among countries and regions of the developing world, a differentiation that makes reference to *the* developing world, *the* Third World, or *the* South rather misleading. There are areas of growing wealth and development, such as the oil-rich states or the newly industrialized countries (NICs) of the Pacific Rim, and also areas caught in perpetual stagnation, such as sub-Saharan Africa.

Clearly East Asia and the Pacific have experienced the highest economic growth rates. From 1996 to 1997, prior to the Asian financial crisis, the average annual growth rate in GNP per capita for these countries was an impressive 5.6 percent. Countries in Latin America and the Caribbean averaged growths rates half that, but many of those economies that have gradually emerged from their foreign debt problems are attracting substantial foreign investment. Sub-Saharan Africa is a quite different story — very slow (sometimes negative) growth, failure to attract foreign investment, and crumbling economic and social infrastructures with significant health-care problems (including AIDS), not to mention a breakdown in civil order in a number of countries (in East, West, and Central Africa).

Comparing countries and regions in terms of their levels of development is a difficult exercise. There are differing views about what exactly "development" means, and therefore different measures of it; some refuse to believe that it can be measured at all. This last position notwithstanding, one useful indicator is constructed annually by the UN Development Programme (UNDP): the Human Development Index (HDI). The UNDP's view is that while wealth (as measured by GDP per capita) is of great importance to development, by itself it is not a sufficient basis for thinking about and measuring human development because it does not always capture *social* progress:

> Human development is a process of enlarging people's choices. Enlarging people's choices is achieved by expanding human capabilities and functionings. At all levels of development the three essential capabilities for human development are for people to lead long and healthy lives, to be knowledgeable, and to have access to the resources needed for a decent standard of living. If these basic capabilities are not achieved, many choices are simply not available and many opportunities remain inaccessible. . . . Income is certainly one of the main means of expanding choices and well-being. But it is not the sum total of people's lives.[2]

For example, there are some countries, like oil-rich Kuwait, that rank very high on per capita GDP (Kuwait was the fifth richest in 1995), but whose performance in areas such as education are mediocre at best (Kuwait was 110th in adult literacy). Other states, like the former Soviet republic of Tajikistan, have done well in educating their population (99 percent literacy in 1995), but at the same time are very poor (the bottom 10 percent in per capita GDP). These are extreme examples, but they do suggest the need for an indicator of development that measures more than just wealth.

The UNDP's index of human development takes into account life expectancy, adult literacy, and school enrollment, as well as GDP per capita. Figure 15.2 shows the HDI aggregated for different regions. The North-South gap is again clear from the darker bars on the left side of the chart. In addition, notice that what used to be called the "Second World" — the former Soviet republics and Eastern Europe — because of their communist-ruled governments (and centrally managed economies), also occupy an intermediate position between the first and third worlds when it comes to economic and social development. Turning to the right side of the chart, the HDI suggests that Latin American is the most developed region of the developing world, while South

---

[2] UNDP, "What Is Human Development?" *Human Development Report 1998,* n.d. [cited March 8, 1999]; available at <http://www.undp.org/hdro/ hd.htm>.

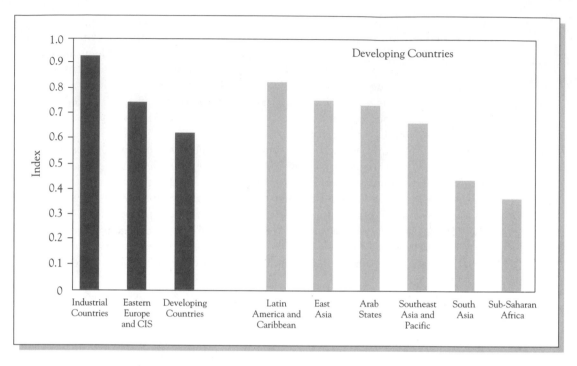

FIGURE 15.2   Human Development by Region, 1995

Note: The human development index is a composite measure based on life expectancy, adult literacy, educational enrollment, and GDP per capita.

Source: Data are from UN Develoment Programme, *Human Development Report 1998* (New York: Oxford Univeristy Press, 1998).

Asia and sub-Saharan Africa lag behind not only the industrialized world, but other regions of the developing world as well.

Some gaps between the North and the South continue to widen — especially differences in wealth and income. From 1980 to 1995 developing countries experienced a higher rate of growth in GNP per capita than industrialized countries. However, the least developed countries actually experienced *negative* economic growth. Many indicators of social development have also shown improvement over time for the developing world as a whole, while at the same time indicating a substantial lag in progress among the poorest states. For example, the infant mortality rate dropped 56 percent from 1960 to 1996 in the developing world, but for the least developed countries the decline was only 36 percent. From 1980 to 1996, there was a 24 percent increase in school enrollment in the developing world; the increase was only 15 percent in the least developed countries. No matter how we group countries for purposes of comparison, it is well to remember that what is often called the "developing world" or the "Third World" is in fact several worlds, with different problems, prospects, and records of performance.

Demographics, Disease, and Disorder

As we will see in the next chapter, recent population growth in much of the world is extraordinary — with over 85 percent of the 2.5 billion people added since 1960 living in the developing countries. The average annual population growth rate for low- and middle-income countries between 1980 and 1996 was 1.8 percent, compared to 0.7 percent for high-income countries. The figure for the developing world hides some much higher rates in certain regions. In the Middle East, Northern Africa, and sub-Saharan Africa the average annual growth in population was almost 3 percent.[3] Greater numbers of people place greater demands on governments for food, housing, health care, and jobs. A basic rule of thumb is that an economy must grow at least as fast as the population just to forestall a degradation in economic and social well-being. Economic growth must clearly exceed population growth for conditions to improve. Economic growth rates for the least developed countries fall drastically short of even matching population growth.

The drag of population is, and will continue to be, a significant obstacle to development in many LDCs. Add the issue of debt and debt servicing, and the obstacles loom even larger. Add additional problems of health care, particularly AIDS, and the task magnifies to daunting proportions. Currently about 24 million people are HIV-positive, and thus expected to die from AIDS, with over 90 percent of the cases in the developing world. Sub-Saharan Africa has been particularly hard hit. According to the World Bank, the infection rate in sub-Saharan Africa is one out of every forty adults; in Zimbabwe, life expectancy has dropped by more than twenty-two years as a result of the AIDS epidemic. Economic and social strains are already evident in Africa, with the costs of health care, lost work days by both AIDS victims and caregivers, and the fact that AIDS kills adults during their most productive years. The majority of Africa's new infections have occurred in the 15–24 age group.[4]

AIDS is truly a case of the poor getting poorer. Robert Kaplan, in a gloomy and controversial portrait of crumbling order in West Africa, sees the region as being isolated by a "wall of disease" that includes AIDS, hepatitis B, tuberculosis, and malaria. The region is for him a microcosm of the way in which "scarcity, crime, overpopulation, tribalism, and disease are rapidly destroying the social fabric of our planet":

> Precisely because much of Africa is set to go over the edge at a time when the Cold War has ended, when environmental and demographic stress in other parts of the globe is becoming critical, and when the post–First World War system of nation-states — not just in the Balkans but perhaps also in the Middle East — is about to be toppled, Africa suggests what war, borders, and ethnic politics will be like a few decades hence.[5]

That is a pessimistic prognosis indeed. Most would like to think that sub-Saharan Africa will narrow the gap with the rest of the developing world, not that the rest of the

---

[3] World Bank, "World Development Indicators 1998," n.d. [cited March 3, 1999]; available at <http://www.worldbank.org/data/pdfs/tab2_1.pdf>.

[4] See World Bank, "Expanding the Response: HIV/AIDS and the World Bank," n.d. [cited March 3, 1999]; available at <http://www.worldbank.org/html/extdr/hivaids/>, and associated fact sheets.

[5] Robert D. Kaplan, "The Coming Anarchy," *Atlantic Monthly* 273, 2 (February 1994): pp. 44–76.

developing world will eventually experience the problems of development and social disorder currently besetting sub-Saharan Africa.

Dependent Development

To some observers, the failure of Western theories of economic and political development to anticipate economic stagnation and political repression in much of the developing world was not surprising. Theorists from Latin America, Africa, and other parts of the world took a view of development that was much more attentive to international and systemic influences on development than was most Western theory. For these people, a crucial flaw in Western theory was its treatment of political and economic development as essentially determined by *domestic* forces. Instead, critics thought, political and economic structures within LDCs were primarily determined by the role LDCs played in the global economy. Without understanding the effect of *foreign* penetration of underdeveloped economies and polities and how that penetration helped shape relations between social classes in those countries, one could understand little.

Some of these theories take a historical perspective that extends back to the establishment of a **world system** in the sixteenth century. The major powers — Spain and Portugal, and later Britain, Holland, and France — had created a world division of labor between themselves, the "center" of the world system, and their colonial territories in the "periphery." Commerce and manufacturing were established largely in the center, and the periphery provided food and raw minerals for the world market. The populations of the periphery were often subjugated and made into landless peasants working on big farms or as slavelike labor in the mines. In some areas, especially in the Caribbean, the original populations were largely exterminated and replaced by slave labor imported from Africa. Governmental control was exercised from the center or, more commonly in those days of slow communication, by the large landowners and urban merchants who sold their products in the world market. Most of the colonial world was thus established as a producer of agricultural products and raw materials for the European center and was ruled by an upper class that imported its manufactured goods from Europe. The local ruling elites had neither the power to resist European penetration and this global division of labor nor an interest in doing so, since they were profiting from the system.[6]

When countries of the periphery became politically sovereign in the nineteenth and twentieth centuries, their ruling elites maintained close economic links with the world economy. In some instances their interests coincided closely with those of

---

[6] The preeminent world-system theorist is Immanuel Wallerstein. See, for example, his *The Capitalist World-Economy* (Cambridge: Cambridge University Press, 1979). Good overviews of this perspective include Alvin Y. So, *Social Change and Development: Modernization, Dependency, and World-System Theories* (Newbury Park, Calif.: Sage, 1990), and Thomas Richard Shannon, *An Introduction to the World-System Perspective* (Boulder, Colo.: Westview, 1989).

European capitalists who came to invest in the periphery, and they prospered by providing services and local expertise to the Europeans. In other instances their interests diverged, but still the peripheral states lacked strong central governments that could effectively resist or control European penetration. There were sometimes deep and violent conflicts between landowners and urban entrepreneurs, between domestic and foreign capitalists. Nevertheless, the masses of people in the countryside usually remained poor and powerless. Sharp inequalities in income distribution meant that, except in a few big countries (Argentina, Mexico, Brazil, and much later India), there could be no large mass market for domestically manufactured goods. The result was economic stagnation and relegation to the role of primary producer for the world economy.

In some areas where significant local industry had existed before the colonial era, that industry was stifled. The most famous instance is nineteenth-century India. The British colonial government deliberately destroyed the Indian textile industry; it built a railway system through India with the express purpose of opening up the country so that the textile manufactures of Lancashire could be sold to the Indian population. Another well-known case is that of the Belgian Congo in the late nineteenth century, where the colonial rulers wanted to use the local population as a labor force in the mines. Streams were poisoned, so that the Africans could not live from fishing. They were then required to pay taxes in money, and they could earn money to pay taxes only by working — for very low wages.

There are important differences of interpretation when it comes to the colonial era. In discussing imperialism in Chapter 8, we found that although there are conflicting theories about just *how* important economic motives were in promoting imperialism and precisely *what* economic mechanisms were involved (a search for markets, for raw materials, or for outlets for surplus capital), economic motives in general were a major influence. A world division of labor between an industrial center and a periphery producing primary goods (with some states in a "semi-peripheral" status) did arise. Associated with this division of labor were powerful groups and classes in all parts of the world with a great stake in maintaining the basic structure. However, what these historical facts meant for patterns of development in the twentieth century, what the significance is of some of the exceptions to the general picture that did exist, and what the prospects are for LDC development in the twenty-first century are issues involving much more controversy.

Contemporary Dependence

In the view of some radical theorists, less-developed countries dependent on the world market face great obstacles in developing advanced, diversified economies. Economies dependent upon exports of agricultural and raw materials were especially sensitive (and vulnerable) to market forces. Wage rates were suppressed, price inflation was persistent, and the market values of primary exports were diminishing even as they fluctuated. What is more, their political institutions were too weak to deal effectively with these deteriorating economic conditions.

Figure 15.3 shows the fluctuation and deterioration in the **terms of trade** for some principal commodity exports of LDCs. By terms of trade we mean essentially what can

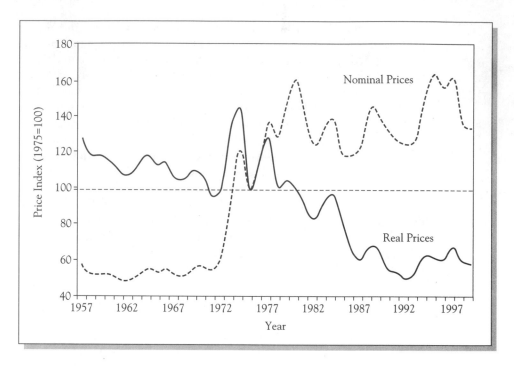

FIGURE 15.3   Primary Commodity Prices, 1957–1999

Note: The dashed line shows the nominal price index for nonfuel commodities exported by developing countries; the solid line is the price index for nonfuel commodities deflated by the price index for manufactures exported by industrialized countries.

Source: Computed from data released by the International Monetary Fund, *World Economic Outlook* (Washington, D.C.: International Monetary Fund, 1983 and subsequent years).

be obtained for one's exports. If the relative terms of trade improve for an LDC, it can obtain a greater volume or value of manufactured imports in exchange for a given amount of the primary commodity it exports. The graph shows the relative value of all primary commodities other than oil (that is, minerals and agricultural products) exported by developing countries from 1957 to 1999. The dashed line represents the market value of commodities over time: prices increased sharply in the 1970s (to keep up with rising oil prices), and although they have maintained roughly the same level since then, they have been subject to wide fluctuation. The solid line tells a more complete story, however — the terms of trade. It represents the value of nonfuel commodities *relative to* manufactured goods exported by developing countries. From the mid-1970s commodity prices fell steadily relative to the prices of manufactures, and only in the 1990s did the decline seem to show signs of leveling off.

Drops of 25 percent or more from one year to the next for cocoa, rubber, sugar, copper, lead, and zinc have been common. With prices fluctuating like that, producers have a very hard time planning future production and sales. Bad weather may reduce the volume of exports but drive up the price of what is left. Producers who increase their acreage or mining capacity to take advantage of higher prices in future years may go too far, creating an excess supply that lowers prices and earnings instead of raising them. Countries that depend heavily on earnings from commodity exports to provide foreign exchange for development can be hit hard. If export earnings fall, key development plans may have to be eliminated or postponed or loans may have to be obtained.

Most big, populous countries can have reasonably diversified economies and therefore are not too vulnerable to fluctuations in commodity prices. In addition, a number of big and middle-sized LDCs have become fairly industrialized; South Korea, Taiwan, Mexico, and Brazil are examples of industrializing states that are no longer very dependent on commodity exports. But some middle-sized countries and many small ones have been very dependent on commodity prices, and often on a single commodity. In the early 1970s, when commodity prices were at an all-time high relative to the costs of imported manufactures, Zaire derived 68 percent of all its export earnings from copper, and 47 percent of Egypt's earnings came from cotton. As real commodity prices fell, these and other countries — for example, Cuba (sugar), Ghana (cocoa), Sri Lanka (tea), Panama (bananas), and Bolivia (tin) — experienced economic difficulties, which were often severe.

To eliminate excessive reliance on commodity exports, many countries adopted a strategy of promoting industrial development that would substitute domestic manufactures for imported ones (called "import substitution industrialization," or ISI). For the larger countries with a reasonably big domestic market, this worked for a while. However, the limits of import substitution soon became apparent: these still were relatively poor countries, with an income distribution heavily favoring the rich and therefore without mass markets for consumer goods. Even the reasonably big domestic markets were, because of their poverty and inequality, much smaller than in European countries of comparable populations. Import substitution policies also often meant subsidizing and protecting new domestic industries, or required foreign loans and direct investment by multinational corporations. With the expansion of regional trading arrangements (see Chapter 14), developing countries find themselves attracting large-scale foreign investment in low-wage manufacturing industries. These industries produce both for the LDC market and for foreign trade. The LDC governments are urged to "get the prices right" by moving toward greater utilization of the free market, selling off state-owned industries, and cutting subsidies to inefficient producers. They also are urged toward greater governmental openness and accountability in order to reduce corruption and other impediments to economic efficiency. All of this may begin to shift levels of wealth and power in their societies, raising the possibility of serious political conflict.

Distorted Development

Radical international political-economists who have analyzed these problems are often referred to as **dependency** theorists, and many have hailed from the developing world, especially Latin America, where the problems of underdevelopment were more "real" than for analysts in the industrialized West.[7] Important differences exist among them. Some see LDCs as doomed to stagnation; others see possibilities of "dependent development" that could make possible rapid growth in GNP per capita, albeit in economies that are fundamentally distorted and highly inegalitarian. Writers differ on the relative importance of domestic class relations as contrasted with external forces. While all would qualify as radical theorists, their theories derive from varying mixtures of liberal economics and Marxist analysis. Yet despite their differences, all dependency theorists agree that economic, social, and political conditions in peripheral societies are inextricably linked and that realist emphasis on the nation-state level of analysis often ignores penetration by transnational and international actors in the global system. Poor countries are dependent on rich countries when the two-way aspects of interdependence are minimal. They are *unequally vulnerable;* there is only a very lopsided interdependence. Acts by the governments of developed-center countries or by MNCs based in those countries affect what happens in peripheral countries much more than almost any action in a peripheral country (especially a small, poor one) can affect what happens in a rich industrialized country. Poor countries are dependent, penetrated, and vulnerable — hardly the unitary, independent actors implied by some realist theories.

Nearly all developing countries are now deeply penetrated by, and in important ways dependent on, the industrial world and especially the world economy. Dependency can take a variety of economic, political, and cultural forms at different periods in a country's development, but its basic structure has been portrayed by radical theorists as in Figure 15.4. Here an economy in the periphery is in a dependent relationship with an economy in the center. Within each of these economies there is also a center and a periphery, representing something like the capitalist and proletariat classes, respectively, that are key to Marxist theories — but with an important geographic dimension: the center is mostly urban, the periphery rural. In the national economy, these classes/regions are in conflict (hence the dashed circles separating them in the diagram). Continuing profits for urban industrialists and large landowners require the suppression of workers' wages, whether in the factories or on the farms; urban centers develop at the expense of the rural hinterland. In the global economy, there exists a harmony of interests (the solid line) connecting capitalists in the center (the North) and their counterparts in the periphery (the South). The former naturally gain from the unequal center-periphery economic relationship, but the latter also enrich themselves as a class (many profit as exporters) even if their national economy as a whole fails to prosper. Last, and again at the level of the global economy, there is a conflict of interest between the working classes. The higher wages and better working conditions enjoyed by laborers in the center are made possible by dismal wages and conditions in the

---

[7] A classic study is Andre Gunder Frank, *Capitalism and Underdevelopment in Latin America* (New York: Monthly Review Press, 1967). One respected dependency theorist, Fernando Henrique Cardoso, was elected president of Brazil in 1994; see his *Dependency and Development in Latin America* (Berkeley: University of California Press, 1979), coauthored with Enzo Faletto. A good collection of dependence theory and related perspectives is Samir Amin, Andre G. Frank, Immanuel Wallerstein, and Giovanni Arrighi, *Dynamics of Global Crisis* (New York: Monthly Review Press, 1982). For reviews of the literature, see Robert A. Packenham, *The Dependency Movement: Scholarship and Politics in Dependency Studies* (Cambridge, Mass.: Harvard University Press, 1992), and So, *Social Change and Development.*

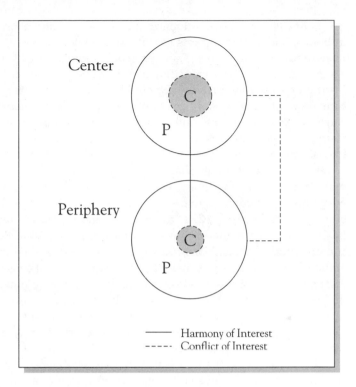

FIGURE 15.4   Structure of Imperialism and Dependency

Source: Adapted from Johan Galtung, "A Structural Theory of Imperialism," *Journal of Peace Research* 8, 2 (1971): pp. 81–117, Figure 1.

periphery. This is an extremely simplified rendition, to be sure, but it does capture the essence of many radical theories of dependency.

Economic penetration of the South by the North can be accomplished by financial or technological means. MNCs often establish subsidiaries involved in mining (Kennecott Copper in Chile, British Petroleum in Iran), agriculture (United Fruit in Guatemala, Firestone Rubber in Liberia), manufacturing (Volkswagen in Brazil), or commerce (Sears, Roebuck in Korea). Subsidiaries of MNCs typically use technology developed in the industrial economies, often after some delay as part of a "product cycle."[8] Previous production processes are transferred to the periphery, where labor is cheaper, after a new process is introduced in the global center. MNC subsidiaries, therefore, are likely to import capital equipment (computers, transport vehicles, and other machinery) from the advanced countries. Local manufacturing facilities are likely to use the processes developed in the center, which thus carry foreign patents, licenses, copyrights, and trademarks.

---

[8] The idea of the product cycle is developed by Raymond Vernon in *Sovereignty at Bay: The Multinational Spread of U.S. Enterprises* (New York: Basic Books, 1971).

Political and cultural influences may come in material or symbolic "packages" — in books, television programs (reruns or news via satellite), newspapers and magazines, and motion pictures. They may come more abstractly, through people who become "carriers" of foreign cultures. Young people are sent to foreign educational institutions and return having adopted important elements of Western industrial culture: ways of thinking and behaving, ideologies, values, and appreciation of Western consumer goods. Tourists coming into the peripheral countries also bring their cultural values. Students may dislike many aspects of the countries in which they study, and tourists may inspire hatred as well as envy or emulation, yet exposure to the cultures of advanced countries deeply shapes and often overwhelms local cultural values. People may come to want consumer goods that are readily available in advanced industrial economies but affordable to only a small minority in poor countries: private automobiles, air conditioners, VCRs, camcorders, and so on. Manufacturing enterprises in LDCs may thus turn toward this small market of upper-middle-class Westernized consumers, producing familiar products with well-established technologies, rather than aiming for a working-class market with many potential consumers but little purchasing power. This means, in effect, that industrial and commercial interests support a distribution of income that favors the well-to-do classes rather than an egalitarian distribution of income that would produce a mass market for basic consumer goods (bread rather than beef, mass transit rather than private cars, and village doctors rather than urban medical specialists).

By all these means, social values in the global periphery regarding consumption and production become deeply conditioned by penetration from the center. Radical theorists have branded this process "neo-imperialism" — or, to emphasize the corrupting influence of Western consumerism, "coca-colonization."

The Debt Problem

Foreign capital tends to flow primarily to the dynamic sectors of a peripheral country's economy, thus spurring uneven development by reinforcing those sectors while ignoring backward sectors and increasing the wages of only a small but skilled part of the labor force. The effects of penetration and dependence are complex, are often indirect, and vary greatly in different kinds of countries. A country's previous colonial history, its size, its relative level of wealth, and its natural resources all influence the results. In the short run, foreign investment and foreign aid usually stimulate growth, but growth will be hindered if foreign corporations ultimately send much of the profits back to the countries where MNCs have their headquarters. Growth is also reduced through repayment of debts to foreign governments and banks. Thus, in the long run, repatriation of profits by MNCs and the effects of large-scale public debts can sharply reduce growth.

At the end of 1998 the foreign debt of all LDCs stood at about $1,800 billion. That represented one-third the entire gross domestic product of those countries. As we can see from Figure 15.5, the ballooning of LDC debt burden — external debt as a share of GDP — can be attributed to borrowing by commodity exporters. The so-called "Third World debt crisis" of the 1980s accompanied the fall in world commodity prices (recall Figure 15.3). Loans were required to compensate for losses resulting from a deteriora-

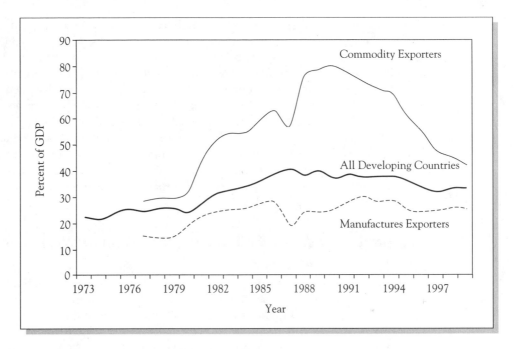

FIGURE 15.5 Third World Debt, 1973–1999

Source: International Monetary Fund, *World Economic Outlook* (Washington, D.C.: International Monetary Fund, various years).

tion in the terms of trade, a problem that did not affect LDC exporters of manufactured goods. When commodity prices began to stabilize in the 1990s, the debt ratio started to decline. The debt burden has not evaporated, however. Annual debt repayment (interest and amortization) alone laid claim to over 20 percent of export earnings throughout the 1990s. The situation is especially bad in Latin America, where debt payments have consistently accounted for about 40 percent of the region's exports. Some countries, in fact, simply have not been able to make their interest payments. Brazil, for example, has on several occasions negotiated a rescheduling of debt payments in order to avoid defaulting on loans made by international agencies and commercial banks. Russia and the countries of central and eastern Europe — "economies in transition" — are also saddled with high levels of debt. In 1998 their external debt represented 30 percent of their economies' gross output and debt-service payments amounted to 15 percent of export earnings.[9]

Servicing the external debt costs about as much as LDC governments spend on education and about twice as much as they spend on health care. It is not hard to see why citizens in heavily indebted countries often feel a great deal of resentment toward

[9] International Monetary Fund, *World Economic Outlook 1998* (Washington, D.C.: International Monetary Fund, 1998).

foreign lenders, whether commercial or public. In Chapter 13 we indicated that the IMF is an important player in international finance and development, as a lender and as an international agency that confers upon debtors its seal of approval. In making loans the IMF typically insists on "structural adjustment." The government is asked to curb its social spending and adopt other belt-tightening measures designed to control inflation and to otherwise channel government resources away from economically inefficient public projects. When governments agree to IMF conditionality, they also establish their credibility with private foreign lenders, so more is at stake than funding from the IMF itself. Yet the political costs can be severe. Structural adjustment has often bred social unrest as popular programs are scaled back or terminated altogether.[10] As we shall see later in this chapter, economic discipline may require political discipline — that is, repression.

Beyond Dependence: Self-Reliance and Basic Needs

Dependency theorists and LDCs governments have proposed and tried various alternative policies to avoid the worst effects of dependence. The most radical alternative is **self-reliance**, which implies shifting economic connections from the core countries, the MNCs, and Western aid-giving agencies — in other words, cutting the ties of foreign penetration and dependence. LDCs have tried to build up trade and technical exchange among themselves, especially where domestic markets are too small for economies of scale and where simple labor-intensive technologies seem appropriate for export to other LDCs. Examples include the Central American Common Market or the Caribbean Community and Common Market.

Some states took self-reliance to the extreme of a near-total withdrawal from the world market and a reduction of all exports and imports to a bare minimum. From the early 1960s until the late 1980s, the government of Burma (now Myanmar) cut most of its ties with the world economy and even sharply reduced tourism, accepting almost complete economic stagnation as the consequence. China, from its break with the Soviet Union in the late 1950s until its new openings to the West in the mid-1970s, also cut foreign economic and cultural contacts to a minimum. China, however, had some economic advantages in its vast population and the diversity of its natural resources. If self-reliance was to work anywhere and allow economic growth to continue, China offered the best opportunity.

Other countries pursued less extreme versions of self-reliance, attempting to reduce, restructure, and control their contacts with the industrial world rather than cut them sharply or entirely. What all these countries had in common, however, was a desire not to replicate the industrial development of the West or to follow in the footsteps of the many developing countries closely linked with the world capitalist economy. Self-reliance was imposed on the populace by radical socialist leaders, often trying to emulate Soviet development policy during the Stalinist era. Incomes of work-

---

[10] Developing countries are not the only ones that have been required to adjust their policies in accordance with IMF dictates. See, for example, Mark D. Harmon, *The British Labour Government and the 1976 IMF Crisis* (New York: St. Martin's, 1997).

DEVELOPMENT AND UNDERDEVELOPMENT: THE NORTH-SOUTH GAP

ers and peasants were kept low to provide a surplus for the government to invest in industry. Being cut off from foreign technology meant backwardness, and being cut off from the competition of the world economy meant inefficiency. Ultimately self-reliance was a complete economic and political disaster. The failure of the "Burmese Way to Socialism" and other ill-conceived programs probably could have been expected, but China's experience was most disappointing for advocates of self-reliance. After running its economy with a minimum of ties to the world market, and experiencing only modest economic growth, China opened up rapidly; it sought foreign trade and investment and expanded economic ties to the West, especially the United States. The impressive economic growth that followed this opening has led some to project China as a possible fourth economic pole, along with the United States, the EU, and Japan.

Advocates for the global South have sometimes been quite forthright in insisting that rich nations have an *obligation* to help LDCs overcome obstacles to development — through aid, debt forgiveness, and other concessions. Such demands frequently offend residents of developed countries, who often respond that they must take care of their own poor citizens before they make giveaways to foreigners. (They could possibly do both; they may in fact do neither.) However, it is important to be aware that the content of these LDC demands is usually not radical, but reformist. That is, they still take for granted the existence of an integrated world economy and do not challenge the most fundamental hierarchical characteristics identified by dependency theorists. They wish to reduce their dependence somewhat and to obtain better terms of trade for their products. However, they are not seeking to overthrow the existing system of international trade and finance, nor are they seeking to withdraw from that system. They are looking to the system for help.

Some countries have industrialized successfully, in ways not anticipated by dependence theory. The East Asian NICs are the best examples. And, as far as the distribution of income between rich and poor, countries like South Korea and Taiwan have been able to do so in a rather egalitarian manner. Both countries implemented vast land-reform programs immediately after World War II — Korea under the American occupation, and Taiwan when Chiang Kai-shek, after losing all of mainland China to the communists, fled with his army to the offshore island. In these countries, war and foreign occupation had broken down the traditional sources of resistance to economic growth and equity. Agrarian reforms and redistribution to the poor provided new incentives and a domestic market for simple manufactured goods. Rapid and sustained economic growth followed. Reducing the power of agricultural interests can also lay the basis for independent labor movements and open the possibility of legitimate political challenge to established power, as it did in much of Europe a century ago.[11]

Korea and Taiwan, of course, were not democracies during most of this period of growth. Other countries, like Malaysia, have been able to achieve moderate equality,

---

[11] See Stephen Haggard, *Pathways from the Periphery: The Politics of Growth in the Newly Industrializing Countries* (Ithaca, N.Y.: Cornell University Press, 1990); Steve Chan, *East Asian Dynamism: Growth, Order, and Security in the Pacific Region,* 2nd ed. (Boulder, Colo.: Westview, 1993); and Dieter Senghaas, *The European Experience: A Historical Critique of Development Theory* (Shakopee, Minn.: Berg, 1982).

decent growth, and partially democratic governments. The choice is made to see that along with economic incentives to entrepreneurs, certain essentials are provided for the mass of the population. Typically this means subsidized rice, health care, education, and transportation. Economists sometimes refer to this as a **basic-needs strategy** of development.

A basic-needs strategy is directed toward raising the living standards of the poorest parts of the population. It is not generally concerned with providing consumer goods for immediate use, which might divert scarce resources from investment and leave everyone no better off when the immediate input of consumer goods has been exhausted. Rather, it tries to build *human capital* that will eventually provide the basis for economic growth. Economists currently studying the impact of equality on growth have shown that investments in such human capital may be as important as investment in industrial facilities. In the Asian NICs, governments have attempted to give poor people both the incentives and capability to improve earnings through land reform, health measures, and, especially, access to high school education. Amartya Sen, one of the economists pioneering in the study of inequality, has stressed the need for enough income to buy food and has helped shift the focus of governments to improving earning power rather than simply food distribution. He has also pointed out glaring inequalities between men and women in the LDCs. Increasing the equality of social and economic benefits across gender, including higher levels of education and political participation for women, helps reduce rates of population growth and thus has a positive impact on economic development. Gender equality is not only a human-rights issue but also an important element of development.[12]

An important starting point for a basic-needs strategy, therefore, is to expand primary and then secondary education, with the expectation that a literate population will be able to acquire the skills needed to operate modern industrial equipment and to employ modern agricultural methods. A second aspect is trying to improve health conditions: bringing doctors or nurses to rural villages rather than allowing medical specialists to concentrate on ministering to the rich in the cities, helping villages obtain clean drinking water and build sanitation systems, and instituting programs of mass inoculation and insect control so that major killer diseases can be nearly eliminated at a very low per-capita cost. Economists have shown that countries with basic-needs policies do not necessarily have lower growth rates even at first, and they usually show fast growth rates later on, when education and better health begin to have positive effects on productivity. People who are healthy work better than people who are sick. Children who are well fed do not experience stunted brain development as a consequence of malnutrition. Moreover, as adults see their own living conditions improve, they become more confident in the future. They become more willing to have their chil-

---

[12] Amartya Sen, *Poverty and Famines: An Essay on Entitlement and Deprivation* (New York: Oxford University Press, 1981). See also Jean Dréze, Amartya Sen, and Athar Hussain, eds., *The Political Economy of Hunger: Selected Essays* (New York: Oxford University Press, 1995). On gender inequities in the context of development, see Cynthia Enloe, *Beaches, Bananas, and Bases: Making Feminist Sense of International Politics* (Berkeley: University of California Press, 1989), chaps. 6–7; see also V. Spike Peterson and Anne Sisson Runyan, *Global Gender Issues* (Boulder, Colo.: Westview, 1993), chap. 4.

dren educated (even at the cost of losing them as productive hands on the farm), and they become more willing to save, to the extent they are able, for the future.[13]

A New International Economic Order?

At the level of international action, the LDCs, especially in the 1970s, attempted to create a program of collective international action to lessen their dependence. Demands for restructuring world trade and industry on terms more favorable to the South became identified with demands for a **new international economic order** (NIEO). These demands included (1) change in the marketing conditions of the world trade in primary commodities, (2) promotion of industrialization in the LDCs, and (3) increased developmental assistance and debt relief.

International Market Reforms

The LDCs have tried to raise and to stabilize the widely fluctuating prices for their exports of agricultural products and minerals. At meetings of the UN Commission on Trade and Development (UNCTAD), which began in 1964 in Geneva, the LDCs pushed for an integrated program for commodities. This program was advocated by a diverse and sometimes very shaky coalition of LDCs known as the Group of 77 (or G-77, which has in fact grown to include more than 130 members). It called for price and production agreements among producers, the creation of international buffer stocks of commodities financed by a common fund, multilateral long-term supply contracts, and other measures to reduce fluctuations in the price of commodity exports.

Some members of the G-77 also called for indexing the price of commodities so that their price would automatically rise with any increase in the price of manufactured goods (much as wages are often tied to the consumer price index in the United States). This last proposal was opposed, however, by many poor countries that were also major commodity importers and by developed countries (which are obviously reluctant to pay higher prices). Although the developed countries have been more open-minded about schemes for stabilizing prices, they have vigorously resisted anything that hinted of indexing. Price changes are necessary for conveying information about changes in market supply and demand. Indexing would be inefficient, encouraging surplus production (as it has for many agricultural commodities like grain and dairy produced in the European Union).

Nevertheless, to argue for maintaining current market conditions purely in the

---

[13] For evidence, see Norman L. Hicks, "Growth vs. Basic Needs: Is There a Trade-Off?" *World Development* 7, 11–12 (1979): pp. 985–994. The 1980 and 1990 editions of the World Bank's *World Development Report* were devoted to the issue of poverty and development. The major report for 2000 is in preparation; see World Bank, "WDR on Poverty and Development 2000/01," n.d. [cited March 9, 1999]; available at <http://www.worldbank.org/poverty/wdrpoverty/index.htm>.

name of free competition is very misleading. Most international markets are, to one degree or another, already quite removed from the economist's model of perfect competition. In the words of a prominent international trade theorist:

> Market rules of the game, and the determination of which markets are allowed to operate, are essentially political decisions. Power, whether military or corporate, abhors an uncontrolled and truly competitive market. It would be an extraordinary world in which asymmetries in military and economic power were not reflected in asymmetries in economic relations.[14]

The clearest example is OPEC, an association of oil-producing countries that for a while took control of the world oil market and changed the terms of trade markedly in their favor. Through coordinated action — in production and distribution (or nondistribution, in the case of embargo) — this **cartel** exercised immense influence over the market price of oil throughout the 1970s.

But many products from industrialized countries are sold in markets that are far from competitive as well. This is especially the case where a developed country receives preferential status for its exports to a former colony. Preferential treatment may result from official government agreements or, more likely, informal arrangements that have solidified over the years. This preferential status especially hurts small LDCs because their domestic markets are not big enough to attract many competitors, which might otherwise undermine these costly arrangements. In addition, some of the most important primary commodities in world trade, like wheat and corn, actually originate in developed countries. Arrangements among national producers and marketers create not a situation of free competition, but one in which there are only a few sellers (oligopolists) who can largely control price and quantity, at least in the short run. Finally, many products sold by LDCs are not sold in markets that are either freely competitive or dominated by the sellers. Rather, markets are often dominated by a few buyers (oligopsonists). Indeed, in most extractive industries, MNCs have the technical expertise to process the material and the marketing organization to sell it. It has been difficult for LDCs to take over such industries completely, from extraction to processing to marketing. These industries can thus be the purview of a relatively small number of MNCs. As buyers of commodities — or as owners of licenses to extract them — *and* as sellers on the world market, they have exercised a great deal of control over market prices.

Relations between MNCs and LDC governments are, however, not the same for all countries, nor are they static. Small and poor countries, as well as being weak in the traditional bases of power, also typically lack negotiating experience and skills. Hence, when they have to bargain with MNCs or with developed countries over international marketing agreements, they often do not get very favorable agreements. One study quoted a standard economic text on the topic and added a comment:

> "In a typical situation, a company earns more abroad than the minimum it would accept and a country's net social benefits from the company's presence are greater than

[14] Carlos Diaz Alejandro, "North-South Relations," *International Organization* 29, 1 (Winter 1975): p. 218.

the minimum it would accept . . . with a wide gap between the maximum and minimum demands by the two parties." Thus viewed, the outside limits of acceptability could be located by means of economic theory but the precise terms of the investment would be a function of the relative bargaining strengths of the two parties. . . . Equilibrium analysis would give way to power analysis, economics to political science.[15]

A study of long-term negotiations between the Chilean government and multinational copper corporations found that in the early years the agreements heavily favored the MNCs. Companies as yet had little invested, the scope of Chilean resources was unknown, and the Chilean government was both very anxious to have the foreign investment and inexperienced in negotiation. Over the years, however, as the MNCs accumulated huge investments (and thus had a lot to lose if the Chilean government nationalized the foreign-owned enterprises) and as the Chileans gained experience, the balance of power and hence the distribution of benefits in subsequent agreements shifted in favor of the Chileans.[16] The power of MNCs has thus prompted host governments to try to control activities and practices that are deemed detrimental to local development (or political power). At the extreme, LDC governments have frequently taken over, or *nationalized,* local subsidiaries of multinational firms. This has been more common in the economically stronger LDCs where the government has some sophisticated administrative capacity and where the export sector's economic performance has been poor.

After the success of OPEC in revolutionizing the world oil market, both LDCs and developed countries expected similar arrangements to arise for other commodities, as the sellers followed OPEC's example to band together in international commodity cartels. But that did not happen, chiefly because the conditions that favored OPEC largely applied to petroleum products alone. First, there existed cultural and political ties among the Arab members of OPEC. Although the importance of this factor can be exaggerated, these ties did at least facilitate the coordinated action that characterized OPEC policy in the early years. Second, there was a lack of ready substitutes for oil, making it very difficult for buyers to refuse to pay the higher prices dictated by the cartel. Third, the rise of OPEC occurred in the context of high global demand for oil and little excess supply. Those conditions did not apply in all commodity markets; they proved temporary even in the oil market. Finally, the hegemonic position of Saudi Arabia, and for a while Iran, within OPEC helped to overcome the free-rider problem. If these two could agree on price and quantity, they could bring along the rest of the suppliers. Even if one or two small exporters did offer cheaper terms, it did not fundamentally upset the imposed price structure; collective action was not undermined by such defections.

No other major commodity cartel has emerged with anything like OPEC's *initial* success. Some effort was made in the bauxite industry (bauxite is the principal ore from

---

[15] Douglas C. Bennett and Kenneth E. Sharpe, *The Transnational Corporation versus the State: The Political Economy of the Mexican Auto Industry* (Princeton, N.J.: Princeton University Press, 1985), p. 80. Bennett and Sharpe quote Charles Kindleberger and Bruce Herrick, *Economic Development,* 3rd ed. (New York: McGraw-Hill, 1977), p. 320.

[16] Theodore H. Moran, *Multinational Corporations and the Politics of Dependence* (Princeton, N.J.: Princeton University Press, 1975).

which aluminum is refined), but all of the above conditions were lacking. Most important, other aluminum-bearing ores exist in many of the developed countries and would be brought into production if the price of bauxite were raised too high. Another complication for many commodities is the existence of stockpiles in the developed countries. It is not enough for a cartel to control a large share of a commodity's production. To set world prices, it must control the market. Market control is not possible when alternatives to a particular commodity are readily available, whether from stockpiles or substitutes controlled by countries outside the cartel. That is, for a commodity cartel to exercise effective influence, target states must be vulnerable, not merely sensitive. The availability of stockpiles and substitutes has discouraged the formation of cartels among non-oil commodity producers. Furthermore, OPEC's clout has waned considerably since the 1970s as these features have also increasingly come to apply to the market for fuel commodities.

Industrialization

Even if LDCs could create many new OPEC-like cartels, such cartels might not be fully in their interests. They would still be specializing in primary commodities and thus denied the potential developmental benefits that come with a shift to manufacturing. At the least, most LDCs want to move into a stage of refining and processing the raw materials they produce. Otherwise, when a nonrenewable resource like a mineral has been exhausted, the country is left with little more than a hole in the ground (and perhaps roads and pipelines leading to the hole). However, if the country shifts to processing or, better, to manufacturing using its raw materials as inputs, it can benefit from "spin-offs" like technical expertise, an infrastructure of communications and transportation, and physical plants and equipment suitable for many uses. The persistent wealth of most developed countries today is based on industry. Processing and industrial diversification seem essential to balanced development, especially in a world where the demand for synthetics has come to replace the demand for so many natural materials.

Exports of technologically advanced manufactured products from industrialized countries are typically subjected to low tariffs by other industrialized countries. But a general reduction of tariffs on imports of, say, automobiles is helpful only to exporters of automobiles. Most LDCs produce simpler manufactured goods and thus do not benefit. Many export refined or processed raw materials or relatively simple and labor-intensive manufactures like textiles. On such goods, tariffs and other restrictions on imports into the industrialized countries are often very high. LDCs can thus be effectively shut out of the world market for those exports. Therefore, they lose the revenue from value added by manufacturing and lose the spin-offs that help stimulate wider development. According to the IMF, other than the "four tigers" of East Asia (Hong Kong, South Korea, Singapore, and Taiwan), only six developing countries could rely on manufactures as their main source of export earnings as of 1998: Brazil, China, India, Malaysia, Pakistan, and Thailand.[17]

In negotiations with the developed countries, LDCs have consistently sought to restructure preferences so they could export more simple manufactures to industrial

---

[17] IMF, *World Economic Outlook 1998.*

countries. Some improvements have been made. Members of the European Community in 1975 signed the Lomé Convention with most of their former colonies, and at about the same time the United States instituted a Generalized System of Preferences (GSP) favoring some simple manufactures from LDCs. Regional free trade areas, such as NAFTA, may also become important. By 1995 developing countries accounted for about one-quarter of world exports of manufactured goods, and just over 20 percent of the manufactured goods imported by the developed world came from LDCs.[18] Many potential LDC exports are in industries that are declining in developed countries, usually because they are low-technology goods requiring labor-intensive production (labor costs are high in the developed countries). The apparel industry, for instance, is endangered in most European countries, as well as in the United States and Japan. In times of recession, when unemployment and the number of business bankruptcies are high, resistance to granting preferences to exports from LDCs is especially great. For this reason, many economists say that an essential requirement for rising prosperity in LDCs is continued prosperity in the developed countries that serve as their markets (developed countries purchased almost 60 percent of their manufactured exports in 1995).

Countries following an outward-oriented development strategy (South Korea, Singapore, Thailand) — often referred to as **export-led industrialization** (ELI) — have experienced faster growth rates than did inward-oriented LDCs (Argentina, Ghana, India, and Tanzania). As changes in exchange rates began to price some Japanese goods out of the world market, goods from the Asian NICs replaced them — often spurred by Japanese capital. The industrial countries have been able to absorb the new manufactured goods exported by the NICs. The NICs' governments have targeted certain industries (in South Korea, steel and the automobile industry) for special government assistance, often with great success. Governments and businesspeople have devised some very clever strategies to get around developed countries' nontariff barriers to their trade. Yet there remains a question as to whether there is room for many more countries to follow in their path. Could world markets absorb enough manufactures from such vast countries as China and India to make much difference in those countries' levels of poverty?

As an alternative or supplement to export-led development, some countries are still pursuing policies of import substitution. For some of the larger LDCs, like Brazil, Mexico, India, and Nigeria, this approach has some promise. Their governments have instituted various requirements for *indigenization* by MNCs; for instance, products must be composed of a certain percentage of locally manufactured components and the firms must have a certain percentage of local ownership or management.

Indigenization requirements, however, do not address questions of whether Western high-technology goods and production processes are appropriate to LDCs. Nor can they do much for small or poor countries that cannot offer large markets for import-substituting manufactures. Efforts at regional economic integration to create larger markets have had mixed results. For instance, ASEAN's Free Trade Area (AFTA)

---

[18] Calculations are based on figures reported in the UN's *International Trade Statistics Yearbook 1996*, vol. 2 (New York: United Nations, 1997); totals include manufactures, machinery, and transport equipment, as well as chemicals.

has had positive results, as has Mercosur for part of South America, but the Latin American Free Trade Association (LAFTA) was not successful. MNCs have found ingenious ways to evade indigenization regulations or to persuade LDCs to admit more manufacturers than would be optimal for their small markets. For example, when the Mexican government was making plans to license a small number of automobile manufacturers to operate in Mexico, some American and Japanese MNCs feared they would be shut out. They persuaded their governments to pressure the Mexican government to include them. In the end, 10 automobile manufacturers were permitted — far too many for the fairly small Mexican market.[19] In some of the worst cases — tractor factories in Russia, shoe companies in Tanzania, shipyards in Poland — state-owned or state-protected industries have been so inefficient that the products were worth less than the raw materials from which they were made.

Economic reforms at home are a key part of recent LDC development strategies. Protective tariffs and quotas for domestic industry are being dismantled, subjecting local industry to the competitive pressures of the world market. Some such industries prove too inefficient to survive competition with imports; others, like the Chilean steel industry, thrive and become efficient exporters of specialty goods. Governments are reducing subsidies to private industry, dismantling some of the maze of government regulations, and selling off government-owned corporations. In 1991 the new government of India announced that it would reduce government regulation and encourage private investment, reversing its longstanding preferences for central planning and government ownership. During the administration of Carlos Salinas de Gortari (1988–1994), the Mexican government privatized $20 billion worth of state enterprises, a policy that continued, albeit at a less vigorous pace, under Ernesto Zedillo.

Debt Relief and Development Assistance

Many LDCs have called for relief from or rescheduling of their foreign debts. For countries facing international bankruptcy, relief is essential. The U.S. government's own trade deficits magnify the problem by attracting much foreign capital that might otherwise flow to LDCs. Many LDCs may never repay the principal on their loans; some cannot even afford to keep up payments on the interest. Some countries that essentially solved their problems of trade dependence through industrialization have fallen back into another form of dependence — debt. If big countries like Mexico or Brazil should default on their payments, big banks in the developed countries, which have lent large sums to LDCs, could go bankrupt. The developed countries thus have a direct interest in keeping the LDCs afloat financially. The Paris Club, a group of mostly OECD creditor countries, provides a multilateral forum for the rescheduling of debt and debt relief. Under the "Naples terms," the Paris Club has allowed debt reductions of up to 67 percent for countries that are extremely indebted (debt-to-export ratio exceeding 350 percent) and extremely poor (less than $500 GNP per capita). Commercial creditors, organized as the London Club, are also involved in negotiating debt relief.

---

[19] Bennett and Sharpe, *The Transnational Corporation versus the State*, pp. 57–59. See also Thomas J. Biersteker, *Multinationals, the State, and Control of the Nigerian Economy* (Princeton, N.J.: Princeton University Press, 1987).

As the immediate debt crisis is surmounted, the need for long-term development assistance returns to center stage. For some of the poorest countries, foreign aid represents a substantial share of their total income. Chad, the Congo Republic, Malawi, Mauritania, Mongolia, and Sierra Leone all received aid equal to more than 20 percent of GNP in 1996; aid to Guinea-Bissau, Mozambique, Nicaragua, and Rwanda exceeded 50 percent. But economic aid can be hard to sell to Western taxpayers far removed from its foreign destinations. Whereas development assistance from the OECD amounted to 0.51 percent of their total GNP in 1960, it had fallen to 0.22 percent by 1997. This occurred despite an earlier agreement by the developed countries to accept a UN target of economic assistance equal to 0.7 percent of their GNP. Countries in the OECD vary considerably in the absolute amount of aid they give, and the burden they are willing to bear. Japan was the largest donor in absolute terms, giving $9.4 billion in development assistance in 1997, but that represented only 0.22 percent of Japanese GNP. Only Denmark, Norway, the Netherlands, and Sweden exceed the UN target for foreign aid; the United States provided a mere 0.09 percent of its GNP, although in absolute terms U.S. foreign aid was second only to Japan ($6.9 billion).[20]

The problem of promoting development in the South will require creative problem solving by the industrial countries as well as by the LDCs themselves. The situation for LDCs has been exacerbated by the end of the cold war. Whatever advantage some LDCs had in the cold war competition for friends and allies — and thus in extracting aid from both the United States and Soviet Union — is gone. Instead, LDCs now find themselves in competition with the Eastern European and the former Soviet republics (often called the "transition economies") for Western aid. The geographic proximity of the former communist areas make them more important to the EU and OECD countries, especially in the movement for European unity and stability. Germany's experience with the ongoing integration of the former East Germany has indicated the scope of the effort needed. Not only do some of the former Soviet republics have significant economic problems (including negative GNP per capita growth rates), they are also states that have moved away from liberalization and in some cases even democracy. The fear that democratic reforms could go the way of some now-scrapped economic reforms has tended to catapult these states to near the top of the Western aid agenda.

Dealing with Financial Crises

The financial crisis that began to unfold in Asia in fall 1997, which we described in Chapter 1, has prompted a reexamination of the global financial system. Debate is ongoing regarding the types of reforms — international and domestic — that might help the "emerging market economies" in Asia and elsewhere weather the next financial

---

[20] Organisation for Economic Co-operation and Development, *Development Co-operation Report 1998* (Paris: Organisation for Economic Co-operation and Development, 1999). For analysis of the humanitarian, strategic, and economic motivations for foreign aid, see Peter J. Schraeder, Steven W. Hook, and Bruce Taylor, "Clarifying the Foreign Aid Puzzle: A Comparison of American, Japanese, French, and Swedish Aid Flows," *World Politics* 50, 2 (January 1998): pp. 294– 323. For a study that places particular emphasis on the humanitarian dimension, see David Halloran Lumsdaine, *Moral Vision in International Politics: The Foreign Aid Regime, 1949–1989* (Princeton, N.J.: Princeton University Press, 1993).

crisis, and the next. Many believe such crises will be increasingly common in the years ahead, especially given some of the transnational economic and financial developments we discussed in the last chapter under the rubric of globalization. The nature and scope of recent currency crises could not have been anticipated by the G-77 when its NIEO framework was coming together in the 1970s, but reforming the global financial system is on the UNCTAD agenda in 2000, which convenes in Bangkok (ground zero for the Asian crisis itself).

The events in Asia demonstrated that financial crises are difficult to contain. International economists now refer to **contagion,** a process of spreading currency crises that may be driven as much by geography and trade patterns as by economic or financial weaknesses in the afflicted countries. At the most fundamental level, the problem is a psychological one —*panic* — and a herd mentality among investors can provoke an exodus of foreign capital that central bankers in emerging markets are virtually powerless to prevent:

> The scenario is similar to shouting "fire" in a theater. A small fire may pose no disaster if patrons quietly, calmly, and resolutely leave a crowded theater. But the same small fire may lead to disaster if patrons panic and trample one another to be the first ones out. Thus, if a debtor starts to weaken, a panicked withdrawal of short-term loans by nervous creditors can immediately lead to illiquidity of the debtor and then to bankruptcy, even if the debtor is fundamentally sound.[21]

LDCs can exhaust their foreign exchange reserves trying to maintain the value of their currencies, but like trying to convince theatergoers that the fire really is a small one, it may not work. Indeed, the fact that an LDC's central bank is making the effort may exacerbate panic among the more jumpy investors.

Dealing with financial crises will depend on how they are ultimately understood, and there is still no consensus on the relative importance of the various factors contributing to the Asian crisis. As we mentioned in Chapter 1, some see the root causes as internal. "Crony capitalism" is the label used to summarize such ills as the loosely regulated banking practices that allowed the accumulation of large amounts of short-term foreign debt and made emerging markets in Asia vulnerable to investor panic. Proposed solutions involve bringing domestic financial practices in line with practices typically adopted in the West. Those who see the causes of financial crises as mostly external point to the rapid liberalization of financial markets in Asia, which led to a flood of foreign investment hoping to profit from the region's impressive economic growth. Their solution would be for governments to exercise more control over the capital flowing into and out of emerging markets in order to guard against another mad dash for the exits. Many on both sides of the debate have scrutinized the practices of the IMF as a lender of last resort. Some would like to abolish the IMF altogether, arguing that the availability of IMF-orchestrated bailouts encourages recklessness on

---

[21] Jeffrey Sachs, "International Economics: Unlocking the Mysteries of Globalization," *Foreign Policy* 110 (Spring 1998): pp. 104–105.

the part of lenders, or "moral hazard." Most, however, see a continuing role for the IMF, even if they cannot yet agree on the most appropriate institutional reforms.[22]

The repercussions of financial crises can be severe. The economies of the countries hit by the Asian crisis went into sustained recession, with negative GDP growth rates in 1998 — between –5 and –8 percent for Hong Kong, Malaysia, South Korea, and Thailand; –15 percent for Indonesia — and possibly in 1999 as well, according to IMF projections. For all of Asia, economic growth in 1998 was expected to be only 1.8 percent, down from 6.6 percent in 1997. Slower growth elsewhere, especially in Latin America, was attributed largely to the Asian crisis (and to subsequent financial turmoil in Brazil), and even where the effects were least felt, in Europe and North America, the decline in industrial production was traceable to withering demand in Asian markets.[23] We shall see in the next section that political stability can be adversely affected by economic downturns. The social upheaval in Indonesia grew out of the Asian crisis, and the financial crisis that engulfed Russia in August 1998 became yet another source of popular resentment directed at the seeming inability of Russian capitalism to deliver on its promises.

Development and Political Freedom

Just as the lack of economic rights is the normal state of affairs in poor countries, so too has been the lack of political rights. Since decolonization resulted in independence for many developing countries in the 1960s, liberal democratic governments have been the exception, authoritarian regimes the rule. Poverty remains a major characteristic of nonfree countries, especially those that have tasted some measure of freedom and then returned to nondemocratic rule. Government coercion and repression — state terrorism — are part of daily life, especially for anyone who dares to challenge the existing distribution of power and wealth.

Dependency and State Repression

Many analysts of different schools of thought — not only radical theorists of dependency but also many quite conventional economists — have recognized problems of distorted development. Dependence theorists nevertheless interpret the phenomena in distinctive ways. They compare this pattern of development with a somewhat idealized image of an economy that is growing rather slowly but in a balanced, integrated, homogeneous manner. Most important for students of international politics, they link foreign penetration and economic distortion with additional distortions in the social

---

[22] See, for example, Robert Wade, "The Coming Fight over Capital Flows," *Foreign Policy* 113 (Winter 1998–99): pp. 41–54; Jeffrey E. Garten, "Lessons for the Next Financial Crisis," *Foreign Affairs* 78, 2 (March/April 1999): pp. 76– 92.
[23] IMF, *World Economic Outlook 1998,* pp. 25, 31.

and political systems. As a consequence, they believe that the economic growth of a periphery country may lead to the establishment not of a liberal democracy but of an authoritarian dictatorship. These theorists see a state bureaucracy that controls the government and perhaps substantial state economic enterprises (in transportation, public utilities, banking, and possibly manufacturing) eager to consolidate its power. According to their view, this state bureaucracy, in alliance with foreign interests and some domestic capitalists, deprives most of the population of basic human rights, both economic rights to decent living conditions and political rights to representation and protest. Violence — direct and structural (as defined in the Chapter 11) — is thus seen as being in large part a consequence of economics and politics in the periphery and the periphery's linkages with the center in the world economy.

How does this process play out? Capital-intensive investment reduces the need for large numbers of workers. By limiting employment to a smaller force of skilled workers, even an expanded industrial sector may employ no more industrial laborers than before expansion. Other workers are left unemployed, only partially employed, or working full-time at unskilled jobs for wages that give them a marginal existence. The larger this reserve army of the unemployed, the greater the downward pressure on wage rates for workers in general (workers who demand too much can readily be replaced). In many instances, MNCs will pay relatively high wages, but high wages in MNC subsidiaries may contribute to increasing income inequalities within the working class because they employ only a portion of the workforce.

These inequalities, as well as enormous inequalities elsewhere in the economy — between the cities and the countryside, between businesspeople or professionals and the unemployed, between large landowners and peasants — may be accompanied by increasing government intervention in the economy. If the government is beholden to either foreign or domestic investors, it will promote their interests by keeping wages down in order to stabilize costs and maximize profits. Whether the state is dominated by capitalists or begins to take on its own major economic role in the public sector, its actions are likely to intensify economic inequalities within society.

We have already encountered the theory that relative deprivation fosters conflict (see Chapter 8). Unequal distributions of the national pie can be a source of resentment, as some groups or classes see others moving ahead rapidly while they themselves gain little or in some instances even slip backward. In highly inegalitarian societies, any appreciable change (either positive or negative) in overall national income will stimulate greater conflict over how the expanded or contracted pie should be divided. This conflict will be especially acute during periods of economic decline.[24] One of the most vivid examples is Uruguay, which until 1973 was a relatively wealthy egalitarian welfare state. But decades of stagnation and economic decline brought severe social tensions, the rise of radical urban guerrilla groups, and ultimately a right-wing military coup to "impose order."

An example of instability in the context of a contracting pie is Chile in the early 1970s. Under President Salvador Allende, a Socialist, Chile experienced economic stagnation and declines in real income in the early 1970s because of mismanagement by

---

[24] E. N. Muller and M. A. Seligson, "Inequality and Insurgency," *American Political Science Review* 81, 2 (June 1987): pp. 425–452.

Allende's government and economic sabotage by Allende's domestic and foreign (especially U.S.) enemies, who wanted to see him fail. When Allende tried to pursue policies of redistributing income at a time of overall decline in growth, the result was work stoppages by key groups, riots, demonstrations, and eventually a right-wing military coup against him. The leader of that coup, General Augusto Pinochet, then instituted an extraordinarily repressive and long-lasting dictatorship. By contrast, an example of social upheaval in the context of an expanding pie is Iran under Muhammad Reza Pahlavi, shah (king) from 1941 to 1978. By the late 1970s Iran had experienced a decade of unprecedented growth in its national income. But these economic rewards were distributed very unequally and left a variety of groups — peasants, urban workers and the urban unemployed, followers of traditional religion, and some intellectuals — very dissatisfied. Many rebelled, culminating in an Islamic revolution and the shah's overthrow.

Foreign economic penetration and coercive government may reinforce each other as local governments become ever more dependent on foreign military assistance — arms transfers, military training, even intervention (overt or covert) — to maintain control over the social unrest that economic developments have created. The condition of peripheral countries in the world economy thus is quite different from that experienced a century or so ago by Europe and North America or even by Japan. Today's LDCs cannot simply copy the development patterns of the industrialized world. Most European countries already had a stronger tradition of representative government than exists in most LDCs, though there are exceptions. (Uruguay, for example, probably had a stronger democratic tradition than did imperial Germany.) Thus, even though most European countries experienced periods during their industrialization when income and wealth were very unequally distributed, most of them ultimately were obliged to make concessions and come to some peaceful terms with their peasants and working classes. Those who waited too long, like the Czar Nicholas II of Russia, lost everything.

The patterns identified by dependency theory have not applied to all countries (nor do all variants of the theory highlight exactly the same patterns). For many LDCs, the inflow of foreign capital may well be essential to the creation of a modern economy. In societies marked by relative equality, economic growth is less likely to foster conflict, as seen in the low levels of violent social conflict in Taiwan. Many economists now argue that the success of the Asian NICs is based in large part on policies that reduce economic inequality, raising the incomes of workers faster than those of economic elites. More generally, some have argued (as we have above) that greater income equality is an important factor in promoting economic and social development growth. One study estimated that reducing the gap between the richest and poorest by one-third could add almost 1 percent to the annual growth rate of per capita income.[25] Nevertheless, dependency theory shows us that the achievement of equitable economic and political development is not merely a matter of promoting foreign investment in LDCs. A recipe for trouble is the combination of economic penetration and military dependence. Together, they tend to magnify economic inequalities, and at the same time give

---

[25] See Sylvia Nasar, "Economics of Equality: A New View," *New York Times*, January 5, 1995.

the state more power to repress dissent. The ultimate result may well be violent rebellion, with often devastating effects on human development.[26]

Development and Democracy — The Chicken and the Egg

Which comes first, development or democracy? Most observers suspected that the acquisition of political power by the world's poor also would be difficult. According to conventional wisdom in political science, the establishment of stable democratic regimes is possible only when certain prerequisites are met. These prerequisites include enough income and wealth to create a literate population, informed by newspapers, radio and television, and other mass media. They also include an economy healthy enough to ensure that a reasonable position in life can be attained through industry, commerce, agriculture, or intellectual activity — that is, by means other than political power and corruption. Private sources of socioeconomic advance provide checks on authoritarian government and provide respectable sources of employment and status for defeated politicians, thereby making it possible for them to accept electoral defeat with reasonably good grace. Economic development is thus not only a way to escape the misery of poverty; it is also a way to promote political liberties.

In comparing countries in the world, the strength of the theory of the economic prerequisites of democracy lies in the fact that high-income industrial countries are, without exception, political democracies. Among them, those with the most recent history of nondemocratic rule — Greece, Portugal, Spain, and Turkey — have the lowest incomes within the OECD. A few of the oil-rich Arab OPEC states, which are not democracies, have very high per-capita incomes, but typically this new wealth has existed alongside an otherwise poor record in regard to *human* development; high rates of literacy or markedly improved living conditions for the whole populace are still missing. Given that some of the worst records on democracy can be found among very poor states, it would seem that there is some validity to the notion that economic underdevelopment is not conducive to political liberalization.

Some analysts have taken the argument a step further, contending that short-term political repression may have to be tolerated for the sake of immediate economic development, after which the prerequisites for democracy will have been established. This "authoritarian-modernizing sequence," to use Robert Dahl's label, has been argued by some to be the basis of the economic development found in China as well as the Asian tigers.[27] Weak government, it is claimed, cannot satisfy the needs of a population that makes major demands on it. Trouble arises from rapid social change and the participation of new groups and classes in politics, coupled with the slower development of political institutions. LDCs typically have large urban centers. Many of their residents have come in from the countryside looking for work, only to remain unemployed or underemployed, living a marginal existence (shantytowns are ubiquitous — in São

---

[26] Terry Boswell and William J. Dixon, "Dependency and Rebellion: A Cross-National Analysis," *American Sociological Review* 55 (August 1990): pp. 540–549; William J. Dixon and Bruce E. Moon, "Domestic Political Conflict and Basic Needs Outcomes: An Empirical Assessment," *Comparative Political Studies* 22, 2 (1989): pp. 178–198.

[27] See, for example, William H. Overholt, *The Rise of China* (New York: Norton, 1993).

Paulo, Santiago, Lima, Johannesburg, and many other cities). Nevertheless, in the city they are exposed to the mass media and see people in the rich sectors of the city living very well. Their expectations rise but are not fulfilled. Because they are in the capital, they can participate in political activity — street demonstrations, riots, and general strikes. The demands of these people, who can be mobilized by activists for political participation, may be nearly impossible for a weak government to meet or repress.[28]

A stable government, the argument goes, requires a strong administrative capacity and political institutions capable of channeling or, if necessary, repressing these popular demands. The institutions of authority might take the form of a mass political party like the Congress party of India, founded in 1885, and the highly capable and well-organized Indian civil service. More commonly, they have been institutions not so clearly associated with democratic rule, more nearly resembling the authoritarian structure of the Ba'ath party in Iraq or a Communist party. The coercive arm of an authoritarian political structure is, of course, an efficient internal security (police) force and the military. In a widely read and controversial study, Samuel Huntington put the argument in these terms:

> Monks and priests can demonstrate, students riot, and workers strike, but no one of these groups has, except in most unusual circumstances, demonstrated any capacity to govern. . . . The military, in contrast, do possess some capacity for generating at least transitory order. . . . The coup is the extreme exercise of direct action against political authority, but it is the means of ending other types of action against that authority and potentially the means of reconstituting political authority. . . . Their job is simply to straighten out the mess and then to get out. Theirs is a temporary dictatorship.[29]

It is not a long step from such an analysis to the argument that traditional Western ideas of political rights and liberties must be put aside in the interest of economic development. Progress often generates political disorder, but further development cannot occur without the imposition of order. Development requires large-scale sacrifice on the part of the masses; without massive foreign assistance, the resources for that investment can be obtained only by reducing consumption. High incomes and social quiescence, however, must be available as an incentive for wealthy investors at home and abroad. In a very poor country with widespread misery, "forced-draft" modernization and widespread income inequalities require government action to repress discontent. Agricultural prices have to be kept low, requiring low wages for farmworkers. The urban employed and unemployed, if they cannot be satisfied, must feel the strong arm of the state so as to discourage disruptive strikes and protests.

According to such views, people in poor countries essentially must choose between political liberty and decent material conditions; they cannot have both, and it is a parochial prejudice to insist on political and civil rights as traditionally defined in the industrialized West. We think these arguments are profoundly wrong. While state

---

[28] Nor can strong governments completely neglect such demands; see, for example, Cathy Lisa Schneider, *Shantytown Protest in Pinochet's Chile* (Philadelphia: Temple University Press, 1995).

[29] Samuel P. Huntington, *Political Order in Changing Societies* (New Haven, Conn.: Yale University Press, 1968), pp. 217, 226.

capacity is important, for a government to be effective it must be able to generate compliance from its people without the threat of coercion — that is, it must have legitimacy.[30]

The Evidence

The trouble with the economic-prerequisites argument — the notion that economic development comes before democracy — is that it only partially fits the facts of recent experience in LDCs. In Latin America and parts of East Asia over the past decade or two, quite a number of democratic governments have emerged, but usually (as in South American countries) as the result of military dictatorships' *failure* to improve their people's living conditions. Having failed to deliver the economic goods, some military rulers seem to have concluded that the economic prerequisites of democracy are not prerequisites after all. In other areas the trend toward an increase in political liberties is harder to discern. Although almost all the former British and French colonies entered their era of independence with governments that were chosen by reasonably free elections and had the forms of parliamentary democracy, today far fewer of them have free competitive elections or the institutions of free speech and free assembly. Some have had stagnant economies; others, very dynamic and fast-growing ones. In many of these countries, however, development has typically been skewed sharply in favor of the rich and has had no appreciable effect on the promotion of political liberties. In some countries the suppression of political liberty has brought economic growth, but in many others it has not.

In direct opposition to these theories of economic and political development is a pattern in some of the more prosperous LDCs that culminated in the early 1970s, when a turn away from democratic government to state terrorism was especially vicious. Uruguay and Chile in the 1960s were relatively rich and had long histories of a stable democracy. Chile had had uninterrupted democratic government since 1927, and Uruguay, since the 1930s. (Along with Argentina and Venezuela, these countries were the most prosperous of the twenty Latin American countries.) The Philippines were fairly prosperous compared with other Asian countries and had a high literacy rate. For several decades the Philippines had developed the institutions and practices of political democracy with free elections, first under American colonial rule and then as an independent state after 1946. Following the economic prerequisites view, all these countries should have been able to maintain and deepen their democratic patterns, but they were not. Their democratic governments were overthrown (in 1973 in Chile and Uruguay, and in 1972 in the Philippines) and replaced by repressive, coercive regimes. Argentina, with a highly sophisticated, literate population and sporadic periods of democratic government, similarly slipped back into authoritarian military rule for almost a decade.

These examples challenge the generalization that there is a strong relationship between the type of political system and the level of economic development, and especially that authoritarian rule promotes economic growth. Table 15.1 lists the ten fastest- and ten slowest-growing economies for the 1980–1995 period. It also shows, for each

---

[30] Robert W. Jackman, *Power without Force: The Political Capacity of Nation-States* (Ann Arbor: University of Michigan Press, 1993).

TABLE 15.1 Development and Freedom, 1980-1995

Country	GNP/Capita Growth (percent)	Human Development	Political Freedom
High Growth			
China	8.6	Medium	Not Free
South Korea	7.5	High	Free
Thailand	6.3	High	Partly Free
Singapore	6.0	High	Partly Free
Botswana	5.4	Medium	Free
Indonesia	4.9	Medium	Partly Free
St. Kitts and Nevis	4.9	High	Free
Bhutan	4.8	Low	Partly Free
Mauritius	4.6	High	Free
St. Vincent	4.5	High	Free
Low Growth			
Côte d'Ivoire	−3.4	Low	Partly Free
Nicaragua	−3.7	Medium	Partly Free
Sâo Tomé and Principe	−3.7	Medium	Partly Free
Niger	−3.9	Low	Not Free
Haiti	−4.0	Low	Not Free
Saudi Arabia	−4.0	Medium	Not Free
Gabon	−4.3	Medium	Not Free
United Arab Emirates	−5.3	High	Partly Free
Dem. Rep. of the Congo	−5.8	Low	Not Free
Qatar	−7.9	High	Partly Free

Sources: The table lists the ten fastest- and ten slowest-growth countries (GNP per capita) for which 1980–1995 data are available. Human development is based on the HDI for 1995 only. Data for GNP per capita growth and human development are from the UNDP's *Human Development Report 1998;* available at <http://www.undp.org/hdro/ectrends.htm>. Political Freedom comes from Freedom House, *Freedom in the World: The Annual Survey of Political Rights and Civil Liberties* (New York: Freedom House, various years), as revised by the authors; categories represent average scores for 1980–1995.

country, the level of human development and political freedom. The experiences of different countries vary enough to make it clear that simple explanations for the data will not do. Yet, if anything, the evidence comes in *against* the argument that rapid growth requires the toleration of huge economic inequalities and political repression. Of the ten countries with per-capita growth rates over 4.5 percent for the 1980 to 1995 period, five were classified as free, four as partly free, and *only one* as not free. The pattern is reversed for those countries with negative growth rates worse than −3.4 percent: five were classified not free, five as partly free, and *none* as free. Of the five free countries in the list, four had high levels of human development in 1995; the other (Botswana) was classified as medium human development. In contrast, none of the six nonfree countries were characterized as having high levels of human development in 1995; half were low-development countries and half medium-development.

What generalizations can we make about the relationship between development and democracy? First, economic development and democracy are strongly correlated. The causal relationship seems to be from development to democracy, rather than in the other direction — and this, at least, is consistent with the economic prerequisites argument. A high level of development makes it easier to sustain democracy. Rich countries tend to be democratic. In many countries, such as Taiwan and South Korea, greater political liberalization and the relaxation of governmental repression have followed substantial economic growth. There are exceptions, however. Some quite rich countries, like Singapore, are still not very democratic, and rapid economic growth in China has not yet produced notable political liberalization or greater respect for political liberties. And democracy is rare, but not unknown, in some very poor countries. Even in many countries that are not democratic in the Western sense there are different means and different degrees of enabling the majority of the populace to have some control over their government, at least at the local level. The cases of real democracy in very poor countries show that, in the right social, economic, and cultural circumstances, mass poverty need not prevent the establishment of democracy. Furthermore, countries that have reached a reasonably high level of income under a democratic government seem never to slip back into authoritarian rule.[31]

Second, in contradiction to some variants of the economic-prerequisites argument, there is little evidence that authoritarian rule promotes economic development. For every authoritarian government that represses political opposition while promoting growth, there are several dictatorial "kleptocracies"; that is, governments run by a tiny elite far more interested in stealing from the people than in stimulating general economic development. (President Mobuto made himself a multibillionaire while impoverishing the rest of Zaire.) The notion that political opposition *must* be repressed in the interest of development, while a convenient justification for authoritarian rule, belies the facts. "There is no evidence that, on average, a democracy with civil liberties is costly in terms of economic development."[32]

---

[31] Adam Przeworski, Michael Alvarez, José Antonio Cheibub, and Fernando Limongi, "What Makes Democracies Endure?" *Journal of Democracy* 7, 1 (January 1996): pp. 39–55.

[32] Alberto Alesina and Roberto Perotti, "The Political Economy of Growth: A Critical Survey of the Recent Literature," *World Bank Economic Review* 8, 3 (September 1994): p. 354. Other reviews of the social science literature on economic and political development can be found in Ross Burkhart and

Finally, a vicious cycle operates from political instability to low economic growth and back again. Poor countries are often socially and politically unstable, with serious ethnic conflicts and weak or arbitrary governments that do not protect property rights. Instability reduces the incentives to save and invest, thereby reducing the capacities for economic growth. Low growth then reinforces the instabilities. Transitions from dictatorial regimes to democratic ones may produce periods of slow economic growth, ultimately endangering the new and fragile democracy. Wise policies and external assistance can help to ease and shorten the economic pain of transition. A "civic tradition" of respect and tolerance — an underpinning of democracy — encourages political stability and, in turn, enhances the prospects for economic growth.

Economic stagnation had brought about the collapse of many authoritarian governments by the end of the twentieth century. They came to power to get the economy moving, and they failed. With the economic failure, their peoples would no longer put up with governments that were politically repressive and could not deliver the material goods. Throughout the world, authoritarian regimes have been discredited. Communist and right-wing military dictatorships have shared the same fate. The result gives democracy a chance. But if less-developed countries cannot solve their economic problems — the need for growth, with equity — their democratic governments are not likely to be tolerated indefinitely. This reaction can already be seen in some of the former Soviet republics. Without a better life, their people will lose faith in democratic government, just as they did in dictatorships. The prospects for growth, equity, and liberty in the LDCs are thus thoroughly intertwined.

The developing world is enormously diverse in many ways: in culture, in degree and kind of ties to the rest of the world, in political systems, in resources, and in levels of economic activity. Theories of development and of dependence are important but partial tools for trying to understand what is happening there. The phenomena are so complex that they defy easy generalization. LDC governments are concerned not only with gaining a higher standard of living for their people, but also with enhancing their own state power. Some of the demands for assistance simply reflect this desire to strengthen the instruments of central governmental authority.[33] Any theory has to address the effects of different developmental contexts and experiences. World resources and social conditions are changing rapidly. The menu of choice presented to leaders of LDCs is constrained by the hierarchical nature of the international political and economic system, by numerous transnational linkages (political, financial, commercial, and cultural), and by the relative strength of various groups and social classes within those countries.

The body of tested theory to support reliable policy recommendations for the less-developed countries is very small. The lives of billions of people — their hopes for

Michael Lewis-Beck, "Comparative Democracy: The Economic Development Thesis," *American Political Science Review* 88, 4 (December 1994): pp. 903–910; Adam Przeworski and Fernando Limongi, "Political Regimes and Economic Growth," *Journal of Economic Perspectives* 7, 3 (Summer 1993): pp. 51–70; John F. Helliwell, "Empirical Linkages between Democracy and Economic Growth," *British Journal of Political Science* 24 (1994): pp. 175–198; and Mansoor Moaddel, "Political Conflict in the World Economy: A Cross-National Analysis of Modernization and World System Theories," *American Sociological Review* 59 (1994): pp. 276–303.
[33] Stephen Krasner, *Structural Conflict: The Third World Against Global Liberalism* (Berkeley: University of California Press, 1985).

relief from the physical misery of poverty and for the implementation of political liberties — are at stake. A responsible analyst, therefore, must tread a treacherous line between irresponsibly ignoring the desperate problems of these people and irresponsibly offering ill-conceived "solutions" that others (not the analysts) will have to live with. A responsible social scientist in a rich industrialized country cannot become, in the words of the West Indian novelist V.S. Naipaul,

> one of those who continue to simplify the world and reduce other men to a cause, the people who substitute doctrine for knowledge and irritation for concern, the revolutionaries who visit centres of revolution with return air tickets[,] . . . the people who wish themselves on societies more fragile than their own, all those people who in the end do no more than celebrate their own security.[34]

Conclusion to Part III

Part III of this book has examined various topics in international political economy. The three major perspectives that helped to organize the arguments and debates covered in Parts I and II — realism, liberalism, and radicalism — also come into play, whether we are talking about the economics of international politics or the politics of international economics. The political economy of national security has more to do with the former, and here the three perspectives tend to focus our attention on different aspects of world politics, rather than offering different explanations for the same aspect or phenomenon. For realists, economic instruments of influence are among the many tools of statecraft available to leaders pursuing the national interest in a dangerous world. Radicals and liberals pay more attention to the domestic politics and economics of national security. While radicals concentrate on the rise of the military-industrial complex as an imperative of capitalism, liberals have wondered about the adverse economic impact of high levels of military spending and more generally about the misallocation of resources in societies where the military-industrial complex wields disproportionate political influence.

The politics of international economic relations has become an important area of inquiry in the study of world politics, no less central than questions of war and peace. Indeed, distinguishing these two subfields can be difficult. Early liberals like Smith and Ricardo, who theorized about the gains from trade, hoped for additional benefits: the tendency of trading states to remain at peace. The founders of the movement toward European unification had peace and stability very much in mind when they hatched their plans for economic integration among states that had fought repeated and increasingly destructive wars on the European continent. Realists, too, recognize that peace and a thickening web of economic transactions go together, all the more so when there exists in the international system a hegemonic state that can shoulder the extra burden required to encourage or enforce adherence to free-trade practices. The

---

[34] V. S. Naipaul, "The Killings in Trinidad: Part Two," Sunday *Times* (London), May 19, 1974, p. 41.

significance of international institutions and regimes — multilateral or regional — and particularly their capacity to constrain the political-economic behavior of member states has and will in all likelihood continue to divide the realist and liberal views.

Perhaps the most significant contribution of the radical perspective in world politics has been to expose the downside of international economic transactions and interdependence — at least for one group of actors, the global South. The persistence of economic and human underdevelopment owes in part to exploitative transnational linkages connecting the center and periphery of the world economy. There are many doorsteps on which to lay the blame for the North-South gap — states and nonstate actors, foreign and domestic — and there is enough variability in the experiences of less-developed countries to argue against any single model of development. However, theories of economic dependency have heightened our awareness of the plight of those left behind by the development process and suggest that our obligations to those who are less fortunate should not be delimited by our own national borders. The scourge of global poverty serves to remind us that in an international system characterized by sovereign equality, some states are indeed more equal than others. Sovereignty has it limits, and we explore a few more of these in the next chapter.

IV

CHALLENGES FOR THE NEW MILLENNIUM

This natural inequality of the two powers of population and of production in the earth forms the great difficulty that to me appears insurmountable in the way to the perfectibility of society.
— T. R. MALTHUS

It is equally impossible to pronounce for or against the future realization of an event which cannot take place but at an era when the human race will have attained improvements.
— MARQUIS DE CONDORCET

16

Limits of Sovereignty: Humanity and the Commons

Collective Goods and Collective "Bads"

Interdependence, in its various forms, confronts us with a set of important problems in the global system that constrain all international and transnational actors. In this chapter we shall discuss some of the many ecological issues facing the human race at the global level. Ecology — the study of the relationships between living things and their physical and biological environments — naturally draws our attention to global interdependencies. Some of these are closely related to matters of economic and human development, as discussed in the last chapter. Others have to do with demography, geology, geography, climatology, and other fields of study outside the immediate expertise of most social scientists. While there is still some debate within various scientific communities regarding the seriousness of the ecological challenges that have accompanied us into the twenty-first century, there is also a widespread feeling that humanity ought not wait for a definitive resolution of these scientific debates before taking action to curb our self-destructive patterns of consumption and waste.

Scholars interested in world order and alternative world futures try to teach us why we should be aware of and interested in global interdependence and emerging transnational ecological problems. To appreciate this, we need to see where we fit in the global system. Figure 16.1 presents the world system as a set of nested subsystems. Individuals tend to give most of their attention to immediate, personal concerns (their families, neighborhoods, and local systems); our typical area of awareness is really quite limited. However, to become aware of and concerned with, and then to solve, the sorts of issues discussed in this chapter, we must expand our perspectives both in space (to the world system) and in time (to at least the next fifty to one hundred years). Over twenty-five years ago Ervin Laszlo, a futurist and student of world order, observed, "World order reform starts at home: with the ideas and values we entertain, the objectives we pursue, the leaders we elect, and the way we talk with and influence those around us."[1]

This observation is even more relevant today with the information revolution and the technologically driven growth of both interdependence and the perceptions of interdependence. With the increased attention to transnational relations and regimes

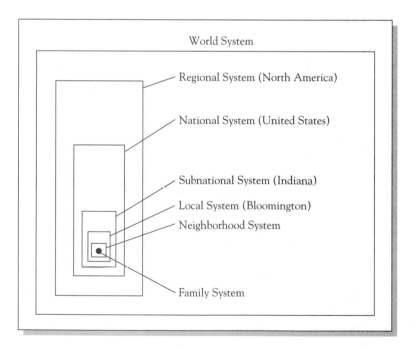

FIGURE 16.1   Nested Human Systems

Source: Adapted from Ervin Laslo, *A Strategy for the Future: The Systems Approach to World Order* (New York: Braziller, 1974).

---

[1] Ervin Laszlo, *A Strategy for the Future: The Systems Approach to World Order* (New York: Braziller, 1974), p. 79.

in the study of world politics, the decreasing concern about East-West security issues, and the growing importance of economic and ecological issues, the interconnectedness of systems and issues has become central. The Club of Rome (gathering since 1968 to study the nature and consequences of global interconnectedness) has addressed itself to the "world problematique" — the complex of contemporary problems facing humankind — and the consequent "predicament of mankind." With the persistence of environmental threats and their appearance in newer and more dangerous forms — acid rain, ozone holes, global warming, soil erosion and degradation, deforestation — interest in the ecological problematique became revitalized in the late 1980s and early 1990s and now has a secure place on the agenda of state leaders, IGOs, and civic groups.[2]

Externalities and "Forced Riders"

In Chapter 13 we introduced the concept of collective goods, which has been useful for understanding some of the issues discussed in subsequent chapters. Recall that individuals acquire private goods if the "price" is right, based on some calculation of the costs and benefits involved. The market mechanism works pretty well for many goods, but not for all; indeed, it can work rather poorly for some goods, such as collective defense or the maintenance of a free-trade regime. In these cases, individual members of the collective (an alliance, a community of trading states) have an incentive to shirk because they believe they can benefit from the collective good without incurring any costs.

We have discussed how the free-rider problem has been overcome in world politics, but it is important to remember that the problem emerges from the individual pursuit of self-interest. It is not always the case that the group suffers from the self-interested behavior of its members. For example, suppose Jones buys a cat for the purpose of killing mice on her property. Jones has acquired a private good: a rodent-free dwelling. But mice were also infesting the property of Jones's neighbor Smith, and by controlling the proliferation of mice Jones's cat has produced a benefit for Smith as well, and at no cost to Smith. The benefit for Smith is external to the private good acquired by Jones — it is an **externality**. During the nineteenth century, to protect the security of its colonial possessions and its profitable trade with them, Britain policed the sea lanes of the Western Hemisphere and prevented intervention by other European powers. Like Jones's cat, the British navy provided a private good for Britain, but also positive externalities to the young United States, which also benefited from the conditions of secure trade.

Externalities often are not positive. Jones's new car, while a private good in the sense that she owns it and can use it as she sees fit, is also bright red. Smith, whose front window looks directly onto Jones's driveway, becomes sick at the sight of bright red. Smith thus incurs costs from Jones's car, and with none of the benefits: he may look out his window and get sick, or pull the shades and deprive himself of the natural sunlight. When a state decides to build a nuclear power plant, it takes into account the

---

[2] A good general introduction to the politics of global ecology is Gareth Porter and Janet Welsh Brown, *Global Environmental Politics,* 2nd ed. (Boulder, Colo.: Westview, 1996).

benefits and the costs, including the risks of nuclear accidents. In 1986, one of the Soviet Union's nuclear plants at Chernobyl experienced an explosion and gradual meltdown, causing death and disease due to contamination in the surrounding area (the republics of Ukraine, Belarus, and Russia). But the Soviet Union's European neighbors to the west were also exposed to radioactive fallout from the accident. They could not simply pull the shades.

Industrial production usually creates some form of pollution as an externality. Pollution is jointly supplied, since the foul air that one person breathes is breathed by others as well. It is also nonexcludable; individual residents in a polluted area cannot lead pollution-free lives unless they leave the area (in which case they exit the group). Thus, the externality of pollution has the basic characteristics of a collective good, though it seems more appropriate to call it a "collective bad." There are many other forms of production and consumption in modern society that create negative externalities, many of which we discuss in this chapter. They all exhibit collective-goods problems, especially as a consequence of nonexcludability. Just as a free rider cannot be excluded from the collective benefits of alliance security or a stable monetary system, neither can a member of the group avoid the costs of pollution, resource depletion, or other collective outcomes that result from the individual pursuit of self interest. They are "forced riders." Here we are back to the idea of vulnerability in interdependence, and the conflicts of interest that negative externalities generate. Unfortunately, sovereignty does not mix well with externalities: "The principle of sovereignty in effect establishes rules of liability that put the burden of externalities on those who *suffer from them.*"[3]

The Tragedy of the Commons

As we saw from the prisoner's dilemma, behavior that appears rational from each individual's point of view can lead to an outcome that is suboptimal for all. This dilemma manifests itself as the mistreatment of common property, and such behavior is not unique to modern society. Aristotle wrote: "What is common to the greatest number has the least care bestowed upon it. Everyone thinks chiefly of his own, hardly at all of the common interest."[4] The best example of this form of defection or free riding is what Garrett Hardin has called the **tragedy of the commons.** Hardin describes a pasture, the commons, that belongs to all the members of a group:

> The tragedy of the commons develops in this way. Picture a pasture open to all. It is to be expected that each herdsman will try to keep as many cattle as possible on the commons. Such an arrangement may work reasonably satisfactorily for centuries because tribal wars, poaching, and disease keep the numbers of both man and beast well below the carrying capacity of the land. Finally, however, comes the day of reckoning, that is, the day when the long-desired goal of social stability becomes a reality. At this point, the inherent logic of the commons remorselessly generates tragedy.

---

[3] Robert O. Keohane, *After Hegemony: Cooperation and Discord in the World Political Economy* (Princeton, N.J.: Princeton University Press, 1984), p. 86 (emphasis added).

[4] Aristotle, *The Politics,* trans. Sir Ernest Barker, ed. R. F. Stalley (Oxford: Oxford University Press, 1995), book II, chap. 3.

As a rational being, each herdsman seeks to maximize his gain. Explicitly or implicitly, more or less consciously, he asks, "What is the utility to me of adding one more animal to my herd?" This utility has one negative and one positive component. The positive component is a function of the increment of one animal. Since the herdsman receives all the proceeds from the sale of the additional animal, the positive utility is nearly +1. The negative component is a function of the additional overgrazing created by one more animal. Since, however, the effects of overgrazing are shared by all the herdsmen, the negative utility for any particular decision-making herdsman is only a fraction of 1.

Adding together the component partial utilities, the rational herdsman concludes that the only sensible course for him to pursue is to add another animal to his herd. And another; and another. . . . But this is the conclusion reached by each and every rational herdsman sharing a commons. Therein is the tragedy. Each man is locked into a system that compels him to increase his herd without limiting — in a world that is limited. Ruin is the destination toward which all men rush, each pursuing his own best interest in a society that believes in the freedom of the commons. Freedom in a commons brings ruin to all.[5]

For Hardin, the commons is a jointly supplied and nonexcludable collective good. The tragedy of the commons is the other side of the free-rider problem. When there are free riders, a collective good may not be provided. In the tragedy of the commons, although individuals follow the logic of rational self-interest, the result is the destruction of a collective good that already exists. The commons can be seen as a collective good as long as usage levels remain low, when the use by an additional member does not reduce its usefulness to others. The tragedy occurs when usage increases so that the good, while still nonexcludable (by definition it is held in common), is now no longer indivisible. The collective good is being used up or is deteriorating, and people do not see or understand the change. Some may see the problem but, as Aristotle noted, do not feel responsible for their own behavior as part of the problem. Hardin has pointed out that a commons often leads people to ignore their responsibilities (but not their rights to use or exploit the commons). The greater the likelihood that the violator of a social norm governing the commons can remain anonymous and avoid rebuke from others in the collective, the larger the temptation to defect from those norms. Thus, we have tax evaders, those who have few qualms about shoplifting from large retail merchandisers, and people who cut into long lines at ticket windows or in traffic jams. The goods they exploit *appear* to be indivisible (and infinite), and the costs distributed among the rest of us may be small at first — minor tax or price hikes, slightly longer delays — but as socially irresponsible behavior becomes more widespread, those costs increase. The challenge becomes reversing the tide of defection before social norms collapse and the commons are destroyed.

In world politics the types of goods most often involved in commons situations are called **common-pool resources.** These are natural resources that do not belong to any specific state, that do not fall under a state's sovereign jurisdiction. They include the

---

[5] Garrett Hardin, "The Tragedy of the Commons," *Science* 162 (1968): p. 1244; see also Garrett Hardin and John Baden, eds., *Managing the Commons* (San Francisco: Freeman, 1977).

deep seabed, the high seas, and their fisheries; outer space; the atmosphere, including the ozone layer; and the electromagnetic frequency spectrum for broadcasting. Many people see the natural resources that exist on earth, even those within national boundaries (such as rainforests and the species inhabiting them), as part of the "global commons." There are many such examples, including all of the nonrenewable energy resources like oil, natural gas, and coal. But who owns or has jurisdiction over such resources? Who should? By custom and law such resources are usually privately owned by those with legal title to the land that encompasses them — "possession is nine-tenths of the law." Thus, one major way to resolve conflicts of interest arising over common-pool resources is by reference to *property rights.*

Some analysts feel that coercion can occur only with a central authority given enforcement powers and that this is the only way to solve collective-goods problems. Calls for some form of world government have been made on this basis. While such calls may be extreme, many issues can be handled by creating international organizations with functional authority over certain matters. For example, according to the UN Convention on the Law of the Sea (UNCLOS), signed in 1982 and now ratified by more than 130 countries, the common resources of the deep seabed, such as the metal-rich manganese or nickel nodules, were to be "owned" by the newly created International Seabed Authority.[6]

Another way of managing the commons is to foster individual responsibility by converting parts of the commons into enclosed areas. The English enclosure movement of the early nineteenth century, for example, eliminated what remained of the commons pastureland. Such "privatization" of collective goods is directed at the problems arising from jointness of supply. Recipients must treat these enclosures with care, or else they will destroy their own property. For example, one provision of the Law of the Sea Treaty is the designation of exclusive economic zones (EEZs), which extend coastal jurisdiction to 200 miles for economic purposes. The aim was to undermine the temptation to free-ride by giving states an exclusive economic stake in their portion of the commons. Nationals of one state may lawfully navigate but may not fish or extract minerals from the EEZs of other states, and if they plunder their own zones they impose costs primarily on themselves. In this way, a large part of the continental shelf and seabed and over 40 percent of the high seas have been put under regulation and restriction.

UNCLOS is an example of an international regime created to help manage common-pool resources. International management regimes act to establish order in areas of market failure — where market mechanisms do not work and the tragedy of the commons is a potential threat. Many are about property rights. They involve such issues as *who* is allowed to use some resource, how much of the resource is available ("harvesting capacity") and the rate at which it can be used, and how its benefits are to be distributed among the participants. Another example is the North Pacific Fur Seal regime, based around a 1957 convention negotiated by the United States, the Soviet Union, Japan, and Canada. To prevent extinction of the seals, the agreement banned open-sea hunting, limited hunting to certain islands, and set quotas for yearly har-

---

[6] See Oran R. Young, *International Cooperation: Building Regimes for Natural Resources and the Environment* (Ithaca, N.Y.: Cornell University Press, 1989), esp. chap. 5, on fisheries and seabed mining.

vests — with a North Pacific Fur Seal Commission determining what the maximum yearly harvest would be. More interesting, Japan and Canada agreed to abstain from hunting seals, in return for being given a share of the profits by the United States and Russia.[7]

Both of these examples illustrate the interaction of rules, law, international organizations, and states. If issue areas are characterized by interdependence, sets of governing arrangements will help the actors to collaborate and coordinate their actions. Collaboration and coordination help states and other international actors avoid the temptation to defect or free ride; instead they are steered toward cooperation and, hopefully, socially optimal outcomes. International regimes foster collaboration and coordination by changing the structure of payoffs, making cooperation more beneficial and defection more costly. Regimes can allow for "side payments," as in sharing the fur seal profits with nonharvesters, and can reduce "transaction costs" by establishing and maintaining an institutional framework for negotiation and conflict resolution. "International regimes do not substitute for reciprocity; rather they reinforce and institutionalize it[,] . . . delegitimizing defection and thereby making it more costly."[8]

Sustainable Development

We now face ecological and environmental problems very different from those in the past. The growth of the world's population and the corresponding expansion of economic activity has alerted people to the fact that the earth is finite and that the limits of its *carrying capacity* can be reached. Resources that were adequate at lower absolute levels of demand are inadequate at higher levels. Exponential growth sharpens the interconnectedness of the problems that characterize the "world problematique." It challenges our ability to pursue human economic and social development while at the same time preserving the ecological systems upon which human development depends. Such a balance has been referred to as **sustainable development.**

> Sustainability requires decent and equitable living within the means of nature. Not living within our ecological means will lead to the destruction of humanity's only home. Having insufficient natural resources, not living decently and equitably will cause conflict and degrade our social fabric. . . . [P]eople are part of nature, and depend on its steady supply of the basic requirements for life.[9]

---

[7] Per Magnus Wijkman, "Managing the Global Commons," *International Organization* 36 (Summer 1982): 511–536.

[8] See Arthur A. Stein, "Coordination and Collaboration: Regimes in an Anarchic World," in Stephen D. Krasner, ed., *International Regimes* (Ithaca, N.Y.: Cornell University Press, 1983). The quote is from Robert Axelrod and Robert Keohane, "Achieving Cooperation under Anarchy: Strategies and Limitations," in Kenneth A. Oye, ed., *Cooperation under Anarchy* (Princeton, N.J.: Princeton University Press), p. 250. On regimes and the global commons, see Elinor Ostrom, *Governing the Commons: The Evolution of Institutions for Collective Action* (New York: Cambridge University Press, 1990); Robert O. Keohane, Marc A. Levy, and Peter M. Haas, *Institutions for the Earth: Sources of International Environmental Protection* (Cambridge, Mass.: MIT Press, 1993); and Young, *International Cooperation.*

[9] Mathis Wackernagel et al., "Ecological Footprints of Nations: How Much Nature Do They Use? — How Much Nature Do They Have?" March 1997 [cited March 23, 1999]; available at <http://www.ecouncil.ac.cr/rio/focus/report/english/footprint/>; Introduction.

It is also possible that the earth's carrying capacity is not only limited, but is actually being reduced through the disruption of natural ecosystems that have either been destroyed or are only slowly regenerating. Examples include overfarming in many areas, the southward spread of the Sahara Desert, and the destruction of the Amazon rainforest. In the past, when a tribe exhausted the productive capacity of an area, it simply moved on or died off. Today, the threatened ecosystem is not local but global. If our global ecosystem is damaged or destroyed, there is nowhere else to go. As both a concept and policy guide, sustainable development has achieved wide popularity. It means different things to different people, but common to all definitions is the notion that we need to address environmental concerns simultaneously with more traditional concerns of economic growth, whether locally or globally. The basic message is that environmental resources *are* finite and that ecosystems will collapse if resource utilization and destruction exceed regenerative capacity.[10]

Most of the major issues identified with the problem of sustainable development were introduced by the Club of Rome in the early 1970s in their limits-to-growth perspective. This often controversial series of books provided an outline of the ecological problematique: (1) the exponential nature of the growth of population and human demands on the environment; (2) the finite limits to global resources (even if we cannot agree exactly on what those limits are); (3) the intricate interdependence among population, capital investment, and the factors that influence growth (such as food, resources, and pollution), including the possibility that working to solve one problem may very well create others; and (4) the long delays in the feedback processes, that is, the long time lag between the release of pollutants or creation of other ecological damage and our realization that damage has been done.[11]

More recently, environmental scholars have developed a measure called an "ecological footprint" designed to give some sense of the land and water area required to sustain indefinitely a given population — that is, to produce what the population consumes and to absorb the waste it generates. Ideally, of course, a community's ecological footprint would correspond to the carrying capacity of the area it occupies, but that is rarely the case. A study commissioned by the Earth Council estimated that the ecological footprint of the earth today is about 13.6 billion hectares, but that its ecological capacity is only 10.6 billion hectares. That is an ecological *deficit* of about one-half hectare (1.24 acres) for every person on the planet. Japan, Italy, Britain, Germany, and the United States are countries with large ecological deficits, in both absolute and per capita terms (more than 2 hectares per person). Countries like Australia, New Zealand, Finland, Sweden, and Ireland have large per capita surpluses (between 1.5 and 4.5 hectares), but their absolute surpluses don't even begin to offset deficits elsewhere.[12]

---

[10] See, for example, see the annual editions of Lester R. Brown and colleagues, *State of the World* (New York: Norton, annual).

[11] There have been over twenty reports sponsored by the Club of Rome, the first and most renowned being Donella H. Meadows, Dennis L. Meadows, Jorgen Randers, and William W. Behrens, *The Limits to Growth* (New York: New American Library, 1972).

[12] Wackernagel et al., "Ecological Footprints of Nations," Table 1. See also Mathis Wackernagel and William E. Rees, *Our Ecological Footprint: Reducing Human Impact on the Earth* (Gabriola Island, Canada: New Society Publishers, 1996).

The limits to growth, and thus sustainable development, can be addressed in two ways: weaken the forces of growth, or expand the limits. There are two distinct views on these problems. One is pessimistic, as epitomized by the Club of Rome, and holds that the ecosystem is fragile and thus difficult to control and manage, that it has been damaged when we have tried to control it, and that technology will not solve our problems. This is sometimes called the *neo-Malthusian* perspective, after British economist Thomas Robert Malthus, whose *Essay on the Principle of Population,* written in 1798, warned of a looming demographic disaster if population growth rates continued to outpace the growth in food supplies. Malthusians are "inclusionist" in that they see humankind as an important and integral part of the interdependent global ecological system. In contrast, a more optimistic view holds that ecological problems are solvable through human ingenuity and technological innovation. It reflects an abiding faith that market mechanisms will drive the more efficient use of scarce resources and the substitution of more abundant resources (including synthetic ones) before the supply of scarce resources expires. This view is "exclusionist" in the sense that humans are effectively outside the confines of the global ecostructure and are able to manipulate its limits through scientific advance and technological development. Adherents to this perspective have been called *cornucopians*.[13]

Population and Demographics

Many people feel that at the heart of all ecological issues is the question of population. Three central problems arise from the pressures of population growth. The first was highlighted by Malthus: the dwindling of world food supplies. The possibility of starvation is not the only Malthusian outcome. If population growth strains food resources, then malnutrition will continue to limit the mental and physical development of children and the energies and abilities of adults — in other words, the *quality* of the population. The second problem is discontent resulting from deprivation. It pertains to the resentment felt among people who find themselves on the short end of an inequitable distribution of resources (including food) brought about by uneven patterns of population growth. As we discussed in Chapter 8, discontent caused by feelings of relative deprivation drives various ideological and political movements, especially those seeking revolutionary change. The uneven distribution of population growth in LDCs, especially the tremendous growth of urban populations (and attendant air- and water-pollution problems), exacerbates this trend. The third problem, perhaps most emphasized, is ecological. Increases in population inevitably increase the demands for natural resources, thus generating ever greater environmental decay.

---

[13] See, for example, Julian L. Simon, *The Ultimate Resource* 2 (Princeton, N.J.: Princeton University Press, 1996); see also Julian L. Simon and Herman Kahn, eds., *The Resourceful Earth* (Oxford: Blackwell, 1984).

The Population Explosion

The revolutions in industrial production technology, along with the medical and hygienic advances responsible for much of the increase in population, have combined to increase human demands and the attendant problems of pollution and resource depletion. Statistics abound on the consumption of natural resources (especially nonrenewable resources) and the production of pollution. But if scientific and technological advance has been more or less continuous throughout human history, what accounts for the fact that the ecological problems we face today seem to have rather suddenly burst into view? One answer is that the problems have always been around, but only recently have we started to take them seriously. However, another answer has to do with the important phenomenon of *exponential growth,* which is very much consistent with the "now you don't see it, now you do" nature of these problems. Exponential growth occurs when some quantity continuously increases by a constant percentage over a given period of time — when, for example, a population grows by 2 percent every year. This is the principle at work when we deposit money in a savings account so that it will grow through compound interest. It is also a very common process in all sorts of natural biological systems.

Common as it is, exponential growth can provide very surprising results; we do not think a problem exists until it hits us between the eyes. Two stories presented in the Club of Rome's initial major study, *The Limits to Growth,* illustrate how exponential growth can generate large numbers very quickly:

> There is an old Persian legend about a clever courtier who presented a beautiful chessboard to his king and requested only that the king give him in return 1 grain of rice for the first square on the board, 2 grains for the second square, 4 grains for the third, and so forth. The king readily agreed and ordered rice to be brought from his stores. The fourth square of the chessboard required eight grains, the tenth square 512 grains, the fifteenth required 16,384, and the twenty-first square gave the courtier more than a million gains of rice. By the fortieth square a million million rice grains had to be brought from the storerooms. The king's entire rice supply was exhausted long before he reached the sixty-fourth square.

The other story is a French riddle for children, which illustrates the suddenness and surprise of exponential growth:

> Suppose you own a pond on which a water lily is growing. The lily plant doubles in size each day. If the lily were allowed to grow unchecked, it would completely cover the pond in 30 days, choking off the other forms of life in the water. For a long time the lily plant seems small, and so you decide not to worry about cutting it back until it covers half the pond. On what day will that be? On the twenty-ninth day, of course. You have one day to save your pond.[14]

Both these stories demonstrate the explosive effects of 100 percent growth rates; at each interval — the next square on the chessboard, the next day in the life of the

---

[14] Meadows et al., *The Limits to Growth,* pp. 36–37.

pond — the numbers double. Of course, human populations don't exhibit 100 percent growth rates, but analysts have found it useful to think of exponential growth in terms of *doubling time*. From 1990 to 2000 the average annual growth rate of the world's population was 1.4 percent; at that rate the world population will double in just fifty years. If we think we have political, social, and economic problems with the present population of about 6 billion, imagine the problems with a population reaching twice that size by the year 2050. Fortunately, however, demographers do not expect a continuation of present exponential growth rates in population. Figure 16.2 shows the actual and projected growth in world population. During the nineteenth century annual growth rates were around 0.5 percent. Growth rates were twice that by the 1930s, and had risen to 2 percent by the 1960s — cutting doubling time in half, then in half again. Growth rates have declined from their peak in the 1960s, but as the dashed line in the figure indicates, if we are to avoid the disastrous consequences of a doubling of world population by 2050, those growth rates will have to continue to decline. Currently, the UN projects that population will stabilize by about 2200, at which time it will stand at 11.6 billion people, just under twice the number of souls inhabiting the earth today. This is *not* a

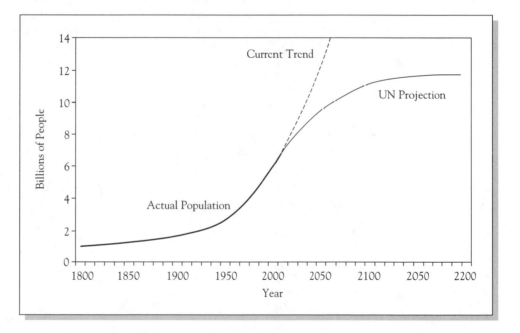

FIGURE 16.2 Actual and Projected World Population, 1800–2200

Sources: Years 1800–1949, 2051–2200: United Nations Population Division, "World Population Growth from Year 0 to Stabilization," 1994 [cited March 17, 1999]; available at <gopher://gopher.undp.org:70/00/ungophers/popin/wdtrends/histor>. Years 1950–2050: United States Bureau of the Census, "Total Midyear Population for the World: 1950–2050," December 28, 1998 [cited March 17, 1999]; available at <http://www.census.gov/ipc/www/worldpop.html>. Some years have been interpolated. Current trend calculated by authors based on an annual growth rate of 1.4 percent.

pessimistic projection, for it is based on an anticipated *reversal* of exponential growth. As the economist Kenneth Boulding observed, "Anyone who believes that exponential growth can continue indefinitely in a finite world is either a madman or an economist."

The Demographic Transition

It took from 1800 to 1930 to add 1 billion people to the world's population; the most recent billion was added in a little more than a decade. The present burst in population growth is due mostly to the drastic reduction in death rates caused by the public health improvements made in the past 200 years. Developing societies go through a **demographic transition,** as illustrated by Figure 16.3. In the first stage, typified by Europe prior to the Industrial Revolution, birthrates and death rates are relatively high. Medicine and health care are underdeveloped; death rates are high, and so are birthrates (in order to provide enough laborers for what is primarily an agrarian economy). By the middle of the eighteenth century, death rates were dropping in Europe due to advances in medicine and sanitation. At this second stage, birthrates remain high because large families remain an asset for agricultural production, which is still central in economies in the early phases of industrialization. This is a period of rapid population growth, given the widening gap between birthrates and death rates. In stage three, industrialization, urbanization, and the entry of women into the workforce decrease the incentives for large families; birthrates drop and death rates level off as access to basic health care becomes nearly universal. Population growth rates begin to

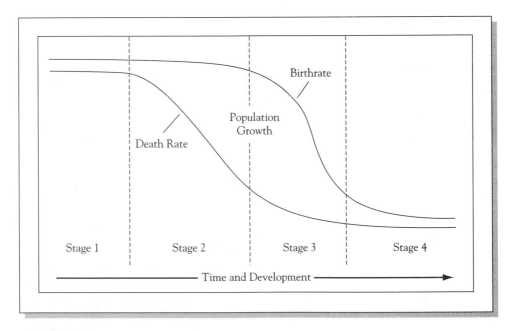

FIGURE 16.3   The Demographic Transition

fall. The last stage in the transition is marked by the stabilization of birth- and death rates at fairly low levels, and Europe and the rest of the industrialized world are presently at this stage.

Table 16.1 shows the total population, birth- and death rates, growth rates, and doubling time for the world, for industrialized and developing countries, and for geographic regions. Clearly, different groups of countries are at different stages in the demographic transition. The industrialized world as a whole has reached the final stage where birth- and death rates are at very low levels and doubling time is high. In

TABLE 16.1 Population, Growth, and Doubling Time, 2000					
Region	Population (millions)	Birthrate (per 1,000)	Death Rate (per 1,000)	Growth Rate (percent)	Doubling Time (years)
World	6,082	22	9	1.4	50
Industrialized countries	1,181	11	10	0.3	233
Developing countries	4,901	25	9	1.7	41
excluding China and Taiwan	3,616	29	10	1.9	37
Africa	798	38	14	2.5	28
Asia	3,451	22	8	1.4	50
Europe and former Soviet Union	799	11	11	0.1	700
Latin America and Caribbean	523	23	7	1.7	41
Middle East	175	31	9	2.6	27
North America	306	14	7	1.0	70
Oceania	30	18	7	1.3	54

Note: Birth- and death rates are for 1998; population growth rates are average annual rates for 1990–2000. Doubling rates calculated by the authors as 70 ÷ growth rate.
Source: U.S. Bureau of the Census, *World Population Profile: 1998* (Washington, D.C.: U.S. Government Printing Office, 1999), tables A-2, A-3.

the developing world, however, high birthrates combined with low death rates suggest that these countries are still in transition; they account not only for most of the
world's population, but also for nearly all of the world's population growth. The gap
between birth- and death rates is even higher if China is excluded (it has cut birthrates
dramatically, often through draconian measures). In Africa and the Middle East, where
birthrates are the highest, population growth is the highest. Notice that there is much
less variability in death rates across the different groups of countries than variability in
birthrates. That is because advances in medicine, developed in societies further along
in the demographic transition, are rather quickly adopted by societies at earlier stages
(those with higher birthrates). For an "importer" of medical advances, in effect, the
death-rate curve in Figure 16.3 turns more sharply downward in stage two, and when
this is not accompanied by commensurate decline in the birthrate, the period of rapid
population growth lengthens. Thus, there have been numerous campaigns by governments, IGOs, and NGOs to educate people in these societies about birth control and
benefits of smaller family size. The aim is to accelerate the decline in birthrates made
necessary by the accelerated decline in death rates.

We need to look at more than birth- and death rates. To get a true picture of population growth, we have to look at the *population composition* of a country; that is, the
numbers of people in different age groups and the fertility rates for those categories. As
child and infant mortality rates fall, a country's population becomes younger and a
greater proportion of women are of childbearing age. Figure 16.4 shows the population
composition for developing and industrialized countries, both in 1998 and as projected
for the year 2025. The developing countries, with well over one billion females under
the age of fifteen, have the potential for much greater population growth in the future.
Many women have yet to reach childbearing age in the LDCs, and in the years ahead a
large portion of the populace will be reproducing: the larger group now at childbearing
age and those who have yet to reach that age (the broad base of the age pyramid). What
is more, although projections for 2025 show a gradual aging of the population in the
developing world (the swollen ranks in the middle), there will still be more females of
childbearing age than there are today. Even if future parents were to merely replace
themselves with two children, so many people have yet to do this that the population
of the LDCs will continue to grow for some time. By contrast, the composition of the
population in the industrialized world is relatively balanced by age group, suggesting
no further growth.

This is an important aspect of the idea of "deadly delays." We need to look at least
fifty years ahead. The longer population control is delayed, the more people of childbearing age will enter the population. In the future when population growth is indeed
level — that is, there is no growth — the absolute level of population will be much
higher. That means that the absolute number of people will continue to grow for
decades after a population control policy is initiated. The uneven rate of population
growth is a major factor in the food trade patterns of North America and Latin America. In 1950, both regions had approximately the same population (166 million). However, the rapid increase in the Latin American population and the emphasis in
commercial agriculture on exports have forced Latin America to become a net importer
of basic foodstuffs, while North America exports food. Countries in Latin America now
have almost 70 percent more mouths to feed than in North America.

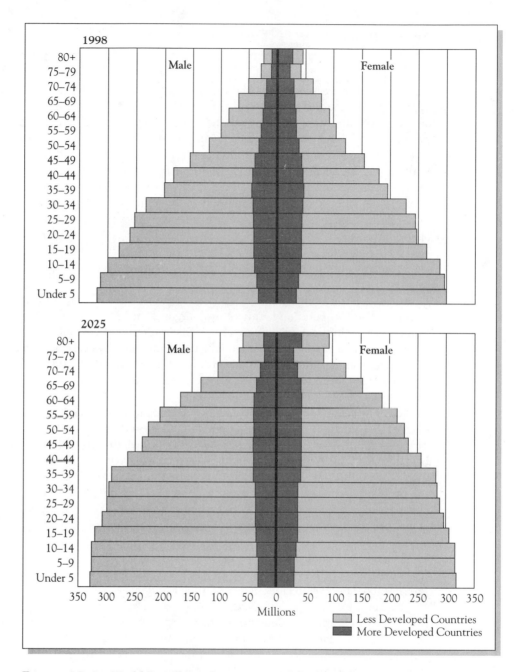

FIGURE 16.4 World Population Composition, 1998 and 2025

Source: U.S. Bureau of the Census, *World Population Profile: 1998* (Washington, D. C.: U.S. Government Printing Office, 1999), figure 17.

Resource Depletion

The inclusionist perspective of Malthusians has given rise to a common metaphor in environmental studies: **spaceship earth.** As Boulding put it, "the earth has become a single spaceship, without unlimited reservoirs of anything, either for extraction or for pollution, and in which, therefore, man must find his place in a cyclical system capable of continuous reproduction."[15] Population growth, combined with the demands for maintaining high standards of living in the rich countries and demands for development and industrialization in the poor ones, has put great pressures on the world's supply of resources. Moreover, although we have made some initial forays along the "final frontier," it may be quite some time before we come across any supply depots for spaceship earth.

Food

As much as 40 percent of the world population suffers from some form of undernourishment. The UN Food and Agricultural Organization (FAO) has estimated that 800 million people in the developing world — 200 million of them children — suffer from *chronic* (continuing) undernutrition, which stunts their physical and mental development and makes it difficult to pursue ordinary human activities. This is despite the fact that global food production is rising, whether measured in the aggregate or on a per capita basis.[16]

The FAO estimates that almost all of the best arable land (1.35 billion hectares) is currently cultivated; the remaining arable land would be very costly to prepare for growing food. Every year much arable land is lost to cultivation (5 to 7 million hectares), perhaps permanently, through the expansion of roads and urban areas and, increasingly, through various forms of land degradation. Deforestation contributes to the problem because forests help to prevent topsoil erosion, and although the expansion of pastures for grazing has been an important cause of deforestation, pastureland is less productive than arable land in terms of the number of people a plot of a given size can feed. Agricultural scientists try to keep up with population growth and loss of arable land by introducing new seeds, fertilizers, and pesticides to raise the productivity of existing land. Nevertheless, it is a hard race, and the new technologies consume a great deal of energy and cause new pollution problems as well.

Part of the problem in assessing the carrying capacity of the world's food resources lies in the definition of "adequate nourishment." Obviously, "adequate" means a certain minimum intake of calories, protein, vitamins, and minerals. It does not, however, require that everyone adopt the dietary habits of people living in the industrial countries, where diets are heavy in meat and other animal products (a steer must take in six

---

[15] Kenneth Boulding, "The Economics of the Coming Spaceship Earth," in Henry Jarrett, ed., *Environmental Quality in a Growing Economy* (Baltimore: Johns Hopkins University Press, 1966), p. 9.
[16] United Nations Food and Agriculture Organization, "Agriculture and Food Security," November 1996 [cited March 22, 1999]; available at <http://www.fao.org/wfs/fs/e/img/Agricu-e.pdf>.

to eight pounds of grain to produce one pound of beef). Thus, we see the virtue of development programs that stress meeting the basic needs of everyone and avoiding a distribution of income and consumption skewed heavily in favor of people in the rich countries or the rich people in poor countries. From 1992 to 1994, the average daily intake for people in the developed world was about 3,200 calories, while in the developing world it was just over 2,500 calories; the protein gap was 98 versus 64 grams.[17] Inequalities in levels of "food security" raise serious ethical questions, some of which we explore later in this chapter.

A global food paradox has also appeared. By the mid-1980s world food production had reached record levels; indeed, because so much food was produced, prices fell, leading to ever higher subsidies from governments to farmers in the United States, Europe, and even the then-Soviet Union. During this same period China became self-sufficient in grain (exporting corn to Japan) and India found itself with a grain surplus. Through improved biotechnology, food production was increased dramatically: American farmers get five times the yield of fifty years ago. Because of new frost-resistant breeds of corn, the corn belt in the United States now extends 250 miles farther north than it did in the mid-1970s. The development of aquaculture — the use of fish farms — has been particularly important in China and India. Although agricultural production is likely to grow faster than world population for the next few decades, the growth per person will drop significantly. The FAO estimates that over the 1990–2010 period, the average annual increase in per capita production will be 0.25 percent, down from 0.54 percent during the 1970–1990 period. Partly this will come about because many people already eat as much as they need and want, but there are many others who cannot afford to pay the prices that would otherwise stimulate increased food production.[18]

Four decades of increasing food production have not eliminated the problems of malnourishment or even starvation. In the short term, yearly harvest fluctuations cause food crises in particular areas. Weather conditions make the world grain crop volatile, and, as seen in 1993, in any one year the grain harvest can drop as much as 5 percent. Still, the larger problem is getting the financial resources needed to produce the food, to pay for the energy needed to produce the food, and to buy the food that is available. The amount of food on the world market may even depress local prices, reducing the money and food available in local areas (as local producers stop producing). Situations of malnutrition and starvation derive primarily from *political* factors that affect the distribution of food: civil war and insurgency (as in Africa) preventing food from getting to certain areas, government decisions to reward and punish certain regions or groups within the state, or urban demands for cheap food.

More generally, in many LDCs food-distribution facilities are terribly inadequate. Food may rot on the piers of a port city or be eaten by pests on the farms. International food assistance is sometimes diverted by corrupt officials who sell the food for profit. Further, development patterns oriented toward the export market — big commercial

---

[17] World Resources Institute et al., *World Resources 1998–99: Environmental Change and Human Health* (New York: Oxford University Press, 1998), table 10.3.

[18] United Nations Food and Agriculture Organization, "Agriculture and Food Security."

crops like cotton, coffee, sugar, fruit, and flowers — may bring in foreign exchange, enabling the rich to buy luxuries or giving LDC governments the finances needed for industrial development. However, when subsistence farms are converted into big commercial establishments raising cash crops, an immediate food deficit is created. Laborers who used to raise their own food must now use part of their earnings to buy food. Part of this problem could be eased by development programs aimed at strengthening small farmers, who could raise some crops for sale but keep a part of their land for raising their own food.

Land reform and technical assistance to small farmers are receiving increasing attention by international lending organizations like the World Bank, but political and economic resistance to a major reorientation of agricultural development is nevertheless very great. International cooperation has also been channeled through the FAO and other agencies. Agencies such as the World Food Council help keep track of and aid in the deliveries of food, and the Agricultural Development Fund helps developing countries increase production. Yet such activity (a world "food regime") only begins to meet the problems — problems requiring a global approach along with investment and food aid, an effective population policy, and balanced economic development within and among the regions of the world.

Natural Resources

Many studies indicate that the use of the world's resources is growing exponentially and that in many areas and for many resources it is growing at a rate faster than the growth in population. For example, while world population has increased three and a half times since 1890, industrial energy use per capita has increased over seven times and total world energy use has grown *fourteen* times. According to World Bank figures, from 1980 to 1995, commercial energy use increased almost 30 percent globally; the increase in low and middle income countries was 42 percent. This is good news for economic development but bad news for world resources.[19]

Every additional human being and every additional demand for every new item produced place demands on the earth's mineral and energy resources. Figures on known reserves of minerals and other nonrenewable resources are deceptive. Many parts of the world are not yet fully explored, so new reserves of many minerals will undoubtedly be found. (Geologists sometimes make estimates of these "probable" and "possible" reserves.) Known bodies of resources may be too difficult or too expensive to tap into, given current knowledge and prices. New technology may be developed for extracting the materials, and a rise in prices may make it profitable to exploit deposits that previously were too costly to mine. Thus, known reserves can be greatly expanded even without any exploration. This has happened with some petroleum

---

[19] World Bank, *World Development Report 1998/99: Knowledge for Development* (Washington, D.C.: World Bank, 1998), Table 10. See also the special issue of *Scientific American,* September 1990, on "Energy for Planet Earth," especially John P. Holdren, "Energy in Transition," pp. 156–163. For an analysis of energy consumption and global patterns of industrialization, see Joshua S. Goldstein, Xiaoming Huang, and Burcu Akan, "Energy in the World Economy, 1950–1992," *International Studies Quarterly* 41, 2 (June 1997): pp. 241–266.

deposits in the United States, where oil fields that were no longer profitable could once again yield valuable supplies when prices rose.

Still, there are limits. The World Resources Institute and others report that at current rates of usage, proved reserves would supply the world's petroleum needs for forty years and natural gas needs for sixty years. Clearly, at some point the world's fuel supplies really will be exhausted, even allowing for further exploration. Long before that happens, they will become too expensive to use except for very special purposes for which there are no acceptable substitutes. If the world expands its reserves of minerals chiefly by making them very expensive, it will have made a very dubious bargain.

It is important to understand that industrialized countries use far more resources than do the overpopulated LDCs. Industrialized countries account for about 20 percent of the world's population, yet consume almost 70 percent of all commercial energy. Thus, a cutback in resource consumption in the developed world could reduce the projected usage rates of nonrenewable resources and increase the lifespan of world's remaining reserves. The United States, with about 5 percent of the world's population, has accounted for about 60 percent of the world's consumption of natural gas, as well as 25 to 30 percent of petroleum, aluminum, copper, and lead (see Table 16.2). It

TABLE 16.2   Mineral Consumption, 1994

Mineral	Largest Consumer	Share of World Consumption (percent)	World Reserve Base Life (years)
Aluminum (bauxite)	United States	26.8	252
Cadmium	Japan	36.1	n.a.
Copper	United States	24.1	62
Iron Ore	China	23.0	233
Lead	United States	25.7	47
Mercury	United States	18.2	83
Nickel	Japan	18.7	137
Tin	United States	15.5	59
Zinc	United States	16.1	48

Note: World reserve base life assumes continuing annual production at 1994 levels; n.a. = not available.

Source: World Resources Institute et al., *World Resources 1996–97* (New York: Oxford University Press, 1996), table 12.4.

accounts for more than a quarter of the world's total energy consumption, and 20 percent of that has to be imported. China, on the other hand, with 20 percent of the world's population, is responsible for only about 10 percent of the world's energy consumption, while India, with 16 percent of the population, accounts for just 3 percent.

Another resource, which is often neglected because it is not strictly nonrenewable, is water. Only about 2 to 3 percent of the world's water is fresh water, and most of that is in the icecaps. Less than 1 percent of the world's water is fresh water that is readily available for human consumption, directly or indirectly, given current levels of technology: rivers, lakes, water in soil and plants, and vapor in the atmosphere. Though water is a scarce resource, usage is rapidly increasing to meet human consumption and food-production demands. Water must not only be available but also be of sufficiently high quality for drinking, washing, and growing food. While desalination of seawater has become more widespread among countries that can afford it, the quality of fresh water is being threatened by a wide range of human-generated pollutants, from sewage to industrial waste to chemical outputs from mining and agriculture.

Vast quantities of water are needed for opening up new farmland, reclaiming old land, maintaining the land in use, and supporting the ongoing "green revolution" in overpopulated areas. To produce 1 pound of grain requires 60 to 225 gallons of water, and the production of 1 pound of beef requires 2,500 to 6,000 gallons. Industrial activities also require great quantities of water: 1 ton of steel requires 65,000 gallons, and 1 automobile requires 100,000 gallons. Water usage grows faster than population (it is estimated that the former will triple as population doubles). Demand will rise most quickly in the industrialized areas.

We began by examining population growth, but many analysts begin with and stress energy consumption, calling energy "the master resource." With enough energy, other resources can be mined or otherwise acquired, processed, substituted, or recycled. In other words, the limits to these resources can be relaxed. Increasing food production or cleaning up polluted air and water also requires expending large amounts of energy. Economic development and growth in national wealth correlate with the use of energy; consequently, poor countries will require more energy to develop. A vicious cycle emerges here: birthrates tend to drop and stabilize as countries develop economically, but for this to happen, more energy is needed. Meanwhile, the added population creates demands that devour additional energy and wealth just to maintain the current level of usage. This means that very large amounts of energy must be devoted to the less developed areas.

The drain on the global commons is highly uneven. While population increases in the developing world drive resource consumption, by far the greatest drain occurs in the developed states. Strategies should therefore include changes in lifestyles, as well as changes in the structure of the manufacturing economy: eliminating planned obsolescence, designing longer-lasting and more easily repaired products, recycling, and ceasing to produce products that wind up in rubbish mountains. The current pattern of production and distribution in the industrialized countries probably cannot be maintained even there; an attempt to imitate it worldwide would cause ecological disaster. The *growth* in energy consumption does seem to be leveling off, in part because of effective conservation (especially in Europe and Japan). From 1973, the year of the initial OPEC "oil shock," to 1995 the average annual growth in commercial energy consumption in high income countries was 1.3 percent (0.6 percent per capita). Compare that to the 6.9 percent annual growth rate in energy consumption by low- and middle-income countries (6.1 percent per capita).[20] Clearly, given a conducive set of circumstances and incentives, countries can curb (and have) their excessive patterns of resource consumption.

Individual actions and attitudes can be important. Some people in the developed countries are slowly changing their habits to reduce consumption and to conserve energy. However, the problems of collective goods continue to hamper those efforts when people emphasize their own self-interest, as most people do most of the time. Preserving the commons for posterity is certainly not foremost in the minds of individuals inclined to ask, "What has posterity ever done for me?" Altruism alone cannot produce the necessary sacrifices; we still need a combination of raised costs (money and otherwise) and a heightened awareness of the effects of our actions. Short- and medium-term strategies, including resource substitution, can allow the development not only of new lifestyles but also of whole processes, technologies, and synthetic materials. Short- and medium-term strategies must therefore bring the world through a difficult period of transition to a point where longer-run thinking has taken root. Very basic changes must be made in resource usage, population growth, and substitutes for exhausted resources. Changes in behavior must occur across all levels of analysis: individual, group, economic enterprise, society, region, and the world system as a whole.

Environmental Decay

The interdependent relationship among population, economic growth, energy consumption, and pollution pointed out by early Malthusians produces a dilemma that is again coming to the forefront of attention. One way to control population growth is through economic and human development; yet to maintain high standards of living in the developed world and improve standards in LDCs means higher energy usage and the creation of ever higher levels of pollution. Other consequences of development we are only beginning to appreciate. Destruction of the natural habitats of other species obviously represents a negative externality for them, and that may be reason enough to work for their preservation. But it is also likely that the extinction of nonhuman species, whether plant or animal, will have repercussions for human well-being.

---

[20] Calculations based on figures in the World Bank's *World Development Indicators on CD-ROM 1998* [electronic database].

Pollution

Pollution can be anything from a bother or an inconvenience to an immediate danger to animal, plant, and human life. It can destroy precious food and water resources and make many of the limited resources of the earth unusable. The *Limits to Growth* made four main points about pollution:

1. The few kinds of pollution that actually have been measured over time seem to be increasing exponentially.

2. We have almost no knowledge about where the upper limits to these pollution growth curves might be.

3. The presence of natural delays in ecological processes increases the probability of underestimating the control measures necessary, and therefore of inadvertently reaching those upper limits.

4. Many pollutants are globally distributed; their harmful effects appear long distances from their points of generation.[21]

The increasing use of nonrenewable fuels, as well as the manufacture of chemicals and other industrial products, is producing rising levels of pollution worldwide. Burning fossil fuels produces carbon dioxide, carbon monoxide, sulfur oxides, nitrogen oxides, hydrocarbons, and solid particles. These are emitted into the air and water of our planet. Some of these emissions produce acid rain. They settle into or are washed into the soil and into the plants and animals that live in polluted areas. Water is also damaged by thermal pollution: heat from industrial processes and nuclear energy reactors disrupts the ecological balance of rivers, streams, and lakes. In addition, nuclear power produces radioactive wastes, which could become the most dangerous pollutants of all. Some of the most difficult, controversial, and critical issues involved with nuclear power concern accidents — Chernobyl is the most striking example — that leak radiation into the ecosystem around the nuclear power plant. Equally difficult is the problem of disposing of the highly radioactive wastes that nuclear power plants produce. Many countries simply have no safe disposal sites or viable disposal policies. Hence, this is a problem demanding international cooperation.

The spread of pollutants throughout the ecosystem is one of the major indications of global interdependence. For example, lead emitted into the air by the industrial countries has been found in the Greenland icecap. Large deposits of DDT (a chemical pesticide, now banned in the U.S. and elsewhere) have been found in the bodies of whales that have lived almost entirely in the Antarctic region. Increases in the carbon dioxide content of the atmosphere (resulting especially from the burning of fossil fuels) create the *greenhouse effect,* which traps heat inside the atmosphere. The result is **global warming,** a gradual increase in world temperatures. Estimates vary, but the UN's Intergovernmental Panel on Climate Change (IPCC) projects that global temperatures will rise by 1 to 3.5 degrees Celsius (1.8 to 6.3 degrees Fahrenheit) over the next 100 years. Climate will change in erratic and unpredictable ways: forests will move pole-

---

[21] Meadows et al., *The Limits to Growth,* pp. 78–80.

ward; arid zones in the middle of continents will grow and make grain cultivation uneconomical; the icecaps will melt and the sea level will rise, drowning low-lying coastal areas. The increased frequency and duration of heatwaves will claim more lives, as will malaria, dengue, and other diseases carried by mosquitos and rodents that will proliferate along with warmer and damper climates. Harmful effects will be different at different latitudes and in different regions.[22] Scientists agree on the general outlines, though not the details, of what will happen, but they disagree as to what should be done about it. Energy conservation and, perhaps ironically, greater emphasis on nuclear energy will be required.

Figure 16.5 shows the trend in carbon dioxide (CO_2) emissions since 1990, as well as the concentration of CO_2 in the atmosphere since 1965. Like population, CO_2 emissions increased exponentially through the early 1970s, although the rate of increase seems to have slowed somewhat since then. The growing atmospheric concentration of CO_2, on the other hand, shows little sign of slowing. Here is another example of

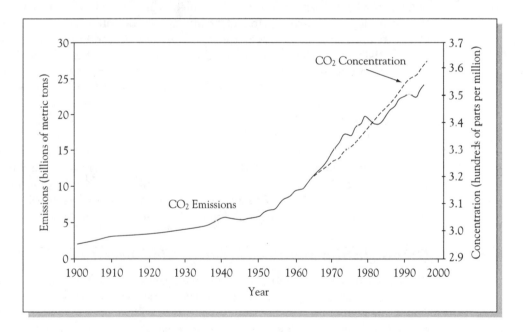

FIGURE 16.5   Carbon Dioxide Emisssions and Concentrations, 1900–1996

Source: World Resources Institute et al., *World Resources 1998–99: Environmental Change and Human Health* (New York: Oxford University Press, 1998). Tables 16.3, 16.4. Emissions data were interpolated for some years prior to 1950.

---

[22] Intergovernmental Panel on Climate Change (IPCC), *Climate Change 1995: The Science of Climate Change* (Cambridge: Cambridge University Press, 1996). See also IPCC, "The Regional Impacts of Climate Change: An Assessment of Vulnerability," November 1997 [cited March 26, 1999]; available at <http://www.ipcc.ch/special/regional.pdf>.

"deadly delays"; the environmental damage wrought by our behavior may last long after that destructive behavior has been curbed.

Over the past decade state leaders have been mobilized into action. The UN Framework Convention on Climate Change (UNFCC) was signed at the Conference on Environment and Development (the "Earth Summit") in Rio de Janeiro in 1992, and it adopted as a goal the reduction of greenhouse emissions to 1990 levels by the year 2000. Binding targets for emissions were generally opposed by the United States, but by the end of 1998 it had come around and signed the 1997 Kyoto Protocol to the UNFCC, which does obligate its industrialized signatories to reduce greenhouse emissions somewhat below 1990 levels not later than 2012, with "demonstrable progress" shown by 2005. By 1995, thirteen of the thirty-five obligated countries had already met their targets.[23]

Pollutants are also responsible for punching the holes that have appeared in the earth's atmospheric **ozone layer** over Antarctica. Ozone at ground level is a health hazard, but the ozone layer miles above the surface is crucial to life on earth because it helps to screen out cancer-causing ultraviolet radiation from the sun. The thinning of the ozone layer is partly the result of the use of chlorofluorocarbons (CFCs), now mostly banned from use in spray cans but still widely used in plastics and refrigeration. In 1987, twenty-five major producing countries signed the Montreal Protocol to cut worldwide production of these chemicals by 50 percent by 1998. It was a fairly impressive agreement, given the difficulties: delay caused by vested economic interests, uncertainty about the scientific evidence, and the reluctance of LDCs to pay for more expensive substitutes. In 1990 in London, an agreement was reached to end *all* production of chemicals that destroy the ozone layer by the year 2000; the 1992 Copenhagen amendment moved this date up to 1996 for industrialized countries. The London agreement came about only through compromise, which included the industrial countries setting up a fund to help developing countries pay for the phasing in of CFC substitutes. By 1999 almost 170 states had ratified the Montreal Protocol, and a majority of these had also ratified the London and Copenhagen amendments.

Deforestation and the Threat to Biodiversity

Both ozone depletion and global warming are compounded by another form of environmental degradation — **deforestation.** The World Resources Institute estimates that "eighty percent of the forests that originally covered the earth have been cleared, fragmented, or otherwise degraded." Of those large, relatively undisturbed "frontier forests" that remain — mainly in the Amazon Basin, Central Africa, Canada, and Russia — 40 percent are now threatened. Large areas of the Amazon and other rainforests are being cleared in the interests of commercial development and of settling new farmers pushed out of their former homes by the South American population explosion. Tropical rainforests, once estimated to have covered 16 percent of the world's terrestrial

---

[23] For a critique of the Kyoto arrangement, especially the exclusion of developing countries from the regime, see Richard N. Cooper, "Toward a Real Global Warming Treaty," *Foreign Affairs* 77, 2 (March/April 1998): pp. 66–79.

surface, now cover only 7 percent. One-fifth of all tropical forest cover was lost between 1960 and 1990; Asia lost about one-third. Overall, global deforestation (the *net* loss) is occurring at a rate of 0.3 percent per year — 0.7 percent per year in tropical areas.[24]

When forests are cleared for farming, the ecosystem is damaged in multiple ways. Trees that absorbed carbon dioxide from the atmosphere are eliminated, but also destroyed are the habitats of many other species, in some cases pushing them to the point of extinction. Such a loss represents a reduction in biological diversity, or **biodiversity,** the number and variety of living things on earth. Again, estimates vary, but scientists believe that thousands of species become extinct each year due to human activities and that the earth could lose 2 to 8 percent of its species over the next twenty-five years.

> While these extinctions are an environmental tragedy, they also have profound implications for economic and social development. At least 40 percent of the world's economy and 80 per cent of the needs of the poor are derived from biological resources. In addition, the richer the diversity of life, the greater the opportunity for medical discoveries, economic development, and adaptive responses to such new challenges as climate change.[25]

Deforestation, like other forms of environmental degradation, involves *local* decisions that cause *global* problems, and the problems cannot be dealt with only by restraint at the national level. They require agreement among nations and changes by international development agencies like the World Bank in the kind of projects they support and encourage. At the 1992 Earth Summit, more than 156 states signed the Convention on Biological Diversity, and by the beginning of 1999 it had been ratified by 175. Signatories agreed to safeguard biodiversity within their borders and expressed a commitment to find ways to share the benefits of biodiversity (like profits from medicines derived from tropical trees) as well as the costs of species protection. The United States was the only developed nation not to sign the treaty in Rio, the main concern being that intellectual property rights were not adequately dealt with, although the Clinton administration did sign in 1993. The treaty has not been ratified by the U.S. Senate, however, and some in the U.S. biotechnology sector worry that developing countries will begin to deny them access to protected areas for purposes of "biological prospecting."

Dilemmas of Development

To prevent even further destruction of tropical rainforests, programs of "debt-for-nature swaps" have been worked out. Governments of developed countries and international organizations forgive a large portion of a developing country's foreign debt in

---

[24] World Resources Institute et al., *World Resources 1998–99,* table 11.1. For information on frontier forests, including regional overviews, see World Resources Institute, "Frontier Regions," n.d. [cited March 27, 1999]; available at <http://www.wri.org/ffi/frontier/>.

[25] United Nations Environment Programme, "The Convention about Life on Earth," December 1998 [cited March 27, 1999]; available at <http://www.biodiv.org/conv/leaflet.html>.

return for its commitment to give permanent legal protection to large tracts of forest. As with developed countries paying for CFC substitutes, agreements for debt relief, trade, and aid to save tropical forests are an example of using side payments to get actors to cooperate in a tragedy-of-the-commons situation.

Such actions come none too soon. Costa Rica provides an example of some of the problems. For its size, it has the largest system of protected land and national parks in the world (45 percent of its forest area, 15 percent of its total land area). Yet it also has had one of the highest rates of deforestation in the world (3.1 percent annually). In essence, everything that is not protected is being cut at breath-taking speed. Banana growing vividly illustrates the dilemmas of Costa Rican development. The country has long been a big banana producer, and the government hopes to make it the region's foremost banana exporter. Multinational corporations are powerful actors in the domestic politics of this small and not wealthy country. Great plantations provide jobs at good wages, but the environmental effects of clear-cutting forests for cultivation, subsequent exhaustion of the land, and widespread pollution are immense. Bananas are not a free lunch.

Tourism is Costa Rica's third largest industry, thanks to the country's political stability, its great and varied natural beauty, and the park system. But its ecological assets are being endangered. The same coral reef that begins far north in Mexico's Yucatan peninsula extends all the way down Costa Rica's east coast and had been a major tourist attraction. Now most of the reef in Costa Rica is dead, a sad remnant of what still remains in the Yucatan and Belize. The runoff of silt and pesticides from coastal banana plantations has killed it. Tourism itself can be a mixed blessing, however. Costa Rica is not yet plagued by wall-to-wall high-rise hotels, but they may soon come. Some Costa Ricans are trying to promote "ecotourism" as an alternative. This entails building small-scale units that blend with rather than dominate the natural landscape, employing residents as managers and as guides who can interpret local culture and ecology, and promoting direct and relatively close contact with the indigenous people. A central aim is the education of tourists about ecological problems and possibilities. Tourism of this form is not for everyone, either tourists or hosts. It cannot provide anything like the number of jobs that mass tourism provides, and visitors' contacts with the local culture will remain fairly superficial. But perhaps ecotourism can interact with Costa Rica's efforts to preserve large segments of its natural environment.

Obligations and Rights

Resource depletion and environmental degradation are externalities produced by population growth and economic development and are clear examples of collective "bads." Individual states cannot avoid being affected by these ecological developments; individual state action cannot overcome them. Collective action is required. Since the late 1980s some impressive movement toward action on ecological issues has taken place, led by IGOs (like the UN Environment Programme and the World Bank's Environment Department), NGOs, and various transnational environmental groups (like Greenpeace). Green groups and green thinking have proliferated around the globe, creating the core of a growing environmental regime.[26] This, of course, is what is needed to deal with collective goods problems arising from global interdependence. A primary dilemma, however, is sustainable development — containing ecological damage must somehow be reconciled with the need for greater global equity and the need to improve living conditions in the LDCs.

International Distributive Justice

Earlier in this chapter we discussed the UN Convention on the Law of the Sea. In addition to creating exclusive economic zones, UNCLOS established an International Seabed Authority to manage the resources beyond the 200–mile limit in order to preserve the "common heritage of mankind." Here, however, the LDCs and the developed states held two different views on how the seabed commons should be regulated. LDCs wanted the International Seabed Authority (and its operational arm, the Enterprise) to control all exploitation of the seabed. Developed states, the United States in the forefront, desired national control. With their own sophisticated mining industries, the United States, Britain, Germany, and others wanted relatively free access and limited control by the authority.

The Law of the Sea process illustrates several previously discussed topics. As we saw in Chapter 15, differences in wealth and development, past colonial relationships, and dominance or dependence complicate the uneven distribution of resources and the use of those resources around the world. To develop, the global South needs vast amounts of resources, energy, capital, and aid. In the process of developing they will add considerably to the consumption of nonrenewable resources and will also generate a great deal of environmental degradation. Given Western opposition to the mining and wealth-sharing provisions of the Law of the Sea, as well as analogous positions taken in other contexts, the view that certain states in the North are trying to keep the South in an underdeveloped and subordinate position is not altogether unjustified. This view is reinforced when ecologically minded people tell LDCs that they should not aim for similar levels of development as the rich countries in light of the environmental consequences. In short, we have a collective-action problem complicated further by a history of colonialism and exploitation.

It is clear that development strategies based on more equity within nations and modest transfers of wealth between nations could greatly improve the conditions of the world's poor. The relationship between per capita income and measures of social health like life expectancy and child mortality, for example, is very strong at the poor end of the spectrum: small increases in wealth have big effects. Figure 16.6 shows the relationship between GNP per capita and child mortality for eighty-five countries classified by the World Bank as low or lower-middle income (each is represented as a dot on the graph). The curve is a way of summarizing the relationship, even though most

---

[26] See, for example, Paul Wapner, *Environmental Activism and World Civic Politics* (Albany: State University of New York Press, 1996). James Pinkerton refers to the greening of domestic and international politics as "enviromanticism"; see his somewhat cynical piece, "Enviromanticism: The Poetry of Nature as Political Force," *Foreign Affairs* 76, 3 (May/June 1997): pp. 2–7.

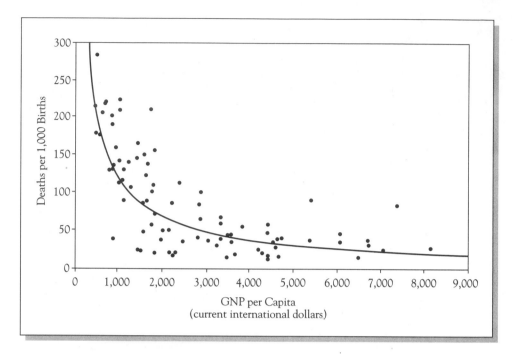

FIGURE 16.6   Child Mortality in Relation to Income in the Poorer Countries, 1996

Note: Child mortality is the number of deaths under the age of five; gross national product (GNP) per capita is measured using purchasing power parities. The counties represented are classified by the World Bank as low or lower-middle income. The relationship between child mortality and income can be written mathematically as: ln(mortality) = 10.5 − 0.83 × ln(GNP/capita).

Source: Based on data in World Bank, *World Development Indicators on CD-ROM, 1998* [electronic database].

countries do not fall exactly on the curve. The steepness of the curve at low levels of income per capita suggests that each increment of additional wealth can substantially reduce the incidence of child death under the age of five. For instance, an increase in per capita GNP from $500 to $1,000 is associated with a decrease of 93 child deaths per 1,000 births. At higher levels of income, the effect is much reduced (an increase from, say, $7,500 to $8,000 yields a decrease of only 1 death per 1,000). This pattern implies that major improvements in health and living conditions for the poor could be brought about at a price not requiring major sacrifices by people in the rich countries, especially if the world's neediest are targeted.

    Of course, the calculation of costs and benefits for transferring wealth from rich to poor is much more complicated than this simple illustration suggests. Presumably, any program to bring about a greater degree of international distributive justice would not be satisfied with merely lifting the world's poorest out of their desperate circumstances. The expressed goal is usually a more substantial improvement in levels of economic and social development, and that brings with it ecological costs. In his controversial "case against helping the poor," Garrett Hardin challenges the spaceship-earth analogy:

> The spaceship metaphor can be dangerous when used by misguided idealists to justify suicidal policies for sharing our resources through uncontrolled immigration and foreign aid. In their enthusiastic but unrealistic generosity, they confuse the ethics of a spaceship with those of a lifeboat. . . . Metaphorically each rich nation can be seen as a lifeboat full of comparatively rich people. In the ocean outside each lifeboat swim the poor of the world, who would like to get it, or at least share some of the wealth. . . . [W]e must recognize the limited capacity of any lifeboat.

Hardin asks us to imagine that our lifeboats are almost full — there is some room left, but certainly not enough for all of those in the water. Obviously, not everyone can be brought aboard, for we would all sink in the process. However, even filling our lifeboats to capacity by helping at least some of those in need is problematic because, says Hardin, we need the extra space as a "safety factor." Our survival demands that we admit no one into the lifeboat. Hardin's **lifeboat ethics** are abhorrent to many, as he recognizes, but they are addressed to the tragedy of the commons. Foreign aid undermines the incentives that would otherwise bring about changes in behavior that are required if the world's resources and environment are to be preserved for posterity. For Hardin the chief problem is population growth and there may be no better alternative than "population control the crude way" — famine.[27]

Fortunately, most people don't see the trade-off in such stark terms (and perhaps neither does Hardin). The lifeboat may be a reasonable analogy, but we might imagine it as filled with many people, including quite a few first-class passengers with all their luggage. We could bring some more into the boat and still preserve our safety factor, as long as we are willing to toss some of the golf clubs and guns overboard. Those we cannot bring aboard we can help become better swimmers or, better, assist in building their own lifeboats with extra room for emergencies. This is the sort of multitrack approach that seems to best characterize the varied efforts of governments, international agencies, and private groups on behalf of the world's poor.

The Limits of Sovereignty

Such issues raise old and ever-present ethical questions about what responsibility each of us owes others.[28] We typically feel the greatest responsibility for those in our immediate systems (recall Figure 16.1). Our families and close friends get the highest

---

[27] See Garrett Hardin, "Lifeboat Ethics: The Case against Helping the Poor," *Psychology Today* 8 (1974): pp. 38–43, 124–126; excerpt from p. 38. For early critiques, see Onora O'Neill, "Lifeboat Earth," *Philosophy and Public Affairs* 4, 3 (Spring 1975): pp. 273–292; and Marvin Soroos, "The Commons and Lifeboat as Guides for International Ecological Policy," *International Studies Quarterly* 21 (1977): pp. 647–674.

[28] See, for example, the essays in William Aiken and Hugh LaFollette, eds., *World Hunger and Morality*, 2nd ed. (Upper Saddle River, N.J.: Prentice Hall, 1996); see also Amartya Sen, *Poverty and Famines: An Essay on Entitlement and Deprivation* (New York: Oxford University Press, 1981), and John Rawls, "The Law of Peoples," in Stephen Shute and Susan Hardy, eds., *On Human Rights* (New York: Basic Books, 1993), pp. 41–82.

priority; our fellow nationals may occupy some sort of middle ground; and inhabitants farther away, about whom we know little, receive the lowest priority. Yet, given such enormous differences in well-being, to what degree is it just to ignore what could be done?

We have addressed issues of *human rights* at various points in this book. In Chapter 10 we discussed international law and pointed out that the rights of noncombatants during wartime are firmly anchored in just war theory and in the actual conduct of war (by most states most of the time). We examined the relationship between democratic governance and peace in Chapter 11 and suggested that the possession of civil and political rights (like free speech, association, and representation) can act to restrain aggressive foreign policies toward other states where the citizenry possesses similar rights. There is a third area that has been recognized as a domain of international human rights — the right to economic and social well-being. The right to life and liberty require restraint on the part of individuals or governments in a position to deny them; they are "negative" rights which grant *freedoms* (from death, censorship, political imprisonment, and so on). The right to economic and social well-being, on the other hand, whether defined in terms of basic human needs or a more substantial level of human development, is a "positive" right. When one or more individuals do not possess a certain level of well-being, their rights entail *obligations* on the part of others, or so it would seem.[29]

The problem is that the notion of international obligation can be somewhat alien to the Western way of thinking, especially with its emphasis on individual freedoms, and it is the West that is generally in the best position to help. Aid to the poor is viewed as charitable, even noble if it involves significant sacrifice on the part of the giver. However, one is obliged to help only by one's own conscience, and although very many people are obliged, many others are not.[30] Another problem is sovereignty. The principle of nonintervention precludes our assisting the needy in other countries unless we are invited to do so by their governments. Invitations are often extended, but a continuing impediment to effective foreign aid is that there are few strings attached, since strings can be an affront to sovereignty. Thus, donors may be forced to sit idly by while their donations rot on the docks because civil war prevents their distribution, while dictators build themselves lavish presidential palaces as they accept assistance on behalf of their impoverished people, while militaries procure state-of-the-art jet fighters with money freed up by foreign economic aid. If sovereignty and the assertion of *states' rights* have undermined international scrutiny even in such extreme cases (though this is changing), then it is not hard to imagine the difficulties encountered by those who would scrutinize population growth or environmentally costly economic development. Foreign aid can be difficult to sell to Western publics for this reason. Sovereignty does not foster a sense of international obligation.

---

[29] See Jack Donnelly, *International Human Rights* (Boulder, Colo.: Westview, 1993), esp. chap. 2.

[30] For empirical evidence suggesting that conscience and obligation have motivated advocates of foreign aid, see David Halloran Lumsdaine, *Moral Vision in International Politics: The Foreign Aid Regime, 1949–1989* (Princeton, N.J.: Princeton University Press, 1993); esp. chap. 5.

Problems of global poverty and the tragedy of the commons make clear the limits of sovereignty. All states are not equal; geography and history have seen to that. A global ethics based on individual freedoms is empty without some semblance of equal opportunity. A global ethics based on well-being or basic needs will fail without a more pervasive sense of international obligation. And neither is attentive to the rights of posterity. We live within borders of both space and time, and we need to look beyond them. Our obligation is to humanity — ourselves, those who inhabit other parts of the globe, and those still to come. Recognizing that obligation, and translating it into state policy and individual behavior, is the most significant challenge for the new millennium.

17

Which Global Future?

Three Futures

We study the past in order to understand the present. In the previous chapters we have taken up many important issues in international politics and have shown that social scientists continue to accumulate quite a bit of knowledge about the way states and nonstate actors interact in a complex world system. But we have also tried to convey the different perspectives and understandings that guide the study of world politics, even when the topic of investigation is the same. Thus, military conflict, international norms, globalization, economic development, and the many other topics we consider under the rubric of world politics are accompanied by multiple explanations of cause and effect, and in some cases varying normative judgments about right and wrong, just and unjust. Organizing these competing explanations and judgments using the frameworks of realism, liberalism, and radicalism can be a useful way to keep them all straight.

If there are multiple interpretations of the past and competing explanations of the present, then it follows that there is more than one view of the future. Mindful of that, in this brief closing chapter we will not try to answer the question, which global future? Instead, we shall present three different visions of the future offered by scholars over the past decade, each of which is obviously speculative. All three are in some ways controversial; those who dare to gaze into the crystal ball, however well informed, almost always invite criticism and controversy. They are not necessarily realist versus liberal versus radical views of the future, although there are stronger traces of certain perspectives in certain of these global futures. Where we see them, we will try to highlight them, but mostly we want to sketch these alternative futures without much further embellishment. Based on your own understanding of world politics, along with your observation of contemporary world affairs, you will be in a good position to evaluate these scenarios for yourself.

The West Has Won

In Chapter 11 we discussed the prevalence of peaceful relations among democracies, and we mentioned the argument put forth by Francis Fukuyama regarding the "end of history." Despite the ominous allusions, the "end of history" really is a vision of the future. The argument is that Western ideas about the most appropriate forms of both political and economic interaction — democracy and capitalism — have demonstrated their superiority over all others, and that this is about as good as it gets. Fukuyama's claim is that Western liberalism has triumphed over competing social arrangements; hence the label "triumphalism" applied to this argument by many skeptics.[1]

The concept of the end of history comes from the work of German idealist philosopher G. W. F. Hegel, who wrote that human progress results from the competition of ideas. Ideas condition our behavior, our relationships with each other, our material well-being. There are competing sets of ideas, or ideologies, that purport to outline the best forms of social organization, but the superior ones will emerge to propel societies along the road of human betterment and progress. Eventually we will get to the end of that road — not Armageddon, but the point at which our particular economic and political arrangements can be improved no further. The history of human progress, for Hegel, was the history of these competing ideas and ideologies. That is not to say that someday human progress would come to an abrupt halt, but rather that humankind will have discovered a form of social organization superior to all others for purposes of freeing human potential. That would mark the end of history.

As Fukuyama points out, Hegel actually thought history was coming to an end in the early nineteenth century as Napoleon's armies were conquering Europe and thereby demonstrating the superiority of the French Revolutionary ideals of liberty and equality. Napoleon, of course, was defeated, although the ideals of political liberty continued to resonate in Europe and America. There would be two major challenges to liberalism in the twentieth century, however: fascism and communism. Fascism was defeated by force of arms during World War II, but its practical and moral bankruptcy was evident by its failure to reemerge after the war as a viable alternative to political

---

[1] See Francis Fukuyama, "The End of History?" *The National Interest* (Summer 1989): pp. 3–18, and Fukuyama, *The End of History and the Last Man* (New York: Free Press, 1992).

and economic liberalism. Communism has been a more serious challenge. As an alternative to Western liberalism, communist — or at least socialist — forms of governance have been more widespread and more durable than fascism ever was. Still, that socialism was in retreat was clear to Fukuyama (and everyone else) when he first presented his view of the future in 1989. Since then socialism has fully collapsed in Russia and Eastern Europe, while market reforms continue to eat away at socialist economics in China.

For Fukuyama, the end of the twentieth century was when we truly arrived at the end of history. Western liberalism in the form of capitalism and democracy are on the march globally. Capitalism and democracy as currently implemented in the West are by no means perfect, but the remaining ills of Western society — economic inequality, racism, and so on — can be attended to within a liberal social order; they are not inherent in capitalist democracy. Neither is the end of history signaled by the universal adoption of capitalist democracy worldwide. Clearly that is not the case today. What is important, for Fukuyama, is that no other set of ideals currently vie with Western liberalism for the hearts and minds of humanity. Even countries like China that hold tenaciously to certain nonliberal principles (for example, in politics) do not actively promote them as humankind's destiny. Western liberalism, on the other hand, is understood and promoted in such terms. True, there are many societies "still in history," but political and economic liberalization is the way to human progress and ultimately they, too, will follow that path. The challengers have been defeated; the west has won.

What Fukuyama and others refer to as Western liberalism is not exactly the same as the term we have used in this book to describe a particular perspective on world politics. Still, there is a great deal of overlap. The liberal approach to world politics does indeed have its roots in political and economic liberalism, as we noted in Chapter 2 when we introduced the three perspectives and in Chapter 12 when we re-introduced them in the context of international political economy. The most obvious affinity between the liberal view of world politics and Fukuyama's vision of the future is that for Fukuyama the end of history brings with it the same sort of peace and stability observed by democratic-peace theorists. As described in Chapter 11, this is a peace among democracies only, reinforced by economic interdependence and international institutions, not among autocratic regimes or between autocracies and democracies. Many of those adopting the liberal perspective would not subscribe to Fukuyama's triumphalism, but there is no denying a common framework that sees domestic politics and society as important influences on foreign affairs.

The Coming Culture Clash

Others are far less sanguine about the Western triumph. Rejecting the idea that history has ended, Samuel Huntington instead points to the coming "clash of civilizations." He does not dispute the end of ideological rivalry, as predicted by Fukuyama. He also remains unconvinced that geo-economic competition will replace it as a source of global conflict, as many others have argued. Conflict will indeed be a feature of world politics in the new millennium, but it is civilizations that will come to blows, not ideological or economic blocs. And the main axis of political conflict in the future is likely to be that between "the West and the Rest."[2]

The civilizational entities to which Huntington refers are the Western, Latin American, African, Islamic, Confucian (or Sinic), Hindu, Orthodox, Buddhist, and Japanese civilizations. These will not necessarily replace nation-states as the central actors in world politics, but they will increasingly provide the glue that brings some states together and pushes others apart. History, language, tradition, and especially religion both unite and divide peoples. With the ideological rivalry of the cold war gone, the iron curtain that divided Europe will be replaced by a "velvet curtain" in Europe and elsewhere, and these fault lines between civilizations will be the battlegrounds of the future. In Europe the velvet curtain is actually somewhat east of the old iron curtain, with Finland, the Baltic states, Poland, the Czech and Slovak Republics, Hungary, Slovenia, and Croatia now to the west and the remainder of the former Soviet bloc plus Greece and Turkey to the east. This fault line separates Western Christianity from Orthodox Christianity and Islam.

Contemporary events in Europe both support and refute Huntington's culture-clash thesis. The expansion of NATO has brought Poland, the Czech Republic, and Hungary into the Western orbit. Many also take seriously the possibility that the other former Warsaw Pact territories west of Huntington's velvet curtain, especially the Baltic states and Slovenia, will join the alliance in a subsequent eastward expansion. The military conflict between Christian Croats and Orthodox Serbs in Croatia fits Huntington's thesis, too, as does the NATO military campaign against Yugoslavia. One problem with the civilizational explanation in each of these cases is that alongside the intracultural cooperation and intercultural conflict are their opposites. In the case of NATO expansion, enthusiasts would like NATO to open its doors to countries east of Europe's cultural fault line as well: Ukraine and Romania, for example, and someday even Russia. (The EU is taking tentative steps in the same direction.) In the Balkans, shared anti-Western sentiments do not provide much in the way of cultural affinities between Muslims and Orthodox Christians, as Huntington is well aware. Here the violent conflicts between Muslims and Serbs in Bosnia and between Muslims and Serbs in Kosovo were themselves accompanied by "civilizational rallying." Both conflicts have also seen NATO assisting embattled members of what Huntington considers to be perhaps the most anti-Western of civilizations, the Islamic world.

Huntington identifies a "crescent-shaped Islamic bloc of nations" from northern Africa to central Asia. The struggle between the Western and Islamic civilization has been going on since the seventh century when the Moors crossed the Strait of Gibraltar and conquered Spain. Conflicts accompanying the rise of Arab nationalism and, more recently, Islamic fundamentalism — both defined largely in opposition to the legacy of Western colonialism in the Middle East and Northern Africa — are simply the most recent manifestations of a long-standing and deep-seated civilizational struggle. There

---

[2] See Samuel P. Huntington, "The Clash of Civilizations?" *Foreign Affairs* 72, 3 (Summer 1993): pp. 22–49; and Huntington, *The Clash of Civilizations and the Remaking of World Order* (New York: Simon & Schuster, 1996).

are fault lines dividing the Islamic civilization from non-Western civilizations as well; as Huntington puts it, "Islam has bloody borders." He implies that the deep historical roots of this struggle ensure it will continue. However, if some Islamic countries should become more democratic, they need not be less Islamic, and in light of our discussion in Chapter 11 we might expect them to become less conflict-prone.

An Islamic-Confucian connection also figures into this scenario for the future, although for Huntington the connection seems to be restricted more to the realm of power and interests than to cultural affinity. Here he focuses mostly on weapons acquisition, including arms transfers from the East to the Middle East, as well as the Western bias of prevailing approaches to arms control, which are rejected by nations in the Islamic-Confucian bloc. Thus, despite the talk of cultures and civilizations — not central in the vocabulary of realism — this vision of the future does have strong realist overtones. What we can expect in the new millennium, following Huntington, is more power balancing — not so much by interest-maximizing states but by culturally bound states called "civilizations."

An entertaining yet insightful critique of Huntington's thesis, put to verse, includes these apt lines:

> As he explores these culture wars, he seems to be inviting
> What used to be a weakness of the school of "realist" writing,
> Ascribing to a concept, like a culture or a state,
> A physical reality which doesn't quite equate.
> This realist bard from Harvard Yard distorts important factors,
> Converting complex cultures into unitary actors;
> What Morgenthau and Wolfers did with power among nations,
> Huntington has nearly done with full-scale civilizations.[3]

These observations, along with the mixed support for the culture-clash argument, should prod us to look more closely at what "civilization" means in the context of realism and other perspectives. Civilizations differ from one another in their political and economic institutions, and in the preferences and behavior patterns of their citizens. Huntington asserts that the Western commitment to democracy and market capitalism makes it distinctive from many other civilizations, and especially the Islamic one. But institutions and preferences are not immutable, and sometimes they can be changed drastically. After World War II a "new" Germany and Japan became democratic and many of their citizens took up pacifist views about international relations. Germany and Japan remained deeply attached to their civilizations, but their behavior in world politics shifted radically. Other countries (like Russia) have radically changed their institutions and shifted their international behavior. Even when civilizations do roughly correspond with regional configurations of democracy and markets, how much more does the concept of civilization add to our understanding of why countries fight each other?

---

[3] Frederick S. Tipson, "Culture Clash-ification: A Verse to Huntington's Curse," *Foreign Affairs* 76, 2 (March/April 1997): p. 168.

Globalization and Fragmentation

A third global future contains elements of both Fukuyama's end of history and Huntington's clash of civilizations. For Benjamin Barber there are two simultaneous trends in world politics, globalization and fragmentation. Globalization, as we discussed in Chapter 14, involves the declining significance of international borders for the flow of goods, capital, people, and ideas. More to the point, globalization seems to be dominated by the flow of *Western* goods, capital, people, and ideas, which is what Fukuyama finds so compelling. For Barber, the icons of globalization include MTV, Macintosh, and McDonald's, which lend themselves to a convenient shorthand for the process he describes — "McWorld." At the same time, there is a counter-tendency. This involves fragmentation, a tribalization or "Lebanonization" of nation-states, with new divisions emerging between peoples. Since these divisions, like those identified by Huntington, are defined by cultural and religious differences, Barber uses the term "Jihad" — an Arabic word meaning spiritual and religious struggle — to summarize this tendency in world politics. The future, then, will be characterized by the clash of these two trends, "Jihad vs. McWorld."[4]

As does Huntington's culture clash, Barber's Jihad conjures up a rather gloomy vision of the future. Unlike Huntington, however, Barber sees this culture clash as a more thoroughly local and fragmenting phenomenon, without the sort of unifying cultural affinities that bring states together into larger civilizational blocs in Huntington's future. The progressive tendencies of Barber's McWorld resemble those that Fukuyama associates with Western liberalism, but Barber sees no end of history in sight. Jihad won't become McWorld; in fact, Jihad may be partly brought about by the alienating impact of McWorld, especially among non-Western peoples. Furthermore, Barber fears that neither McWorld nor Jihad bode well for the future of democracy. Consumerism supplants participatory politics and human rights on the list of social priorities in McWorld, for democratic ideals cannot be allowed to impede the march toward domestic market reforms, free trade, and foreign investment. Jihad is even more explicitly antidemocratic. Not only is there a willingness to defer to local demagogues, but the exclusion of outsiders from the political community can take on ruthless proportions, as in the case of "ethnic cleansing" in the Balkans. Jihad is not multiculturalism.

"Jihad vs. McWorld" is not exactly a radical vision of the future, as we have characterized the radical view of world politics in this book, but the theme of global capitalism's alienating effects as well as the struggle against its universalizing tendencies is also one found in radical scholarship. However, Barber does not expect that McWorld will come crashing down as a result of its own internal contradictions (nor do many

---

[4] See Benjamin R. Barber, "Jihad vs. McWorld," *Atlantic Monthly* (March 1992): pp. 53–61, and Barber, *Jihad vs. McWorld* (New York: Times Books, 1995). As we mentioned in previous chapters, these trends have also been documented and discussed by James Rosenau. See his *Turbulence and World Politics: A Theory of Change and Continuity* (Princeton, N.J.: Princeton University Press, 1990), and his *Along the Domestic-Foreign Frontier: Exploring Governance in a Turbulent World* (Cambridge: Cambridge University Press, 1997).

radical scholars, really). Instead, he hopes for a "confederal option," in which democratic ideals can be shored up in the face of antidemocratic trends associated with both globalization and fragmentation. So do we.

A Final Word

In this book we have discussed the different levels at which world politics is analyzed and the variety of interactions and interdependencies that constitute both challenges and opportunities for the new millennium. We have examined the behavior of individual states and the consequences of their pursuit of self-interests narrowly defined. These interests derive from political processes in various governments and societies: organizational and bureaucratic dynamics, domestic interest groups like big business or peace activists, and public opinion in general. The outcomes of these political processes help determine whether states will "defect" in the prisoner's dilemma situations that pervade world politics. The outcomes of these political processes may also encourage states to free ride in the context of multilateral efforts at cooperation, expecting to benefit from collective goods like environmental preservation without making any of the sacrifices. While scholars may concentrate on one or another level for purposes of analysis, all the levels are linked. They create a complex set of interrelationships that present each of us — state leaders and ordinary citizens — with a menu for choice.

The three theoretical perspectives that have surfaced throughout this book — realism, liberalism, and radicalism — are not merely worldviews possessed by distant observers. They motivate the policies advocated by domestic groups and pursued by state leaders. These policies not only vary among states, but are held variously by the same states over time. Of some periods of history we might say that world politics was marked by a high degree of competition, as highlighted by realists: alliance formation, arms races, frequent crises and wars deriving from unstable balances of power or economic conflicts. Other periods, often following wars, witness creative challenges to established political practices and ways of thinking. New approaches to conflict resolution or the creation of new international organizations and regimes have often been associated with an increased willingness to apply liberal or radical solutions to recurring problems in world politics. We may not be fully trapped in a realist world where the central principle is the competitive pursuit of power.

Despite numerous challenges to sovereignty, the Westphalian state system is still with us, and nation-states continue to play on center stage. Yet the actions of individuals do have an impact on the future. We each have conceptions of our interests, and the inclusion of the interests of others in our calculations will make a difference. After all, our interests are reflected in the demands we make on our governments. Politics and society — domestic and international — may be slow to change, but they do change, and often for the better.

You may recall the famous opening lines of Charles Dickens's *A Tale of Two Cities:*

It was the best of times, it was the worst of times, it was the age of wisdom, it was the age of foolishness, it was the epoch of belief, it was the epoch of incredulity, it was the season of Light, it was the season of Darkness, it was the spring of hope, it was the winter of despair, we had everything before us, we had nothing before us.

These lines refer to the social and psychological upheavals associated with revolutionary change at the end of the eighteenth century. Revolutions are periods fraught with problems and the dangers they pose, but also with opportunities for significant progress if those problems can be solved. We, too, live in a period of change — some might even say revolutionary change. At the dawn of the new millennium, we see a series of challenges to peace, liberty, and human development in an increasingly interdependent world. But we also see progress: the erosion of some long-standing global and regional rivalries, the spread of democracy, and an ever-rising standard of living for much of the world's people. The challenges are indeed daunting, but the possibilities are enormous. We hope you will come away from this book with a deeper understanding of what the world looks like and how it works, and a commitment to make it better.

APPENDIX A

CHRONOLOGY OF WORLD EVENTS

1804	Napoleon becomes emperor of France.
1812	Napoleon invades Russia: disastrous campaign ultimately leads to French defeat.
1814–1815	Congress of Vienna: victorious powers reconstitute European order.
1823	Monroe Doctrine: President James Monroe declares the Western Hemisphere "off limits" to European interference.
1846	Mexican war: the United States defeats Mexico, annexes New Mexico and California (war ends February 1848).
1848	Communist Manifesto published by Karl Marx and Friedrich Engels. Antimonarchical liberal revolutions in France, Prussia, Austria-Hungary, and the Italian states.
1852	Napoleon III establishes the Second French Empire.
1853	Japan opened to the West by American Commodore Matthew Perry.
1854–1856	Crimean War: France and Britain ally with Turkey against Russia.
1857–1858	Sepoy rebellion: Indian soldiers revolt against British rule in India.
1859	Construction begins on Suez Canal (completed in 1869).
1861	Kingdom of Italy established after process of unification led by Sardinia; emancipation of serfs in Russia; U.S. Civil War (1861–1865).
1864	First International organized by Marx in London.
1864–1870	Lopez War: Argentina, Brazil, and Uruguay virtually destroy Paraguay.
1867	British North America Act creates Canada as a confederation. Marx publishes *Capital*. United States purchases Alaska from Russia.
1870–1871	Franco-Prussian war: German states, led by Prussia, invade and defeat France (completing a process of German unification that included the 1864 Second Schleswig-Holstein War against Denmark and the 1866 Seven Weeks' War against Austria).
1871	German empire established under leadership of Prussia; Wilhelm I becomes kaiser.
1878	Congress of Berlin: European powers meet to thwart Russia and carve up Ottoman Empire.
1882	Triple Alliance is formed by Germany, Austria-Hungary, and Italy.
1894–1895	Sino-Japanese War: Japan defeats China and becomes an imperial power with acquisition of Taiwan.
1898	Spanish-American War: the United States defeats Spain, acquires the Philippines, and becomes a great power.
1899	"Open Door" policy forced on China by the Western powers. Boer War (1899–1902) between British and Dutch settlers begins in South Africa.
1900	Boxer rebellion: forces of the European powers, Japan, and the United States sent to China to put down revolt against foreign penetration.
1904–1907	Entente Cordiale signed between France and England. (1907: Russia joins and Triple Entente is formed.) Russo-Japanese War: Japan defeats Russia, becomes great power (1904–1905).

1911	Chinese Revolution led by Sun Yat-sen removes emperor and establishes a republic.
1912–1913	First and Second Balkan wars drive Turkey from Europe.
1914	June: Assassination of Archduke Franz Ferdinand of Austria-Hungary. August: World War I breaks out between Triple Entente and Central Powers; Panama Canal opens.
1917	April: United States enters World War I on the side of the Allies. November: Bolshevik Revolution in Russia, led by Vladimir Ilyich Lenin.
1918	March: Treaty of Brest-Litovsk; Bolshevik government of Russia signs separate peace with Germany. November: Armistice signed; World War I ends.
1919	Treaty of Versailles negotiated by victors of World War I (signed by Germans in June).
1920	January: League of Nations, created by Treaty of Versailles, established in Geneva; United States does not join.
1922	October: Benito Mussolini and Fascist party come to power in Italy. December: Union of Soviet Socialist Republics is officially created, the first communist state.
1923	October: Kemal Ataturk's westernized Turkish Republic officially proclaimed.
1924	January: Lenin dies; Joseph Stalin emerges as Soviet leader.
1929	October: Great Depression begins with the collapse of the New York stock market.
1931	September: Japan occupies Manchuria.
1933	January: Adolph Hitler comes to power in Germany.
1934–1935	Mao Zedong leads the Red Army on the Long March in China.
1936	July: Spanish Civil War begins; clash between fascists and communists is a precursor of World War II (Spanish Civil War ends January 1939 with fascist Francisco Franco as ruler of Spain). November: Rome-Berlin-Tokyo Axis formed (formalized in 1937 treaty).
1938	September: Munich agreement — French and British appease Germany over claims to Czechoslovakia.
1939	August: Germany and the Soviet Union sign a nonaggression pact. September: Germany invades Poland, World War II begins.
1941	December: Japan attacks Pearl Harbor, United States enters World War II.
1944	July: Bretton Woods meeting establishes postwar economic system.
1945	February: Yalta Conference — Churchill, Roosevelt, and Stalin plan postwar Europe. March: Arab League established. May 8: V-E (Victory in Europe) Day marking German surrender. June: UN charter signed in San Francisco. August: Hiroshima destroyed by first atomic bomb used in war; August 15, V-J (Victory in Japan) Day, Japanese surrender.
1947	June: Marshall Plan for economic recovery of Europe proposed. August: British leave Indian subcontinent; India and Pakistan separate and become independent.
1948	February: Communists seize power in Czechoslovakia. May: Israel established as an independent state; first Arab-Israeli war (ends January 1949); Organization of American States (OAS) established. June: Berlin blockade; Soviets bar Western access to Berlin (Allies supply city by airlift, blockade ends May 1949).
1949	April: North Atlantic Treaty Organization (NATO) established. August: Soviet Union explodes its first atomic weapon. October: People's Republic of China proclaimed.

1950   June: North Korea invades the South; Korean War begins. October: Communist China enters Korean War.

1951   March: European Coal and Steel Community formed (forerunner of European Economic Community).

1952   November: United States explodes the first hydrogen (thermonuclear) bomb.

1953   March: Stalin dies. July: Korean armistice signed.

1954   July: Geneva settlement ends French rule in Indochina; Vietnam divided into North and South. September: Southeast Asia Treaty Organization (SEATO) formed.

1955   May: West Germany joins NATO; Warsaw Treaty Organization (Warsaw Pact) established.

1956   July: Gamal Abdal Nasser nationalizes Suez Canal. October: Hungarian revolt against communist rule crushed by Soviet troops. October–November: Britain, France, and Israel invade Egypt (Suez War).

1957   March: European Economic Community (Common Market) established by the Treaty of Rome. October: Soviet Union launches Sputnik, first artificial satellite.

1958   June: Charles de Gaulle takes over leadership of France (elected president in January 1959). July: United States sends troops to Lebanon, Britain sends troops to Jordan to forestall radical takeovers.

1959   January: Fidel Castro leads the overthrow of President Fulgencio Batista in Cuba.

1960   February: France explodes an atomic weapon. July: The Republic of the Congo becomes independent; civil war begins.

1961   April: United States sponsors unsuccessful Bay of Pigs invasion of Cuba. August: East Germany builds the Berlin Wall.

1962   October: Cuban missile crisis. October–November: China and India fight border war.

1963   November: President John F. Kennedy assassinated in Dallas.

1964   October: Nikita Khrushchev deposed by Leonid Brezhnev and Aleksei Kosygin; China explodes its first atomic bomb.

1965   April: United States sends troops to Dominican Republic to prevent radical takeover. July: President Lyndon B. Johnson announces major U.S. buildup of 125,000 troops in Vietnam. September: War between India and Pakistan over Kashmir begins. November: White-dominated government of Rhodesia unilaterally declares independence from Britain; UN imposes economic sanctions.

1966   April: Mao-inspired Cultural Revolution begins in China.

1967   May: Biafran civil war begins; Nigerian government ultimately defeats attempt at secession (ends January 1970). June: Six-Day War between Israel and Egypt, Jordan, and Syria.

1968   July: Nonproliferation treaty signed by United States, the Soviet Union, and Britain. September: Soviet and Warsaw Pact troops invade Czechoslovakia.

1969   March: Soviet-Chinese conflict erupts into border fighting at the Ussuri River. July: American astronaut Neil Armstrong is the first human being to walk on the moon.

1970   September: Marxist Salvador Allende elected president of Chile (killed during a coup to overthrow his government in September 1973).

1971   October: People's Republic of China admitted to United Nations. December: Bangladesh established by breakaway of East Pakistan after civil war and India-Pakistan War.

1972   January: Britain, the Republic of Ireland, and Denmark join European Economic Community. February: U.S. President Richard Nixon visits People's Republic of China. May: United States and the Soviet Union sign strategic arms limitation treaty (SALT I).

1973   June: East and West Germany establish diplomatic relations. October: Yom Kippur War between Israel and Egypt and Syria (ends in November). November: Arab members of OPEC embargo oil to United States, Japan, and Western Europe and begin series of price hikes.

1974   May: India explodes nuclear device. August: Nixon resigns as president of United States after Watergate affair.

1975   April: Serious fighting begins in civil war in Lebanon; Saigon taken by communist forces, and Indochina War ends with collapse of U.S.-backed South Vietnam and Cambodia. June: Indira Gandhi imposes emergency rule in India and arrests opposition. August: European Agreement on Security and Cooperation signed in Helsinki. November: Angola becomes independent from Portugal after long guerrilla war; struggle between liberation movements supported by different countries (including Cuban troops).

1976   September: Mao Zedong dies.

1977   March: Gandhi allows free elections in India; opposition wins. August: United States and Panama sign treaty to cede Panama Canal to Panama (ratified March 1978). November: Egyptian president Anwar Sadat makes dramatic trip to Israel.

1978   August: China and Japan sign treaty of peace and friendship. December: United States and People's Republic of China establish full diplomatic relations.

1979   January: Shah resigns in Iran; Ayatollah Khomeini forms revolutionary government in February. February: War breaks out between two communist states as China invades Vietnam. March: Egyptian-Israeli peace treaty signed at Camp David. June: President Jimmy Carter and Brezhnev sign SALT II in Vienna. July: Sandinista rebels overthrow dictator Anastasio Somoza in Nicaragua. November: Iranian "students" and government seize U.S. embassy personnel as hostages. December: Soviet troops invade Afghanistan; agreement reached on independence for Zimbabwe (Rhodesia) under black government; UN-imposed economic sanctions lifted.

1980   September: Iraq attacks Iran. October: Strikes by Polish workers' union (Solidarity) force extensive concessions from government. November: "Gang of Four" put on trial in China amid criticism of Mao Zedong; Ronald Reagan elected president, says United States will observe, but not ratify, SALT II.

1981   January: Greece joins European Economic Community. October: Sadat assassinated by Muslim extremists; succeeded by Vice President Hosni Mubarak. December: General Wojciech Jaruzelski declares martial law in Poland and arrests Solidarity members; United States imposes economic sanctions on Poland and the Soviet Union.

1982   April: Argentina seizes Falkland Islands; British naval and air force retakes them by June. May: Spain becomes sixteenth member of NATO. November: Brazil holds free congressional elections; Brezhnev dies, is succeeded by Yuri Andropov, in turn by Konstantin Chernenko (February 1984). December: Final act of the Law of the Sea Convention signed by 117 states, not including the United States.

1983   September: Korean Airlines civilian passenger plane shot down by the Soviet Union over Soviet territory. October: Nearly 300 French and U.S. troops of peacekeeping force killed by terrorist bombs in Lebanon; United States invades Grenada to overthrow Marxist government. December: Brazil reaches agreement to reschedule debt.

1984   October: Prime Minister Indira Gandhi assassinated.

1985   March: Chernenko dies, is succeeded by Mikhail Gorbachev; civilian government restored in Brazil.

1986   January: Spain and Portugal join European Community; U.S. space shuttle Challenger explodes. May: Nuclear accident at Chernobyl power station in the Soviet Union.

1987   January: Gorbachev calls for glasnost and political reforms; United States and the Soviet Union sign INF Treaty to eliminate intermediate range missiles in December. September: Treaty to protect the ozone layer is approved.

1988   May: Soviet troops begin withdrawal from Afghanistan. August: Iran and Iraq agree to cease-fire.

1989   April: Chinese students rally in Beijing, marking onset of democracy movement (in June pro-democracy movement is crushed as troops kill thousands). November: Berlin Wall falls; subsequently, barriers to the West are thrown open throughout Eastern Europe.

1990   February: South African government legalizes the African National Congress and Nelson Mandela is freed from jail. March: Communist party loses its monopoly in the Soviet Union; Namibia becomes independent. August: Iraq invades Kuwait; UN votes a trade embargo against Iraq. October: East and West Germany unite. November: The UN authorizes the use of force against Iraq; CSCE summit meeting ends the cold war with conventional arms agreement (Warsaw Pact dissolves in July 1991).

1991   January: UN coalition, led by the United States, launches air war against Iraq; retakes Kuwait in four-day ground campaign in February. June: South Africa repeals land laws that are central to apartheid; fighting erupts in Yugoslavia over Slovenian and Croatian secession; Boris Yeltsin elected president of the Russian Republic. August: Attempted KGB/military coup to oust Gorbachev fails. November: Macedonia secedes from Yugoslavia. December: European Community leaders agree to closer integration; Union of Soviet Socialist Republics dissolved.

1992   March: Referendum among South African whites endorses new constitution and end to minority rule; Bosnia secedes from Yugoslavia and fighting erupts between Bosnian Muslims, Serbs, and Croats. June: Earth Summit held in Rio de Janeiro, Brazil. December: First U.S. troops in Operation Restore Hope arrive in Somalia; United States, Canada, and Mexico sign NAFTA treaty.

1993   January: United States and Russia sign START II nuclear arms agreement. September: Israeli Prime Minister Rabin and PLO Chairman Arafat agree to framework for interim Palestinian self-rule. November: European Community's Maastricht Treaty goes into effect. December: The Uruguay Round of GATT officially concludes; a joint Irish-British framework for peace in Northern Ireland is issued (IRA announces cease-fire in August 1994).

1994   January: NATO endorses "partnership for peace" plan, which would include former Warsaw Pact members. March: United States ends peacekeeping mission in Somalia; Bosnian Muslims and Croats join forces against Serbs. April: Civil war and massive ethnic violence breaks out in Rwanda. May: Nelson Mandela and ANC emerge victorious in South Africa's first universal suffrage elections; PLO assumes self-rule in Gaza and parts of the West Bank. July: Israel and Jordan formally end state of war; UN Security Council approves U. S . -led invasion of Haiti to restore democracy (Aristide reinstated as president in October). December: Russian army invades breakaway republic of Chechnya.

1995   January: The World Trade Organization (WTO) begins its work as successor to GATT; Austria, Finland, and Sweden officially enter the European Union, bringing EU membership to fifteen. May: Representatives of over 170 countries approve the indefinite extension of the Nonproliferation Treaty; NATO launches air attacks against Bosnian Serb positions for ceasefire violations (more attacks would follow). July: The United States opens full diplomatic relations with Vietnam. August: Croatian armed forces reoccupy Serbian controlled regions, prompting a mass exodus of Serb refugees. November: Dayton Accord ends fighting in Bosnia, creating a Muslim-Croat federation and a Serb republic.

1996　　January: Yasir Arafat is elected president of the Palestinian Authority; February: Cuban jet downs two US civilian planes. May: Russia and Chechnyan rebels agree to a cease-fire. June: Truck bomb kills nineteen Americans at U.S. Air Force housing area in Saudi Arabia. September: U.S. launches air strikes against Iraq after Iraqi military seizes Kurdish town under UN protection; Elections are held in Bosnia. November: 500,000 refugees return to Rwanda; Pope John Paul II visits Cuba. December: Kofi Annan is named Secretary General of the UN; Peru rebels seize 600 at Japanese Envoy' s residence; Agreement signed by the Guatemalan government and leftist rebels to end thirty-six years of civil war.

1997　　January: Israel and Palestinians agree on Hebron withdrawal. February: Deng Xiaoping, China's "paramount leader," dies at age ninety-two. May: NATO-Russia agreement clears way for NATO expansion to the east; Mobutu Sese Seko, longtime dictator of Zaire, is overthrown by rebel forces, who rename the country the Democratic Republic of Congo. June: Russia joins the Group of Seven economic summit. July: Britain returns Hong Kong to China; Czech Republic, Hungary, and Poland invited to join NATO (they formally join in March 1999); a currency crisis in Thailand provides the spark that would later ignite a wider Asian financial crisis. December: 125 countries sign a treaty banning landmines.

1998　　April: Britain and Ireland sign peace accord on Northern Ireland to end the thirty-year conflict. May: India and then Pakistan explode five underground nuclear devices; protests triggered by Indonesian financial crisis force Suharto's resignation after thirty-two years in office. July: UN General Assembly votes to create a permanent International Criminal Court to prosecute genocide and other crimes against humanity. August: Car bombs simultaneous explode at U.S. embassies in Kenya and Tanzania, killing twenty-two. October: Former Chilean dictator Augusto Pinochet is arrested in Britain on a Spanish warrant charging genocide. December: Weapons inspection regime collapses in Iraq, prompting U.S. and British air strikes.

1999　　January: Eleven EU currencies are locked to the euro and the European Central Bank begins its work. March: NATO begins prolonged air assault against Yugoslavia in response to continued attacks against ethnic Albanians in Kosovo; the EU's entire European Commission resigns following charges of mismanagement and corruption. April: India and then Pakistan test-launch intermediate-range ballistic missiles. June: NATO suspends bombing campaign in Yugoslavia; peace settlement provides for NATO and other peacekeeping forces in Kosovo, as well as substantial autonomy for the province.

APPENDIX B

CHARACTERISTICS OF STATES
IN THE CONTEMPORARY INTERNATIONAL SYSTEM

Appendix B lists all of the independent states in the International system as of January 1999, along with some of their key demographic, economic, social, and political characteristics. Unless noted otherwise, data are from the World Bank's *World Development Indicators CDROM 1999* [electronic database] (Washington, D.C.: World Bank, 1999), available on the Web at <http://www.worldbank.org/data/>. Some data missing from the World Bank's compilation come from the U.S. Central Intelligence Agency's *World Factbook 1998* (Washington, D.C.: U.S. Central Intelligence Agency, 1998), on the Web at <http://www.odci.gov/cia/publications/factbook/>. Two dots (..) indicate that data are not available.

1. *Year of Independence:* This is the year of independence for all states that became independent after 1816 (the conclusion of the Napoleonic Wars). If no date is provided, the state was independent before 1816.

2. *Population:* Figures are for 1997, in millions.

3. *Area:* Area is reported in thousands of square kilometers (one square kilometer = 0.386 square miles).

4. *GNP:* Gross national product (GNP) represents the sum of all economic activity undertaken by nationals of a given country, whether at home or abroad, in 1997. Figures are in billions of "international" dollars, calculated using purchasing power parity (PPP) rates. For each country, the dollar amount reported is equivalent to the value of that same economic activity if undertaken in the United States.

5. *GNP/Capita:* This is the sum of all economic activity undertaken by the average national of a given country in 1997, computed as GNP divided by population and expressed in thousands of international dollars.

6. *Trade:* Trade is the sum of all merchandise exports and imports as a percentage of gross domestic product (GDP) in 1997. GDP is the value of all economic activity within the state's boundaries, whether by nationals or nonnationals, converted to international dollars. Trade percentages will be very high if much of what the state exports is produced outside its territory.

7. *Military Spending:* This shows how much was spent on the military establishment in 1995 in millions of dollars. Figures generally exclude expenditures on internal policing. Data are from the U.S. Arms Control and Disarmament Agency, *World Military Expenditures and Arms Transfers 1996* (Washington, D. C.: U.S. Government Printing Office, 1997), on the Web at <http://www.acda.gov/wmeat96/wmeat96.htm>.

8. *Under-5 Mortality:* This mortality rate represents the number of children under five years of age who would die in 1997 for every 1,000 live births. When the figure is divided by 10, it can be interpreted as the probability that a child born in 1997 will die within five years if prevailing conditions remain unchanged.

9. *Life Expectancy:* This is the expected life span for a child born in 1995. Data come from the UN Development Program (UNDP), *Human Develoment Report 1998* (New York: Oxford University Press, 1998), on the Web at <http://www.undp.org/hdro/indicators.html>.

10. *Adult Literacy:* Figures show the the percentage of the population aged fifteen and above who can read and write a short, simple statement about their everyday life. Data are for 1995 and come from the UNDP's *Human Development Report 1998.*

11. CO_2 *Emissions:* Carbon dioxide emissions, the largest component of greenhouse gases, are a byproduct of burning fossil fuels. Each figure is therefore an indicator of both atmospheric pollution and energy consumption. Data are for 1996, expressed in millions of metric tons.

12. *Status of Freedom:* Based on a number of indicators of political rights and civil liberties, states are labeled as free (F), partly free (PF), or not free (NF) in 1996. Data are from Freedom House, *Freedom in the World: The Annual Survey of Political Rights and Civil Liberties, 1997–1998* (New York: Freedom House, 1998), on the Web at <http://www.freedomhouse.org/>. Some data have been modified by the authors.

Country	Year of Independence	Population (millions)	Area (1,000 km²)	GNP ($ billions, PPP)	GNP/Capita ($ thousands, PPP)	Trade (% of GDP, PPP)	Military Spending ($ millions)	Under-5 Mortality (per 1,000 births)	Life Expectancy (years)	Adult Literacy (% of 15 and over)	CO_2 Emissions (million metric tons)	Status of Freedom
Afghanistan	..	25.0	652	19	0.8	1	..	..	45	32	1.2	NF
Albania	1912	3.3	29	7	2.2	11	45	40	71	85	1.9	PF
Algeria	1962	29.3	2,382	124	4.3	17	1,238	39	68	62	94.3	NF
Andorra	..	0.1	0.5	1	18.0	87	..	..	84	..	..	F
Angola	1975	11.7	1,247	10	0.8	39	225	209	47	42	5.1	NF
Antigua and Barbuda	1981	0.1	0.4	0.6	8.7	84	..	22	75	95	0.3	PF
Argentina	1816	35.7	2,780	360	10.1	15	4,684	24	73	96	129.9	F
Armenia	1991	3.8	30	10	2.5	12	79	..	71	99	3.7	PF
Australia	1920	18.5	7,741	362	19.5	35	8,401	7	78	99	306.6	F
Austria	1918	8.1	84	178	22.0	69	2,106	7	77	99	59.3	F
Azerbaijan	1991	7.6	87	12	1.5	13	304	23	71	96	30.0	NF
Bahamas	1973	0.3	14	5	19.4	27	23	23	73	98	1.7	F
Bahrain	1971	0.6	0.7	8	13.7	101	273	22	72	85	10.6	NF
Bangladesh	1972	123.6	144	135	1.1	8	502	104	57	38	23.0	PF
Barbados	1966	0.3	0.4	3	10.9	36	13	12	76	97	0.8	F
Belarus	1991	10.3	208	49	4.8	32	331	..	69	98	61.7	NF
Belgium	1830	10.2	33	235	23.1	140	4,449	7	77	99	106.0	F
Belize	1981	0.2	23	0.9	4.1	63	9	44	74	70	0.4	F
Benin	1960	5.8	113	7	1.3	17	24	149	54	37	0.7	F
Bhutan	1949	0.7	47	1	0.7	14	..	127	52	42	0.3	NF
Bolivia	1825	7.8	1,099	22	2.8	14	132	96	61	83	10.1	F
Bosnia & Herzegovina	1992	2.3	51	4	1.7	28	..	..	63	..	3.1	PF
Botswana	1966	1.5	582	11	7.4	78	225	88	52	70	2.1	F
Brazil	1822	163.7	8,547	1,039	6.4	12	10,900	44	67	83	273.4	PF
Brunei	1984	0.3	6	5	18.0	98	269	11	75	88	5.1	NF
Bulgaria	1908	8.3	111	32	3.9	25	1,073	24	71	98	55.3	F

Country												
Burkina Faso	1960	10.5	274	11	1.0	10	68	169	46	19	1.0	PF
Burundi	1962	6.4	28	4	0.6	5	46	200	45	35	0.2	NF
Cambodia	1953	10.5	181	13	1.3	13	90	147	53	65	0.5	NF
Cameroon	1960	13.9	475	25	1.8	12	102	78	55	63	3.5	NF
Canada	1920	30.3	9,971	659	21.8	63	9,077	8	79	99	409.4	F
Cape Verde	1975	0.4	4	1	3.0	46	4	..	66	72	0.1	F
Central African Republic	1960	3.4	623	4	1.3	2	..	160	48	60	0.2	PF
Chad	1960	7.2	1,284	7	1.0	3	34	182	47	48	0.1	NF
Chile	1818	14.6	757	179	12.2	19	2,243	13	75	95	48.8	F
China	..	1,227.2	9,597	3,770	3.1	9	63,510	39	69	82	3,363.5	NF
Colombia	1818	40.0	1,139	263	6.6	10	2,000	30	70	91	65.3	PF
Comoros	1975	0.5	2	0.8	1.5	20	3	..	57	57	0.1	PF
Congo	1960	2.7	342	3	1.3	185	48	145	51	75	5.0	NF
Congo, Dem Rep.	1960	46.7	2,345	36	0.8	17	17	148	52	77	2.3	PF
Costa Rica	1820	3.5	51	23	6.5	238	50	15	77	95	4.7	F
Côte d'Ivoire	1960	14.2	322	24	1.7	147	98	140	52	40	13.1	NF
Croatia	1992	4.8	57	23	4.9	54	2,114	10	72	98	17.5	PF
Cuba	1902	11.1	111	17	1.5	30	350	9	76	96	31.2	NF
Cyprus	1960	0.7	9	11	13.5	47	495	10	77	94	5.4	F
Czech Republic	1918	10.3	79	107	10.4	44	2,368	8	72	99	126.7	F
Denmark	..	5.3	43	124	23.5	75	3,118	6	75	99	56.6	F
Djibouti	1977	0.6	23	0.5	1.2	46	22	157	49	46	0.4	NF
Dominica	1978	0.1	0.8	0.3	4.0	..	..	20	73	94	0.1	F
Dominican Republic	1844	8.1	49	38	4.7	177	154	47	70	82	12.9	PF
Ecuador	1830	11.9	284	56	4.7	18	611	39	70	90	24.5	F
Egypt	1922	60.3	1,001	186	3.1	3	2,653	66	65	51	97.9	NF
El Salvador	1821	5.9	21	17	2.9	67	101	39	69	72	4.0	PF
Equatorial Guinea	1968	0.4	28	0.7	1.5	..	2	173	49	79	0.1	NF
Eritrea	1993	3.8	118	4	1.0	26	40	95	50	25	..	PF

Country	Year of Independence	Population (millions)	Area (1,000 km²)	GNP ($ billions, PPP)	GNP/Capita ($ thousands, PPP)	Trade (% of GDP, PPP)	Military Spending ($ millions)	Under-5 Mortality (per 1,000 births)	Life Expectancy (years)	Adult Literacy (% of 15 and over)	CO₂ Emissions (million metric tons)	Status of Freedom
Estonia	1991	1.5	45	7	5.1	92	118	13	69	99	16.4	F
Ethiopia	..	59.8	1,104	30	0.5	7	118	175	49	36	3.4	PF
Fiji	1971	0.8	18	3	3.9	31	32	24	72	92	0.8	PF
Finland	1919	5.1	338	101	19.7	67	2,381	5	76	99	59.2	F
France	..	58.6	552	1,301	22.2	44	47,770	6	79	99	361.8	F
Gabon	1960	1.2	268	8	6.6	50	104	136	55	63	3.7	PF
Gambia	1965	1.2	11	2	1.4	205	15	107	46	39	0.2	NF
Georgia	1991	5.4	70	11	2.0	11	194	21	73	99	3.0	PF
Germany	1871	82.1	357	1,737	21.2	54	41,160	6	76	99	861.2	F
Ghana	1957	18.0	239	29	1.6	17	87	102	57	65	4.0	PF
Greece	1828	10.5	132	132	12.5	28	5,056	9	78	97	80.6	F
Grenada	1974	0.1	0.3	0.5	4.8	51	..	31	72	98	0.2	PF
Guatemala	1839	10.5	109	43	4.1	17	191	55	66	65	6.8	PF
Guinea	1958	6.9	246	12	1.8	14	51	182	46	36	1.1	NF
Guinea-Bissau	1974	1.1	36	1	1.0	8	7	220	43	55	0.2	PF
Guyana	1966	0.8	215	2	2.8	63	7	83	64	98	1.0	F
Haiti	..	7.5	28	9	1.3	12	59	125	55	45	1.1	PF
Honduras	1821	6.0	112	14	2.3	51	51	48	69	73	4.0	F
Hungary	1918	10.2	93	71	7.0	55	961	12	69	99	59.5	F
Iceland	1944	0.3	103	6	21.0	67	0	..	79	99	2.2	F
India	1947	962.4	3,288	1,599	1.7	4	7,831	88	62	52	997.4	PF
Indonesia	1949	200.4	1,905	679	3.4	14	3,398	60	64	84	245.1	NF
Iran	..	60.9	1,633	347	5.7	58	4,191	35	69	69	266.7	NF
Iraq	1932	21.8	438	43	2.0	..	1,965	140	59	58	91.4	NF
Ireland	1922	3.7	70	64	17.4	121	689	7	76	99	34.9	F
Israel	1948	5.8	21	103	17.7	49	8,734	8	78	95	52.3	F

Country											
Italy	1861	57.5	301	1,156	20.1	38	19,380	7	78	98	403.2	F
Jamaica	1962	2.6	11	9	3.3	56	28	14	74	85	10.1	F
Japan	..	126.1	378	3,076	24.4	25	50,240	6	80	99	1,167.7	F
Jordan	1946	4.4	89	15	3.4	35	481	35	69	87	..	PF
Kazakhstan	1991	15.8	2,717	56	3.5	19	426	29	68	99	173.8	NF
Kenya	1963	28.6	580	33	1.2	15	173	112	54	78	6.8	NF
Kiribati	1979	0.1	0.7	0.1	0.8	71	..	..	60	90	0.02	F
Korea, Dem Rep.	1948	22.9	121	..	..	..	6,000	74	72	95	254.3	NF
Korea, Rep.	1948	46.0	99	618	13.4	120	14,410	11	72	98	408.1	F
Kuwait	1961	1.8	18	46	22.3	67	3,488	13	75	79	..	PF
Kyrgyzstan	1991	4.6	199	10	2.2	14	..	..	68	97	6.1	PF
Laos	1949	4.8	237	6	1.3	42	72	128	52	57	0.3	NF
Latvia	1991	2.5	65	10	4.0	45	74	19	68	99	9.3	F
Lebanon	1946	4.1	10	25	6.1	33	410	32	69	92	14.2	PF
Lesotho	1966	2.0	30	5	2.5	26	28	137	58	71	..	PF
Liberia	1822	2.9	111	3	1.0	..	45	..	47	38	0.3	NF
Libya	1952	5.2	1,760	38	6.7	..	1,599	30	64	76	40.6	NF
Liechtenstein	..	0.03	0.2	0.7	23.0	..	..	..	78	99	..	F
Lithuania	1991	3.7	65	15	4.1	57	78	13	70	99	13.8	F
Luxembourg	..	0.4	3	13	33.7	122	142	..	76	99	8.3	F
Macedonia, FYR	1991	2.0	26	6	3.2	140	63	17	72	94	12.7	PF
Madagascar	1960	14.1	587	13	0.9	11	28	158	58	46	1.2	PF
Malawi	1964	10.3	118	7	0.7	20	21	224	41	56	0.7	F
Malaysia	1957	21.7	330	168	7.7	90	2,444	14	71	84	119.1	PF
Maldives	1965	0.3	0.3	0.9	3.3	72	..	76	63	93	0.3	NF
Mali	1960	10.3	1,240	7	0.7	18	43	235	47	31	0.5	F
Malta	1964	0.4	0.3	5	13.4	92	32	..	77	91	1.8	F
Marshall Islands	1986	0.1	0.2	0.1	1.7	92	..	..	64	91	..	F
Mauritania	1960	2.5	1,026	4	1.7	26	33	149	53	38	2.9	NF

Country	Year of Independence	Population (millions)	Area (1,000 km²)	GNP ($ billions, PPP)	GNP/Capita ($ thousands, PPP)	Trade (% of GDP, PPP)	Military Spending ($ millions)	Under-5 Mortality (per 1,000 births)	Life Expectancy (years)	Adult Literacy (% of 15 and over)	CO$_2$ Emissions (million metric tons)	Status of Freedom
Mauritius	1968	1.1	2	11	9.2	36	14	23	71	83	1.7	F
Mexico	1821	94.3	1,958	765	8.1	29	2,321	38	72	90	348.1	PF
Micronesia, Fed. States	1986	0.1	0.7	0.2	1.8	110	..	..	68	89	..	F
Moldova	1991	4.3	34	6	1.5	32	222	24	68	99	12.1	PF
Monaco	..	0.03	0.002	0.8	25.0	..	..	..	78	..	..	F
Mongolia	1921	2.5	1,567	4	1.5	30	20	68	65	83	8.9	F
Morocco	1956	27.3	447	88	3.2	14	1,375	67	66	44	27.9	PF
Mozambique	1975	16.6	802	12	0.7	12	69	201	46	40	1.0	PF
Myanmar	1948	43.9	677	56	1.2	4	1,833	131	59	83	7.3	NF
Namibia	1990	1.6	824	8	5.1	48	64	101	56	76	..	F
Nauru	1968	0.01	0.03	0.1	10.0	46	..	..	67	..	..	F
Nepal	..	22.3	147	24	1.1	4	42	117	56	28	1.6	PF
Netherlands	..	15.6	41	332	21.3	113	8,012	7	78	99	155.2	F
New Zealand	1920	3.8	271	59	15.8	44	740	7	77	99	29.8	F
Nicaragua	1821	4.7	130	9	1.8	20	34	57	68	66	2.9	PF
Niger	1960	9.8	1,267	8	0.8	8	21	320	48	14	1.1	NF
Nigeria	1960	117.9	924	102	0.9	17	..	122	51	57	83.3	NF
Niue	1974	1.6	0.3	0.002	1.2	..	..	..	..	95	..	F
Norway	1905	4.4	324	107	24.3	77	3,508	6	78	99	67.0	F
Oman	1970	2.3	212	17	8.0	44	1,735	28	70	59	15.1	NF
Pakistan	1947	128.5	796	202	1.6	10	3,740	136	63	38	94.3	PF
Palau	1994	0.02	0.5	0.2	8.8	54	..	..	68	92	0.2	F
Panama	1903	2.7	76	19	6.9	27	97	26	73	91	6.7	F
Papua New Guinea	1975	4.5	463	12	2.7	36	107	82	57	72	2.4	PF
Paraguay	..	5.1	407	20	3.9	27	121	28	69	92	3.7	PF
Peru	1824	24.4	1,285	112	4.6	14	989	52	68	89	26.2	PF

Country												
Philippines	1946	73.5	300	270	3.7	31	1,151	41	67	95	63.2	F
Poland	1919	38.7	323	251	6.5	27	4,887	12	71	99	356.8	F
Portugal	..	9.9	92	141	14.2	41	2,690	8	75	90	47.9	F
Qatar	1971	0.7	11.	11	16.7	96	330	21	71	79	29.1	NF
Romania	1878	22.6	238	96	4.3	20	2,520	26	70	98	119.3	F
Russia	..	147.3	17,075	631	4.3	21	76,000	25	66	99	1,579.5	PF
Rwanda	1962	7.9	26	5	0.7	9	118	209	42	61	0.5	NF
Saint Kitts and Nevis	1983	0.04	0.3	0.3	7.8	73	..	38	69	90	0.1	F
Saint Lucia	1979	0.2	0.6	0.8	5.0	59	5	22	71	82	0.2	F
Saint Vincent and Gren.	1979	0.1	0.3	0.5	4.1	67	..	23	72	82	0.1	F
Samoa	1962	0.2	3	0.6	3.6	24	..	53	68	98	0.1	F
San Marino	..	0.03	0.1	0.5	20.0	..	4	..	81	96	..	F
São Tomé and Principe	1975	0.1	1	0.2	1.0	16	..	80	69	75	0.1	F
Saudi Arabia	1902	20.1	2,150	211	10.5	50	17,210	28	71	63	267.8	NF
Senegal	1960	8.8	197	15	1.7	11	76	110	50	33	3.1	PF
Seychelles	1976	0.1	0.5	0.6	7.0	53	14	19	72	88	0.2	PF
Sierra Leone	1961	4.7	72	2	0.4	23	41	286	35	31	0.4	PF
Singapore	1965	3.1	0.6	91	29.2	291	3,970	6	77	91	65.8	PF
Slovak Republic	1993	5.4	49	42	7.9	51	577	..	71	99	39.6	PF
Slovenia	1991	2.0	20	24	11.9	76	344	6	73	96	13.0	F
Solomon Islands	1978	0.4	29	0.9	2.3	25	..	29	71	62	0.2	F
Somalia	1960	8.8	638	8	0.6	5	..	..	47	24	0.02	NF
South Africa	1920	40.6	1,221	292	7.2	21	2,895	65	64	82	292.7	F
Spain	..	39.3	506	617	15.7	36	8,652	7	78	97	232.5	F
Sri Lanka	1948	18.6	66	46	2.5	22	585	19	73	90	7.1	PF
Sudan	1956	27.7	2,506	38	1.4	5	..	115	52	46	3.5	NF
Suriname	1975	0.4	163	1	3.4	64	38	31	71	93	2.1	PF
Swaziland	1968	1.0	17	4	3.7	51	27	97	59	77	0.3	PF
Sweden	..	8.8	450	168	19.0	85	6,042	5	78	99	54.1	F

Country	Year of Independence	Population (millions)	Area (1,000 km²)	GNP ($ billions, PPP)	GNP/Capita ($ thousands, PPP)	Trade (% of GDP, PPP)	Military Spending ($ millions)	Under-5 Mortality (per 1,000 births)	Life Expectancy (years)	Adult Literacy (% of 15 and over)	CO_2 Emissions (million metric tons)	Status of Freedom
Switzerland	..	7.1	41	188	26.6	85	5,034	6	78	99	44.2	F
Syria	1944	14.9	185	45	3.0	21	3,563	38	68	71	44.3	NF
Taiwan	1949	21.9	36	308	14.2	77	13,140	..	77	86	..	F
Tajikistan	1991	6.0	143	7	1.1	22	209	36	67	99	5.8	NF
Tanzania	1964	31.3	945	19	0.6	15	69	136	51	68	2.4	PF
Thailand	..	60.6	513	393	6.5	30	4,014	38	70	94	205.4	PF
Togo	1960	4.3	57	6	1.5	23	28	138	51	52	0.8	NF
Tonga	1970	0.1	0.7	0.2	2.3	41	..	..	70	99	0.1	PF
Trinidad and Tobago	1962	1.3	5	8	6.5	60	82	15	73	98	22.2	F
Tunisia	1956	9.2	164	47	5.1	26	345	33	69	67	16.2	PF
Turkey	..	63.7	775	412	6.5	19	6,606	50	69	82	178.3	PF
Turkmenistan	1991	4.7	488	7	1.4	32	196	50	65	98	34.2	NF
Tuvalu	1978	0.01	0.03	0.008	0.8	80	..	..	64	..	..	F
Uganda	1962	20.3	241	24	1.2	6	126	162	41	62	1.0	PF
Ukraine	1991	50.7	604	110	2.2	39	3,588	17	69	98	397.3	PF
United Arab Emirates	1971	2.6	84	54	24.0	106	1,880	11	74	79	81.8	PF
United Kingdom	..	59.0	245	1,222	20.7	48	33,400	7	77	99	557.0	F
United States	..	267.6	9,364	7,783	29.1	20	277,800	..	76	99	5,301.0	F
Uruguay	1825	3.3	177	30	9.1	22	410	20	73	97	5.6	F
Uzbekistan	1991	23.7	447	61	2.5	13	2,062	31	68	99	95.0	NF
Vanuatu	1980	0.2	12	0.6	3.2	55	..	53	66	64	0.1	F
Venezuela	1821	22.8	912	197	8.7	21	854	25	72	91	144.5	F
Vietnam	1954	76.7	332	122	1.6	19	544	40	66	94	37.6	NF
Yemen	1990	16.1	528	12	0.7	33	407	137	57	38	..	NF
Yugoslavia, Fed. Rep.	1878	10.6	102	24	2.3	37	..	20	73	93	..	NF
Zambia	1964	9.4	753	9	0.9	25	102	189	43	78	2.4	PF
Zimbabwe	1980	11.5	391	26	2.2	20	231	108	49	85	18.4	PF

Table 3.1 World Bank's Classification of States, 1996. *Source:* World Bank, *World Development Indicators, 1998.* Copyright © 1998 by World Bank. Reprinted by permission.

Figure 3.1 Growth of States, IGOs, and NGOs, 1900–1997. *Source:* States from the POLITY Project, "POLITY Data Archive III," 31 March 1998, <http://www.colorado.edu/IBS/GAD/spacetime/data/Polity.html> (18 August 1998). Reprinted by permission of the Harvard MIT Data Center. IGOs and NGOs compiled from Union of International Associations, *Yearbook of International Organizations.* (Brussels: UIA, various years). Reprinted by permission.

Table 4.1 Relative Strength of Major Powers and Their Coalitions, 1960 and 1989. *Source:* Revised version of "The Penn World Table (Mark 5): An Expanded Set of International Comparisons, 1950–1988.," QJE 106:2. Reprinted by permission of the National Bureau for Economic Research. Military Expenditures for 1960 are from Stockholm International Peace Research Institute, *SIPRI Yearbook 1980: World Armaments and Disarmaments* (London: Taylor and Francis, 1981). Reprinted by permission of the Stockholm International Peace Research Institute.

Table 5.1 State Capabilities: Rankings and Correlations, 1995–1996. *Source:* Rankings for geographic, economic and quality-of-life indicators are based on data from the World Bank, *World Development Indicators, 1998.* (New York: Oxford University Press, 1998). Copyright © 1998 by World Bank. Reprinted by permission.

Figure 6.1 An Environmental Model for Foreign Policy Analysis. *Source:* Maria Papadakis and Harvey Starr, "Opportunity, Willingness, and Small States: The Relationship between Environment and Foreign Policy," in Charles F. Hermann, Charles W. Kegley, and James N. Rosenau, eds., *New Directions in the Study of Foreign Policy.* Copyright © 1987 by International Thomson Publishing Services. Reprinted by permission.

Table 6.1 Foreign Policy Attitudes of American Elites after the Cold War. *Source:* Select Data from Shoon Kathleen Murray, *Anchors against Change: American Opinion Leaders' Beliefs after the Cold War* (Ann Arbor: University of Michigan Press, 1996), Table 5.24.

Figure 6.2 American Public Opinion on Defense Spending, 1946–1992. *Source:* 1946–1964 data computed from Bruce Russett, "The Revolt of the Masses; Public Opinion on Military Expenditures," in Russett, ed., *Peace, War, and Numbers,* pp. 301–306. Copyright © 1972 by Bruce Russett. Reprinted by permission of Sage Publications, Inc. 1965–1990 data from Thomas Hartley and Bruce Russett, "Public Opinion and the Common Defense: Who Governs Military Spending in the United States?" from *American Political Science Review* 86,4 (1992), 905–915. 1991–1992 data from Jonathan M. Feldman, "Public Choice, Foreign Policy Crises, and Military Spending," in Lloyd J. Dumas, ed., *The Socio-Economics of Conversion from War to Peace* (Armonk, NY: Sharpe, 1995), pp. 233–264.

Figure 7.1 A Decision Cube (American perspective). *Source:* Modified from Charles F. Hermann, "International Crisis as a Situational Variable," in James N. Rosenau, ed., *International Politics and Foreign Policy,* revised edition. Adapted with the permission of The Free Press, a Division of Simon & Schuster, Inc. Copyright © 1969 by The Free Press.

Table 7.1 Factors Affecting Foreign Policy and Their Susceptibility to Change. Adapted from James N. Rosenau, "The Study of Foreign Policy," in James N. Rosenau, Kenneth Thompson, and Gavin Boyd, eds., *World Politics.* Adapted with the permission of The Free Press, a Division of Simon & Schuster, Inc. Copyright © 1976 by The Free Press.

Table 8.2 Global War in the Contemporary State System. *Source:* Jack S. Levy, *War in the Modern Great Power System, 1495–1975.* Copyright © 1985 by Jack S. Levy. Reprinted with permission of The University Press of Kentucky.

Table 8.3 Issues in War and Major Armed Intervention, 1648–1998. *Source:* Compiled from Kaelvi J. Holsti, *Peace and War: Armed Conflicts and International Order, 1648–1989*, Tables 3.1, 5.1, 7.1, 9.1, and 11.1. Reprinted by permission of Cambridge University Press.

Figure 8.1 Decision Tree Depicting an International Interaction Game. *Source:* Adapted from Bruce Bueno de Mesquita and David Lalman, *War and Reason: Domestic and International Imperatives* (1992), p. 30. Copyright © 1992 by Bruce Bueno de Mesquita and David Lalman. Reprinted by permission of Yale University Press.

Table 8.4 Ethnopolitical Groups: Rebellion and War, 1990–1995. *Source:* Compiled from data released by the Minorities at Risk Project, Center for International Development and Conflict Management, University of Maryland, "Tracking the Status and Condition of Ethnopolitical Groups Around the Globe," 22 March 1998, <http://www.bsos.umd.edu/cidcm/mar/> (4 August 1998).

Table 8.5 Armed Conflict in 1997. *Source:* Data compiled by the Uppsala Conflict Data Project, Department of Peace and Conflict Research, Uppsala University, and published in Peter Wallensteen and Margareta Sollenberg, "Armed Conflict and Regional Conflict Complexes," *Journal of Peace Research* 35, 5 (1998). Reprinted by permission of the Sage Publications Ltd. and the authors, Peter Wallensteen and Margareta Sollenberg.

Figure 8.2 International Terrorism, 1968–1997. *Source:* 1981 and 1984 reports reprinted in Robert A. Friedlander, ed., *Terrorism: Documents of International and Local Controls*, vols. 4 and 6. Copyright © 1984, 1992 by Oceana Publications, Inc. Reprinted by permission.

Figure 9.1 American and Soviet/Russian Military Expenditures, 1954–1995. *Source:* For 1954–1962, Stockholm International Peace Research Institute, *World Armaments and Disarmament*, various years (New York: Oxford University Press). Copyright © Stockholm International Peace Research Institute. Reprinted by permission.

Table 9.1 Global Military Presence, 1997. Compiled from International Institute for Strategic Studies, *The Military Balance 1997/1998*. Copyright © 1998 International Institute for Strategic Studies. Reprinted by permission of Oxford University Press.

Figure 9.2 The Rise and Decline in Superpower Offensive Nuclear Forces, 1945–1996. *Source:* Natural Resources Defense Council Nuclear Program, "US and USSR/Russian Strategic Offensive Nuclear Forces, 1945–1996," January 1997, <http://www.nrdc.org/nrdcpro/nudb/dainx.html> (16 September 1998). Copyright © 1997 by the Natural Resources Defense Council. Reprinted by permission of the Natural Resources Defense Council.

Table 9.2 American and Russian Strategic Nuclear Forces, 1998. *Source:* William M. Arkin, Robert S. Norris, and Joshua Handler, *Taking Stock: Worldwide Nuclear Deployments, 1998*. Copyright © 1998 by the Natural Resources Defense Council. Reprinted by permission of the Natural Resources Defense Council.

Table 10.1 Formal Declarations on the Laws of War. *Source:* Compiled from W. Michael Reisman and Chris T. Antoniou, eds., *The Laws of War: A Comprehensive Collection of Primary Documents on International Laws Governing Armed Conflict.* Copyright © 1994 by Vintage Books. Reprinted by permission of Random House.

Figure 11.1 A Crisis Subgame: Democracies and Dictatorships. *Source:* Adapted from Bruce Bueno de Mesquita and David Lalman, *War and Reason: Domestic and International Imperatives* (New Haven, CT: Yale University Press, 1992), p. 159. Copyright © 1992 by Bruce Bueno de Mesquita and David Lalman. Reprinted by permission of Yale University Press.

Figure 11.2 Kant's Prescription for Perpetual Peace. *Source:* Bruce Russett, "A Neo-Kantian Perspective: Democracy, Interdependence, and International Organizations in Building

Figure 15.1 North–South Human Development Gap, 1995–1996. *Source:* Data from the United Nations Development Programme, *Human Development Report, 1998.* Copyright © 1998 by the United Nations Development Programme. Reprinted by permission of Oxford University Press.

Figure 15.2 Human Development by Region, 1995. Data from United Nations Development Programme, *Human Development Report, 1998.* Copyright © by the United Nations Development Programme. Reprinted by permission of Oxford University Press.

Figure 15.3 Primary Commodity Prices, 1957–1999. *Source:* Computed from data released by the International Monetary Fund, *World Economic Outlook.* Copyright © 1983 by the International Monetary Fund. Reprinted by permission of the International Monetary Fund.

Figure 15.4 Structure of Imperialism and Dependency. *Source:* Adapted from Galtung, J. "A structural theory of imperialism" in *Journal of Peace Research,* Vol. 8 (2), 1971, pp. 81–117. Copyright © 1971 by John Galtung. Reprinted by permission of Sage Publications and the author.

Figure 15.5 Third World Debt, 1973–1999. *Source:* International Monetary Fund, *World Economic Outlook.* Copyright © by the International Monetary Fund. Reprinted by permission of the International Monetary Fund.

Table 15.1 Development and Freedom, 1980–1995. *Source:* Data for GNP per capita growth and human development are from the *Human Development Report, 1998* by the UNOP. Copyright © 1999 by the United Nations Development Programme. Used by permission of Oxford University Press.

Figure 16.1 Nested Human Systems. *Source:* Adapted from Ervin Laslo, *A Strategy for the Future: The Systems Approach to World Order.* Copyright © 1974 by Ervin Laslo. Reprinted by permission of Braziller.

Table 16.2 Mineral Consumption, 1994. *Source:* World Resources Institute, et al., *World Resources 1996–1997* (New York: Oxford University Press, 1996). Table 12.4 World reserve base life assumes continuing annual production at 1994 levels. Reprinted by permission of the World Resources Institute.

Figure 16.5 Carbon Dioxide Emissions and Concentrations, 1900–1996. *Source:* World Resources Institute, et al., *World Resources 1996–99: Environmental Change and Human Health* (New York: Oxford University Press, 1998), Tables 16.3 and 16.4. Reprinted by permission of the World Resources Institute.

Figure 16.6 Child Mortality in Relation to Income in Poorer Countries, 1996. *Source:* Based on data in World Bank, *World Development Indicators on CD-ROM* [electronic database]. Reprinted by permission of World Bank.

INDEX

Note: Page numbers in *italics* indicate figures; those in **boldface** indicate defintions; those followed by t indicate tables; and those followed by n indicate footnotes.